Exploring Culturally Diverse Literature for Children and Adolescents

Learning to Listen in New Ways

Darwin L. Henderson

University of Cincinnati

Jill P. May

Purdue University

Boston • New York • San Francisco
Mexico City • Montreal • Toronto • London • Madrid • Munich • Paris
Hong Kong • Singapore • Tokyo • Cape Town • Sydney

Senior Series Editor: *Aurora Martínez Ramos*
Editorial Assistant: *Erin Beatty*
Executive Marketing Manager: *Amy Cronin Jordan*
Production Editor: *Anna Socrates*
Editorial-Production Service: *Omegatype Typography, Inc.*
Manufacturing Buyer: *Andrew Turso*
Composition and Prepress Buyer: *Linda Cox*
Cover Administrator: *Kristina Mose-Libon*
Electronic Composition: *Omegatype Typography, Inc.*

For related titles and support materials, visit our online catalog at www.ablongman.com.

Between the time Website information is gathered and then published, it is not unusual for some sites to have closed. Also, the transcription of URLs can result in typographical errors. The publisher would appreciate notification where these errors occur so that they may be corrected in subsequent editions.

Library of Congress Cataloging-in-Publication Data

Henderson, Darwin L.
  Exploring culturally diverse literature for children and adolescents : learning to listen in
  new ways / Darwin L. Henderson, Jill P. May
     p. cm.
  Includes bibliographical references and index.
  ISBN 0-205-36640-6
    1. Children—Books and reading—United States. 2. Teenagers—Books and reading—United
  States. 3. Children's literature—Study and teaching—United States. 4. Young adult
  literature—Study and teaching—United States. 5. Multiculturalism—Study and
  teaching—United States. 6. Pluralism (Social sciences)—Study and teaching—United States.
  I. Henderson, Darwin L. II. May, Jill P.

  Z1037.A1E98 2005
  028.5'5—dc22

                                                                                      2004044493

Printed in the United States of America

10   9   8   7   6   5   4   3   09   08   07   06   05

Exploring Culturally Diverse Literature for Children and Adolescents

To my mother Edith and my brother Bill
DLH

To the women in my family who have taught
me much, and to my father's spirit,
which still lives with his family
JPM

Finally, to Bob, mentor, friend, and dearest companion,
who has traveled with us on each step of this journey
JPM and DLH

Contents

Practice

PART TWO • *Toward a New Perspective: Learning to Interpret Culturally Diverse Literature*   137

Theory

Practice

Introduction

We have edited *Exploring Culturally Diverse Literature for Children and Adolescents: Learning to Listen in New Ways* because we believe there is a void in the discussion of literature and its literary heritage in the fields of children's and adolescent literature. For some time, as close professional and personal friends, we discussed the need to approach children's and adolescent literature as a dynamic representation of community. Finally, we decided to ask others to join our conversations. Our aim was to look beyond those books that have won awards such as the Newbery and the Caldecott or are listed on canonical publications such as the Children's Literature Association Touchstones List and to consider how diverse writing styles in children's and adolescent literature might be discussed for their literary merits. Because we believe that teachers and literary scholars will best be able to enter into a new dialogue about literature's place in the world of our young readers when they understand how stories are tied to specific cultural and sociopolitical histories, we asked various professionals in children's and adolescent literature and education for personal thoughts about ways to evaluate this literature. We also asked them to consider what new discussions might best fit with contemporary literary theory and classroom practices. Our hope was to open a new dialogue about the possibilities of exploring literature as a communal sign. We wanted our colleagues to voice their ideals for sharing literature's cultural significance as its literary potential. The project has reached closure with the book you have in your hands. We believe it holds a new perspective on what might be considered canonical in teaching with and about children's and adolescent literature.

When we looked at the various professional books available on multicultural texts in the children's and adolescent literature, we were impressed with the well-founded arguments that children's and adult literature should be inclusive and the positive suggestions for classroom activities inspired by multicultural literature. At the same time, we noticed a lack of conversations about the literary structures embedded in diverse literary forms, the ways cultural aesthetics have been represented in ethnocentric stories, and the need for studies that analyze children's interactions with new literary symbols and signs in their classroom literature explorations. Our conclusion was that though much has been written about literature from different viewpoints, little has been said about the ideals for exploring divergent literary codes or the strengths in centering young people's discussions on individual patterns and motifs accepted by a particular group. The problem with earlier explorations is they lack communication about the imperatives of cultural aesthetics in children's and adolescent literary appreciation. We wanted our authors to fit their discussions into a larger framework that would advocate for theory's use in classroom practice.

The best trips we may be able to afford our young readers can be found in literature. However, unguided journeys into new lands may not change these readers' perspectives. Often, young people have not experienced or studied lots of diverse literary patterns, and they have not visited lots of diverse cultural localities; they need to explore literature with adults who understand how the *mythos* of a particular group helps to shape story patterns. The authors of the theoretical pieces in this book have often identified these patterns and suggested new ways of discussing diverse literature published for and read by youthful readers. Even when the authors are looking at negative aspects of the published literature we share in our classrooms, their emphasis has been on expanding the American literary canon; they all suggest new ways of approaching the acts of reading, interpreting, and sharing literature written for, by, and about diverse populations within American society. Our professional colleagues offer enlightenment concerning cultural diversity and its representations in the literature written for children and adolescents; their insights will help us reframe our current discussions of literary interpretation and literacy.

This book's organization is designed to fit within Peter Elbow's call for change in the teaching of literature. Elbow suggested a literary approach that allowed for "personal tone and talk about feelings" (260). Furthermore, Elbow argued that interpretation should be "always open, never settled, always dependent on the interpreter" (246). Our authors were selected because they held beliefs about contemporary literacy practices within education and had earlier advocated that teachers use new interpretative tools as they guided youngsters in their readings of culturally diverse literature. We asked that our contributors reexamine the theory and practice they were most familiar with and extend earlier established guidelines. Their disclosures concerning theory and practice represent personally considered narratives about the need to expand both the books we share and the ways we talk about their literary significance: How did they feel about the literature available? How would they choose to approach it? What would be the responses of youthful audiences when they were introduced to new literary patterns?

Once our authors responded, we determined to focus this discussion under the broader rubrics of *difference* while placing pieces together that addressed similar literary structures. Therefore, we did not place the essays into rigid ethnic, religious, or sociopolitical subgroups. Within the divisions found in *Exploring Culturally Diverse Literature for Children and Adolescents: Learning to Listen in New Ways,* contributors discuss the theory for and possible ways to practice literary analysis and discussion with children and adolescents. Our goal in this design has been to present new perspectives about literary analysis in ways that suggest a beginning dialogic discussion of *literary difference.* We believe the book's structure fits with Clifford Geertz's early call for understanding how the lived experience differs from the studied one. As Geertz says, "The problem of the integration of cultural life becomes one of making it possible for people inhabiting different worlds to have a genuine, and reciprocal, impact on one another" (161). Theory has been placed first.

Peter Elbow penned his commentary about literary and writerly approaches to teaching with literature at the end of the 1987 English Coalition Conference, a meeting sponsored by eight professional organizations in English: the College English Association, the Conference on English Education, the College Language Association, the Conference on

College Composition and Communication, Modern Language Association, the Conference of Secondary School English Department Chairs, and the National Council of Teachers of English. As MLA's designated writer of an "executive report" for the meeting, Elbow observed how teachers at all levels might approach the literature shared in schools. In the end, Elbow argued that theory should be the framework for spirited discussions about literature. This would change professional perspectives on literature's place in the curriculum at all levels of education, refocusing the canon on theory into practice rather than books in the curriculum:

> [. . .] most of the intellectual enterprises that are connected in any way to "English" seem to be happy to think of themselves as engaged in theory—literary theory, critical theory, composition and rhetorical theory, cultural theory, learning theory, reading or reception theory, language or linguistic theory, and cognitive theory. The emphasis on theory itself seems to make people less contentious even if their theories are at complete odds with each other. [. . .] When we translate theory to the human level and I think this was the main accomplishment of the conference in this realm—it amounts to accepting differences among people and among positions, indeed, sanctioning and rewarding them as good things: celebrating diversity, not trying to get everyone to be the same, framing and taming conflicts. (61–62)

Elbow's words emphasize our intent to engage an intellectual conversation about the meanings of literature, the purpose of literacy education, and the ways to identify *difference* and to celebrate its artistic significance. Therefore, some of our authors discuss the *roots of difference,* and these essayists go beyond what is traditionally thought to be children's or adolescent literary concerns.

Gerald Graff was also a participant in the English Coalition Conference; he has argued continually for a debate in our reading principles and practices that would center itself on theory. Graff has maintained that honest and open explorations of the controversies articulated within various theoretical approaches would strengthen our students' learning experiences, allowing them to understand that all texts can be read from multiple perspectives. Graff has agitated for an integration of diverse opinions within our discussions of shared texts, commenting that adults cannot teach about any book or idea without engaging the ideas and theories of others who disagree with them. He concluded, "I believe I am a better teacher because I am able to take my colleagues as reference points in my classroom" (114). We have not asked our authors to agree with anyone else; rather, we have asked that they participate in a dynamic debate concerning those sensitive issues that have been voiced within the academy and have caused debate among scholars and teachers about finding, evaluating, and exploring culturally diverse texts.

As co-editors, we hoped to begin each section with an introductory discussion that might suggest how past literary and cultural history have caused adults to unconsciously accept a framework for reading children's and adolescent literature. Throughout, we have explored a literary periphery we felt highlighted the connections between the papers that followed. These introductions were designed to work as stepping-stones into the wider discussion that follows. We believe, as Northrop Frye stated in *The Educated Imagination,* "literature follows after a mythology" (110). We have purposefully asked our contributors to consider what it means to "reading differently" when teachers turn to the controversial issues of ethnicity and displacement. We hope that their writings will cause you to consider literature's role in personal identity: How can (or should) classroom teachers explore issues of religious practices, cultural representation, and persecution as they discuss literary texts?

American Indian advocate Vine Deloria, Jr. once wrote:

> There must be a drive within each minority group to understand its own uniqueness. This can only be done by examining what experiences were relevant to the group, not what experiences of white America the group wishes itself to be represented in. [. . .] Self-awareness of each group must define a series of histories about the American experience. (42–43)

It is Vine Deloria, Jr.'s early call for a revisionist way of reading that frames our writers' explorations as they petition for each group's right to define itself so that "the ideological basis for portraying the members of any group will depend on that group's values" (Deloria 43–44). David Mura has written about the Japanese American experience, commenting that it is one of the three most ignored omissions in American history. He alludes to two other groups that have failed to be recognized during past Eurocentric control of the canon:

> Knowing the history behind the camps, knowing that during the internment the lives of many Japanese-Americans, particularly the Issei (first generation), were permanently disrupted; knowing the internment caused the loss of millions of dollars of property, I, as a Japanese-American, feel a kinship to both Black and Native Americans that I do not feel with white Americans. (138)

We hope to open a dialogue that includes diversity. Indeed, as Juan Bruce-Nova asserted, "It is no longer a matter of absorbing 'foreign' expressions within a national literature but of heeding an insistent, multivoiced call for the restructuring of the canon into a polyglot, pluralistic expression of many nations within a common frontier" (199). We hope that the pieces in this book will cause you to consider several groups who live on the edges of border politics: How are these "invisible children" and their families represented in contemporary literature? How can teachers discuss these books with children who live inside and outside the borderland?

Virginia Hamilton argued effectively for the sole right of the Black author to pen the Black experience when she stated,

> Black people are an oppressed people. There is little black writing that is not socially conscious and race-conscious writing. There is no other way but this way for a black writer to be considered a writer of truth in this society. The very substance of our thinking is of struggle, becoming, and change. There is a thesis and antithesis in search of synthesis. All of my young characters live within a fictional order, and it is largely a black social order that is characterized by tension, insecurity, and struggle. The final analysis is one of growing consciousness. That is what history teaches us, or should. (91)

Our authors ask us to consider important issues of selection and privilege in our literary analysis: Who determines how history will fit in the books for young readers? How has gender been represented in children's and adolescent literature? Is literature political? What is the role of the author and the illustrator to the cultural story? What can we do to help English language learners learn about American literature?

As you finish reading *Exploring Culturally Diverse Literature for Children and Adolescents: Learning to Listen in New Ways,* you might wonder how the parts all fit together. Some of our authors seem to conflict with the opinion of another. This, we feel, is good scholarship. Divergence brings critical analysis and causes us to consider new ways to interpret the literature we share. We have hoped to encourage you, our reader, to enter into a more divergent dialogue without privileging one voice over another. This was how we have learned to converse whenever we are together. We have begun to consider how important cultural and historical research has been in our formulation of the book's introductions and conclusions. We have learned to listen and determine how to evaluate literature in new ways. We have endorsed the prospect of different people coming to different conclusions about the texts they read.

This idea of a reader's privilege beyond ethnicity, we both agree, is a conversation that is so new and so raw it needs to be opened in our field. As you close this book, we ask you to consider Bakhtin's argument made in his discussion of the novel. Bakhtin wrote:

> The novel [. . .] is, by its very nature, not canonic. It is plasticity itself. It is a genre that is ever questing, ever examining itself and subjecting its established forms to review. Such, indeed, is the only possibility open to a genre that structures itself in a zone of direct contact with developing reality. (39)

Isn't criticism just like that too? Surely, as we read and critique, we are questing for a definition of community, searching for the author's meaning of reality, trying to establish what conventions have shaped our reviews so that we can learn to listen and respond to a new ideas in positive ways.

Works Cited

Bakhtin, Mikhail M. 1981. *The Dialogic Imagination: Four Essays.* Ed. Michael Holquist. Translated by Caryl Emerson and Michael Holquist. Austin: University of Texas Press.

Bruce-Nova, Juan. "Canonical and Noncanonical Texts: A Chicano Case Study." *Redefining American Literary History.* Ed. A. LaVonne Brown Ruoff and Jerry W. Ward. New York: Modern Language Association, 1990: 196–209.

Deloria, Vine, Jr. *We Talk, You Listen: New Tribes, New Turf.* New York: Dell Publishing, 1970.

Elbow, Peter. *What Is English?* New York: Modern Language Association of America, 1990.

Frye, Northrop. *The Educated Imagination.* Bloomington, IN: Indiana University Press, 1964.

Geertz, Clifford. *Local Knowledge: Further Essays in Interpretative Anthropology.* New York: Basic Books, 1983.

Graff, Gerard. *Beyond the Culture Wars: How Teaching the Conflicts Can Revitalize American Education.* New York: W. W. Norton, 1992.

Hamilton, Virginia. "Hagi, Mose, and Drysolongso." *The Zena Sutherland Lectures, 1983–1992.* Ed. Betsy Hearne. New York: Clarion Books, 1993. 75–91.

King, Debra. *Deep Talk: Reading African-American Literary Names.* Charlottesville, VA: University Press of Virginia, 1998.

Mura, David. "Strangers in the Village." *The Graywolf Annual Five: Multi-Cultural Literacy.* Ed. Rick Simonson and Scott Walker. St. Paul, MN: Graywolf Press, 1988.

Redefining American Literary History. Ed. A. LaVonne Brown Ruoff and Jerry W. Ward. New York: Modern Language Association, 1990. 262–87.

Acknowledgments

This book would not be in your hands if we had not had strong colleagues in the field who agreed to write papers and to suffer through our lengthy suggestions for editing their manuscripts. Every author's piece represents lots of collaborative conversations about our book's overall intent, our need to have "readable pieces" that undergraduates and graduates in education, English, and library science could understand, and our demand for high scholastic standards. Those who chose to stay with us through the editing process must be acknowledged for sharing their content knowledge, personal visions, and intellectual fortitude.

Each section of the book begins with a poem by Christian Knoeller and a framing illustration by Beth May. Somewhere in the middle of our editing, we asked Christian if, as a published, award-winning poet, he would be willing to help us frame our sections with poetry and illustration. That way, we felt, readers could see how artists take concrete concepts and create visual and oral imagery for their audiences. Beth May had already illustrated a book while she was in Africa (*Esiku Limmwe.* Gambsberg Macmillan, 2000), and we asked if she would meet with Christian to discuss his poetry and how they might combine their work as a frame for the sections, especially since Beth had already read and critiqued each of the essays. Luckily, they both agreed. We wish to thank them for their efforts.

We would like to thank our individual universities for their continued support on this project. Several people at both universities played some role in sustaining our efforts throughout the three-year process. Darwin wishes to acknowledge his department head, Glen Markle, for his professional guidance throughout this time. Jill wishes to thank colleagues Jim Greenan and Jim Lehman for providing academic forums in which we could talk about the book manuscripts with colleagues at Purdue University. Support staff and graduate students also played key roles. In particular, we would like to recognize the secretarial help afforded by Ann Loebhard at the University of Cincinnati and Bonnie Nowakowski at Purdue University. Both Ann and Bonnie supervised several mailings to the contributors and kept us on top of problems as they arose. Kelly Neyland, a graduate student in literacy at the University of Cincinnati, work closely with Darwin. They checked all manuscripts for copyright compliance, and Kelly checked the papers' bibliographies for MLA citations. We would also like to thank the reviewers: Ian W. Andrews, Eastern Michigan University; Karen Coats, Illinois State University; and H. Richard Milner, Vanderbilt University.

Jill would like to thank her family for their continued support of her academic projects. In particular, she would like to thank Bob and Beth, her husband and youngest daughter. As a returning Peace Corps worker who taught teachers about language arts methodology, children's literature, and English grammar rules in Nambia, Beth spent her first summer home acting as "first reader" and grammatical editor for the entire manuscript.

Darwin and Jill thank her for reading and tagging questionable phrases and use of jargonese in each paper. Although not all of her comments are embedded in the final pieces, many are. Bob listened to several drafts of introductions and "final notes." He was our razor-sharp "first critic" who kept us honest. For that we thank him. We also thank him for cooking and cajoling us along during these past three years.

At the bitter end, when some final edited manuscripts arrived in Mac format, Bonnie contacted Steve Wellinski, a former graduate student in literacy and language at Purdue University with computer expertise who is now a faculty member at Illinois State University, and he "broke the code" for us. Jill owes Bonnie and Steve a special thanks because they helped her in a real time of need.

Exploring Culturally Diverse Literature for Children and Adolescents

Part I

In the Beginning: Recognizing Diversity in Children's and Adolescent Literature

Learning to Speak Again

We define ourselves by such boundaries
as oceans make, learning each other's words
first for fish and for wine, then for colors

and for grace. Between us, currents cross
and Pacific, warming water and shore,
drawing us together. Yet no simple

geography charts the confluence of
our lives. From a bluff above
the beach, buffeted by the wind, we watch

once more for whales migrating south turn
of the year. Here, we again learn to speak
a language of gestures made or

not made, the vocabulary of
leave-taking and loss. Together
there are such worlds to be named.

—Christian Knoeller[1]

American critic Frederick Turner has noted that although early writers in the United States often mimicked the literary patterns of Europe, by the 1890s literature written by U.S. authors decidedly pictured the American country as both picturesque and rough. Immigrants were depicted as honest but simple folk who had settled this new land on the beliefs of freedom, individual independence, and economic aggregation, earnestly working to civilize the large continent. The enemies in these accounts were often the wild beasts found in the woods and the unenlightened Natives. Nationalism, individual rights (for those not deemed aboriginal), and Christianity were represented as positive forces in this new world. These early writers established the American myth of the hero's journey into an unplowed backwoods inhabited by savage Indians. This was touted as the common American pathway within westward expansionism. James Fennimore Cooper's fictional heroes followed these mythic patterns.[2]

When Ralph Waldo Emerson called for a literature that addressed the issues of poverty, children's lives, and the everyday household experiences of settlers in 1837, he suggested writing observational, introspective, regional literature that was connected to a place.[3] Probably the book that best answered Emerson's call was Thoreau's *Walden*. Turner says, "*Walden* in its narrative of one man's confrontation with the discrete facts of a particular place—hoot owls, the colors of pond ice, the hum of summer insects, golden pickerel beneath green waters—tells all who will listen that America, the New World, is first and last a grand spiritual opportunity" (39). Thoreau was writing more introspectively than the earlier Americans. He once declared,

> Why should we be in such haste to succeed, and in such desperate enterprises? If a man does not keep pace with his companions, perhaps it is because he hears a different drummer. Let him stop to the music which he hear, however measured or far away. It is not important that he should mature as soon as an apple tree or an oak. (589)

Thoreau's observations about nature's part in the larger world established a narrative style for writing about the natural world that was neither scientific nor expansive. Thoreau's writing was reflexive, subjective, and personal. There could be harsh descriptions of daily conditions and odes to nature in the same breath. And although he might find a sympathetic ear in the common public, the last thing he wanted was to engage in speaking tours for an adoring public. Thoreau sought solitude in the woods behind his home town, deeming this his habitat and seeing civilization as a place to be visited. In many ways his voice today would be termed feminine.[4] He had chosen to seclude himself from industry, to remain private, and to share his inner thoughts in his journal, perhaps talking to it more than to a reading audience.

Scholars have spent much time considering whether Emily Dickinson's poetry was written for the people she knew and loved or whether it was something she was compelled to write in order to understand herself and her circumstances. Many would agree that Dickinson was not limited to describing the natural world that surrounded her. Her poems are largely untitled, as if written in her journal while observing her world. Dickinson can speak of the cycle of life as if she were describing an event in her quiet life:

> I stepped from Plank to Plank
> A slow and cautious way
> The Stars about my Head I felt
> About my Feet the Sea.

> I knew not but the next
> Would be my final inch—
> This gave me that precarious Gait
> Some call Experience.[5] (106)

Dickinson survived when other poets—men as well as women—were lost. She witnessed her natural world within a subjective analysis of the environment around her: The changing seasons, the cyclical pattern of nature in life to death experiences, and the need to carefully observe the smallest creatures in order to understand God's creation are all embedded in her many poems. Unlike Thoreau and many of his male counterparts, she did not name her countryside. But it is well known in the world of women: The backyard garden, the skies at night and the sea in the distance, the forbidden edge of the forest, and the bedroom window where the rising sun as well as the passing of another day are visually experienced.

Archibald MacLeish commented that Emily Dickinson is probably a part of the American literary canon because of her personal style with its unique approach to poetic format and descriptive language. He claimed that Dickinson speaks to her audience. As for perspective, he concluded:

> Poem after poem—more than a hundred and fifty of them—begins with the word "I," the talker's word. She is already in the poem before she begins it, as a child is already in the adventure before he finds a word to speak of it. To put it in other terms, few poets [. . .] have written more *dramatically* than Emily Dickinson, more in the locutions of dramatic speech, words born living on the tongue, written as though spoken. [. . .] Something is being *said* to you and *you* have no choice but to hear. (19–20)

Literary scholars Ruland and Bradbury insist that Dickinson's entry into the canon of American literature depended on her discipline as a writer, her craft as a poet, and her capacity to view her scenes without sentimentality (172–178).

Both Thoreau and Dickinson offer readers subjective re-visions of America, and they continue to be republished. Since neither received immediate fame in their own time, they might be surprised if they could stand at the front of any number of bookstores and survey not only the reprints of their writings in a prominent display but also mugs with their pictures on them, posters with quotations from their writings, Post-it notes with Thoreau and Dickinson witticisms. As Hans Robert Jauss has pointed out, literary works can be judged by their popularity at the particular moment when they are released (or in Dickinson's case written), but they also can be best appreciated later: "There are works that at the moment of their appearance are not yet directed at any specific audience, but that break through the familiar horizon of literary expectations so completely that an audience can only gradually develop for them" (25).[6]

Children's literature contains an American landscape that is also a subjective version of America and its peoples. At first glance, we observe a secure "universal landscape" we might wish to enter; at the same time, these texts and illustrations defy earlier depictions of many American cultural scenes stereotyped by mainstream Americans. American picture books reveal the complexity of the literary representations found in books for youth;

they are the collaborative efforts of women and men who are redefining America with divergent visions of nature, space, and civilization. These artists and authors have often restructured the popular imagery of the United States to present a country with cultural, economic, and/or social difference within its regions for youthful readers.

Picture books hold versions of America that depend on two traditions, subjective description of a historical and social place and artistic landscape painting of a particular setting at a particular moment. Robert Scholes and Robert Kellogg have noted, "Illustration differs from representation in narrative art in that it does not seek to reproduce actuality but to present selected aspects of the actual, essences referable for their meaning not to historical, psychological, or sociological truth but to ethical and metaphysical truth" (88). Children's literature contains an ethics of cultural diversity that is revolutionary and timeless. The following two picture books can be explored as representations of the diversity found in children's and adolescent literature.

Cynthia Rylant and Barry Moser successfully combine their creative images of the rural American South in *Appalachia: The Voices of Sleeping Birds.* Both were born in the South and understand the ideals of the people represented in their book. Yet, they are coming at the process of depicting the Appalachian South from slightly different perspectives. Rylant has commented, "I grew up in West Virginia and what happened to me deeply affects what I write" (qtd. in Olendorf & Telgen 167). Moser grew up in the South but he now lives in the North; he has illustrated texts set not only in the United States but also in the illusive land of fantasy. He once observed, "A text I choose must seed my mind and have a market" (qtd. in Olendorf & Telgen 121).

The textual imagery of Appalachia found in *Appalachia: The Voices of Sleeping Birds* begins prior to Rylant's narrative with a quote from James Agee's *Knoxville: Summer 1915,* which contains Rylant's subtitle: "[. . .] All my people are larger bodies than mine, quiet, with voices gentle and meaningless like the voices of sleeping birds" (unpaged). Once the beginning text is read, it becomes obvious that Cythnia Rylant is not writing for the people in Appalachia. Instead, she is "talking" to others as a former resident of the region who grew up in her maternal grandparents' home. When discussing her writing, Rylant has said, "The tone of my works reflects the way they spoke, the simplicity of their language, and, I hope, the depth of their own hearts" (qtd. in Olendorf & Telgen 167). Richard Sennett once commented, "Ethnicity is a sense of identity established by awareness of difference, and this awareness of difference comes through a history of displacement" (198). Rylant's text describes within new rhetorical patterns the southern mountain scenes and society that most Americans have stereotyped as "backward areas" with "hillbillies" and "white trash." Throughout, she is defining herself as a member of a sociocultural group that has been misrepresented in American culture. Rylant is asking her reader to view Appalachian life in a new, fresh way, while playing on the earlier established stereotypes of coal miners with homes full of dogs, tired women, and several children. She writes:

> In a certain part of the country called Appalachia you will find dogs named Prince or King living in little towns with names like Coal City and Sally's Backbone. These dogs run free, being country dogs, and their legs are full of muscles from running rabbits up mountains or from following boys who push old bikes against the hill roads they call hollows. They are mostly good dogs and can be trusted.

The owners of these dogs who live in Appalachia have names like Mamie and Boyd and Oley, and they probably have lived in Appalachia all of their lives. Many of them were born in coal camps in tiny houses which stood on poles and on the sides of which you could draw a face with your finger because coal dust had settled on their walls like snow. The owners of these dogs grew up more used to trees than sky and inside them had this feeling of mystery about the rest of the world they couldn't see because mountains came up so close to them and blocked their view like a person standing in the doorway. They weren't sure about going beyond these mountains, going until the land becomes flat or ocean, and so they stayed where they knew for sure how the sun would come up in the morning and set again at night. (*Appalachia: The Voices of Sleeping Birds*)

In their contemporary descriptions of coal mining's rebirth in Virginia during the 1980s, reporters James A. Baker and Douglas Pardue suggested that the American public saw the region from the lenses of the 1960s when "Appalachia became synomous with poverty, despite vast coal wealth lying beneath its mountains" (4). Rylant rhetorically describes the mountain people in a more poetic fashion, creating a vocal stance that someone from the region might use when explaining the people's link to the terrain to an outsider.

First, Cynthia Rylant acknowledges the established American social prejudices against these hill people. Then she displaces these earlier stereotypes with social and economic statements about the people who live in Appalachia. In *Appalachia: The Voices of Sleeping Birds,* Rylant is arguing against the earlier renditions of Appalachian poverty by redefining the people. She asserts, "Most of them are thinkers, because these mountains inspire that, but they could never find the words to tell you of these thoughts they have." Her goal is to help her reader understand that while the stereotypic imagery of the southern Appalachians may contain threads of truth about the lifestyles of the ordinary Appalachian families in these rural surroundings, this is not a complete picture. Her prose is direct and rhetorically defiant without being antagonistic.

Barry Moser, the Tennessee boy who attended art programs in the South and became a typographer and illustrator, uses real Appalachian people and actual photographs from the Depression as his models. The notes at the book's end tell the reader that Moser grew up in the shadow of a mountain in Tennessee, that the boy standing in front of an Appalachian grocery store is a cameo of his brother Tommy, and that both of his grandfathers owned country grocery stores in the South.

Barry Moser's water color illustrations contain vignettes of the people in the countryside, usually with their backs toward the audience. The people in the scenes selected for Moser's interpretation of Appalachia suggest a particularized and closed community that excludes the viewer from their social activities. Moser uses the icons discussed by Rylant. Dogs are depicted throughout, following the hunter home, stretching on the earth, sleeping under the porch, leading the children in work and play. Because many of Moser's depictions are not quite centered, they feel like "candid shots" of people who have not posed for a photographer, of rooms not cleaned and arranged for guests. Moser recreates the isolation and regionalism of the setting without suggesting that this world is discordant. In fact, there is a sense of unity in Rylant's text and Moser's illustrations that comes from their melding of public and private interpretations of Appalachia. According to Mark Roskill, artists link the public aspects of their imagery through structure and presentation, making the newness accessible to "'unprivileged' viewers who possess and bring to the work nothing more than a built-in receptivity" (40). The private aspects of these scenes, in turn, are ones that are accessible only through an awareness of cultural particularization and its relationship to land in Appalachia.

African American children's literature has largely depicted families living in urban and suburban settings in the South and Midwest. Authors and illustrators have also created southern visions with rural plantation settings in the Deep South, but they have rarely placed their scenes outside of the historical slavery territories. Yet, African American families resided and continue to reside on farmland in Texas and Oklahoma.

Joyce Carol Thomas and Floyd Cooper grew up in Oklahoma, one of the areas rarely found in children's picture books with African American imagery. Their picture book *Brown Honey in Broomwheat Tea* represents the human conditions, habits, and customs of an African American family living in harmony with the earth. Thomas and Cooper have graphically encoded this family's lifestyle as both rural and southwestern in their collaborative work. Furthermore, the textual and visual imagery in their book carries icons of African Americans in rural settings: The family does not interact socially with White society; they take pride in the earth's tones and count it as a part of their identity; they live as extended family of three generations who use oral signification and cultural reframing to define their heritage. The images created by Thomas and Cooper fit within nineteenth-century illustrator and art lecturer Walter Crane's early description of art: a work "so closely connected with life and thought, so bound up with human conditions, habits, and customs." Crane wrote that art in illustrated books cannot be separated from life:

> [. . .] so intimately and vividly do they reflect every phase and change of that unceasing movement—the ebb and flow of human progress amid the focus of nature we call history— that it is hardly possible even for the most careless stroller, taking any of the by-paths, not to be led insensibly to speculate on their hidden sources, and an origin perhaps common to them all. (1)

Brown Honey in Broomwheat Tea is a powerful collection of quiet poems affirming African American traditions of communal independence, color allusions, and storytelling. Thomas does not name Oklahoma, but it is situated in the text through Thomas's descriptive language. Color, the natural horizon, and the "homeplace" become the boundaries for Thomas as she enters into a cyclical description of family within a first-person narrative. Each poem is an affirmation of self and family, but within several of the poems there is a secondary message of caution. Thomas continually signifies about race relations in the Southwest in her poetry. Her use of color, space, and metaphor suggest that African Americans must be wary of Whites and they must appreciate their need for separate standards in aesthetic beauty. According to African American educator and literary scholar Carol D. Lee, this tradition defines African American cultural stories. Lee asserts, "*Signifying,* a form of discourse in the African American community, is full of irony, double entendre, satire, and metaphorical language" (612). These literary devices are found in Thomas's poetry.

Thomas begins with the simple definition, "Broomwheat tea: good for what ails you, especially when poured by loving hands." Immediately, Thomas suggests that all hands are not equally good for the narrator. She follows with the poem "Cherish Me"[7] and establishes the natural link between nature and the African American people. Within this poem, there is also an ironic plea for understanding. Thomas writes:

> I sprang up from mother earth
> > She clothed me in her own clothes
> I was nourished by father sun
> > He glazed the pottery of my skin
> I am beautiful by design
> > The patterns of night in my hair
> > The pattern of music in my rhythm
> As you would cherish a thing of beauty
> > Cherish me[8]

Carol Lee has explained that African American verbal tradition places great value on figurative language, and she argues, "African American adolescents routinely participate in signifying speech events in which they must immediately interpret accurately the double entendre and ironies of each turn of talk" (612). Thomas implies that this family's history is joined to the history of slavery. In her poem "Family Tree" Thomas creates a forest that has been violated, "stepped on, broken." She defines the earth in warm, rich tones—red clay, brown honey, broomwheat tea, gold dust—using colors to create new codes within short poems.

These colors play in Floyd Cooper's impressionistic illustrations. The narrator smiles out at her audience from the cover. She is the color of broomwheat tea, which Thomas has described as "liquid ambrosia with fire." The fall leaves around her are umber-red. The sunshine is caught in the girl's hair, and it is luminous. Furthermore, there is an implied sense of a family's stories in Thomas's text, and Cooper's illustrations visualize one family in multiple scenes, talking and sharing time in their house and on its porch, walking in the nearby fields, or visiting the family tree. And Cooper's eerie illustration of the family tree suggests ghosts from the past are still intermingled with the contemporary setting. Thus, Cooper's visual links give Thomas's poetry continuity, texture, and plot. His illustrative style supports her use of double entendre and figurative language. Together, these two artists have constructed a unified vision of an African American southwestern landscape rich with joy and laughter while forewarning of possible family despair.

In his history of American painting and sculpture Matthew Baigell talks about artists working toward self-discovery and political expression. Victor Burgin claims that art in the twentieth century became "a field of signifying practices, perhaps centered on a medium but certainly not bounded by it" (39). John Arthur's descriptions of contemporary landscape painting include observations of American artists who use artistic conventions in their painting to "communicate by reflecting the spirit of its epoch" (10). When describing the value of painting, Salim Kemal and Ivan Gaskell wrote,

> [. . .] painting is a fiction, but it is a very distinctive kind of fiction because it does not so much contrast with reality as incorporate it, structure and reconstitute it, in ways

permitted by its medium. [. . .] Painting, like literature, does not seek to provide such an exact correspondence but instead extracts and reintegrates the features of the world into its own structures. (5)

When we began this exploration, we said that several versions of American landscape found within the picture book format hold cultural, economic, and/or social ideals of topography, everyman, and civilization. They also suggest a sharing of gender power within the picture book industry. Two women have textually redefined American family landscapes for the picture book audience. The male illustrators who have brought these visions alive share their sense of geographical place and socioeconomic culture. They all have created an American landscape they know and love.

What makes any artistic work distinctively modern is the illustrators' understandings of illustration as a metapicture. Such work, according to W. J. T. Mitchell, theorizes about a larger world (82). Mitchell writes, "The collaboration of word and image engenders what Foucault calls a 'calligram,' a composite text image that 'brings a text and a shape as close together as possible'" (69). These books go beyond traditional Anglo-American landscapes, creating a "reinhabitization" of our history and our practices. They ask us to stop, recognize, and reflect on nonstereotypic representations of America.

The papers in this section are also asking us to reconsider how we recognize and "read" difference in our stories and illustrations. Barbara Lehman shows us how subjectivity can influence our reactions to our literature, and she suggests that reading about religious difference can be a complex activity. Christian Knoeller argues for diversity in our interpretations of the stories written by and about American Indians, and he identifies the importance of place in their writings. April Komenaka acknowledges that the American picture book versions of "The Crane Wife" are not always authentic to the original; yet, for her they are sometimes deeply insightful in their illustrative allusions to cultural understanding. In contrast, Margaret Chang details American misrepresentations of Chinese artifacts and culture in picture books. Taken together, these pieces suggest that we must do more than read and enjoy stories representing other cultures. We must research the art and legends depicted in picture books if we hope to choose good books to share with children. Nancy Tolson's discussion of the Black Aesthetic sets us up for further explorations of Black children's literature throughout the book. Tolson takes a strong stance about reading as the "other," a stance that we will revisit in the last section of *Exploring Culturally Diverse Literature for Children and Adolescents.* Hopefully, Tolson's writing will suggest that you will gain much if you reconsider earlier arguments while you read later pieces on similar topics found in the various sections of this book. May's discussion looks at issues of race, gender, internationalism, and intragenerational communication, which she finds reflected in two children's classics, *The Adventures of Tom Sawyer* and *The Secret Garden.* Like Tolson, May has presented ideas that can be linked to others as you read, sometimes for their strong differences in their theoretical approaches as well as for their agreement in literary interpretations.

Our first three practical pieces suggest ways to test theory: Charles Elster has researched readers' responses to the Golem legend and, thus, answers Barbara Lehman's call for careful subjective readings of difference. Olha Tsarskovska suggests ways to help new immigrants become successful readers that might help novice cultural critics begin teaching reading with less trepidation. And Trudy Nelson demonstrates that a thoughtful and concerned teacher can successfully pick good literature and encourage students to independently become compassionate American citizens who read and think about others who are living in worlds very different from their own.

Notes

1. Reprinted by permission of Christian Knoeller.

2. Cooper himself wrote, "I have never seen a nation so much alike in my life, as the people of the United States, and what is more, they are not only like each other, but they are remarkably like that which common sense tells them they ought to resemble. [. . .] In short, it is not possible to conceive a state of society in which more of the attributes of plain good sense, or fewer of the artificial absurdities of life are to be found, than here" (1828. *Notions of the Americans.* State University of New York Press, 1991).

3. Several literary scholars have pointed to Emerson's Harvard lecture, "The American Scholar," as a turning point in our understanding of an American way of writing. Ruland and Bradbury write, "Emerson's statement of the innocent vision at work in a natural world was meant as a new beginning for himself and all Americans, and that is what it eventually came to be seen" (119). Turner recalls Emerson writing in his journal about the writer's need to embrace both the beauty and awfulness of nature by living "in its forms [. . .] in order to rise" (19). Herbert Leibowitz notes that Emerson did not equate traveling out of one's community with the makings of great writing (68).

4. Lawrence Buell has addressed recent scholarship, suggesting that Thoreau's *Walden* is the writing of a frustrated gay man who overtly denied his feelings and placed them instead on the landscape. Buell remarks, "One ought to expect an extraordinary individual like Thoreau and an extraordinary book like *Walden* to comprise many strands and also to expect some of these to set both author and book at odds with 'normality'; otherwise nothing extraordinary would have been produced" (525).

5. Reprinted by permission of the publishers and the Trustees of Amherst College from *The Poems of Emily Dickinson,* Thomas H. Johnson, ed., Cambridge, Mass.: The Belknap Press of Harvard University Press, copyright © 1951, 1955, 1979 by the President and Fellows of Harvard College.

6. An interesting essay on Dickinson, written by Jane Langton, has been placed in the selection of poems illustrated by Nancy Ekholm Burkert (*Poems by Emily Dickinson.* Little, Brown and Company, 1980). Both Langton and Burkert are known for their work in children's literature. Langton's essay appears to be for adults, but the book has the appearance of one published for adolescents. Langton writes, "Poetry was her natural speech, and she took her calling as poet with intense seriousness. But over and over again she must have faced the truth that others did not" (39). Langton's conclusions complement those of other critics cited earlier. Dickinson spoke with her reader, even if she wasn't sure who that reader might ever be.

7. Neither of the picture books discussed has pagination. Therefore, our discussion does not include page numbers.

8. Copyright © 1993 by Joyce Carol Thomas. Used by permission of HarperCollins Publishers.

Works Cited

Arthur, John. *Spirit of Place: Contemporary Landscape Painting and the American Tradition.* Boston: Bulfinch Press, 1989.

Baigell, Matthew. *A Concise History of American Painting and Sculpture.* New York: Harper & Row, 1984.

Baker, James A. and Douglas Pardue. "Virginia's Coalfields: A New Day." Roanoke, VA: *Roanoke Times and World News* July 1981: 4+.

Buell, Lawrence. *The Environmental Imagination: Thoreau, Nature Writing, and the Formation of American Culture.* Cambridge: Harvard University Press, 1995.

Burgin, Victor. *The End of Art Theory: Criticism and Postmodernity.* Atlantic Highlands, NJ: Humanities Press International, Inc., 1986.

Crane, Walter. *The Decorative Illustration of Books.* 3rd ed. London: G. Bell and Sons, Ltd., 1905.

Dickinson, Emily. *Acts of Light: Poems by Emily Dickinson.* Illus. Nancy Ekholm Burkert. Boston: Little, Brown and Company, 1980.

Jauss, Hans Robert. *Toward an Aesthetic of Reception.* Trans. Timothy Bahti. Minneapolis: University of Minnesota, 1982.

Kemal, Salim and Ivan Gaskell. "Interest, Values, and Explanations." *Exploration and Value in the Arts.* Ed. Salim Kemal and Ivan Gaskell. New York: Cambridge University Press,

Langton, Jane. "An Appreciation." *Poems by Emily Dickinson.* Boston: Little, Brown, 1980. 1–43.

Lee, Carol D. "A Culturally Based Cognitive Apprenticeship: Teaching African American High School Students Skills in Literary Interpretation." *Reading Research Quarterly* 30: 4 (1995): 608–30.

Leibowitz, Herbert. *Fabricating Lives: Explorations in American Autobiography.* New York: New Directions Books, 1989.

MacLeish, Archibald. "The Private World." *Emily Dickinson: Three Views.* Amherst: Amherst College Press, 1960. 13–26.

MacLeod, Anne Scott. *American Childhood: Essays on Children's Literature of the Nineteenth and Twentieth Centuries.* Athens: The University of Georgia Press, 1994.

Mitchell, W. J. T. *Picture Theory: Essays on Verbal and Visual Representation.* Chicago: University of Chicago Press, 1994.

Olendorf, Donna and Diane Telgen, eds. "Barry Moser." *Something about the Author.* Vol. 56. Detroit, MI: Gale Research Inc., 1989.

Olendorf, Donna and Diane Telgen, eds. "Cynthia Rylant." *Something about the Author.* Vol. 44. Detroit, MI: Gale Research Inc., 1986.

Roskill, Mark W. *The Interpretation of Pictures.* Amherst: University of Massachusetts Press, 1989.

Ruland, Richard and Malcolm Bradbury. *From Puritanism to Postmodernism: A History of American Literature.* New York: Penguin Books, 1991.

Rylant, Cynthia. *Appalachia: The Voices of Sleeping Birds.* Illus. Barry Moser. San Diego: Harcourt Brace Jovanovich, Publishers, 1991.

Thomas, Joyce Carol. *Brown Honey in Broomwheat Tea.* Illus. Floyd Cooper. New York: HarperCollins, 1993.

———. *Marked by Fire.* New York: Avon, 1982.

Scholes, Robert and Robert Kellogg. *The Nature of Narrative.* New York: Oxford University Press, 1966.

Sennett, Richard. "The Rhetoric of Ethnic Identity." *The Ends of Rhetoric: History, Theory, Practice.* Ed. John Bender and David E. Wellbery. Stanford: Stanford University Press, 1990.

Thoreau, Henry David. "Walden." *American Poetry and Prose.* Ed. Norman Foerster. Boston: Houghton Mifflin Company, 1957. 553–92.

Turner, Frederick. *Spirit of Place: The Making of an American Literary Landscape.* Washington, DC: Island Press, 1989.

1

Religious Representation in Children's Literature

Disclosure through Character, Perspective, and Authority

Barbara A. Lehman

My interest in the topic of religious representation started when I read Carolyn Meyer's *Gideon's People,* a young adult historical novel about an encounter between an Orthodox Jewish boy and an Old Order Amish youth. I found myself not only strongly attracted to the story but also deeply troubled by its depiction of the Amish (about which I will elaborate more fully later). However, it's also important to admit that I am not a neutral reader in this case. My Mennonite heritage and continuing identification with the faith certainly influenced my response. Amish and Mennonites have a common origin in the sixteenth-century Anabaptist movement in Germany, Alsace, and Switzerland. The Amish, led by and subsequently named after Jacob Ammann, split from the main group in 1694 over the practice of "shunning" (*Meidung*) in excommunication. Today Old Order Amish and mainstream Mennonites have evolved differently in many practices, such as dress and avoidance of modern conveniences, but continue to share other fundamental doctrines, such as believers' baptism and nonparticipation in the military. Although without direct Amish contacts, I may be no more well qualified to evaluate the authenticity of a story about them than any other non-Amish reader, with our common theological history I feel a special sense of kinship toward them.

With this background, I started to ask questions about the author, which, in turn, led me to consider myself as the reader (hence, the context I provide in my introduction). I realized that critical issues of authenticity and arguments over insider versus outsider status run both ways between the author and the reader. In discussions of multicultural literature, considerable debate has surrounded issues of authorship. Rudine Sims Bishop and others have cogently articulated the considerations surrounding whether persons outside a culture can write authentically about that culture. These concerns are no less critical for children's literature depicting diverse religions.

Authors who write outside their own religion have a special obligation not only to verify the accuracy of facts underpinning realistic fiction but also to create authentically the more subtle nuances or impressions of the religion being depicted. Thus, both the author's knowledge about and her relationship to the religion are important considerations. While writer Kathryn Lasky abhors the "literary version of ethnic cleansing" (4)—authors only writing about their own culture—she agrees that "great stories are told from the inside out" (5). This is exactly what writers outside a religion must capture: the insider's voice. For ethnicities or religious groups that do not or cannot write about themselves, it is the only alternative. For example, as Elizabeth Jared explains, Old Order Amish do not write about themselves, and literature about the Amish "is for children and adults who are not members of this culture.[. . .] Thus, there are few 'insider' perspectives or purposes for these books within the culture itself" (233–234).

Indeed, Amish discouragement of such literature may be related to Amish objections to photographs or faces on dolls (see John A. Hostetler), which is based on biblical prohibition of graven images, at least in part, as representations of rather than reality itself. Likewise, *written* representations are viewed as a kind of idolatry, or at least worldly.

On the other hand, readers also are obligated to read critically. Perry Nodelman terms this "reading against a text" (120), or questioning the values a text implies, whereas Daniel Hade calls it "reading multiculturally" (251), which he stresses is a *reading* (rather than writing) issue. As readers, we need to question the author's (and our own) assumptions. Where are biases (including our own) and stereotypes? How much information about the religion is shared by the author and why? What images are shown? How do these enhance the story? How do they affect the reader's view of the religion? Where are the "silences" or gaps in the narrative? What do these imply? What is the author's (and our) relationship to the religion being depicted?

Essentially, what Jon Stott has termed "otherness" and "ourness" can be examined from both sides of the transaction: the author's and the reader's. I believe it is useful to probe who is the "our" and who is the "other" in children's literature as revealed through the aspects of character, perspective, and authority. How does the author develop the characters, and how does the reader identify with them? What are the characters' perspectives about other characters and religions? How do those influence or compare with the reader's perspectives? What knowledge and relationship—or authority—do the author and reader bring to the religion?

In this essay, I explore these dimensions across three novels that represent religion: *Gideon's People* by Carolyn Meyer, *Habibi* by Naomi Shihab Nye, and *The Storyteller's Beads* by Jane Kurtz. Each book uniquely juxtaposes two contrasting religions through the relationships developed between young characters, which highlight, to paraphrase Stott, that one person's "otherness" is someone else's "ourness." In discussing each book, I analyze how the author portrays the characters, their perspectives about each other and their respective religions, and information about the religious cultures. I also offer my critical reading of each consideration, beginning with *Gideon's People.*

Carolyn Meyer's novel, set in early twentieth century Lancaster County, Pennsylvania, depicts the relationship between a twelve-year-old Orthodox Jewish boy and a sixteen-year-old Old Order Amish youth. When a Jewish peddler's horse causes an accident that injures the peddler's son Isaac, the boy is left to heal with the Amish family on whose farm the accident happens. During several weeks of recovery, Isaac comes to know Gideon, the Amish teenager, and his sister Annie, who is Isaac's age. Gradually, Isaac learns that Gideon's relationship with his father ("Datt") is contentious and that Gideon chafes so much under the strict Amish *Ordnung* (rules) that he is plotting to run away to live with his more liberal Amish uncle in central Pennsylvania. Meanwhile, Isaac copes with his own homesickness, the strange Amish language, and their *treyf* (unkosher) food. When Gideon finally returns a recovered Isaac to Isaac's family in Lancaster city, the roles are reversed, and Gideon briefly experiences Isaac's religion and culture.

Meyer, the author of many fiction and nonfiction books for children and young adults, was born in Lewistown, Pennsylvania (close to the area where Gideon's uncle lives), a region with a sizable Amish population. Meyer's heritage is German American, as are the Amish, although she identifies her religion as Episcopalian in *Something about the Author* (Olendorf and Telgen). One of her nonfiction works is *Amish People: Plain Living in a Complex World,* published in 1977, which she researched by reading (especially books by noted scholar of Amish life, John A. Hostetler), spending time in Lancaster County, visiting Amish families, and asking questions. She frames information in *Amish People* around a "fictitious but typical character" (9) named Samuel Beiler, who is closely reflected in Gideon's character, although with a different resolution to their common dilemmas.

The two main characters in *Gideon's People,* Gideon and Isaac, both carry Biblical names, a reflection of religion's importance in their lives, but Gideon, the older youth, is portrayed as anomalous in his culture. He is curious and loves to learn. Unlike his brothers, Gideon wishes school lasted all year; he asks about remote places like Russia and New York and about the Jewish religion; and the adventure of pirates and buried treasure makes Robert Louis Stevenson's *Treasure Island* one of his prize (though forbidden) possessions. He feels suffocated by strict Amish church rules and wants "to find out certain things about himself" (233). Because he asks too many questions and thinks too much, his father calls him *Dopplig* (or "dreamy"), and he is "the only son who had not inherited Datt's flame-red hair" (33).

Despite his differences, Gideon also is depicted as helpful, responsible, and honorable. He makes a crutch for Isaac and arranges for him to deliver the tools Gideon promised to buy for Datt, rather than using the money to buy a train ticket. He make no promises to Annie that he may not be able to keep about returning, but he writes both to Annie and his parents to let them know he arrived safely at his uncle's.

Isaac, at twelve-going-on-thirteen, is at a younger developmental stage, more egocentric, and less complex emotionally. His primary concern is with wanting to be treated as grown-up, responsible, and independent by his parents. Thrilled to accompany his father for the first time on his peddler's rounds, he is annoyed by his mother's parting warning that Jakob should watch what Isaac eats because Isaac doesn't "know *treyf* [unclean food]" (54). He wishes he could reassure his parents that he kept the Sabbath rules and eating *kosher* while he recuperated at the Amish farm. He dreams of the day he will take over his father's business, and when he returns home, he proudly displays his new responsibility for the horse and wagon. Thus, Isaac and Gideon respond very differently to their religious strictures, perhaps mostly due to their developmental stages.

As a critical reader, I find myself asking questions about the author's portrayal of character in these contrasting religious cultures. First, who is more developed? I believe that Gideon's character receives more attention and development in this narrative. He is conflicted about his decision, which requires considerable treatment to convey why he would want to take the drastic step of leaving his family yet feel ambivalent about doing so. He also seems to be the most multidimensional character in the book, the one who contends with the most complex set of issues. Isaac's needs and desires are much simpler to grasp, the resolution of which is his happy return to a safe, loving home environment.

Thus, when I ask with whom I more strongly identify, I respond easily that it's Gideon, although this identification perhaps also attributes to my stronger identification with Gideon's background or to the age of Gideon's character being more interesting to me as an adult than is Isaac's stage of development. The title, *Gideon's People,* appears to focus appropriately on Gideon's character as being more dominant. It really is his story, and Isaac's parallel narrative highlights Gideon's by providing contrast, rather than being central.

At the same time, I have trouble reconciling the two father figures who sharply differ in their characterization and relationship with their sons. The elder Stoltzfus is stern and silent except for his sharp, violent temper, and I never see any positive interaction between him and Gideon. Ezra belittles Gideon and dismisses his competence, even directing his other son to double-check the job he assigned to Gideon of assessing damage to the peddler's wagon. He uses physical punishment liberally in addition to verbal chastisement on a son old enough to be his peer in size. Thus, Ezra's character—and the father–son relationship—seems negative and one-dimensional to me. Isaac's father, Jakob, in contrast, is excitable, talkative, and demonstrative of his love and acceptance for Isaac. He worries about Isaac's injury and rejoices at his safe return home. He exuberantly hugs his son, tells him repeatedly how concerned he was, and even kisses Gideon, whom he has just met, on both cheeks. He also demonstrates faith in his son's competence by taking him along as assistant on his peddler's rounds. The two parents could not be more different, and I, as reader, felt as repulsed by Gideon's father as I was attracted to Isaac's father. There is no doubt in which family I would want to belong, which by extension negatively influences my perception of the Amish religion and the possibility of Gideon's (or for that matter anyone's) being happy in it. This perception disturbs my prior conception (stereotype?) of Amish culture and my closer identification and engagement with Gideon's character.

The narrative's overall point of view is third person, but chapters alternately provide Isaac's and Gideon's or Annie's perspectives and offer clues regarding the author's perspective. In roughly equal measure, the Jewish and Amish viewpoints, represented by the characters' thoughts toward each other, note similar peculiarities: the "Dutch" and Yiddish languages that sound both similar and "mixed-up" (10) to the other person; the oddness of each other's appearances (which ironically may strike outsiders as similar); the unfamiliar foods of each culture; and the different rules that each religion must follow. Here, as noted earlier, each perspective reaches a different conclusion. Gideon wonders if Isaac doesn't "get fed up with the rules and want to leave it all" (160) as he does, and Isaac, while admitting that he does sometimes tire of rules, ultimately sees them as important and valued symbols of his religion.

In addition to their parallel impressions, Isaac focuses considerably on the Amish silence at mealtimes and contrasts it with his family's lively discussions. This typical silence becomes extended in his mind to the less usual practice of shunning, in which the family and entire Amish community literally do not speak to an Amish person who breaks the rules. Isaac finds such treatment (which will be Gideon's fate) appalling. Isaac also equates the normal Amish silence as a sign of Gideon's unhealthy relationship with Datt and contrasts his own father's joyful expression with the "dour Ezra Stoltzfus" (225). Isaac's view—and the book's dominant perspective—is summed up by his thought, "*. . . in our family, everything is fine.* It was Gideon's people that troubled him" (italics in original 228). Ironically (because I find Gideon's character to be more developed, as discussed earlier), such wording makes Isaac seem the "our" in this story, while Gideon is the "other."

Although Meyer appears to have gotten many things right in her depiction of the Amish religion and culture (as will be discussed later), I believe that her portrayal of their use of silence is very much that of an outsider. Unlike the negative connotation that she gives it in this story, according to John A. Hostetler, silence is a positive force "used not in opposition to others, but with others" (389). Words, which cannot be taken back once spoken, can do harm, whereas "silence can aid in the restoration of good human relationships" (388) and show forgiveness. The Amish value harmony and avoid conflict, and silence contributes to these ends. Even shunning, the most extreme use of silence, is viewed by the Amish as the pacifist's response to disobedience, rather than using verbal or physical confrontation. The perspective offered through Isaac on Amish silence, although certainly one legitimate view, is entirely negative and is not balanced by any of the positive qualities of Hostetler's interpretation. Yet Meyer skillfully interweaves information about the Old Order Amish and Orthodox Jewish religions to support her narrative. Because these are both cultures with which typical readers may be unfamiliar, she provides considerable background material to enhance our understanding. Several areas are particularly noteworthy: Amish and Jewish rules or laws, views toward outsiders, religious practices, and temperament.

Both religions are known for their well-defined, strict rules or laws. For Old Order Amish, the rules of the church (*Ordnung*) govern everything from clothing style and color, hair length, and the use of modern conveniences, such as telephones, electricity, or automobiles, to behavior after baptism. Likewise, Orthodox Jewish laws govern dress and hairstyle (such as the earlocks, or *payess*), but especially food. Not only is pork forbidden as unclean, but so are any pork products such as lard (used widely in Amish cooking), mixing milk and meat together, and butchering meat without kosher rituals. These Jewish laws puzzle the Amish, who have no comparable rules regarding food.

In essence, rules and laws are the means for both religions to separate themselves from outsiders. For Amish, separation from "worldly" practices and lifestyles is commanded in the Bible. Meyer explains: "Be ye not unequally yoked together with unbelievers" (23) and "Be ye not conformed to this world" (126). For Jewish believers, their laws distinguish between observant Jews and Gentiles. Both groups share a history of persecution for their beliefs, which resulted in their emigration to America from Europe and Russia; both groups rebuilt their ways of life in a new land surrounded by a secular culture.

Amish religion, in addition to rules about appearance, is highlighted primarily through three practices: their strict observance of the Sabbath, baptism as the rite of passage for young persons to join the church and promise to obey the *Ordnung,* and shunning (*Meidung*) in which a disobedient church member is excluded from all social contact with other members (including family or spouse). A greater range of Orthodox Jewish religious practices is mentioned, in addition to the intricacies of food laws and a more detailed discussion of the Sabbath observance: recitation of prayers for the dead, the *pushke* (cup for charity), daily prayer rituals, the *mezuzah* (sacred scroll attached to a home's doorjamb), Passover preparations, and ritual circumcision. Comparable to Amish baptism practice, the Jewish bar mitzvah at age thirteen is a rite of passage to adulthood.

Finally, there are stark comparisons in temperament between the Amish and Jewish cultures as dramatized by the personalities of Ezra and Jakob, the two fathers. The Amish are depicted as sober, even stern, quick to anger and to use "smackings" as punishment for children's misbehavior, and obedient (or concealing disobedience) toward authority. They not only use silence as a deliberate practice through shunning but also as a way of dealing with much everyday socialization: They never discuss courtship until it is formally announced, meals are generally silent except to discuss the day's work, and they even discourage questions and intellectual discourse. Isaac cannot imagine the harshness of the beatings that Gideon endures, whereas Isaac's family (and culture) is characterized by curiosity and eagerness to learn, open-armed welcome and acceptance for strangers, enthusiastic praise for accomplishments, and demonstrative affection.

My critical reading of this information stems first from the question, how accurately and fully is each religion depicted? Meyer appears to be thorough and knowledgeable in her research about these religions, for both of which she is an outsider. At least, she includes much information quite naturally throughout the narrative and in a manner that should be understandable to young readers. For example, she includes this amusing detail about an Amishman's name: "Daniel Miller [. . .], known as Salty Dan, because he had once put salt instead of sugar into his coffee at a barn raising [. . .]" (184). Note its similarity to Hostetler's anecdote: "Gravy Dan stuck with one Amishman when he poured gravy instead of cream into his coffee at a threshing dinner table" (246). My concerns in this area center on what aspects of the religious cultures are emphasized and what is omitted and, because of my own relationship and knowledge, focus on the author's depiction of the Amish.

First, the tone I detect toward rules and laws in either religion differs. Gideon dwells on the restrictiveness and arbitrariness of his religion's rules, and although he can recite the scriptural basis for some when questioned by Isaac, he clearly questions much of the *Ordnung* and its value. His conclusion is that it doesn't make sense for him, and therefore, he must leave his community. Isaac, on the other hand, grasps the value and reasonableness of his religious laws. Although he feels like they may hurt his assimilation into American culture, he reaches a different choice about whether to abide by the rules. He even observes the laws when there is no one to watch whether he does so, while there are several instances of Amish covertly disobeying their rules, which are presented as positive examples of resistance to authority. In contrast, Isaac's friend Abie is viewed disapprovingly when he breaks kosher laws and cuts his *payess.*

Second, the completely negative portrayal of shunning troubles me. Repeatedly, the *Meidung* is depicted as a permanent state that even extends into eternity from which there is no reunion unless the banned member repents and asks forgiveness. The only options are to leave the community or live with the consequences. John Hostetler, however, explains that a member who confesses his sin is forgiven unconditionally, he is fully restored in the church, and the transgression is never spoken of again—a positive use of the Amish way of silence. The problem for me is not that shunning is controversial but that this book makes no attempt to show its redeeming value. Thus, although I appreciate the generally high quality of research that went into this novel, in several respects, it seems unfair in its depiction of the Old Order Amish.

Turning to the other two novels, I provide similar analyses of the authors' portrayals and my critical reading. Lacking the same level of authority (i.e., knowledge and relationship) with the religions depicted in these books that I may have about the Amish, my discussion is less detailed but extends my overall thesis.

In *Habibi,* fourteen-year-old Liyana lives in present-day St. Louis, Missouri, with her brother, Palestinian father, and American mother. Naomi Shihab Nye shows how Liyana's life is uprooted when her father suddenly decides to move the family to Jerusalem in closer proximity to his family roots. There Liyana slowly adjusts to life in an unfamiliar land with her large extended Palestinian family, attending a trilingual Armenian school, and facing a bewildering, often violent, political scene. She also falls for a boy, Omer, who she first assumes is Arab but later discovers is Jewish. Their developing relationship provides each teenager with positive glimpses of a different culture and religion that are often viewed as enemies.

This novel draws autobiographically on Nye's own life, with her Palestinian father, American mother, and the family's experiences of moving from St. Louis to Jerusalem, where they lived for several years while Nye was in high school. Like Liyana's family, described as "spiritual" and not traditionally religious, Nye cites her religion as "Independent" in *Something about the Author.* A poet and anthologist, Nye views her writing as portraying "the idea of connections. 'I see that as one of the primary themes to all my work'" (qtd. in Hile 171).

Nye's treatment of character, characters' perspectives, and religious cultural information in *Habibi* particularly interests me. Liyana, the novel's protagonist, has two overriding preoccupations: a teenager's interest in the opposite sex and longing for friends and life in St. Louis. The story's opening sentence sets the stage for both traits: "Liyana Abboud had just tasted her first kiss when her parents announced they were leaving the country" (1). How she comes to view her situation in a positive light is a main theme of the novel. Her talents for closely observing and writing about events and people play a major role in her adjustment. Omer, the Israeli youth, is portrayed as sensitive, thoughtful, open to new ideas, and interested in art and literature. However, he is much less well rounded, and much of the character description focuses on his physical attributes—"He smelled like cinnamon" (123); "the straight line of his jaw" (147); his rich voice—and his sense of humor (which closely matches Liyana's).

These two friends share the same desire for peace between Israelis and Palestinians. However, they have different perspectives on the Jewish concept of being a "chosen" people: Omer struggles to explain the Jewish belief in being chosen as "a historical way of—looking at ourselves—and things" (170). But Liyana flatly rejects that stating, "I think as long as anybody feels *chosen,* the problems will get worse" (171). Liyana also identifies with Palestinian suffering and challenges Omer that past Jewish suffering should make Jews more sensitive to the suffering of others, to which he agrees. She notices language like "occupied territories" for Palestinian lands and searches for a postcard labeled with "Palestine" instead of "Israel." Omer, for his part, has no other friends who live on the Ramallah road, and he realizes during his first visit to the West Bank that "these lands don't seem abandoned" (239) and are more beautiful than he imagined.

The information about the contrasting religious cultures is much more extensive for Palestinians than for Israelis. For example, the author shows readers that not all Palestinians are Muslim; although Poppy's extended family is, Liyana's immediate family subscribes to no one religion. As Poppy says, "The worst foolish thing is when a religion wants you to say it's the only right one. Or the best one" (169). At the same time, Muslim rituals practiced in Sitti's village and their cultural restrictions on what women wear or how young men and women meet and court are presented through Liyana's eyes as she tries to adjust to her new environment. Little information about the Jewish religion appears because Omer is not an observant Jew.

The way that Palestinians and Israelis are depicted on a secular level offers a sharp contrast. Palestinians are the victims of discrimination, and Israelis clearly are the oppressors. Palestinians are harassed in many facets of their lives: being held up going through customs, being stopped and searched at Israeli checkpoints, having the family home ravaged by soldiers looking for Liyana's cousin, and describing how Khaled, one of their friends who lives in a nearby refugee camp, is shot and Poppy is arrested by soldiers looking for the person who bombed a market. Other than Omer, there are no Jewish characters in the novel except for the Israeli military, and they intimidate and brutalize innocent Palestinians. Numerous Palestinians express their desire for peace throughout the story, but Omer is the only Israeli who does.

What does my critical reading suggest about the author's representation of two cultures in relation to the reader who is living outside both? Because Liyana's character and perspective are more fully developed and defined in this narrative, I feel stronger identification with her and her point of view on issues. In my mind, the narrative is clearly hers, and she is the "our," while Omer is the "other," albeit sympathetic, character. This is reinforced by the positive portrayal of Palestinians and their plight and overwhelmingly negative portrayal of Israelis, which (except for Omer) are reduced to the military. Thus, my instinct to sympathize with the underdog further supports my identification with their (and Liyana's) story. Neither the Muslim nor Jewish religion receives much treatment on which to base a judgment of how accurately each is depicted. However, this lack of information and the represented characters' views regarding religion in general suggest that the author believes that traditional religion holds more harmful than reconciling potential for peaceful human coexistence, while nonreligious persons are more able to forge positive cross-cultural relationships.

I now turn to the final book. Set in Ethiopia in the 1980s, Jane Kurtz's *The Story-teller's Beads* portrays two girls' escape to the Sudan from oppression in their war-torn country. Sahay, of the Kemant religion, and Rahel, a blind Beta-Israel girl (or Ethiopian Jew), meet on the journey and initially avoid each other. In fact, the Kemant people, while persecuted by the dominant Amharic ethnic group, also despise and fear the Falasha, as they refer to the Beta-Israel, who, in turn, are persecuted by and wary of all other ethnic groups and religions. However, when each girl loses her only other family member near the journey's end, they are thrown together to survive and eventually grow to care deeply for each other after they arrive at the refugee camp. When the opportunity arises for Rahel to join the Israeli rescue of Ethiopian Jews, she includes Sahay as her "sister." Thus, the Biblical story of Nahomey and Hirute (Naomi and Ruth) provides a strong parallel motif for the girls' experiences.

Jane Kurtz, also the reteller of several Ethiopian folktales, does not identify her own religion, but she does reveal in *Something about the Author* that, from the age of two, she lived for many years with her Presbyterian missionary parents in Ethiopia. She states that her identification with her adopted land was so strong that "Ethiopia was home and I generally felt like a stranger among my peers in the United States" (qtd. in Hedblad 119) when she returned there for visits.

How might the author's background influence her portrayal of character, characters' perspectives, and religious cultural information in this novel? Sahay and Rahel share some character similarities. They are both determined and even stubborn in their efforts to survive and attain their goals of freedom. At the same time, they both fear the dangers of their journey and show tremendous courage through adversity. They are ambivalent about leaving their homes and long for loved ones lost or left behind. Their relationship gradually develops into one of mutual admiration and caring for each other.

However, there are significant differences between the two characters' portrayals. Although both girls fear the unknown, Sahay seems more frightened, and many of her fears are based on superstitions, such as the evil eye of strangers or believing that a hyena could be a Falasha in disguise. Rahel, on the other hand, is not only determined but also assertive and decisive—leaving no doubt that she is the leader of the two girls. In addition, she is imaginative and inquisitive, a skilled storyteller and musician. Her stories and flute songs provide strength and comfort when the girls' future seems most bleak.

In terms of the characters' perspectives, Sahay's views regarding Rahel and her religion are specific and detailed. She refers to Rahel as *Falasha,* or alien stranger; she fears that she will be polluted by traveling with Falasha; and she thinks that the Falasha practice witchcraft. Rahel, in contrast, offers little perspective toward Sahay and her religion, other than to find her annoying and to recognize that Sahay dislikes her. Rahel has a strong sense of identity as Beta-Israel, and she insists that Sahay show respect by using that term rather than Falasha.

The author presents information about the religions through the narrative and in a historical note at the end. Both the Kemant and Beta-Israel are persecuted by dominant ethnic groups, such as the Amhara, and are from the same Agau ethnic group with the same historical roots in Ethiopia. The Beta-Israel practice Judaism, whereas the Kemant "have their own unique blend of beliefs drawn from Christianity, Judaism, and spirit worship"

(147). Both religions observe the same Sabbath and other feast days, and believers pray facing Jerusalem. Both groups sew the same star of David on their clothes, and both keep to their separate communities away from the Amhara and from each other.

Beyond these similarities, however, and a description of one religious ritual in a sacred grove, little information is offered about the Kemant. Sahay and Rahel discover some common religious stories, but many more Beta-Israel stories and sayings are interwoven throughout the narrative's motif of the storyteller's beads. These are the parting gift from Rahel's grandmother, which symbolize stories that will help Rahel remain connected to her family and religion. The Beta-Israel also hold the Jewish view of themselves as "God's chosen people" (34) and place great importance on their eventual return to Jerusalem, or *aliyah,* as a sacred promise that will be fulfilled.

From my critical reading, although both Sahay and Rahel are equally well-developed characters, not only is Rahel the leader of the two, but she also is the more admirable and strong. Therefore, the story seems to be primarily hers, and she ultimately holds more power in this relationship even though her religion is more despised. Just as Isaac's perspective in *Gideon's People* contained more observations about Amish religion and practices, Sahay's viewpoint offers more insights about Rahel and her religion than the reverse. However, instead of contributing to my sense that Sahay is the "our" in this story and Rahel is the "other" (as I experienced regarding Isaac and Gideon), I felt the opposite. In addition, the greater depth of knowledge offered about the Beta-Israel religion added to my overall sense of identification with it. In reality, I have no ties to either religion, although possibly the familiarity of the Biblical stories recounted by Rahel resonate more with my Judeo-Christian subconscious, whereas the Christian aspects of the Kemant religion were largely undeveloped. Thus, the author's emphasis on the similarities between the Kemant and Beta-Israel beliefs and a brief glimpse of Kemant spirit worship provide little information (or perhaps I overlooked embedded information) from which I might gain understanding and insights about the Kemant religion in its own right. My view of Beta-Israel as "our" religion in this narrative also seems underscored by the title, which signifies this religion's stories.

I selected these three novels representing contrasting religions because they offer potential for exploring how authors disclose religious cultures through portrayal of character, characters' perspectives, and authority (information based on knowledge and relationship). I now return to the idea that author and reader bear a dual responsibility to be sensitive to religious representations in children's literature, as required by all multicultural literature. Authors are obligated to "get it right" when portraying religion and, even if they are not part of the religion, to try to capture the insider's voice. However, authors also need freedom to make artistic choices in their writing craft. This freedom, in turn, bestows an obligation on readers to read critically. Hade states, "It is a matter of *reading* the book [the author] did write" (246). A resisting reader will develop a dialectic with the text, asking questions about what the author has written or omitted and why, examining power relationships among characters and what their perspectives reveal, and weighing the author's against the reader's (or other) authority. Moreover (especially if we are outsiders to a religious culture ourselves), we need to read and compare multiple texts (including nonfiction) about the same religion to gain a sense of accuracy and authenticity. We should avoid depending on a single book to tell us the whole story about the religion, because that only gives us one author's version. For example, if we grant Carolyn Meyer the artistic freedom to present one image of Old Order Amish in the story she wants to tell, we cannot allow her representation to be the only one we receive about that religious culture.

Thus, critical reading is literary criticism within sociocultural contexts. Active (critical) readers, Jill May notes, "must learn to read in new ways" (83), as described previously. According to Anna Soter, this means that teachers "are faced with new critical challenges if we intend to use literature representative of different cultures [or religions] in our classrooms" (215). Simply, we must teach our students (from elementary to graduate levels) to read critically. One of the best ways we can do this is by modeling our own critical reading of the books we read and discuss with students, which is what I have tried to do in this essay.

My final comment relates to this last point. My critical reading of these three novels should be just a beginning, for it is only one, undoubtedly flawed and certainly not definitive, view. As a community of readers, we can all broaden our perspectives by reading widely, talking with other readers about their insights, challenging our own biases, assumptions, and misconceptions, and offering each other our authority on the religious cultures being represented.

Works Cited

Bishop, Rudine Sims. "Selecting Literature for a Multicultural Curriculum." *Using Multiethnic Literature in the K–8 Classroom.* Ed. Violet J. Harris. Norwood, MA: Christopher-Gordon Publishers, 1997. 1–19.

Hade, Daniel D. "Reading Multiculturally." *Using Multiethnic Literature in the K–8 Classroom.* Ed. Violet J. Harris. Norwood, MA: Christopher-Gordon Publishers, 1997. 233–256.

Hedblad, A., ed. *Something about the Author.* Vol. 91. Detroit: Gale Research, 1997.

Hile, K. S., ed. *Something about the Author.* Vol. 86. Detroit: Gale Research, 1996.

Hostetler, John A. *Amish Society.* 4th ed. Baltimore: Johns Hopkins University Press, 1993.

Jared, Elizabeth J. "Amish Literature for Children." *The New Advocate* 12:3 (Summer 1999): 233–240.

Kurtz, Jane. *The Storyteller's Beads.* San Diego, CA: Harcourt Brace, 1998.

Lasky, Kathryn. "To Stingo with Love: An Author's Perspective on Writing Outside One's Culture." *The New Advocate* 9:1 (Winter 1996): 1–7.

May, Jill P. *Children's Literature and Critical Theory.* New York: Oxford University Press, 1995.

Meyer, Carolyn. *Amish People: Plain Living in a Complex World.* New York: Atheneum, 1977.

———. *Gideon's People.* San Diego, CA: Harcourt Brace, 1996.

Nodelman, Perry. *The Pleasures of Children's Literature.* 2nd ed. White Plains, NY: Longman Publishers, 1996.

Nye, Naomi Shihab. *Habibi.* New York: Simon & Schuster, 1997.

Olendorf, Donna and Diane Telgen, eds. *Something about the Author.* Vol. 70. Detroit, MI: Gale Research Inc, 1993.

Soter, Anna O. "Reading Literature of Other Cultures: Some Issues in Critical Interpretation." *Reading Across Cultures: Teaching Literature in a Diverse Society.* Ed. Theresa Rogers and Anna O. Soter. New York: Teachers College Press, 1997. 213–229.

Stott, Jon C. "Otherness and Ourness: A Multicultural Approach to Children's Literature." *The CLA Bulletin* 17:3 (Fall 1991): 2–9.

Telgen, D., ed. *Something about the Author.* Vol. 70. Detroit: Gale Research, 1993.

2

"Not One Voice, but Many"

Reading Contemporary Native American Writers

Christian Knoeller

> Lately I write, trying to combine sound and memory,
> searching for that significance once heard and nearly lost.
> It was within the tall pines, speaking.
> There was one voice under the wind.[1]
>
> —Paula Gunn Allen

> As I write, I create myself again and again. Re-Create. And
> breathe. And I see that I am not one voice, but many. [. . .]
> I feel strongly that I have a responsibility to all the sources that
> I am: to all past and future ancestors, to my home country, to all
> places that I touch down on and that are myself, to all voices.
>
> —Joy Harjo

The writing of contemporary Native American authors is both abundant and diverse, encompassing a number of genres and reflecting a variety of tribal cultures. To date, this rich literature has been largely neglected in the schools. Instead, stereotypes about Native Americans still prevail. Yet there are many interesting and compelling works by contemporary Native American writers well worth considering for classroom use, works that address poignant and timely themes such as intercultural interaction and social identity. This chapter will survey a range of such writing, including young adult novels. First, I consider how contemporary Native American writing can contribute to an expanded canon of American literature—as well as its relation to tribal traditions of oral storytelling. I discuss several recurrent themes that seem central to this work, especially place, language, memory, and change. I also address issues of historical misrepresentation and outright stereotypes. In addition, I examine one young adult novel in detail to explore approaches for introducing such texts to students. The focus throughout remains on writing by Native Americans themselves, rather than books about them by others. How might the voices of Native American authors enrich the curriculum, and how do such additions fit or conflict with previous definitions of "American" literature?

While writing this chapter, I visited the impressive Museum of Art in Birmingham, Alabama. At the heart of its American collection is a huge landscape of Yosemite painted in 1865 by Albert Bierstadt, whose work famously romanticized the pristine and typically unpeopled grandeur of the American West. This magnificent canvas is flanked on either side by a pair of early twentieth-century bronzes depicting conventional Indian images: an "End of the Trail" brave on horseback and a "noble savage" bust of an Indian chief. Richard Hill Sr., an art critic of Tuscarora descent, describes such stereotypical icons as "noble in appearance and melancholy in attitude. In this manifestation of the vanishing Indian stereotype, Native Americans face an uncertain future as white civilization advances westward" (145). Although the museum separately exhibits an extensive collection of pre-Columbian and later Native American artifacts, tellingly it is the stereotypic sculpture of white artists that has been canonized to represent the "Indian" in "American art." A literature curriculum missing Native American voices runs a similar risk of silencing and misrepresenting cultural traditions.

Introducing the writing of contemporary Native Americans to young adult readers in a classroom setting places it in relation to existing curricula and thereby of traditionally taught literary works—a defacto "canon" that has proven remarkably resilient and static (Applebee). Although admittedly the literary canon has expanded "exponentially" over the last several decades (Hamill 33), many voices are still too often neglected in the classroom (e.g., Gunn Allen *Studies*). Laguna Pueblo poet, novelist, and critic Paula Gunn Allen acknowledges that with the rapid expansion of literary canons, "a teacher of American Literature is hard put to know where to begin [. . .] so many voices telling one huge, complex, multitudinous story," yet ultimately she exhorts us to "open ourselves to multiplicity" (*Off* 145–46, 162).

Some literary historians have viewed canonicity in terms of Bakhtinian theory, particularly *polyphony,* the presence of multiple voices. In *The Voice in the Margin: Native American Literature and the Canon,* critic Arnold Krupat argues that critical recognition constitutes a pluralistic impulse, a contemporary emphasis on diversity. According to Krupat, recognizing the "legitimate claims of otherness and difference" involves embracing not only a diversity of works but also the dialog and "plurality of voices" present in individual texts ("Dialogic" 65). Achieving such critical reception requires Native American writers to "confront the notion of voice brought to the text by the reader, to carve out a space within the Anglocized discourse for a different voice, an Indian voice" (Carr 199). Moreover, as Muscogee poet Joy Harjo reminds us, every contemporary Native American writer is likely to possess "not one voice, but many," and to accept a personal "responsibility [. . .] to all voices" ("Bio-Poetics" 9). Such fidelities run deeper than prevailing literary tastes.

Indeed, Native American works clearly contribute to the polyphonic quality of an evolving canon. The last several decades have witnessed a veritable renaissance among writers in the Native community. It is worth considering its growing reputation during the last fifty years. Interestingly, a single work and the prominent honors it garnered proved a seminal event, inspiring other Native Americans to write. Momaday's Pulitzer Prize–winning *House Made of Dawn* signaled the beginning of broad critical acceptance of such writing. Momaday's contribution is indeed monumental, as Krupat observes: "Momaday has become almost an iconic figure for those interested in Native American literature" (*Voice* 13). Literary theorist Catherine Rainwater actually dates the advent of contemporary Native American writing from that book: "Since 1968, the publication date of N. Scott Momaday's *House Made of Dawn,* a new generation of Native American storytellers has chosen writing over the oral storytelling tradition" (xii). Momaday himself describes the impact of *House:* "the publishing world found it had an audience it was not aware of" (Isernhagen 35). Without a doubt, Momaday's first novel heralded a turning point. The abundance of Native American writing available today is a result.

The achievement of that novel, moreover, coupled with its critical success, inspired others to write. Gunn Allen is just one of the present generation of Native American authors who credits Momaday for making the "space" for others to write: "I wouldn't be writing now if Momaday hadn't done [*House Made of Dawn* . . .] it brought *my land* back to me" (qtd. in Bruchac *Survival* 11). Subsequently, small presses, such as Greenfield Review Press and the Blue Cloud Quarterly, as well as such venerable institutions as the University of New Mexico Press, the University of Arizona Press, the University of California at Los Angeles Native American Studies Program, and the Institute of American Indian Arts in Santa Fe have championed a whole generation of new writers. Such programs are only one especially visible sign of a widespread grassroots movement that has called attention to emerging writers, some of whom have since gone on to gain considerable recognition nationally. As Acoma Pueblo poet, essayist, and editor Simon Ortiz has observed, "Since the 1960s, contemporary Native written expression has gained a wide and large audience. It has received serious critical attention [. . .] and has earned considerable recognition, but it still needs to be heard in every corner of the Americas" (*Speaking* xii). Yet other literary historians suggest that although high-profile, national prizes have helped deliver major works by Native Americans to a mass market, too often commercial publishers and general readership are even today still influenced by stereotypical media depictions (Coltelli 6). As editors Jill May and Darwin Henderson contend, "Perhaps Native American writers are not plentiful in the catalogs of the mainstream houses publishing children's and adolescent literature because they write stories that fit their [own] historical understandings," rather than conforming to popular stereotypes (personal communication). Yet having published initially beyond the reach of commercial publishing houses—and marketing forces governing mainstream publication and literary politics—arguably has contributed to both the authenticity and diversity of voices.

One way to evaluate the place of Native American writing in relation to the traditional canon is to examine connections between the two. After all, interpreting Native American writing involves situating it in relation to American literature more generally, a question of *literary* history. Native American poetics—connected with translation and publication of traditional cultural materials such as songs and chants collected by anthropologists and linguists—has long had a presence as part of a national literature broadly defined. Contemporary anthologists such as Jerome Rothenberg have also sought to popularize such traditional oral literatures for a general readership, following better than a century of attempts at translation (1972; see Krupat *Voice* for a detailed history). Collections, such as those assembled by John Bierhorst (e.g., *In the Trail of the Wind, The Red Swan,* and *Four Masterworks of American Indian Literature*), although widely read, raise serious questions—acknowledged by the editor—about the translation of oral traditions, and how such "texts" are to be rendered on the page in English (May 78). Influential anthropological linguists such as Dell Hymes (1981) have called for retranslation of the vast corpus of such ethnographic texts to more accurately reflect both the substance and form of the originals. Similarly, folklorists Larry Evers and Barre Toelken exhort those "engaged in the study of Native American oral traditions to continue opening up the mutually responsive, mutually responsible dialogues that will bring forth hundreds of other tribal literatures and languages of America" (12). After all, even early Indian "autobiographies" have been viewed by critics such as Krupat as "bicultural composite authorship" (qtd. in Wiget *Native* 56) since "the Euro-American editor [was] responsible for fixing the text in writing" (Krupat *Voice* 55). Accordingly, critics such as Catherine Rainwater emphasize the authenticity of contemporary works by Native Americans, in contrast with materials written about them by others: "Written and published works (as opposed to yesteryear's ethnographic and 'as told to' accounts) give Indian people control over the knowledge they impart as well as the means of imparting it" (9).

In *Sing with the Heart of a Bear: Fusions of Native and American Poetry, 1890–1999,* literary critic Kenneth Lincoln suggests that the true influence of Native American poetics on American letters is in fact far more pervasive than previously recognized. Lincoln claims that a variety of canonized authors such as "major" modernist poets show traces of influence stemming from Native American sources. More recently, a number of contemporary poets, particularly those in the American West and Pacific Northwest as well as some associated with the San Francisco Renaissance movement, have drawn to varying degrees on Native American influences as well. For example, poet Gary Snyder's Pulitzer Prize–winning *Turtle Island* frequently alludes to Native cultural traditions. Although Native American writers such as Ray Young Bear have sometimes decried imitation by Whites of Native American verse, perhaps such works represent the flip side of the same coin: literary artifacts from the "zone" of contact between Native American and European cultures. Questions of appropriation or authenticity aside, such experimentation by contemporary non-Native writers with "Native-like" subjects and style, although at times admittedly romanticized, is indicative of overt influence. Such influence—and dialogue—moves in both directions, of course, as Native American authors freely appropriate and adapt European literary forms and voices.

Perhaps stylistic resemblances in the poetry of non-Native writers to Native American oral poetics (e.g., a lack of written conventions including punctuation and capitalization) can best be viewed not in terms of influence so much as a *dialogue* between and across literary traditions. I believe that ultimately such a dialogue of *mutual* influence may well have helped to pave the way for wider critical recognition and broader overall readership for Native American writers. Native American critics themselves have long questioned whether such influences have not in fact been greatly underestimated (e.g., Gunn Allen, Young Bear). Such a revisionist literary history would certainly bolster arguments based on the virtue of polyphony, generally, and better representation of the silenced voices of marginalized perspectives. Bakhtin's theories of polyphony, after all, suggest that there is no escaping such linguistic pluralism. Distinguishing the cultural origins and authenticity of constituent voices only adds to the challenge and rewards of engaging these works. There is no mistaking the highly polyphonic character of American literature as a whole—or the importance of Native American voices. For the purpose of classroom use, Native American writing provides a uniquely multifaceted cultural perspective that rightfully holds an integral place in our national literature. Consequently, incorporating works by Native American authors themselves, and perhaps especially contemporary writers, is arguably long overdue.

In order for teachers to distinguish among texts that misrepresent and romanticize versus those that are more culturally "authentic," it is helpful to consult Native American authors themselves. Indeed, the perspectives of Native American critics and theorists can enrich our appreciation of such literature. Introducing this volume, May and Henderson invoke historian Vine Deloria Jr.'s "call for a revisionist way of reading" emphasizing that a "self-awareness of each [cultural] group must define a series of histories about the American experience." Scholars of Native American oral tradition, the "literature" of storytelling, such as Toelken, also champion this view. Krupat argues in *The Voice on the Margin: Native American Literature and the Canon,* whether or not one personally "adopts" any given cultural perspective, "the strongest *ethical* case can be made for taking the subject's own view of things seriously" (12). As May contends, "Critics from divergent ethnic groups lament that many interpretations about their people and their literature have been penned by authors who are not members of the group depicted. [. . .] they suggest that much is lost by denying the minority its own voice in literature" (76). Importantly, contemporary Native American writers themselves, such as Gunn Allen, also challenge us as readers, students, and teachers of "American Indian literature to look at this literature from the point of view of its people" (*Studies* 21).

Gunn Allen cautions against conventional misrepresentations of Native cultures. Historian Robert Berkhofer Jr.'s seminal *The White Man's Indian* traces the history of such images and stereotypes from the arrival of Columbus to modern times. Admittedly, sensational and sentimental images still linger today. Such oversimplifications miss the diversity among Native peoples; as Gunn Allen observes: "there were no 'Indians' for one thing; there were a multitude of tribes and nations who often had no more in common than the other inhabitants of the Eastern Hemisphere have with one another" ("Forward" 118–19). In fact, Gunn Allen speaks in terms of analyzing the "cultural diversity" found among the works of various Native American novelists, given the range of their individual tribal affiliations (Coltelli 18). Erdrich emphasizes that although contemporary Native American writers are primarily English speaking, "they all come out of different heritage, background, a different worldview, a different mythology" (qtd. in Coltelli 47). Accordingly, May and Henderson exhort us to consider "the ways the reader is allowed to see Native diversity" in literary representations of "American Indians" (conversations with the editors).

Historically, portrayals of Native Americans from a European perspective are fraught with stereotypical and contradictory "images," alternately romanticized and demonized:

"sometimes [Native Americans] were pictured as virulently dangerous [. . .] sometimes they were pictured as innocent, physically beautiful, generous, mild mannered submissive, and gentle" (Gunn Allen "Forward" 118). Visual images dating from the age of exploration represented Native Americans in distorted ways and neoclassical styles. As Chippewa author and literary theorist Gerald Vizenor observes, "these drawings were the first images and representatives of natives [. . .] 'portraying' savagism for an international audience" (*Fugitive* 149–51). European artists and writers since colonial times have in effect partially *imagined* the "Indians" they depict. Native Americans have conveniently provided the European imagination with both "a romantic symbol of the settling of the North American continent" and "the symbol of the savage other" (Carr 192). Gunn Allen concludes, "the attributes of the 'Indians' were as often a projection of the viewer as an aspect of the viewed" ("Forward" 119). Such historic misrepresentations underscore the importance of reading the writing of Native Americans themselves.

Distorted visual images of "Indians" are, of course, still with us. In "Developed Identities," Tuscarora Richard W. Hill, Sr. explores the perpetuation of stereotypical images of Indians in popular culture through literature and lore—but particularly through conventional and stylized visual images. Such images shape our expectations: "People do not seem to be Indians unless they match our ideas of appropriate dress and appearance" (145). And once such images became pervasive, they have persisted through sheer repetition.

Historically, even "documentary" photographs can become ensnared in such stereotypes. Nineteenth-century photographers, such as Edward Curtis, and painters, such as George Catlin, who purported to document the "traditions" of Native American peoples, sometimes altered their "Indian" subjects in order to more convincingly portray stereotypes such as "the noble savage as the antithesis of civilization" (Vizenor *Fugitive* 160–61). Curtis reportedly posed Indian subjects in contrived ways, "removed evidence of Western contact," and even altered photographic negatives to preserve the appearance of "tradition," albeit idealized. Ironically, as Vizenor points out, subsequent generations of Native Americans have sometimes appeased the expectations of tourists by mimicking such old photos (Coltelli 170–71). That is, living Indians sometimes conform to prevalent stereotypes to serve commercial purposes, perpetuating the "cultural clichés that predominate American popular culture" (Hill 139). Clearly, even photographs do not necessarily provide a reliable record, since they can so readily conform to stereotypes. Susan Sontag, a critic who has written on the art and symbolism of photographs, also describes questionable practices such as "paying the Indians to pose and getting them to revise their ceremonies" (qtd. in Vizenor *Fugitive* 162–63). Consequently, photographs can be misleading, particularly when rendering cultural traditions in anachronistic ways, intentionally leaving out any trace of change (Vizenor *Fugitive* 152). Similarly, not even well-meaning anthropological accounts are always trustworthy when attempting to describe a culture in a "purer," pre-existing form, untainted by contact with the modern world. Such primitive depictions can be partially fiction, especially in the face of rapid cultural change.

Problems of misrepresentation and stereotyping crop up repeatedly in literary works about Native Americans by others. As Hill notes, stereotypical visual images of Native Americans "illustrate a universal melodrama that exists only in the viewer's mind, one created by reading about James Fenimore Cooper's Indians, Longfellow's Hiawatha, and the fall of Custer, and by watching too many westerns on television and in movie theaters" (155). Ironically, such stereotypes provide a backdrop when we read authentic Native American writing today. Although Native Americans are not the only ones, of course, to be depicted in romanticized ways, these stereotypes seem particularly pervasive and resilient historically, to the point of eclipsing more authentic representations, including the works of contemporary Native American writers that only relatively recently have received serious critical reception and broad popular acceptance. Anthropologist Tom Carr argues that "hearing Indian voices is difficult for mainstream peoples, precisely because those peoples are inclined to permit only a certain Indian voice, one that confirms what they expect to find" (199). Gunn Allen points out that historically preconceptions, such as those "created by dime novels, by writers like James Fenimore Cooper, Daniel DeFoe, and such, and by Hollywood," have made it more difficult for Native American authors to gain recognition—or, indeed, to get published in the first place (qtd. in Coltelli 27).

Contemporary Native American writing diverges from such limited stereotypes and allows us to rethink cultural identity in all its diversity and complexity. Yet as May has argued, "publishers and authors of books about American Indians and their encounters with the Europeans have often given young readers a distorted perspective [. . . and] have left out the Indian viewpoint in favor of images of New World's early settlers" (72). Stereotypical depictions have long flourished as a "vast and conspicuous silence marked by the absence of Native people's voice" (Rainwater 134). As Rainwater claims, "Native American [writers] are also 'reinventing' tribal people following their long consignment to silence and stereotypical representation within mainstream culture" (ix). In "Sending a Voice: The Emergence of Contemporary Native American Poetry," literary critic Andrew Wiget views Native American writers in just such terms: overcoming both silence and misrepresentations by "an act of self-naming" (qtd. in Yancey xviii).

Indeed, contemporary Native American authors view their own writing as a way to undo such inherited stereotypes. Gloria Bird, for example, tribal member of the Spokane Reservation, explains her autobiographical essays in terms of correcting just such conventional misrepresentations: "We have been constructed as 'Indians' [. . .] falling prey to the romanticism of 'Indians' who have been appropriated to serve other needs. For instance, the Noble Savage of pop culture and American literature [. . .] if I view that representation of Native people as a distortion, my alternative is to offer another version of self to counter that one" (48).

The absence, historically, of Native American writers in the literary canon ultimately can be viewed in terms of voice. Native American activist Donald Grinde claims that in the wake of protracted battles, repeated defeats, and loss of their lands, "Indian people were *silenced*, that they became *voiceless*" (paraphrased in Freisinger 246). Introducing an anthology of writing by a new generation of Native American authors, Abnaki writer and editor Joseph Bruchac hailed "a new era in which voices which have been traditionally silent (or silenced) are being heard" (qtd. in Lincoln *Native* 73). A dramatically different vision of cultural history and identity is encountered in the writing of contemporary Native Americans themselves, a vision rooted in direct experience of tradition and transition, and one enriched by many voices: voices of landscape and place, voices of elders and ancestors, voices of culture and self.

Once we decide to incorporate Native American voices in the literature curriculum, we are faced with new challenges. After identifying works that portray Native American cultures in authentic ways (a question to be addressed later in this chapter), how are we to help students interpret them? How, for instance, do Native American writers conceive of the dynamics of cultural identity? And how might such issues be addressed when contemporary Native American literature is introduced in the classroom? To begin, students might focus on themes that Native American writers and critics themselves see as central.

Native American writing almost inevitably involves historical dimensions. Recurring themes of place—and of displacement—are frequent motifs in this literature. Why is place such an important theme for Native American writers? I recall listening decades ago, on the deck of an Alaska Marine Highway vessel, to a Tlingit elder naming the headlands and islands that we passed, recounting stories that belonged to these places and to his people. As he spoke, these three—story, people, and place—seemed inextricably linked. Native American authors such as Ortiz have made similar claims: "Speaking for the sake of the land and the people means speaking for the inextricable relationship and interconnection between them. Land and people are interdependent" (*Speaking* xii). Harjo goes as far as to claim "the strongest [American] writers have always been the ones with well defined sense of place [. . .] knowing of landscape as something alive with personality, breathing. Alive with names, alive with events, nonlinear" (Coltelli 63–64). There is the geographic or physical landscape and the interior or spiritual landscape. This landscape is historicized, a landscape enriched by cultural memory—a storied landscape.

Historically, place has been central to oral tradition, the stories passed down in Native cultures. Having no written language, much of a tribe's history took an oral form that must be remembered and retold from one generation to the next. Connections to landscape and place are common to both oral tradition and written narrative (Gunn Allen *Studies* 219; Jahner). An emphasis on landscape and place—and its relationship to cultural identity—has in effect been carried over from oral tradition to literary texts. Momaday places *relationship* to landscape at the heart of Native worldviews. He describes a process of "reciprocal appropriation" involving both the imagination and an ancient "racial" memory ("Native"). Throughout the essay "Native American Attitudes to the Environment," Momaday contends that connections between landscape and culture are deep-seated in collective memory and reflected in tribal storytelling traditions. Moreover, Momaday explains that such a culturally based "sense of place" links contemporary writers to oral tradition:

> [. . .] spiritual investment in landscape [. . .] characterizes much of American Indian oral tradition. Probably writing too, more recently, because the writing, I think, springs in a natural way from oral tradition and the sense of place is crucial to both. (qtd. in Coltelli 91)

Admittedly, written literary genres such as the novel are a considerably different form than oral storytelling per se, yet a number of traditional elements—including themes of place—can be echoed, embedded, and "transformed." Novels can readily draw on oral tradition to "fashion their own unique versions of traditional stories that conform to the aesthetic criteria," to varying degrees, of contemporary literary forms (Rainwater 133). It is important, therefore, to view contemporary Native American writing in relation to the cultural history of oral tradition, particularly its emphasis on place.

How do contemporary Native American authors talk about the importance of place to their writing? Some such as Ortiz, Silko, and Harjo claim that their identities and voices as writers are directly related to place. Simon Ortiz, perhaps echoing Momaday, confides that connection to place is crucial to his perspective and *voice* as a Native American writer: "As an influence—in fact as an essential element—in the development of my writing, my Native voice has come from the concept of the necessary and essential relationship of land and people" (*Speaking* xviii). When interpreting works by Native American authors, it is essential to consider themes connected to place—since, by their own account, place shapes cultural identity in profound ways.

Historical relationships among place, culture, and self are by no means simple ones. Indeed, the relationship of cultural identity to place can be especially complex for contemporary Native Americans who have moved among and been shaped by several tribal traditions. The presence and interaction of multiple cultural traditions, after all, can readily be seen in even a single geographical region. Gunn Allen points out extraordinary Native and non-Native diversity in the Southwest both historically and today. She writes that such "regional identity [. . .] is confluential" (*Off* 229–31). Gunn Allen describes her sense of how multiple influences shape her cultural identity—and her writing: "My poetry has a haunted sense [. . .] that comes directly from being split, not in two but in twenty, and never being able reconcile all the *places* that I am" (qtd. in Bruchac *Survival* 18). Gunn Allen has also described her own mixed-blood heritage and the many national, ethnic, linguistic, cultural, and religious traditions reflected by the members of her extended family (Coltelli 16–17). Lincoln refers to Gunn Allen's heritage as "Laguna-English-Arabic-Spanish-Lakota-German upbringing on the edges of Pueblos, 'a confluence of cultures'" (*Native* 9). How do Native American writers cope with such diverse influences? One way is by writing about their own experiences of social identity and cultural change. Indeed, it is important to remain alert to such themes—as well as the dialogue between Native and European voices—in their work.

Momaday comments on the role of change among Native American cultures historically:

> Virtually all Native Americans have a history of great change. [. . .] Change has been their survival; their adaptability has enabled them to survive. So when we talk about preserving a heritage or culture, this is not exclusive of change by any means. Quite the reverse. The last thing, the most dangerous and destructive thing that the Indian can do, is to remain static, become a museum piece. So when we talk about preserving the culture we are really talking about change. (qtd. in Isernhagen 40–41)

Ortiz similarly explains how change itself has emerged as a motif in his work: "As a writer whose native landscape has changed, in some instances drastically and traumatically, I've focused on this change as a topic in most of my writings" (*Speaking* xvii). These writers are not alone in viewing their own social identities in terms of change. Harjo also writes of identity as connected to place and to change.

I am from Oklahoma. But that isn't my only name. I am Creek and other Oklahoma/Arkansas people. I am a woman, many women. The namings can go on and on and it is frustrating to name someone or something when in the *real* world all is in motion, in a state of change. ("Bio-Poetics" 8)

Other than place, themes emerging out of oral storytelling traditions include the profound importance of memory and language. Native American writers often see language and memory as metaphors for survival. In his seminal essay about a traditional Kiowa story entitled the "The Arrowmaker," Momaday describes how oral tradition necessarily relies on human memory. Spoken language is, of course, the medium for oral tradition. Without writing, the perpetuation of tribal history and culture depends on retelling stories that have been handed down and must be remembered. Much of the culture in an oral society can be lost in a single generation if the storytelling tradition is disrupted.

Native American writers such as Momaday and scholars such as Lincoln point to the power of language itself as an essential element of both Native American oral tradition and subsequent written literature. In fact, the power of language can be viewed as a central theme not only for specific stories such as "Arrowmaker" but also for oral tradition overall: "Language defines a people [. . .] the people are born into and die out of a language" (Lincoln *Native* 45). Such losses are especially poignant given the number of Native American languages that have become endangered or extinct, due in part to educational policies that favor linguistic assimilation. Indeed, both memory and language have powerful roles, practically and symbolically, in preserving Native American identities. Like Momaday, other contemporary Native American authors such as Harjo and Silko also acknowledge that memory is central to one's identity and one's writing. As readers we would do well to remember how elements of tribal storytelling traditions are echoed in such writing today.

What then is the relationship between oral tradition and contemporary written forms? Arguably it is one of similarity as well as difference. Critics such as Lincoln characterize connections between oral and written literatures as "the long cultural odyssey into written contemporary poetry, fiction, essay, drama" (*Native* 2). Momaday claims that "the things that inform oral tradition [. . .] are the things that ought to inform the best literature [. . .] they share, I think, the same qualities [. . .] the writer who is writing a novel, say, is engaged in pretty much the same activity, it seems to me, as the storyteller who is telling a story in the oral tradition" (qtd. in Coltelli 93). Momaday's own fiction, as Chickasaw poet Linda Hogan notes, makes connections fluidly between oral tradition and written literature in part by its attention to *language* itself: "*House Made of Dawn* draws on American Indian oral tradition in which words function as part of the poetic processes of creation, transformation, and restoration" (169).

Many contemporary Native American writers seem keenly self-aware of their role as tradition bearers, perpetuating the legacy of tribal worldviews in light of lived experience, while addressing a diverse, modern-day audience. As Momaday reminds us, "we are all [. . .] at the most fundamental level what we imagine ourselves to be" ("Native" 80). What do Native American writers imagine as the possibilities of culture and identity in a contemporary landscape, whether reservation or metropolis, Laguna Pueblo or Los Angeles? And what rewards await young adult readers in the pages of their works?

Several contemporary Native Americans have written works expressly for young adult readers, including novels by Abnaki author Joseph Bruchac, Chippewa Louise Erdrich, and Modoc Michael Dorris. Noteworthy among their books are Erdrich's *The Birchbark House* (1999); Bruchac's *The Heart of a Chief* (1998), *Eagle Song* (1997), and *Children of the Longhouse* (1996); and Dorris' *Guests* (1994) and *Morning Girl* (1992). A number of Native American writers have also produced stunning multigenre works, such as *The Way to Rainy Mountain, The Names,* and *In the Bear's House* by N. Scott Momaday; *Storyteller* by Leslie Marmon Silko; *A Map to the Next World* and *The Woman Who Fell from the Sky* by Joy Harjo; and *throwing fire at the Sun, water at the Moon* [*sic*] by Anita Endrezze. Many of these works intersperse text with visual images such as paintings, drawings, and photographs, often to explore an interlocking set of themes relating to place, naming, story, and memory.

How can student readers be guided to deepen their appreciation of such works? One fruitful approach is to focus on themes emblematic of Native American literature generally: When reading *Morning Girl,* for example, pay attention to Native American reverence for storytelling and naming, as well as themes of social identity and intercultural contact. By providing a reading of this novel along these lines, I will illustrate how to help students approach interpreting such works.

Morning Girl alternates chapter by chapter between the voices of two characters who serve as the book's narrators, both children: the siblings Star Boy and Morning Girl. Curiously, this interweaving of gendered voices might seem to parallel the remarkable process of co-authorship Dorris frequently shared with his wife, Louise Erdrich. Star Boy describes the importance of storytelling and memory as he witnesses a powerful storm, a storm that might metaphorically foreshadow the arrival of whites in the work's final pages: "I watched the way you watch when you know you want to remember: Slowly, even though everything was going fast. Carefully, even though everything was confusing. In some part of me I thought that if I noticed each piece of what I saw, I could someday put it all together in a story" (40). Here we sense the importance of story, especially in an oral culture, for ordering experience—for *making* sense of even the seemingly incomprehensible.

Stories, Dorris seems to suggest, both warn us and guide us: according to Star Boy, "there are stories that small children believe, stories about strange happenings, stories that tonight I tried very hard not to tell myself" (59). Yet Star Boy survives the terror of the storm by recalling the voice of his grandfather telling him "stories about the sort of man I would grow up to be" (43). For the Native American, as Momaday's seminal essay "The Man Made of Words" explains, stories protect by revealing and preserving cultural identity—just as Star Boy is protected by the memory of his grandfather's words. Indeed, folklorists such as Toelken characterize the performance of stories from oral tradition as "a process which uses words and tones to touch off shared values among culturally associated people: it is a culturally structured way of thinking and experiencing together the patterns that make us real" (*Anguish* 143). Stories, especially in oral traditions, embody knowledge of a collective past, a shared history, important for cultural survival in the present and in the future. As Harjo has claimed, "I have a responsibility to all the sources that I am: to all past and future ancestors" ("Bio-Poetics" 9).

Morning Girl also explores identity in terms of how one is *seen*. In a lovely, lyrical passage the narrator contemplates how perceiving oneself involves multiple perspectives: "The water is never still enough. Just when I can almost see my face [. . .] picture I can remember [. . .] Star Boy tosses a pebble into my reflection and I break into shining pieces. It makes no sense to him that I'm curious about what people see when they look at me" (30). The two characters view this question differently: How is one defined in part by relationship to others? It is hardly the first time the two siblings do not see eye to eye, for as Morning Girl confides, "I don't know how my brother came to see everything so upside down from me" (3):

> "They see *you*," he said as if that answered my question. We were searching for ripe fruit on the trees behind our house.
>   *"But what is me?" I asked him. "I wouldn't recognize myself unless I was sitting on the bottom of a quiet pool, looking up at me looking down."* (31)

Later, this idea of seeing oneself is echoed when Morning Girl is first startled but then reassured to find herself reflected, literally, in her father's eyes. Such visual images provide an almost archetypal metaphor for self-perception, akin to the myth of Narcissus. Such imagery can readily evoke a variety of allusions. Critic Robert Alter considers such questions from the perspective of comparative literature in *Canon and Creativity,* a study of intertextuality between Biblical and both classical and contemporary literatures. He shows how an image as recurrent as reflections on water can echo scriptural sources such as Genesis, which "sets off a whole train of associations [. . .] the starlight reflected in the water thus intimates a renewal of creation" (43). The point is that works such as *Morning Girl* by Native American authors need not be taught in isolation. Rather, they can readily be woven into thematic units, and students can be encouraged to make connections among texts for themselves.

Like many Native American authors, including Gunn Allen and Harjo, Dorris depicts identity as both fragmented and relational. The question of how we are perceived by others, as we will see, takes on profound intercultural overtones at the novel's close. Finding one's true identity, in this work, is intimately bound up with the process of naming, another recurrent theme in contemporary Native American literature generally. Morning Girl muses on the power and mystery of names, which, like identity itself, involves multiplicity: "Names are strange and special gifts. There are names you give to yourself and names you show to the world, names that stay for a short while and names that remain with you forever, names that come from things you do and names that you receive as presents from other people" (52). Such attention to naming echoes works by other Native Americans, notably Momaday's multigenre memoir *The Names.* In Momaday's account, themes of place, ancestry, story, and names intertwine. Like Momaday, Dorris explores the interplay of identity and history, a relationship mediated by stories and names. Likewise, in his novel *Fool's Crow,* Blackfoot novelist and poet James Welch explores naming as a stylistic device that linguistically signals "an older (but for the reader newer) way of knowing" (Gish qtd. in Isernhagen 19). Harjo's poem "She had some Horses" is yet another example of a work that explores the mystery of naming: "She had horses who called themselves, 'horse.'

/ She had horses who called themselves, 'spirit,' and kept / their voices secret and to themselves. / She had horses who had no names / She had horses who had books of names" (11). Like Harjo, Dorris portrays the act of naming as the interplay of inner and outer, self and other.

Yet naming plays an even more central role as the novel unfolds, as the family considers names for an unborn child. Morning Girl's parents contemplate the power of naming, explaining that "People choose their own name, or it chooses them" (18) but that "She's not a real person until she has a name, not a human being, not your sister or my daughter" (16). Momaday claims that "in the Native American worldview, the idea of naming is coincidental with creation; that when you bestow a name upon someone or something you at the same time invest it with being" (qtd. in Coltelli 92), or simply that "naming confers being" (qtd. in Rainwater x). Soon all are deeply disappointed by news, as Morning Girl understands it, that "the new sister didn't come" (21). Yet just before the story ends, Morning Girl remembers: "It seemed to me wrong that she had received no name. Grandmother said that we hadn't known her well enough [. . .] and yet I did know her [. . .] and found exactly the right one: She Listens. Now she was real" (67). Here we glimpse the nearly metaphysical power ascribed by many Native traditions to naming—and to language itself.

It is at this very moment that Morning Girl beholds a bewildering sight: the first arrival of Europeans on her island, identified only by the book's epilogue, excerpted from the log Columbus had actually kept. Tellingly, the Spaniards cannot comprehend her words of welcome, nor she their "impossible language." Ironically, Columbus's entry ends with his wish to carry several Natives back to Spain, "in order that they may learn to speak." Yet the unspeakable chasm between them only begins with language. Morning Girl, who wondered poignantly with her brother about how each of us is perceived, "what people see when they look at me," is met by stares of utter disbelief. Importantly, as readers we see this encounter through indigenous eyes.

How might we lead student readers to perceive themes in a particular work for themselves as emblematic of those often found in Native American writing? Before reading *Morning Girl,* they might examine the meanings of personal names in their own families, and perhaps contrast this with Native American naming traditions. They might also recount especially memorable stories—whether oral or written—learned as children, and consider their purpose and import. Interpretation of the work can be further enhanced by exploring historical and cultural contexts. Preceding or while reading, for example, students might research related historical topics such as European voyages of "discovery," written accounts of initial contact with Native American "Indians," or information about the folkways of specific peoples indigenous to the Caribbean referred to in the novel. Indeed, given the significance of history in such works, reading Native American literature provides an ideal opportunity for interdisciplinary teaching and learning—and, as May and Henderson advocate, can enable "discussions about the past and present in Native cultures" (personal communication). In these ways, student readers can better grasp the historical and cultural dimensions of this work and others like it. Moreover, reading the writing of contemporary Native Americans with an awareness of recurrent, cultural motifs can deepen appreciation for the significance of these works, as well as their contribution to our national literature.

In the case of *Morning Girl,* for example, students can learn to explore themes of social identity and intercultural contact as well as considering the meaning of cultural practices such as storytelling and naming.

By contrast, a number of accomplished, non-Native authors such as Will Hobbs and Gary Paulsen have also written novels for young readers that depict Native American characters and communities. Several center on adolescent protagonists in contemporary settings. Others, such as the lavishly illustrated *Crow and Weasel* by National Book Award winning author Barry Lopez, go to remarkable lengths to render traditional cultural customs and philosophies in responsible ways while addressing themes of intercultural contact. When presenting in a classroom context, it is essential not to conflate such work with the writing of Native Americans themselves. If student readers are alerted to the social identity and cultural background of authors in advance, introducing such works provides an excellent opportunity to discuss questions of representation and authenticity, as well as unromanticized depictions of realistic situations and contemporary issues.

One study of Native American high school students suggests that a number of such books—by non-Native authors such as Beatrice Culleton, Rob MacGregor, Phyllis Reynolds Naylor, James Bennett, Jon Hassler, Paul Pitts, Ron Querry, and Jean Craighead George as well as Hobbs and Paulsen—are perceived as being credible and true to life, though differences in interpretation reflecting specific tribal traditions sometimes arise. Cynthia Leung worked with a book club at a boarding school for Native Americans in North Dakota. Student readers identified specific topics and themes that interested them most, including "traditional American Indian ceremonies and beliefs" as well as "American Indian identity" generally (Leung n.p.). In addition, relationships to grandparents and "tribal elders" stood out to them in many of the novels. Leung reports that the high school students viewed a number of young adult novels by non-Native authors as plausible, accurate, and, with few exceptions, culturally acceptable. These student readers naturally recognized where texts represented traditions and practices specific to individual Native American tribes and communities that differ from their own (the school enrolls students from a variety of tribes), an insight echoed by literary critics who emphasize pluralism within ethnic groupings as diverse as "Native Americans" (e.g., Rainwater 68, 134). As Erdrich observes, "writing is different from tribe to tribe, the images are different from tribe to tribe" (qtd. in Coltelli 48). Yet, importantly, Leung's study establishes perceptions of "authenticity" and cultural representation of young adult novels by non-Native authors *from the perspective of Native American students.*

How do non-Native authors approach writing about Native American characters? In his essay "Navigating by the Stars," Will Hobbs, author of better than a dozen young adult novels, especially adventure stories, describes his view:

> A great personal favorite among my characters is Johnny Raven, the Dene elder in Far North. Johnny made it possible for two teenage boys, Gabe and Raymond, to survive through November and December in the backcountry of Canada's Northwest Territories, and now they're going to have to try and go on without him. Here Johnny is speaking after he's dead, through the letter that the boys discovered on his body . . . "And so I say to you 'Take care of the land, take care of yourself, take care of each other.'"

Hobbs goes on in the essay to describe visiting junior high schools:

> In one of the schools, right across from the library was a banner that declared, "TAKE CARE OF THE LAND, TAKE CARE OF YOURSELF, TAKE CARE OF EACH OTHER." I realized at that moment that Johnny Raven's message and mine are the same, that if there is a theme running through all of my novels, that is what it would be. (58)

Hobbs reveals from the perspective of a non-Native how such writing is necessarily multivoiced, blending the author's own beliefs with the words of characters, including those of Native descent, as they are represented in his works. Clearly, student readers need to recognize the distinction between writing by Native Americans and works about them by others. Yet so long as these issues are addressed openly, some young adult novels by non-Native authors arguably have a valid place in the literature classroom and could conceivably complement works by contemporary Native American writers themselves.

The writing of contemporary Native Americans might also be approached in the classroom through various creative and imaginative activities. Maria Offer, for instance, reports on such strategies for teaching *Two Old Women* by Velma Wallis, an Alaska Native from the Athabaskan village of Fort Yukon. Using literature circles with her middle school students, Offer encouraged creative response to the novel, a story that depicts the "struggles and sacrifices" of women in a traditional culture enduring the harsh winters of the far North. Students not only drew pictures of scenes but also co-authored a dramatic script, which was subsequently performed for younger students, other teachers, and community members (26–27). Offer concludes that such collaborative and imaginative projects deeply engaged students with the work—and took on profound intergenerational dimensions, especially because the book had originally been recommended to her by parents in the community of Angoon, a largely Tlingit village on Admiralty Island in southeastern Alaska, where she teaches.

Works published by Native American writers well worth considering for classroom use, beyond those books written expressly for young adult readers, include major novels by Joseph Bruchac, Louise Erdrich, Linda Hogan, N. Scott Momaday, Leslie Marmon Silko, Gerald Vizenor, and James Welch, among others. Prior to writing *The Birchbark House* for young adult readers, for example, Erdrich published a number of highly acclaimed novels, notably *Tracks* and *Love Medicine*. The novels are complex in their structure and fresh in their perspective. Although teachers need to be aware of sexual content, with discretion, the strikingly original voice of these works offers provocative reading. For readers new to this author, *Tracks* is a sensible place to begin and a likely choice for the classroom.

Other excellent prospects include a number of books by the late Blackfoot novelist and poet James Welch such as his acclaimed early novel *Winter in the Blood,* the more recent *Fool's Crow,* and the sometimes unsettling *The Death of Jim Loney*. The latter novel traces the tragic life and decline of its adolescent protagonist in the years immediately following high school during which ultimately "he defines himself [. . . and] dies a warrior's death" (Gunn Allen "Interview" 20). Welch depicts the difficulties faced by Native American youth with unflinching realism—what Lincoln views as a "stunning honesty" emblematic of the "courage and candor" of many Native American writers generally (*Sing* 79). The readability level of the text makes it readily accessible to middle school students. Critics such as Wiget recognize how "through his clean, deceptively simple prose [. . .] Welch's narrative voice speaks of a great and intimate love for both the land and the people about which he writes" (*Native* 94). As Welch described in an interview, the character Loney "hasn't done anything positive with his life ever since high school ended. He was a basketball player; he was a smart young man" who begins, tragically, to "drift" (qtd. in Coltelli 192). The plot is straightforward and the language unembellished, much like his earlier work. According to Gunn Allen, Welch's first novel *Winter in the Blood* concerns personal identity and gaining one's name. Moreover, the work "transposes" traditional ways into a contemporary, American context (Coltelli 21). That book initially established Welch's reputation as an important novelist in the 1970s. Welch himself has acknowledged that the protagonists of both novels are characters searching, perhaps unconsciously, for "something that will give some meaning to their lives." Though far different from traditional vision quests, he says, "maybe the search itself will reveal something that will give meaning to his life" (qtd. in Coltelli 187). *The Death of Jim Loney* evokes themes such as coming of age and cultural identity that easily link to other young adult and "classic" literature.

Finally, Erdrich's nonfiction memoir *Books and Islands in Ojibwe Country* touches on deep human bonds to family and place as well as tribal history. The prose is highly accessible and organized into brief passages, making it conducive to excerpting for classroom use. In what might be termed a literary travelogue, the author recounts her journey by canoe through the lake country of southern Ontario, traditionally Ojibwe land. She finds this landscape inscribed, quite literally, with history and symbolism, petroglyph and narrative. She reflects on the role of writing, broadly defined, beginning with the derivation of the tribe's name, *Ojibwe,* possibly from "Ozhibii'ige, which is 'to write.' Ojibwe people were great writers from way back and synthesized the oral and written tradition by keeping mnemonic scrolls of inscribed birchbark. The first paper, the first books" (11). Likening petroglyphs to texts, she introduces the work's predominant metaphor: "People have probably been writing books in North America since at least 2000 B.C. Or painting islands. You could think of the lakes as libraries" (5). Erdrich senses a profound cultural continuity in the fact that these ancient depictions are still legible: "Since the writing or drawings that those ancient people left still make sense to people living in Lake of the Woods today, one must conclude that they weren't ancestors of the modern Ojibwe. They were and are the modern Ojibwe" (6).

In such a tradition, connection to place is quintessential. In a work that is by turns personal and philosophical, Erdrich ultimately considers her own place as an author in relation to indigenous language—and thereby to the landscape itself:

> Ojibwemoin is one of the few surviving languages that evolved to the present here in North America. For an American writer, it seems crucial to at least have a passing familiarity with the language, which is adapted to the land as no other language can possibly be [. . .]. Many of the names and songs associated with these places were revealed to people in dreams and songs—it is a language that most directly reflects a human involvement with the spirit of the land itself. It is the language of the paintings. [. . .] (85)

For these rock paintings, she tells us, "refer to a spiritual *geography,* and are meant to provide teaching and dream guides to generations" (50) (emphasis mine). Moreover, Erdrich views present-day, indigenous art as a natural extension of these ancient paintings: "contemporary Native art is not just influenced by conventions invented by the rock painters, it is a continuation, evidence of the vitality of Ojibwe art" (56). By analogy, as I have argued throughout this chapter, the same might be said of contemporary Native American writing and its relation to oral tradition.

As Mayan writer Victor D. Montejo explains, "The Native writer, then, has a mission: to keep the torch of his or her culture burning, illuminating the ancestors' path and guiding others to understand why Native cultures are distinct and unique on this earth" (213). Such themes of cultural perpetuation pervade much of the writing by contemporary Native Americans. Momaday's *Rainy Mountain* has been described as an emblematic work in just such terms: "the story of that quest for a sense of personal identity—Momaday's search for the self that could integrate past, present, and future [. . .] the imagination's power to transcend time, to transport us through history" (Blaeser 48–52). As readers of whatever age and ancestry, we too get the privilege of glimpsing such cultural riches—as they take shape in our time: to listen for *not one voice, but many.*

Author's Note

The author gratefully acknowledges those who have thoughtfully commented on earlier versions of this chapter including Rachel Groner, Darwin Henderson, Brooke Hunsucker, Alan Jenkins, Kip Kaufman, Julie Knoeller, Jill May, Nancy Peterson, and Jason Splichal.

Notes

1. Paula Gunn Allen. "Recuerdo," *Shadow Country.* Regents of the University of California, 1982. Reprinted by permission.

Works Cited

Alter, Robert. *Canon and Creativity: Modern Writing and the Authority of Scripture.* New Haven: Yale University Press, 2000.

Applebee, Arthur. *A Study of Book-Length Works Taught in High School English Courses.* Albany, NY: Center for the Study of Literature (SUNY), 1988.

Berkhofer, Robert. *The White Man's Indian: Images of the American Indian from Columbus to Present.* New York: Vintage/Random House, 1978.

Bierhorst, John. *The Red Swan: Myths and Tales of American Indians.* New York: Farrar, Straus, and Giroux, 1976.

Bird, Gloria. Breaking the Silence: Writing as "Witness." Ed. Simon Ortiz. *Speaking for the Generations: Native Writers on Writing.* Tuscon, AZ: University of Arizona Press, 1998.

Blaeser, Kimberly. "*The Way to Rainy Mountain:* Momaday's Work in Motion." *Narrative Chance: Postmodern Discourse on Native American Indian Literatures.* Ed. Gerald Vizenor. Albuquerque, NM: University of New Mexico Press, 1989.

Bruchac, Joseph. *The Heart of a Chief.* New York: Penguin-Putnam/Dial Books for Young Readers, 1998.

———. *Eagle Song.* New York: Dial Books for Young Readers, 1997.

———. *Children of the Longhouse.* New York: Dial Books for Young Readers, 1996.

———. *Survival This Way: Interviews with American Indian Poets.* Tucson, AZ: University of Arizona Press, 1987.

———, ed. "American Indian Writings." *The Greenfield Review* 9.3–4 (1981).

Capps, Walter Holden, ed. *Seeing with a Native Eye: Essays on Native American Religion.* New York: Harper & Row, 1976.

Carr, Tom. "Varieties of the 'Other': Voice and Native American Culture." *Voices on Voice: Perspectives, Definitions, Inquiry.* Ed. Kathleen Blake Yancey. Urbana, IL: National Council of Teachers of English, 1994. 191–201.

Coltelli, Laura. *Winged Words: American Indian Writers Speak.* Lincoln, NE: University of Nebraska Press, 1990.

Deloria, Vine, Jr. *We Talk, You Listen: New Tribes, New Turf.* New York: Dell Publishing, 1970.

Dorris, Michael. *Guests.* New York: Hyperion Books for Children, 1994.

———. *Morning Girl.* New York: Hyperion Books for Children, 1992.

Endrezze, Anita. *throwing fire at the Sun, water at the Moon* [*sic*]. Tucson, AZ: The University of Arizona Press, 2000.

Erdrich, Louise. *Books and Islands in Ojibwe Country.* Washington, DC: National Geographic Society, 2003.

———. *The Birchbark House.* New York: Hyperion Books for Children, 1999.

———. *Love Medicine.* New York: HarperPerennial Library, 1993.

———. *Tracks.* New York: HarperCollins, 1989.

Erdrich, Louise and Michael Dorris. "Interview." *Winged Words: American Indian Writers Speak.* Laura Coltelli: Lincoln, NE: University of Nebraska Press, 1990. 41–54.

Evers, Larry and Barre Toelken. *Native American Oral Traditions: Collaboration and Interpretation.* Logan, UT: Utah State University Press, 2001.

Freisinger, Randall. "Voicing the Self: Toward a Pedagogy of Resistance in a Postmodern Age." *Voices on Voice: Perspectives, Definitions, Inquiry.* Ed. Kathleen Blake Yancey. Urbana, IL: National Council of Teachers of English, 1994. 242–74.

Gunn Allen, Paula. *Off the Reservation: Reflections on Boundary-Busting, Border-Crossing, Loose Canons.* Boston, MA: Beacon Press, 1999.

———. "Interview." *Winged Words: American Indian Writers Speak.* Laura Coltelli: Lincoln, NE: University of Nebraska Press, 1990. 11–40.

———. "I Climb the Mesa in my Dreams." Interview. *Survival This Way: Interviews with American Indian Poets.* Joseph Bruchac: Tucson, AZ: University of Arizona Press, 1987. 1–21.

———, ed. *Studies in American Indian Literature: Critical Essays and Course Designs.* New York: Modern Language Association, 1983.

———. *Shadow Country.* Berkeley, CA: University of California Press (Publication of the American Indian Series), 1982.

———. "Forward to 'Song of the Sky'." *The Greenfield Review* 9.3–4 (1981): 117–21.

Hamill, Sam. *Crossing the Yellow River.* Rochester, NY: BOA Editions, 2000.

Harjo, Joy. *A Map to the Next World.* New York: W. W. Norton & Company, 2000.

———. *The Woman Who Fell from the Sky.* New York: W. W. Norton & Company, 1994.

———. "Interview." *Winged Words: American Indian Writers Speak.* Laura Coltelli: Lincoln, NE: University of Nebraska Press, 1990. 71–88.

———. "Bio-Poetic Sketch for *Greenfield Review.*" *The Greenfield Review* 9.3–4 (1981): 8–9.

———. *What Moon Drove Me to This?* New York: I Reed Books, 1979.

Hill, Richard. "Developed Identities: Seeing the Stereotypes and Beyond." *Spirit Capture: Photographs from the National Museum of the American Indian.* Ed. Tim Johnson. Washington: Smithsonian Institution, 1998.

Hobbs, Will. "Navigating by the Stars." *Reading Their World: The Young Adult Novel in the Classroom.* Ed. Virginia Monseau and Gary Salvner. Portsmouth, NH: Heinemann, 2000. 52–59.

Hogan, Linda. "Who Puts Together." *Studies in American Indian Literature: Critical Essays and Course Designs.* Ed. Paula Gunn Allen. New York: Modern Language Association, 1983.

Hymes, Dell. *"In Vain We Tried to Tell You": Essays in Native American Ethnopoetics.* Philadelphia: University of Pennsylvania Press, 1981.

Isernhagen, Hartwig. *Momaday, Vizenor, Armstrong: Conversations on American Indian Writing.* Norman: University of Oklahoma Press, 1999.

Jahner, Elaine. "A Critical Approach to American Indian Literature." *Studies in American Indian Literature: Critical Essays and Course Designs.* Ed. Paula Gunn Allen. New York: Modern Language Association, 1983.

Krupat, Arnold. *The Voice in the Margin: Native American Literature and the Canon.* Berkeley, CA: University of California Press, 1989.

———. "The Dialogic of Silko's Storyteller." *Narrative Chance: Postmodern Discourse on Native American Indian Literatures.* Ed. Gerald Vizenor. Albuquerque, NM: University of New Mexico Press, 1989.

Leung, Cynthia. "Young Adult Novels about Contemporary American Indians: An Action Research Project to Identify Culturally Realistic Texts." National Council of Teachers of English Spring Conference. Birmingham, Alabama, 30 March 2001.

Lincoln, Kenneth. *Sing with the Heart of a Bear: Fusions of Native and American Poetry, 1890–1999.* Berkeley, CA: University of California Press, 2000.

———. *Native American Renaissance.* Berkeley, CA: University of California Press, 1983.

Lopez, Barry. *Crow and Weasel.* San Francisco: North Point, 1989.

May, Jill. *Children's Literature and Critical Theory.* New York: Oxford University Press, 1995.

Momaday, N. Scott. *In the Bear's House.* New York: St. Martin's Griffin, 1999.

———. "Interview." *Winged Words: American Indian Writers Speak.* Laura Coltelli: Lincoln, NE: University of Nebraska Press, 1990. 89–102.

———. "Native American Attitudes to the Environment." *Seeing with a Native Eye: Essays on Native American Religion.* Ed. Walter Holden Capps. New York: Harper & Row, 1976a. 79–85.

———. *The Names.* New York: Harper & Row, 1976b.

———. "The Man Made of Words." *Indian Voices: The First Convocation of American Indian Scholars.* San Francisco: Indian Historian Press, 1970.

———. *The Way to Rainy Mountain.* Albuquerque, NM: University of New Mexico Press, 1969.

———. *House Made of Dawn.* New York: Harper & Row, 1968.

Montejo, Victor D. "The Stones Will Speak Again." *Speaking for the Generations: Native Writers on Writing.* Ed. Simon Ortiz. Tucson, AZ: University of Arizona Press, 1998. 196–216.

Offer, Maria. "Listening to Voices: Integrating Standards and Culturally Relevant Content." *Bread Loaf Teacher Network Magazine.* Middlebury, VT: Middlebury College/Bread Loaf School of English, 2001.

Ortiz, Simon. *Speaking for the Generations: Native Writers on Writing.* Tucson, AZ: University of Arizona Press, 1998.

Rainwater, Catherine. *Dreams of Fiery Stars: The Transformations of Native American Fiction.* Philadelphia: University of Pennsylvania Press, 1999.

Rothenberg, Jerome. *Shaking the Pumpkin: Traditional Poetry of the Indian North Americans.* New York: Doubleday & Company, 1972.

Silko, Leslie Marmon. *Storyteller.* New York: Seaver Books, 1981.

———. *Ceremony.* New York: Viking, 1977.

———. "Interview." *Winged Words: American Indian Writers Speak.* Laura Coltelli: Lincoln, NE: University of Nebraska Press, 1990. 135–54.

Snyder, Gary. *Turtle Island.* New York: New Directions, 1974.

Toelken, Barre. *The Anguish of Snails: Native American Folklore in the West.* Logan, UT: Utah State University Press, 2003.

Vizenor, Gerald. *Fugitive Poses: Native American Indian Scenes of Absence and Presence.* Lincoln, NE: University of Nebraska Press, 1998.

———. "Interview." *Winged Words: American Indian Writers Speak.* Laura Coltelli: Lincoln, NE: University of Nebraska Press, 1990. 155–84.

————, ed. *Narrative Chance: Postmodern Discourse on Native American Indian Literatures.* Albuquerque, NM: University of New Mexico Press, 1989.

Wallis, Velma. *Two Old Women.* New York: HarperPerennial Library, 1994.

Welch, James. *Fool's Crow.* New York: Penguin USA, 1987.

————. "Interview." *Winged Words: American Indian Writers Speak.* Laura Coltelli: Lincoln, NE: University of Nebraska Press, 1990. 185–200.

————. *The Death of Jim Loney.* New York: Harper and Row, 1979.

————. *Winter in the Blood.* New York: Harper and Row, 1974.

Wiget, Andrew. *Native American Literature.* Boston: Twayne Publishers, 1985.

————. "Sending a Voice: The Emergence of Contemporary Native American Poetry." *College English* 46.6 (1984): 598–609.

Yancey, Kathleen Blake, ed. *Voices on Voice: Perspectives, Definitions, Inquiry.* Urbana, IL: National Council of Teachers of English, 1994.

Young Bear, Ray. "Staying Afloat in a Chaotic World: A Conversation with Ray Young Bear." *Callaloo* 17.2 (1994): 205–12.

3

Transforming "The Crane Wife"

Western Readings and Renderings of "Tsuru-Nyobo"

April Komenaka

"*Tsuru-nyobo*" is a favorite folktale in Japan, recorded by folklorists in oral form in rural regions as recently as 1940. It continues to be fruitful and vigorous in the culture where new variants have arisen that reflect the social and economic changes of the twentieth century. In the United States, the story and its best-known variant, "The Crane Maiden" ("*Tsuru no ongaeshi*"), have appeared in a number of English translations or adaptations, including several picture book versions. The story features motifs familiar to Western readers—a supernatural spouse, a good-hearted but foolish peasant, magical weaving, an interdiction against looking—but in a distinctively Japanese narrative.

American readers who know little about Japanese culture can find much that is familiar and meaningful in the traditional story, especially when interpreted by a skilled American translator like Katherine Paterson, and most especially when it is presented with illustrations that sweeten the sense of otherness so often experienced when reading across cultures. At the same time, readings of the story are enriched by some acquaintance with the home culture, with Western folktales, and with folklore scholarship such as that of Vladimir Propp's work with Russian folktales. And, as Molly Bang has demonstrated in her 1983 picture book *Dawn*, pictorial elements interacting with verbal narrative can recast the traditional story to reflect contemporary American concerns about marriage and about relations between the various human "races."

Here are the common elements of the tale's variants. A poor and lonely peasant finds a crane downed by an arrow in its wing (or trapped in a snare), tends to it, and releases it. Later a beautiful woman comes to his hut and offers to marry him. To help support the household, she weaves bolts of beautiful cloth for him to sell, asking at the same time that he not look into the room where she weaves. She works hard and grows increasingly frail, and the husband worries about her health. A rich man (or envious neighbor) tells him that more of the cloth will make him wealthy; in some versions, he asks how the wife can weave without any supplies. After some resistance, the exhausted wife agrees to weave more and reminds her husband not to look in on her. One day, overcome by curiosity or concern, he looks into the weaving room. He discovers at the loom a crane, drawing feathers from its bleeding breast and weaving them into the cloth. The crane explains that she is the crane that he once rescued, that she had come to repay his kindness by becoming his wife, and that she must now leave him. She flies away. In one important variant, the distraught husband searches everywhere for his crane wife and finally finds her living as queen of the cranes, still featherless. The cranes give him a feast but send him home alone.

Unlike the best-known Western fairy tales, "The Crane Wife" cannot be read as a tale of finding one's way in the world, freeing oneself of parental bonds, or achieving sexual maturity. The peasant and the mysterious woman are married early in the story, and the main part of the story takes place in their home. Unlike such Western tales, the story involves no clear "dichotomy between hero and villain" and does not unfold along a "trajectory of rags to riches, from feeble dependence to royal autonomy, from the dissolution of one nuclear family to the formation of a new one" (Tatar 71–72). Instead, there are two obligations to be met: the crane must repay the peasant's kindness, and she does; and the husband ought to comply with his wife's urgent request, but he does not. Unlike Western tales, which involve the trials through which a hero earns a felicitous marriage, "The Crane Wife" revolves about the trials and transactions of marriage itself. With the husband's invasive act, the marriage dissolves and the wife returns to her own realm. In the context of Japanese narrative expectations, this resolution is morally appropriate and aesthetically satisfying.

A standard source in English is *Folktales of Japan,* Robert Adams's translation of selections from Keigo Seki's scholarly compilation of traditional Japanese folktales, *Nihon no Mukashi-Banashi.* Seki's version includes the search for the lost wife. Molly Bang's translation, "The Cloth of a Thousand Feathers" in her collection *Men from the Village Deep in the Mountains,* follows the Seki text closely but heightens the husband's concern over his wife's health and concludes with the departure of the crane. In the Sumiko Yagawa and Katherine Paterson rendering, Suekichi Akaba's illustrations provide such visual detail and cultural depth that an American reader will feel that theirs is the definitive version. Molly Bang returned to the tale in the picture book *Dawn* but situates it in nineteenth-century New England, gives the couple a daughter, replaces the anonymous folktale narrator with a first-person participant-narrator, and uses the ironic interplay of text and picture to develop Western themes.

An adult American can read "The Crane Wife," especially the Yagawa-Paterson version, without knowing much at all about Japanese culture. Among the familiar themes implicit in the story are those of appearance versus reality, associated with tales of transformation and animal spouses such as "Beauty and the Beast," and the irresistible temptation to see or know what is forbidden, apparent in stories from Genesis and classical mythology through "Bluebeard," *Frankenstein,* and many contemporary science fiction novels.

The crane wife herself is engaging. She is active, decisive, and ethically exacting. Although the peasant sets the plot in motion by rescuing the crane, and the invidious outsider prompts his foolish act, the crane-woman is responsible for the substance of the tale. She returns to her rescuer to repay his single act of kindness by bringing love and comfort into his life. She is marvelously skilled. She contributes to the household, and she sets the conditions under which she will work. Her one request is that she must have "a room of her own." When her husband opens the door to that room, she is not angry at him, but she offers no second chance and no alternative: she must leave him. (There are variant reasons for her departure; these will be discussed later.) He, not she, is bereft.

The husband is a kind, simple man, but he is inferior in refinement and spirit to his mysterious wife. It is his impulsive kindness that leads him to rescue the crane. When the woman appears at his door, he is fully aware of the disparity between his own humble status and her beauty. In the Seki and Bang versions, he tries to dissuade her from sharing his impoverished life. In the Yagawa version, he is too delighted to offer resistance. In all of these versions, it is his simplicity and naïveté that make him vulnerable to the urgings of the greedy or envious merchant/neighbor. Finally, he breaks his promise for simple reasons. In some versions he looks because he is worried about his wife's long days at the loom; in others, it is because he is curious about how she can weave without thread.

The key events are spaced to suggest growing tenderness in the marriage and the passage of at least months, if not years. The first weaving comes after the two have been together for some time and have established a happy relationship. Eventually it is revealed that the unworldly beauty of the cloth is produced by the feathers drawn in loving self-sacrifice from the wife's own body. In the context of her strength of character, her willingness to endure such suffering suggests to the Western reader not masochism but passion.

The story concludes decisively: having explained herself, the crane flies off into the distance. The poor, foolish husband is left with the bolt of cloth he had begged for so insistently but without the wife who had produced it and everything else that had made his life so briefly happy and prosperous. Many wives in many other cultures have undoubtedly fantasized about leaving defective husbands with such dignity and such finality.

For a reader with some acquaintance with Japanese culture and with Western folklore scholarship, the crane wife story becomes a hypertext with links through common structural properties and motifs to familiar Western folktales as well as to such exotic sites as the distinctively Japanese aesthetic principle of *awaré,* the Japanese ethical and social institution of *on,* and certain aspects of Japanese folk cosmology.

Like any folktale, "The Crane Wife" adheres to a narrative pattern reflecting the values of the culture in which it is found. Folktales preferred and promoted in American culture typically follow an upward path, foster hope and aspiration, and assert (without examining the claim) that marriage between deserving people will be permanent and happy. One group of tales that does not conform to this pattern and is not popular in the United States, though it has long been current in European and other cultures, is that of the swan maiden, which like the crane wife story, involves a nonhuman wife and a doomed marriage (Leavy). Whatever functions this pattern may serve in other cultures, in "The Crane Wife" and many other Japanese tales, it evokes a sense of *awaré*—of "melancholy beauty"—a feature prized in Japanese literature and graphic arts. *Awaré* grows out of a conventional chain of associations: life is transient and mutable, love is fragile, the seasons pass, and the best one can do is to appreciate each brief moment of beauty and to savor the sadness one feels as the moment passes (Befu 178, Ueda 200–01). In most stories involving a nonhuman wife, the marriage is happy—until the final, abrupt break. In terms of narrative expectation, it must be so, in order that the inevitable departure of the wife will be *mono no awaré*—an occasion of deep poignancy.

The tale is governed by a second structuring principle: equilibrium is disturbed early in the story and is reestablished in the end. Lüthi points out that the order/disorder/order structure also governs Western tales: the evil stepmother is an expression of disorder; at the end, she is punished and all is well in the world (*Fairy Tale* 55). This correction is simultaneous with the once-humble hero's accession to marriage and wealth. By contrast, in the Japanese supernatural-spouse tale, the return to equilibrium or the natural order means that all creatures are once again in their proper—that is to say, original—places. Kawai's reading is that "the crane wife tries to establish [a permanent] position in the human world, preserving her tie with nature in secrecy. [. . . She] creates her position by proposing marriage and by working." However, her position is untenable; the balance is too precarious, and the marriage must fail (124).

To continue in structural terms, the story contains at least sixteen of Vladimir Propp's thirty-one functions of the folktale. Propp (64–65) points out that certain of the functions occur in pairs, including the Interdiction/Violation pair (functions 2 and 3) and the Lack Felt/Lack Resolved pair (functions 9 and 19). So fundamental is such pairing to the structure of Western tales that, as Tatar points out, "As soon as we learn about the dire consequences that will attend the mere touching of a spindle, we know that Briar Rose will somehow search out and find the only spindle left in her father's kingdom" (165). In many Japanese tales involving a supernatural wife, the interdiction/violation pair is prominent. Algarin, Kawai, and Yanagita summarize a number of such tales in which the interdiction against looking is motivated by the wife's desire to prolong the marriage: she believes that once the human husband realizes that she is actually a fox, snake, or crane, he will stop loving her and she will have to leave. Therefore, the focus is not on his violating her proscription (which would anger or disappoint her) but on his discovering her true nature (which forces her to leave in shame).

The Japanese tale gives prominence to two pairs of events. Bracketing the marriage is the transformation of the crane into a woman and her later resumption of her natural form (function 29). Propp does not include the first transfiguration as a function. As Lüthi points out, in Western tales, including Propp's Russian tales, "the emphasis lies clearly not on the enchantment but on the disenchantment; the source of the enchantment, where the responsibilities lie, is of less interest [. . .] than the actual need for disenchantment" (143). In the Japanese tale, however, the "source of the enchantment," the adoption of the human form, is as crucial as the disenchantment. Both are intimately linked with the second prominent pair of events: the rescue, which generates an obligation (function 8a, Lack) and the appearance of the crane woman and her commitment to make her rescuer happy, which initiates the process of repaying the obligation (function 19).

In Japanese society, obligation or *on* is a powerful and pervasive concern. A person (*onjin*) who provides a benefit or benevolence to another person imposes *on* upon the recipient, who is compelled to discharge the debt (*ongaeshi*) in order to restore balance to the relationship. The *on* relationship may exist between two persons by virtue of familial relations: thus, a child is permanently indebted to his or her parents. Or it may be occasioned accidentally: if one is rescued from drowning, for example, the rescuer becomes a lifelong *onjin* (Lebra 90–91). In addition to the bonds imposed by *on* between two individuals as a result of a specific act, the Japanese recognize a generalized, informal, diffuse reciprocity, perhaps connected to Buddhism. A person should be kind and sympathetic not only toward other humans but also toward animals. Such generalized benevolence imposes generalized obligation: a common form of this vague sense of obligation is "overall compliance, submission, or loyalty" (Lebra 102). When the peasant rescues the crane, he is exercising generalized benevolence toward an animal. Certainly, he does not expect any return for his kindness. But the crane assumes the obligation and views him as a lifelong *onjin.*

However, the husband's later violation closes off the wife's obligation by making it impossible for her to continue living with him. In Seki's extended version, the husband tries to find his wife again. Apparently, knowing she is a crane does not after all terminate his love (or his dependence on her contributions). When he does find her, she is queen of the cranes, still featherless. He is sent home alone. It is made clear that the crane has returned to her own kind and that the husband must remain with his.

The transformations of the crane wife can be read to involve the natural order. Ironically, it is virtuous acts that have destabilized that order—the peasant's rescue and the crane's acceptance of *on,* including her assumption of a form that is unnatural but most gratifying to her *onjin.* And, ironically too, order is restored by the husband's wrongful act.

To return to the Proppian analysis: Propp hypothesized that not only would every fairy tale contain at least some of the thirty-one functions but also that the functions would always occur in the same sequence (22–23). In the Japanese tale, not surprisingly, the paired functions do retain their sequencing: interdiction, then violation; lack felt, lack resolved. And the final phase of the tale also follows Propp's sequencing: recognition (23), transfiguration (29), punishment (30), and (end of) marriage (31). However, as is clear from Table 3.1, in the Japanese tale the Proppian functions fall into phases that adhere to Propp's sequencing, but these phases are ordered differently.

The Japanese story contains two parallel plots defined in terms of two sets of Proppian characters. In one, the hero is the peasant/husband, the helper or desired one is the crane/wife, and the villain is the merchant/neighbor. In the other, the hero is the crane/wife, and the two male figures are ambiguous. Such multiplicity and ambiguity are allowed for by Propp (66). The structural parity of the two plots is appropriate for a story about the mutuality and reciprocity needed to hold together a marriage. Early in the marriage, the couple are happy in their sufficiency and their union. When money is needed, the wife offers her weaving as a gift to her husband and as her contribution to the family welfare. The interdiction against looking is at this point a request that she be allowed to work in complete privacy, an acknowledgment that she has "a room of her own." The marriage is altered by the entry of the villain, the outsider who persuades the husband to view his wife as a producer of income and her beautiful cloth as a commodity. The couple begins to uncouple: the weaving is performed under duress, and the interdiction becomes burdensome.

TABLE 3.1 *Proppian Functions in "The Crane Wife"*

Function	Description	Level	Events in "The Crane Wife"
8	Lack/debt is established	Level 1	Crane owes life to peasant
19	Debt repayment begins		Woman appears and asks to become peasant's wife
9	(Secondary) Lack is felt by family	Level 2	Couple very poor
2	Interdiction		"Don't look into my room"
19	(Secondary) Lack is resolved		Wife's weaving brings prosperity
4	Villain reconnoiters	Level 3	"Who makes this cloth?"
5	Villain gains information		"My wife weaves the cloth"
6	Villain sets trap/deceives		"Get her to weave more cloth"
7	Victim is taken in		Husband demands more cloth
3	Violation; Debt is closed	Level 2; Level 1	Husband looks into wife's room
27	Recognition	Level 1	Wife is seen as shape-shifting crane
29	Transfiguration		Crane shape is permanent
30	Punishment		Husband loses wife
31	Marriage		Marriage ends, crane returns to her own kind

The Yagawa/Paterson version makes this shift in the relationship explicit. The wife is puzzled by her husband's demand for more cloth, asking "Why in the world would anyone need so much money as that? Isn't it plenty to be able to live together, just the two of us?" She yields because she cannot bear his unhappiness. In the meantime, the husband has lost his naiveté: "Why did the young woman appear to grow thinner each time she wove? What was going on between those paper doors? How could she weave such beautiful cloth when she never seemed to buy any thread?"

The husband's violation of the wife's interdiction (function 3) leads to the closure of other Proppian pairs, with different twists. The wife is released from her obligation to her husband (function 19), resumes her natural form (29), and terminates the marriage (31). The husband, as agent of the villain (as a violator), is punished (30).

Just as they produce distinctive cultural variants, cultural differences produce variations in the management of the motifs of the tale. In the most widely known Western tales, the hero or his or her spouse is a human being long ago turned into an animal or forced to assume animal disguise by a malevolent figure. By contrast, in the Japanese tales, the non-human spouse has assumed human form voluntarily. The Aarne-Thompson cross-cultural compilation of tale types includes the large group B600–B699 "Marriage of Person to Animal." Such liaisons are regarded in many cultures as troubled. Among the category of tales with a tabu motif are listed these subcategories: C31, Offending supernatural wife; C35, Offending animal wife; C31.1.2, Looking at supernatural wife in certain occasions; and C441, Mentioning the original form of the transformed person.

Toshio Ogawa suggests that animal spouse tales reflect cultural views of a biological hierarchy. In the West, human beings are considered closer to the divine than are animals, and cross-species coupling is tabu. Thus, in Western tales the enchanted hero or intended spouse must resume human form before the wedding can take place. The disenchantment having occurred, the tales end with the promise of a long and happy marriage. In tales of animistic cultures, in which certain animals are equal in importance and power to human beings, marriage between animals and humans may be viable and permanent. In Japanese tales in which the wife is nonhuman, she adopts human form before proposing marriage. In all such tales, the marriage is happy, but the wife's true nature is discovered and she terminates the marriage (cited by Kawai 118–20). Other Japanese tales featuring wives who turn out to be wild ducks or geese, foxes, snakes, frogs, or fish follow the same pattern as the crane wife story: the future husband saves the animal, the animal reappears in human form and proposes marriage, the wife prohibits looking, the wife's true nature is revealed, and the wife departs (Kawai 110).

It is not only animal wives whose happy marriages ultimately fail. In a common variant of the crane wife story, the crane is saved by a childless elderly couple and joins their household as a young girl. The rest of the story unfolds as in the original version. Other Japanese tales of supernatural wives include "*Yuki-Onna*" ("Snow Wife"), "*Aoyagi*" ("Green Willow"), and "The Wife from Heaven." In "Snow Wife," a snow witch kills a woodsman but spares his young companion when he promises never to mention the incident. She comes to him later as a beautiful young woman; they live happily together, producing ten children, until he innocently mentions once having seen a snow witch. Enraged, she leaves him. In "Green Willow," a young courtier marries a beautiful peasant woman and lives happily with her for some years. One day he finds her dying. She explains that she is the spirit of a willow tree that has just been cut down (Martin).

Such tales would seem to reflect not only the *awaré* principle but also Japanese folk beliefs, a blend of imported Buddhism and Taoism with native Shinto, in which "all natural phenomena, animate or inanimate [. . .] are at least potentially capable [of serving as] receptacles in which spirits reside" (Befu 101). There is little attempt to establish a systematic hierarchy of gods, spirits, or souls; all are referred to as *kami,* and all are revered. However, Shinto recognizes that human beings are a distinct group. Similarly, Buddhists teach that existence in animal form is lower than human existence, and enlightenment can only come to human beings. Thus, a wife who is not human might expect that her husband will cease to love her if he discovers her true nature.

It is tempting to highlight as characteristically Japanese the self-sacrifice made emblematic in the wife's tearing of feathers from her own bosom. However, the joining of weaving with suffering is found in folktales the world over. Carole Scott points out that methods of production of clothing are often associated with "the sacrifices demanded of the (usually female) workers who transform vegetable or animal products into valuable commodities," and with transformations of people out of or into human form (152). There are striking parallels between the crane wife and the sisters in the Grimms' "The Six

Swans" and Andersen's "The Wild Swans," who can save their brothers only by producing shirts for them at great pain and risk to themselves.

The crane wife's weaving takes place in a forbidden chamber, another common folktale motif. When the last wife of Bluebeard looks into the forbidden room, she finds that it is filled with the bloody bodies of his previous wives. In psychoanalytic terms, the forbidden chamber represents the vagina, and the bloody contents suggest menstruation, therefore, sexual maturity. That access is forbidden to the wife in Bluebeard's absence, Dundes proposes, indicates that the chamber represents adultery. In the crane wife story, the husband is forbidden access while the wife is present and the wife herself is bloody, suggesting menstruation and perhaps the Shinto association of spilled blood and menstrual blood with pollution. A connection between blood, suffering, and shame is apparent in such literary works as the Japanese *no* drama *Kurozaka*. There, a woman forbids a visiting priest from looking into her bedroom; he disobeys and finds the room is full of bloody corpses. She pursues him but is finally vanquished. As she departs, she says, "Hide as I did in this black grave, how miserable I became! How shameful!" Kawai points out that the emphasis is on her feelings of shame rather than on anger at his breaking his promise (23).

The crane wife, when discovered at her loom, is naked or bloody or both. She has sacrificed her white feathers and she has endured pain. The Seki version refers to the crane as "naked," and her speech implies humiliation and inferiority. "I have finished the cloth, but since you have seen who I really am, I am afraid that you can no longer love me. I must return to my home. I am not a person but a crane whom you rescued" (80). In the Yagawa text, the crane is "smeared with blood," and a fine thread of red is worked through the cloth. Although her farewell speech is tender rather than ashamed, the crane tells her husband that she must leave exactly because he has "looked upon [her] in [her] suffering."

The interdiction against looking is tied also to the wife's power and her ability to contribute to the household. Aside from its association with sexuality and/or impurity, the forbidden room is also the weaving room, the place of the wife at the center of the family. It is also the secret place in which she can draw from her other body the means to create things of unearthly beauty that far exceed her husband's power to match or to understand. Thus, the key motifs of the story—the obligation that must be repaid, the interdiction and violation, the weaving and self-sacrifice, the nonhuman spouse—all converge in the forbidden chamber. Quite apart from Japanese cultural considerations, such economy of motif and internal association, such "clarity, exactness, positiveness, and precision" make "The Crane Wife" an instance of the fairy tale as a work of art (Lüthi 57).

Having established the cultural matrix in which "The Crane Wife" developed as an oral tale and continues to flourish and diversify in printed and picture book versions, I now turn to two contemporary picture book adaptations of the story, one traditional Japanese in pictorial style and narrative structure, the other American. As Perry Nodelman observes of picture book versions of fairy tales, they give "human faces to the disturbingly strange or symbolically ideal," so that reader-viewers are forced to "confront the implications of these characters in terms of our acquaintances and of ourselves, in a way that our own vaguely mysterious imaginings never could" (282). Beyond the contributions of the pictures alone, it is in the subtle interactions of textual narrative and pictorial codes that complex and surprising cultural meanings are developed.

In *The Crane Wife,* Suekichi Akaba's pictures work with the textual narrative (Katherine Paterson's translation of Sumiko Yagawa's retelling) to induce in an American reader the sense of a universe governed by principles rather different from those with which he or she is familiar. In *Dawn,* author and illustrator Molly Bang turns the crane wife into a wildgoose wife, moves the story to Cape Cod, and plays texts and pictures against each other to portray the familial ironies underlying a domestic tragedy of a kind familiar to that American reader.

Akaba's illustrations use a combination of water color, gouache, and black ink applied *sumi-e* style to rice paper, the texture of which is apparent in a number of the pictures. Text and picture are distributed across fifteen double-page panels. As described earlier in this discussion, the text, perhaps by the choice of the American translator, makes explicit in dialogue both the tenderness and the tension between the mismatched husband and wife. The pictorial narrative locates the relationship in a vast but benevolent natural world and enables the reader-viewer to perceive these human figures both intimately and as figures of *musashi* ("long-ago magic times"). Akaba achieves this by employing a style that Nodelman would characterize as comprised of an "absence of a clearly defined viewpoint and of internal framing devices, great contrasts of scale, [. . .] and a firm sense of the picture as surface" (86). Akaba's strong shifts in scale and space emphasize the small place of human existence in the immense, life-infused universe.

The human world and the natural world are kept visually distinct. The human figures are rendered in strong color, and interior scenes are done on textured buff rice paper. The woman is white-skinned, slender, always turned gracefully toward her husband or her loom. The husband is brown-skinned, sturdy, broad-faced, a true bumpkin. When she presents herself at her future husband's door, the small human figures and little hut are almost buried in swirls of snow. The exterior scenes are dominated by large, curving mounds of pale snow, beginning with the opening spread, where large pale grey snowdrops drift across creamy snow, and ending with the final two spreads of long, low snowy hills below a large, vividly blue sky.

The pictures imply that the man and the crane woman are together for just one winter in the long cycle of life: the intersection of their separate worlds is brief, sweet, and finally conflicted, motivated by good intention but doomed by human frailty and by difference.

In *Dawn,* Molly Bang has Americanized setting and character and has invested the story with contemporary themes. There is a Cape Cod catboat on the front cover and a blue-and-white quilt on the marriage bed. Instead of an elegant white and black crane, there is a brown Canada goose. Instead of a stocky Hokkaido farmer, the hero is a slender, fair-haired boat maker. The woman is dark-skinned and distinctly ethnic, possibly Native American, Caribbean, African, or Oceanic. The young boat maker and his once-mysterious wife have a child whom they name Dawn. Finally, rather than an anonymous narrator, the boat maker himself tells the story years later, the sad story of how, out of ignorance, ambition, and impatience, he lost his wife and his child's mother.

In *Dawn,* the textual narrative indicates that the husband has appropriated the family story, but the pictures repeatedly subvert his telling by revealing his obtuseness—in the retelling as in the living—and also reveal the limitations of any purely verbal, monologic, monophonic account of anything so complex as the relations between man and woman. In the Akaba-Yagawa-Paterson book, blocks of text are incorporated into the pictorial composition, and text and picture parallel and deepen each other. In *Dawn,* however, picture and text are on separate, facing pages (with three exceptions, discussed later) and operate in ironic counterpoint. The traditional crane wife theme of seeking to see what should not be seen is replaced in *Dawn* by the theme of *not* seeing or knowing what should be seen or known. Each double-page spread displays a pair of contrasting accounts of an event, one pictorial and one verbal. The full-page picture on one side shows what "really" happened; across it is a page of text in which the husband reports the event from his own perspective.

Bang uses two kinds of full-page pictures. Half are monochrome pencil drawings that overflow a bit from simple line borders. The rest are intensely colored acrylic paintings, each with an ornate frame showing designs of feathers, vegetation, or brocade; in some cases, the picture has the formal feel of a posed photograph. The figures in all of the pictures tend to be of uniform size, and there is little background detail. Nodelman points out that in many picture books, formally framed pictures like these imply "a clearly positioned viewer that makes the self and its perceptions central" (86) and that such a picture "can inform us that the viewpoint of a character as conveyed by the text [. . .] is limited or one-sided" (235).

Several of the same scenes occur in both Bang and Akaba, but Bang's pictures comment ironically on the father's story and reveal a second, tacit story—that of the wife and daughter. The motif of not seeing/not knowing is developed most dramatically in two picture-text pairs. In the first, the young woman presents herself at the shipbuilder's door and offers to work as a weaver of sails. We see her as he must have seen her. Framed by the doorway, she stands face-on, head tilted, brown-skinned, long-necked and round-shouldered, wrapped in a brown cloak and slightly duck-toed. Her silhouette is that of a large, graceful bird. The picture is framed with brown feathers. It is obvious to the reader-viewer who and what she is. Her identity, however, was a mystery to the young boat maker. In the facing text, the father recalls that he had noticed a scar on the young woman's arm but had failed to connect it with the injury to the goose he had recently rescued. Excusing himself, he says, "How could I know what it was from?"

In the second revealing picture, the young wife is shown in bed just after giving birth, smiling at her husband, the new baby beside her. The reader-viewer notices the broken shell of a very large egg protruding from under the bed. Because there is no reference to the broken shell in the facing text that reports the husband's absence during the moment of birth, we can infer that he had not noticed the shell or, seeing it, had failed to apprehend its significance.

The turning point of all variants of "The Crane Wife" is the moral seduction of the husband by the outsider. Akaba's double-page representation of the scene is exactly halfway through the book. On the right page the neighbor whispers into the husband's ear, while in the far upper corner of the left page, we see the wife listening, in shadows, from behind the door. This is the only split illustration in the book, another signal of the importance of the scene.

In the full-color representation in *Dawn,* all four of the narrative figures are present. The husband and the rich man stand over the plans for the splendid racing schooner that the young man will build and, he hopes, for which his wife will weave the sails. The wife and daughter go about their business outside the door. The top-hatted villain looks strikingly like Gustave Dore's Bluebeard leering out from under his plumed hat and down at his bride/

victim. In that famous illustration, Bluebeard simultaneously offers the girl the keys to his castle and warns her not to open the door to the one forbidden room. The girl gazes down intently at the keys, hands outstretched; it is obvious to us that she is already planning to open the door, and that he means her to. Similarly, in *Dawn,* the rich man lays out the plans for the great ship before the rapt young husband—like Bluebeard's wife, the intended dupe—while gazing lustfully and covertly at the wife and child. Unlike her husband and Bluebeard's wife, and like the crane wife, the young mother sees the unfolding disaster: she looks back at the two men, solemnly observing her bedazzled husband and the hovering outsider.

Dawn also alludes to the contemporary phenomena of unconscious racism and sexism. Although the husband never refers to it, he and his wife are shown to be of different races. His narration makes it clear that in their relationship, which he perceives as having been completely loving, she is the seen object and he is the seeing subject. She is the sole figure in six of the fourteen pictures, including two in bird form. In all six, she is positioned and framed as she would be if the reader-viewer were looking at her through her husband's eyes.

Moreover, he speaks while she is silent. In the Japanese versions, the crane wife is given her own voice, a full participant in the dialogue, and even utters the definitive final words, the ones that explain everything. In *Dawn,* the wife is never heard by the audience; the story is told by the husband/father, who summarizes what he considers to be the gist of his wife's speeches. Finally, in bird form, she is completely wordless, expressing her distress by flapping her wings and "beating at [her husband] with her beak." Dawn herself speaks only at the end, but with those words—"I'll bring her back, Father. I'll go in the boat you made for us. We'll be back in the spring, when the geese come north again"—she takes the story from her father and reframes it as her own story.

The themes of seeing/not seeing/being seen and of speaking/not speaking give some answers to the question that an American reader is likely to ask of both the traditional story and of *Dawn:* "Why can't she just tell him up front exactly who she is?" The husband's monologic style as well as his self-reported behavior toward his wife (and his daughter) indicate that he would not have heard her. Moreover, the pictures reveal that she had shown him signs of her true or other nature again and again, but he had simply never noticed. If the husband had been properly attentive and perceptive, he would have recognized her at the outset. If the husband's flaws in "The Crane Wife" were curiosity, greed, or a lack of appreciation for the seriousness of her request, the husband's flaw in *Dawn* is a limited ability to receive and process input, both verbal and visual.

The final loss in the Japanese tale is alleviated by broadening the perspective from the marriage of individuals to the affirmation of the natural order. The American tale turns from the past (the father's limited vision, the inequity of the marriage) to the future as embodied in the vigorous, mixed-blood daughter. On two double-page spreads, a very young Dawn is shown on the same page as the text, looking across her father's words to the facing picture. In the first she is watching her parents heatedly discussing the rich man's demands, and in the second she watches her father struggling to hold on to the great bird. Clearly, she has long seen the relations between her parents from her own perspective and has her own understanding of their story.

The physical book itself fosters this duality of voices and diversity of perspective. The front cover shows Dawn sailing alone in a little sailboat, perhaps setting out (like the husband of the crane wife) in search of her mother. The back cover shows the father, his hair now grey, bending protectively over a Canada goose. The picture reunites the two figures in the second double-page spread in the book, in which the young boat maker on the left page and the injured goose on the right page gaze across the words at each other. The implication of these cover pictures and the title of the book is that the story of her parents is less than, and contained in, the story of their child.

We know that traditional tales like "The Crane Wife" have continued to flourish, essential clusters of figures and motifs persisting and permuting across centuries and cultures. Contemporary technologies of photography, graphic reproduction, publication, and commercial distribution have made it possible to produce beautiful and well-written picture books and make them available to a large public. The crane wife story is perpetuated in and enriched by the new picture book medium in a form approximating its traditional setting and cultural spirit, and in a transformation embodying the setting and spirit of a new culture.

Works Cited

Algarin, Joanne P. *Japanese Folk Literature: A Core Collection and Reference Guide.* New York: Bowker, 1982.

Bang, Molly. *Dawn.* New York: William Morrow, 1983.

——. *Men from the Village Deep in the Mountains and Other Japanese Folk Tales.* Trans. and illus. Molly Garrett Bang. New York: Macmillan, 1977.

Befu, Harumi. *Japan: An Anthropological Introduction.* San Francisco: Chandler, 1971.

Dundes, Alan. *Folklore Matters.* Knoxville: University of Tennessee Press, 1989.

Grimm, Jacob and Wilhelm Grimm. *The Complete Tales of the Brothers Grimm.* Trans. and ed. Jack Zipes. New York: Bantam, 1992.

Kawai, Hayao. *The Japanese Psyche: Major Motifs in the Fairy Tales of Japan.* Trans. Hayao Kawai and Sachiko Reece. Dallas, TX: Spring, 1988.

Leavy, Barbara Fass. *In Search of the Swan Maiden: A Narrative on Folklore and Gender.* New York: New York University Press, 1994.

Lebra, Takie S. *Japanese Patterns of Behavior.* Honolulu: University of Hawaii Press, 1976.

Lüthi, Max. *The Fairy Tale as Art Form and Portrait of Man.* Trans. Jon Erickson. Bloomington, IN: Indiana University Press, 1984.

Martin, Rafe. *The Mysterious Tales of Japan.* Illus. Tatsuro Kiuchi. New York: Putnam, 1996.

Nodelman, Perry. *Words about Pictures: The Narrative Art of Children's Picture Books.* Athens, GA: University of Georgia Press, 1988.

Propp, Vladimir. *Morphology of the Folktale.* 2nd ed. Trans. Laurence Scott. Austin, TX: University of Texas Press, 1968.

Scott, Carole. "Magical Dress: Clothing and Transformation in Folk Tales." *Children's Literature Quarterly* 21 (Winter 1996–97): 151–57.

Seki, Keigo. "Folktales of Japan." Trans. Robert J. Adams. *Folktales of the World.* Toronto: University of Toronto Press, 1963.

Tatar, Maria. *The Hard Facts of the Grimms' Fairy Tales.* Princeton: Princeton, NJ: Princeton University Press, 1987.

Thompson, Stith. *The Folktale.* New York: Dryden, 1951.

Ueda, Makoto. *Literary and Art Theories in Japan.* Cleveland, OH: Western Reserve University, 1967.

Yagawa, Sumiko. *The Crane Wife.* Illus. Suekichi Akaba. Trans. Katherine Paterson. New York: William Morrow, 1981.

Yanagita, Kunio. *Guide to the Japanese Folktale.* Ed. and trans. Fanny H. Mayer. Bloomington, IN: Indiana University Press, 1986.

4

Daydreams of Cathay

Images of China in Modern American Children's Books

Margaret Chang

> Ever since the [. . .] travels of Marco Polo, mention of China has evoked images of a mysteriously magnificent land. (Ruffa 52)

> [. . .] I have written with two ends in mind: one, to present [. . .] intellectual genealogy [. . .] in a way that has not been done; two, to criticize—with the hope of stirring discussion—the often unquestioned assumptions on which [the] work for the most part depends. (Said 24)

Eighteenth- and nineteenth-century Europeans had a passion for "things Chinese." Landscape gardening, porcelain patterns, wallpaper and furniture designs, as well as painting and book illustration in the Rococo and Romantic periods depict a collective daydream of a mysteriously magnificent land known as China. Wealthy aristocrats from Great Britain to Italy, and most importantly in France, commissioned, bought, and built in this elaborate, eclectic style art historians have termed *chinoiserie*. European writers, too, freely used the China they imagined as a setting for philosophical fantasies and fables. In the introduction to his 1716 play produced in London, Aaron Hill wrote: "our distance from, and dark ideas of, the Chinese Nation [. . .] tempted me to fix my scene in so remote a location. The fable is fictitious and the characters are all imaginary" (qtd. in Honour 126).

Following Hugh Honour, an authority on chinoiserie, I shall call the landscape of this European daydream "Cathay," Marco Polo's name for China. Chinoiserie has been a persistent influence on twentieth-century American children's books. Writers for children continue to assume "distance from, and dark ideas of the Chinese Nation," or to twist elements from Chinese traditional literature entirely out of context. Illustrators of texts with a Chinese setting may substitute the intellectual genealogy of chinoiserie for the heritage of Chinese art. Critics and reviewers, like the teacher Jane Ruffa in *Book Links* January 1997, find themselves comfortably situated in the "mysteriously magnificent" landscape of Cathay.

Chinoiserie is a branch of Orientalism, as defined by Edward W. Said. In his book of the same title, which examined British and French academic writing about Islam from the late eighteenth century to the present day, Said describes an all-too-human mind-set that needs to control and contain the Other, the Foreign. He repeatedly describes Orientalism as a European invention that represents, quoting V. G. Kiernan, "Europe's collective day-dream of the Orient," with its own set of unconscious assumptions:

> Everyone who writes about the Orient must locate himself vis-à-vis the Orient; translated into his text, this location includes the kind of narrative voice he adopts, the type of structure he builds, the kinds of images, themes, motifs that circulate in his text—all of which add up to deliberate ways of addressing the reader, containing the Orient, and finally, representing it or speaking on its behalf. (20)

I would add, quoting Zhang Longxi, "For the West [. . .] China as a land in the Far East becomes traditionally the image of the ultimate Other" (110). Both writers shed light on the underlying assumptions of certain writers who interpret China for American children. I wish to examine some examples from this body of work, excluding realistic fiction and nonfiction and concentrating on picture books and fantasies. Said reminds us that "things to look at are style, figures of speech, setting, narrative devices, historical and social circumstances, *not* the correctness of the representation nor its fidelity to some great original" (21).

Said also reminds us that European notions of the Orient tell us more about Europeans than they do about the Orient (12), just as European chinoiserie tells us more about Europe than it does about China. The basic premise common to Orientalism and its more frivolous offshoot, chinoiserie, is the intellectual authority of the West. When a European writer sets an original fantasy in China, the writer's presumption is that the Chinese cannot speak for themselves, that a Westerner must speak for them. The Western gaze is turned on the Orient and controls the images in broad generalizations with a subtext affirming Western dominance and moral superiority. This intellectual authority allows authors and artists to describe the Chinese in general terms, stereotyping them, if you will, and certainly undermining both their individuality and common humanity. Eventually, what Said calls the "imaginative demonology of 'the mysterious Orient' " (26) emerges as the overarching image: China as exotic, barbaric, inscrutable, glamorous, splendid, cruel, and sometimes incomprehensibly silly.

Said's notion of "imaginative geography" (49) links European chinoiserie with the country depicted in many stories for children about China. Imaginative geography is accompanied by a preoccupation with the past. Cathay is a nostalgic never-never land concocted from fabrications and misperceptions by past writers from Marco Polo to the fictitious John Mandeville. As Said shows, this imaginary past takes on a life of its own, one that subsequent writers refer back to, refine, and embellish, giving ignorance a superstructure that bears a diminishing relationship to fact. We see an outsider's fascination with past exotic customs, such as the kow-tow, and an indiscriminate clutter of motifs and architectural elements from East and West, emphasizing the bizarre and the picturesque. Time seems to stand still.

Said shows how scholarly European ideas of the Orient were formed in ancient, "classical" texts, and how these ideas had no reference to modern realities, even when the scholar visited the country he studied. Children's book writers and artists shaped by the intellectual genealogy of chinoiserie maintain this fixed Western gaze, able to see only what has been written or described previously, not what is before the eye. It is worth quoting Said's "principal dogmas of Orientalism" as a background for modern fantasies set in China:

> [. . .] one is the absolute and systematic difference between the West, which is rational, developed, humane, superior, and the Orient, which is aberrant, undeveloped, inferior. Another [. . .] is that abstractions about the Orient [. . .] are always preferable to direct evidence drawn from modern [. . .] realities. A third [. . .] is that the Orient is eternal, uniform, and incapable of defining itself. [. . .] A fourth [. . .] is that the Orient is at bottom something either to be feared [. . .] or controlled. (301)

At the beginning of the eighteenth century, China seemed a remote and mysterious land, described by medieval travelers, ruled by a wise and just monarch, "where flourished a civilization more elegant and humane, more sophisticated and highly wrought than any the West [had] ever seen" (Honour 7). During the nineteenth century, contacts with China increased. Merchants, priests, and military men went to China, more to exploit and convert than understand and interpret (Dooley 95). Knowing nothing of Chinese art, they favored the fantastic, the whimsical, the grotesque over objects valued by Chinese connoisseurs.

Let's explore the landscape of Cathay as depicted in European chinoiserie and the art for modern American children's picture books. Hugh Honour describes this landscape in his book *Chinoiserie, the Vision of Cathay.* I will give a few examples of picture books that fit his description, hoping to help armchair travelers know when the images they see descend from the intellectual genealogy of chinoiserie.

Honour calls Cathay "[. . .] a continent of immeasurable extent lying just beyond the eastern confines of the known world" (5). The ancestral authority for this exotic landscape, marked by snowy mountains and "dreaming pagodas," (6) is Bernard Picart (1673–1733), a French Protestant and popular illustrator of his day. Among his many illustrated books is a four-volume work bearing the English title *The Ceremonies and Religious Customs of the Idolatrous Nations; together with historical annotations and several curious discourses, equally instructive and entertaining* [. . .]. The work was first published in Holland in 1723 and stayed in print for about one hundred years. Picart portrayed Chinese worshippers kow-towing to grotesque and fantastic statues while the familiar snowy mountains rise in the background.

Picart's ignorance is understandable, but it is interesting to find illustrations very similar to his in the modern picture book *Everyone Knows What a Dragon Looks Like.* Jay Williams's text is a whimsical fantasy set in Cathay. Mercer Mayer's art shares with Picart's many elements of chinoiserie: Western architectural elements, corrupt characters, distorted images of deities, and, inevitably, the kow-tow, all arranged in an overripe, jumbled composition that is one of the hallmarks of European depictions of Cathay. The Williams/Mayer creation is the most egregious and ubiquitous example of chinoiserie available today.

Honour notes that "porcelain painters are the most reliable topographers" (5–6) of Cathay. Chinese porcelain was prized by Europeans from its earliest introduction, and before long, Europeans were trying to copy the technology, as well as the blue and white designs. Art historians differ about the origin of the design we know as "Blue Willow," but they all agree that the story of the blue willow plate, often assumed to be Chinese, is in fact an English creation. The brilliant colors and images of Chinese life executed on European porcelain painting in the eighteenth and nineteenth centuries have certainly influenced twentieth-century book illustration.

Steeped in these images, as well as those from tapestries and wallpaper, Honour catalogs the exotic flora and fauna of Cathay. Fantastic, oversized flowers and plants flourish there. Exotic animals, like peacocks and dragons, turn up regularly. Peacocks, native to India and ornamental in China as they are in America, seem extraordinarily abundant in Cathay. The Chinese masters in the exhibition *Splendors of Imperial China; Treasures from the National Palace Museum, Taipei,* shown at the Metropolitan Museum in 1996, painted familiar birds: eagles and sparrows, chickens and geese. In this huge collection of Chinese masterpieces, only one peacock appeared. It stood in the courtyard of a wealthy merchant, symbolizing a pretentious display of wealth. Considering how rarely Chinese artists depict the peacock, it is amazing how often that gaudy bird or its feathers turn up in picture books for children about China. Marilee Heyer's hyperventilated illustrations for an authentic Chinese folktale, *Weaving of a Dream,* depicts many fantastic—and frightening—animals, including a strange variety of peacock on page 13. I read pictures of peacocks or their feathers as an emblem of the exotic, glamorous, mysterious Orient.

When Honour says of Cathay: "Huge and fiery dragons lurk in every mountain cave" (6), he could have been describing Mercer Mayer's illustrations of the title character in *Everyone Knows What a Dragon Looks Like.* Exotic dragons come in many guises. One recent descendant of the porcelain dragons of chinoiserie is the title character in Elizabeth Steckman's *Silk Peony, Parade Dragon.* The story is set in a timeless ancient past, when a rude mandarin comes to Mrs. Ming's dragon farm to rent a dragon for the New Year's Day parade. He chooses Silk Peony, a female dragon, who turns out to be the star of the parade. Breathing fire, she frightens the obnoxious, powerful mandarin into proper behavior. Never mind that dragons from Chinese traditional literature guard bodies of water, breathe clouds and mist, or that they usually symbolize the male emperor. This original fantasy imagined by a Pennsylvania storyteller is distinctly American in tone and spirit, emphasizing the ascendance of spunky females while suggesting China as imagined in a Western operetta.

Honour tells us that "the inhabitants of Cathay are small and neat. Hats, shoes, and cheekbones are worn high, while moustaches, pigtails, and finger-nails are encouraged to grow to inordinate length. Their similarity of appearance—like so much else about them—is proverbial [. . .]" (6). Characters fitting this description move with artificial gesture and studied grace through the illustrations for *The Perfect Peach,* dressed in a hilarious mix of Chinese and Japanese costumes. The plot of Clair Huchet Bishop's *The*

Five Chinese Brothers turns on the brothers' proverbial similarity of appearance, reinforced by Wiese's illustrations.

Honour's characterization of the inhabitants of Cathay as "a peace-loving, and, perhaps, an effete race [who] avoid martial combat save when ancestral voices are heard prophesying war and Tartar warriors clad in clinking amour swoop down on them from beyond the mountains" (6) could have been written about Mercer Mayer's illustrations, pages 21 and 23, of *Everyone Knows What a Dragon Looks Like.* Although making picturesque war sometimes occupies the people of Cathay, their major occupation is the pursuit of leisure. Drinking tea, watching goldfish, playing games, or letting their fingernails grow, the inhabitants of Cathay seem to live without useful work. "This luxurious people has created a style of architecture to suit its leisured life," Honour explains. "In a country of perpetual spring [. . .] no very substantial buildings are needed, and the climate permits a long duration to the flimsiest construction" (7). The wise man in Arnold Lobel's version of a Chinese fable, *Ming Lo Moves the Mountain,* lives in just such an insubstantial building.

Honour ends his vision of Cathay by saying that "some memory lingers on of this bizarre land to the east of the world where most European values were turned topsy-turvy" (7). Surely the most bizarre fantasy written for children about China is Isaac Singer's *The Topsy-Turvy Emperor of China.* The illustrations, by William Pène du Bois, seem to be a tongue-in-cheek homage to Picart. Presented as a literal depiction of China, they are mean-spirited and offensive.

Said's idea of Orientalism and Honour's description of Cathay provide a background for text as well as art. Although the inhabitants of Cathay are too weak and silly to threaten us, Said's notion of fear and control underlies the text of some Western fantasies set in China. Before I discuss twentieth-century writing, I would like to consider the most famous "fictitious fable" set in China, Hans Christian Andersen's *The Nightingale.* The Danish author used the imaginary landscape of Cathay as a background for his diatribe about artificial, mechanical rules governing art, which worked against spontaneity and naturalism. Published in 1845 and translated into English the following year, the story told of the conflict between a real nightingale and a clockwork imitation for the soul of the Emperor of China. Patricia Dooley, in a seminal article examining something over forty illustrated editions of the story, notes, "The symbolic China of the tale is a compound of both the 'real' [i.e., stereotyped] China known to Europeans and the created world of Andersen's romantic imagination" (96). *The Nightingale* was a tribute to a singer Andersen loved, the Victorian sensation Jenny Lind, known as "The Swedish Nightingale."

Since Andersen, writers for children have freely used the China they imagined as a setting for philosophical fables and fantasies. Unfortunately, few were as gifted as Andersen nor so honest about what they were doing as Aaron Hill. Eighty years after *The Nightingale,* the American publisher Dutton brought out *Shen of the Sea* by Arthur Bowie Chrisman. American critics and librarians were so enchanted with the book that they awarded it the Newbery Medal for 1926. They might have had difficulty meeting educated Chinese, for the 1882 Exclusion Act was then in full force. Prohibiting but a few Chinese from entering the United States, it would not be repealed until 1943. Furthermore, a 1924 act of Congress prohibited American citizens of Chinese descent from bringing their wives and children into the United States (Hoobler 122).

It is interesting to compare *The Nightingale* with *Shen of the Sea.* Both were lauded by critics in the years after their publication. Andersen and Chrisman each locates himself, to use Said's phrase, vis-à-vis the Orient, but their locations are very different. Andersen's story transcends its time and literary roots in chinoiserie, whereas Chrisman's tales are mired in the mind-set of the Exclusion Laws. Chrisman assumed the intellectual authority to speak for China, while caricaturing its inhabitants as "aberrant, undeveloped, inferior" (Said 301). Unfortunately, Chrisman's stance is more common than Andersen's.

Andersen's first words, "In China, you know, the Emperor is Chinese and all his subjects are Chinese too," (1965, 1) locate the writer at a great distance from the setting of his story. By describing the Emperor's porcelain palace and garden where flowers were hung with tiny bells, Andersen reminds us, with subtle, almost self-mocking humor, that "the fable is fictitious and the characters [. . .] all imaginary." In contrast, Chrisman, in the title story of his collection of pseudo-traditional tales, pretends to locate himself within a topsy-turvy landscape and, thus, give it credence:

> Any reliable geography will tell you that Kua Hai is below sea level. And that, I know, is a fact, for I, lazily seated in my garden, have often gazed at sailing ships [. . .] wide-staring-eyed junks as they fetched into the Bay of the Sharp-Horned Moon, and to view them I had to raise my eyes. It is very true. (29)

Andersen's diction is colloquial, natural, in keeping with the theme of his story. Characters who speak with exaggerated formality, like the chamberlain (or chief courtier, depending on the translation), are ridiculed as pompous and pretentious. Chrisman, following a hoary tradition, succumbs to the temptation to translate the honorifics embedded in slangy, staccato spoken Chinese into absurdly polite dialogue and ludicrously formal diction, spiced with fractured Chinese phrases transliterated. Chrisman enjoys making jokes with Chinese names. A father calls his son, "Ah Mee." In Chinese, "Ah" is a meaningless syllable placed before the given name of a servant or inferior. A father would never use it for his son.

Western writers since Chrisman's time have continued to amuse their readers with ludicrous invented Chinese names. A Chinese cat is called "Kitty Ho" (Zimelman 8) and a first-born son named "Tikki tikki tembo-no sa rembo-chari bari ruchi-pip peri pembo" (Mosel 9). Furthermore, Chrisman's introduction of Western elements into the story recalls chinoiserie's melange of Western and Chinese architectural elements. Chinese drink milk, long for jam, and eat with a knife and fork. Chrisman explains the invention of chopsticks in the tale of a Chinese king who ate with a knife, fork, and spoon until these implements were used as weapons against him. Then "he [. . .] ate with the aid of two harmless, delicate little sticks" (68). Again, European values are turned topsy-turvy, with the Chinese cast as aberrant, undeveloped, and inferior.

One of Chrisman's stories, "Contrary Chueh Chun," faintly echoes the old Chinese story "The Man at the Border Lost His Horse." Since Chrisman, Western writers have had no compunction about twisting Chinese traditional literature beyond recognition. Winifred Morris's *The Future of Yen-Tzu* presents a topsy-turvy version of the lost horse story, complete with such whimsical honorifics for the emperor as "Your Irascible Amazement."

Another Chinese fable twisted out of shape in an American picture book is "How the Fool Moved Mountains." Mao Zedong and the Communist Party used this fable, widely known in China, to extort the Chinese people to undertake difficult tasks. An elderly fool finds the mountain range in front of his house inconvenient and decides to get rid of it. Helped by his family and a neighbor's child, he carries baskets filled with stones and earth from the mountain out to the sea. One trip takes them several months. When a wise man reproaches him, the fool replies that persevering through generations will accomplish the task (*Ancient Chinese Fables* 3–4). Chinese understand that the fool in this story has more insight than the wise man because he believes that he can accomplish anything if he works long enough.

Arnold Lobel's *Ming Lo Moves the Mountain* turns the fable into a "noodlehead" story. Ming Lo wants to move the mountain and goes to a wise man for help. The wise man suggests several useless solutions, including an offering of cakes and bread (introducing Western culinary staples in the eclectic tradition of chinoiserie) to the spirit of the mountain, before proposing a solution that fools Ming Lo into moving away from the mountain. The Chinese meaning is totally subverted.

In "The Nightingale," Andersen creates characters recognizable in their common humanity, in their universal delusions and longing. Chrisman, however, caricatures the Chinese people as incomprehensibly silly. Their whimsical, irrational behavior establishes them firmly as the mysterious, inscrutable Other. Later writers continue his stance.

I do not know if *Shen of the Sea* was influenced by Alice Ritchie's collection of original fantasy stories, *The Treasure of Li Po,* published in England in 1940 and America in 1949. Ritchie worked as a sales representative for her English publisher, Hogarth Press. I have been unable to determine how much she knew about traditional Chinese literature or whether she had ever been to China. She named the character in the title story after China's most famous poet but made him a basket maker.

Like Chrisman's, Ritchie's stories delighted reviewers and were widely used by library storytellers. Everyone understood quite clearly that they were humorous original fantasies set in China and written by a European. May Hill Arbuthnot included the most popular of Ritchie's stories, "Two of Everything" in her folktale anthology, *Time for Old Magic,* noting that it could *not* be called a true folktale (206). In this story, Ritchie drew on a situation from traditional Chinese literature, the magical doubling of wives, which occurs in a Chinese opera titled *The Carp-Fish Chase,* retold as "The Two Miss Peonys" in Linda Fang's recent collection of authentic Chinese tales, *The Ch'i-Lin Purse.*

Though Chrisman and Ritchie are long forgotten as writers, their vision of Cathay is a persistent influence on children's literature. For writers, illustrators, and publishers working into the twenty-first century, the assumptions of chinoiserie raise questions about artistic integrity. As Eleanor Cameron once noted, one characteristic of a well-written fantasy is "an overwhelming sense of place" (157). E. B. White's intimate knowledge of life on an American farm helps make *Charlotte's Web* a touchstone. Susan Cooper's knowledge of the Welsh countryside adds substance to her heroic fantasy *The Grey King.* There is a caveat often addressed to fantasy writers: if you posit a talking animal or space alien, you must always ask yourself, "Why is this character not a human being?" There must be a good reason, a reason integral to the narrative trajectory of the story. "Because it's cute" is not a good reason.

Likewise, at this time there must be better reasons than Aaron Hill's to set original fantasies in China. It is a real country, with a long, continuous cultural tradition, not mysterious, magnificent, mythical, exotic, or silly to its own inhabitants. Writers and artists should think long and hard before they take up pen or brush, questioning their assumptions, and remembering that they are working in a pervasive intellectual genealogy. Could the story just as well take place in an imaginary country or another planet?

Critics, reviewers, librarians, and teachers must also be aware of the intellectual genealogy of chinoiserie. If we feel a responsibility to present a culture accurately to children, it is important that we recognize and evaluate chinoiserie for what it is, a Western art form. Too often critics, reviewers, teachers, and librarians accept its genealogy without question. For example, Mingshui Cai's article, "Images of Chinese and Chinese Americans Mirrored in Picture Books," does not differentiate between folktales drawn from Chinese traditional literature and "modern folktales written by American authors" (169). I maintain that there is a crucial difference.

Original fantasies set in China that have, at best, a remote connection to Chinese culture are regularly recommended by teachers and librarians earnestly trying to enhance cultural understanding. Lily Toy Hong's truncated retelling of Alice Ritchie's "Two of Everything" from *The Treasure of Li Po* was published in a picture book version without attribution to Ritchie by Whitman in 1993. The Library of Congress assigned it the number 398.21, giving it the Dewey decimal status of Chinese traditional literature, and as such it received starred reviews in *Booklist, Kirkus,* and *School Library Journal.* How easily a piece of chinoiserie became a Chinese folk tale!

Another example comes from *Book Links,* January 1996 (Scales 40). Included on a list of folktales suggested for use with Laurence Yep's outstanding novel about a Chinese American girl, *Child of the Owl,* is Marianna Mayer's picture book version of *Turandot.* Loosely based on a tale of Persian origin, retold in an eighteenth-century Italian play and two twentieth-century Italian operas, this title belongs in a bibliography of Italian literature, not Chinese folklore.

Not all textbook writers are as discriminating as May Hill Arbuthnot. Liz Rothlein's *The Literature Connection: Using Children's Books in the Classroom* describes a thematic unit on China intended to make primary school students "familiar with Chinese culture" (334). The fanciful explanation of names in *Tikki Tikki Tembo* is accepted with deadpan literalness as an accurate piece of Chinese history.

Chinese listeners may have been surprised to hear Madeleine Albright, later to become the first female U.S. Secretary of State, quote an American picture book in her remarks to the Fourth World Conference on Women in Bejing on September 6, 1995. The five-line verse, which Albright calls an old Chinese poem, ended with the lines "But what can we do with a girl like you?" (676). It appears in Thomas Handforth's *Mei Lei,* a picture book set in old Bejing that was awarded a Caldecott medal in 1939. The verse was first introduced to English speakers in an 1896 anthology collected around Beijing by Guido Vitale, an Italian diplomat. Isaac Taylor Headland of Beijing University drew on Vitale's work for his larger 1900 collection *Chinese Mother Goose Rhymes,* aimed at a child audience, and from there it passed into modern picture books. Vitale characterized the tone of the verse as playful (198), but Albright recited it indignantly. Evidently, she took it to represent wholesale victimization of Chinese women, a simplistic view of women's history promulgated by twentieth-century reformers in China, from Western missionaries to Chinese Communists. This image of suffering Chinese women is very persistent, yet even a brief investigation of the large body of Chinese poetry by women writers would give a far more complex, nuanced view and one that the Chinese audience might recognize.

Discerning critics, reviewers, teachers, and librarians should distinguish between stories set in mysterious, magnificent Cathay and those set in the country that is a fourteen-hour jet ride across the Pacific. Both can be used and discussed with children. We Westerners must remember that the reason Cathay is so comfortably familiar is that we created it. Adult intermediaries must read source notes carefully and seek out literature in translation. Many writers, notably Laurence Yep and Ed Young, are building bridges between China's literary tradition and American children. There is enough authentic Chinese art in urban museums or art libraries to introduce the uninitiated to the Chinese sensibility.

American children must know that the never-never land of the blue willow plate is very far from the China of the Tang or Ming dynasties, from the China of Mao Zedong and Deng Xiaoping. Chinoiserie, charming and entertaining as it is, shrouds in a veil of misinformation our children's first impressions of a complex and ancient civilization that is already playing an important role on the world stage.

Bibliography

These books, mostly published for children, are drawn from Chinese literature or depict Chinese history in a form Chinese themselves might recognize. Also useful are *Ancient Chinese Fables* and Handforth's *Mei Lei.*

Background Notes

Chang, Margaret and Raymond. *Speaking of Chinese.* New York: Norton, 2001.
Mahy, Margaret. *The Seven Chinese Brothers.* Illus. Jean and Mou-sien Tseng. New York: Scholastic, 1990.
Rumford, James. *The Cloudmakers.* Boston: Houghton Mifflin, 1996.

Mined from Chinese Literature

Bedard, Michael. *The Painted Wall and Other Strange Tales.* Toronto: Tundra, 2003.
Bruya, Brian. *The Dao of Zhuangzi; More Music of Nature.* New York: Anchor, 1997.
Chuang Tzu: Basic Writings. Trans. Burton Watson. New York: Columbia University Press, 1996.
Da Chen. *Wandering Warrior.* New York: Delacorte, 2003.
Fang, Linda. *The Ch'i-Lin Purse: A Collection of Ancient Chinese Stories.* Illus. Jeanne M. Lee. New York: Farrar, Straus and Giroux, 1995.
Freedman, Russell. *Confucius: The Golden Rule.* Illus. Fréderick Clément. New York: Arthur A. Levine/ Scholastic, 2002.
Ji-li Jiang. *The Magical Monkey King: Mischief in Heaven.* Illus. Hui Hui Su-Kennedy. New York: Harper-Collins, 2002.
Kherdian, David. *Monkey; Journey to the West.* Illus. Hokusai and others. Boston and New York: Shambala, 2000.
Lao Tzu/Tao Te Ching; A Book About the Way and the Power of the Way. Trans. Ursula K. Le Guin in collaboration with J. P. Seaton. New York: Shambala, 1997.
Maples in the Mist: Children's Poems from the Tang Dynasty. Trans. Minfong Ho. Illus. Jean & Mou-Sien Tseng. New York: Lothrop, Lee, and Shepard, 1996.

McCully, Emily Arnold. *Beautiful Warrior: the Legend of the Nun's Kung Fu*. New York: Scholastic/Arthur A. Levine, 1998.

Shepard, Aaron. *Lady White Snake: A Tale from Chinese Opera*. Illus. Song Nan Zhang. Union City, CA: Pan Asian, 2001.

Siyu, Liu and Orel Protopopescu. *A Thousand Peaks: Poems from China*. Illus. Siyu Liu. Berkeley, CA: Pacific View Press, 2002.

The Song of Mu Lan. Trans. and illus. Jeanne M. Lee. Arden, NC: Front Street, 1995.

Yep, Laurence. *The Butterfly Boy*. Illus. Jeanne M. Lee. New York: Farrar, Straus and Giroux, 1993.

———. *Dragon of the Lost Sea*, 1982; *Dragon Steel*, 1985; *Dragon Cauldron*, 1991; *Dragon War*, 1992. New York: HarperCollins.

———. *Lady of Ch'iao Kuo: Warrior of the South*. New York: Scholastic, 2001.

———. *The Man Who Tricked a Ghost*. Illus. Isadore Seltzer. Mahwah, NJ: Bridgewater Press, 1993.

Young, Ed. *Night Visitors*. New York: Philomel, 1995.

Chinese Traditional Literature Art and Festivals

Ai-Ling Louie. *Yeh-shen: a Cinderella Story from China*. Illus. Ed Young. New York: Philomel, 1982.

Bang, Molly Garrett. *Tye May and the Magic Brush*. New York: Greenwillow, 1981.

Chinese Folktales. Adapt. Howard Giskin. Lincolnwood, IL: NTC Publishing Group, 1997.

Simonds, Nina and Leslie Swartz. *Moonbeams, Dumplings, & Dragon Boats: A Treasury of Chinese Holiday Tales, Activities, and Recipes*. Illus. Meilo So. San Diego, CA: Harcourt/Gulliver, 2002.

Stepanchuk, Carol. *Red Eggs and Dragon Boats: Celebrating Chinese Festivals*. Berkeley, CA: Pacific View Press, 1993.

Traditional Chinese Folktales. Adapt. Yin-lien Chin and others. Illus. Lu Wang. M. E. Sharpe, 1989.

East Meets West

Chang, Margaret and Raymond. *In the Eye of War*. New York: Margaret K. McElderry/Macmillan, 1990.

Da Chen. *China's Son: Growing Up in the Cultural Revolution*. New York: Delacorte, 2001.

Fritz, Jean. *China Homecoming*, 1985; *Homesick, My Own Story*, 1982. New York: Putnam.

Ji-Li Jiang. *Red Scarf Girl*. New York: HarperCollins, 1997.

Namioka, Lensey. *Ties That Bind, Ties That Break*, 1999: *An Ocean Apart, A World Away*, 2002. New York: Delacorte.

Partridge, Elizabeth. *Oranges on Gold Mountain*. Illus. Aki Sogabe. New York: Dutton, 2001.

Paterson, Katherine. *Rebels of the Heavenly Kingdom*. New York: Dutton/Lodestar, 1983.

Russell, Ching Yueng. *First Apple*, 1994; *Water Ghost,* 1995; *Lichee Tree*, 1997; *Child Bride*, 1999. Honesdale, PA: Boyd's Mills Press.

Song Nan Zhang. *A Little Tiger in the Chinese Night*. Toronto: Tundra, 1993.

Yee, Paul. *Dead Man's Gold and Other Stories*. Illus. Harvey Chan. Toronto: Groundwood Books, 2002.

Yep, Laurence. *Serpent's Children*, 1984; *Mountain Light*, 1985. New York: HarperCollins.

Today's China

Tsubakiyama, Margaret Holloway. *Mei-Mei Loves the Morning*. Illus. Cornelius Van Wright and Ying-Hwa Hu. Morton Grove, IL: Albert Whitman, 1999.

Wu, Priscilla. *The Abacus Contest: Stories from Taiwan and China*. Illus. Xio-jun Li. Golden, CO: Fulcrum Kids, 1996.

Works Cited

Albright, Madeleine K. "Remarks to the Fourth World Conference on Women, Bejing, China, September 6, 1995." *U.S. Department of State Dispatch* 6 (September 4, 1995): 674–76.

Arbuthnot, May Hill and Mark Taylor. *Time for Old Magic*. Glenview, IL: Scott, Foresman, 1970.

Dooley, Patricia, "Porcelain, Pigtails, Pagodas: Images of China in 19th and 20th Century Illustrated Editions of 'The Nightingale.' " *Proceedings of the Annual Conference of the Children's Literature Association* 6 (1979): 94–105.

Cai, Mingshui. "Images of Chinese and Chinese Americans Mirrored in Picture Books." *Children's Literature in Education* 25 (1994): 169–91.

Cameron, Eleanor. "The Eternal Moment." *Children's Literature Association Quarterly* 9 (Winter 1984–85): 157–64.

Honour, Hugh. *Chinoiserie, the Vision of Cathay.* London: J. Murray, 1961.

Picart, Bernard. *The Ceremonies and Religious Customs of the Idolatrous Nations: together with historical annotations and several curious discourses, equally instructive and entertaining . . .* V. IV, part II. London: James Bettenham for Claude du Bose, 1735.

Rothlein, Liz and Anita Meyer Meinbach. *The Literature Connection; Using Children's Books in the Classroom.* Glenview, Illinois: Scott, Foresman, 1991.

Ruffa, Jane. "Reading the World: China." *Book Links* (January 1997): 52–57.

Said, Edward W. *Orientalism.* London: Penguin Books, 1995.

Scales, Pat. "Laurence Yep's *Child of the Owl.*" *Book Links* (January 1996): 36–41.

Vitale, Guido (Baron). *Pekinese Rhymes.* Peking: Pei-T'ang Press, 1986.

Zhang Longxi. "The Myth of the *Other:* China in the Eyes of the West." *Critical Inquiry* 15 (Autumn 1988): 108–31.

Children's Literature

Ancient Chinese Fables. Trans. Yang Xianyi, Gladys Yang, and others. Illus. Feng Zikai. Bejing: Foreign Languages Press, 1981.

Andersen, Hans Christian. *The Nightingale.* Trans. Eva Le Gallienne. Illus. Nancy Ekholm Burkert. New York: Harper and Row, 1965.

Bishop, Claire Huchet. *The Five Chinese Brothers.* Illus. Kurt Wiese. New York: Coward-McCann, 1938.

Chrisman, Arthur Bowie. *Shen of the Sea: Chinese Stories for Children.* Illus. Else Hasselriis. 1925. New York: E. P. Dutton, 1968.

Fang, Linda. *The Ch'i-Lin Purse: a Collection of Ancient Chinese Stories.* Illus. Jeanne M. Lee. New York: Farrar, Straus and Giroux, 1995.

Handforth, Thomas. *Mei Lei.* New York: Doubleday, 1938.

Headland, Isaac Taylor. *Chinese Mother Goose Rhymes.* New York: Fleming H. Revell Company, 1900.

Heyer, Marilee. *Weaving of a Dream.* New York: Viking, 1986.

Hong, Lily Toy. *Two of Everything.* Morton Grove, IL: Albert Whitman, 1993.

Hoobler, Dorothy and Thomas. *The Chinese American Family Album.* New York: Oxford University Press, 1994.

Lobel, Arnold. *Ming Lo Moves the Mountain.* New York: Scholastic, 1982.

Mayer, Marianna. *Turandot.* Illus. Winslow Pels. New York: Morrow Junior Books, 1995.

Morris, Winifred. *The Future of Yen-Tzu.* Illus. Friso Henstra. New York: Atheneum, 1992.

Mosel, Arlene. *Tikki Tikki Tembo.* Illus. Blair Lent. New York: Holt, Rinehart and Winston, 1968.

Ritchie, Alice. *The Treasure of Li Po.* Illus. T. Ritchie [Marjorie Tulip Parsons]. New York: Harcourt, Brace, and World, 1949.

Schwartz, Stephen. *The Perfect Peach.* Illus. Leonard B. Lubin. Boston: Little, Brown, 1977.

Singer, Isaac Bashevis. *The Topsy-Turvy Emperor of China.* Translated from the Yiddish by the author and Elizabeth Shub. Illus. William Pène du Bois. New York: Harper and Row, 1971.

Steckman, Elizabeth. *Silk Peony, Parade Dragon.* Illus. Carol Inouye. Honesdale, PA: Boyd's Mills, 1977.

Williams, Jay. *Everyone Knows What a Dragon Looks Like.* Illus. Mercer Mayer. New York: Four Winds, 1976.

Zimelman, Nathan. *The Great Adventure of Wo Ti.* Illus. Julie Downing. New York: Macmillan, 1992.

5

The Black Aesthetic within Black Children's Literature

Nancy D. Tolson

> *We must give our own story to the world.*
> —Carter G. Woodson, *Negro Makers of History* 1928

Imagine a child being snatched away from his mother immediately after birth. This child has never seen or physically touched his mother. This child was not able to suck upon her breast or get lulled to sleep in her arms. Instead, this child is given scraps to nourish his body and falls unconscious from exhaustion from being overworked. But this child recognizes his siblings who were also taken in the same way. They gather together when possible and whisper memories they share from when they were within the womb. They recall that when their mother danced; they danced; when she sang, they listened; and while she talked, walked, worked, and ate, they felt her soul and were nourished by her. They soothe themselves with her memory and carry joy with them because they know they resemble her.

The Black Aesthetic is the artistic expression that interprets the Black experience in the New World. It is the artistry of a people denied so much for so long after their awakening. The Black Aesthetic is art that told others Blacks were and are not bastard children; they know their mother and celebrate her existence through every artistic movement they create. And at the same moment, the Black Aesthetic says Blacks really don't care what others think about them as long as they are able to think for themselves. It is what Langston Hughes states in "The Negro Artist and the Racial Mountain":

> We younger Negro artists who create now intend to express our individual dark-skinned selves without fear or shame. If white people are pleased we are glad. If they are not, it doesn't matter. We know we are beautiful. And ugly too. The tom-tom cries and the tom-tom laughs. If colored people are pleased we are glad. If they are not, their pleasure doesn't matter either.

> We build our temples for tomorrow, strong as we know how, and we stand on top of the mountain, free within ourselves. (309)

This creative movement began when Black artists started creating written, visual, and aural art for and about Black people. The Black Aesthetic was not created for Whites to understand or critique; it was a cultural connection from Blacks to Blacks. This creativity moved away from "standards" set down by Whites and moved toward cultural independence. Writer/poet Margaret Walker Alexander defines the Black Aesthetic as being "indigenous to Black people, having its roots in ancient Black Africa and characterized by certain marked traits seen throughout the Diaspora or the modern world" (100).

Black children's literature is based on this aesthetic theory. This literature allows Black writers to create words that can be poured on the rich-fertile soil of the Black child's mind. Former Black children have created words and illustrations to tell victorious stories of the past, give lessons for the future, and bring laughter to the present. The purpose of Black children's literature was to build the self-esteem of the Black child, to have Black achievements and creativity culturally instilled within them so Black children will strive to achieve what is best for them. A good story would be able to inspire Black children to read more, especially when the images inside that story present positive Black role models. This literature would be able to magnify the various experiences within Black culture that demonstrate historical beauty and wealth; it is the fuel to start the creativity and sense of self in a Black child. This literature also has the ability to assist non-Black children in their understandings of another part of America. Illustrator/author Ashley Bryan explains the way his work reflects who he is and at the same moment who he is reflects his work:

> No matter what my source, I feel that, as an African American, rooted in the study and love of Black culture, my identity is revealed in whatever I create. Through my work I reach out to offer, to take in, to initiate dialogue. As I speak, I am listening to you. I have been sharing with you my sources—resources from which I work. They are variously presented as family, friends, neighbors, schools, world cultures. [. . .] These are the tender bridges that link past to present and my stories to yours. ("A Tender Bridge" 301)

There is a long ignored history of the Black Aesthetic in children's literature that is not often included in children's literature textbooks. It needs to be acknowledged.

> The younger Generation comes, bringing its gifts.
> —*Alain Locke,* The New Negro, *1925*

As early as the 1920s, Black leaders began to create literature for Black children aimed at inspiring them to become high achievers. *The Brownies' Book,* a magazine written for and dedicated to "the children of the Sun," was created by scholar and political activist, W.E.B. Du Bois and writer Jessie Fauset. *The Brownies' Book* was the youth's version of *The Crisis,* which was the magazine formulated for the National Association for the Advancement of Colored People (NAACP). Renown Negro writers contributed historical and geographical essays, fictional stories, and poetry to *The Brownies' Book*. This magazine overflowed with photographs of Negro children from all across the United States. Dianne Johnson states that *The Brownies' Book* encouraged children to dream: "each issue of the magazine included stories of people, famous and not famous, who accomplished much with their lives. The editors also encouraged children by suggesting books they could read to help them know more about history and to prepare for the future" (15). Jessie Fauset made it clear when writing the dedication who *The Brownies' Book* wished to have as its primary audience:

> *To Children, who with eager look*
> *Scanned vainly library shelf and nook,*
> *For the History or Song or Story*
> *That told of Colored People's glory—*
> *We dedicate The Brownies' Book.*[1]

During the 1920s many new Black voices emerged with a new way to express and celebrate their culture. This was the beginning of a Black Arts movement. In his article, "Negro Youth Speaks," Alain Locke introduced several of the fresh young "New Negro" artists who were a part of this *new* aesthetic style that was called the Harlem Renaissance to Black readers of 1925. Locke explained the style of these new artists:

> It has brought with it, first of all, that wholesome, welcome virtue of finding beauty in one-self; the younger generation can no longer be twitted as "cultural nondescripts" or accused of "being out of love with their own nativity." They have instinctive love and pride of race, and, spirituality compensating for the present lacks of America, ardent respect and love for Africa, the motherland. (52–53)

Carter G. Woodson, founder of the Association for the Study of Negro Life and History and advocate of the first Negro History Week, wanted to instill pride and build self-esteem in Negro youth. The Associated Publishers, a Black publishing company that began in 1927, was backed by Black authors, educators, and historical scholars such as Woodson and Charles Wesley. The company was able to publish informative books teaching the history and culture of Blacks, but it alone was not large enough to remove the negative depictions of Blacks from the minds of children throughout the United States during this time. By the 1930s and early 1940s, there was a literary crusade that involved scholars, politicians, and community social groups being led by children's librarian Augusta Baker. Baker wanted to raise the standards of books for and about Black boys and girls at the 135th Street Branch Library in Harlem. She and the others began a crusade that coincided with the "New Negro" stance. The purpose of this crusade was to increase the positive image of Negroes with literary role models Black children could aspire to emulate. Baker believed it was important to promote an image that could generate self-esteem for Harlem children as well as other Black children living in the United States. She advocated that this literature not be didactic as Sunday School literature published prior to the Harlem Renaissance had been. The purpose of this movement was to have positive and enjoyable images to enjoy available in all facets of the child's literary experience.

White publishers had to be attacked during this crusade in order to develop better books for Black children. It would take decades before many publishing companies would include Black images at all, but Baker's crusade pushed other librarians who were serving areas highly populated by Blacks. The images of Blacks that did appear inside children's books were derogatory and offensive, and even when positive Black images did appear inside the pages of children's picture books these images often showed Blacks in servitude positions and were created by White illustrators with stories by White writers about Black characters as subservient persons. The majority of American children's books promoted a strong White Aesthetic that literary critic Addison Gayle, Jr. has defined:

> The distinction between whiteness as beautiful (good) and blackness as ugly (evil) appears early in the literature of the middle ages—in Morality Plays of England. Heavily influenced by both Platonism and Christianity, these plays set forth the distinctions that exist today. To be white was to be pure, good, universal, and beautiful; to be black was to be impure, evil, parochial, and ugly.
>
> The characters of the plots of these plays followed this basic format. The villain is always evil, in most cases the devil; the protagonist, or hero, is always good, in most cases, angels or disciples. The plot then is simple; good (light) triumphs over the forces of evil (dark). (*The Black Aesthetic* 40)

During the Harlem Renaissance, established Black authors had better chances to write for children and get their books published because they already were working within the publishing establishment. Langston Hughes and Arna Bontemps, separately and collaboratively, began writing books for children, starting with *Popo and Fifina: Children of Haiti* (1932). They continued to write books for Black children throughout their careers. In a 1939 letter to Langston Hughes, Bontemps states, "seems like we're going to be the models for future generations of writers for children and students of that literature" (qtd. in Nichols 35).

> Imagination, by definition, is freedom.
> —*Carolyn Fowler,* Black Arts and Black Aesthetic, *1976*

By the post–World War II era the literary mood of Negro writers was influenced by the severe pain of racism throughout the United States. Writers such as James Baldwin, Richard Wright, and Ralph Ellison voiced their thoughts about racism in their writings. As junior novelists slowly appeared, a few books containing true-to-life images of Black experiences emerged, including the racial struggles for equality in America. Jesse Jackson, Ellen Tarry, Shirley Graham (Du Bois), and Lorenz Graham wrote both nonfiction and fiction books for children. Black authors who wrote children's fiction about Blacks were not being published in abundance, but their few books that were published honestly addressed the truth about Black conditions across the country. Jesse Jackson began writing stories he hoped would motivate the reading skills of troubled youth, especially troubled boys. As a former probation officer, Jackson realized that slow readers or nonreaders sometimes could not find reading material that would keep them interested. They needed stories they felt related to their lives. Jackson hoped that *Call Me Charley* could hold the attention of these young readers. Jackson stated, "I decided that I wanted to write stories that kids would read because they wanted to. I felt reading should be an enjoyable experience" (67). *Call Me Charley* begins with the Black protagonist, Charles Moss, being introduced to a few of the White boys on his paper route. This beginning unfriendly scene sets the pace for the remainder of Jackson's realistic drama containing honest images and true-to-life Black/White experiences:

> George looked from Tom to Charles. His gray eyes were slits. He picked up a stick. "Tom, let's show Sambo?"
> My name is Charles," the boy repeated. "Sometimes I'm Charley. Nobody calls me Sambo and gets away with it." He dropped the paper he was rolling and moved closer to George. George swung back with the stick. (8)

Jackson's junior novel became a popular title for Black youth in the late 1940s.

Lorenz Graham's junior novel *South Town* did not romanticize life in the rural South; Graham wrote about the struggle of a Black family that stands up to the bigots in their town. *South Town* was not immediately accepted by publishers, but Graham fought to maintain his honest portrayal of his protagonist and his family:

> I was told there was unanimous agreement that my book would have to be re-written. The Negro characters in my story were too much like other people. I countered that Negroes are like other people. I offered to change the plot, to add to or to remove portions of the story, but I refused to change the character of the people. (History 192)

David Williams's first encounter with Travis, a White soldier back from the Korean War, contained realism not often included in historical novels about the American South during that era. Travis talks to David about his experience in Korea, which included Black medics who came to the rescue of many wounded soldiers, while walking down the road. Travis describes the medics as Black angels with stretchers:

> People are all kinds of fools. I don't suppose I was ever so glad to see anyone in my life as I was to see that colored fellow that helped me in Korea. It makes me mad now when I see colored folks put off in the Jim Crow car and stuff like that. (55)

Graham's plot shows the emotional pains and triumphs of Blacks within the fictional setting of South Town. This highly imaginative novel reflected the racism that many Blacks experienced during the 1950s. Graham wanted this junior novel published so youthful readers could see the truth about Black families in the South. Graham later recalled:

> I was writing about people who were singing "We shall overcome!" The parents of my central character uphold ambition and hope. I pointed out that there were many such families. (History 193)

However, at this time, many Black writers found that publishers preferred to print stories about the Black experience as written by White authors. They realized that these stories were not coming from the community, that inside the community, spirited change was being built on the realizations of Black struggles, past and present. These authors understood that though publishers would rather have a Black story told by a White writer the Black Aesthetic would not be found in stories that tried to mimic experience through observed incidents or assumed knowledge. Stories about racism and Black lives would be ones their authors had experienced. As essayist Julian Mayfield explained:

> [. . .] deep in their guts they cannot feel what we have felt. Their eyes cannot see what our eyes have seen, and what the eyes of all those generations of dead and dying old black men and women saw, from slave ships to cotton fields to ghetto obsolescence; the crushing of manhood spirit in childhood, the destruction of what was pure and beautiful and godlike in ourselves before we could see it. (31)

> Black Art is the aesthetic and spiritual sister of the Black Power concept.
> —*Larry Neal,* "The Black Arts Movement": The Black Aesthetic, *1971*

In the 1960s the civil rights movement pushed for equality for Blacks, and it became a highlight of Black activity. Youths marched for the civil rights their parents had not yet acquired. Discrimination was made visible in all facets of American society. According to James A. Emanuel, the 1960s changed Black youth in America: " the nonviolent black youth, who had to pass through the valley of the angry 'white backlash' into morass of public espionage, private harassment, and racist assassination, grew inevitably into a new breed of men" (208). Riots, marches, and demonstrations situated the mood and progress during this monumental decade. Young Black voices protested in the streets across the United States, and, standing alongside the Black political leaders of this decade, young Black voices would not be silenced by Whites engaged in brutal beatings, shootings, and bombings. The 1960s brought change in American race relations.

In these years the Black Arts Movement began. Black writers and poets were applauded for their truthful use of expressive Black language. John Henrik Clarke argued that change must take place in the literature created by Blacks: "In the next phase of Afro-American writing, a literature of celebration must be created—not a celebration of oppression, but a celebration of survival in spite of it" (645). The literary observations of Addison Gayle Jr., Larry Neal, Darwin Turner, and other Black critics identified and defined Black Aesthetics. Their writings exposed the civil unrest caused by White attitudes and actions toward Black Americans; these authors celebrated being Black and wrote creative commentaries that reported American history and contemporary actions not being televised. Black leaders inspired Black people to stand up and fight back even when they were silenced for telling the truth. The Black Arts Movement, while not the first awakening of artistic Black expression, was the strongest. Authors used strong language to cut into the deep emotional outpouring and openly expressed new Black views about current events. A Black consciousness became visible across America as Black people chose to wear African clothing, and natural hairstyles and to create music once more that sent out messages of freedom, telling Blacks to "Say It Loud, I'm Black and I'm Proud."[2]

American publishing was forced to face its part in past discrimination. Publishers could no longer disregard the fact that Black children were ignored in children's literature or that White imagery dominated the books created for children. America saw a flurry of studies that showed how children observed a completely White world in their literature. These studies demonstrated that both White and Black children were being negatively affected. Publishers had no choice but to begin publishing more children's books that were written by and about Blacks. Thus, by the mid-sixties Black children were being represented in picture books and junior novels. Research in the Black Aesthetic articulated the literary elements featured in Black children's literature, books focused on the identity of the Black child. Inspired Black writers and illustrators created positive imagery for the Black children who daily faced turmoil and chaos. These new publications with their straightforward Black perspective showed Black children how beautiful they were and demonstrated that they should be proud of their heritage.

In 1969, Virginia Hamilton marked a change in heroism and Black identity by defining the beauty of a Black woman through an African image in her junior novel *Zeely*. Hamilton created a story and setting without racial conflict that centered its plot around the awakening of a young Black girl to the truth about racism and Black pride. Using literary frames found in the Black Aesthetic, Hamilton wove folklore into a contemporary story so that her protagonist and her reader could grasp how Black folk art tradition mixed realism with imaginative metaphors. Virginia Hamilton gave children the traditions Zora Neale Hurston had given adult readers during the Harlem Renaissance. *Zeely* tells of a young Black girl who decides to change her name to Geeder and to change her brother John Perry's name to Toeboy while they are visiting relatives during the summer. When Geeder meets Zeely Tayber, whose father Nat Tayber rents land from Geeder's uncle's and keeps hogs there, Geeder becomes intrigued with Zeely's beauty:

> Zeely Tayber was more than six and a half feet tall, thin and deeply dark as a pole of Ceylon ebony. She wore a long smock that reached to her ankles. Her arms, hands, and feet were bare, and her thin, oblong head didn't seem to fit quite right on her shoulders.
>
> She had very high cheekbones and her eyes seemed to turn inward on themselves. Geeder couldn't say what expression she saw on Zeely's face. She knew only that it was calm, that it had pride in it, and that the face was the most beautiful she had ever seen. (42)

Thus, Black beauty is defined positively without any relation to White ideals. Geeder's fascination in Zeely is accentuated when she finds an old magazine that has an article on the Watusi people of Africa. When Geeder turns to a picture of a Mututsi woman of royal birth that resembles Zeely, she is convinced that Zeely Tayber is part of a royal lineage. Hamilton's interweaving of folk literature, cultural imagery, and orality is exceptional; within her plot she introduces slave songs and stories about reaching freedom. Within Zeely, Virginia Hamilton's character (and indirectly her audience) comes "to grips with the cultural ramifications of the African presence in America" (Neal 85).

In the late 1960s, John Steptoe became one of the pioneers of Black children's picture books. Steptoe's first book, *Stevie,* was published in 1969, and it soon became one of the first widely acclaimed prominent picture books created by a Black artist. Steptoe was able to capture the voice and imagery that many Black children knew, bringing a valid representation of Black identity to the picture book format. When reviewing literature for and about Black children, Judy Richardson stated, "The dialogue is so realistic that the reader might feel he's overhearing an actual conversation between two children" (396). The August 29, 1969, issue of *Life* contained three illustrations and the complete text of *Stevie* along with an article about the young John Steptoe. Steptoe introduced his frustrations and ideals to this wider audience:

> I have been taught Western ideas of what a painter is, what painting is, and that stifles me because I am not a Western man. I have never felt I was a citizen of the U.S.A.—this country doesn't speak to me. To be a black man in this society means finding out who I am. So I have got to stay on my own, get out from under induced values and discover who I am at the base. (59)

Steptoe continued to create new experiences in stories that gave life to the voice of the Black child during the 1970s and 1980s. Other new Black writers brought in new perspectives and images of Blacks that provided more positive imagery on the Black child in society. These honest depictions awakened the field of children's literature to a new set of literary standards. Black writers and illustrators were celebrating the Black experience and Black Arts through their creations. Camille Yarbrough, Eloise Greenfield, Ashley Bryan, Tom Feelings, and others created stories and images that honored the Black child's experiences and cultural identity. They created stories that could inspire Black children; they sent these children across the oceans to discover who they were and where they had come from. Several of these stories announced to these children that they, too, had a homeland. Artists and authors brought back stories as they visited Africa and created books that allowed Black children to recognize their place of cultural birth, to read about Africa with pride, and wonder about the oral stories that began so long ago. Julius Lester explained that he was writing for Black children:

> I must address myself to blacks, to write books that hopefully will give black children the strength and pride that have been deliberately kept from them. It will be a long time before the mass of whites look upon black children as blacks and as individuals. I do not exist in this country as an individual. I am a black. (72)

Yarbrough's *Cornrows* contained the unified spirit between this distant homeland and America within her characterization of a grandmother and mother who conjure up stories of Africa to explain the significance of various cornrow styles for their children and grandchildren Sister (Shirley Ann) and Brother (Mike). While they tell their stories, the visions they manifest come alive in Carole Byard's artwork; the audience watches as two children listen and get their hair braided into beautiful cornrow styles. *Cornrows* replicates Black inner pride and outer beauty through two folk art traditions, storytelling and cornrowing:

> *I delight in tellin you, my child—*
> *yes, you please me when you ask it—*
> *it's a hairstyle that's call* suku.
> *in Yoruba, it means* basket.[3]

Eloise Greenfield's *Africa Dream*, first published in 1977, is a poetic expression of the spiritual connectivity between African and Black people and culture throughout time. In

Greenfield's rhythmic story, a child describes a wonderful journey she took while sleeping that allowed her to see and touch her ancestors in Africa. The words are accompanied by graceful black and white sketches by Carole Byard. These images are ornamented across the pages with Egyptian symbols and images that surround the child's ancestral dream:

> *I went all the way to Africa*
> *In a dream one night*
> *I crossed over the ocean*
> *In a slow, smooth jump*[4]

Ashley Bryan's *The Dancing Granny,* published the same year, is a wonderful commemoration to Black folklore. Bryan's images with swaying hips and flinging arms dance across the pages; they can be physically copied by the youthful reader. Bryan pinpoints the origin of the Black Aesthetic within its first cultural aesthetic form—folklore. He combines words and illustrations to fit Ron Karenga's second characteristic of Black Art: "it must be from the people and must be returned to the people in a form more beautiful and colorful than it was in real life" (34). Bryan took oral tales from the people and from the inspiration of his grandmother's telling of tales:

> Adults pass stories orally, and authors use this material in their work. That is the round. We move from the voice to the book and back again to the voice. The oral tradition feeds into literature, and thus the stories of all peoples with a written language exist today in books.
> When I work with an African story motif, I try to evoke the oral tradition in the written tale. The presence of the storyteller now needs written equivalents. I work from the family of African-American poets to inform the prose of my retelling of stories. (Tender Bridge 300)

Tom Feelings captured the strong Black features in children within *Something on My Mind.* Feelings visibly placed the Black Aesthetic in a picture book format when he created images of Black children with semi-smiles and far away glances. Feelings wanted to magnify the beauty of these children in order to privilege their existence. He used two main colors in his artwork, showing both the joy and sorrow of Black life in an American setting (694). He purposefully reflected a double consciousness in his drawings:

> In America my colors were muted, monochromatic, and somber. In Africa they became more vivid and alive, as though they had light radiating from within. This light is what I brought back to America for young Black children to see and feel. I put it into all the books whose setting took place in America. In 1966, armed with this new energy and a full portfolio of strong, positive Black imagery, I returned to the America and a world of children's book publishing that was no longer lily white. (689)

Nikki Grimes' rhythmic prose completed the complexity of Black experience found in Feelings's artwork.

Mildred D. Taylor broke through the lily white world of children's literature that Feelings described with a monumental junior novel in 1976. *Roll of Thunder, Hear My Cry* is a family saga that shows the strength and love within a Black family and the bitterness of racism that surrounds them. Taylor has shared stories of the Logan family for the past twenty-five years, writing nine realistic fiction books based on her family's history. *Roll of Thunder, Hear My Cry* continues to receive recognition throughout the country; today it is part of the children's literary canon.

In *Shadow & Substance,* Rudine Sims surveyed 150 contemporary fiction stories about Blacks written and published between 1965 and 1979. She reported that out of the 104 different authors who wrote the books, only 34 were Black writers who "produced books of the culturally conscious/self-affirming type" (104). Sims sought to expose the importance of writing culturally conscious fiction for Black children and developing a body of literature that "presents an image of Afro-Americans as courageous survivors with a strong sense of community and cultural affinity and with positive feelings about being Black" (105).

> And just like the color of our skin varies in shades of black, so does our vision.
> —*Terry McMillan,* Breaking Ice, *1990*

The 1980s and the 1990s brought forth a new image and a new Black aesthetic concept. Terry McMillan has described the attitude of Black authors who have turned to writing fiction during this period in terms of a growing awareness about the elements of the Black Aesthetic:

> For many of us, writing is our reaction to injustices, absurdities, beauty. It's our way of registering our complaints or affirmations. The best are not didactic. They do not scream out "message," nor are they abstractions. Our stories are our personal response. What we want to specify. What we see. What we feel. Our wide angle lens—our close-up look. And even if the story doesn't quite pinpoint the solution or the answer, it is the exploration itself that is often worth the trip. (xxii)

Newer fiction has questioned beauty and an earlier acceptance of standards for appearance within Black culture. Problems within recently constructed plots have not been easily solved, and plots do not necessarily contain happy-ever-after endings. The protagonists end their journeys with new insights and with hope that they have learned the truth about their possibilities. In 1987 *An Enchanted Hair Tale,* written by Alexis De Veaux and illustrated by Cheryl Hanna, appeared. This book centers its drama on a male protagonist with dreadlocks. Sudan, who looks different from other Blacks, feels the pain of difference within his own community, though he does not strive to fit in and look like everyone else. What Sudan wants is to be able to be accepted for who he is, not what he looks like. Images of a pyramid, lions sailing away in rowboats, zebras, and crescent moons complement the story, reminding the reader that Sudan is tied to his African beginnings. In Phil Mendez's *The Black Snowman,* published two years later, a Black snowman conjures up African images during the night and informs the young protagonist Jacob of his impressive African heritage. At first, Jacob considers everything black to be negative because he has not been taught any differently. When a magic piece of kente cloth is wrapped around a dirty snowman and the snowman informs Jacob about Africa, Jacob becomes enlightened. Both books take their readers back to the African beginnings of Black history.

Thank You, Dr. Martin Luther King, Jr.!, by Eleanora E. Tate, was published in 1990. Tate sets her story in the South; her female protagonist is embarrassed to be Black because she does not consider that Black is beautiful. Tate's main character believes that beauty only appears in White images like a Barbie doll. Therefore, Mary Elouise considers Black History month the worst time of the year until Miss Imani comes to her school and begins to talk with her about her African heritage. Because she has never been taught anything positive about Africa, she is uncertain until Big Momma reframes American history for her:

> Shoot, our ancestors didn't jump in line over in Africa to sign up to be slaves for over here like they were looking for jobs. No! They had their own homes and families. But some evil Europeans and some evil Americans and some evil English and some evil Africans got together and put the finger on other Africans. (171)

Tate and Mendez express the painful omission of Black history and its effect on Black children, whether the omission is the history of Blacks within the United States or of African history. These books correct the long held negative images of Blacks earlier created by Whites. Tate and Mendez reform history for their contemporary youthful audiences.

> May they understand that we are not what we say. We are what we do.
> —*Mildred Pitts Walter, "Social Responsibility," 1991*

The Black Aesthetic within Black children's books continued to evolve throughout the 1990s and into the new millennium. As Zora Neale Hurston stated, "Whatever the Negro does of his own volition he embellishes" (227). Black children's literature has been able to embellish the Black Aesthetic. Black authors and artists of children's picture books have incorporated the Black folk art tradition. Artists such as Faith Ringgold have moved cultural artistry such as quilt making into a modern picture book format and have exposed issues of racism and family pride. Artists such as Christopher Myers and Javaka Steptoe have both adapted the artistic style of collage art earlier found in the artwork of Romare Bearden in their picture book presentations. They have returned to the poetic stance of writers like Langston Hughes in their choices of texts. For instance, Christopher Myers uses his father Walter Dean Myers's poetic words with the photomontages for a combined interpretation of today's Harlem in *Harlem* while Javaka Steptoe's multiple art forms complement the poetry about fathers that was contributed by several Black poets on the topic of fathers. Steptoe uses nails, buttons, dirt, pennies, wood, and seeds as elements in his work. Finally, Steptoe acknowledges his father's contribution to his career in a poem dedicated to his artistic father, John Steptoe (1950–1989):

> *I became the words I ate in you.*
> *For better or worse*
> *the apple doesn't fall far from the tree.*[5]

Angela Johnson's *Heaven* again alludes to the seeds of regeneration that may be scattered but still are close to their beginnings. Set in Heaven, Ohio, Johnson depicts a place where wrongs are healed through time. The main issues addressed within *Heaven* concern ways

Black families handle crisis. Johnson has reemphasized Terry McMillan's explanation on the new Black Aesthetic:

> We do not feel the need to create and justify our existence anymore. We are here. We are proud. And most of us no longer feel the need to prove anything to white folks. If anything, we're trying to make sense of ourselves to ourselves. (xxi)

Black authors today address social injustice and Black creativity. In Walter Dean Myers's award-winning novel *Monster,* published in 1999, sixteen-year-old Steve Harmon is awaiting trial for felony murder. He begins to write a screenplay, a creative outlet that allows him to deal with his fears and frustrations. Myers uses multiple texts to draw his reader into the drama: As Steve Harmon sets up scenes, cues camera takes, and inserts dialogue, he writes journal descriptions of how he is feeling and what it is like inside detention:

> Wednesday, July 8
>
> They take away your shoelaces and your belt so you can't kill yourself no matter how bad it is. I guess making you live is part of the punishment. It's funny, but when I'm sitting in the courtroom, I don't feel like I'm involved in the case. It's like the lawyers and the judge and everybody are doing a job that involves me, but I don't have a role. It's only when I go back to the cells that I know I'm involved. (59)

Throughout this literary history of the Black Aesthetic, Black authors and artists speak first to Black children. However, they have addressed other children within their books. Because they are speaking to multiple audiences with one voice, they create sympathetic Black protagonists who face realistic problems of race and American history. At times, they seem difficult for the outsider to comprehend; this is due to the many years of silence. Dianne Johnson explains:

> This heritage and its implications cannot always be understood fully by White authors. The point here is that part of the legacy of African American experience is a justified sensitivity of African American writers, illustrators, critics, educators, and reading audiences towards past misrepresentations of themselves—a sensitivity which will persist until there exists a balance and range of various African American images available in children's books. (9)

Black writers are still finding new ways to express the consciousness of a Black child who is aware of world events. The Black Aesthetic is evolving in form and format. Yet, it is connected to the past authors because of shared Black experiences. Tony Medina and R. Gregory Christie created the poetic tales of DeShawn Williams, a little Black boy living in the hood in *DeShawn Days.* Many Black children familiar with their literature will relate him to Robert in John Steptoe's *Stevie.* Medina's work and personal voice make him a contemporary model for Black children because he has based the story on his experiences, and, thus, he becomes a role model for children who want to make their dreams become reality. He tells his youthful audience:

A writer is a great thing to be because you get to paint pictures, tell stories, create worlds, and express your feelings—all with words. It just takes imagination. DeShawn uses his imagination to see things differently and to help others. Maybe his experiences will inspire you to write poems, paint pictures, sing songs, or help others, too! (unpaged)

Black art is not created just for art's sake; it is designed to move and motivate other Blacks. The Black Aesthetic promotes the distinctiveness of Black expression, and it erases Black stereotypes created by the White media. The Black artist must be able to paint a vision of a beautiful culture with a spirituality that outshines the dysfunctional imagery published for centuries. Black writers and illustrators must control art that interprets Black lives. Within Black children's literature there is history, politics, and theory. Within Black children's literature there is creativity, beauty, and also a variety of cultural identities that break the stereotypes of the Black image for children and adults to experience and learn from.

Notes

1. Reprinted by permission of Oxford University Press.
2. Taken from the James Brown album *Say It Loud: I'm Black and I'm Proud* (Polydor, 1969).
3. From *Cornrows* by Camille Yarbrough, illustrated by Carole Byard, copyright © 1979 by Camille Yarbrough, text. Used by permission Coward-McCann, A Division of Penguin Young Readers Group, A Member of Penguin Group (USA) Inc., 345 Hudson Street, New York, NY 10014. All rights reserved.
4. Copyright © 1977 by Eloise Greenfield. Used by permission of HarperCollins Publishers.
5. "Seeds," a poem from the collection *In Daddy's Arms I Am Tall*. Text copyright © 1997 by Javaka Steptoe. Permission arranged with Lee & Low Books, New York, 10016. Lee & Low Books, Inc.

Works Cited

Bergman, Peter M. *The Chronological History of the Negro in America.* New York: Harper and Row, 1969.

Bradley, Darcey H. "John Steptoe: Retrospective of an Imagemaker." *The New Advocate* 4 (1991): 11–23.

Bryan, Ashley. *The Dancing Granny.* New York: Aladdin Paperbacks, 1977.

———. "A Tender Bridge." *Journal of Youth Services in Libraries* (September 1990): 295–302.

Clarke, John Henrik. "The Origin and Growth of Afro-American Literature." *Black Voices: An Anthology of Afro-American Literature.* Ed. Abraham Chapman. New York: Mentor Book, 1968. 632–44.

Cooperative Children's Book Center. "Children's Books by and about People of Color Published in the United States." School of Education University of Wisconsin-Madison. www.education.wisc.edu/ccbc/pcstats.htm.

De Veaux, Alexis. *An Enchanted Hair Tale.* Illus. Cheryl Hanna. New York: Harper & Row, 1987.

Emanuel, James A. "Blackness Can: A Quest for Aesthetics." *The Black Aesthetic.* Ed. Addison Gayle. Garden City, NY: Anchor Books, 1971.

Feelings, Tom. "The Artist at Work: Technique and the Artist's Vision." *The Horn Book Magazine.* (November/December 1985): 685–95.

Gayle, Addison, Jr. *Black Expression.* Ed. Addison Gayle. New York: Weybright and Talley, Inc., 1969.

———. "Cultural Strangulation: Black Literature and the White Aesthetic." *The Black Aesthetic.* Ed. Addison Gayle, Garden City, NY: Anchor Books, 1971.

Graham, Lorenz B. *South Town.* Chicago, Follett Publishing Co., 1958.

———. "A History of Black Writing for Children in the USA." *Towards Understanding: Children's Literature for Southern Africa.* Cape Town: Maskew Miller Longmen, 1988.

Greenfield, Eloise. *She Come Bringing Me That Little Baby Girl.* Illus. John Steptoe. New York: HarperCollins, 1974.

————. "Something to Shout About." *The Horn Book Magazine* (December 1975): 624–26.

————. *Africa Dream.* Illus. Carole Byard. New York: HarperCollins, 1977.

————. *Honey, I Love, and Other Love Poems.* Illus. Diane and Leo Dillon. New York: Crowell, 1978.

Grimes, Nikki. *Something on My Mind.* Illus. Tom Feelings. New York: Dial Press, 1978.

Hamilton, Virginia. *Zeely.* Illus. Symeon Shimin. New York: Collier Books, 1967.

Horning, Kathleen T. "The Contributions of Alternative Press Publishers to Multicultural Literature for Children." *Library Trends* (Winter 1993): 524–40.

Hughes, Langston. *The First Book of Jazz.* Hopewell: The Ecco Press, 1955.

Hurston, Zora Neale. "Characteristics of Negro Expression." *Voices from the Harlem Renaissance.* Ed. Nathan Irvin Huggins. New York: Oxford University Press, 1995.

Jackson, Jesse. *Call Me Charley.* New York: Harper & Brothers, 1945.

Johnson, Angela. *Heaven.* New York: Simon & Schuster Books for Young Readers, 1998.

Johnson, Dianne. *Telling Tales: The Pedagogy and Promise of African American Literature for Youth.* New York: Greenwood Press, 1990.

Johnson-Feelings, Dianne, Ed. *The Best of The Brownies' Book.* New York: Oxford University Press, 1996.

Joans, Ted. *A Black Manifesto in Jazz Poetry and Prose* (Signature Series 8). London: Calder & Boyars, 1971.

Lester, Julius. "Black and White: An Exchange." *Black Perspective.* Ed. Alma Murray. New York: Scholastic, 1971. 65–72.

Locke, Alain. "Negro Youth Speaks." *The New Negro: An Interpretation.* New York: Albert and Charles Boni, 1925.

Mayfield, Julian. "You Touch My Black Aesthetic and I'll Touch Yours." *The Black Aesthetic.* Ed. Addison Gayle, Garden City, NY: Anchor Books, 1971.

McMillan, Terry. *Breaking Ice: An Anthology of Contemporary African-American Fiction.* New York: Penguin Books, 1990.

Medina, Tony. *DeShawn Days.* Illus. R. Gregory Christie. New York: Lee & Low Books, 2001.

Mendez, Phil. *The Black Snowman.* Illus. Carole Byard. New York: Scholastic, Inc, 1989.

Myers, Walter Dean. *Harlem.* Illus. Christopher Myers. New York: Scholastic, 1997.

————. *Monster.* Illus. Christopher Myers. New York: HarperCollins Publishers, 1999.

Morrison, Toni. *playing in the dark: whiteness and the literary imagination.* New York: Vintage Books, 1993.

Neal, Larry. "The Black Arts Movement." *The Black Aesthetic.* Ed. Addison Gayle. Garden City, NY: Anchor Books, 1971.

Nichols, Charles H. Ed. *Arna Bontemps—Langston Hughes Letters, 1925–1967.* New York: Paragon House, 1980.

O'Neal, John. "Black Arts: Notebook." *The Black Aesthetic.* Ed. Addison Gayle. Garden City, NY: Anchor Books, 1971.

Parks, Carole A. "Goodbye Black Sambo: Black Writers Forge New Images in Children's Literature." *Ebony* (November 1972): 60–70.

Rampersad, Arnold. *The Life of Langston Hughes, Volume II: 1941–1967, I Dream a World.* New York: Oxford University Press, 1988.

Richardson, Judy. "Black Children's Books: An Overview." *The Journal of Negro Education* (Summer 1973): 380–400.

Ringgold, Faith. *Tar Beach.* New York: Crown Publishers, Inc., 1991.

Sims, Rudine. *Shadow & Substance.* Urbana, IL: National Council for Teachers of English, 1982.

Steptoe, Javaka. *In Daddy's Arms I Am Tall: African Americans Celebrating Fathers.* New York: Lee & Low Books, Inc., 1997.

Steptoe, John. *Stevie.* New York: Harper & Row, Publishers, 1969.

Tate, Eleanora E. *Thank You, Dr. Martin Luther King, Jr.* New York: Bantam, 1990.

Taylor, Mildred D. *Roll of Thunder, Hear My Cry.* New York: Dial Press, 1976.

Walker Alexander, Margaret. "Some Aspects of the Black Aesthetic." *Freedomways* (Second Quarter 1976): 95–102.

Walter, Mildred Pitts. "Social Responsibility." *The Horn Book* (January/February 1991): 51.

Yarbrough, Camille. *Cornrows.* Illus. Carole Byard. New York: Coward, McCann & Geoghegan, 1979.

6

Linguistic Secrets

Subjective Attitudes about Race and Gender in Children's Literature

Jill P. May

In 1985, when the Children's Literature Association published the first of three edited volumes of critical essays about the books the organization had selected as "touchstones" in children's literature, Perry Nodelman wrote in his "Introduction" that the books were selected as literary models useful for judging new publications in the field. Nodelman called the selection committee professionals who "had the undeniable arrogance to proclaim that these books are, indeed, the touchstones for children's literature" (2). He admitted that the list itself was being questioned by some who deemed lists that named the "best books" as "elistist: attempts by one segment of humanity to impose its tastes on others with less power" (9). And he wrote,

> A quick glance through the ChLA list reveals the justice of that criticism. The books almost exclusively represent European traditions of most well-off North Americans. These myths and legends and poems and novels are the literary equipment of well-educated people destined for economic and social success—and so are the values they express. Taken as a whole, in fact, these books are rather singlemindedly concerned with the joys of acceptance of one's lot—with coming to an accommodation with what already is. (10)

Nodelman argued that this list was not designed to reflect children's pleasures; instead, it defined what was best studied by adults who taught and critiqued children's literature. Good books, he concluded, would reach their child audiences and become the sorts of experiences they sought. These books would be "a means of exploring the imaginative playfulness that makes us human" (12).

At that time no Black authors were selected for the association's list, nor were there many authors who had not been published first in either England or North America. In fact, within the first of three *Touchstones* volumes, only three authors who wrote of other cultures were included, and only one of those was truly a book beyond the Anglo-Saxon canon: *The Adventures of Pinocchio,* an Italian classic had reached the shores of North America in 1892. Yet, the Pinocchio of America and the original literary hero are vastly different. As Richard Wunderlich and Thomas J. Morrisey suggest, Carlo Collodi's *The Adventures of Pinocchio* probably would not be recognized in its original form by many American readers. They commented, "*Pinocchio* has been so frequently altered that one has to wonder whether North Americans do actually regard the real novel as a classic, or whether it is one or more of the reformed versions they revere" (58).

Kipling's Mowgli books and the *Just So Stories* were also included on the Children's Literature Association's list, books Celia Catlett Anderson called a combination of history and fantasy. Because Kipling was not Indian, his children's stories must be considered British reflections of native Indians residing in the British Empire. As Anderson pointed out in her essay, Kipling was a nineteenth-century author who determined that civilization was in contrast with naturalism:

> For Kipling, freedom implies order. Though not overtly political, *The Jungle Books* [*sic*] convey his belief in a hierarchial world where men are judged good or evil according to their willingness to submit to a legitimate community. There is a clear hierarchy in Mowgli's jungle. [. . .] The jungle is a microcosm of human society. This is what I meant in saying that *The Jungle Books* are really about civilization. (121)

Kipling was born in 1865 in India, and he resided there until he was sent to England at the age of six. Most of his schooling happened in England; he returned to India in 1882 but he left again in 1889 (Said 132–33). He lived in India for less than fifteen years altogether; yet, this was the land he would often depict in his novels. Kipling's upper-class friends enjoyed reading his stories about the natives of India, a land he depicted as inhabited by primitive people. When discussing Kipling's other masterpiece, *Kim,* Edward Said wrote:

> Does Kipling portray the Indians as inferior, or as somehow equal but different? Obviously, an Indian reader will give an answer that focuses on some factors more than others (for example, Kipling's stereotypical views—some would call them racialist—on the Oriental character), whereas English and American readers will stress his affection for Indian life on the Grand Trunk Road. [. . .] We must not forget that the book is after all a novel in a line of novels, that there is more than one history in it to be remembered, that imperial experience while often regarded as exclusively political also entered into cultural and aesthetic life of the metropolitan West as well. (135–36)

Kipling's body of writing has always been positioned in children's and adolescent literature. Much of what he wrote was for youthful readers. As Edmund Wilson has noted, Kipling settled with his family in Vermont and wrote nine children's books while there, including the two Jungle Books and his *Just So Stories* (53). However, Kipling never wrote stories about Indians who were masters of their own fate. J. S. Bratton has commented that Kipling's real heroes were from the aristocracy: "they define themselves by birth, by the profession of arms, by the practice of certain sports and games, notably hunting, and by adherence to a set of rules of personal behaviour which can loosely be designated chivalric" (81).

Kipling was not Indian; he was British. And he was not writing for children alone. When discussing writing *Rewards and Fairies,* Kipling acknowledged his understanding of audience duality in children's literature. He commented in his autobiography:

> Yet, since the tales had to be read by children, before people realised that they were meant for grown-ups; and since they had to be a sort of balance to, as well as a seal upon, some aspects of my 'Imperialistic' outpost in the past, I worked on the material in three or four overlaid tints and textures, which might or might not reveal themselves according to the shifting light of sex, youth, and experience. (182–83)

Said suggests that this imperialistic attitude conveys issues of race and gender: "In the field or on the open road, two men can come to each other's rescue more credibly than if a woman were along" (138).

Race, audience, and gender have played important roles in children's and adolescent literature. If the reader is young, and race or gender is underwritten into the text with certain cultural assumptions, then the reader is taught a codified way of approaching difference. That way is built on acknowledging continuing difference. Critics have often been loath to approach such issues. As Toni Morrison says, "in matters of race, silence and evasion have historically ruled literary discourse. Evasion has fostered another, substitute language in which the issues are encoded, foreclosing open debate" (9). Children read the silences along with the overt oppressive scenes, and they decode the meaning of equity and humanity in the conversations of the characters in their books.

Two other books on the ChLA list are more indicative of classical silence against racism and gender stereotypes. Both *The Secret Garden* by Frances Hodgson Burnett and *The Adventures of Tom Sawyer* by Mark Twain are discussed in Volume One of *Touchstones.* In her article on *The Secret Garden,* Heather Murray asks, "What are we to make of a woman-authored text which so validates the status quo, which erases the presence of the lower-class boy of the moors, and so disposes of its heroine? [. . .] Is Mary, in her middle place, a mediator between classes and sexes, between nature and culture; or is she simply, now, a young woman?" (40–41). Mary does see that race is an issue even in the moors where she goes to live once her parents die in India. When Mary asks "in her imperious little Indian way" if Martha is her servant, she learns that she is not. Mary says, "It is different in India," and Martha responds, "Eh! I can see it's different [. . .]. I dare say it's because there's such a lot o' blacks there instead o' respectable white people" (27). Burnett never contradicts this first image of the Black Indian as somehow responsible for Mary's bad temper. Thus, Burnett leaves her youthful reader with racial assumptions that are never corrected.

Language is encoded in children's and adolescent literature, and it shapes ways of reading and of acting within contemporary society. Children learn that discourse is powerful as they read about characters their own age, and they assume certain stances that relate to gender and to race. *The Adventures of Tom Sawyer* is set in America during slavery times. Unlike *Huckleberry Finn,* it does not deal directly with issues of Black subservience or slavery, but it does convey a very negative stance concerning American Indians. Twain's story implies that Indians are less honorable than the others when he has his two young protagonists talk of "Injun Joe" as a "murderin' half breed" and then he writes about the ensuing murder of two men:

> "Look here, what does this mean?" said the doctor. "You required your pay in advance and I've paid you."
>
> "Yes, and you done more than that," said Injun Joe, approaching the doctor, who was now standing. "Five years ago you drove me away from your father's kitchen one night [. . .] and you said I warn't there for any good; and when I swore I'd get even with you if it took a hundred years, your father had me jailed as a vagrant. Did you think I'd forget? The Injun blood ain't in me for nothing. And now I've *got* you, and you got to *settle,* you know!" (68–69)

One could argue that the death of the doctor is justified in this recollection, but when the Indian sees the doctor kill his compatriot and then kills the doctor, he mutters, "That score is settled—damn you" (69), implying that the Indian is unremorseful about his compatriot's death and is willing to commit revengeful murder. Young readers of the text are left with a negative image of American Indians.

Both Twain and Burnett were probably aware of issues of control in dialogue. They demonstrate in their stories that children naturally "fool around" within their speech acts as they determine how to "master" the conventions of discourse within intergenerational conversation. They quickly learn to use the ruse of naive innocence within their oral narratives. When they engage in intergenerational conversations, they ask straightforward questions and make implicit assertions in their linguistic structures. While listening to their elders express particular beliefs about childhood and children's play, youngsters circuitously learn how to encode their interactions with adults in order to win approval for their everyday activities. Children quickly discover that they will be successful when they can communicate with adults about their immediate needs and gain approval for their social actions. Therefore, children articulate learned cultural attitudes about society, childhood, and child play in their interchanges with adults.

Authors writing for children claim an identity with the youthful reader. They also assume an adult reader. As Francis Molson noted, Mark Twain created *Tom Sawyer* prior to *Huckleberry Finn* as a "boy's book" that he hoped adults would also read (262). *Tom Sawyer*'s first audience, it would seem, would be the boys and girls who read it. The primary audience for any book is encoded in the author's use of perspective, but a secondary—and often more powerful—audience is assumed for books published as children's literature. This secondary audience also meets the child narrative in his literature. When discussing the relevance of children's narrative structure in adult books, Mary Jane Hurst commented, "the forms and functions of children's discourse are frequently restricted by the nature of their audience and their relationship to that audience" (97). Later, she argued that children's interactions in their conversations uncover the dramatic movement of the plot and the authorial emphasis in the story. She concluded that there was a difference in the authorial stance when the author assumed a child would be the preferred audience:

The fundamental differences in the uses of children's narratives arise from a distinction in the role of the child in the fiction, on whether the adult is recreating a child's perspective on life or whether the adult is elaborating an adult point of view by contrasting it with a child's. [. . .] For example, in *Huckleberry Finn* Clemens's primary goal is to establish Huck's world view and Huck's perspective on life, but he cannot achieve his aim without contrasting Huck's point of view with that of the adults he encounters. (108)

Thus, when we consider the child characters in literature written expressly for a youthful audience, we need to take into account their literary discourse; children as speakers determine the author's perception of children's possibilities within contemporary society.

Throughout children's literature, authors suggest that children gain power within their intergenerational discourse. As has been established in earlier discussions of Black Aesthetics, oral inferences can change the dominance from one group to another. Linguistic performance becomes political; oral language allows a less powerful speaker to recreate the power structure in his or her favor. When Myron C. Tuman discussed the importance of studying communication acts, he argued that future cultural literacy will rely on discerning how others use language to gain control within communication. Tuman has suggested that the implied meanings embedded within the speaker's oral communication are as significant as the overt ones easily deciphered by those engaged within a conversation. "How important," he asks, "will it be [. . .] to voice our thoughts and to understand those of others? Even more important, how likely are we to see any point in such an activity?" (5).

Conversation in children's literature contains clues about children's understanding of language as a controlling device in society. As the youthful audience watches the author's characters interact, they learn strategies for dialogue with the adults in their everyday experiences. As children read their novels, they identify modes of verbal sparring that can control adults in their discourse with children. Young readers see their heroes incorporate culturally encoded language within their interactions and they see how discourse works as a persuasive genre. Children who are readers observe certain linguistic patterns they can use when engaging adults in conversations. They indirectly begin to understand the power of language. If they choose, they can imitate these literary constructions in their language and adopt the attitudes presented in the author's representations. Narrative is an important element in children's literature because literary conversation breaks the codes of adult values; furthermore, it identifies and defines the oral structures of generational and gender-specific linguistics.

Children's authors have written about the secondary world of the child, and they have asserted that youthful heroes can manipulate power in ways not often understood by the adults they address. As Erik Christian Haugaard writes, "Every child knows that lies come in various sizes and that they are not equally reprehensible. There are lies to get one out of trouble, and their seriousness depends upon the nature of the trouble. Then there is bragging [. . .]. There are many kinds of lies, and a child knows them all" [. . .] (292).

Youngsters in children's literature are often depicted as skillful manipulators of conversations who define their needs and achieve their goals by negotiating permission for activities they know are not normally permitted within adult rules. Furthermore, a number of stories that have been defined as classics have plots that abound with encoded language of youthful protagonists. As J. D. Stahl points out, children's literature uses secrecy to define what youthful characters will do in reaction to the adult values and activities about them (41).

The Secret Garden and *The Adventures of Tom Sawyer* were placed on the ChLA list because they were considered long-standing classical texts; they demonstrate how youthful heroes generate the right to do what they want through language. In both cases, the youthful protagonist lives with an adult who did not choose to have the child in the household. Twain's Tom Sawyer is being raised by his mother's sister, and Burnett's Mary Lennox is residing on her uncle's estate. Both children engage these adults in conversations, testing and/or expanding the conditions they face. However, their encounters with adults are quite different. Whereas Tom is continually in trouble because he is caught boasting, lying, and storytelling, Mary sparingly uses language to control the events in her environment.

Neither Tom nor Mary see their caretakers as compassionate adults. Rather, they see them as judges and jury for their actions. Both youthful characters often prefer to remain silent rather than explain their actions; they understand that ambiguity will leave room for approval of their behavior by the adults who determine what they may or may not do, and they use language to reconstruct their possibilities within the adult world. Both children know how to control adults within their conversations: they use vagueness when answering a question in order to gain approval for their goals. When Tom is forced to paint the fence because he has "told a tale" to his aunt, he talks his playmates into painting it for him. However, when Tom wants to be excused from further work, he knows better than to tell Aunt Polly how he got the fence painted so quickly. Aunt Polly wants Tom to become a good boy so that she can be proud of him. She continually listens to Tom's excuses, hoping that his tales are true. Twain writes,

> He said: "Mayn't I go and play now, aunt?"
> "What, a'ready? How much have you done?"
> "It's all done, aunt."
> "Tom, don't lie to me—I can't bear it."
> "I ain't, aunt; it *is* all done."
> Aunt Polly placed small trust in such evidence. She went out to see for herself; and she would have been content to find twenty per cent of Tom's statement true. When she found the entire fence whitewashed, and not only whitewashed but elaborately coated and recoated, and even a streak added to the ground, her astonishment was almost unspeakable. She said:
> "Well, I never! There's no getting round it, you *can* work when you're a mind to, Tom." (23)

Mary Lennox knows that she is not wanted in the household where she resides. Her uncle will not see her when she arrives at his manor house, and she is told that he doesn't wish to meet her. When Mrs. Medlock takes Mary to her room, she says, "Well, here you are! This room and the next are where you'll live—and you must keep to them. Don't you forget that!" (23). Mary is locked away from her guardian, shut off from the activity of the house. Her only real companion is Martha, a local girl who works as a maid in the house. Older than Mary but poorer in education and stature, they cannot be equals. Martha is both a conspirator for and against Mary. She gets Mary a jump rope and tells her of Mr. Craven's past, but she refuses to break any trusts she has with her real employer, Mrs. Medlock. For instance, when Mary hears noises in the night and asks about them, she is told by Martha, "It's th' wind. Sometimes it sounds like as if some one was lost on th' moor an' wailin'. It's got all sorts o' sounds" (50). Because Mary knows that the sounds are coming inside the house, she learns not to trust Martha's verbal explanations of the happenings in the house.

Left with no one to confide in, Mary chooses silence as her solace. And she begins to make her own rules based on the earlier acquired knowledge that no one in the household cares about her existence. On a rainy day, she determines to go exploring, though she knows it is forbidden for her to roam the halls. Burnett writes, "Why shouldn't she go and see how many doors she could count? It would be something to do this morning when she could not go out" (54). During her wanderings, she discovers the noises are coming from one of the corridors in the house. However, she is met by Mrs. Medlock who denies that anyone is concealed and is informed, "you stay where you're told to stay or you'll find yourself locked up. The master had better get you a governess, same as he said he would. You're one that needs some one to look sharp after you. I've got enough to do" (58). Thus, Mary knows that she cannot talk directly with any adult in the house about her needs or discoveries, and when she meets her uncle, she simply says, "might I have a bit of earth?" Unaware that the servants have explained how the garden behind the wall has been locked up and forbidden to all who live at the house, her uncle answers, "You can have as much earth as you want. [. . .] When you see a bit of earth you want, [. . .] take it, child, and make it come alive." Mary presses her uncle further, asking, "May I take it anywhere—if it's not wanted?" Not knowing exactly what Mary means to do, her uncle replies, "Anywhere" (117–18).

Indirectly both youthful characters understand that they are using language ambiguously in order to break rules earlier established by the adults in control, and they engage these adults in discourses that give them power over their surroundings. They are not directly confronting the rights of authority of those adults; instead they gain permission to break an already established adult rule by allowing the adults to interpret their meanings without full explanations of their intended actions. Tom has been directed to paint the fence himself in order to learn not to be dishonest, but he immediately encodes his understanding of the crime and the punishment in his conversation with Aunt Polly. Mary reminds her uncle that she needs fresh air in order to grow strong, and she asks for land. Both children have learned how to cryptogram their conversations for power. Their use of language allows them to participate in play they know to be forbidden.

Children's conversations within their play show that learned systems of discourse give children power over one another. Then they use language in other ways. Because they have more than one peer, their conversations reflect their burgeoning awareness of the communal power found within imaginative linguistic structures.

Authors of stories with youthful heroes also place literary allusions in their play to suggest that literature plays a part in cultural power. For instance, Tom has read about Robin Hood and pirates, so when he plays with his male friends, he instructs them on the rules for their play. Thus, using his prior literary knowledge, Tom controls the group's play and sets up the boundaries for their activities. Tom talks his comrades into running away from home and becoming pirates rather than hermits by explaining the differences between their lives as boys and the lives of these two adult groups:

> "It's just the life for me," said Tom. "You don't have to get up mornings, and you don't have to go to school, and wash, and all that blame foolishness. You see a pirate don't have to do

anything, Joe, when he's ashore, but a hermit he has to be praying considerable, and then he don't have any fun, anyway, all by himself that way." (92)

After Tom has convinced his friends that they should become pirates, Huck asks, "What does pirates have to do?" Tom replies,

"Oh, they have just a bully time—take ships and burn them, and get the money and bury it in awful places in their island where there's ghosts and things to watch it, and kill everybody in the ships—make 'em walk a plank." (93)

Tom's cultural explanation of the rules that control the lives of pirates and hermits is based on characteristics found in his books. He uses descriptive language to gain acceptance of his ideas and to lead a rebellion against the already established adult social rules for boys in his small Missouri community. Furthermore, Tom manipulates the ideals found in literature to shape his play. And he positions his imaginative authority by using earlier read details found in the plots of children's stories. However, Tom does not "see" minorities in a subjective light. Instead, he accepts society's attitudes about Injun Joe. In the end, Twain substantiates Tom's attidues, showing his Indian character as an evil man.

In contrast, authors also depict children as participants in socially constructed conversations that allude to the significance of communal gender practices. When Tom wants to communicate with Becky, he assumes the cultural rules of adult society within his home town. Tom has not read adult romance literature, so he must engage in linguistic structures he has observed within his community between males and females. Tom and Becky get lost in the cave, and Tom uses silence to shape Becky's response to their situation:

[. . .] By and by Becky suggested that they move on again. Tom was silent a moment; then he said:
   "Becky, can you bear it if I tell you something?"
   Becky's face paled, but she thought she could.
   "Well, then, Becky, we must stay here, where there's water to drink. That little piece is our last candle." (195)

Tom's language is defined by his audience. He cajoles adults and distorts the truth in order to win verbal battles. Tom listens carefully to the adults he communicates with, and he forms his responses to fit their expectations. His interactions with adults demonstrate his growing awareness that he inhabits a secondary child-inhabited world with divergent goals. Tom's playful imagination with his group of male friends depends on his literary understanding. He alludes to stereotypic characteristics of literary groups not found in his small community. He accepts racial stereotypes, but he also creates a secondary existence that is adventurous and alien to his small town with its schools and church services. Finally, Tom's interactions with Becky reveal his understanding of the community's already established gender roles. As Tom ventures past his role of young trickster, he becomes the male protector and the instructor. Becky leans on him and seeks protection.

Mary's life is more complicated. Once in England, she is in a situation that is cold and unfriendly. No one seems interested in the realities of India. Humanism is most identified with the servants, and they become her role models. Her only real companions are two boys, one a cottager's son who roams about freely and the other her invalid cousin who is kept under lock and key. She learns how to share language from Dickon. When Dickon explains the natural world to Mary, Burnett writes,

> She wished she could talk as he did. His speech was so quick and easy. It sounded as if he liked her and was not the least afraid she would not like him, though he was only a common moor boy, in patched clothes and with a funny face and a rough rusty-red head. (96)

Dickon affirms Mary's right to venture into the garden where they work on its regrowth, though they both know it has been locked up and entry forbidden by Mr. Craven, Mary's uncle. Once in the garden, Dickon is part of Mary's secret world: "Eh!" he almost whispered, "it is a queer place! It's like as if a body was in a dream" (100).

In Burnett's world, peer communication and child play come from nature rather than books. When Mary meets Colin, she finds that he does not know about the world outside, though he is "always reading and looking at pictures in splendid books" (127). When Mary tells him of the secret garden, he determines that he will make the servants open it up for him. However, Mary swears him to secrecy by telling him what she is sure might be arranged:

> "If you won't make them take you to the garden," pleaded Mary, "perhaps—I feel almost sure I can find out how to get in sometime. And then—if the doctor wants you to go out in your chair, and if you can always do what you want to do, perhaps—perhaps we might find some boy who would push you, and we could go alone and it would always be a secret garden." (131)

Though Mary's stories of the garden and its rebirth that drive Colin outside, Dickon is the person who assures him that he will get well. And it is the desire to work as a laborer in the garden that appeals to Colin. Dickon says, "Us'll have thee walkin' about here an' diggin' same as other folk afore long," and Colin answers, "Walk! . . . Dig! Shall I?" (219).

Both books demonstrate that in children's fiction male language is more powerful and controlling than female language. In both cases, however, the girls are allowed to manipulate the adults who can help them shape their future through secrets. After she and Tom are rescued from their cave expedition, Becky tells her father "in strict confidence" about the time he took her punishment at school, thus convincing her father that Tom's lying was "a noble, a generous, a magnanimous lie—a lie that was worthy to hold up its head and march through history" (214–15), and Becky has won her upper-class father's approval for her attentions to an orphan. Mary's indirect request to enter the secret garden changes the fate of Colin and his father. Mary heals the son for the father, and in the end, though she does not appear in the final pages, she has proven the remark of an observant servant who still sees Mary as a spirited outsider:

> "Well, there's one thing pretty sure," said Mrs. Medlock. "If he does live and that Indian child stays here I'll warrant she teaches him that the whole orange does not belong to him, as Mrs. Sowerby says. And he'll be likely to find out the size of his own quarter." (207)

Although Mary is still identified by a servant as "the other" and is, thus, considered subordinate to the servants because she has come from the outposts of the Empire, she has made herself a home within this English manor, and she has opened its doors to the cottagers in ways they were never opened before.

If children's language in children's literature is gender coded, it is also honest. These stories suggest that adults code their speech to show power, whether that power is one of race or gender, and that at the same time children are taught ways to indirectly communicate with their superiors in order to succeed despite the cultural codes of sex and race. These two classics show us the sorts of worlds children create when they encode their speech and use ambiguity to bridge the gaps between adult expectations and their desires. Furthermore, children's literature shows both the benefits and the disadvantages of "living within the book" when interacting with peers. As these fictional children manipulate language to recreate their worlds, they learn to voice their thoughts in ways that others—both adults and peers—comprehend, often just at the moment they break the cultural codes of past generations. They allude to past linguistic codes found in everyday life and in literature as they move from playing with language to controlling it. Mary Jane Hurst has commented that children in literature reflect adult concerns about the loss of innocence and their growing place within society. She comments, "Language is a key which opens many doors. An understanding of fictional children's language leads to discoveries about various critical questions" (2). The secret codes of language in childhood interactions with adults and in their play, as depicted in children's literature, become the linguistic training ground for youngsters who read and emulate their favorite heroes within society. Thus, children's literature holds linguistic bridges between the generational and gendered constraints of childhood, and its study can help all readers better understand oral literacy and its implications for social power. At the same moment, unbroken cultural attitudes about race and ethnicity that are written into the discourse between servant and child or between child and adult can suggest to youthful readers that all barriers cannot—or perhaps should not—be broken.

Works Cited

Anderson, Celia Catlett. "Kipling's Mowgli and Just So Stories: The Vine of Fact and Fantasy." Vol. 1 of *Touchstones: Reflections on the Best in Children's Literature.* Ed. Perry Nodelman. West Lafayette, IN: ChLA Publications, 1985. 113–23.

Bratton, J. S. "Of England, Home and Duty." *Imperialism and Popular Culture.* Ed. John MacKenzie. Manchester, England: Manchester University Press, 1986. 73–112.

Burnett, Frances Hodgson. *The Secret Garden.* New York: Dell Publishing Company, 1938.

Haugaard, Erik Christian. "Truth, the Child, and Literature." *Innocence & Experience: Essays & Conversations on Children's Literature.* Comp. Barbara Harrison and Gregory Maguire. New York: Lothrop, Lee & Shepard, 1987. 292–302.

Hurst, Mary Jane. *The Voice of the Child in American Literature: Linguistic Approaches to Fictional Child Language.* Lexington, KY: The University Press of Kentucky, 1990.

Kipling, Rudyard. *Something of Myself: For My Friends Known and Unknown.* New York: Charles Scribners Sons, 1937.

Molson, Francis. "Mark Twain's *The Adventures of Tom Sawyer*: More Than a Warm Up." Vol. 1 of *Touchstones: Reflections on the Best in Children's Literature.* Ed. Perry Nodelman. West Lafayette, IN: ChLA Publications, 1985. 262–69.

Morrison, Toni. *playing in the dark: whiteness and the literary imagination.* Cambridge, MA: Harvard University Press, 1992.

Murray, Heather. "Frances Hodgson Burnett's *The Secret Garden*: The Organ(ic)ized World." Vol. 1 of *Touchstones: Reflections on the Best in Children's Literature.* Ed. Perry Nodelman. West Lafayette, IN: ChLA Publications, 1985. 30–43.

Nodelman, Perry. "Introduction: Matthew Arnold, a Teddy Bear, and a List of Touchstones." Vol. 1 of *Touchstones: Reflections on the Best in Children's Literature.* Ed. Perry Nodelman. West Lafayette, IN: ChLA Publications, 1985. 1–12.

Said, Edward W. *Culture and Imperialism.* New York: Knopf, 1993.

Stahl, J. D. "The Imaginative Uses of Secrecy in Children's Literature." *Only Connect: Readings on Children's Literature.* 3rd ed. Ed. Sheila Egoff, Gordon Stubbs, Ralph Ashley, and Wendy Sutton. Toronto: Oxford University Press, 1996. 39–47.

Tuman, Myron C. *A Preface to Literacy: An Inquiry into Pedagogy, Practice, and Progress.* Tuscaloosa: The University of Alabama Press, 1987.

Twain, Mark. *The Adventures of Tom Sawyer.* New York: New American Library, 1980.

Wilson, Edmund. "The Kipling That Nobody Read." (1941) *Kipling's Mind and Art: Selected Critical Essays.* Ed. A. Rutherford. Stanford, CA: Stanford University Press, 1964. 17–69.

Wunderlich, Richard and Thomas J. Morrisey. "*The Adventures of Pinocchio:* A Classic Book of Choices." Vol. 1 of *Touchstones: Reflections on the Best in Children's Literature.* Ed. Perry Nodelman. West Lafayette, IN: ChLA Publications, 1985. 53–63.

7

The Legend of the Golem in Popular Culture and Children's Literature

Charles A. Elster

The legend of the golem—a nonhuman being who is created out of earth by a holy rabbi to protect a Jewish community from danger—contains a combination of ancient and modern elements. It evolved within Jewish rabbinic traditions and folklore and was redefined by modern Jewish writers to reflect nineteenth- and twentieth-century Jewish experience. More recently, the golem legend has entered mainstream modern children's literature and popular culture. As legends evolve, they create new forms and meanings in each age in the originating cultural group as well as in the evolving literature of other cultural groups that adopt and adapt them. In this chapter I want to show the layers of Jewish and non-Jewish traditions and stories in the modern golem stories, to explore universal and Jewish themes in the golem story and related stories in modern literature and popular culture, and to analyze the responses of Jewish and non-Jewish readers. I want to show what happens to a legend from a particular group as it is adapted in literary incarnations by and for those outside that particular group. And, finally, I want to suggest that teachers can use their understanding of how literary pieces are reframed and revisited in children's literature and popular culture to open their classrooms to a mixture of ancient and modern themes and stories in the responses of their students.

I.

The evolution of the golem legend in Jewish tradition spans biblical, postbiblical, medieval, and modern times.[1] It contains two stories: that of the creation of a living creature, and the creature becoming God's agent in protecting the Jews from oppressors. The sources of the legend are in biblical and postbiblical texts, and in rabbinic and popular Jewish traditions. The legend began in postbiblical rabbinic interpretation of two biblical passages and was adapted into popular forms in medieval and postmedieval Europe, especially in the late nineteenth and early twentieth centuries.

The original concept of a golem was of an unformed being or incomplete human. The word *golem* appears only once in the Bible: in Psalm 139:16,[2] the psalmist addresses God as his maker, the one who knows him intimately, even in his initial, half-formed state (golem). According to rabbinic interpretation, the psalmist compares himself here to Adam, the first human God created (Genesis 1:26–27 and 2:7). Rabbinic interpretation of the Bible in the postbiblical Talmud describes Adam as a golem—a soulless being, a "clod" of earth without speech—before God breathed the spirit of life into him. Like the golem, Adam was made of earth (the Hebrew word for "earth" is *adamah*). And like the golem, Adam was, according to some traditions, of gigantic size.[3]

The Talmud describes the creation of golems by prophets and pious rabbis—including Abraham and Jeremiah—as a demonstration of their piety and knowledge of sacred text. In the Talmudic sources, the golem sometimes functions as a servant. This rabbinic tradition grows out of Jewish attitude toward divine and human acts of creation; an act of golem making is an imitation by humans of God's creative powers. As God rested from his labor on the seventh day, so humans are commanded to rest on the Sabbath; as God created the world, so humans are encouraged to be creative. God purposely left the world incomplete and imperfect, and it is the role of humans to perfect or complete the world (*tikkun olam*). In Jewish tradition, human acts of creation are imitations of God's creative acts.

The manner of golem making—through the use of Hebrew letters and words—also grows out of Jewish attitudes toward sacred knowledge and language. It rests on a Jewish scholarly tradition in which rabbis and rabbinic students, through the intense study and interpretation of sacred texts and their commentaries, seek religious and legal messages. This tradition recognizes the special creative power of spoken words and written letters. In both Old Testament and New Testament tales of creation, God speaks the world into being: "In the Beginning [. . .] God said, 'Let there be light' " (Genesis 1:1–3); "In the beginning was the Word, and the Word was with God, and the Word was God" (John 1:1). Out of this tradition arose the belief that righteous humans can speak a life into being. Golem making in medieval and modern retellings is based on the *kaballah,* the mystical tradition in Judaism. In kabbalistic readings of the Bible and its secret messages, the Hebrew language, especially in its written form, has a special power, and the Torah (The Law, the first five books of the Bible) contains a blueprint in hidden form for the whole universe. Secret formulas for golem making are contained in the kabalistic text *The Book of Creation* (Scholem 167).

Based on these rabbinic and kabbalistic traditions, popular versions of the golem legend evolved in medieval and postmedieval Europe during times when Jews experienced intense persecution living in the Diaspora (the scattering of the Jews from Palestine following the destruction of the Second Temple by the Romans in 70 of the Common Era). Jews were often forbidden to own property or weapons, forced to live in segregated communities (ghettos), and sometimes subject to attacks by Christian mobs (*pogroms*). When persecution and annihilation were central facts of life for the Jewish communities of Europe, the golem came to represent a savior of the Jews from persecution by intolerant neighbors. In the eighteenth century, the legend of the golem became especially attached to the figure of Rabbi Loew ben Bezalel of Prague (1512?–1609), called the Maharal, despite the fact that Rabbi Loew was not known as a kaballist but as a strict rationalist (Goldsmith 29, Ozick 100).

The appearance of the golem as God's tool for saving the Jews from disaster reflects a central motif in Jewish religious belief. The theme of God saving the Jews from disaster appears in the most central of Jewish myths, the Exodus from Egypt: God sends Moses as a savior to deliver the Jews from Egyptian bondage, to give God's law to the Jews, to reaffirm the Jews' covenant with God, and to lead them to their homeland in Canaan (later Palestine). The story of the Exodus is retold each year in the *seder,* the ritual banquet of the spring holiday of Pesach (Passover). It is no accident that the golem story in its modern versions takes place at Passover time. The connection to the Passover holiday has a narrative motive because the golem comes to protect the Jews from Christian retribution for the Blood Lie, the belief that Jews used the blood of Christian children to make the Passover *matzoh* (unleavened bread). At the same time, the Passover setting underscores the parallelism between the Jews' deliverance from Egypt and their deliverance from their oppressors in Prague. Rabbi Loew and his golem play the part of Moses at Pesach time.[4] He also reflects the Jewish belief in an ultimate savior, or Messiah, who will redeem the Jews and the whole world at the end of time, which is also found in the Christian belief of Jesus as the Messiah.

The basic golem legend was written down by the Grimm brothers and I. L. Peretz in the nineteenth century, but the major modern literary sources of the golem legend are Yudi Rosenberg's *The Golem or the Miraculous Deeds of Rabbi Liva,* published in Hebrew in Warsaw in 1909, Gustav Meyrink's *The Golem,* and Maurice Bloch's *Legends of the Golem,* published in German in 1919. Bloch's version was the most complete and literary, collecting a variety of legends, and weaving them into a literary presentation, and it brought the golem legends to a wider, non-Jewish audience. These literary reworkings of the legend provide the model for modern children's book retellings. The golem legend has remained part of popular culture, appearing in many stage and film versions in the early twentieth century.

Despite the fact that modern versions of the golem legend are set in Prague in the late Middle Ages (a time of persecution and restrictions for Jews), they reflect more directly the precarious world of Eastern European Jews who were often persecuted and subjected to pogroms in the late nineteenth and early twentieth centuries when the modern versions were being compiled.

The theme of deliverance from destruction takes on special poignancy in the aftermath of the Holocaust: no savior—whether golem or Messiah—came to the aid of the Jews who were annihilated. Elie Wiesel's retelling of the earlier tales is most poignantly evocative of the Holocaust:

> Ah, if only the Golem were still among us. [. . .] I would sleep more peacefully. Why did the Maharal take him from us? Did he really believe that the era of suffering and injustice was a thing of the past? That we no longer needed a protector, a shield? Tell me, please: our Maharal who knew everything, did he not know that exile, after him, would become harder than before, even more cruel? That the burden would become heavier, more bloody? He could have left us his Golem; he should have. (17)

The theme of protection by a God-sent or secular superhero has strong modern appeal.[5] The savior motif is also seen in modern comic book and popular media superheroes. It contains an important thematic link between the original Jewish golem legend and its modern, popular culture versions. The superhero is often flawed or vulnerable in the way that the golem is with his magical, but erasable, written words. Superheroes are secular counterparts of the religious savior—saving others from danger on the metaphysical plane—who occurs in the Jewish messiah myth and the Christian story of Jesus.

The golem legend was presented to the wider culture of world literature in the nineteenth century by romantic folklorists and writers, such as the Grimm brothers and Mary Shelley.[6] The German folklorist Jacob Grimm and the Yiddish short story writer I. L. Peretz both retold the golem tale in the nineteenth century.[7] As the Jewish golem legend evolved in the nineteenth and twentieth centuries, other stories of the creation of artificial life came to be mingled with the story of the golem. The most well known of these is *Frankenstein, or the Modern Prometheus,* a romantic novel composed by Mary Shelley and published in 1818. The golem is replaced by the Creature, a monstrous, human-like being who rebels against his human creator. Shelley explored the parent–child drama, the rage of the rejected child, and the romantic theme of the limitations of rational knowledge.

Another theme has had special resonance in modern times: the power, dangers, and limits of technology, and the relationship of technology to the people who create it. This technology theme appears in Hans Christian Andersen's well-known story "The Nightingale" where a mechanical bird competes with a live nightingale. It also appears in the story of a mechanical flying horse in "The Enchanted Horse" in Andrew Lang's edited version of *The Arabian Nights.* The golem has been compared to the atom bomb, cloning, and the computer—he could be the runaway computer in Stanley Kubrick's film *2001: A Space Odyssey.* David Wisniewski reports that he first got the idea for the golem book from reading a book about robots (Peck and Hendershot 458). A more benign form of the monster technology motif appears in the "Sorcerer's Apprentice" segment of Walt Disney's classic animated film *Fantasia,* which is based on a ballad by the romantic German writer Goethe (Scholem 203). In this story, a magician's assistant makes magic that he is unable to stop. The motif of magical power gone awry also appears in the Greek legend of King Midas's "golden touch" (Graves 281–85) and in Tomie De Paola's picture book *Strega Nona,* whose foolish apprentice attempts to operate a magic pasta pot.

A second universal theme that grew out of the romantic tradition of the Frankenstein motif and came to be mixed with modern stories of the golem has to do with the meaning of growing up and becoming "real" or accepted into the larger community. Frankenstein's Creature is a prime example of this motif; the connections between the Creature and the golem become inescapable in modern responses. The puppet Pinocchio in Carlo Collodi's novel and the Walt Disney film version, the toy rabbit in Margary Williams's children's classic *The Velveteen Rabbit, or How Toys Become Real,* and the Scarecrow and Tin Woodman in R. Frank Baum's *The Wizard of Oz* and the subsequent Hollywood film version are examples of this motif. Another poignant example is Robin Williams's portrayal of a robot longing to be human in Chris Columbus's recent film *Bicentennial Man.*

A dark side of the romantic theme of creation and human experience was expressed in the figure the "double." The golem is Rabbi Loew's double—he does the deeds of protecting the Jews that are motivated by Rabbi Loew's desire to protect them.[8] The Creature is the double of Doctor Frankenstein—he is a personification, on the one hand, of the doctor's "inhuman" side and, on the other hand, of his desire for love and recognition. This theme was popular in nineteenth-century literature as it explored the human sense of self in pathological forms: Nikolai Gogol's "The Nose," published in 1836, Feodor Dosto-evsky's "The Double," published in 1846, Robert Louis Stevenson's *The Strange Case of Dr. Jekyll and Mr. Hyde,* published in 1886, and Oscar Wilde's *The Picture of Dorian Gray,* published in 1890.

The two themes of the creature yearning for life and the danger that a creation might go out of control are united in the image of the child, rejected by the parent, who turns violent and destructive. In Shelley's novel and the later Frankenstein film adaptation of 1931, it is only after the "parent" rejects the "child" that the child turns violent and vengeful. In James Whale's *Frankenstein,* Dr. Frankenstein attempts to kill the creature by lethal injection after realizing that the creature is imperfect. Subsequent modern retellings of the golem legend also feature the golem resisting Rabbi Loew's intention to end its life.

The creature in Whale's *Frankenstein* also displays a poignant appreciation of nature. When he is first brought to life, the creature, who has lived in darkness, sees a shaft of sunlight and childishly raises his hands toward it, attempting to grasp it; thus, he is immediately seen as attempting to grasp life. In another crucial scene, he accepts a flower from a little girl, sniffs it appreciatively, and smiles. The Creature is a sympathetic character in this version, and he is childlike in his responses to his environment.

Frankenstein's Creature, the "bicentennial man" and the golem are all poignant characters who, while considered monstrous, are also tragic because they are denied full human rights. Ironically, the Jews treat the golem as not quite human, just as they are treated by the Gentiles, but they do not see themselves playing the same role as their oppressors. On a deeper level, the golem, yearning for but denied full humanity, could represent the Jews. On an ethical level, this motif can be read against the philosopher Martin Buber's distinction between I–thou and I–it relationships. In Buber's distinction, we can engage with other people fully as people (an I–thou relationship), or we treat them as tools or means to an end (an I–it relationship). From this perspective, the golem legend represents the experience of being treated as a tool, and it is this aspect that can be disturbing for modern readers.

Like all oral traditions adapted into literature, the golem legend has accumulated and recombined historical layers of stories and motifs. Modern retellings of the golem legend contain three layers of thematic and cultural material. The earliest layer is the Jewish tradition of golem making and the theme of divine and human creative power. The second layer contains the theme of deliverance of the oppressed by a just savior, which is central to Jewish and Christian theology, and later secular superhero mythologies. The third layer of thematic material comes from outside the Jewish tradition, from early modern experience and the romantic tradition, and it contains two themes: on the one hand, the power and dangers of technology, especially relevant in the modern age of factories, pollution, technological dehumanization, and doomsday military technology, and on the other hand, the creation of the authentic human self and the plight of the child and other powerless individuals within the social order.

II.

The golem has appeared recently in literature for adults in the short story "Puttermesser and Xanthippe" by the Jewish American writer Cynthia Ozick; in poems by Jorge Luis Borges and John Hollander (reprinted in Goldsmith); in the recent Pulitzer Prize–winning novel, *The Amazing Adventures of Kavalier and Clay,* by the American writer Michael Chabon; in James Sturm's recent comic-book format story of a Jewish baseball team, *The Golem's Mighty Swing;* and in an episode of the popular TV show, *The X-Files.* At least six children's book retellings of the golem legend have appeared in English since the 1970s. Four versions of the legend are in novel (chapter book) form: the Caldecott honor book *The Golem: A Jewish Legend,* by Beverly Brodsky McDermott, published in 1978; Barbara Rogasky's *The Golem,* published in 1982; Elie Wiesel's *The Golem: The Story of a Legend,* published in 1983; and the Nobel Prize–winning Yiddish writer Isaac Bashevis Singer's *The Golem,* illustrated by Uri Shulevitz, published in 1982. There have also been two picture book versions of the legend: Mark Podwal's *Golem: A Giant Made of Mud,* published in 1995; and the Caldecott Award–winning *Golem* written and illustrated by David Wisniewski, published in 1997. I will focus especially on Singer's chapter book and Wisniewski's picture book because they are the most widely known, widely available, and widely admired of the recent retellings: Wisniewski's picture book is a recipient of the Caldecott Medal and I. B. Singer is recognized as perhaps the master Jewish storyteller of the twentieth century. The two books also represent different types of retellings: an extended novel (Singer) versus a condensed picture book (Wisniewski), one told by an insider (Singer), and one by an outsider (Wisniewski).

Both Singer's and Wisniewski's retellings incorporate the two stories associated with the golem: savior from danger, and a human-like creature who yearns for life. In both books, these two stories are presented sequentially: the golem saves the Jews, the golem leads its own life and is destroyed. These two stories also represent two distinct points of view—that of Rabbi Loew, God's agent who creates a golem to protect the community, and that of the golem, a creature desiring to experience the life humans enjoy.

Singer's and Wisniewski's books contrast extended and condensed versions of these two golem stories. Singer's novelistic version of the legend includes more content than Wisniewski's. It includes multiple episodes related to the persecution of the Jews, focusing around the trial of a righteous Jew, Eliezer Polner, who is framed by Count Bratislawski, who is greatly indebted to Eliezer, and tried for abducting and murdering a Christian child. The golem finds the girl and arrests Bratislawski's henchmen. In the Wisniewski version, the deliverance of the Jews focuses around the threat by a mob of townspeople of a pogrom against the entire Jewish community. The golem protects the Jews by violently repelling the mob.

Likewise, Singer's version gives a more extended retelling of the second story: the golem's desire for life and his eventual destruction. Both books represent the golem's child-like appreciation of life. Wisniewski's retelling emphasizes the poignancy of the golem's feelings.

> "The sun is rising." said Golem. "The sky changes from black to blue. It is very beautiful."
> Rabbi Loew sighed. How simple Golem was! The smallest thing—the scent of a rose, the flight of a pigeon—filled him with wonder.
> "Joseph!" he replied. "Finish your work. Then you can watch the sun rise." (unpaged)

Singer's version is more humorous. The golem plays with real soldiers like toys, barges into a school, and wants to learn to read. He develops an appetite and sexual feelings:

> Besides her maid, Genendel [Rabbi Loew's wife] kept an orphan girl, Miriam, who helped with the household chores. The golem sat down on the floor. He seemed tired. Miriam asked, "Joseph, are you hungry?"
> "Hungry," the golem repeated.
> Miriam brought him bread, onions and radishes. The golem gulped them all down in no time. Miriam smiled. She said, "Where did you put all that food?"
> "Food," the golem echoed. Suddenly he said, "Miriam nice girl."
> Miriam began to laugh. "Hey, golem, I didn't know that you notice girls."
> "Miriam nice girl," the golem said.
> If another man had said this to Miriam, she would have gotten red in the face. In those times girls were known to be shy. But, before a golem Miriam felt no embarrassment. She asked playfully, "Would you want me for a bride?"
> "Yes, bride." He gazed at her with large eyes. Suddenly he did something that star-tled Miriam. He lifted her up and kissed her. His lips were as scratchy as a horseradish grinder. Miriam screamed and the golem exclaimed, "Miriam golem bride." He put her down and clapped his huge hands. (72–73)

Singer's version depicts the golem's childlike desire for a full life that includes sexuality. The golem's potential to dangerously demand what he sees others have is sometimes represented by his phenomenal growth. In Podwal's picture book, *Golem: A Giant Made of Mud,* the motif of phenomenal growth is represented from a comic perspective. In Wis-niewski's book the golem's growth has an emotional-moral dimension: he grows larger as the dangerous mob comes closer to the ghetto.

Another, more traditional Jewish perspective on the destruction of the golem reflects Jewish concern that created images (idols) might be worshiped in place of God. It also provides a motivation for the eventual destruction of the golem that may not be evident to its modern readers. In Singer's version, the golem begins to disobey and rebel when Rabbi Loew uses him for ordinary tasks beyond the divine task he was created to fulfill. Singer and Wisniewski both depict the golem's attempt to avoid the rabbi's intention of taking away his life. Wisniewski's retelling portrays a creature who knows he has fulfilled his purpose but wishes to remain alive:

> The Rabbi found Golem in the cemetery, gazing at the tombstones. "Joseph," he said softly. "Come here."

"No," said Golem.

"Why not?" asked the rabbi

"The Jews are safe," said Golem. "Now you will return me to the earth."

"Yes," said Rabbi Loew. "Your purpose is at an end." [. . .]

Golem leaned down to him. "Then I shall not obey you," he said.

"You have no choice, Joseph." The rabbi lashed out with his staff, erasing the first letter—*aleph*—from the word on Golem's forehead. At this, *emet*—Truth—became *met:* Death.

Golem staggered and fell to his knees. "Oh, Father!" he pleaded. "Do not do this to me!" Even as he lifted his mighty hands, they were dissolving.

"Please!" Golem cried. "Please let me live! I did all that you asked of me! Life is so . . . precious . . . to me!" With that, he collapsed into clay. (unpaged)

Singer's version of the golem's rebellion is more extended and more steeped in ancient motifs. Rabbi Loew uses the girl Miriam to lure the golem to his death. She gets him drunk on wine so that the rabbi can erase the aleph from his forehead and end his life. Singer's story echoes *The Odyssey* of Homer, where Odysseus uses wine to lull the Cyclops Polyphemus to sleep before blinding him (146–47). Singer also echoes motifs of the Biblical story of Samson and Delilah and the ancient Babylonian "Epic of Gilgamesh" when a woman is used to tame the "wild man" Enkidu (Gaster 22–23). Enkidu, like Adam and the golem, was formed of clay, and like the golem he was formed for a purpose: to combat the oppressive King Gilgamesh (Gaster 21). In Wegener's film, *Der Golem,* the golem perishes when he picks up a little girl and she playfully pulls the magic word from his chest, a scene that is repeated in James Whale's later *Frankenstein*.

As readers (and viewers) read, view, and respond to modern versions of the golem legend and its related images, they can foreground one or more of these themes, one or more of these points of view. The modern texts combine multiple themes, both Jewish and universal, and multiple points of view, including that of Rabbi Loew and that of the golem. Modern readers use a repertoire of Jewish and non-Jewish meanings to re-articulate and re-combine what they have experienced prior to these texts.

III.

Could it be that the themes and insights generated by youthful readers exposed to these modern versions are aligned to particular cultural and literary traditions from inside and outside the Jewish culture? Do young audiences choose viewpoints and foregroundings of certain stories over others as a reflection of their cultural, developmental, and personal identities? With these questions in mind, I studied the responses of three groups of readers: Jewish eighth and ninth graders in a religious school class where I taught, non-Jewish undergraduate education students (preservice teachers in training) in a class on children's literature, and non-Jewish teacher-graduate students in a class I taught on teaching reading and writing. The first two groups of readers live in the Midwest, whereas the graduate students live in California.[9]

The teenage Jewish students' readings took place during a religious school class on modern Jewish experiences, and it was explicitly connected to themes in that experience.

The students—mostly from Reform Jewish backgrounds—had an introductory lesson about the kaballah. Then I read Wisniewski's book aloud to the students as they modeled clay golems around a table. After reading, I asked them to write their responses. Then I read them an excerpt from I. B. Singer's *The Golem,* the part where the golem draws water from a well but does not know when to stop, flooding the town. I also showed the students the "Sorcerer's Apprentice" segment from Walt Disney's film *Fantasia* and asked them to write a response comparing the video and the Singer story. The following week, I showed them excerpts from Paul Wegener's silent film *Der Golem* and from James Whale's *Frankenstein* film. I then asked them to write responses, comparing the Frankenstein and golem stories.

In sharing the story with undergraduate and graduate students, I used only Wisniewski's book, because it is shorter and striking as a book. First we discussed the cut-paper illustration technique. Students then received and read a two-page handout of notes on the Jewish background of the book, briefly describing Jewish life in the Diaspora, the Kaballah, and the holiday of Passover. Students then divided into small groups and read the book aloud (most taking turns, many commenting and discussing as they went along). They composed short "Think and Write" notes partway through the reading and after reading, and they wrote responses to six questions after the reading.[10]

The responses of the teenage and adult readers make reference to the two stories inherent in modern retellings of the legend—the story of the golem saving the Jews from danger, and the story of the golem's yearning for human life. These readers also related these two golem stories to other stories they were familiar with and to themes found throughout literature. These readers recognized the golem not only as a helper for the Jews but also as one of the class of powerful beings, whether God or a superhero, helping those in need. They also recognized the theme of the creation of life—both its potential and its dangers—including the golem's own yearning for life and, more broadly, the theme of the child striving to be recognized as a fully formed human being.

The responses—as documented through their writing—show how readers can take various perspectives, foreground various stories, and recombine literary and popular cultural traditions. Five strong voices came out of grouping the written responses thematically: golem as superhero; being the golem; Jewish and Christian perspectives; aesthetic experiences; and failure to step in.[11]

Golem as Superhero

One of the strongest voices of response was heard when readers wrote about the protector or savior theme and its manifestations in Jewish, Christian, literary stories, and popular culture. Universal themes identified by graduate and undergraduate college students included the hero helping those in need, helping the needy by means of divine intervention, and oppression and resistance. The intertextual comparison they most commonly made was between the golem and superheroes: 97 percent of undergraduates and 62 percent of graduate students did so. The reasons given for considering the golem as a superhero included having special powers; helping the weak, fighting crime; receiving no reward from helping; being "normal until help is needed," and having a "key vulnerability." Some students compared the golem to the comic book and TV show hero the Incredible Hulk, either because of the resemblance in Wisniewksi's illustrations or because the golem was "capable of helping the community but misunderstood by them." Several students compared the golem to Superman and Batman.

Some students compared the golem to savior figures from the Bible, literature, or film. Most of these comparisons were to biblical characters: Jesus ("savior"), Moses ("led the Israelites"), the Messiah, and Goliath ("or was he bad?"). Two non-biblical comparisons were made to Aslan, a savior figure from C. S. Lewis's *Narnia* series, and to "the woodsman in 'Little Red Riding Hood.' " A few students compared the golem to other giants in literature and film who were not necessarily savior figures, including the BFG (from Roald Dahl's novel of the same name), and Hagrid, the giant gamekeeper in J. K. Rowling's popular *Harry Potter* novels.

When writing about the savior theme, many readers focused on the plight of the oppressed people needing to be protected by a superhero or a god:

- "a group of people need help and the hero saves the day" (UG)
- "people calling on a supernatural force for help in battle" (G)
- "Golem is an all-powerful creature like Jesus, superheroes, heroes in traditional WASP literature. These people, creatures, etc. save the people from persecution, the bad guys, evil, etc." (UG)

Some students identified with Rabbi Loew, as the true helper of his threatened people:

- "He was a leader and helped solve the problem of his community. [. . .]" (UG)
- "I thought most about the Rabbi. I wondered if he regretted making Golem, then I wondered if he regretted killing him." (G)

Being the Golem

A second strong voice in the written responses was heard as readers identified the golem as a sympathetic character striving to live. Among the Jewish teenagers, especially the girls, identification with the golem and indignation that he was treated unfairly emerged as a major theme:

Amy: I think creating the Golem to protect the Jews was a good idea. It kept them safe from harm. But I think it was wrong in the end how they destroyed the Golem because I think if the Jews didn't need protection the Golem would have kept to himself and not hurt anyone.

Leslie: It's sad that the golem had to die. He helped them so much, and all they had to thank him with is death. It wasn't very kind of them.

Sharon: I think that although Golem was made for the protection of the Jews that Rabbi could have treated him better.

Boruch: Those people were cruel. Golem was like a child, filled with wonder, and they killed him! And even the best funeral in the world can't make up for that. They should have written Shalom [peace] on his forehead instead of death.

> ***Steven:*** It wasn't much of a children's story. Very tragic. Golem understood and appreciated life more than anyone else but he had to be destroyed anyway. Isn't it ironic?
>
> ***Leo:*** I like the way Joseph was able to appreciate life and beauty. I also liked how they said Kaddish [the prayer for the dead] over him, even though he wasn't really human.

These young teenagers identified with the injustice done to the golem (child) by his creators (parents). This intergenerational conflict connects directly with these young readers' developmental concerns and family dynamics. Some of the older college readers were also indignant:

- "I was sympathetic to the golem at the end and disappointed that the Rabbi called him forth as a protector and then dismissed his value after he was no longer needed." (UG)
- "I just fell for him. I thought about how it must feel to want to live and to not come back." (UG)
- "Golem wanted to keep human just like Pinocchio wanted to be made into a real boy." (UG)
- "I was more interested in the second half of the book [which focuses on the life of the golem]." (UG)

The responses of two of the teenagers shift the focus from the golem as life-seeking child to the underlying conflict between parent and child, creator and creation:

> ***Boruch:*** Both Rabbi Loew and Dr. Frankenstein created monsters, people who were alive and yet still dead. At the end they both got scared of their creations and killed it. Rabbi Loew made it to protect the Jews. Dr. Frankenstein made it to show everyone he could. But in the end they both were killed because they were so strong. Humans are scared of what we can't control, and these creations were out of our grasp.
>
> ***Michael:*** I feel like the golem was just like this lump of clay that I was molding [while listening to the story] to make it perfect, then it looked horrible so I smashed it.

Boruch's response to the story shows a capacity for a high level of abstraction: "Humans are scared of what they can't control." Michael's response is more concrete, connected to his work with the clay during the reading. He describes how he depicted the role of Dr. Frankenstein as creator and destroyer, even imagining his motives. The dynamic between the golem and his creator, between child and parent, certainly had an impact on many of the readers.

Jewish and Christian Perspectives

A third strong voice in the written responses emphasized the intertextual connections between the golem legend and Jewish and Christian texts and traditions. The Jewish teenagers read as cultural insiders who appreciated Rabbi Loew's holy motives and were able to contrast his motive for creating the golem with those of Dr. Frankenstein:

> *Amy:* Both Dr. Frankenstein and Rabbi Loew wanted to create life. Dr. Frankenstein created the monster to prove that he could create life. Rabbi Loew created the Golem to defend the Jews.
>
> *Ron:* Dr F is a crazy man. He should be sent to prison, but Rabbi Loew was smart and he created the golem for a good cause. Rabbi Loew created the golem to save the Jews but Frankenstein was just crazy.
>
> *Jonathan:* I think he'll be back. The temple probably sank to the ground and some day someone will find it and save us.

In contrast, the non-Jewish undergraduates and graduate students experienced the story in the context of their own textual and religious traditions, especially the story of the sacrifice of Jesus.

- "This reminds me of the idea of the Messiah coming and coming again someday. It is hard to relate to the idea of a Messiah made out of clay because I am a Christian and believe in Jesus." (UG)
- "A mix between Frankenstein and the creation of Adam from the Bible. The golem was the savior as Jesus was and then crucified. It shows Jewish beliefs of faith and that God will come and save them when they need it." (UG)
- "Savior who is sacrificed" (G)
- "He gives but does not receive in return." (UG)
- "He did as his 'father' told him and then had to die once his purpose was fulfilled— much like Jesus Christ." (G)
- "Golem could be a 'Jesus' of Jewish people." (UG)
- "I thought that the name Joseph as odd to use since that was Jesus' father's name." (UG)
- The expression of going back to earth when he dies is something said in the Bible. (UG)

The Christian readers, especially those from the Midwest, connected this story to Jesus, and they could use this connection to appreciate underlying Judeo-Christian motifs. The Jewish teenagers, in contrast, were indignant at the sacrifice of the golem, since self-sacrifice is not within their religious tradition.

Personal Responses

A fourth strong voice in the responses described readers' personal and aesthetic experiences with the book, showing appreciation of the story or illustrations. These responses often blended together elements of the text and illustrations with popular culture and literary or religious traditions.

- "Throughout the story, I kept thinking the golem looked like The Incredible Hulk! The illustrations really show the fierceness of the golem during the riot. On the last page the letters of truth show through the rubble of the old song books in the attic." (UG)
- "So far [halfway through] the book reminded me of when God created Adam. But this version comes across as scary and mysterious. The illustrations set the mood." (UG)
- "The book was very predictable and followed the patterns of a fairy tale. Happy ending—one character sets out on a journey and saves the day (or town) and returns home." (UG)

> ***Boruch:***   The Golem and the broom both had the same single-minded purpose, but one had cooler music. The pictures [in the book] were definitely cool, though.
>
> ***Leo:***   I liked the book better than the movie because it was more realistic, the Golem was really a Golem in the story, but in the movie it was a broom. The movie was too comical and the book had cooler pictures.
>
> ***Jonathan:***   The golem is also cool.
>
> ***Dan:***   I liked the story. It was exciting.

Failure to Step In

It is important that I mention a fifth strong voice in the responses—that of readers who failed to enter into the world of the legend, as has been earlier noted in my work and the work of Victoria Purcell-Gates, either because they did not understand or appreciate the story and its characters or because they responded to it only as a purveyor of culture. Jewish names and vocabulary seemed to interfere with engagement of the book for many non-Jewish readers. The following responses came from the "Think and Write" responses of the non-Jewish undergraduate students.

- "I still don't like the book. It seems very depressing to me, and I really don't think that children will understand what is going on in the text." (UG)
- "Didn't enjoy it. The words were hard to pronounce. The story was much like Frankenstein, but not as enjoyable." (UG)
- "This book is informative and lets the readers know about Jewish culture." (UG)
- "The book was very hard to follow. I think before reading this we must learn about Jewish culture."

Some students explained why they failed to identify with any of the characters:

- "because I am an outsider to this type of situation" (UG)
- "I was too busy trying to follow the story and understand it" (UG)

The responses of the readers in this study reveal the influence of age, culture, and experience. The young Jewish teenagers identified with the golem's yearning for life and full acceptance into the human community, something they were immediately experiencing. The older non-Jewish students related to the theme of someone who is willing to help others. The older readers identified with the Rabbi because he was a leader; the younger readers identified with the golem because he was naïve, helpful, and life-seeking. Individual self-realization was more important for the young teenagers, whereas for the college readers, awareness of the need to save a minority group from persecution seemed to be the central theme. The responses of the Jewish teenagers represented a developmental connection to the needs of the child and to a Jewish cultural emphasis on social justice, whereas those of the university students represented their strong Christian beliefs in a savior who is sacrificed for the people he came to help.

Conclusions: Cultures, Legends, and Literatures

Literary experience and literary learning through multicultural literature give voice, ideally, to both universal and culturally specific themes. In the golem legend, universal themes of personal growth, child and parent relations, the human's relationship to technology, and minority survival make the story accessible to all. At the same time, when reading "modern multicultural" texts, readers often interpret the story according to their own religious, ethnic, and cultural experiences. When readers select a variety of stories, themes, and motifs to foreground in their responses, they face the possibility of "familiarizing the unfamiliar." Readers who are not aware of a story's cultural roots will miss the Jewish significance of the story's structure, with its complex history, religious allusions, and culture-specific themes that are related to but not identical with mainstream Christian traditions.

In this study, the readers who identified most with the Rabbi chose the story of the civic helper and righteous savior as the most compelling one. The "savior" theme that the golem personified was connected with other saviors, both religious (Moses, Jesus, Messiah) and secular (superheroes, fairy tale heroes). Those readers who identified with the golem chose the story of the child's yearning for life as the most compelling story. The "creation of life" theme in its Jewish golem form—which supplies the mechanism for the savior theme and the persona for the childhood growth theme—necessarily blends, for modern readers, with the Frankenstein story made popular in films and popular culture. Readers' responses grow out of their familiarity and engagement with these various traditions, stories, and themes.

For teachers, the legend of the golem could easily contribute to an integrated Holocaust literature–social studies curriculum, which is widely mandated in the United States. The theme of deliverance from destruction by God's intervention in the golem legend could be explicitly connected to the Holocaust, especially through Elie Wiesel's retelling. But there is a danger that, with study of the Holocaust as the primary reference point students have to Jews and Judaism, Jewish identity can come to be equated with victimhood. On the other hand, study of the cycle of golem legends could encompass the layers of culture-specific knowledge of history, texts, language, and other traditions that lie behind the Jewish themes of the legend: the history of Jewish migrations and persecution, the role of rabbis in Jewish communities, Jewish ethical teachings, the role of prayer, sacred texts, and the Hebrew language, and the mystical tradition of the *kaballah*.

In modern multicultural literature, images, themes, and voices from particular cultural traditions are refocused; often they are simplified, transformed, and appropriated into another group's literature. However, as the history of the golem legend shows, those images, themes, and voices had already been layered and redefined within the original cultural group. To insist too rigidly on the distinction between "in-group" and "cross-group" borrowing threatens to misrepresent particular cultures as unified, rather than as a collection of competing traditions.

Literature has evolved from stories and poems that were first transmitted orally within cultural groups. Once these oral myths and legends enter written literature, their unique traditions are adapted to new audiences and assimilated with other traditions in the creation of a new literature. This is part of the literary process. Indeed, one can only guess at what reincarnations the golem will undergo in future visual, oral, and written stories.

Notes

1. Scholarly sources on the golem in modern literature and film include Arnold Goldsmith's *The Golem Remembered, 1909–1980: Variations of a Jewish Legend.* Detroit: Wayne State University Press, 1981, and Byron Sherwin's *The Golem Legend: Origins and Implications.* Lantham, MD: University Press of America, 1985. The evolution of the legend in Jewish culture, particularly its connection to the kaballah, is illuminated by Gershon Scholem in his chapter "The Idea of the Golem" in *On the Kaballah and Its Symbolism* (tr. Ralph Mannheim). New York: Schocken Books, 1963.

2. I have included Psalm 139 (*Tanakh, The Holy Scriptures: The New JPS Translation.* Philadelphia, PA: Jewish Publication Society, 1983) so that readers can appreciate the context of the original biblical source of the legend (ellipses represent omitted verses).

> Lord, You have examined me and know me.
>> When I sit down or stand up, you know it
>> You discern my thoughts from afar . . .
> If I take wing with the dawn to come to rest on the western horizon
>> Even there your hand will be guiding me
>> Your right hand will be holding me fast [. . .]
> It was you who created my conscience
>> You fashioned me in my mother's womb . . .
> My frame was not concealed from you when I was shaped
>> in a hidden place
>> Knit together in the recesses of the earth
> Your eyes saw *my unformed limbs* [my golem];
>> They were all recorded in Your book
>> In the time they were formed
>> To the very last one of them . . .
> Examine me, O God, and know my mind;
>> Probe me and know my thoughts
> See if I have vexatious ways
>> And guide me in ways everlasting.
>> (Tanakh, 1273–4)

3. Folklorists Robert Graves and Raphael Patain describe myths and legends that surround canonical biblical stories in *Hebrew Myths: The Book of Genesis.* Garden City, NY: Doubleday & Company, 1964. Gershon Scholem reports that in a midrash (talmudic story) from the second or third century, Adam "is de-

scribed as a golem of cosmic size and strength, to whom, while he was still in this speechless and inanimate state, God showed all future generations to the end of time" ("the idea" 161).

4. The same theme of deliverance appears in the Book of Esther, which is retold and reenacted during another Jewish holiday, Purim. In the Purim story, the Jews of ancient Persia are threatened with annihilation by the wicked government official, Haman. They are ultimately saved from destruction by the intercession of the Jewish queen Esther and her uncle Mordechai. The golem is a savior figure like Moses, Mordechai, and Esther.

5. An ancient non-Jewish legend of protection by an artificial being is the legend of Talos, a bronze creature created by the god Hephaestus who protected the island of Crete from its enemies. It is recounted by Robert Graves in *Greek Myths, vol. I.* Baltimore, MD: Penguin, 1955, 314–15. Superhero protectors from ancient myth include Hercules and Theseus.

6. I am not willing to confirm Mary Shelley's link to the golem since I have found no direct connection between the Frankenstein story written by Mary Shelley in 1811 and the golem legend. In fact, Shelley refers more directly to the myth of Prometheus as her source: Prometheus, rather than the gods themselves, was the creator of (imperfect) mankind in Greek myth. Prometheus was also the one who stole fire (knowledge) from heaven. This contains a more explicit and Christian sense of certain knowledge being forbidden and dangerous in ways that is not part of the Jewish perspective. The indirect link between Frankenstein and the golem is through references to Victor Frankenstein's study of the alchemists Albertus Magnus and Paracelsus, who were near contemporaries of Judah Loew and who are likely to have had knowledge of the kaballah:

> When I arrived home my first care was to procure the whole works of [Cornelius Agrippa], and afterwards of Paracelsus and Albertus Magnus. I read and studied the wild fancies of these writers with delight, they appeared to me treasures known to few beside myself; [. . .] I declared my discoveries to Elizabeth [. . .] under a promise of strict secrecy, but she did not interest herself in the subject, and I was left by her to pursue my studies alone. (Shelley 57–58)

The golem and Frankenstein legends are most clearly connected in the early twentieth-century theater and films of Eastern and Central Europe, where, according to Goldsmith, numerous versions of both stories were staged and filmed (see Goldsmith, Arnold. *The Golem Remembered, 1909–1980: Variations of a Jewish Legend.* Detroit: Wayne State University Press, 1981, and Sherwin, Byron. *The Golem Legend: Origins and Implications.* Lantham, MD: University Press of America, 1985).

7. The I. L. Peretz version is in Irving Howe and Eliezer Greenberg's *A Treasury of Yiddish Stories.* New York: Viking Press, 1953, 245–46. The Grimm version is quoted in Scholem's chapter.

8. The theme of the double is made explicit in Elie Wiesel's version of the legend:

> But even more striking was [the Golem's] shadow, which followed the Maharal's as if refusing to let go; sometimes in the street at night or in the enchanted forest, the two shadows would unite for a second and you could feel them living a life of their own which filled you with terror. (33–34)

9. As part of the orientation to the legend, I asked the non-Jewish readers how much knowledge they had about Judaism before reading the story. The graduate students, who lived in the more ethnically diverse San Francisco Bay area, had more knowledge of Jewish culture than the undergraduates, who lived in the more homogeneous Midwest. The majority of undergraduates (70%) reported having little knowledge about Jewish culture, a minority (27%) had a medium amount, and none had a good deal of knowledge. Most graduate students (77%) reported having a moderate amount of knowledge about Jewish culture. Two graduate students reported having little knowledge (15%), and one reported having a good deal of knowledge. Only two or three of the undergraduate or graduate students were already familiar with the book.

10. The response questions that students wrote to were (1) What themes do you see in *Golem*? In what way is this a universal story? In what way is it a uniquely Jewish story? (2) With whom did you identify? What aspects of the book led to this identification? (3) Compare *Golem* to (a) Frankenstein, (b) superheroes, (c) fairy tale characters or other legendary characters, or (d) other characters he reminds you of. (4) What elements of Jewish culture and experience are included in *Golem*? Are there any terms, ideas, or parts of the story that you find hard to understand? Does the text attempt to define or clarify these ideas?

How? (5) Is this a satisfying book for you? Why or why not? What did/didn't you enjoy about the book? (6) In general, how much knowledge do you feel you have about Jewish culture? (Check one: little or none, medium, a good deal.)

11. Responses from undergraduate students (UG) and graduate students (G) are given without names. The Jewish teenagers are referred to by pseudonyms.

Works Cited

Andersen, Hans Christian. "The Nightingale." *Hans Christian Andersen: The Complete Fairy Tales and Stories.* Trans. Erik Haugaard. New York: Doubleday, 1974.

Baum, L. Frank. *The Wizard of Oz.* New York: Dover Publications, 1960.

Bloch, Chayim. *The Golem: Legends of the Ghetto of Prague.* Trans. Harry Schneiderman. Vienna: John N. Vernay, 1925.

Borges, Jorge Luis. "The Golem." Trans. Anthony Kerrigan. *The Golem Remembered, 1909–1980: Variations of a Jewish Legend.* Ed. Arnold Goldsmith. Detroit: Wayne State University Press, 1981, 160–62.

Buber, Martin. *I and Thou.* New York: Scribner, 1958.

Chabon, Michael. *The Amazing Adventures of Kavalier and Clay.* New York: Random House, 2000.

Chapman, Abraham. "Introduction." *Jewish-American Literature: An Anthology.* New York: New American Library, 1974. xxi–lxiii.

Collodi, Carlo. *Pinocchio.* New York: Puffin, 1996.

De Paolo, Tomie. *Strega Nona.* Upper Saddle River, NJ: Prentice-Hall, 1975.

Dahl, Roald. *The BFG.* New York: Puffin Books, 1982.

Dostoevsky, Feodor. "The Double." *Three Short Novels of Dostoevsky.* Trans. Constance Garnett. Ed. Avrahm Yarmolinsky. Garden City, NY: Doubleday & Company, 1960. 1–176.

Elster, Charles. "Entering and Opening the World of a Poem." *Language Arts* (2000) 78: 71–77.

Gaster, Theodor. "The Adventures of Gilgamesh." In *The Oldest Stories in the World.* Boston: Beacon Press, 1952. 21–51.

Gogal, Nikolai. "The Nose." *The Diary of a Madman and Other Stories.* Trans. Andrew McAndrew. New York: New American Library, 1960.

Goldsmith, Arnold. *The Golem Remembered, 1909–1980: Variations of a Jewish Legend.* Detroit: Wayne State University, 1981.

Graves, Robert. "Midas." *Greek Myths, vol. I.* Baltimore: Penguin, 1955. 280–85.

Hollander, John. "Letter to Jorge Luis Borges Apropos of the Golem." *The Golem Remembered, 1909–1980: Variations of a Jewish Legend.* Ed: Arnold Goldsmith. Detroit: Wayne State University Press, 1981. 164–66.

Homer. *The Odyssey of Homer: A Modern Translation.* Trans. Richmond Lattimore. New York: Harper & Row, 1967.

Lang, Andrew, ed. "The Enchanted Horse." *The Arabian Nights Entertainments.* New York: Dover, 1969. 358–89.

McDermott, Beverly Brodsky. *The Golem: A Jewish Legend.* Philadelphia: J. B. Lippincott, 1976.

Meyrink, Gustav. *The Golem.* Prague: Mudra, 1972.

Ozick, Cynthia. "Puttermesser and Xanthippe." *Levitation: Five Fictions.* New York: E. P. Dutton, 1977. 75–158.

Peck, Jackie and Judy Hendershot. "Golem Comes to Life: A Conversation with David Wisniewski, Winner of the 1997 Caldecott Award." *The Reading Teacher* (1998) 51: 456–62.

Podwal, Mark. *Golem: A Giant Made of Mud.* New York: Greenwillow Books, 1995.

Purcell-Gates, Victoria. "On the Outside Looking In: A Study of Remedial Readers' Meaning-Making While Reading Literature." *Journal of Reading Behavior* (1991) 23: 235–50.

Rogasky, Barbara. *The Golem.* Illus. Trina S. Hyman. New York: Holiday House, 1982.

Rosenberg, Yudl. "The Golem or the Miraculous Deeds of Rabbi Liva." *The Great Works of Jewish Fantasy and Occult.* Ed. Joachim Neugroschel. Woodstock, VT: The Overlook Press, 1987, 162–225.

Scholem, Gershon. *On the Kaballah and Its Symbolism.* Trans. Ralph Manheim. New York: Schocken Press, 1963.

Shelley, Mary. "Frankenstein, or the Modern Prometheus." *The Essential Frankenstein.* Ed. Leonard Wolf. New York: Byron Preiss/Penguin, 1983.

Singer, Isaac Bashevis. *The Golem.* Illus. Uri Shulevitz. New York: Farrar Strauss Giroux, 1982.

Stevenson, Robert Louis. *The Strange Case of Dr. Jekyll and Mr. Hyde.* New York: New American Library, 1994.

Sturm, James. *The Golem's Mighty Swing.* Montreal, Canada: Drawn and Quarterly Books, 2001.

Wiesel, Elie. *The Golem: The Story of a Legend.* Illus. Mark Podwal. New York: Summit Books, 1983.

Wilde, Oscar. *The Picture of Dorian Gray.* New York: Modern Library, 1992.

Williams, Margary. *The Velveteen Rabbit, or How Toys Become Real.* New York: Doubleday, 1969.

Wisniewski, David. *Golem.* New York: Clarion Books, 1997.

Films and Videos

Bicentennial Man. Dir. Chris Columbus. Perf. Robin Williams, Sam Neill, Columbia Pictures, 1999.

Fantasia. ("The Sorcerer's Apprentice" sequence). Dir. Walt Disney, animated. Walt Disney Studios, 1940.

Frankenstein. Dir. James Whale. Perf. Boris Karloff, Colin Clive, and Mae Clark. Universal Pictures, 1931.

Der Golem. Dir. Paul Wegener. Perf. Paul Wegener, 1922.

Pinocchio. Dir. Walt Disney, animated. Walt Disney Studios, 1939.

2001: A Space Odyssey. Dir. Stanley Kubrick. Perf. Keir Dullea, 1969.

The Wizard of Oz. Dir. Victor Fleming. Perf. Judy Garland, Ray Bolger, Jack Haley, Bert Lahr, Margaret Hamilton, Frank Morgan. MGM, 1939.

"Kaddish." *The X-Files.* Twentieth Century Fox.

8

Picture Books and ESL Students

Theoretical and Practical Implications for Elementary School Classroom Teachers

Olha Tsarykovska

This paper is about the ways children's literature can be used to teach non-English-speaking students English literacy in the elementary classroom. I wish to focus my attention on picture books and their significance in working with ESL (English as second language) students to promote their comprehension, speaking, reading, and writing skills in English. I will also explore different kinds of picture books that could be effectively used with ESL students and selection criteria and guides for their evaluation from the perspective of their relevance to the students' levels of proficiency.

The purpose of this paper is (a) to reveal the importance of the topic to regular classroom teachers, (b) to examine advantages of using picture books with elementary school ESL students, and (c) to come up with guidelines for evaluating picture books that would help teachers choose appropriate reading materials for working with non-English-speaking students on a daily basis to promote their second language literacy skills. At the end of the paper I will explore the importance of images in illustrations in books for ESL students.

I.

The immigration of people in the modern world has a profound effect on literacy education in their host countries. Immigration brings a speech community into a new language environment. U.S. schools have to help non-English-speaking children acquire literacy skills. During the last decade, 14 percent of the U.S. school-age population lived in homes where a language other than English was dominant. In 80 percent of the states, the number of ESL speakers has increased (Watts-Taffe and Truscott 258). Thus, all schools must be prepared to meet the challenge of an increasingly diverse student population that contains many students who are not proficient in English. Teachers should be ready to teach these children English literacy skills in different ways, using techniques and strategies other than those used with first language speakers. However, along the way classroom teachers will confront many problems: (a) inadequate teacher training in dealing with ESL students, (b) use of an outdated methodology, (c) the absence of textbooks designed for different language students, (d) the large differences in language acquisition and communication patterns of these students, and (e) the different cognitive schemata of diverse students (Flatley and Rutland 276).

Besides the issues of decoding and communicating, educators must consider how children become literate. Watts-Taffe and Truscott have summarized the main points teachers should keep in mind while working with ESL students: (a) reading, writing, listening, speaking, and thinking develop in an integrated manner; (b) language and thought are socially constructed; (c) language learning proceeds best when children use language in meaningful contexts with meaningful purposes; (d) meaningful language use is influenced by an individual's prior experience, culture, motivation, and goals; (e) language learning proceeds best when children are encouraged to take risks, experiment, and make mistakes; and (f) modeling and scaffolding are critical to successful language learning (260). In fact, carefully chosen children's literature can do all this while helping ESL students acquire and practice English literacy skills in a nonthreatening situation.

During my internship at one of the area elementary schools, I noticed an activity that seems to be part of the daily school routine in American elementary school classrooms: Teachers were reading picture books to a group of students. Ukrainian and Russian elementary schools do not use the practice in literacy education, and so I was interested in its purposes. I was told by the teachers I worked with that it was a popular method when teaching all students about literacy and fostering their language skills. However, although there were several non-English-speaking children among the students, the teachers did not pay special attention to their needed skills that could help them understand the shared stories. There were activities they could pursue before, during, or after the reading, but they did not. I wondered why. Sharing picture books seemed a way to assist non-English-speaking students as they acquired English literacy skills in the classroom. Most were given individualized instruction when they were pulled out for special English classes, but this did not seem to be tied to oral readings by the teachers. As work in both first and second language acquisition has shown, "purposive direct instruction is not the only way by which [students] 'get proficient' in language" (Appelt 69). The more opportunities students have to hear, read, and practice language, the more language they can produce and understand.

In "Whole Language and Children's Literature," Bernice Cullinan has justified the choice of narrative texts, saying, "we remember the past in narrative, we plan the future in narrative, and we dream in narrative. Narrative is the way we organize our minds. In order really to live, we make up stories about ourselves and others, about the past and future" (426). Thus, we use language to represent and structure our world. We create stories of our lives using the framework of our individual belief systems. Each story is a cultural universal for its teller and listeners. Furthermore, listening to stories helps children remember cultural rules and events. Stories make ordinary events memorable. And stories are powerful because they provide the schema for listening and learning.

Children's picture books offer a natural and interesting way to teach literacy skills acquisition. They often contain predictable, repetitive patterns that reinforce cultural vocabulary and linguistic structures, and they provide introductions to relevant ethnic mores for young learners. Quality literature can present a multitude of discussion topics that will grab children's attention and allow them to link the events recounted to those in their own lives. Carefully chosen children's literature allows ESL students to develop their literacy skills in an entertaining, meaningful context, and this naturally encourages them to repeat many of the predictable words and phrases. Therefore, picture books have a number of advantages for use with ESL elementary school students. They are:

- Usually short
- Written in a language that is structurally simple
- Cover a wide content range
- Often presented from a young child's perspective
- Found in most elementary school and public libraries that have good picture book collections of different levels

Picture books, especially, hold exceptional opportunities for supporting students with diverse language proficiencies and reading levels and for assisting them to actively participate in daily classroom activities. These books also contain cultural information, are short in length, usually have a small amount of text, and use illustrations that can guide the students' comprehension of new situations and beliefs.

When selecting literature for ESL students, teachers will need to consider the following usual qualities of good literature:

- Good books expand awareness.
- Good books provide an enjoyable read that does not overtly teach or moralize.
- Good books embody quality.
- Good books have integrity.
- Good books show originality (Hadaway, Vardell, and Young 64).

Moreover, teachers need to consider elements particular to a specific population of ESL students. These include (a) clarity of presentation, (b) use of illustrations, (c) number of new concepts, (d) number of new words, (e) familiarity of subject matter, (f) author's style, and (g) length of the book (Hadaway et al. 57–58). It may be even more helpful for the teacher to choose from the different variations of picture book format currently available, including (a) ABC and counting books, (b) concept books, (c) wordless picture books, (d) predictable books, (e) picture storybooks, and (f) poems.

ABC books may be used to teach the alphabet to children and also to introduce a variety of objects, images, or terms. For instance, *Eating the Alphabet* by Ehlert introduces fruits and vegetables for each letter of the alphabet. *Illuminations* by Hunt is an alphabet book that is really more appropriate for older students. It introduces vocabulary and concepts related to the Middle Ages.

Counting books also have a built-in structure. Often this is simply counting from one to ten, but sometimes counting books include zero, sets, multiples, and so on. Making counting books can also be fun for students. *The M&M's Brand Counting Book* by Mc-Grath is an enjoyable thematic counting book.

Concept books are really nonfiction books for young children, the purpose of which is to teach and present information, not to tell a story. The best concept books are very simple and highly visual. They usually deal with such challenging topics as color, direction, time, proportion, and the like. Hoban's *26 Letters and 99 Cents* introduces letters, objects, colors, and American coins.

Wordless picture books are picture books that have no or very few words; the pictures are the books. Such books generally tell a story through illustrations alone. For instance, *Tuesday* by Wiesner, *Window* by Baker, and *Good Dog, Carl* by Day do not use words and challenge students to create or narrate their own text. This can provide an excellent opportunity for storytelling, writing captions, developing oral fluency, assessing visual literacy, and developing language skills.

Predictable books with repeated refrains are especially appropriate for younger ESL students, because these books allow them to function quickly as readers of English text. Stories are made comprehensible by illustrations, repeated language patterns, and by predictable story structure as in *Brown Bear, What Do You See?* by Martin, Jr. or *I Went Walking* by Williams.

Still, I admit that choosing effective reading material for students learning a new language is a difficult struggle for teachers. America's diverse classrooms require a wide range of language, topics, and literary styles that only books can provide. Nevertheless, because ESL students are often learning the reading and writing process for the first time while learning English, teachers seem to worry that students will not be able to handle authentic materials that they would use with children from homes where English is spoken. Huck, Hepler, and Hickman (220) have suggested the following guidelines for evaluating picture books:

Content
- How appropriate is the content of the book for its intended age and interest level of the children?
- Is this a book that will appeal to children, or is it written for adults?
- Is the language cognitively demanding?
- Does the text have structures that will support children's understanding?
- Are the characters well developed?
- Are sex, race, or any other cultural stereotypes avoided?

Illustrations
- In what ways do the illustrations help to create the meaning of the text?
- Do the pictures contain enough details? Are these details authentic?

- Do the illustrations extend the text in any way? Do they provide clues to the actions of the story?
- Are the pictures accurate and consistent with the text?

Medium and Style of Illustrations
- How has the illustrator used shapes and colors to represent the story?
- Is the style of illustrations appropriate for the story?
- How has the illustrator created balance in composition?

Format
- Does the size of the book seem appropriate for the level of ESL students?
- In what way does the title page anticipate the story to come?

Comparison with Others
- How is this book similar to or different from other works by this author/illustrator?
- How is this story similar to or different from other books with the same subject or theme?
- What comments have reviewers made about the book? Do you agree or disagree with them?
- What has the writer/illustrator said about his/her work?
- Will this book support students' acquisition of English? (220)

I wish to suggest further possibilities that fit with the work of Hadaway, Vardall, and Terrell:

Non-English speakers could benefit from picture books containing illustrations that retell the story. They would also benefit from oral readings by a teacher who is willing to be expressive and to use gestures and props to help them as they read books to these children.

Beginning English speakers should hear stories with typical story structures. They will learn best if the stories seem to follow familiar patterns, and they will enjoy listening to stories best when the illustrations correlate with the text. Illustrations should support the story line. In the beginning of language learning, short stories are most effective, and predictable plots with repetition are best because they allow ESL students to frame the English language as they listen to simple phrases repeated in the story. Is is essential that teachers look for linguistic structures that might be difficult. Idioms and dialect that might confuse students should be discussed with them.

Intermediate ESL students are ready to attack new words and concepts. They will be less dependent on illustrations to retell them what they hear. Many will prefer longer stories and will want more text than will be found in books with text and illustrations contained within a two-page spread. In this case, it is best to look for stories that are framed by a familiar plot structure or topic. Then the children can feel safe as they explore new language that is not encoded in the book's illustrations. When sharing unfamiliar patterns with these children, the teacher should seek books with simple language, little text, and illustrations that support the text. Again, linguistic repetition is desirable. Teachers need to consider what ideas might seem culturally strange to the children and be prepared to discuss why a certain story has been created. New words in these books can be used as vocabulary for the children, especially when combined with dictionary skills.

Advanced ESL students are becoming part of the learning community. They need fewer illustrations, can attend to and understand longer and more complex texts, but will still need teacher support with new linguistic structures, allusions to cultural attitudes and practices that they are not familiar with, and aid in building their English vocabulary.

If children's picture books chosen for ESL students are not carefully selected, teachers will find the children in their classroom struggling and will watch as they become frustrated and/or silent during classroom interactions. Teachers need to carefully plan if they hope to assist immigrant students. Several factors concerning linguistic competency must be considered when selecting picture books: (a) the students' levels of spoken and written languages, (b) the variances in story structure between diverse ethnic populations, and (c) the style of illustrations presented in the text.

Language must be carefully considered in selecting picture books for ESL students. This does not mean that texts need to be simplified by limiting the length of sentences, the number of words within the text, or the number of syllables in words. Rather, "texts should support meaning by being predictable" (Rigg and Allen 59). For instance, folktales with their conventional beginnings and endings and recurring characters help children predict both the actions and the language of the story. Thus, children just learning a new language should be able to decode the text as they practice retelling folklore, play with language in oral responses to the stories they hear, and experiment in their written work about the stories they share in the classroom.

The format of a typical picture book allows limited English speakers to predict the actions and events in the plots. This practice usually reduces students' cognitive load and allows them to focus their attention on the language and the ways it is used in telling stories. Rigg and Allen have stressed the importance of illustrations in the teacher's choice of picture books. They feel that the illustrator plays a significant role in helping children attach meaning to the text, which is absolutely crucial to ESL students' acquisition of English literacy skills, and they claim that the basal reader is incomparable to picture books when working with ESL children. If textbooks include pictures, their placement and size are usually changed to accommodate the format of the reading book. This is a hindrance to the second language learner who relies on the illustrations as a second code to a new linguistic system. The dimensions of a good picture book are an important part of its structure. Often the format of a picture book allows the illustrator to create, for example, a sense of the length of a trip, as is seen in *The Ox-Cart Man* by Hall, or a sense of a frightening power, as shown in *Foolish Rabbit's Big Mistake* by Martin. Thus, "picture books not only provide experience with printed language, they also provide a variety of eye-catching, interesting illustrations which capture a child's attention" (Moe 24).

However, although the significance of illustrations has long been recognized, little research has been done on the different types of images in picture books and how they can be more fully exploited in teaching English to children just learning a new language. This is an important issue to consider because the generic structure of the stories, the linguistic choices made by the writer, and the visual choices made by the illustrator closely interact with the verbal text. The more fully the illustrations depict each significant stage in the text as well as the major participants, the processes in which they engage, and the circumstances surrounding their activities the more support ESL students will have in linking the visual and the verbal texts and, thereby, enhance their level of comprehension.

Astorga's study on the text–image interaction in picture books and second language learning paid special attention to how and to what extent the visual images represented the meanings communicated by the verbal text. She assumed that "visual communication has its own grammar, that images are amenable to rational accounts and analysis, and that language and visual communication both realise [*sic*] the same fundamental and far-reaching systems of meaning that constitute our culture, each by means of its own specific forms and independently" (212–13). For her analysis, Astorga also used two basic image–text relations identified by Barthes: (a) elaboration (when the verbal text restates the meanings of the image or vice versa, with word and image in an equal relation) and (b) relay (when the verbal text extends the meanings of the image or vice versa, with word and image in a complimentary relation) (213). Written stories used in second language learning have the undeniable value of providing the context through which children can acquire the new language by being exposed to the sentence patterns and rhythms of English. At the same time, the language can be a barrier that prevents the ESL children from getting into the story. Then pictures illustrating the verbal text become powerful aids. They facilitate the decoding process by making the language of the story not only meaningful but also memorable. Besides, when both text and image are simultaneously shared, the image will be the first to engage the child's attention. ESL students need teachers who help them make connections between the images and words printed on the page, and, who, as a result, are encouraged to consider the interdependence of two cultural frameworks while they are reading.

According to Astorga, the pictorial code can serve three major functions: (a) the ideational function (to represent experience), (b) the interpersonal function (to develop a relationship between illustrator and audience), and (c) the textual function (to provide cohesive links) (214). Astorga considered the ideational function to be of a primary significance because it was realized through a variety of participants (animate-inanimate), processes (material, mental, verbal, behavioral, relational, and existential), and circumstances (how? where? when?) and was the first to attract the child's attention. All the images realizing the ideational meanings could be categorized into two groups: (a) conceptual images and (b) presentational images (214–15). Teachers should select good reading materials appropriate to children with limited English skills that allow the children chances to differentiate between the ideas found in the text and their visual representations.

Conceptual images are those that "represent the meaning of a participant, its stable and visible essence, and define it as a member of a class" (214). These images have a didactic function as they serve to explain what things are like. Such images are usually found in textbooks, manuals, and scientific papers. They are meant to be studied carefully, not simply looked at. Conceptual images usually represent existential (there was) and relational (was) processes. In other words, the main function of the image is to identify and describe someone or something within the text. They record the text.

Presentational images are those that deal with actions and events. Their main function is to show a particular moment in time or an event. These images are mainly found in stories. They are meant to be understood unconsciously, not intellectually. Presentational images usually represent material (ran), behavioral (swallowed), and mental (wondered) processes. They record actions.

The next step when helping children learn to analyze a picture book from the perspective of images in illustrations is to teach them to look for setting. The presence or absence of setting is a distinguishing feature. It is not necessary to have a clearly defined setting in the conceptional stage, but it is absolutely obligatory in presentational images: "A picture of an action or interaction without a setting acquires a conceptual aspect [. . .] the more defined the setting is in conceptual images, the more the picture will blend the conceptual and the presentational" (Astorga 215). Thus, setting, characterization, and plot become essential story components.

The following step would be to find out which speech functions images represent. Astorga used four of the primary speech functions developed by Halliday: (a) offering information (statement), (b) offering goods and services (offer), (c) demanding information (question), and (d) demanding goods and services (command). In the majority of cases images will represent only one speech function. According to Astorga, "our society has not developed images to the extent where they have the capacity to realise [*sic*] a large number of speech acts" (217). Thus, I can conclude that when there is a relation of elaboration in the picture book, the verbal text is brought closer to the reader through the visual images that fulfill the same functions as those of gestures, mimicry, gaze, and body posture used in spoken interaction.

Keeping all this information in mind, the teacher could ask ESL students to compare how each stage is represented both visually and verbally in the books they share. This practice will cause ESL students to explore the language as carefully as the images used in picture books. For example, they may be asked to analyze the picture in order to determine whether the written text and visual text convey the same meanings about the characters and the setting. Or they may be asked to examine the pictures that illustrate the action stages and compare the events that the visual images depict with those that are verbally recounted. Or the students may be asked to examine the pictures with the purpose of determining which processes (e.g., actions, behaviors, etc.) are/are not visually communicated. The same procedure may be done with characters and setting. The procedures recommended previously may develop ESL children's literacy abilities further.

Because I believe that pictures are useful and necessary not only at the stage when children are introduced to a story for the first time, but also later when the aim is to develop children's strategies in remembering, retrieving, and using the language of the stories in their everyday life, I urge teachers to make sure pictures are paid attention to and included in postreading assignments.

The steps in analyzing text–image relations in picture books chosen for ESL students mentioned previously do not exhaust all the criteria teachers may look for. The following questions may assist them in developing their own parameters for assessing the function that visual images have in illustrated stories:

- Do images illustrate every stage of the story?
- What type of text–image relations (elaboration or relay) is more frequent in the story?
- Which clauses have matching images and which don't?

- If there are gaps in the written text (events that are not recounted), are they filled by the visual images and vice versa?
- What role do images have in the interactive stages of the story?
- Do presentational images represent the characters in the same role as in the text (actor, sender, sayer)?
- Do presentational images communicate all the events that are recounted in the text? (Astorga 222)

The preceding list, which is by no means exhaustive, helps as teachers develop literacy skills needed to help ESL students deal with the relations. They will be better able to help ESL children acquire appropriate strategies to become active participants in their literacy classrooms.

Throughout the process of reading picture books, many skills can be taught and developed. The teacher should not simply emphasize reading and writing skills; she also may engage new language learners in oral discussions about the representations of ethnicity and culture available in their picture book stories. Gradually these children will lose their fear of reading and discussing an English text. They will be motivated to connect the books to their lives and to consider the linguistically and culturally different ways authors and illustrators use when telling others about themselves. Rather than reducing language to a series of isolated rules and skill sequences with texts that are simplified, literature-rich classrooms can offer teachers and students rich language experiences that correspond to visual literacy and oral competency while exploring relevant and interesting texts.

Works Cited

Appelt, Jane E. "Not Just for Little Kids: The Picture Book in ESL Classes." *TESL Canada Journal* 2 (1984): 67–78.

Astorga, Maria C. "The Text–Image Interaction and Second Language Learning." *The Australian Journal of Language and Literacy* 22 (1999): 212–33.

Baker, Jeannie. *Window.* New York: Greenwillow, 1991.

Cullinan, Bernice E. "Whole Language and Children's Literature." *Language Arts* 69 (1992): 426–30.

Day, Alexandra. *Good Dog, Carl.* San Marcos: Green Tiger Press, 1985.

Ehlert, Lois. *Eating the Alphabet.* New York: Trumpet Club, 1989.

Flatley, Joannis K. and Adele D. Rutland. "Using Wordless Picture Books to Teach Linguistically/Culturally Different Students." *The Reading Teacher* 40 (1986): 276–81.

Goldsmith, Arnold. *The Golem Remembered, 1909–1980: Variations of a Jewish Legend.* Detroit: Wayne State University, 1981.

Hadaway, Nancy L., Vardell, Sylvia M., and Terrell A. Young. *Literature-Based Instruction with English Language Learners.* Boston: Allyn and Bacon, 2002.

Hall, Donald. *Ox-Cart Man.* New York: The Viking Press, 1979.

Hoban, Tana. *26 Letters and 99 Cents.* New York: Greenwillow, 1987.

Huck, Charlotte S., Hepler, Susan, and Janet Hickman. *Children's Literature in the Elementary School.* New York: Holt, Rinehart and Winston, Inc., 1987.

Hunt, Jonathan. *Illuminations.* New York: Bradbury, 1989.

Martin, Bill, Jr. *Brown Bear, What Do You See?* New York: Henry Holt, 1970.

Martin, Rafe. *Foolish Rabbit's Big Mistake.* New York: G. P. Putnam's Sons, 1985.

McGrath, Barbara B. *The M&M's Brand Counting Book.* Watertown: Charlesbridge, 1994.

Moe, Alden J. "Using Picture Books for Reading Vocabulary Development." *Using Literature in the Elementary Classroom.* Ed. J. Stewig and S. Sebesta. Urbana, IL: National Council of Teachers of English, 1989. 23–34.

Rigg, Pat and Virginia G. Allen. *When They Don't All Speak English.* Urbana, IL: National Council of Teachers of English, 1989.

Rosenberg, Yudl. "The Golem or the Miraculous Deeds of Rabbi Liva." *The Great Works of Jewish Fantasy and Occult.* Ed. Joachim Neugroschel. Woodstock, VT: The Overlook Press, 1987, 162–225.

Scholem, Gershon. *On the Kaballah and Its Symbolism.* Trans. Ralph Mannheim. New York: Schocken Books, 1963.

Watts-Taffe, Susan and Diane M. Truscott. "Using What We Know About Language and Literacy Development for ESL Students in the Mainstream Classroom." *Language Arts* 77 (2000): 258–64.

Wiesner, David. *Tuesday.* New York: Clarion, 1991.

Williams, Sue. *I Went Walking.* San Diego: Harcourt Brace Jovanovich, 1990.

9

Building Empathy and Character

Children Reading and Responding to Literature

Trudy Nelson

As a fifth-grade teacher, I find my greatest challenge and my greatest sense of satisfaction come from teaching reading. Helping children develop into readers who are engaged in what they are doing is an exciting process. The most simplistic prescription for achieving this goal is to allow the students to read often from a variety of quality literature. In the process of discovering the wonderful literature available at this age level, they gain another reward that they do not often see coming: the chance to learn more about the diverse world where they live. Fifth grade is an exciting grade when children can begin to discover that there is a world beyond their own family and community, one that is not often a just world in which to exist. Once their sense of social conscience begins to develop through the discoveries they make when reading and hearing good literature, they are on the road to being lifelong readers who are more aware of their world. Multicultural literature and historical fiction are genres that can help children with these discoveries. According to Donna Norton,

> Children gain knowledge about the people, values, beliefs, hardships, and physical surroundings common to various periods [through literature . . .]. As characters in historical fiction from many different time periods face and overcome their problems, children may discover universal truths, identify feelings and behaviors that encourage them to consider alternative ways to handle their own problems, empathize with viewpoints that are different from their own, and realize that history consists of many people who have learned to work together. (523)

The classrooms where I have taught—from the Philadelphia suburbs to a small town in Maine to a small city in Indiana—have not been culturally diverse. They all have been predominantly White and middle class. Many of the children have been culturally isolated. In Maine, what the children knew about Blacks or Hispanics usually was from watching television news about Boston, a city 250 miles away, or from the views of their parents who also, for the most part, had lived most of their lives in Maine. The area in suburban Philadelphia was only slightly more culturally diverse and was still predominantly White. Their views of Blacks and Hispanics were also formed by television news, but they usually only heard the negative issues and attitudes of Philadelphia and its nearby small cities. My experience in Indiana has not changed my experiences in my classroom. Because I faced similar issues in these three regional schools, I want to focus on my work as a teacher in the most recent setting, Indiana.

In Indiana, my classroom currently has little diversity, but there is a growing Hispanic population in the area. Most of my students' views on cultural diversity form from their families' views, and many parents do work in culturally diverse workplaces. Hispanic, Japanese, and Black cultures are represented in the surrounding area with its growing industrial base and the presence of a major university. Both draw people from diverse ethnic backgrounds. In the past two years, I have gone from a classroom with no Hispanic Americans to having four Hispanic children. Two of these four children are recent immigrants from Mexico. I have had no African American students in my classroom, but each year there have been two African American students among the three fifth grades. The school's population is not diverse; most students are Caucasian whose middle-class parents work in a variety of occupations, including being self-employed, working at local factories as executives and laborers, as teachers or administrators in the schools, and as university staff. Rarely are they faculty.

When my students enter my classroom in August, they often comment on the amount of books in the classroom. My philosophy is that every child should have a book for daily silent reading, and each child should be reading at least fifteen minutes every evening at home unless there is a large amount of other homework to do. Every year there are one or two students who are self-motivated and read profusely for pleasure on their own, both at home and after finishing other assignments in school. They never need to be encouraged to read. Still, most children admit they do not read at home, which indicates to me that they only read when books are assigned. At the beginning of the school year, these children do not take books out of my collection and read when they have finished their other work unless I request that they do. At parent conference time, I usually find out they are not reading for fifteen minutes a night. I explain to parents that they do indeed have homework every night and that is to be reading for at least fifteen minutes. Sadly, many parents understand this in terms of how that affects their child's reading grade. I have had comments from several parents indicating that they feel their child is not "a reader." I try to explain that our goal is to help every child become a reader and that at this age perhaps their child has not yet discovered what books have to offer or has not been given the opportunity to read the many self-selected books necessary to make this discovery.

I feel one of the most important goals I give my students is to read a variety of books. I want them to record something about each book in their reading logs. In my classroom, the average student reads approximately thirty books by the end of the school year. Several children will read up to sixty books. These books include novels, nonfiction, and picture books for older readers. (One exceptional student during this two-year period read 110 novels and eight picture books. She wrote about each of these books in her reading log.) Student entries in their logs may take the form of critiques or summaries. They might ask questions about what took place in a particular story or even suggest a new ending. Most of the books are self-selected. When the children are assigned a novel, I choose it because it fits within a curriculum theme. Individual book selection is still possible at this time, but I ask that students also select books that fit within the theme. Several books, such as *The Pinballs* by Betsy Byars, *Number the Stars* by Lois Lowry, or novellas like Mildred Taylor's *Song of the Trees,* are assigned each year to the entire class. The students' responses to assigned books are more formal; book discussions are required for our shared literature.

Throughout the year, I emphasize to the students that they are to read, write an entry in their reading log, and then select another book. They do not have to do a formal "book report" or project for every book they read. I periodically check their logs, so they do not have to report to me each time they finish a book. Because I have read most of the hundreds of books available to them in our room, I can discuss titles with them when I do have book conferences, and I can recommend others to them. I know many teachers feel they cannot read every book available for children, and I agree, but I find my teaching is energized by reading as many children's books as I can. During the first quarter, I periodically give "book talks" to introduce various stories from our classroom library. After a few weeks, I also urge other students to tell us about books that they really enjoy. Other students' recommendations are very effective in getting classmates to read a book. Shared experiences further encourage reading. For instance, after reading aloud *Roll of Thunder, Hear My Cry,* I gave the class multiple copies of Mildred Taylor's short books, *The Well, The Friendship, The Gold Cadillac, Mississippi Bridge,* and *Song of the Trees.* These books were read quickly and enthusiastically. As some students talked about Mildred Taylor's stories, others grew eager to read more of her literature based on the recommendations of their fellow students.

At the end of the first quarter, I conference with each child about his or her reading log and progress as an independent reader, and we set goals for the next quarter. At that time, many students realize that although they have free choice of reading material, I expect them to read a large quantity of high-quality literature written by respected children's and adolescent authors. We discuss their selections, and I make suggestions for other genres and types of books that they might enjoy. I believe my guidance to new literacy styles is important. Few children choose historical fiction in the beginning of the quarter. However, after reading Mildred Taylor's books, more children seek books in the historical fiction genre.

It is important to have high-quality literature surrounding the students in the classroom, and when selecting books for the classroom library it is also important to consider children's interests. Children may not ask you to order historical fiction books because they may equate the word *historical* with a school textbook. If you are able to give insight to the stories and adventures, mostly of children, found in historical fiction literature, you can interest them in this genre. Most children are hooked on books for their stories, not what they can learn! I also look for award-winning books such as the Newbery Award and the Coretta Scott King Award winners. These awards are not guarantees of student interest. I have found that some of these books appear to be awarded on adult criteria rather than student interest. Again, reading the books yourself will help you understand your students' reactions to them.

It is important to consider your rationale in choosing literature for the classroom. I want to find good stories for my students, but I also want to connect them to history in the grade where they are introduced to American history. I know that anyone can get too much of one thing so I look for other genres such as biographies, mysteries, and science fiction to round out my collection. I want them to become readers, so I look for a variety of high-interest books at a variety of reading levels. A child learns to read by reading. If only "fifth grade reading level" books were available, my students who may not be reading at that level would not be reading at all. My students who are reading at higher levels would find few books to interest and challenge them. I also look for books that are high interest but above my average students' reading level to use as readalouds. Along with these books, I find companion books that students may want to read after hearing a book by that author or about a certain theme or topic. For example, after reading *Roll of Thunder, Hear My Cry,* students eagerly seek out Mildred Taylor's novellas such as *The Well, The Friendship, The Gold Cadillac,* and *Mississippi Bridge.* Other readalouds that have been class favorites are *Where the Red Fern Grows* by Wilson Rawls, *The True Confessions of Charlotte Doyle* by Avi, and *My Brother Sam Is Dead* by James and Christopher Collier.

After becoming aware of the rich availability of quality literature for children, I began collecting books for my classroom. In my classroom, we have theme books and those read by the whole class. Because the majority of the books read by the students are self-selected texts that are read at school and at home, I have a large library of books available to my students. I have been fortunate to work in schools with school boards and parents who support funds for excellent school libraries. I also know that when students are exposed to book titles throughout the day, they tend to become interested and pick up books to read more often. I now have a collection of hundreds of books. Not only are they on bookshelves, but I also have two turning bookracks where the book covers face the students to capture their interest. I have picture books for older readers, novels, and nonfiction books throughout the room. Building this collection has been exciting and definitely worthwhile.

In building my library, I have used many sources. There are many journals that give excellent book reviews. My favorite source for books is the National Council for the Social Studies' "Notable Social Studies Trade Books for Young People" found in the May/June issue of its journal, *Social Education.* The Notable Book lists for the past four years are found on the website for the National Council for the Social Studies (www.socialstudies.org). This annotated list divides the books into categories: Biography; Contemporary Concerns; Environment; Energy and Ecology; Folk Tales, Myths and Legends; Geography, People and Places; History, Life and Culture in the Americas; Reference; Social Interactions and Relationships; and World History and Culture. This list is developed with the cooperation of the Children's Book Council, a professional group that sponsors National Children's Book Week and Young People's Poetry Week. The website of the Children's Book Council is also very informative (www.cbcbooks.org). One helpful part of its website is a list of seventy-five authors and illustrators that everyone "should know." This is divided by age level and gives a brief description of the author and illustrator and lists some of their works. They also have annotated bibliographies of newly published works and award winners.

Other book lists available for teachers are in *Book Links* and *Horn Book Magazine*. *Book Links* is published every two months by the American Library Association. *Horn Book Magazine* is published six times a year and contains reviews of books, articles about literature, and interviews with authors. Both of these give outstanding reviews, and they are often available in professional school and public libraries. Children's literature book lists can also be found on Internet searches by simply entering the keywords "children's literature."

Joining organizations that can connect you with authors will prove invaluable. There are conferences hosting guest authors such as those conducted by the International Reading Association, the National Council of Teachers of English, and state reading associations. Information on these conferences is in member journals or sent to librarians. Belonging to these organizations also gives you access to additional publications. For example, the National Council for the Social Studies publishes "bulletins" that are extremely informative booklets. *Linking Literature with Life: The NCSS Standards and Children's Literature for the Middle Grades* and *Children's Literature in Social Studies: Teaching to the Standards* are two very helpful sources. They give helpful information on using literature to teach social studies, and they contain annotated book lists divided by the themes of social studies.

I am fortunate to be in an area that has a group known as TELL—Teachers Encouraging a Love for Literature. This group, sponsored by local teachers, brings four authors or illustrators a year to workshops at local schools for students at the schools, and then to a Saturday workshop for teachers and interested citizens and parents. We have been honored to have such noted authors and illustrators as Patricia Polacco, Jerry Pinkney, Robert San Souci, Lois Lowry, and Kathryn Lasky. Nearby Purdue University has sponsored programs that have brought in Russell Freedman, Milton Meltzer, and Ted Lewin. Listening to authors and illustrators can give teachers new perspectives on their work and the process of writing and illustrating. This in turn should empower teachers to bring to their students new perspectives and new teaching ideas when using the books that have been presented.

Another source of new book titles is found by regularly browsing the local bookstores for recent publications. I regularly look for some favorite authors in the fiction and picture books sections and for topics in both social studies and science. Going to a bookstore without a definite title in mind to purchase has led to great discoveries for my classroom library. For example, my discovery of Eve Bunting's picture book, *So Far from the Sea,* illustrated by Chris Soentpiet, has been an invaluable addition to my teaching about the Japanese American Internment during World War II. The artist has given the story full-color pictures, but as the family recalls the time of internment, the pictures turn to black and white, much like photos that may have been taken during the time period of the internment. Students are able to get a visual image and go back into time. This book, combined with novels such as *Journey Home* by Yoshiko Uchida and *I Am an American: A True*

Story of Japanese Internment by Jerry Stanley, gives comprehensive coverage to this important topic.

The student book order clubs that arrive monthly are another good source of books for the room. With any order, teachers collect points that can be used for free books. This has greatly enhanced my library. I also personally buy books if I don't have points but have found some interesting new titles. Recently I discovered in my Scholastic book order form the title *Darkness Over Denmark: The Danish Resistance and the Rescue of the Jews* by Ellen Levine. This proved to be an excellent companion book to use when the class reads *Number the Stars* by Lois Lowry and when I read aloud *Behind the Bedroom Wall* by Laura Williams. Other Holocaust books have also been purchased through my book orders to help stock my classroom library for self-selected books.

Finally, one of the best sources of good literature for students can be found when teachers talk to their colleagues. When teachers find good books that enhance the curriculum or when they see children's reactions to books, they need to tell their fellow teachers about these titles, especially when they are written for their own grade level. Although personally reading as many children's books as I can, I find there are still too many books available and too little time to read as many as I may want. Getting reviews from students and fellow teachers is important in building a library that the students will actually read and enjoy.

I find a critical aspect in helping students become engaged as readers is to model reading and literary discussions as a teacher. I own literally hundreds of novels and picture books for older readers; because I have read most of these books, I periodically give reviews of several books. Students gradually find themselves reading without being assigned the task. They see my enthusiasm for the stories I have read and appreciate my joy in reading. It is not hard to draw fifth graders into my excitement for the books and authors featured in our classroom. Because they are given at least twenty minutes a day for independent reading, they learn how to read independently. Another ten to twenty minutes is set aside for read-aloud time. As a shared literary experience, this is one of the most valued times for myself and the students.

I choose the books I will read for their challenging vocabulary, but they must also have exceptional stories to tell. I also choose books that let students enter into worlds they could not have discovered in their everyday experiences or in their textbook reading. My first book selection in my fifth-grade classes has traditionally been Mildred Taylor's *Roll of Thunder, Hear My Cry*. As my students listen, they discover that not all children have or are given the same opportunities to learn. They listen to a story that shows racial pride, individual determination, community loyalty, and family love. They also hear about hatred, injustice, and prejudice. Although this is not a short book, the students always sit engrossed throughout my reading of the entire story.

After my most recent reading, the class "retold" the story while I listed the events they named. They recalled the book with excitement and animation and left few details out. They were then asked to show what "life skills" at least five characters did or did not display, using examples from the story. As a class, we determined that "life skills" included such traits as caring, responsibility, trustworthiness, respectfulness, and acting as a good citizen. The students' answers, when considering Taylor's novel, were thoughtful and reflective; their conversation showed that they could analyze these character traits, even though some students do not seem to fully understand the meaning of these traits. The children revealed a consensus about certain characters.

Mama and Papa were perceived as holding all the foregoing traits. The children felt that these adults cared for their children, their neighbors, the land, and the Berry family who had been targeted by the "nightmen." They understood that these adults also cared about T.J., even though he had caused them to set fire to the land they so valued in order to divert some men from harming T.J. My students argued that Mama and Papa could be trusted by their neighbors to shop for them in Vicksburg, and that Mama showed respect for her neighbors when she visited the Berrys' home after Mr. Berry was burned. Thus, the children reasoned that Mama and Papa were good citizens because they wanted justice for T.J., helped their neighbors shop in Vicksburg, and urged families to keep their children away from the Wallace store. Some of the children's misconceptions came from their misunderstanding of our "life skills" vocabulary words. One child thought that Mama and Papa were respectful for putting out the fire. Another child felt Mama was responsible when she lost her job and she was trustworthy when Papa came home with a broken leg.

T.J. was described by the children as being irresponsible because he cheated on tests, stole, got out of doing chores, and told the Wallaces that Mama covered the inside binding of the textbooks to hide the fact that these books were given to their school after being considered in too poor condition by the school board for White students. They felt T.J. was not trustworthy because he framed Stacy when he cheated, lied to Mrs. Logan, tricked Stacy out of his new coat, and told the school board about the covered books. They also wrote that he didn't show caring because he let his brother Claude and his friend Stacy take the blame for things he did. He was not a good citizen because he robbed the store, and he didn't think about things before he acted. Again, some children had misconceptions about the traits we were discussing. One child wrote that T.J. was a good citizen because he went to the Logan house and told Cassie what R.W. and Melvin had done to him. Another child stated that he was trustworthy because he told the truth when he was hurt.

The class analysis of Cassie indicated that some children understood that respect needs to be earned. Several children wrote that Cassie was respectful to some Whites, indicating that Lillian Jean's actions of forcing Cassie to apologize for bumping into her and Mr. Barnett's refusal to help the children before White customers did not warrant Cassie's respect. Another child said Cassie thought that she was respectful, but the Whites felt she was not because she wouldn't get off the sidewalk to apologize to Lillian Jean. Children said that Cassie was respectful to her parents, her grandmother, and Jeremy, Lillian Jean's brother, who tried to be her friend.

Children chose four characters to analyze from a list that included Cassie, Mama and Papa, Big Ma, Mr. Morrison, T. J., Lillian Jean, Mr. Jamison, R. W., Melvin, and Jeremy Simms. Other than a few misconceptions on what the values of caring, responsibility, trustworthiness, respect, and citizenship meant, most students realistically analyzed what attributes characters demonstrated. Taylor's richly drawn characterization allowed children to deeply consider the multiple facets of each character. They saw good and evil in both Whites and Blacks.

When the students read self-selected books by Mildred Taylor, they were asked to respond with three questions:

1. Did anything in this story surprise you?
2. Do you think the events in this story could really happen? Explain.
3. Why do you think people are mean to each other when they look different from them?

Children were generally surprised at the people's cruelty to one another and the extreme experiences people might have to endure for their beliefs. Students reading *The Friendship* were surprised that John Wallace would actually shoot his boyhood friend Tom Bee because Tom was Black and John Wallace wanted the other Whites to see him control Tom when he called John by his first name. One child was surprised that Tom wouldn't stop calling John by his first name. Mildred Taylor's *Song of the Trees* depicted the convictions of a Black man when he agreed to blow up all the trees on his land and die rather than let Mr. Anderson have the trees. This amazed my students. Several children were also surprised that someone would cut down trees before asking the owner's permission and then try to get permission by threatening the family. Some children were struck by the fact that Mr. Anderson hit Little Man when he tried to stop Mr. Anderson from cutting the trees. One child commented that he never knew people were so mean in the past.

Mildred Taylor's mimetic language allowed these readers to consider the realism in the story. Most students felt the events in each of these stories could really have happened, but some did not think these things could happen today. Several children talked about racial prejudice during the Depression. However, most children did not limit the behaviors Taylor depicted to the Depression, and they stated that there is still prejudice against people because of the color of their skin. One child wrote that there are still White people who don't respect Blacks. These students believed that people would try to cheat others, as Mr. Anderson did when he offered so little money for the trees he wanted to cut. The only action several students thought was not realistic was Taylor's portrayal of a boy traveling alone on a mule to Louisiana to get his father. However, the children were beginning to trust the author's voice. For instance, one child wrote that in the beginning Taylor said this was a true story, and she believed it.

I wanted the children to understand that Taylor was illustrating racial hatred, so I asked, "Why do you think people are mean to each other when they look different from them?" After their reading, several commented that they thought White people are prejudiced because it makes them feel bigger or more important than others they encounter. And they related this literature to themselves when they stated it makes them feel good to put someone down. They acknowledged that people who show prejudice get "respect" from others who feel the same way, but they understood that prejudiced people are hated by those persons whom they mistreat. Race again played into their answers. One student wrote that Whites might have been scared of the Blacks. One child wrote that some people think America belongs to the Whites. Another said, "maybe they were raised like that" (prejudiced), or that "perhaps their mom and dad were prejudiced." Mildred Taylor's strong characterization, dramatic plots, and implied messages helped these students begin to grapple with abstract issues of racism and citizenship in America.

I want the children to understand that intolerance is found in many situations, so I share books from various perspectives. Another readaloud I use is *Crazy Lady* by Jane Leslie Conly. As they listen, children can recognize a different form of prejudice that they may have experienced or observed. This author deals with issues of physical difference, parental neglect, and peer acceptance. Ronald is mentally handicapped, and he is cared for by his loving but alcoholic mother. The neighborhood children continually taunt and tease them. One neighborhood child, Vernon, suddenly finds himself forced to befriend Maxine and Ronald. Along the way, he discovers their positive qualities and becomes their true friend. Sadly, Ronald is taken away from his mother in the end of the book and forced to live with relatives in another state. When we reached this event, the students felt the pain of Ronald's separation from his mother and the neighborhood.

After reading *Crazy Lady,* I asked these same students to describe whose attitudes had changed in this story. Most children believed Vernon's feelings had changed through his experiences with Maxine and her son Ronald. They explained that he had first taunted Maxine and Ronald and laughed at them, but when he spent time with them he realized they were people who had good qualities. They also mentioned how the neighborhood children became more supportive of Ronald when they helped raise money for Ronald's sneakers. They mentioned that Vernon had discovered one of his neighborhood friends had a brother who was also mentally handicapped but had been too ashamed to let anyone know. They noticed that once Vernon befriended Ronald, Jerry became more open about his brother.

Because Conly is dealing with the realities of difference, her ending is not romantic. Ronald does not get to stay with his mother. The students' written responses showed their mixed feelings over this realistic ending. Maxine signed the papers so that Ronald could live with relatives in another state. Most thought that it was best for Maxine to sign the papers allowing Ronald to live with out-of-state relatives because she could not stay sober and periodically left Ronald alone with only the neighbors watching him. The children empathized with Ronald's mother, and they saw opportunities for Ronald to stay in this environment. Some felt that Maxine loved Ronald and should be given another chance. They pointed out that many of the neighbors willingly helped with Ronald. Conly's characterization allowed the students to develop an understanding about two handicaps—alcoholism and retardation—and to explore the importance of family love and community caring.

Each student read *The Pinballs* by Betsy Byars, a realistic novel depicting three foster children who are cared for by a childless couple, once we had completed *Crazy Lady.* I wanted the children to personally respond, so I asked them to write journal entries after every twenty-five pages. They were asked to write a short summary of what was happening, what they thought the characters were feeling in the section, and what they were feeling about what had happened.

The students did not have to be reminded to read this book. They appeared hooked after they had read the first chapters describing how the protagonists became foster children. These youngsters showed great empathy for the characters in this book. Their entries often explained how the plot made them sad, yet they wanted to continue to read Byars's drama. During our classroom discussions, they showed an appreciation for the lives they led in comparison to the troubled ones of these foster children.

I have used these books more than once. Recently, we finished reading *Crazy Lady* and *The Pinballs* in December. As a class project we had a "No-Bake Bake Sale" where students brought in money that would normally be spent on ingredients for bake sale items. They donated their money to Family Services, asking that Christmas presents be purchased for a local foster child. They raised $75 to buy presents for a ten-year-old boy in our community. The students were eager to participate and were excited to help someone whose life may have been filled with disappointment. They felt the boy might be in a similar situation, and they believed he might be facing situations like the characters in the stories we had read.

I do not share all books on a topic at once. Instead, I try to create an awareness of certain topics, like racial prejudice, by the end of the year. Fifth graders have a limited understanding of the historical roots of Black/White relations. Although I want their background to be deepened through their reading, I do not want them to feel overwhelmed as they learn. Once I have shared the last two books, I am able to return to issues of American history and Black history. In December I read *Christmas in the Big House, Christmas in the Quarters* by Fred and Patricia McKissack, a historical representation of the lives of the slaves in comparison to those of the master and his family during the Christmas season. Throughout our shared reading, the students note the differences between the celebration in the master's house and the slave quarters. They also learn about traditions of both groups that have continued throughout the years. While listening to the McKissacks' presentation, the students glimpse one harsh historical reality of slavery: some slaves were dispassionately sold by their master at the season's end.

Each year I have randomly assigned students to react as either an enslaved person or as someone from the "big house." We have already discussed the fact that slaves were not taught to read or write, but I explain that for literary purposes those who are telling their experiences from the slaves' viewpoints will have the skill to read and write. Each student has been asked to write a letter or journal entry about the events that took place during the holiday season or after the New Year. Many children attempted to write in the dialect they heard in the story because they wanted to share the voice of their character. What has been difficult for these children, and what we have needed to discuss, was placing people's beliefs about ethical behavior in their historical narratives. Many children who found they were from the "big house" wrote how wrong their parents were and how they would free the enslaved. They wrote that everyone was equal and it was wrong to treat people differently. Still, some said they were relieved not to be enslaved. As we talked about whether the children really would have disagreed with their parents and why children in Antebellum times would probably not have taken the view that slave children were equal to them, I was able to teach about the McKissacks' careful construction of an accurate historical perspective in their writing and to suggest that as they wrote they also should avoid evaluating the past in terms of present-day understanding of past events. Their stories were to realistically depict times past. I hope that my children will begin to see that authors write to show conditions, and we cannot interpret the author's accurate use of history as the attitudes of the author.

Though I do not teach Black History only during Black History Month, I do use this time to return to our shared readings and discussions on the Black experience in the United

States. Most fifth-grade students have heard of Martin Luther King, Jr. and have had stories read to them about him. During Black History Month, I try to find other people's life stories to read aloud. I feel it is important for children to view the realities of the past, so I present nonfiction information in different formats. One set of books I have used is *The Story of Ruby Bridges* by Robert Coles and *Through My Eyes* by Ruby Bridges. Coles tells how young Ruby Bridges was the first Black child in the New Orleans schools when she entered as a first grader. His overview of her life allows the class to explore issues of school integration. I then show them *Ruby Bridges* with actual photographs of young Ruby during the events that took place. The reality of *The Story of Ruby Bridges* hits home when the class sees the photographs. I do not read this entire book, but I do go through the pictures, retelling the events. The autobiographical account, *Ruby Bridges,* has proved to be one of the most popular books with my students when they are choosing books for self-selected reading. One year, almost a third of the class read this book, mostly breaking it into short sections; students were most fascinated by the pictures showing incidents of prejudice when the students were escorted to school by the National Guard. They find the book's format engrossing because the actual photographs of Ruby, her teacher, and her school bring history to life. Historical events are placed into their growing perspectives of Black/White relations first established by the books of Mildred Taylor and the McKissacks.

Children need background knowledge before they comprehend and appreciate many books set in historical time periods. By the time it is Black History Month, our class has already read books by Mildred Taylor, giving them insight into the Depression. Because I hope they will explore many perspectives about Black/White relations in the United States, I have built my picture book collection extensively around the African American experience. I find that many of my picture books for older readers, which might have been read prior to that time, are more popular once my class turns to a study of Black History. The collection contains historical fiction, legends, biography, and historical accounts of Black History. Although these books are picture books, they are not simplistic representations of the past. They allow my students opportunities to see conditions of economic suffering and to view social injustice from America's past. *Uncle Jed's Barbershop,* written by Margaree King Mitchell and illustrated by James Ransome, is very popular because it presents still another perspective they have never considered. This story is set in the segregated South of the 1920s. Uncle Jed travels the county to cut his customers' hair as he saves for his own barbershop. Many setbacks delay his dream. As they explore Mitchell's carefully crafted story and Ransome's realistic, positive illustrations, the students see a man who is caring and persevering, but they also see the cruelties of segregation and the hardships of the Great Depression. In *My Name Is York,* written by Elizabeth Van Steenwyk and illustrated by Bill Farnsworth, the journey of Lewis and Clark is told by Clark's enslaved servant, York. Students learn about this historical expansion of America while they discover the history of a man who contributed much to the expedition but has only recently been placed in literature for young people. The students learn that Clark never granted York his dream of freedom, adding another perspective in our discussions of the journey of Lewis and Clark, the attitudes of racism and paternalism our leaders had during that time, and our nation's racial history prior to the Civil War. *Minty: A Story of Young Harriet Tubman,* a fictionalized biography written by Alan Schroeder and illustrated by Jerry Pinkney, tells the story of Harriet Tubman's childhood and her dream to be free. Only in the author's note do we read about her actual escape as an adult and her return to help others flee to freedom. Based on earlier presentations about Harriet Tubman, *Minty* helps students understand the fierce desire Harriet had to be free and to learn more about slavery's injustice. This also gives my students some insight concerning Tubman's acquired "necessary knowledge" that helped her successfully escape from the South to the North, and it introduces a Black woman often left out of children's American history textbooks.

I want children to see African American independence and perseverance, so I hope they will read the books that depict African American people after the Civil War. *Vision of Beauty: The Story of Sarah Breedlove Walker,* written by Kathryn Lasky and illustrated by Nneka Bennett, and *The Wagon,* written by Tony Johnston and illustrated by James Ransome, are "success stories" for children. In *Vision of Beauty,* students read about the rise of a child born just after slavery who is orphaned at age seven and later becomes a successful businesswoman, creating hair and beauty products for Black women. Not only did Sarah Walker contribute to the economic and cultural life of the community, but she also stood up for the rights of women and Black citizens. *The Wagon* tells of a Carolina family whose carpenter father builds a wagon for his master; the wagon is symbolic as a chariot that will take them away to freedom when, at the end of the Civil War and the death of President Lincoln, the wagon takes the family to Washington and the funeral of President Lincoln. Because this fictional story shows that slaves dreamed of leaving their lives behind and traveling to freedom, the students can place African American metaphors of travel, flight, and freedom into their earlier understandings of the dreams of an oppressed people.

Short story collections help students read more than one interpretation of the past. They are both entertained and enlightened by the stories of Virginia Hamilton in *The People Could Fly: American Black Folktales.* They not only enjoy Tar Baby, Bruh Rabbit, Bruh Fox, and other characters, but they also further learn how stories can express the culture and feelings of those who told them. Hamilton introduces them to African folklore roots that have become part of Black Aesthetics. *Many Thousand Gone: African Americans from Slavery to Freedom* by Virginia Hamilton recounts, in short story form, the experiences of Africans taken into slavery, those who attempted escape, and those who were successful. Stories of the Nat Turner Rebellion, Solomon Northup, Frederick Douglass, and Harriet Tubman are only a few of the captivating accounts in this book.

The made-for-television video *The Ernest Green Story* is an excellent companion for *Ruby Bridges* because it heightens student understanding of the Civil Rights Movement and the integration of Central High School in Little Rock, Arkansas. Based on our follow-up written responses and discussion of this movie, I saw the obvious impact the production had on the students. An important part of our discussion concerned the racial slurs the children hear in the movie and the signs carried by the protestors to integration. My students expressed their outrage and professed to understand how wrong prejudice is; still, I keep in mind that they are ten and eleven years old. We have had several incidents of racial slurs toward the Black students at our school. One incident involved a derogatory remark directed toward a girl in another room. I watched several children in my room come in from recess quite upset, and one child was in tears. They told me about the incident and said they were upset because she was their friend. They knew how badly this incident had hurt her. Another incident in a different class of fifth graders involved one of my students who, in anger against another child in a playground dispute, decided to "try out" a racial slur that was used in *Roll of Thunder, Hear My Cry.* The student called another White child a "nigger." I had no African American students in my class, so the response of the class was generally one of disbelief. One girl commented that she couldn't believe anyone in our class would say that after all we had learned about prejudice. When I spoke with the child, he did show remorse for his actions. I think it is likely that children "try out" inappropriate vocabulary after hearing it from adults, the media, and seeing it written. But I feel if the children hear the words through the historical context of literature and discuss why people used these terms and how hurtful they would be today, children will be less likely to use negative expressions without also having it affect their consciences. Although the one incident in my class was upsetting, I was pleased to watch the remainder of the students react in unison against verbal name-calling.

During our unit on the Holocaust, I read *Behind the Bedroom Wall,* written by Laura Williams, to the class. This is the story of thirteen-year-old Korinna, who is an enthusiastic participant in the Hitler Youth Movement. She discovers that her parents are hiding a young Jewish girl and her mother behind her own bedroom wall. Readers witness the conflict within her to be a good German citizen and her love for her parents. She almost turns her parents in for the "good of the fatherland," until she makes some discoveries about her own friends. This book has helped my students understand what the Jews went through during the Holocaust, and it has also helped them understand that people can be brainwashed into doing what they would normally think inconceivable. While I read this book, the students read *Number the Stars* by Lois Lowry. Again, they saw the injustices suffered by the Jews in World War II, but they also witnessed the humanity of the Danish people in their daring rescue of the Jewish population.

At the end of the year, I asked my students three questions: Please think back on some of the books I have read to you, such as *Roll of Thunder, Hear My Cry, Christmas in the Big House, Christmas in the Quarters, The Story of Ruby Bridges, Crazy Lady,* and *Behind the Bedroom Wall.* (1) Do you see anything these stories have in common? (2) Why do you think I chose to read these particular books to you? (3) Do you feel that since entering fifth grade you have learned anything from these books, and if so, what would that be?

Students recognized that all of the stories show people who have prejudiced attitudes about others. All five books contain someone who is discriminated against because of race, religion, or disabilities. My students discussed how people are mistreated and demonstrated that they understood people can use bad judgment. Children recognized that prejudice has happened in different time periods. They mentioned that most of the stories had an embedded history. They realized that these stories were about things that really happened or could happen.

Students responded interestingly concerning my reasons for choosing these books. Some students said that I wanted to teach them about prejudice and show that it was wrong. One said, "We learned history and how people have been treated." Another student understood the connection between pleasure reading and experience. He wrote that I chose the books to help them learn about history and read some good stories at the same time. Others realized that they gained empathy. Most thought the stories showed them how badly people feel when they are discriminated against because of things they can't control. Children stated that everyone is different, and they argued that people should not be treated badly if they are different. One student wrote that I read the books because I wanted the students to know that people were, and still are, unfairly treated, and that I chose this literature to show them that they should not do such things.

Finally, in answering what they thought they had learned in fifth grade, I discovered students might have a variety of answers, but they carried the same themes:

- It is wrong to be prejudiced.
- People have been treated unfairly for things they can't control. Some people think less of others because they are different. There are many different customs, languages, and religions. Everyone should accept that as the way of life.
- Lots of people are mistreated for no particular reason at all except for the fact that some people think that they are better than others.
- They had never heard how people treated each other in the ways these books depicted. As they read, they learned some history and something of human nature.

When I choose the books I share, I hope to develop better readers, better students of history, and better citizens in a multicultural society. As I share historical fiction, a genre I find most exciting for fifth graders, I can see my students exploring cultural history in a narrative form. I want to explore images of the past that are controversial. This is different from those classes that depend on history textbooks that tell facts. Fictional narratives help students understand people, their motives, and their perspectives. Nonfictional accounts can help children view people in history with more compassion and understanding, and they can help them explore their developing views about how to fit in the society where they live. According to Tunnel and Jacobs, "Teaching children at an early age about the [positive] differences and similarities between people will not singularly ensure a more gentle and tolerant society, but might act as a prerequisite to one" (193). Tunnel and Jacobs quote James Baldwin in support of the use of literature to combat prejudice: "Literature is indispensable to the world. [. . .] The world changes according to the way people see it, and if you alter, even by a millimeter, the way a person looks at reality, then you change it" (193). It is my hope that sharing literature helps my students view the people of the world with more tolerance, understanding, and acceptance. If this is so, literature becomes the key for social change.

Works Cited

Avi. *The True Confessions of Charlotte Doyle.* New York: Avon Books, 1990.

Bunting, Eve. *So Far from the Sea.* Illus. by Chris Soentpiet. New York: Clarion Books. 1998.

Bridges, Ruby. *Through My Eyes.* New York: Scholastic, 1999.

Byars, Betsy. *The Pinballs.* New York: Harper Trophy, 1977.

Coles, Robert. *The Story of Ruby Bridges.* Illus. George Ford. New York: Scholastic, 1995.

Collier, James Lincoln and Christopher Collier. *My Brother Sam Is Dead.* New York: Scholastic, 1974.

Conly, Jane L. *Crazy Lady.* New York: Harper Collins, 1993.

Hamilton, Virginia. *The People Could Fly: American Black Folktales.* Illus. Leo. and Diane Dillon. New York: Alfred A. Knopf, 1985.

Hamilton, Virginia. *Many Thousand Gone: African Americans from Slavery to Freedom.* Illus. Leo and Diane Dillon. New York: Alfred A. Knopf, 1993.

Johnston, Tony. *The Wagon.* Illus. James Ransome. New York: Tambourine Books, 1996.

Lasky, Kathryn. *Vision of Beauty: The Story of Sarah Breedlove Walker.* Illus. Nneka Bennett. Cambridge, MA: Candlewick Press, 2000.

Levine, Ellen. *Darkness over Denmark: The Danish Resistance and the Rescue of the Jews.* New York: Scholastic, 2000.

Lowry, Lois. *Number the Stars.* Boston: Houghton Mifflin, 1989.

McKissack, Patricia and Fred McKissack. *Christmas in the Big House, Christmas in the Quarters.* Illus. John Thompson. New York: Scholastic, 1994.

Mitchell, M. *Uncle Jed's Barbershop.* Illus. James Ransome. New York: Simon and Schuster, 1993.

Norton, Donna. *Through the Eyes of a Child: An Introduction to Children's Literature.* Upper Saddle River, NJ: Merrill, 1999.

Rawls, Wilson. *Where the Red Fern Grows.* New York: Bantam, 1974.

Ryan, Pam Munoz. *Esperanza Rising.* New York: Scholastic, 2000.

Schroeder, Alan. *Minty: A Story of Young Harriet Tubman.* Illus. Jerry Pinkney. New York: Dial Books, 1996.

Stanley, Jerry. *I Am an American: A True Story of Japanese Internment.* New York: Scholastic, 1994.

Taylor, Mildred. *The Friendship.* Illus. Max Ginsburg. New York: Scholastic, 1987.

———. *The Gold Cadillac.* Illus. Michael Hays. New York: Scholastic, 1987.

———. *Mississippi Bridge.* Illus. Max Ginsburg. New York: Dial Books, 1990.

———. *Roll of Thunder, Hear My Cry.* New York: Puffin Books, 1976.

———. *Song of the Trees.* Illus. by Jerry Pinkney. New York: Bantam Doubleday, 1975.

———. *The Well.* New York: Scholastic, 1995.

Tunnell, Michael and Richard Ammon, ed. *The Story of Ourselves: Teaching History Through Children's Literature.* Portsmouth, NH: Heinemann, 1993.

Tunnell, Michael and Joseph Jacobs. *Children's Literature, Briefly.* New York: Prentice Hall, 2000.

Uchida, Yoshiko. *Journey Home.* New York: Atheneum, 1978.

Van Steenwyk, Elizabeth. *My Name Is York.* Illus. Bill Farnsworth. Flagstaff, AZ: Northland Publishing, 1997.

Williams, Laura. *Behind the Bedroom Wall.* New York: Scholastic, 1996.

Searching for Material to Share

One of the challenges we face once we begin to pursue cultural diversity in children's and adolescent literature is finding reliable sources to use as guides for our selections. We ask ourselves, "When is a publication authentic? What causes a particular book to be aesthetically pleasing and historically valuable? What are the contemporary stories that are told in the books being published for children? Who are the illustrators and authors I wish to share with children?" These are difficult questions that we will each find personal answers for as we read, discuss issues and books with one another, and reflect on our experiences.

We are searching for ways to break patterns in our past. The American literary "canon" of children's literature has been dominated by European traditions. Many of us have attended public schools in which this tradition has been used as the yardstick for the evaluation of new children's and adolescent literature. Although authors such as Louisa May Alcott, Frank Baum, Frances Hodgson Burnett, C. S. Lewis, A. A. Milne, Robert Louis Stevenson, and E. B. White are recognized, other writers and their remarkable contributions to a discourse of difference are not. For instance, Howard Pyle's *Otto of the Silver Hand* and Arna Bontemps's *Golden Slippers, an Anthology of Negro Poetry* are largely unavailable to us today. Both hold distinctively divergent stories for youthful readers: Pyle was a Quaker illustrator and writer who recreated British legends and folklore but also looked critically at the inhumanness of medieval war; Arna Bontemps was an African American children's librarian who later became an archivist at Fisk and Yale Universities and was author of several books for all ages, as well as an early proponent of Black art. The loss of their contributions in today's schools and libraries suggest a mislaid history of American writing and publishing and a cultural unawareness about early children's literature.

In 1973 the University of Chicago Press published *The Best in Children's Books: The University of Chicago Guide to Children's Literature, 1966–1972*. In her "Introduction" Zena Sutherland explained that the Center for Children's Books was first launched by the Graduate School of Education in 1945. Teachers and librarians who worked at area schools and libraries met and selected books for review in the *Bulletin of the Center for Children's Books.* Zena Sutherland was the *Bulletin* editor in 1973, and she wrote:

> Because children are forming concepts of themselves and their society and are testing and acquiring ethical values, it is imperative that the books they read foster and nurture opinions and attitudes that are intelligent and flexible. Will the books they read serve to do this? The best ones will. Adults should be wary, however, of their own bias and should evaluate very carefully the author's values and assumptions lest agreement with their own ideas be confused with objectivity. (viii)

Dianne Johnson has pointed out that categories in books have never been as finite as we might wish. Looking at African American children's literature, Johnson commented, "picture books are often collaborative efforts between Black and non-Black writers and illustrators. The confusion even creates room for a multitude of non–African American writers to write what is marketed as literature for/or about Black children. In some cases, these products are successful, but more often they are not" (5–6).

We can be guided in our search for materials in many ways. If we wish to pursue the past, we can look at books listed in Sutherland's edited book to understand past standards in evaluating children's and young adult literature and at journal issues of the now defunct *Bulletin of Interracial Books for Children, Advocate,* and *The New Advocate* in order to understand the evolving literariness of the books published for a youthful audience. When we turn our attention to new publications, we can begin by pursuing the authors and illustrators whose books have been honored in the following awards or on the following websites:

American Book Award for Children's Literature was established by the Before Columbus Foundation. The authors are selected because their work is an "outstanding literary achievement" of culturally diverse writing.

Américas Award for Children's and Young Adult Literature is presented by the Consortium of Latin American Studies Programs to books that are published in English or Spanish and recognize Latin American, Caribbean, or Latino culture. Winners are selected for their distinctive style, cultural contextualization, and possibilities for classroom sharing.

AsianAmericanBooks.com is a site that hopes to "educate the public about the great diversity of the Asian American experience" by distributing good books containing positive images of Asian American life, both past and present.

Christopher Awards for Young People are presented by the Christophers through a nonprofit organization founded in 1945 by Fr. James Keller. Books are selected because they "affirm the highest values of the human spirit" and promote understanding to people of all faiths and of no particular faith.

Coretta Scott King Book Award is given to a children's author and illustrator of African descent whose work has "promoted understanding and appreciation of the 'American Dream.' " These two awards are sponsored by the American Library Association's Social Responsibilities Round Table.

Jane Addams Children's Book Awards are annual awards for a children's book and picture book that promote social justice. The awards are presented by the Women's International League for Peace and Freedom and the Jane Addams Peace Association. The site lists past and present winners.

Jewish Book Council Children's Literature Award and the *Children's Picture Book The Louis Posner Memorial Award,* selected each year by the National Jewish Book Award Committee, are presented each year to books considered to be of exceptional literary quality and of significant Jewish content.

John Steptoe Award for New Talent is given to new writers and illustrators who have not published more than three books and have not been acknowledged previously for their contributions to the field. Sponsored by the American Library Association's Social Responsibilities Round Table, these awards are presented to artists whose books are not Coretta Scott King Award winners.

Mildred L. Batchelder Award is given to an American publisher whose outstanding translation of a foreign children's book has been published in the previous year in the United States. The award is selected by members of the American Library Services for Children Division of the American Library Association in order to encourage American publishers to seek out and publish superior foreign children's books.

Pura Belpré Award winner is selected by the Association for Library Services to Children and the National Association to Promote Library and Information Services to Latinos and the Spanish-Speaking (REFORMA), an ALA Affiliate, and is given to a Latino/Latina writer and illustrator "whose work best portrays, affirms, and celebrates the Latino cultural experience in an outstanding work of literature for children and youth."

Works Cited

Johnson, Dianne. "Introduction." *African American Review: Children's and Young-Adult Issue* 32 (1998): 5–7.
Sutherland, Zena, ed. *The Best in Children's Books: The University of Chicago Guide to Children's Literature, 1966–1972.* Chicago: University of Chicago Press, 1973.

Part II

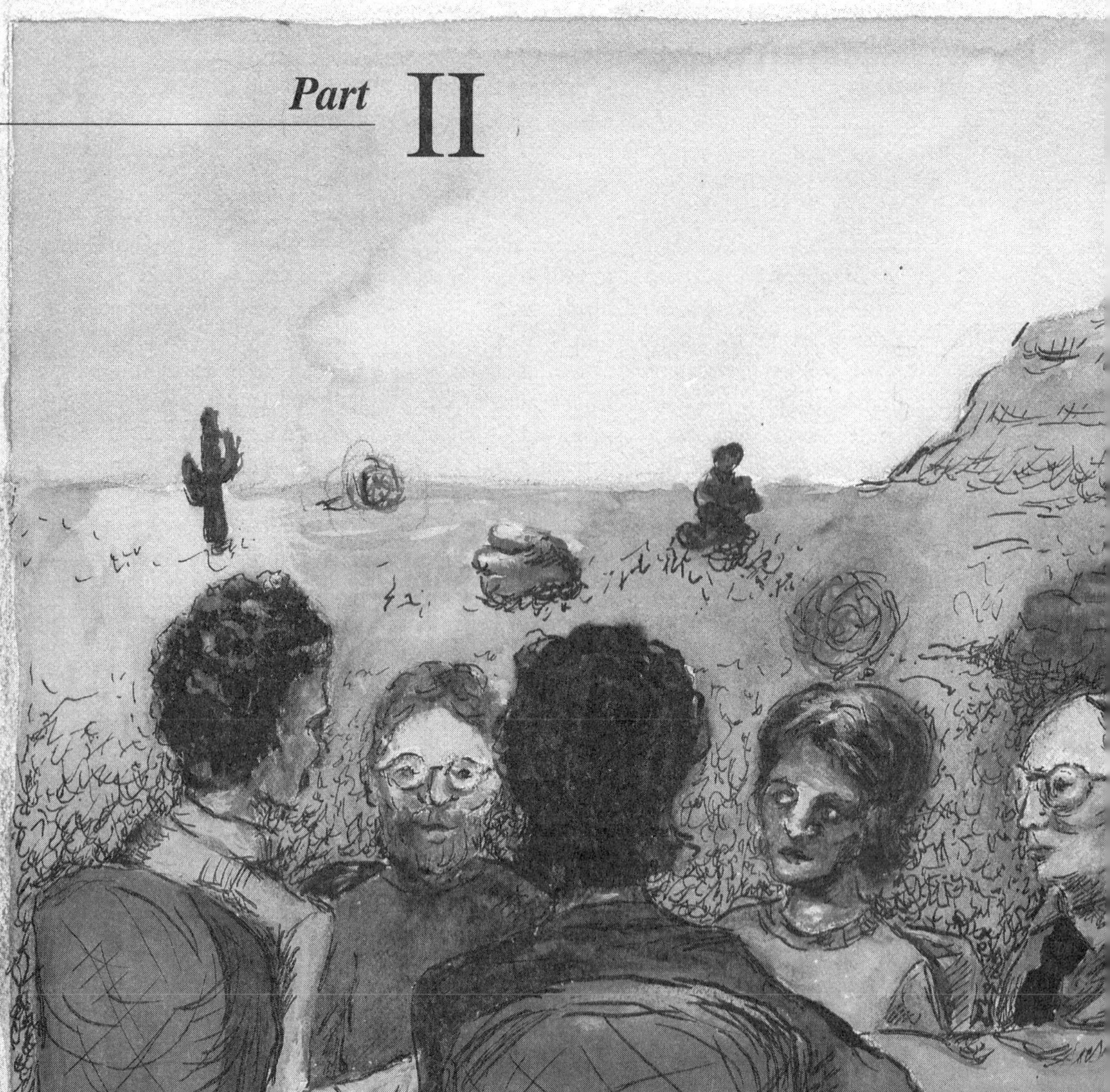

Toward a New Perspective: Learning to Interpret Culturally Diverse Literature

Linguists Gather in the American West

Scholars flock to contemplate
in the exhausting heat of August
all the languages lost in a single
lifetime that once populated
this continent with song.

There is talk of retranslating,
of breaking line in just
the right places,
unearthing the metrics
of a buried people.

—*Christian Knoeller*[1]

We have done most of our work at Jill's house, and often we are at the table in the recreation room, near Jill's computer. Once evening comes, we adjourn to the upstairs. When we've finished preparing dinner with Bob, Jill's husband, the three of us sit down in the dining area and relax. If we look toward the living room space, we can see the tops of the trees in the backyard. If we look the other way, we will see the enclosed patio and small flower garden. Our working world is tranquil, and it reminds us in many ways of our bucolic childhoods. Darwin grew up in a small town in Illinois, whereas Jill grew up in rural settings in Colorado and Wisconsin.

When we began to think about our introduction for this section we were sitting at the table, enjoying the dusk light and looking at a candle holder Jill had recently purchased. The medal moose holding the candle seemed aptly appropriate for the topic. So did the buffalo standing on the nearby fireplace mantle that Jill's father had carved. Both are popular culture images of American wilderness. We began to talk of our heritage and our ties to Native people's history.

Darwin's family has Choctaw roots, so he has always had empathy for American Indian literature. Darwin talked of the links between African American culture and American Indians.[2] Choctaws and Blacks were objectified by Europeans as they settled the South and the West. Both had served as slaves in our history. About a third of the South Carolina slaves were Indians in the early eighteenth century.[3] Growing up in Colorado, Jill's experiences included explorations that we later recognized as the Americanization of Native peoples. As a child in Colorado, she had roamed the mountains, thinking about the first people who had lived there, and she had visited the Denver Art Museum with its extensive collection of Indian and Indian-inspired artwork. Her parents had taken her to see the Cliff Dwellings in the Four Corners, and she had attended an Indian ceremonial dance. Most of what we learned in our families came from personal or cultural experiences. For instance, though Jill remembered that her parents marveled at the dwellings for their architectural design and at these people's fortitude to try farming in such an impoverished area, she did not remember reading much about the people themselves.

We began to think of the language continually used in children's and adolescent books that explained the immigration of Europeans to North America. Children are told that Columbus "discovered" America; that Native peoples were savages or uncivilized; that colonialists and Indians at first lived together and celebrated Thanksgiving in peace. In *N. C. Wyeth's Pilgrims,* Robert San Souci writes,

> The first "Thanksgiving" reminded the Pilgrims of all they had to be thankful for and made them confident that their settlement would endure. Their Indian guests left with pledges of friendship and peace—a peace that lasted many years, until the growth of the colonies created tensions between the two groups. (unpaged)

San Souci's text does allude to the fact that Europeans captured Indians and sold them into slavery when he states that Squanto was "kidnapped by a ship's captain who planned to sell him as a slave." And he mentions that Squanto returned from England to find "that his tribe, the Patuxet, had been wiped out by disease" (unpaged). What San Souci fails to mention is that the disease ravaging through Native peoples was smallpox, and it was brought from Europe. According to Ian K. Steele, "The epidemic also improved English chances to found a colony successfully in what was now an underpopulated area" (84).

Columbus came in search of another country and its man-made materials, and many of the Spanish invasions that followed came in hopes of finding riches in this "new land." The Virginia Company of London came to establish a base where it could plant crops and hunt for a passage to Asia (Steele 39). French, Dutch, and English ships traveled to southern New England to trade with the Natives prior to settlement. And the Pilgrims who arrived in Plymouth were not pacifists who expected to live peacefully with the Natives. They were men and women seeking a new world where they could adhere to their beliefs; they did not practice religious tolerance. They would label the Natives "heathen." Furthermore, they had not heard of peaceful coexistence prior to their arrival: "Some of them had even read Richard Hakluyt's accounts of Elizabethan voyages to America, which included frightful warnings about cannibals and Amerindian treachery" (Steele 85).

San Souci's picture book retelling of Plymouth's history says, "Thanksgiving invites us to recall the Pilgrims' achievements and the original peace and friendship between Native Americans and the early settlers" (unpaged). Perhaps their relations were founded on mutual understanding and peaceful cohabitation, but history does not support such conclusions. Steele discusses the growing need for the colonists to "buy" goods from the Indians to ship to England. They were not simply farming the land; they were building a trading industry through the sale of "wampum" or shell beads that were drilled and threaded into attractive decorative belts and necklaces. Since beads were a status symbol in Abenaki, Massachussetts, and Wampanoag cultures, wampum became an unofficial currency between these groups as well as with the settlers (85–90).

We began to think about two Virginians who are found in several children's biographies because of their importance as "founding fathers" of the new United States government and to consider their beliefs about Native rights. When George Washington was elected the first president, he supported settlement of the land in the Old Northwest, and he endorsed General Henry Knox's proposal that would encourage the settlement of former Continental Army soldiers and officers in these areas. Their appearance, he argued, "would be the most likely means to enable us to purchase upon equitable terms of the Aborigines their right of preoccupancy; and to induce them to relinquish our Territories, and to move to the illimitable regions of the West" (as qtd. in Horsman 6). Washington's mind was changed through his negotiations with others (but especially with General Philip Schuyler of New York); he agreed to pay these Natives to leave the areas of settlement within a specified area. Thus began the U.S. treaties that would gradually take more and more Indian land away from Natives.

Thomas Jefferson's father Peter had traveled in the Alleghenies and in uncharted wilderness areas between Virginia and North Carolina; his ventures are said to have influenced Jefferson's adult interest in obtaining Indian land for settlers. In January 1803, he addressed the U.S. Congress concerning governmental relations with Indians living in unsettled territories. Jefferson proposed a two-pronged process: (1) turning them from their culture of hunters into agrarian farmers who would remain on a particular piece of land and (2) establishing governmental "trading houses" that could "undersell private traders, foreign & domestic, drive them from competition, & thus, with the good will of the Indians, rid ourselves of a description of men who are constantly endeavoring to excite in the Indian mind suspicions, fears & irritations towards us" (qtd. in *Letters of the Lewis and Clark Expedition* 11). In 1803, when Clark was preparing for the Lewis and Clark expedition, which was sponsored by President Thomas Jefferson, he listed areas he hoped to study in relation to the Indians they met: physical history and medicine; morals; religion; traditions and national history; agriculture and domestic economy; fishing and hunting habits; war; amusements; clothing and ornaments; customs and manners.[4] Of religion, he wrote:

> What affinity is there between their religious ceremonies and *those of the ancient Jews*? (italics added)
>> Do they use animal sacrifises [*sic*] in their worship?
>> What are the principal [*sic*] objects of their worship?
>> [. . .]
>> Do they ever use human sacrifices [*sic*] in any case?
>> Do they Mourn for their disceased [*sic*] friends and what [is] their cerimony [*sic*] on
> such occasions?

Clark seems to have considered Jews as different—perhaps more religiously primitive—in comparison to Christian European Americans. At the very least, he recognized their "ancient" beliefs as different from his Christian ones and tied them to animal and human sacrifices.

When Clark met with Natives during the expedition, he recorded their dress and customs. Writing about the Shoshoni village they visited, for instance, he commented on their scarcity of food; their willingness to use their wives and daughters as property; the age when the daughters were given in marriage; and tribal child rearing practices. Clark observed:

> They seldom correct their children particularly the boys who soon become masters of their own acts. they [*sic*] give as a reason that it cows and breaks the sperit [*sic*] of the boy to whip him, and that he never recovers his independence of mind after he is grown. They treat their women but with little rispect [*sic*], and compel them to perform every species of drudgery. [. . .] Some of the women appear to be held more sacred than in any [Native] nation we have seen. I have requested the men to give them no cause for jealousy by having connection with their women without their knowledge, which with them, strange as it may seem is considered as disgracefull [*sic*] to the husbands as clandestine connections of a similar kind are among civilized nations. to [*sic*] prevent this mutual exchange of good offices [*sic*] altogether I know it impossible to effect, particularly on the part of our young men whom some months of abstanence [*sic*] have made very polite to those tawney [*sic*] damsels, no evil has yet resulted and I hope will not from these connections. (208)

Clark's journal contains a good deal of observation and supposition of Native culture. His judgments of Native customs reflect European ideals of family and fidelity. Yet, he suggests that White needs will reign superior to the familial ties established within this new culture, writing that his men will probably engage in sexual relations with the Native women and they will not seek the women's husbands' permission. His men are not judged harshly for this possibility: He simply says that they have been too long without European women and need the company of a woman. Native women are, thus, relegated to a lower role in the cultural hierarchy than are White women. In practice, they become the commercial objects that Clark assumes they are in Native cultures.

Because he had to rely on the interpreters to tell him what the people were saying, Clark may have misinterpreted the people's behavior. Nevertheless, Clark did observe a good deal about the village life when he was entertained in a community. When he returned from the expedition, he was appointed superintendent of Indian affairs for the Louisiana Territory (*Letters of the Lewis and Clark Expedition* 376). According to Donald Jackson, Clark wanted the Native cultures to remain true to their beliefs, and he wrote Jefferson in 1826, "It is to be lamented that this deplorable Situation of the Indians do [*sic*] not Receive more of the humain [*sic*] feelings of this Nation" (qtd. in *Among the Sleeping Giants* 40).

Both Jefferson and Clark were slave owners. Neither had the ability to converse directly with the Natives they met. They lived at a time when White women could not vote or own property after their husband's death. These women also had little chance of gaining a divorce if they were in an abusive marriage. Men's attitudes about *difference* were very paternalistic and overbearing at that time,[5] so it is ironic that the explorers observed Native family life as so offensive because of male dominance.

Numerous books have been published for children dealing with the Lewis and Clark expedition, but we decided, after rereading the journals and the letters and documents edited by Donald Jackson, to discuss a book that had the "official endorsement" of a nationally respected group—the National Council for Social Studies—to see what perspectives concerning the expedition's interactions with Native tribes were considered exemplary. *How We Crossed the West: The Adventures of Lewis & Clark* was published in 1997, and it was placed on the 1998 National Council for Social Studies Notable Books list. This simple picture book edits the journals down to 32 pages, and it only covers the expedition's outward journey. In her note at the book's beginning, Rosalyn Schanzer thanks leaders in the Lewis and Clark Trail Heritage Foundation and the National Geographic Society for their help and support. She explains that the words used throughout her presentation come from the journals and are aided by the use of updated spellings and bracketed explanations. Thus, to the uninformed reader, it would appear that the entries are directly from the Lewis and Clark journals.

On a closer examination, we discovered that Schanzer had placed several observations into one entry and had chosen to use those observations that reflected the Natives as naive or warlike. The two-page spread entitled "Among the Indians" details their encounters with four nations, and each is given little attention. Of the Oto and Missouri nations, Schanzer writes,

> At sunset a part of the Oto and Missouri nations came to camp. Among those Indians, six were chiefs. We sent them some roasted meat. In return they sent us watermelons. Captain Lewis shooting the air gun astonished those natives! (unpaged)

This same encounter takes over ten pages in Clark's journal. Clark's entries show that the expedition is delayed near the Oto (called *Otteaus* in his journal) village in order to "let them know of the Change of Government, the wishes of our government to Cultivate friendship with them, the Objects of our journy [*sic*] and to present them with a flag and Some Small presents" (DeVoto 11). Clark's journal in this section contains numerous stories: a deserter from the party is tracked down and punished in front of the Natives who are visiting the encampment; a Mahar village is found where small pox has ravaged the community and "they put their *wives* & children to *Death* with a view of their all going together to some better Countrey [*sic*]" (19); fires set by the Natives burn on the prairie; when the Indians are gathered for a council of speeches and gift exchanges, they are given "Some Small articles & 8 Carrots of Tobacco, we gave one small Meadel [*sic*] to one of the Chiefs and a Sertificate [*sic*] to the others of their good intentions [. . .] We then gave them a Dram and broke up the Council" (21). There is no mention of watermelon in these pages. Thus, the episode detailed in one paragraph actually was a series of events that began on July 20, 1804 and ended on August 19, and it had information that was incorrect inserted into the "diary entry."

We were appalled to think that White exploration had been rewritten in an abbreviated way for young readers. The complexities of travel across the plains and of meeting peoples in new cultures with diverse language styles had been watered down until not only Lewis and Clark and the American Indians but also all humanity had been flattened in this presentation. Certainly, this had nothing to do with Native cultures. Or did it?

We began to see that the most important element in American Indian representations was perspective, or the ways the reader is allowed to see Native diversity. Native cultures become stereotypes of uncivilized people rather than established societies with *mythos* when they are uniformly viewed as naive and savage. Although we might not fault Lewis and Clark for living within their own century, we can fault contemporary educators who perpetuate an image of aggressive, playful, childlike cultures in that first literature we share with children. We began to understand how American stereotypes infiltrate our children's and adolescent literature. Indeed, when she discusses the earlier Americanization of the southwestern Indians into popular culture's imagery for adults, Leah Dilworth observes:

> Artists, writers, ethnographers, and tourist entrepreneurs had vested interests in presenting Indian cultures, as picturesque subject matter, tourist attractions, collectable data, and sources of souvenirs and art objects. Their imaginings of Indians were instrumental in the formation of cultural identities for the nation and the region, for urban middle-class Americans, and for Native Americans. (20)

When social studies textbooks declare that the American government was founded on concepts of religious and ethnic independence and developed through the ideals of concerned citizenship, they deny American Indian perspectives of history. Many critical theorists who have studied American Indian literature suggest that Native writing is postmodern. Although it might depend on elements that can be found in the traditional literary canon, often it is ironic and deceptive.

Modern Native American literature is very postmodern in its style and intent. When discussing his interpretation of postindian writing, poet playwright Gerald Vizenor playfully explained, "Natives have always been on one road of resistance or another, creating postindian myths and tricky stories in the very ruins of representation and modernity. We are postindian storiers at the curtains of that stubborn simulation of the *indian* as savage, and the *indian* as a pure and curative tradition. The *indian* is a simulation, an invention, and the name could be the last grand prize at a casino" (21). Vizenor has called postindian stories works that can be labeled "survivance" writing. He explains,

> Survival is a response; survivance is a standpoint, a worldview, and a presence. Yes, and there is a sense of dependency in the meaning of the word survival, a dependency on the cause of some action. Dominance is a strong word and stands for historical prominence of such conditions. Many natives are experts on the nuances of dominance, and most histories of natives are themes of dominance and victimry. My stories are about survivance, not victimry. So survivance is resistance and hermeneutics. (93)[6]

Vizenor calls the name *indian* an invention of "Columbus and his rogues" because it enslaved cultures in images that were semantically controlled rather than realistically viewed and/or experienced, and he says that the word should always be printed in italics. In the end, Vizenor argues that children have been given a simulation of *indian* history rather than a true understanding that "Natives are the first diverse cultures of this continent" (179).

In our search for literature that could be shared in the elementary classroom or with a small group of young children, we found *When the Rain Sings: Poems by Young Native Americans* and thought this might be good beginning poetry for children ages eight and older. Each poem could easily be shared with these audiences. As we read Vena A-dae Romero's "I Always Begin with I Remember" we saw much of what our contributors suggest: Native prose and poetry are tied to the European conquest, but Natives had stories and traditions prior to the invasion of Whites. Romero alludes to the past in an ironic way, and as she does, she demonstrates that Native American history is firmly situated in much of the published contemporary Native writing. It is, as Vizenor suggests, written "out of silence, and the unnameable, and the chance to create characters in the nick of time to hear me" (142). Of learning this continent's history, our sixteen-year-old poet writes,

> *I remember the day history almost disappeared.*
> *The day Indian children's mouths were stuffed with English*
>   *Words,*
> *And almost suffocated out of existence,*
> *But they lay hidden in memory until is was safe, almost too*
>   *Late.*[7]

Our ruminations about Native history and its reflection in scholarly and creative writing have helped us understand the significance of exploring important questions: How can we find appropriate details of past and present encounters between diverse groups and place them in literature to share with young audiences? Will we always be uncomfortable with the cultural icons of another culture, or can we learn to read divergently? Shouldn't all people be given literary voices in our canon that reflect their experiences and their beliefs? We believe they should, and we hope this section will help our readers address these questions.

Within the following section, a wide variety of cultural texts are discussed. Shauna Bigham uses the short stories of Zora Neale Hurston, Mildred Taylor, and Joyce Carol

Thomas to discuss the importance of orality in Black women's writing. Cicely Cobb expands Shauna's historical and cultural discussion of Mildred Taylor in her analysis of *Roll of Thunder, Hear My Cry* and *Let the Circle Be Unbroken*. Richard Van Dongen shows us how reading Hispanic literature requires readers to approach the author's storytelling with some discernment concerning multiple cultural histories and their representations in Hispanic literature. Amanda Cockrell lets us see how stories evolve as new authors reframe familiar elements from earlier traditions in their modern fiction for adolescent readers. Lingyan Yang and Zhihui Fang link Chinese and Chinese American history to Laurence Yep's highly acclaimed immigrant and historical fiction novels. Readers might be well advised to refer back to Margaret Chang's article after reading Lingyan and Zhihui's piece. Then they will begin to see the interconnectedness of these discussions and can pinpoint others for themselves. Violet Harris looks at series books with biracial main characters and discusses how they symbolically reflect both hip hop culture and adolescent requirements for heroines who define and break popular attitudes in their adventures. Paula Connolly looks thoughtfully at Jacqueline Woodson's ability to take stereotypical imagery and reconstruct societal issues of race and abuse in her adolescent novels. Our practical pieces are field studies of children's acceptance of the racial and cultural images they find in the books they read. Larry Sipe and Pat Daley observe one teacher's practices of sharing literature in her urban kindergarten class. Jiening Ruan explores the possibilities of Chinese imagery in picture books within her study of three Chinese families living in the United States. Thus, these authors require us to reconsider the literary canon and move toward a new perspective of culturally diverse literature for children and adolescents.

Notes

1. From *Completing the Circle* by Christian Knoeller. Copyright Buttonwood Press, 2000. Reprinted by permission of Buttonwood Press and Christian Knoeller.

2. According to Arrell M. Gibson ("Indians of Mississippi" in *A History of Mississippi, Volume One.* Edited by Richard Aubrey McLenmore. Jackson: University & College Press of Mississippi, 1973), Choctaws had a rich folklore and religious life. They were town dwellers who maintained a government with geographic representation. Located primarily in Mississippi, they traded with the other tribes in the area and, once the Europeans arrived, largely maintained commerce relations with the French. Gibson says that Choctaws intermarried with the British and the French, though more French traders took Choctaw wives than the British. Gibson tells how these families owned Black slaves; the slaves "fed the aristocratic pretensions of the owners in their drive to emulate white planter neighbors" whose slaves "performed labor generally scorned by Indians such as clearing the wilderness and opening fields for agriculture, building roads and bridges, and performing other useful labor which enhanced the value of Indian properties and improvements" (69–81). Between 1795 and 1837, the Choctaw nation relocated west of the Mississippi in Indian Territory as their major food supplies of bear and buffalo disappeared and Whites forced them off their lands. Gibson states, "The Choctaw removal [from Mississippi] was nearly completed by 1840 [. . .] until by 1900 the Choctaw community in Mississippi numbered less than 2,000" (82–89). John Peterson ("Choctaws" in *Encyclopedia of Southern Culture.* Edited by Charles Reagan Wilson and William Ferris. Chapel Hill: University of North Carolina Press, 1989) says, "They were second only to the Cherokees in adopting European institutions" but they were "the first major southern Indian tribe removed to Oklahoma" (425).

3. Darwin and Jill take full advantage of Bob in their conversations because he is an American historian whose research has largely been in southern U.S. history. He added his observation as we talked, and then he ran to his study to validate it. Peter Kolchin's *American Slavery: 1619–1877* states, "Indians also

served as slaves, at first usually victims of military defeat or kidnapping but subsequently also bought and sold on the open market. Such slaves were most numerous in South Carolina, where the governor estimated in 1708 that there were 1,400 Indian slaves in a population of 12,580, but they could be found in all the English colonies." Peter Kolchin, *American Slavery: 1619–1877* (New York: Hill and Wang, 1993) 7.

4. We realized as we talked that we were not experts in the Lewis and Clark expedition and that this was not Bob's area of expertise. However, we knew that this expedition was usually taught as a defining moment in our history in schools. We knew that most teachers in elementary and middle schools did not know much more than we did. Therefore, we determined to approach the expedition in ways the "average citizen" might: What books would be available at the public library? Jill had read Bernard DeVoto's *The Journals of Lewis and Clark* (New York: Houghton Mifflin, 1953) years ago, and she had obtained it from the public library. It could still be found in the West Lafayette Public Library's collection. We decided to use that edition for our work. We also determined to use Stephen E. Ambrose's *Lewis & Clark: Voyage of Discovery* (National Geographic Society, 1998) because this was available in the public library and was aimed at the same audience. Finally, we agreed to use one scholarly book—*Letters of the Lewis and Clark Expedition with Related Documents, 1783–1854* (Donald Jackson, ed. Urbana: University of Illinois Press, 1962)—because we wanted to see what might be found in other official letters and documents that was not written into the other two interpretations of the expedition.

5. We recommend reading Eleanor Flexner's classical study on women in the United States, *Century of Struggle: The Woman's Rights Movement in the United States* (New York: Atheneum, 1970), as background concerning women's positions in the home, workplace, social movements, and education from the *Mayflower*'s arrival until the end of the 1950s.

6. During our reading for this section, we found Vizenor's screenplay "Harold of Orange" (in *Nothing But the Truth: An Anthology of Native American Literature.* Edited by John L. Prudy and James Ruppert. Upper Saddle River, NJ: Prentice Hall, 2001) and the commentary of another playwright, Daniel Daviv Moses (in *Speaking for the Generations: Native Writers on Writing.* Edited by Simon J. Ortiz. Tuscon: University of Arizona Press, 1998). We would highly recommend that the works of these two fine writers be shared in high school and college classes.

7. Reprinted by permission of Vena A-dae Romero.

8. Works cited in the notes throughout the introduction are not listed in this bibliography unless they also appear in the text.

Works Cited[8]

DeVoto, Bernard. *The Journals of Lewis and Clark.* New York: Houghton Mifflin, 1953.

Dilworth, Leah. *Imagining Indians in the Southwest: Persistent Visions of a Primitive Past.* Washington, DC: Smithsonian Institute Press, 1996.

Gale, Dale, ed. *When the Rain Sings: Poems by Young Native Americans.* Washington, DC: National Museum of the American Indian, Smithsonian Institute in Association with Simon & Schuster, 1999.

Horsman, Reginald. *Expansion and American Indian Policy, 1783–1812.* Norman, OK: University of Oklahoma Press, 1992.

Jackson, Donald. *Among the Sleeping Giants: Occasional Pieces on Lewis and Clark.* Urbana, IL: University of Illinois Press, 1987.

———, ed. *Letters of the Lewis and Clark Expedition with Related Documents.* Urbana: University of Illinois Press, 1962.

San Souci, Robert. *N. C. Wyeth's Pilgrims.* San Francisco: Chronicle Books, 1991.

Schanzer, Rosalyn. *How We Crossed the West: The Adventures of Lewis & Clark.* Washington, DC: National Geographic Society, 1997.

Steele, Ian K. *Warpaths: Invasions of North America.* New York: Oxford University Press, 1994.

Vizenor, Gerald and A. Robert Lee. *Postindian Conversations.* Lincoln, NE: University of Nebraska Press, 1999.

10

African American Short Stories and the Oral Tradition

Shauna A. Bigham

Africans brought to slavery a rich culture, which they accommodated and assimilated as they learned the language, customs, and cultures of the slaveholders and other African slaves from other regions. In the South Carolina Sea Islands, slaves made sense of the multiple languages they encountered by creating a creole language (Joyner 222–23). Although some Africans came to slavery from a print culture, slaves were prohibited from learning to read or write. This restriction required that slaves develop oral literacy acts that could be based on the African rhythms of call and response. Today we still see this characteristic in African American writing.

Susan Willis, a critic studying African American female writers, believes their novels are compilations of shorter pieces of writing, which she calls the "four-page formula" (14–15). Willis asserts that this mode of writing embodies the storytelling tradition by establishing the uniquely African American teller–listener relationship. The language used reflects the earlier oral tradition. This is seen in the use of metaphor, by specifying, or name-calling, and the distinct tradition of teller–listener orality (14–21).

This teller–listener relationship is based on the assumptions that history and the culture of the community are privileged topics. It assumes that the metaphor and imagery will be understood and appreciated by those addressed. Wolfgang Iser calls the person who understands the author's intent the implied reader. The implied reader knows and understands the cultural implications and is able to follow the story and appreciate the humor, satire, and irony. For those not familiar with Black history and language use, the story is simply entertaining, without any richer significance or meaning. For the implied reader, it contains layers of meaning. Henry Louis Gates, Jr. agrees with Susan Willis's idea that "Black texts are 'mulattoes' (or 'mulatas'), with a two toned heritage: these texts speak in standard Romance or Germanic languages and literary structures, but almost always speak with a distinct and resonant accent, an accent that Signifies (upon) the various Black vernacular literary traditions" (Gates xxiii).

One of these literary traditions that is often exemplified in the Black short story is the trope of signifying, or talking back and starting trouble by using language. According to Roger D. Abrahams,

> Signifying seems to be a Negro term, in use if not in origin. It can mean any of a number of things; in the case of the toast about the signifying monkey, it certainly refers to the trickster's ability to talk with great innuendo, to carp, cajole, needle, and lie. It can mean in other instances the propensity to talk around a subject, never quite coming to the point. It can mean making fun of a person or situation. Also it can denote speaking with the hands and eyes, and in this respect encompasses a whole complex of expressions and gestures. Thus it is signifying to stir up a fight between neighbors by telling stories; it is signifying to make fun of a policeman by parodying his motions behind his back; it is signifying to ask for a piece of cake by saying, "my brother needs a piece a cake." (54)

Abrahams emphasizes that signifying is a particular way of speaking. It is a technique or method. "Lying," "sounding," and "the dozens," seem to stem from Abrahams's definition. "Lying" refers to telling exaggerated stories or tall tales. "The dozens" involves insults about family members (Cobb 166–67). Sounding is a "friendly verbal dual" (Lee 12) that requires quick, nimble-witted responses in an effort to one-up an opponent. Telling a fictitious story and crediting it to a third party to stir up trouble is also a popular image of signifying.

Whereas Abrahams sees signifying as a technique or method of speaking, Claudia Mitchell-Kernan defines signifying as an attitude toward language. According to Mitchell-Kernan, "Signifying [. . .] also refers to a way of encoding messages or meanings which involves, in most cases, an element of indirection" (311). Thus, signifying is done through irony, metaphor, and figurative speech, thus allowing Black speakers and writers to mask their comments and "move freely between two discursive universes" (Gates 75).

This literary trope derives from Africa and was employed during the African American slave experience. Slaves "signified" when talking with their masters and used metaphor and figurative language in their songs to convey subversive messages (Blassingame 115). In interviews with writers from the Federal Writers Project of the 1930s, ex-slaves told of the ways they signified on others, or directly signified on the interviewer. These interviews reveal a rich use of language that extends from the oral narrative to the written story.

In one interview, Tina Johnson, age 85, explained that she did not know who her father was, but after emancipation she and her brother saw their mother marry. She then goes on to say, "I pulled a good one on a White feller 'bout dat onct. He axed me if I knowed dat my pappy an' mammy wuz married 'fore I wuz borned. I sez ter him dat I wonder if he knows whar his mammy an' pappy wuz married when he wuz borned" (Rawick vol. 15, 22). Johnson's response to the "White feller" implies that his parents were having a sexual relationship before marriage, and his birth was the occasion for them to marry. On the surface her response looks benign. The dialect and sentence structure appear awkward. Assumptions about her intent and intellect may cause the "White feller" to miss that he is being insulted. Hers is a masked and unexpected response.

In a more political context, Samuel S. Taylor of Little Rock, Arkansas, was signifying when he asserted, "We were savages when we came over here. Everything we got and everything we know, good and bad, we got from White folks. Don't know how they can get impatient with us when everything we do they learnt us" (Rawick 10.6, 30). In this remark, Taylor belittles the African slaves and endorses White images of the slaves as savages in order to insult the White man. The White man becomes the originator, model, and instructor of all the negative qualities that the African Americans supposedly have. Thus, it is the White society that has failed.

Not all signifying was used to insult. In Wayman Williams's interview, we glimpse the ways Blacks used language to tease and manipulate their mistress and the northern White school teachers. Williams was a small child when freedom came, and he remembered slavery, Confederate soldiers, working shares, and this incident apparently from Reconstruction:

> Some White school teachers from up North come to teach de chillen, but dey didn't talk like folks here and didn't understan' our talk. Dey didn't know what us mean when us say 'titty' for sister, and 'budder' for brother, and 'nanny' for mammy. Jes' for fun us call ourselves big names to de teacher, some be named General Lee and some Stonewall Jackson. We be one name one day and 'nother name next day. Until she git to know us she couldn't tell de diff'rence, 'cause us all look alike to her. Us have good times tellin' her 'bout Black magic and de conjure. Us tell her night birds full of magic and der feathers roast in ashes work spells what kill evil conjure. If a rabbit run 'cross de path, turn your hat round and wear it hind part befo' to keep bad luck away. A buzzard's claw tie round de baby's neck make teethin' easy. De teacher from de North don't know what to think of all dat. But our old missy, who live here all de time, know all 'bout it. She lets us believe our magic and conjure, 'cause she partly believe it, too. (Rawick vol. 5 pt. 4 184)

Williams signifies to both the northern school teacher, as well as his mistress. The children know that they "all look the same" to the northern White woman and play off the newcomer's obtuseness. Their choice of names—Stonewall Jackson and General Lee—soldiers who gave the North a whipping, reflects a strikingly ironic form of signifying. They are also names the teacher would recognize as not being a slave child's proper name, making her aware that she still did not know the child. The superstition and folk customs, although they could have been authentic, may have been false. Wearing a hat backwards was not a fashion statement in the postslavery times. If the superstition was invented, and the teacher, believing it, wore a hat backwards, she would appear the fool. Likewise, if, at least partially, the children convinced their mistress that they had supernatural powers, they would have found a way to control her behavior.

Perhaps there were moments during the Federal Writers Project interviews when the interviewers caught the irony of the former slaves' comments. However, without a record of the reactions of the interviewers, we must assume the signification was missed by the interviewers, allowing the ex-slaves to "tell them off" without them knowing it. Zora Neale Hurston, who was writing at the time of the WPA interviews, used the same oral traditions in her short stories. However, instead of masking meaning, Hurston expected her use of language play to be understood and appreciated by her audience. Susan Willis writes in *Specifying,* "Hurston's folktales did not become the 'four-page formula'; rather, the modern narrative has the same rhythm, desire for closure, and relationship between teller and listener (in this case, writer and reader) as previously existed in the work camps and on the plantation" (18). Hurston's implied audience would know the rhythms and traditions of the oral stories. Hurston was obviously aware of the importance of specifying in the Black community. In her autobiography *Dust Tracks on the Road,* she calls the trope by name, writing, "I heard somebody, a woman's voice 'specifying' up this line of houses from where I lived and asked who it was" (194). This passage suggests Hurston's primary audience for readers is the Black community who would understand her writing. Yet, Hurston also had to please White publishers who did not share the history and context of her subject. Perhaps her obvious use of signification allowed her to educate them to read the text appropriately. Hurston was a trained anthropologist who had hoped to gather the Black folktales from the South. Her writing in *Of Mules and Men* reflects her work "in the field." Hurston's writing suggests that there was a literary technique and style established within the Black community that had not changed from the earlier established mode of call and response emulated in the oral literature of the community.

In 1974, when Alice Walker was writing a tribute to Hurston after searching for, and finally finding, her grave, Walker lamented the shackles placed on African American women's creativity:

> How was the creativity of the Black woman kept alive, year after year and century after century, when for most of the years Black people have been in America, it was a punishable crime for a Black person to read or write? [. . .] Then you may begin to comprehend the lives of our "crazy," "Sainted" mothers and grandmothers. The agony of the lives of women who might have been Poets, Novelists, Essayists, and Short-Story Writers (over a period of centuries), who died with their real gifts stifled within them. (*Search* 234)

Walker answers her own question by examining her own mother's life. Walker's mother's outlet was her gardening and quilting. Walker takes artistic strength from the adversity Hurston faced, fortifying her resolve, making herself a stronger, more determined writer. Additionally, Walker recognizes the debt she owes her own mother for her quiet influence on Walker's writing. She says, "Yet so many of the stories that I write, that we all write, are my mother's stories. Only recently did I fully realize this: that through years of listening to my mother's stories of her life, I have absorbed not only the stories themselves, but something of the urgency that involves the knowledge that her stories—like her life—must be recorded" (240).

Walker also recorded part of her father's life in her children's picture book *To Hell With Dying.* The youngest of eight children, Walker remembers a father worn down by labor and sickly, not the young, energetic father her older siblings recall (*Living* 13). As a younger man, her father voted for Roosevelt and helped organize other sharecroppers. He was also active in establishing a Black school, believing education was important (13). As an older man, "he seemed fearful of both education and politics and disappointed and resentful as well" (13). Walker's father's disillusionment and health problems are reflected in Mr. Sweet, the story's most significant character. Mr. Sweet is a diabetic and a drunk whom the narrator and her family revive from his death bed. The narrator's father says, "To hell with dying, man. [. . .] These children want Mr. Sweet" (unpaged). This command was followed by the children hugging, kissing, and tickling Mr. Sweet until he laughs and rejoins the living. Whenever Mr. Sweet is drunk and playing the blues on his guitar, the children know they will soon be called to his bedside to revive him. We understand Mr. Sweet's depression because his racial plight has been explained by the narrator.

> Mr. Sweet had been ambitious as a boy, wanted to be a doctor or lawyer or sailor, only to find that Black men fare better if they are not. Since he could become none of these things he turned to fishing as his one earnest career and playing the guitar as his sole claim to doing anything extraordinarily well. His son, the only one that he and his wife, Miss Mary, had, was shiftless as the day is long and spent money as if he were trying to see the bottom of the mint, which Mr. Sweet would tell him was the clean brown of his hand. (unpaged)

In this passage, Walker uses the storytelling attributes of orality and metaphor, while also allowing the narrator to culturally signify life's contradictions through Mr. Sweet. Walker signifies to her primary audience when she reports that Mr. Sweet learned he would fare better if he was not ambitious. Her remark alludes to the general disfranchisement of Blacks as well as to the threat of personal violence. His choice of fishing, thus gaining food without having to work for or pay a White man, allows Mr. Sweet to subvert the economic and political system that holds him back. Additionally, Mr. Sweet is allowed to signify to his son that money is not as noteworthy as skin color. Later, we find out this may not be his son. This separates father from son, allowing Walker to differentiate between shiftless, lazy behavior, and "lazy" behavior that subverts the system. Walker takes the short story form beyond the earlier call and response format, establishing a tone of protest through signification. As a result, Alice Walker's short stories designed for young audiences have been received with less favor than her adult writings.

Mildred D. Taylor, who has won the Newbery Medal for *Roll of Thunder, Hear My Cry,* and the Coretta Scott King Award for her 1987 short story *The Friendship,* also uses signification and irony. Taylor, who uses the characters, conflicts, and family folklore of her youth, bases her stories on events from her father's life.

The Friendship tells the account of the Logan children who witness the shooting of ex-slave Mr. Tom Bee. From the first line in the story, we are warned and forewarned that danger is lurking. Stacey, the oldest Logan child, cautions his brothers and sister, "Now don't y' all go touchin' nothin' "(5). In the next sentence, Cassie, the narrator admits, "After all, we weren't even supposed to be up here" (5). Taylor builds the tension with the introduction of Jeremy Simms, a "sad-eyed" (5) White boy who tries to be friends with the Logans. As adults who know the history of White/Black relationships in the South in the 1930s, we know of the Klan's activities, the segregated schools and public facilities and the repercussions of socializing between the races. Jeremy Simms is trouble.

The Black/White tension is alluded to when Dewberry Wallace, the store owner's son, teases Little Man, the youngest Logan child, about his hands being so dirty Dewberry could plant seeds on them. Thurston Wallace, Dewberry's brother, then suggests they cut off Little Man's hands with an axe. The Logan children make their hasty retreat from the store, but Little Man is still upset about the exchange. Little Man is assured by Stacey that the Wallaces were just teasing. Stacey tries to dispel the lingering worry by saying, "Ah, shoot, boy! You know they can't do no such-a thing!" Taylor continues, "Skeptically Little Man looked to Stacey for affirmation. Stacey nodded. 'They can do plenty all right, but they can't do nothin' like that'" (13). As adult readers, we know what Stacey is referring to. We know the extra-legal control southern Whites exercised. We know what the Wallace boys could do. Stacey's words foreshadow the violence that the Wallace boys and Jeremy Simms's father provoke by demanding that John Wallace "teach" Mr. Tom Bee a lesson.

Taylor uses irony in *The Gold Cadillac* when she again uses a naive child narrator who does not understand the conventions and rules of society to call attention to the racial inequalities of the South and explain history, such as the Civil War, slavery, and segregation. The child narrator's descriptions allow the implied reader to infer a second message or layer to the story. For example, 'lois's description of her mother's reaction to news of a new car foreshadows conflict:

> "Come on, Mother-Dear!" we cried together. "Daddy say come on out and see this new car!"
> "What?" said my mother, her face showing her surprise. "What are you talking about?" (55)

Reading the mother's reaction as implied readers, we realize she has not been consulted about this purchase, and it is not in the budget. This car has not been planned or saved for. Her husband has made financial commitments without consulting his wife. He is in trouble.

Taylor shows how a fancy car can cause both trouble at home and in the larger Black/White community: It signifies racial pride and White prejudice. When the family takes the car South to visit their relatives, they are stopped by the police. The policemen's address to 'lois's father is more than a greeting, and even a northern Black child can feel the racial tension:

> "Whose car is this, boy?" they asked.
> I saw anger in my father's eyes. "It's mine," he said. (74)

The use of the term *boy* is racist and derogatory, and 'lois's description signals the father's understanding of the insult. Even the child reader unaware of the use of the term *boy,* can assume the father is upset about being pulled over and being addressed as if he were a child.

As an adult audience who shares the history and culture of the author, we interpret the father's arrest differently from someone not familiar with the history of the South. His three-hour detention in jail is treated as a natural consequence of receiving a speeding ticket. After the judge arrives, 'lois's father pays the ticket and is released. No further explanation or description of what life in jail for a Black man with White captors is necessary for an implied audience. Taylor has set racial and historical boundaries for her implied audience: Reading between the lines, and knowing the history, this audience will not need a fuller description of outrage over police behavior in the South. We get the implications.

It is irony that lets the author's audience "see over the head of a situation" (Frye 56). The early oral tradition of signifying or using a trope has been a conscious device used to eliminate the effects of White power over Black society. It was also cautious in nature, reflecting the current social relations between races. And it suggests a change in the mode as cultural tales venture from oral performance to written stories. Whereas Federal Writers Project interviewees masked their signifying, Taylor makes hers obvious for an adult White and Black audience. Taylor's written irony makes adult Whites conscious of the unstated and, therefore, uncomfortable. When Taylor employs a call and response trope within her plot, her call reveals Black society's call for equality and White rejection in their response. Thus, Taylor's character Mr. Tom Bee calls for equality but is denied. When he refuses to address John Wallace as anything other than John, he makes the Wallaces face their prejudice and act on it. Taylor's White society uses power to silence the Black society, but it finds it cannot fully achieve its goals of dominance. Blacks are fully aware of their intentions, and they compromise according to their status. 'lois's father's call for economic equality is the purchase of a gold Cadillac. The response to his call is his arrest by White authority figures. Mr. Tom Bee refuses to submit to the pressures of bigotry and faces physical abuse; 'lois's father protects his northern family from southern bigotry by getting rid of the auto. Implicit in these stories is the allusion to power and subsequent warning that the oral tradition of call and response is precarious change. If practiced in the larger society, the call between Blacks and Whites might be answered with violence. Still, the real caller's need has been met. As the author, Taylor has shown that two cultures are not yet equally powerful. Social order is not couched in justice within these stories.

Joyce Carol Thomas has used Black tropes and signification in more positive ways, reaffirming the uniqueness of Black culture and orality. Singing, a particular way of speaking that is often practiced in the Black church, is a metaphor for power in the African American tradition. Singing allows the women in Thomas's "Young Reverend Zelma Lee Moses" (1990) to have a voice and be active in church services. Zelma relies on the support of her congregation and counts on their response to her call to determine her preaching effectiveness. Thomas's use of call and response in "Young Reverend Zelma Lee Moses" illustrates the traditional expectations of the trope within a local community. Zelma is a young woman who has gained notoriety because of her singing, and she is depicted as the naive performer within her church. Zelma's preaching at Perfect Peace Baptist Church involves the audience: they second and respond to her call. Hers is a local voice not aware of newer customs practiced elsewhere. When a visiting choir joins Perfect Peace on Palm Sunday, Zelma Lee is only able to get her "dear Daniel" (117) to shout. Unaware that the visiting Louisiana choir members have fainted instead of shouting to announce their acceptance of religion, Zelma feels as if she has failed:

> She was used to more call and response and certainly more shouting.
> "Why's this church so cold?" she asked.
> Stopped in the middle of her sermon and asked it.
> What she could not see behind her were the visiting choir members being carried off the stage one by one. The entire soprano section of the New Orleans New Baptist Church Youth Choir had danced until they fainted, until only one or two straggly alto voices were left.
> The Sweet Earth congregation gazed so amazed at the rapture and the different shouting styles of the Louisiana choir that they settled back and, instead of joining in the com-

motion, sat transfixed on their chairs like they were in a downtown theater watching a big city show on tour. (118)

Zelma expected orality in call and response; she only understood one kind of support. However, Zelma's desire to make her "dear Daniel" (117) proud causes her to go beyond her normal routine and promise to fly on Easter Sunday. Thus, Thomas is mixing metaphors within her short story. The trope of flying has its roots in slavery, and it refers to the ability to take flight from oppression and ridicule. Slaves used the metaphor in their songs and stories in order to talk and sing about escaping when they were on the plantation. Then and now, flying evokes the image of freedom from oppression. It signifies going beyond local constraints. Although her inability to fly will cause Zelma to change, Thomas alludes to this Black symbol and suggests Zelma's ability to rise above local conditions throughout the tapestry of her story. Flight imagery is used to describe Zelma's preaching when Thomas writes, "Men flocked like butterflies to Zelma's color-rich flower garden, to the sunbows in her throat every time she opened her mouth to preach or sing. Out flew the apricot hues of hollyhock, the gold of the goldenrod, the blue pearl of Jacob's ladder" (112). Crows roost on the tupelo trees outside the church windows to hear Zelma sing. Inside the church, "Melodies lifted them [the congregation] up to a higher place and never let them down" (109). Zelma preaches in response to Psalms 57, 61, and 91, and she speaks of flight:

> Keep me as the apple of thy eye, hide me under the shadow of thy wings. And He shall cover thee with his feathers, and under his wings shalt thou trust: his truth shall be thy shield and buckler. [. . .] Be merciful unto me, O God, be merciful unto me: for my soul trusteth in thee: yea, in the shadow of thy wings will I make my refuge [. . .]. (126)

These scenes hold multiple meanings; they foreshadow her failure to fly and subsequent escape to the bird refuge, and they signal her unspoken love for Daniel. Furthermore, Zelma's singing and ability to raise others' spirits reveals a caring, nurturing, mystical gift that raises the congregation above the temporal world.

Thomas uses several images from the Black community to evoke a sense of call and response: song, dance, the Bible, and food all bring the community together. Thomas calls the reader into her story with descriptions of food as sensual goods created by commonplace people for cultural events. Food, too, has cultural implications of power. It became central to the few holidays experienced by the slaves. Thus, Thomas is using history in a positive way. She is demonstrating that Blacks in Oklahoma understood their past and have developed a culture of church within their community. The church is depicted as the meeting spot for the congregational family. It contains many leaders, each with his or her own role. Though Zelma and her father are the preachers, Mother Augusta serves as the spiritual mother of the church. The women of the congregation open their kitchens to the Louisiana choir and others who come for revival week.

Food, the nourishment of the community, has been continually used by Black female writers to specify the maternal strength of the African American culture that Walker had earlier alluded to in her writings. Thomas's story begins by using it metaphorically to establish community:

> A mother, brown and fluffy as buttermilk biscuits, stood by the muslin-draped window, opening glass jars of yams, okra, tomatoes, spinach, and cabbage and stirred the muted colors in a big, black cast-iron pot. Then she raised the fire until she set the harvest green and red colors of the vegetables bubbling before fitting the heavy lid in place and lowering the flame. (101)

Later, when the choir is fed by the women of the Perfect Peace congregation, Thomas writes:

> The gray-haired, white-capped mothers of the church, mothers of the copper kettles and porcelain pans, kept their kitchens bustling with younger Sweet Earth women. They instructed these sisters of the skillet in the fine art of baking savory chicken-and-dressing and flaky-crusted peach cobblers. (124)

Mother Augusta is the psychic mother of the community and her choir is the ladies of Perfect Peace. Zelma's probable downfall is also foreshadowed when she begins reaching outside of this matriarchal community with its established roles and, thus, angers her congregation. She builds a launch pad without consulting the deacons and takes her clerical robes to "unsanctified, whiskey-drinking folks and had them sew some wings onto her robe" (122). After Zelma's literal fall from grace, Deacon Jones removes the launch pad. Thomas alludes to the ultimate restoring power of the church women when they meet to offer a prayer and begin sewing new holy robes for Zelma, "a child of God" (132). For three days they sing and sew; lining a hymn and lining a hem (132). On the third day, Zelma returns and is welcomed by the congregation. Thomas's female community has used its nesting powers to nurture and restore Zelma to her role as religious leader.

The use of signification in the early slave narratives and later short stories of Hurston, Walker, Taylor, and Thomas illustrate the three evolutionary phases that have been in minority women's literature as identified by Elaine Showalter. Showalter says that minority writers first imitate and internalize the dominant culture's traditions; they then protest and demand minority rights and recognition; and, finally, they break with the dominant tradition by developing new patterns (13). The slave narratives illustrate the first phase of internalization and imitation of White culture as they establish Black patterns of call and response, signification, and metaphorical language. Zora Neale Hurston, Alice Walker, and Mildred D. Taylor exemplify the second stage of protest. Whereas Hurston and Walker have written primarily with an adult audience in mind, Taylor decided to write for young readers. Her writing was motivated by the lack of African American history available in public school history books. As a child, Taylor remembers stories of the adults in her family and their talk:

> [. . . they] would often turn to a history which we heard only at home, a history of Black people told through stories.
>
>   Those stories about the small and often dangerous triumphs of Black people, those stories about human pride and survival in a cruelly racist society were like nothing I read

in the history books or the books I devoured at the local library. There were no Black heroes or heroines in those books [. . .]. ("Newbery" 25)

Taylor protests against American history by providing an alternative perspective for her young readers. Her use of signification and irony calls attention to the unwritten racial undercurrents of U.S. history and unacknowledged mistreatments of African Americans. Although she crafts strong, nurturing African American communities that are healthy and safe in isolation, they are always enveloped by the negative White community that surrounds them.

Thomas has also written with a youthful audience in mind. However, Thomas exorcizes Whites, exemplifying Showalter's third stage. White society is absent because Thomas is creating a voice uniquely African American by enveloping her plot with Black cultural metaphors of the church, singing, food, and flying. Thomas goes beyond the past, offering a text that has autonomous Black women who are the cultural sociologists within an African American community. Because there are no Whites in her story, her signification moves away from traditional response patterns. Thomas has created a uniquely African American text that is a celebration of Black community traditions. It is her use of specifying that takes her writing beyond Showalter's Eurocentric explanation of patterns for White women who hope to fit into the Eurocentric White male tradition. As Willis notes, African American female writers are creating a new utopia:

> [. . . it] depends on the radical reconstitution of domestic life and space. The future takes shape within the walls that have traditionally imprisoned women and defined their social labor: the home. [. . .] it works on the commonplace features of daily life, from household objects to household labor, from childbearing to sexuality. It asks how these might be lifted out of the oppressive and repressive constraints defined by bourgeois society and capitalism. (159)

Thomas's utopia places her writing outside of the three categories earlier defined by Showalter, creating a fourth plateau where female African American writers craft short stories that fit the nurturing practices found within their contemporary mothers' gardens.

Works Cited

Abrahams, Roger D. *Deep Down in the Jungle: Negro Narrative Folklore from the Streets of Philadelphia.* Hatboro: Folklore Associates, 1964.

Blassingame, John W. *The Slave Community.* New York: Oxford University Press, 1979.

Cobb, James C. *The Most Southern Place on Earth: The Mississippi Delta and the Roots of Regional Identity.* New York: Oxford, 1992.

Frye, Northrop. *The Educated Imagination.* Bloomington, IN: Indiana University Press, 1964.

Gates, Henry Louis, Jr. *The Signifying Monkey.* New York: Oxford University Press, 1988.

Hurston, Zora Neale. *Dust Tracks on a Road.* New York: Arno Press, 1969.

———. *Of Mules and Men.* Bloomington, IN: Indiana University Press, 1978.

Joyner, Charles W. *Down by the Riverside: A South Carolina Slave Community.* Urbana, IL: University of Illinois Press, 1984.

Lee, Carol D. *Signifying as a Scaffold for Literary Interpretation.* Urbana, IL: National Council of Teachers of English, 1993.

Mitchell-Kernan, Claudia. "Signifying." *Mother Wit from the Laughing Barrel: Readings in the Interpretation of Afro-American Folklore.* Ed. Alan Dundes. Englewood Cliffs, NJ: Prentice Hall, 1973. 310–28.

Rawick, George P., ed. *The American Slave: A Composite Autobiography.* 19 vols. Westport, CT: Greenwood, 1972.

Showalter, Elaine. *A Literature of Their Own: British Women Novelists from Bronte to Lessing.* Princeton, NJ: Princeton University Press, 1977.

Taylor, Mildred D. *The Friendship and The Gold Cadillac.* New York: Bantam Skylark, 1987.

———. "Newbery Medal Acceptance." *Newbery and Caldecott Medal Books 1976–1985.* Ed. Lee Kingman. Boston: Horn Book, 1986. 21–30.

Thomas, Joyce Carol. "Young Reverend Zelma Lee Moses." *A Gathering of Flowers: Stories About Being Young in America.* Ed. Joyce Carol Thomas. New York: HarperCollins, 1990. 99–134.

Walker, Alice. *Living By the Word.* San Diego: Harcourt Brace Jovanovich, 1988.

———. *In Search of Our Mothers' Gardens.* San Diego: Harcourt Brace Jovanovich, 1983.

———. *To Hell With Dying.* San Diego: Harcourt Brace Jovanovich, 1967.

Willis, Susan. *Specifying: Black Women Writing the American Experience.* Madison, WI: University of Wisconsin Press, 1987.

11

Reading Literature Multiculturally

A Stance to Enhance Reading of Some Hispanic Children's Literature

Richard Van Dongen

Reading and rereading literary works are life-sustaining pleasures that evoke endless wonderment about our multiple worlds. Even though these pleasures are bounded by our experiences through our specific cultural ways of knowing, this "boundedness" need not be rigidly set. Movement out of and across bounded frames of experience can become a part of pleasurable reading and will sustain wonderment about our worlds.

To move out and across such bounded frames of cultural experience, however, we must agree to cross one boundary and into another, fully recognizing that we come with our earlier established values and our familiar story patterns. Undoubtedly, as we widely read or encounter life experiences in zones where different bounded frames push against each other, new perspectives and possibly new lenses for interpreting experience develop. As we read about life in unfamiliar zones, we need to proceed uncritically, withholding the convictions of our culture and its critical judgments for a while; if we respond too quickly to a new place in literature we limit our possibilities of seeing. When taking a deliberate, different stance to look in, to look out, or to look across bounded interactions, we may be amazed at the human possibilities of experience within our reading and our living. Such experiences are the essence of reading and living multiculturally.

I take a stance of reading multiculturally[1] in ways that are discerned in Dow-Anaya y Garcia's 2001 dissertation. Rather than simply reading a multicultural text, I suggest that the reader must actively engage in reading beyond earlier culturally bound experiences and willingly pursue the challenging perspective of the "journey itself." As Rosenblatt suggests, during the reading event the reader's attention "is centered on what he [or she] is living through *during* the reading, during the transaction with the text" (15). Yet, she further illuminates: "No matter how great the potentialities of the text, the reader can make a poem [transaction] only by drawing on his or her own reservoir of past experiences with life and language" (19). The broader and deeper this reservoir is, the more the individual can read multiculturally. Movement out of the comfort zone of one's culture and into the bounded frames of another culture will contribute to the multicultural pleasures of the reading journey itself.

The reading journey contrasts sharply with the act of defining a book as multicultural literature. In order to meet some important needs and to make sure minority literature is visible and available, multicultural literature has often quite appropriately been defined in the United States as literature by and/or about African Americans, Latinos, Hispanics, Asians, or American Indians. In so doing, however, at times I have found contexts in which such multicultural literature is devalued as literature and deemed as only appropriate for minority readers. I have particularly observed this in elementary school contexts in which minority population numbers are either a very high percentage or a very low percentage of the school population. Such multicultural literature should be part of the literary experience of all readers. If all children and adults move toward an active stance of reading multiculturally, the pleasures of reading literature with wonderment can be enhanced.

I will try to demonstrate reading multiculturally by discussing my reading of books by and about Hispanics.[2] I will focus on the richness of Hispanic literature and on how I, as a cultural outsider, can appreciate that richness because I not only draw from my experiences of American mainstream children's literature but also enrich them by looking outside of this boundedness. I will try to make somewhat conscious my frames or boundaries that potentially limit my reading of works steeped with literary allusions to traditions of Hispanic literature and life experiences. I will also try to place myself consciously into a context in which these frames or boundaries push against each other. I will try to prepare myself for my reading of a children's book so that some of my established expectations in literary experience will not block me as I engage with some of the Hispanic traditions; rather, I wish to acknowledge how these traditions will encourage a richer frame if I am mindful. In other words, I will set new expectations of my reading, although these will necessarily be ambiguous and will emerge only while I am in the reading journey. I will try to be aware of the need to withhold quick surface judgments so that I can cross boundaries into these new works and reap the pleasures of reading multiculturally.

I am situated in an area where American mainstream culture and Hispanic cultures live. Therefore, my reading is framed within a definable context in which mainstream U.S. American and Hispanic cultures coexist. In such a context, a bounded zone of Hispanic culture, thought, and literature and a bounded zone of mainstream U.S. American culture, thought, and literature come together in an interactive zone. This "border culture" between two existing groups includes interactions of literature and of daily life that spill over into many geographic identities. My region encompasses border cultures of both northern Mexico and southwestern United States. This is also thought to be the mythic region known as Aztlan.[3] Today in this region the cultural ways of knowing dramatically push up against each other, in a geographic and demographic landscape that frequently creates new possibilities for life experiences and self-expression. A U.S. American/Hispanic border culture might also occur where mainstream U.S. American life is dominant but a strong "minority" Hispanic presence is a vital part of the community. In such regions, wide reading and life experiences can help us withhold judgments when ways of knowing conflict. Stories from border cultures reflect this, often asking readers to move across borders and perspectives and to take on at least the possibility of other perspectives.

People in communities along the United States–Mexico border embrace boundary crossing as a natural, exhilarating way of life; sometimes the movement is for survival as well as pleasure. *True Tales from Another Mexico: The Lynch Mob, the Popsicle Kings, Chalino, and the Bronx* by Sam Quinones shows us this. Such viewpoints can be highlighted in Chicano literature in particular and Hispanic literature in general. A close, reflective reading of Sam Quinones's book or of any such work can be an invaluable preparation for delving into a children's book. In addition, as I engage in a close reading of a new perspective, I have to face my own assumptions about my reading of literature and consider what I hold as expectations of narrative forms, characters, realism, and so on. Therefore, I would encourage readers of children's literature to engage in close readings of adult Chicano literature prior to entering a similar journey found in a children's book.

I will illustrate selective aspects of my close reading of *So Far from God* by Ana Castillo as a way to highlight some general qualities of Hispanic literature that contribute to the literariness of the text and bring delight when reading this particular novel. I will consider what perspectives are needed as I engage in this close reading, and I will then bring my experience to my readings of selected children's works. I will highlight several qualities that should support and illuminate reading other Hispanic texts multiculturally.

So Far from God is a novel set in the small community of Tome, New Mexico. A good way to verify pronunciation of Tome is to go to the "Key to Pronunciation" in a dictionary such as *Cassell's Spanish Dictionary*. Within its very short description, the book describes the regularity of pronunciation of vowels and consonants in Spanish. For the English-only reader, this is delightful; the definition should encourage the non-Spanish speaker to enter Hispanic literature with anticipation. Dual language texts are common in Hispanic literature. Frequently Hispanic writers use Spanish words and phrases, even when they are predominantly writing in English. In the case of Tome, the pronunciation analysis might go something like this:

> The **o** has two sounds. In an open syllable such as in **To** it is pronounced like the **o** in **halo**. The **e** has two sounds. In an open syllable such as **me** it is pronounced like the first **a** in **fatality**. So **Tome is** _____.

My reading of definitions and careful exploration of the text have shown me there are cultural stances in Hispanic literature that I need to understand. I see that I must enter into another bounded frame. For instance, a quick read of Castillo's introduction to the mother and her four daughters by a U.S. American mainstream reader with his or her own reliable assumptions about narrative forms, characters, voice, and realism might misinform the reader about the story's tone and sense of realism. Sofi, the mother, wakes up at midnight to the "howling and neighing of the five dogs, six cats, and four horses." When she checks on her children, she finds her three-year-old daughter is jerking and thrashing about. Sofi screams out, "Ave Maria *Purisima*" because there is something wrong. The other three children and Sofi scream and moan when the baby stops and is still; they know she is dead. The text continues: "It was the saddest *velorio* in Tome in years because it was so sad to bury a child" (italics added 20).

Castillo seamlessly moves in and out of English and Spanish; hers is a natural and effortless Chicana style of communication. This is also true for the fluent bilingual Spanish-English reader. However, with some willingness to embrace the text, the non-Spanish speaker reading the text will be able to enter in to this world as well. The knowledge of the regularity and predictability of the pronunciation should contribute to the English speaker's building comfort. Non-Spanish-speaking teachers reading Hispanic picture books aloud to all children must be able to (and they can) embrace the pronunciation of Spanish comfortably and with confidence.[4] In addition, as in the example of Castillo's surrounding of *velorio* with familiar emotions when a child dies, most Hispanic authors embed vocabulary meanings and text comprehension in the context of the story. Mine is an insight that all good readers continuously and almost automatically use when reading new words in a story.

On the surface, English is strikingly the dominant language in this text, but the Spanish rhythms and shaping of the text are not far from the surface. As a result, the reader unfamiliar with Spanish syntax may take some time before reading comfortably in the groove of the cultural frame. Readers, both bilingual Spanish/English and English only, who persistently move ahead and hold back judgments based on their experienced readings of other fiction will quickly be rewarded as they seep into the dialogic interaction between Spanish and English. Certain patterns of rhythm, flow, and lilt will emerge. Certain language uses of the negative and the double negative in Castillo's writing will be noted, and the reader will understand how they support the cultural community, its language, and its identity within the novel and contribute to the vivid humor—at times outrageous—and the maddeningly complex dilemmas and paradoxes of the human condition.

The story of Sofi and her daughters continues. On the day of the funeral, with the outside temperature at 118 degrees, Father Jerome, for some reason known only to him, asks the two pallbearers to place the small casket on the ground just in front of the church. He advises the crowd that has gathered that God alone knows why we are on earth. This sets Sofi off, and she throws herself on the ground. She wants to know why. Why? Why? Why? Suddenly one of her other daughters, Esperanza, shrieks, and everyone becomes silent as the lid on the casket moves and the little girl inside sits up: She "lifted herself up into the air and landed on the church roof" (23). Castillo soon continues: "Once the baby was able to receive medical attention [in Albuquerque . . .] it was diagnosed that she was in all probability an epileptic" (25). Coming from a traditional mainstream background, I might ask, "How does this explain anything or everything that has happened so far?" This, however, would not be reading multiculturally.

The reader who refuses to see that mythic spiritualism is embedded within the contemporary realism of Castillo's novel will find the story problematic. From my position as a reader who lives in the geographic region where the story takes place, I can see a different stance to take: The setting for this story could be Aztlan, the mythic homeland of the Mexica people that was revived by the Chicano rights activists of the 1960s. Chicano writers and artists have incorporated elements of Aztlan landscape, memory, and cultural and spiritual identities into this contemporary borderland, as Fields and Zamudio-Taylor point out in their recent work.

I am not using this description of Aztlan to explain events in *So Far from God,*[5] but I do suggest that remembering the multicultural boundedness of the region gives me a lens into the literature that may allow me to embrace what on the surface might seem beyond credibility. I can gradually enter into the novel's world with an understanding that I can enjoy the perplexities, the struggles, the contradictions, and the fusion of elements from cultural *mythos* and historical beliefs that alert me to a richly complex cultural, mythic, and spiritual identity embedded in the text. As I read multiculturally, I become engaged in the story's journey.

I offer one more set of literary observations from another powerful Hispanic writer, the Mexican writer Carlos Fuentes. In the "Author's Notes" (unpaged) to his collection of short stories entitled *Burnt Water,* Fuentes reveals the meaning of the title. It is the paradox of *The Encounter,* a stunning cultural/historical observation that continues to ripple throughout the Americas and underlies the psyche of the Hispanic world. This paradox is the Spanish/European encounter with the Western Hemisphere; in 1521 the encounter came to the Mexica peoples. These are the people who at some earlier time wandered south from Aztlan to found and create the great Aztecan civilization. In 1325 the wandering Aztecs founded Tenochtitlan, the oldest city in the Americas, on "a high lagoon guarded by sparkling volcano and [were] conquered in 1521 by the Spanish, who there erected the viceregal city of Mexico on the burnt water of the ancient Indian lake" (Fuentes unpaged). While burning and destroying the city/culture on the lake, the Spanish created a new city/culture. Fuentes explains: "Burnt water, atl tlachinolli: the paradox of the creation is also the paradox of the destruction. The Mexican character never separates life from death, and this too is the sign of the burnt water that presided over the city's destiny in birth and rebirth" (unpaged).

The paradox is used by Fuentes as a structural device for this collection of short stories, which are entirely set in one high-rise imaginary apartment building in Mexico City. Each story centers on the people living on a different floor. The building is, as much of the city is, sinking into the "uneasy mud [of the lake bottom] where the humid god, the Chac-Mool, lives" (unpaged). Chac-Mool continues to live in the basement of this apartment building and, thus, readers of the stories are reminded of such paradoxes as present/history, mythical/contemporary, and rationality/spirituality. These contraries in imagery shape our reading of Fuentes's stories because we always know that the Chac-Mool of Aztecan times still inhabits the basement.

Although not to be overdone or overemphasized, the idea of paradox is another entry lens to take along on the journey of reading some Hispanic literature multiculturally. Bringing together the ideas of border language crossing, Aztlan, and the framing of paradox, I now have several lenses that can be tools, if you will, to move my expectations to new possibilities for me as the reader of Hispanic literature. I will be more ready for the text and can charge ahead—perhaps—using the metaphor of Sandra Cisneros, author of *The House on Mango Street,* in her description and praise for Castillo and her novel, which appeared on the book's back cover:

> "Goddamn! Ana Castillo has gone and done what I always wanted to do—written a Chicana *telenovela*—a novel roaring down Interstate 25 at one hundred and fifteen miles an hour with an almanac of Chicanoismo—saints, martyrs, T.V. mystics, home remedies, little miracles, *dichos,* myths, gossip, recipes—fluttering from the fender like a flag [. . .]. (Penguin paperback edition May 1994)

The paradox of the Americas, the burning and destroying of one civilization while giving life to another, continues to both inspire and to underscore Hispanic literature. Also, the border culture, as is perhaps true for all cultural zones in the Western Hemisphere, is still conflicted by this event. Folk stories of La Llorona written in our contemporary times provide one window to assist readers in interpreting the significance of *The Encounter;* the paradox of life and death comes markedly alive and is dramatically contrasted in various versions of the tale of *The Weeping Woman.*

I have selected three versions to show how past and present merge and contribute to the life/death/still-life metaphor, however brazenly or subtly it might be set. Collectively, these three versions draw on border crossing of language and Aztlan as well as *The Encounter* paradox. Reading multiculturally can collectively heighten appreciation of paradox, language, and mythic underpinnings in these versions. These insights are then accessible for the reader to use during further journeys in reading Hispanic literature multiculturally.

The Legend of La Llorona, by Rudolfo Anaya, places the reader in the year of the 1521 *Encounter.* In 1516, the daughter of the chief in a local village on the Central American sea coast quickly and effortlessly learns the language of some shipwrecked Spanish strangers who survived, made it to the seashore, and continued to live and wander along the coast. When the captain and his soldiers arrive in great ships in 1521, the daughter quickly becomes the interpreter for the village and the captain. The captain asks that she tell him her name. She says Malintzin, but the captain hears with a Spanish ear and he says Malinche, and that is her name from then on. She becomes the interpreter for the captain during his dealings with this village and other villages as well, and joins him as interpreter on the march to Mexico. There are early signs in their human traits that will lead them to their tragedies. Malinche is uncommonly beautiful and also aloof. The captain is ambitious, restless, and strikingly handsome. They fall in love; Malinche becomes his wife and bears him two sons. However, Princess Isabella arrives from Spain to spend time in the captain's viceregal court set up in the conquered city. Although the captain still is attached to his two sons, he is less and less interested in Malinche. Deceit, jealousy, and the betrayal of Princess Isabella and the captain force Malinche to kill her two sons and cast them into the lake.

Anaya ends:

> "Listen," Malinche responded. "Do you hear the cry of my sons? They cry in the waters of the lake. They call for me to come. I go now, transformed by this deed into the eternal mother who cannot sleep until she finds her sons. I will never tire of that search, not until all of my sons are safe in my arms. I, Malinche, princess mother of the Mexicans, will forever be known as the woman who cries for her sons [. . .]."

She turned and disappeared into the dark. For her deed that night, she left behind her grief and her penance, and her wailing cry. (89)

La Llorona, the Weeping Woman; An Hispanic Legend Told in Spanish and English by Hayes is the second version that I want to discuss. Published ten years later, this story is set in a village that could be anywhere in the southwestern border country in the folkloric past:

Long years ago in a humble little village there lived a fine looking girl named Maria,

or

Hace muchisimo años viviá en un pueblo humilde una bella muchacha llamada María. (unpaged)

However, illustrator Vicki Trego Hill visually connects the reader with the roots of *The Encounter* and history of La Malinche by placing a stone face from Aztecan times on the title page and on the first page of the text. On the last page, as Maria becomes La Llorona, Hill creates a close-up of her face with the river in the background to suggest an extraordinary likeness of Maria to the Aztecan stone face at the front of the book. The reader with knowledge of *The Encounter* paradox, the history of Aztlan, and earlier discussion in *Burnt Water* reads the story with more richness of contextuality, drawing deeply into the past, into the cultural identity of the teller, and into the cultural stance that reading multiculturally allows.

Maria eyes a ranchero, a son of a rancher, from the southern plains who rides his horse like a Commanche. She is haughty but tricky—and she convinces the ranchero to marry her. After they have two children and spend some years together, the dashing, restless ranchero leaves their home for longer and longer periods, returning to the life of the plains and to his own wealthy class. Maria sees the ranchero with a beautiful, elegant woman from his wealthy class, and she becomes so jealous and full of despair that she hurls her two children into the river. When she realizes what she has done, she sinks to the ground. The next day she is found dead and is laid to rest where she has fallen. However, at night she comes out from her grave and wanders up and down the river's edge, crying for her children. The illustration at this story's end shows her face with the river in the background. This is Maria, but this is also La Malinche.

In the collection of stories entitled *The Day It Snowed Tortillas: Tales from Spanish New Mexico* the story of La Llorona is set in contemporary Santa Fe with its small river and arroyos. Perhaps the author and illustrator used this contemporary setting to remind children not to play by the river and to get home before dark. The book does seem more didactic. There is a less explicit sense of the underpinnings of La Malinche and Burnt Water. On the other hand, this setting is Santa Fe, the City of the Holy Faith, and the home of La Conquistadora, Our Lady of the Conquest.[6] Again, if I read multiculturally, I can see that the historical and legendary ties are slightly different. La Conquistadora is a wooden statue of the Virgin brought by Spanish colonizers when they came to New Mexico in 1627. The statue was removed in 1680 by the fleeing Spanish during the Pueblo Revolt when all Spanish colonists were driven out of the area. The Spanish returned in 1692, and La Conquistadora returned with them. The statue has been in Santa Fe ever since that time, according to Chavez's account in *La Conquistadora: The Autobiography of an Ancient Statue*. With new understandings about such mythic, spiritual underpinnings, the multicultural reader might find himself or herself shivering as La Llorona cries along the rocky edge of rivers and arroyos, seeking her children. Even today, Hayes maintains, there are children who will tell you a story about nearly being caught by La Llorona when they stayed out too late or played along the river.

Reading multiculturally, I come with my memory of the historical tale about *The Encounter,* understand there are broadly representative legends and motifs for stories in many villages, and recognize there is a specific contemporary town with a literary tradition that is attached to the earlier cultural materials; this will *collectively* bring me closer to Ana Castillo's writing and will give me a better understanding of the story patterns I am encountering: The Chicana writes through mythic Aztlan and melds landscape, memory/history, spirituality, and identity. Thus, the three versions of La Llorona *collectively* encourage me to become engaged within multicultural literature when it achieves such melding.

A closely related paradox to the life/death/still-life allusions in these tales is that of old age and youth, and perhaps even more interestingly of wise children and endearingly wise, but sometimes foolish, viejos. Hispanic writers also play with such characterization counterpoints as depictions of an exceedingly wise child and a wise, but sometimes seemingly less wise, grandfather or abuelo. This paradoxical framing, along with dualism in language, allows a youthful, experienced reader to successfully move toward a rich multicultural (or collective) engagement with a short story by Gary Soto.

In *Baseball in April and Other Stories,* Soto includes the story "Two Dreamers." Hector, a nine-year-old, spends the summer with his grandparents in Fresno, California. Grandfather Luis Molina dreams of selling his house in Fresno and returning with the newfound money to the town of his birth, Jalapa, Mexico. He asks his grandson, without his wife's knowledge, to phone a realty company and inquire about another house. Partly, he hopes to discover how much his own house might be worth, but he also dreams of buying another house to inhabit or sell for a profit. Hector, the wise child, negotiates for his abuelo, calling the realtor and finding out what his abuelo wanted. There are many humorous contradictions in language and events throughout this negotiation, but Hector remains very wise and also recognizes the importance of his grandfather's dreams. He also knows that Abuela will offer both a strong dose of reality when she discovers what they are up to. Within this short story, Soto employs a good deal of language crossing, plays with the ideal of elderly experience in contrast to youthful inexperience, and reveals warm relationships between the two within the tugs and pulls of their adventures. Reading multiculturally allows the reader to enjoy the dualism in the language, the typical elder/youth motifs found in Hispanic traditions and legends, and brings an understanding that the boy and his grandfather are sharing bounded experiences in their adventures.

Rudolofo Anaya, in *The Farolitos of Christmas,* creates the dualism found in Soto in his characterization of a young girl and a grandfather. The paradoxes of age and youth and the depiction of a wise child (who is young but wise beyond her years) are used to build tension as Luz, the very wise child, solves the story's problems: Abuelo is ill and cannot cut and stack the piñon logs that are to be lit on Christmas Eve to outline a path for the pastores who will stop at the house to sing and then to be invited in to eat posole, tamales, and biscochitos. Luz's father joined the Army because World War II is on; her mother received a telegram that he has been wounded and is in a hospital. The time line is revealed by the illustrator Edward Gonzales who depicts Luz crossing out another day on the calendar, something she has done each day since her father left the village of San Juan. December 1944 can be clearly ascertained by the reader. Edward Gonzales is a Hispanic artist, and his work captures a romantic, nostalgic image of the past that depicts what we might like to remember; quite possibly it never existed with such panoramic beauty of landscape, richness of family traditions, and social relationships within the community. Nevertheless, this is a book designed for children. Through text and illustration, the reader deduces that Luz is probably in those intermediate years of the elementary school years. Seemingly, her mother and her abuelo do not solve the problem as to how the family can prepare and light the small fires—luminaries—so that the family can fully participate in the rituals of faith, church, and community. That is up to Luz.

A quick reading of the story might suggest to some readers who are not reading multiculturally that this story holds an unrealistic character too wise for her years and a somewhat helpless family, accompanied by illustrations that are too idyllic, romantic, and overly nostalgic. But a reader on a multicultural journey may ponder: Are the writer and the illustrator Chicano artists of Aztlan? Is this the Aztlan mythic landscape? Is this that homeland of history, spirituality, identity, and landscape? There are paradoxes embedded in the border psyche, and, as in Castillo's work, the hard reality of a historical situation—in this case World War II—becomes a part of Hispanic children's literature with visual and verbal representations of lived Hispanic experiences. There are language shifts from the dominant use of English to Spanish, and there are the underlying rhythms of this linguistic dualism. Rather than perceptions of a stilted English style, a richly layered style accompanies Abuelo as he speaks to Luz: "You look happy mij'ita" (unpaged).

A reader on a multicultural journey may still reject rather than appreciate this particular work, but those judgments will be based on a much richer set of propositions if the reader can read multiculturally. Children who have learned how to take a multicultural stance by reading texts through enlightened engagements may glimpse the more complex, diverse view of the boundless possibilities when reading multicultural literature.

All of the works selected to discuss so far have been fiction or variations of Hispanic folklore. There are other possibilities available. A children's informational book entitled *Fiesta U.S.A.*, by the Hispanic photographer and writer George Ancona, may also both affirm and add insight into a reader's stance for reading multiculturally. The fiestas documented are in San Francisco, New York City, and New Mexican villages. There is new and additional information about farolitos and the processions of Las Posadas in Ancona's photographic essay; *Fiesta U.S.A.* shows how revelers are joined by many non-Hispanic neighbors, who have adopted the fiesta and take part every year. Ancona includes photographic and textual documentation of a New York City Puerto Rican version of La Fiesta de los Reyes Magos celebrated in East Harlem every January 6. There are also the paradoxes of Burnt Water and of life and death never being separate in his depiction of the San Franciscan version of the celebration of El Dia de los Muertos on each November 2, a day known in Hispanic cultures as All Souls' Day. This is the day to honor and remember friends and relatives who have died, but it is also the day to celebrate life. Families build altars in their homes that might include marigolds (flowers of the dead), candied skulls and skeletons of melted sugar, and foods including pan de muertos, sweet breads baked especially for the holiday. Ancona indicates that originally in San Francisco only the Mexican community celebrated but that now many people from all over the city come to march and to remember their friends and loved ones, some who have died of AIDS. Ancona writes: "The musicians begin to play. The marchers light their candles, and the parade is under way. [. . .] It is a carnival of living, joyous people united in their mockery of death" (unpaged).

And then Ancona documents Los Matachines in El Rancho, New Mexico. There is a photograph of a costumed man, a grotesque viejo with a whip who mocks all viejos, wise or foolish. In one photograph there is a young girl dressed in white among the Matachines dancers. Our multicultural reader queries: Is this Abuelo? Is this La Malinche? Is this La Conquistadora? Is this a paradox of the very wise child? El Abuelo explains to the crowd:

> We think Los Matachines originated around the time the Moors invaded Spain in the eighth century. The Spanish conquistadors brought it here, but no one knows for sure how the dance began. It has been performed in both Indian pueblos and Hispanic towns since the sixteenth century. (unpaged)

As the dance begins, the principal dancer, el monarca—the king—enters and he is accompanied by el abuelo, La Malinche, el torito, and the Matachines. The cast for the representation of the arrival in Mexico of Hernan Cortes, the Spanish conqueror of the Aztecs, is now complete. El Abuelo introduces the little girl dressed in white to el monarca. She is called La Malinche, the Aztec princess. In this version, she is the Aztec princess who converts to Catholicism and becomes the interpreter for Cortes. In this portrayal, her dance among the Matachines depicts yet another paradox for the indigenous peoples of the Western Hemisphere, the arrival of Christianity in the "New World." The Burnt Water paradox of life and death is now reset and reinterpreted by yet another generation who will engage in the identity, history, spirituality, and the landscape that inspires a significant force of Hispanic literature. Thus, George Anacona helps the newest reader take a multicultural stance in reading experiences with Hispanic literature.

I hope this small slice of Hispanic literature is viewed only as that, a small slice. The breadth and creativity of the dynamic writers and stories of this literature are far more encompassing and far richer and complex than these vignettes. Yet, I offer these vignettes as small windows to invite new readers on lifelong journeys of reading multiculturally.

Notes

1. I am particularly indebted and privileged to being nudged every so often from a colleague, Donald Zancanella. Through his studies of teachers teaching literature and through his work with students, he has provided the opportunity for many collegial conversations. One of those conversations challenged me to think about reading multiculturally.

2. *Latino* is probably the term used mostly to identify Western Hemispheric cultures with Spanish and Indian roots. However, *Hispanic* is also used and in some areas, such as New Mexico, it seems to be the term most widely used. Because the slice of literature I have chosen to discuss is mainly New Mexican in origin, I will use Hispanic although the context is certainly part of the Latino world.

3. A good description of Aztlan can be found in the museum notes for an exhibit prepared by the Los Angles County Museum of Art, entitled *The Road to Aztlan: Art from a Mythic Homeland.* The notes indicate that the Mexica people, or Aztecs, believed that their ancestors lived in *Aztlan,* an earthly paradise. They

stayed in Aztlan until the twelfth century when their supreme deity led them south on a migration that lasted several generations. In 1325 they arrived in central Mexico, where they founded Tenochtitlan, the city that would become the capital of their empire. In the fifteenth century, Moctezuma, the Mexica ruler, looked to Aztlan for spiritual roots. He sent emissaries in search of the legendary place of origin. According to ancient legend, Aztlan was located somewhere in the American Southwest or northern Mexico. It has become a metaphor for the geographic, historical, and spiritual home of many peoples of Mexico and the Southwest. Chicano writers and artists have used Aztlan as an inspiration in their creativity.

4. Many children's texts provide glossaries for meaning and pronunciation.

5. An important impulse in Hispanic writing is that of paradox, which will be touched on in this chapter. Even the title of this novel carries such an ironic paradox. In the frontispiece, Castillo quotes Porfirio Diaz, the Mexican dictator during the Mexican Civil War, as the source for her title and includes the second half of the quote, which is probably also completed in the minds of many readers of the book: "So far from God, so close to the United States."

6. In 1992, the title of "Our Lady of Peace" was added by Archbishop Robert Sanchez (Archdiocese of Santa Fe website). This was due in part to revisions of political perspectives between American Indian groups and the Hispanic history of the Southwest (personal observation).

Works Cited

Anaya, Rudolfo A. *The Farolitos of Christmas.* Illus. E. Gonzales: New York: Hyperion Books for Children, 1995.

———. *The Legend of La Llorona.* Berkeley, CA: Tonatiuh-Quinto Sol International, 1984.

Anacona, George. *Fiesta U.S.A.* New York: Dutton, 1995.

Archdiocese of Santa Fe. www.archidocesesantafe.org/AboutASF/ASFHistory.htm. 2002.

Castillo, Ana. *So Far from God.* New York: Plume, Penguin Books, 1994.

Chavez, Fray Angelico. *La Conquistadora: The Autobiography of an Ancient Statue.* Santa Fe, NM: Sunstone Press, 1983.

Cisneros, Sandra. *The House on Mango Street.* Houston, TX: Arte Publico Press, 1984.

Dow-Anaya y Garcia, Donna L. "Teachers Using Multicultural Literature and Reader Response to Teach Children Multiculturally." Diss. Albuquerque, NM: University of New Mexico, 2001.

Fields, Virginia M. and Victor Zamudio-Taylor. "Aztlan: Destination and Point of Departure."*The Road to Aztlan: Art from a Mythic Homeland.* Los Angeles: Los Angeles Country Art Museum, 2001.

Fuentes, Carlo. *Burnt Water: Stories by Carlos Fuentes.* Trans. M. S. Peden. New York: Farrar, Straus and Giroux, 1980.

Hayes, Joe. *La Llorona: The Weeping Woman: An Hispanic Legend Told in Spanish and English.* Illus. V. T. Hill. El Paso, TX: Cinco Puntes Press, 1990.

———. *The Day It Snowed Tortillas: Tales from Spanish New Mexico.* Illus. L. Jelinek. Santa Fe, NM: Mariposa Publishing, 1990.

León-Portilla, Miguel. "Aztlan: From Myth to Reality." *The Road to Aztlan: Art from a Mythic Homeland.* Comp. V. F. Fields and V. Zamudio-Taylor. Los Angles: Los Angeles County Art Museum, 2001.

Museum Associates/Los Angeles County Museum of Art. *The Road to Aztlan: Art from a Mythic Homeland. Exhibition Notes Accompanying the Exhibit Itinerary:* (2001). Los Angeles County Museum of Art, May 13–August 26, 2001; The Austin Museum of Art, October 12–December 30, 2001; and the Albuquerque Museum, February 10–April 28, 2001.

Quinones, Sam. *True Tales from Another Mexico: The Lynch Mob, the Popsicle Kings, Chalino, and the Bronx.* Albuquerque, NM: University of New Mexico Press, 2001.

Peers, Edgar Allison, José V. Barragán, Francesco A. Vinayls, and Jorge Arturo Mora, ed. *Cassell's Spanish Dictionary.* New York: Funk & Wagnalls, 1968.

Rosenblatt, Louise. *The Journey Itself.* The Leland B. Jacobs Lecture. Columbia University. New York. April 1981.

Soto, Gary. (1990). "Two Dreamers." *Baseball in April and Other Stories.* San Diego: Harcourt Brace Jovanovich Publishers, 1990. 23–32.

12

When Coyote Leaves the Res

Incarnations of the Trickster from Wile E. to Le Guin[1]

Amanda Cockrell

The trickster is a character who appears across world folklore, often one who is given habitation in an animal body, too sly, too vain, too crafty to be quite human. He appears in Europe as Reynard the Fox and in Africa and the West Indies as Anansi the Spider. Most often in North America he is Old Man Coyote, creator of the world, shaper of mankind, sprinkler of the stars and general troublemaker.

The genuine coyote, *Canis latrans,* the little yellowy-gray wolf of the southwestern desert, takes his name from the Aztec *coyotl,* and he is a logical choice to inhabit the trickster's skin: he is wily, voracious, adaptable, and possessed of an insatiable curiosity. He is a trickster in the wild: a hunting coyote will often play the clown for his prey—holding its attention by dancing on his hind legs, biting his tail, turning backflips, while his partner slinks up from the other direction. He has easily survived the incursions of man upon his territory but despite, and in actual contradiction to, his reputation as a stock-killer, Coyote eats anything, including bumblebees and leather shoelaces. He likes melons, porcupines, mice, dead buzzards and leather gloves left unattended (Dobie 110). But he is most interested in things he has never seen before. To catch a coyote, you can bait your trap with food, or sex, but better yet is something ripe to wallow in or something new to investigate. One coyote hunter reported success with a powder puff saturated with drug store perfume (Dobie 144). And despite bounties on his hide, and the curiosity which leads him to take a bite of things he shouldn't, his tribe is increasing.

Like his original, the Coyote of Native American legend is known for his cunning, is always hungry, and is killed often but never dies. He dislikes work and spends his time thinking up schemes. In a Native American Coyote story the hero either outsmarts someone else or outsmarts himself.

Coyote stories are often teaching tales—Coyote tries to get more than his share of the food or to eat corn without digging his garden first. He insults the powerful or brags that he can perform impossible feats and is squashed for his impertinence. He sleeps with his friends' wives by trickery and steals their dinner before he leaves. He is unreliable and untidy, his jokes are crude and his sexual appetite is insatiable. He is like a dreadful uncle, fascinating in his sheer awfulness, whom you wish would not visit you, but who is the subject of many family stories. In the words of one Navajo father, "If my children hear these stories they'll grow up to be good people" (Toelken 128). These teaching stories carry the implicit moral: Don't be like Coyote. Don't be greedy, lazy, rude; it will only get you into trouble.

But just as often, Old Man Coyote serves as culture hero, creating the world from mud at the bottom of the sea, scattering the stars in the sky, or stealing water from the frog people to give it to mankind. It is this duality which is the hallmark of the trickster. Not a benevolent deity, Coyote eats what falls into his jaws, and anyone who trusts him is taking that risk. Yet he is also the bringer of change, the essence of the creative spirit without which the world would become static and die. He is Picasso's "lie which makes us realize truth" (Hyde 79).

Just as coyotes have not retreated from their turf with the advent of white people and their cities, neither has Old Man Coyote left the world of storytelling. In Maidu artist Harry Fonseca's 1980 acrylic "When Coyote Leaves the Res," the trickster slides into an old role with a new wardrobe: the leader of the pack, clad in black leather jacket with chains and fancy zippers, high-heeled boots and a ring in one gray ear, lounging against a brick wall. His tail is bushy, his stance a swagger. It is easy to imagine the Harley just outside the frame (Bierhorst *Mythology* 119). In "Shuffle Off to Buffalo" Fonseca gives us 20th Century Coyote again, on the cover of the Smithsonian's July 1998 issue of *Native Peoples* magazine, in Uncle Sam hat, striped pants, tailcoat, cane and fancy jogging shoes, dancing his way across a star-filled room.

Canis latrans lives happily in the foothills of Los Angeles, subsisting on rodents and unwary poodles, just as Coyote inhabits the late twentieth century, telling new twentieth-century, and now twenty-first-century stories about himself. As Lewis Hyde says, the trickster is a boundary-crosser (7), and he is not easily encapsulated in the amber of folklore. He is infinitely adaptable, trotting from one form and genre to another, taking all stories and making them his. In the sixteenth century, Spanish adventurers introduced a Spanish translation of Aesop's *Fables* to the Aztecs. One or more Aztec authors translated the stories into their own language, abandoning unfamiliar animals and giving the main roles to creatures they knew, including Coyote and Puma. In 1987, John Bierhorst translated that version into English as *Doctor Coyote,* expanding Coyote's role and collaborating with illustrator Wendy Watson, who gave the book a setting that leaves the landscape looking very like twentieth-century New Mexico and Coyote looking less Aztec than Navajo. In it he retains his trickster's nature, although in the last story we see him on his deathbed, tricking his sons for their own good. He has left them a treasure, he says, that will ensure that they never go hungry. They will find it by digging in the cornfield. Because of these cryptic last words, the coyote sons work the ground diligently, the corn grows tall and plentiful, and they are never hungry. A coyote has to be tricked into doing the sensible thing.

In the *Looney Tunes* and *Merrie Melodies* cartoons produced by Warner Brothers and directed by Chuck Jones, nothing will ever teach Wile E. Coyote to be sensible and dine on mice, or even chickens, like his natural counterparts. He is obsessed with having roadrunner for dinner. However it is interesting to note that someone in the Warner Brothers animation shop has paid attention to *Canis latrans* himself—Wile E. Coyote is anatomically accurate, with yellow eyes and big ears, bigger than a wolf's.

Wile E. is the true descendant of the coyote of legend. In these tales, he perpetually attempts to catch the Roadrunner, employing high explosives as well as native cunning. Instead, he blows himself sky high with his own backfiring bombs, falls from thousand-foot cliffs to flatten himself at the bottom, or otherwise dies a violent death—from which he pops back up as good as new in the next frame, shaking the cinders from his tail. This indestructibility has engendered protests from adults concerned by the level of violence, as well as by the notion conveyed that death is neither real nor permanent. However this coyote remains, if not politically, then certainly mythologically correct. Old Man Coyote is killed often, but never dies.

Grandmother Spider's web slices him into a thousand pieces. But Wind puts him back together and blows breath back into him (Hausman 85–86). He dances with a star, falls from the sky for ten winters and is flattened. It takes many more winters for him to puff himself back up again, but one spring there he is (Erdoes 385–386). He wants to fly with the blackbirds and convinces them to lend him feathers. But he is such a nuisance that they take his feathers away again and he falls once more. He picks himself up and slinks home, embarrassed, but he is never dead (Dobie 284). When Wile E. Coyote is flattened by the latest gadget with which he has been attempting to defeat the Roadrunner, he is only telling the latest tale of Old Man Coyote's indestructibility.

Hyde suggests that in trickster myth creative intelligence derives from appetite (17, 76). Certainly appetite for roadrunner fuels Wile E.'s ingenuity, and the gadgets themselves are creations which only Coyote could imagine—one is constructed of an electric motor, a refrigerator, a meat grinder and skis; another a street-cleaner's wagon, a weather balloon and an electric fan. In one of the few cartoons in which Wile E. actually speaks, we see him in pursuit of Bugs Bunny rather than the Roadrunner. (Perhaps because Bugs also speaks and the Roadrunner doesn't.) In this episode he has a laboratory of his own in which he invents and patents elaborate gadgets, rather than buying the components from the Acme Company, his usual supplier. Given the power of speech, he brags loudly about his genius, a trait which can be traced directly to the Old Man Coyote of legend.

When magic finds its way into these cartoons, it is trickster magic, magic gone wrong, magic folded back in upon itself. In a typical episode, Wile E. constructs a false painting of a bridge to disguise the fact that the real bridge has fallen into a chasm, hoping that the Roadrunner will run off the end and be killed. Instead the Roadrunner runs *into* the painting and continues along the nonexistent bridge. But Wile E., attempting to follow, plummets into space. In another episode, he paints a tunnel onto a rock face, hoping that the Roadrunner will run into it and knock himself unconscious. Instead, the Roadrunner runs *through* the painted tunnel. When Wile E. tries to follow, he smacks himself flat against its surface. It is as if the act of painting a thing has made it real enough to bear the weight of the Roadrunner but not its author, in the same way that some traditions hold that telling a story may give it a life of its own.[2] In other variations on the false road, a truck comes out of the tunnel and flattens the coyote, or a train roars down the painted trestle and runs him over. The story has opened the road between our world and some other one, and now new things may come down it.[3]

The Coyote of legend has begun to make a magical realist appearance in late twentieth-century fiction. In Ursula K. Le Guin's novelette, "Buffalo Gals, Won't You Come Out Tonight?" Coyote, seen in a rare female incarnation, takes a lost human child into the dream-time world of the animals. The child, Gal, waking from a desert plane crash which has blinded her in one eye and killed the pilot taking her to her father, finds a coyote standing over her, talking to her. She follows it and soon begins to see the coyote as a woman with yellow-gray hair. Coyote Mother takes Gal into the desert where the animal people live and gives her the sight to see them as people and not creatures. They bestow on her an eye made of pine gum, parallel to a number of Coyote tales in which new eyes are made in this fashion, and perhaps it is this eye which lends her new vision. Chickadee becomes a round little woman with a black cap on her head; Horned Toad Child a pale, solitary playmate; Rattler a yellow-eyed dancer in a diamond-patterned cloak. In return, each animal sees Gal as a young member of his or her own particular species. They are quite aware that she is not. That is just that way that vision works, they tell her. To them, the places that humans inhabit appear as holes in the landscape, full of a white mist, inhabited by things unknowable.

Coyote's maternal instincts are no better than one would expect: her house is filthy and full of fleas, and she has sex with anyone, including her sons from previous litters (advising Gal not to have boys if she can help it). But she protects Gal, after her fashion, and feeds her, and when the child begins to yearn for the human people who are her own, Coyote goes with her. Coyote can see between the worlds, move between them, into the human places and out again, although often enough with a shotgun blast at her tail. On the edges of the human world, Gal's vision blinks between that of a human child and the sight of the animal people, but Coyote sees clearly. She just doesn't have any sense. Coyote never does. She finds the poisoned carcass of a lamb and, while Gal warns her not to, bolts down the bait, and dies in agony. It is Grandmother Spider who sends Gal back to the human world, telling her not to worry about Coyote. Coyote gets killed all the time, she says.

The Coyote of Christopher Moore's novel *Coyote Blue* personifies the protagonist Sam Hunter's need to go home to the country of his birth and become himself again. But because he is Coyote and not somebody's fairy godmother, his appearances are marked by upheaval and outrage. His first manifestation gets Sam thrown out of his condominium complex for harboring an illegal "dog." In this excerpt, the security chief, Spagnola, reads Sam his log book:

> "Nine A.M.: Mrs. Feldstein calls to report that a wolf has just urinated on her wisterias. I ignored that one. Nine oh-five: Mrs. Feldstein reports that the wolf is forcibly having sex with her Persian cat. I went on that call myself, just to see it. Nine ten: Mrs. Feldstein reports that the wolf ate the Persian after having his way with it. There was some blood and fur on her walk when I got there, but no wolf."
>
> "Is this thing a wolf?" Sam asked.
>
> "I don't think so. I've only seen it from below your deck. It has the right coloring for a coyote, but it's too damn big. [. . .] Okay. Ten fourteen: Mrs. Narada reports that her cat has been attacked by a large dog. Now I send all the boys out looking, but they don't find anything until eleven. Then one of them calls in that a big dog has just bitten holes in the

tires on his golf cart and run off. Eleven thirty: Dr. Epstein makes his first lost-nap call: dog howling. Eleven thirty-five: Mrs. Norcross is putting the kids out on the deck for some burgers when a big dog jumps over the rail, eats the burgers, growls at the kids, runs off. First mention of lawsuits."

"Kids? We've got her right there," Sam said. "Kids aren't allowed."

"Her grandkids are visiting from Michigan. She filed the proper papers." Spagnola took a deep breath and started into the log again. "Eleven forty-one: large dog craps in Dr. Yamata's Aston Martin. Twelve oh-three: dog eats two, count 'em, two of Mrs. Wittingham's Siamese cats. She just lost her husband last week; this sort of put her over the edge. We had to call Dr. Yamata in off the putting green to give her a sedative. The personal-injury lawyer in the unit next to hers was home for lunch and he came over to help." (48–49)

Coyote's appetites are always ravenous and his sexuality is not subtle. In Coyote stories, the penis is an organ capable of stretching to enormous length and is detachable to boot. There are numerous tales in which Coyote seduces females of all species, often borrowing someone else's penis to do so or taking off his own while pretending to be a woman. In one scene of *Coyote Blue* he becomes female and hands Sam his penis to hold. But with the exception of Le Guin's story, this transformation is generally a matter of trickery, and he reverts to his male persona.[4]

The issue of why Coyote is nearly always male is interesting. Hyde suggests that it may be because his creativity is non-procreative. "It should be noted that the trickster's fabled sex drive rarely leads to any offspring. Tricksters do not make new life, they rearrange that which is already at hand" (341).[5] So his sexuality serves another purpose, perhaps the same as that of fertility deities. He does not reproduce himself, but encourages others to do so. In addition he offers the chance to make trouble, and thus change, into the bargain. Hyde cites another story involving a transvestite marriage and a false vulva made of elk liver (221).[6] Certainly the exploding love affair is a Coyote gift. Thomas Moore says that "[i]t is the nature of sex, maybe its purpose, to blast some holes in our thinking, our planning, our moralisms—sex is life in all its boldness" (28).

As Hyde suggests, Coyote is neither the muscle-bound hero nor the ascetic male who "develops the muscles of self-restraint" (342). Like Richard Fariña's "Hard-Loving Loser," he is "the schoolyard failure who never kept his cool, went to flicks alone, and lost out all around, or nearly. Catching what he could, he practiced subtler arts than surfing, and mothers wondered why their daughters smiled" (album notes). Hyde calls him "the lithe and small-bodied escape artist, [who] doesn't win the way the big guys do, but [who] doesn't suffer the way they do either, and [who] enjoys pleasures they find too risky" (342). In twentieth-century terms, his sexual role is that of that perennial seducer of the female heart, the Bad Boy.

Yet because Trickster is defined by his duality, the other end of the Coyote character scale is that of world creator, preserver. In Moore's novel, Coyote proves to be the brother of Anubis, dog-headed god of the Egyptian underworld, not too far a departure from the legends which make him brother of Wolf. His purpose is to see that someone tells his stories and therefore keeps his people alive. Like Le Guin's Coyote, this one too dies at the end of the novel, this time to rescue a child who will be his next storyteller. Again we are given the clear hint that he will not stay dead.

Coyote figures as the creator of the world in a number of tales, and in Thomas King's novel *Green Grass, Running Water,* the origins of the Christian God are traced to one of Coyote's dreams, which just got a little out of hand:

> So, that Coyote is dreaming and pretty soon, one of those dreams gets loose and runs around. Makes a lot of noise.
>> Hooray, says that silly Dream, Coyote dream. I'm in charge of the world. [. . .]
>> "No," says Coyote. "You can't be Coyote. But you can be a dog."
>> Are dogs smart? says that Dream.
>> "You bet," says Coyote. "Dogs are good. They are almost as good as Coyote."
>> Okay, says that Dream. I can do that.
> But when the Coyote Dream thinks about being a dog, it gets everything mixed up. It gets everything backwards. [. . .]
>> I am god, says that Dog Dream.
>> "Isn't that cute," says Coyote. "That Dog Dream is a contrary. That Dog Dream has everything backward."
>> But why am I little god? shouts that god.
>> "Not so loud," says Coyote. "You're hurting my ears."
>> I don't want to be a little god, says that god. I want to be a big god!
>> "What a noise," says Coyote. "This dog has no manners."
>> *Big one!*
>> "Okay, okay," says Coyote. "Just stop shouting."
>> There, says that G O D. That's better.
>> "Now you've done it," I says.
>> "Everything's under control," says Coyote. "Don't panic." (1–3)

Here Coyote is portrayed as both creator and reshaper, of the world and of human destinies. He travels with four old Indians who appear periodically to "fix the world," including re-arranging old John Wayne movies so that the Indians win. Their fix is accompanied each time by a retelling of the world's origins, and, because Coyote can never resist dancing and singing just a little, some overwhelming natural disaster. Under their influence, a Black-foot Sun Dance ceremony gathers in a number of tribal members whose subconscious, like Sam Hunter's, knows they need to be there, whatever their conscious inclinations. And in a wry comment on the retelling of an already altered history, their voyage works its way through a 448-page pun on Columbus's discovery of a land previously quite adequately discovered by its inhabitants, involving a Nissan, a Pinto, and a Karmann-Ghia.

Similarly, the Coyote who appears in Charles de Lint's tales of urban fantasy, *The Ivory and the Horn,* inhabits those who feel the need to tell their story and the stories of their tribe and nation. Often enough it is under the influence of whiskey and desperation, getting drunk and picking a fight with a lamppost, too long gone from the reservation into a bleak city where things were supposed to be better and are not. But this Coyote makes a drum and a dancing circle and a fire, and in a while he has made community of the scattered vagrants and hookers and drunks who live on the tarnished edge of the city. And after he is killed in a knife fight in jail, the community is still there. Coyote makes trouble, but he made the world to begin with, and so he lives in the people of his creation.[7]

Coyote appears in multiple guises (again including that of God) in John P. Spivey's 1997 poem, "Coyote Genesis." Here he is first God, then Coyote, then the Snake, playing all roles interchangeably. In this account, God, or "whatever it [is]", gets bored:

> *So whatever it was became a brown coyote,*
> *Stopped for a moment to appreciate his form reflected*
> *In a nearby puddle,*
> *Farted twice,*
> *Licked his balls, then told the newcomers,*
> *"Don't eat that fruit," and trotted off.*

He then becomes enamored of his own penis, which becomes an emerald green snake, tells them to go ahead and eat the fruit, and then watches the results. Here and in King's novel, Coyote crosses into Christian mythology as easily as he absorbed the Egyptians' Anubis.

Old Man Coyote is never still. Duality is in his nature. Gerald Hausman calls his role that of "universal, creator, destroyer, rebuilder" (xix). Joseph Campbell assigns his power to the figure of the shaman, the free-lance mystic, more dangerous than members of the more orderly priesthoods (275). C. G. Jung calls him "an old river-bed in which water still flows" and assigns him the role of the collective "shadow," both bestial and divine, that human ability to achieve glory and ignominy simultaneously, knowledge of which "breaks up under the impact of civilization, leaving traces in folklore which are difficult to recognize" (142). (If we look, we may find him in the pyramid scheme, presidential sex scandals, and advertising.) Both the trickster and the tricked, both life and death, bringer of gifts and exploding cigars, he is the shape-shifter, the agent and personification of change. Neither good nor evil, he is simply that which is. According to Jung, "[a]lthough he is not really evil, he does the most atrocious things from sheer unconsciousness" [. . .] (144).

That ambiguous aspect makes him a difficult character for children's authors. Most mainstream picture books in which Coyote appears are retellings of traditional Native American tales, unfortunately simplified. Lost is the ambiguity of the mythological archetype. And lost is his role as world creator. His crudity, his sexual appetite, his vulgar behavior are all tidied up in the way that European fairy tales have been tidied. He is a clean coyote. Norman Williamson has suggested that adaptations of Native American stories by the dominant culture can only be successful (from the dominant culture's point of view) if they become "tales" which meet the criteria of the written literature of that culture (70). As Perry Nodelman argues, although many adults may laugh about vulgar subjects, and even accept their children's laughter,

> What they do not accept is the presence of such laughter within the narrow confines of children's literature. The relative silence of children's literature about such subjects is most significant simply because it reveals the often huge gulf between childhood as depicted in children's literature and the lives and interests of real children. [. . .] elimination has been eliminated, all evidence of animality and mutability has been eliminated, in order to satisfy an adult nostalgia for a supposed time of freedom from pain and limitation, a time of purity and innocence that never was. (108)

The sexual component of many unadulterated Coyote stories caused the first white people who heard them to label them as pagan and evil (Toelken 208), which is a short step from equating the trickster with the devil. And certainly the nostalgia of which Nodelman speaks leaves little room for the uncomfortable ambiguity of polytheism which Hyde claims a trickster tale requires (9–10).

In the picture book *And Me, Coyote!* by Betty Baker, rather than creating the world, he only helps World Maker to do so. When it is time to create man, all the animals try, each one attempting to make the man like itself, and succeed only in making a conglomerate creature that is ridiculous and useless. Then World Maker does it properly. This version strips its Miwok original (Dobie 267–69) of Coyote's creator role in favor of the vaguely defined World Maker, whom the illustrations portray as looking like man, only larger, much like the Old Testament God. Tom Pohrt's picture book *Coyote Goes Walking* is closer to the mythological Coyote. Here he remakes the world after a first failed world, tries to imitate the woodpecker to his embarrassment and discomfiture, and insults the spirit of Bull Buffalo through sheer bad manners. But there is very little of the trickster's ingenuity here. Closest perhaps is Jon Scieszka's *The True Story of the Three Little Pigs, by A. Wolf,* in which the Wolf explains how it was all just a mistake—he sneezed and that straw house fell down, and that poor pig was killed, and, well you can't just leave food lying around, can you? That's wasteful. This sounds like the true Coyote, even in this lupine guise. He is hungry, not benevolent, ambiguous in his intentions, prone to brag about his cleverness, and scornful of the pigs' stupidity. Whatever Scieszka's original intentions, he has achieved a true Coyote story.[8]

The Trickster element is the theme of Andre Norton's young adult book *Fur Magic,* and it too, has a contemporary setting, although it is less successful than Le Guin, King or Moore in its attempt to fit the wild world of Coyote into the world of Christian understanding, in which only one true god is allowed. Norton personifies Coyote as the Changer, the force which "turns the world over," ending the rule of animals, and beginning the rule of man. But Norton both gives this transformation the flavor of original sin—the animal people were truer, simpler, better—and at the same time portrays them as anthropomorphic in their wars, their tribes and alliances.

Of the Changer, the boy Cory is first told, "He never wanted things to be the same. It was in him to change them around." Left alone in the countryside, Cory meets the old Indian Black Elk, who speaks with an unfortunate movie-Indian grammar, but is ancient and powerful, full of knowledge of the old ways. For an inadvertent sin, Black Elk changes Cory into a beaver, to learn the ways of the animal people in the time before the world turned over.

In the course of his adventures, the beaver Cory must battle the Changer himself, a man/coyote to whom Norton has given *green* eyes as long as he stays in his half-human shape. The Changer is busily making a man from clay and making a bad job of it. He cannot make the clay take the right form and only achieves a properly molded man when Cory appears to serve as his model. Even then the head is only a ball, not a true human head. This Coyote is evil, and his intent is to enslave mankind to the animal people and to his own ends. He is thwarted in his attempt when Cory calls down the Thunderbird, who imposes on the Changer Coyote the will of what he calls The One Above—the only power great enough to create man. The Changer Coyote is left on his knees before the power of The One Above; and defeated, he loses all human aspect, becoming only a "great yellow-white beast who stood there. It was all animal, and the yellow eyes, the teeth from which his snarling lips curled away, promised only death" (169). We note here that, having lost all his human attributes, the Changer now has the coyote's properly yellow eyes. But this beast cannot cross the running water of the stream in which Cory hides, and so from its bank he promises Cory the things he wants most—return to his own form—and then threatens what he most fears—entrapment in the beaver form. Cory wins by shoving the Changer's medicine bundle into the sunlight, where the sun's rays destroy it and transform Cory to his own shape again.

Here Norton, like Baker, takes away Coyote's status as creator of mankind and gives it to The One Above, the only true god,[9] couching Cory's victory in the Christian symbolism of running water and sunlight. In doing so, Coyote trades his original role for that of a lesser avatar of Satan the tempter. This Christian overlay leaves us without true understanding of the nature of Coyote, who is not evil but only the agent of change; as Hyde says, not *im*moral but *a*moral (10).

It is mostly in the Coyote of the adult authors, except that of *Spiritwalk,* that he retains his original role as the incarnation of the wild lands, and thus his value to us. He is not a comfortable deity, which may have influenced Norton's urge to ally him with the forces of evil. But he is something we need. He does not fall in love, but he is powerfully sexual, another uncomfortable aspect which Norton, like Williamson's adapters and authors of folk tale retellings for younger children, chooses to ignore. He encourages procreation, the replenishment of the earth. He is Life, which, of course, contains Death. An archetypal trickster, he is the North American equivalent of Shiva, Lord of the Dance and balancer of the world. Both creator and destroyer, he thus fills a primal niche in our mythological subconscious, and it should not surprise us that, like *Canis latrans,* we cannot make him go away.

Notes

1. This article appeared in *Journal of the Fantastic in the Arts* (Vol. 10, Issue 1, Winter 1998) and is reprinted with the permission of the journal editors.

2. In one story Coyote creates the animals merely by naming them (Erdoes and Ortiz 90).

3. In an episode of *The Simpsons,* Homer Simpson goes to a chili cook-off and eats "Guatemalan insanity peppers," which appear to be a thinly disguised, and more politically and socially acceptable, substitute for peyote. The effect might best be described as Wile E. Coyote meets Carlos Casteneda. Homer finds himself transported to a surrealistic Southwest, where Coyote materializes to be his spirit guide. Find your true desire, Coyote tells him. When Homer asks if he should get rid of all his possessions, Coyote says, "Oh, no, you should get more of them," and bites him. In a bow to *Looney Tunes,* Homer's vision ends with being run over by a "ghost train" that materializes out of nowhere.

4. Coyote dons the guise which serves him. He also appears twice at crucial moments in *Coyote Blue* as a fat, white vacuum cleaner salesman.

5. There are a few tales in which Coyote has children. Hyde cites a Nez Percé story in which Coyote goes to the land of the dead to look for his daughter (83); in the Kwakiutl story "Always-Living-at-the-Coast," he marries and has a son (Erdoes and Ortiz 362); and Dobie records a Zuni tale in which he has a wife and many pups (297).

6. Joseph Campbell cites a story in which Coyote turns into a girl and actually does become pregnant (417).

7. Coyote as he appears in de Lint's long novel *Spiritwalk* is less successful than Le Guin's or Moore's or King's Coyote or de Lint's Coyote of "Coyote Stories." In *Spiritwalk,* he is a coyote-headed man, Whiskey Jack, one incarnation of the force who is Old Man Coyote, Anansi the Spider, Robin Goodfel-

low, and multiple other tricksters from world mythology. But de Lint endows his world of urban fantasy with so much overlapping magic that any real sense of it is lost. In this book everyone seems to have powers; enchanted talismans and magical portals litter the streets; goblins and elves sit under every bush. The heroine goes on study vacations in parallel dimensions with her tame Druidic bard. With this much magic floating about there is very little sense of wonder each time it appears, and Coyote becomes so diluted that he even falls in love, and pontificates about learning from one's mistakes. At that point he ceases to be Trickster. When the Bad Boy is domesticated, marries and settles down, we don't hear from him again. As Hyde says, "awakened conscience is the potential end of the narrative" (220–21).

8. Susan Lowell's *The Three Little Javalinas* is a straightforward retelling, given a Southwestern setting and Southwestern substitutions for pigs and wolf. Here Coyote is credited with "magic" that doesn't always work, but otherwise he is the traditional wolf of the original.

9. Most Native American traditions include the idea of a "Great Mystery Spirit" (one of a number of awkward and largely inaccurate translations for a concept of God), who is a force above all others, an ultimate creator. But they are rarely vain enough to insist that only this All-Powerful could create humans or the world as we know it. That is a task more often left to Coyote or other lesser avatars.

Works Cited

Baker, Betty. *And Me, Coyote!* Illus. Maria Horvath. New York: Macmillan, 1982.

Bierhorst, John. *Doctor Coyote: A Native American Aesop's Fables.* Illus. Wendy Watson. New York: Macmillan, 1987.

———. *The Mythology of North America.* New York: William Morrow, 1985.

Campbell, Joseph. *The Masks of God: Primitive Mythology.* New York: Viking, 1959.

de Lint, Charles. "Coyote Stories." *The Ivory and the Horn.* New York: Tor, 1995. 319–26.

———. *Spiritwalk.* New York: Tor, 1992.

Dobie, J. Frank. *The Voice of the Coyote.* 1949. Bison Books, 1961.

Erdoes, Richard and Alfonso Ortiz, ed. *American Indian Myths and Legends.* New York: Pantheon, 1984.

Fariña, Richard. "Hard-Loving Loser." *Reflections in a Crystal Wind.* Santa Monica, CA: Vanguard, 1966.

Groening, Matt, creator; written by Ken Keeler, directed by Jim Reardon. "El Viaje Misterioso de Nuestro Homer" ("The Mysterious Voyage of Homer"), *The Simpsons.* Production Code: 3F24, original airdate on Fox Television: Jan. 5, 1996.

Hausman, Gerald. *Tunkashila.* New York: St. Martin's Press, 1993.

Hyde, Lewis. *Trickster Makes This World.* New York: Farrar, Straus and Giroux, 1998.

Jones, Chuck, director. *Looney Tunes.* Burbank, CA: Warner Brothers, cartoon compilations, 1993.

Jung, C. G. *Four Archetypes.* Princeton, NJ: Princeton University Press, 1970.

King, Thomas. *Green Grass, Running Water.* New York: Houghton Mifflin, 1993; Bantam, 1994.

Le Guin, Ursula K. "Buffalo Gals, Won't You Come Out Tonight?" *Buffalo Gals and Other Animal Presences.* New York: Plume, 1988. 17–51.

Lowell, Susan. *The Three Little Javalinas.* Illus. Jim Harris. Flagstaff, AZ: Rising Moon, 1992.

Moore, Christopher. *Coyote Blue.* New York: Simon & Schuster, 1994.

Moore, Thomas. "An Erotic Way of Life." *The Sun* (June 1998): 28.

Nodelman, Perry. "Eliminating the Evidence." *Children's Literature Association Quarterly* 11.3 (Fall 1986): 106–08.

Norton, Andre. *Fur Magic.* New York: World Publishing, 1968.

Pohrt, Tom. *Coyote Goes Walking.* New York: Farrar Straus Giroux, 1995.

Scieszka, Jon. *The True Story of the Three Little Pigs, by A. Wolf.* Illus. Lane Smith. New York: Viking, 1989.

Spivey, John R. "Coyote Genesis." *The Sun* (January 1997): 15.

Toelken, Barre. *The Dynamics of Folklore.* Logan, UT: Utah State University Press, 1996.

Williamson, Norman. "The 'Indian Tales': Are They Fish or Fowl?" *Children's Literature Association Quarterly* 12.2 (Summer 1987): 70–73.

13

Rainbow Literature, Rainbow Children, Rainbow Cultures, and Rainbow Histories

The Chinese and Chinese American Adolescent Heroines in Laurence Yep's Selected Novels

Lingyan Yang and Zhihui Fang

Arguably the best creative artist in Chinese American children's and adolescent literature, Laurence Yep is important to the canon of contemporary American children's literature. Winner of numerous prestigious awards, Yep has authored more than forty novels, fantasies, and collections of folkloric fables. However, rigorous studies of Yep's remarkable accomplishments, especially of his creative literary style, his powerful integration of Chinese and Chinese American histories in his texts, and his enormous contributions to contemporary American multicultural children's and adolescent literature, are yet to be produced. What are uniquely Chinese, Chinese American, and American about Yep's writing? What kind of adolescent heroines and heroes, or *rainbow children,* has he portrayed? How has he reinvented the Chinese and Chinese American legends and myths to create a unique Chinese American aesthetics for children? What historical elements has he deployed and how? Why is Yep's work central to contemporary American multicultural children's and adolescent literature?

To answer these questions, we will utilize Asian American and Asian diasporic feminist cultural criticism (Yang) as we interpret Laurence Yep's making of the contemporary

Chinese American children's and adolescent literature. Specifically, we will analyze Yep's creation of the narratives on, about, or by the adolescent heroines in his novels, *The Serpent's Children, Mountain Light, Child of the Owl,* and *The Star Fisher.* We will particularly examine Yep's reinvention of Chinese and Chinese American legends, histories, and myths.

One hallmark of Yep's work is his masterful juxtaposition of gender, genre, culture, history, and storytelling. His work represents the pinnacle of what we call *rainbow literature:* colorful, stimulating, enriching, "heterogeneous, hybrid, and multiple" (Lowe, "Heterogeneous" 24). Our rigorous interpretation of his work simultaneously emphasizes the feminist consciousness, "the critical consciousness" (Said, *The World* 5), the aesthetic consciousness, "the historical consciousness" (White v), the multicultural consciousness, and "the political consciousness" (Mohanty 33). While reading Laurence Yep's Chinese American children's and adolescent literature through the feminist consciousness, we refer to the Chinese and Chinese American adolescent female narrators, narrative voices and protagonists, attending to how gender, power, and genre interreact to illuminate the girls' challenges of the multiple patriarchal social and symbolic orders.

"The critical consciousness" is borrowed from Edward Said, a leading contemporary cultural critic. It requires us to utilize contemporary critical cultural theories to emphasize rigorous critical thinking and to refuse reductionism in reading contemporary Asian American literature in the global context.[1] According to Etienne Balibar, a contemporary French Marxist philosopher, such a critical consciousness "combines philosophical reflection with historical synthesis, and [. . . attempts] conceptual recasting with the analysis of political problems that are more than urgent today" (1). We will use Hayden White's "the historical consciousness" because it allows us to articulate the complex and heterogeneous Chinese, Chinese American, and American women's histories, which we call the *rainbow histories,* and which contextualize Laurence Yep's writings, but especially his Chinese American historical novels for children. We are also interested in how his Chinese and Chinese American adolescent girls employ feminist narrative voices and subject formations that contribute directly to the reader's understanding of Chinese diasporic and Chinese American global feminist historical consciousness. Our aesthetic consciousness allows us to express our keen interests in presenting the complex and sophisticated materials embedded in Yep's skillful writing as he uses literary elements, styles, and rhetorical devices, such as allegory, symbolism, imagery, and metaphor. It also enables us to focus on Yep's reinvention of an array of Chinese and Chinese American legends and myths central to his creation of the adolescent female personae in his narrative voice. Multicultural consciousness is defined by our insistence on situating the readings of Yep's literature within the Chinese American, Chinese, and American multicultures, which we call the *rainbow cultures.* The multicultural consciousness is central to Yep's writing as well as to our reading of the *rainbow literature* of the contemporary Chinese American, Asian American, or American children's literature.

Finally, our "political consciousness," as defined by Chandra T. Mohanty, a postcolonial feminist critic, reflects our belief that no production or interpretation of children's literature is innocent or apolitical. We have not subordinated our literary criticism and appraisal of Yep's literature to rigid political dogmas. However, we cannot divorce reading Yep's texts from the larger contexts of Asian American cultural politics or from our understandings of the contemporary American racial, economic, sexual, ethnic, and transnational political dynamics that we believe have situated Yep's creative storytelling. We wish to demonstrate that Yep has fearlessly contested and unmasked the complex power relations and hierarchies of gender, race, class, ethnicity, and nationality found in contemporary society. Therefore, we read Yep's fiction as never innocent, always depicting remarkable rainbow children.

I.

> And once a serpent sets her mind on something, she doesn't give up—whether she's fighting or loving someone. (*The Serpent's Children* 18)

The Serpent's Children and *Mountain Light* are the first two historical novels from Laurence Yep's ambitious multigenerational "Golden Mountain Chronicles." The chronicles narrate the Young family's history of struggle and emigration from the Three Willows Village in China's Guangdong Province in the past one hundred and fifty years and follows their heroic immigration to and survival in the Land of the Gold in America. The chronicles include *The Serpent's Children, Mountain Light, Dragon's Gate, Dragonwings, Child of the Owl, Sea Glass,* and *Thief of Hearts.*

We choose to focus our historical analysis on *The Serpent's Children* and *Mountain Light.* We believe that Cassia Young, the adolescent girl-warrior heroine in these two novels, is one of Yep's most unique and unforgettable feminist characterizations. She is unusually fascinating in her representation of Chinese culture and history: antipatriarchal, anticolonial, antiracialist, and proemigration to America. Set in 1849, *The Serpent's Children* begins when Cassia is an eight-year-old Chinese girl narrator and protagonist; she is then cast as the teenage protagonist in *Mountain Light,* a story set in the half-colonial and half-feudal agrarian Three Willows Village, Guangdong Province, China, during 1855. Yep presents Cassia, her family, and her people in a sympathetic manner that significantly contributes to contemporary American multicultural children's literature. We believe that Yep's historical novels contain well-crafted intersections between literary representation and historical contextualization and between Chinese legends and historical details. Yep fictionalizes Cassia's life and ordeals in mid-nineteenth-century China *before* the Young family's immigration to America and *before* the birth of Chinese American children's literary tradition. As Laurence Yep himself emphasizes, he begins the "Golden Mountain Chronicles" with these two historical novels because Cassia's stories provide the familial, local, national, and global historical pretext and context for the Young family's "love affair with America:"

> Most books of that time viewed the evolution of Chinese Americans from either the Chinese side or the American side, but I wanted to do both. Through the Young family, I tried to show how rebellions, wars, and famine in China forced many to make the dangerous voyage to America. ("Author's Note" unpaged)

Yep's deliberate and skillful juxtaposition of literature and history is one of the most significant aesthetic achievements in his historical novels for children. Yep seamlessly interweaves everyday events and storytelling in *The Serpent's Children* and *Mountain Light,* using an enormous amount of historical background of nineteenth-century China. To the readers who are unfamiliar with Chinese history, these historical events will appear extremely difficult and challenging to comprehend. However, relating this historical knowledge about "the rebellions, wars and famine in China" is so important to Yep that the American-born Chinese American author himself spent a lot of time and energy researching them "to discover my identity as a Chinese" (Afterword, *The Serpent's Children* 276). Therefore, we will interpret Yep's aesthetic accomplishments in his style, examining his utilization of legends, metaphor, symbolism, and myth and his effective characterization of his feminist young protagonist while explaining clearly the key historical knowledge needed to supplement the youthful reader's understanding.

In both novels, Laurence Yep carefully reinvents the legend of the White Serpent to signify Cassia Young's distinctive feminist consciousness and her feminist resistance against all forms, institutions, and techniques of patriarchy in nineteenth-century Chinese women's history. "The Legend of the White Serpent" was originally a popular Chinese traditional folkloric legend that has been frequently adapted in numerous Chinese opera forms, such as in *Peking Opera* (Wu et al. 107; Siao and Alley 80–83). Yep reconstructs the melodramatic romantic love story between the white she-serpent and the young scholar of Xu Spirit and turns it into Cassia's favorite "talk-story" (Kingston 19) from her deceased mother. He emphasizes the quintessentially feminist archetypal image and metaphor of the White Serpent, who is beautiful and loving, yet still fiercely strong and independent. Thus, Yep's reinvented legend nurtures Cassia to be who she is and empowers her to battle against all obstacles, such as patriarchal oppressions, British colonialism, poverty, and the loss of family members.

The legend of the White Serpent enables Yep to effectively characterize Cassia Young as a feminist girl warrior in *The Serpent's Children* and a young "woman warrior" in *Mountain Light*. The White Serpent boldly claims her existential legitimacy, her right to live, and her right to love. She believes that she is equal to humans in spirit, emotion, and strength. She refuses to allow the ultramoralist and ultrapatriarchal Buddhist monk master, whom Yep changes into a religionless priest, to categorize her as a species inferior to human beings or unfit to marry Xu Spirit. Yep arms his young protagonist, Cassia, with this imagery so that readers will believe she can heroically resist the patriarchal politics, practice, and institution of foot binding forced on her by her senior relatives in the village after her mother's death:

> Aunt Patience's palm cupped Lily's foot. "It's shaped just like a lotus blossom, delicate and perfect [. . .] Every man will turn to stare at you as you walk by on feet as dainty as Lily's [. . .] It's you and I who walk like buffalo, not like real women."
> I still found it hard to believe that my uncle and aunt intended Lily's fate for me. "But I want to be able to go for long walks and to run," I shouted. (43–44)

Yep skillfully reshapes the White Serpent legend so that his protagonist Cassia can use this story to counter the oppressive social, sexual, and symbolic apparatus of foot binding utilized to control, dominate, police, and confine Chinese female sexuality. Cassia achieves this through refuting the foot-binding metaphor of the "lotus blossom." Yep's young heroine despises the "delicate and perfect" imagery of the "lotus blossom" because it produces the problematic "ideal" Chinese femininity and reduces the female social and sexual identity to the metonymy of the deformed body part of bound feet. She refuses to deform, denaturalize, or destroy her natural female body into an object of male perverted erotic desire or a public sexual spectacle. Cassia, thus, refuses to let the patriarchal ideology of foot binding confine her social space strictly to the three inches of domesticity. With feet bound, girls or women cannot run away from male control. Yep's Cassia wants "to be able to go for long walks and to run." She demands total freedom. She is determined to control her own destiny and formulate her own female identity.

By allowing his protagonist to see the irony of this practice, Yep forcefully unmasks the foot-binding metaphor of the "lotus blossom" as merely employed to control women's bodies and imprison women within the assigned patriarchal sexual, social, and symbolic power hierarchy. Beneath the façade of the visually exquisite and sexually pleasing metonymy of the "lotus blossom" lies the brutal foot-binding sexual politics of systematically restricting women's movement to performing the domestic functions of cooking, cleaning, reproducing, and satisfying men's erotic appetites. Yep's protagonist vigorously battles against the violent technology of patriarchal power and its meticulous maintenance procedures, which require many years of grotesque and consistent binding, deforming, bone breaking, rebinding, unbinding, and brainwashing of little girls. Cassia refuses from day one to be bound.

Yep skillfully introduces the legend of the White Serpent, showing the war of the sexes between the heroic white serpent and the tyrannical evil monk master. In Yep's telling, the Buddhist monk master propagates his ascetic, asexual, and institutionalized religious dogma to dictate and censor love, erotic or platonic, between an ordinary human of Xu Spirit and the fantastic White Serpent. The White Serpent summons her army of ocean creatures with her power of the feminine hereditary magic and wages war against the monk master's masculine orthodox magic. Passionately claiming her freedom of love, of sexuality, and of being an independent female self, the White Serpent fearlessly battles the monk master to liberate her husband, who is imprisoned in the Temple of the Golden Mountain, and to reclaim her captured serpent's child.

Inspired by the tale of the White Serpent's legendarily strong willpower and magic, the eight-year-old Cassia publicly wages her own war against the violent metaphor and brutal practice of foot binding:

> "You can't do this to me!" When I fell down, I began to scramble on my hands and knees into the courtyard.
>   I let out one shrill scream of horror and frustration and scratched, kicked, hit and bit her. And I can't describe the satisfaction I felt when I heard the matchmaker shriek. (*The Serpent's Children* 46–47)

Yep's portrayal of this mid-nineteenth-century Chinese girl as a warrior image defies the Euro-American stereotype of adolescent girls as victims who are saved by charming princes in shining armors. Such characterization also refutes the Euro-American stereotype of Chinese and Chinese American adolescent girls as the demure, obedient, and exotic Oriental porcelain dolls. Cassia's body, emotion, spirit, and soul are not bound to these things. Like the action heroine of the White Serpent in the legend, Yep effectively uses a series of action verbs to depict Cassia as relentless in her resistance against the collective coercive forces that would bind her feet, her tongue, and her spirit. Interestingly, Cassia not only fights against her senior male relatives or patriarchs but also "scratched, kicked, hit and bit" the village females who are agents in the foot-binding process. Thus, Yep consciously critiques the complex and problematic female complicity with, participation in, and implementation of the very patriarchal power structures in Chinese women's history.

Yep reinvents the legend of the White Serpent not only to create the feminist metaphor to empower Cassia to resist the sexual and social institution of foot binding in mid-nineteenth-century Southern China. The literary legend also enables Yep's heroine to bridge symbolically the Chinese feminist history and Chinese American feminist history for the contemporary audience of the rainbow children of Asian American, American, and world constituencies.

Hybridizing the worlds of the serpents and humans, the serpent's baby child in the legend allegorizes Yep's own Chinese American hybrid authorial cultural identity and symbolizes his making of the unique, new, and hybrid literary tradition of Chinese American children's literature. Yep also reinvents the name and image of the serpent's husband and father to the serpent's child from Xu Spirit to a nameless "wanderer." In fact, Yep frequently uses such Asian American male sojourner protagonists in exile as central images in his Chinese American children's literature. Such archetypal wanderer personas appear in the legend of the Owl in *Child of the Owl* and in his title fable of "The Rainbow People" in *The Rainbow People.*

The Temple of the Golden Mountain remains in both the original and Yep's legends the primal location for the war of sexes between the resistant feminist white serpent and the patriarchal and self-righteous Buddhist monk master. However, Yep deliberately and acutely makes visible the pun of the "Temple of the Golden Mountain" to signify the Golden Mountain of America as the future destiny of Foxfire, Cassia's younger brother and another serpent's child (*The Serpent's Children* 17). The Temple of the Golden Mountain also symbolizes the literary significance of Yep's reinvented feminist legend of the White Serpent in Asian American children's literature.

In both historical novels, Laurence Yep characterizes Cassia Young not only as the feminist and antipatriarchal serpent's child empowered by her mother's "talk-story" of the legend of the White Serpent but also as a girl martial artist and an anti-British-colonial patriot like her father, Gallant. Gallant is a master of martial arts and a revolutionary in the anticolonial and anti-Manchu-rule peasant uprising called the Taiping Rebellion. As a diligent, disciplined, and excellent pupil of Gallant in the martial arts, young Cassia champions in the alleged masculine discipline and distinguishes herself as a more capable martial artist than her fragile younger brother, Foxfire. Although Cassia is a loyal believer and supporter of the anticolonial rebellion just like her parents, the rebellion "Work" is supposed to be her father's territory and another male-dominated discipline. Cassia learns to fight to love like the White Serpent and to love to fight like her father. Yep's positive portrayal of Cassia in these historical novels deconstructs the fiction depicting Chinese and Chinese American girls as "the second sex" (de Beauvoir):

[. . .] But I could feel the old familiar resentment welling up inside me whenever the subject of my sex was brought up. It's one thing for a woman to do all sorts of heroics in a story; it's quite another for a girl to practice the martial arts with the boys—and beat them. (*The Serpent's Children* 99)

On numerous occasions Yep depicts young Cassia as a precociously responsible protector and savior—though she is sometimes vulnerable—of her family, her clan, her friends, and even her men. As Cassia's dying mother commands at the beginning of *The Serpent's Children:* "Your brother and father [. . .]. Their minds are so busy walking in the clouds that their feet would trip over the first pebble if we weren't there to guide them. [. . .] You are the strong one. Take care of them" (34–35). Immediately, eight-year-old Cassia becomes the emotional center and nurturer for her men. She is often the only farmer in the family's fields, the breadwinner, and economic provider for the household. When Dusty comes from neighboring feuding Phoenix Village to challenge Cassia's Three Willows Village, it is little Cassia who stands up to help her father defend the honor of her clan. As Gallant praises her in front the villagers, "My daughter's a better warrior than any of you" (97). When the Manchu soldiers are chasing Gallant and Cassia, the daughter fights with her father until he dies in her arms (*Mountain Light* 43–49). In times of famine, when Cassia's own fellow villagers in Three Willows Village try to persecute her "stranger" (*kejia*) friends, Tiny and Aster, simply because of their cultural differences, it is Cassia again who fights to help her friends escape (166–67).

It is obvious that Yep depicts Cassia's Chinese adolescent femininity not only with her domestic and private love for her family, herself, and her body—like her beloved, strong, and selfless mother—but also with his heroine's masculine commitment to her country, her people, and her clan—like her anticolonial patriotic father—in the public history of Chinese nationalism. Thus, Yep's feminist portrayal of Cassia blurs the very dividing lines between femininity and masculinity, between private and public discourses, and between the supposedly local and feminist resistance against foot binding and the assumed national and masculinist rebellion against British colonialism.

Meanwhile, Yep complicates Cassia's relationship with her father by having Cassia recognize the paradoxes and contradictions of Gallant's "gendered," "classed," and "racialized" anticolonial and anti-Manchu revolutionary legacies (Lowe *Immigrant Acts* 1–36). Gallant's seemingly sacred nationalist "Work" remains a problematically male-dominated, male-privileged, and exclusively male patriarchal institution despite its patriotic and decolonization politics. For example, the Young women, both Cassia's mother and Cassia, share the same nationalist ideal of ridding China of both the barbaric British colonial "demons" and the barbaric Manchus (*The Serpent's Children* 2). However, only the Young men are eligible to participate in the nationalist "Work." Although Cassia is not allowed to share the hype of anticolonial glory in its beginning, she still has to shoulder the burden of nurturing and sustaining the broken, disillusioned, and bitter men like Gallant after the failure and bankruptcy of his politics of nationalism.

Yep also portrays Cassia's disillusionment with the gendered truth of the sexually unevenly divided domestic labor within Gallant's anticolonial nationalist enterprise. As often the only laboring force in the family's fields, the Young women—little Cassia and her mother—provide material stability and economic possibilities for Gallant's costly dream of revolution and Foxfire's dream of Golden Mountains. Yep critiques this sexual inequality with humor and poignancy: "'Why did Heaven give men such strong backs and such weak minds if they hate to work?' I grumbled. Aster shrugged and went back to her hoeing. 'You forget that Heaven also gave them sisters and wives'" (*The Serpent's Children* 121). When the men in the Young family are gone to be busy revolutionaries, little Cassia farms their crops, feeds Foxfire, and keeps the family together, especially after her mother's abrupt death. Gallant returns as the defeated rebel, and he resumes his position of authoritative patriarch and master of martial arts.

Yep further deepens his feminist characterization of Cassia by linking her own sexual victimization by the sexual/social institution of foot binding with her critique of father's "racialization" (Lowe *Immigrant Acts* 14) by the British colonial white supremacy. The barbaric British colonial "demons" bring guns, which are a white Eurocentric phallic symbol that signifies white colonial political, military, economic, and sexual power that Cassia and her father resist. Father's "crippled" limp after his return symbolizes the crippled and disabled masculine apparatus of mid-nineteenth-century Chinese nationalism by the British white racialist masculine capitalist colonialism (*The Serpent's Children* 101). Yep places Cassia's negotiation with her father's anticolonial legacy within the context of the historical aftermath of the first Opium War (1839–1842), which is the colonial war between resisting Manchu imperial China in Qing Dynasty and the nineteenth-century global colonial power of Great Britain. Cassia's family struggle realistically chronicles Chinese history. Britain leads numerous Western powers in the nineteenth century to try to colonize China in the name of "opening her" to the Western Enlightenment ideals of capitalism, modernity, progress, science, technology, and democracy.

In the eyes of little Cassia, Gallant's grand nationalist slogan of the double missions of anti-British-colonial and anti-Manchu-minority rule reflects the profound irony of Chinese nationalism as a racialized history of betrayal and failure. Isolated from the popular lives, needs, and support of the people, Gallant's elitist revolutionary cause is misunderstood, dismissed, or publicly mocked by the very villagers he attempts to protect. Cassia tells how the British colonial guns have ironically disarmed her father's impotent revolution and caused her father's anxiety, symbolizing the literary metaphor of white penis racially castrating Gallant's native Chinese spear of resistance on the Chinese native soil. Yep's literary representation of Cassia Young's complex antipatriarchal, anticolonial, and antiracialist Chinese adolescent feminist subjectivity in mid-nineteenth-century China in the two historical novels, thus, provides the transnational historical pretext and context for the formation of the Chinese American female adolescent immigrant subjectivity later in America.

Yep's feminist historical consciousness is also reflected in the metaphor of "the light" in the title of *Mountain Light*. He transforms "the light" *from* Gallant's *nationalist metaphor* for the Chinese mandarin ethnic absolutist rule *to* Cassia's inclusive *humanist metaphor* for "the light . . . coming from each of us" (*Mountain Light* 270). Yep uses Cassia as his voice to demonstrate that the "light" in *Mountain Light* and in Gallant's Chinese nationalist slogan of "restoring the light" "is more than a pun on the name of an old dynasty, just as the Darkness is more than a pun on the name of the Manchus. There is a whole world of darkness around us that's trying to put out the Light in each of us" (23).

With such humanistic rethinking, Cassia critiques the complex national interethnic power struggles and conflicts between the ruling Manchu minority in Qing Dynasty and the mandarin or Han majority and reflects on the limits of the multiple local tribal feuds and relations. Gallant's obsessive "Work" to "banish the darkness" of Manchu minority rule is symptomatic of a popular collective desire for the political norm of majority rule in the form of Chinese ethnic absolutism and ethnic chauvinism. Such nationalism condemns and demonizes the nomadic, ethnic, and conquering Manchu as not Chinese enough and mobilizes its majority citizens, such as Gallant, to drive the Manchu out of the "imagined communities" (Anderson) of the nation of China. Yep's layered metaphor of "the light" contrasts further with the economically dark times of drought and famine and forecasts the bright emergence of the global myth of America as the Golden Mountain represented by Cassia's younger brother, Foxfire.

Laurence Yep further utilizes the humorous food symbolism of Cassia's "weed soup" to depict realistically the extremely difficult economic and historical conditions that Cassia and her family endure during the time of famine in mid-nineteenth-century southern China: "'But it's all so tasty.' Father stuffed a spoonful of weeds bravely into his mouth and proceeded to chew it with immense enthusiasm" (*The Serpent's Children* 150–51). Yep's effective and comical food symbolism foreshadows the historical pretext for the birth of the myth of the Golden Mountain of America and the genesis of Chinese emigration pursued by Foxfire, who is dissatisfied by this bleak socioeconomic life style of the weed soup in Three Willows Village. This soup, consisting of the tasteless and nonnutritious wild weed boiled in water, meets Cassia's and Gallant's "immense enthusiasm." However, such humor cannot overcome the bitter reality of poverty in the lives of Cassia, her family, and her people. Although the Young family has been farming rice for generations, Cassia laments that her family can only afford to eat weeds in the time of drought and famine. "As I gathered weeds and ferns, it was maddening to think of the rice we had grown but were unable to keep" (148). The excessive eating of "weed soup" results in starvation and death in the village. Cassia witnesses Peony, another teenage girl in the village, being sold by her family to the brothels so she can survive (154). Cassia, her father, and the whole clan are further disheartened when her father's revolutionary comrade, Spider, turns into a bandit who loots, threatens, and robs her already starving family and clan. Historically, poverty was caused by the socioeconomic consequences of the Opium War, taxes for the corrupted imperial Qing government, and natural disasters such as drought and famine. Are there better alternatives of survival than the "weed soup" for Cassia's family and people?

Yep's social and symbolic alternative to the "weed soup" for Cassia's family is to allow Cassia's brother, Foxfire Young, to take a chance with the new myth called the Golden Mountain of America. Yep creates a vividly hilarious moment when the mythical "gold of the mountain" in Foxfire's daydreams turns into the shocking reality of power in the twenty strings of gold he sends home. The whole village festively celebrates such deliciously golden surprises. Golden Mountain is no longer a foolish alien fairy tale. It becomes a metaphor of hope: "Whether they actually took the risk or not, the golden mountain was something that gave them new hope in the middle of their misery—like people trapped inside a black cave who suddenly see a little pinpoint of light" (*The Serpent's Children* 255).

Yep depicts the myth of the Golden Mountain as an economic alternative to the extreme poverty for Cassia's people and implies that there could be possibilities of prosperity and survival in America. Indeed, "emigration therefore became not just a means to a better life, but a lifeline" (S. Chan 8). Yep also turns the Golden Mountain across the Pacific into a political alternative to Gallant's failed nationalist revolutionary dreams. As Cassia sees it, the Golden Mountain myth symbolizes for Foxfire an active engagement with the Enlightenment history of modernity in the West. As a forced alternative to Chinese nationalism, feudalism, poverty, and Western colonialism, Chinese emigration brings Third World natives like Foxfire and Third World histories closer to the metropolitan center of Western empires like America and closer to the very thought of the Western master historical discourse of modernity.

The myth of the Golden Mountain is not simply an Asian American myth. It is, first and foremost, a Chinese myth born out of and deeply rooted in mid-nineteenth-century Chinese social, historical, political, and economic contexts. In Yep's novels, the myth of the Golden Mountain as the literary metaphor for the history of Chinese emigration perhaps signifies that modernity is no longer a historical monopoly of the West. Rather, with the eager and active participation of Chinese emigrants out of China and Chinese American immigrants into America to begin an Asian American history, modernity becomes a hybrid and global historical consciousness. Therefore, on one hand, the Golden Mountain myth symbolizes the profound, forced, and unwilling transformation of modernity of the Chinese natives and Chinese emigrant laborers in Yep's historical novels. On the other, the very histories of modernity and America are simultaneously and profoundly transformed by the new makers and participants, such as Foxfire, of the myth, and by the very native Third World national and local histories and memories that these Chinese American immigrants bring transpacifically to their new home. The birth of the myth of Golden Mountain also marks the genesis of Chinese American literary, cultural, political, economic, and intellectual histories, which we call the rainbow histories. Curiously, the historically significant myth of Golden Mountain is as much a masculine institution as is Chinese nationalism. Once again Cassia and many Chinese girls or women are prevented from actively and legitimately participating in it. Ultimately, Foxfire's voyage to America is still a gendered alternative to his father's gendered nationalist predicament.

One of the unique and significant literary achievements of Yep's two historical novels is his epical realistic portrayal of Foxfire and the Chinese American laborers' historical transpacific emigrant "voyage out" (Woolf) of China and immigrant "voyage in" (Said) via sea to the Golden Mountain of America. Yep achieves this by juxtaposing Cassia's feminine narrative voice with the masculine stories and narrative voice in the letters sent home from America by her Pacific-crossing men—first Foxfire Young, her younger brother in *The Serpent's Children,* then Squeaky Lau, her boyfriend in *Mountain Light.* Using the first-person narrative, Yep effectively describes the violent bath forced on emigrant laborers aboard the ship:

> Suddenly a team of sailors took up the hose while another group gathered around a pump and began to work it [. . .].
> Water suddenly spurted from the hose. The column played down the line too fast for us to dodge. It felt like someone had struck me in the chest, and when I gasped, I took in a mouthful of saltwater. I began to choke. (200–01)

Yep's passionate representation of the epical transpacific immigrant voyages of Cassia's men as well as all heroic Chinese American emigrant laborers (*kuli*) in these two historical novels is significant because it is one of the first in Chinese American, Asian

American, and American literature. It also represents another perspective of American history. Yep recovers and reconstructs the symbolic voices of Cassia's men, who paid high prices and overcame an enormous amount of hardship and suffering to follow their dreams of coming to America. Their historical transpacific voyage is long and turbulent. But eventually they were triumphant. Cassia and we the readers learn that these men have endured hunger, racial abuse, disease, storm, fights, starvation, boredom, loneliness, and above all, the threat of death. Yep realistically depicts racial beating and whipping by the British or American sailors aboard these ships of dreams, something that historically was as frequent and random *during* the voyages as the survivors of the cross-Pacific Asian American voyage will encounter, endure, and counter *after* they have docked in America.

What Lisa Lowe calls the "proletarianization" of Asian American laborers did not start after they landed in the capitalist, racialist, and masculinist America (*Immigrant Acts* 15). Rather, it started in the half-colonial and half-feudal mid-nineteenth-century China, where peasants or farmers were driven from their land and were driven out of possibilities of survival by the multiple political economic forces. Such proletarianization certainly continued during the Chinese emigrant kulis' transpacific voyages on the ships. Its injustice simply intensified and accelerated after the Chinese American immigrant laborers entered the American economic labor market in the mid-nineteenth century.

At the end of the epical journey crossing the Pacific, Cassia's men—Foxfire and Squeaky—are portrayed by Yep as the new Chinese Americans. They decide that America is still their new destiny and home despite all the hardships endured. These Chinese men's heroism, optimism, and hope for a better future in the new land of America finally triumph over racism, exploitation, and a bumpy voyage. Planting the seeds of the Chinese and Chinese American myth of the Golden Mountain firmly on the beautiful land of America, Foxfire and Squeaky diligently and shrewdly participate in the American myth of opening and claiming the "virgin soil" of the American western frontier in California (*Mountain Light* 218). Simultaneously, they begin writing a new chapter in the distinctively Chinese American literary and historical traditions by participating in building the Chinese American "new communities" (Chinatown) Yep fondly and humorously translates as the "Tang People's Town" (*The Serpent's Children* 213–17).

The Chinese American literature and history, thus, begin.

II.

I didn't have to be just like a Chinese owl. I could be like an American one too. (*Child of the Owl* 214)

In *Child of the Owl* and *The Star Fisher,* Laurence Yep deftly constructs the new and unique Chinese American adolescent female immigrant subjectivity in Casey Young and Joan Lee as he retells the Chinese legend of the owl and the legend of the star fisher. Both legends function as allegories of the "between-the-worlds" (Ling) Chinese American immigrant experience of Casey and Joan, Yep's two adolescent female narrators and protagonists. The child of the owl and the child of the star fisher in the legends hybridize and mediate between the seemingly foreign mystical worlds of owls/star fishers in the sky and the very ordinary human secular world. They also allegorize the contradictions that American-born Casey and Joan must negotiate between the Chinese cultures of their families and the American culture that surrounds them. The fantastic settings of the jungle of owls and the sky of the star fisher fairies who fish for the stars allegorize the Chinese culture, the ethnic home Casey and Joan must reconnect with through family stories and mythic representations. As the stories evolve, Casey and Joan learn that their Chinese heritage can be powerful in its intangible imagery, even though the Chinese culture is fantastic yet distant like the owl's jungle or the star fisher's sky in the legends.

Neither Casey nor Joan has the powerful or beautiful wings of an owl or star fisher. However, their magical wings of language combined with imaginations often soar high as they metaphorically journey into the sky of freedom, cultural understanding, and hope. Their creativity, coupled with their enormously rich cultural heritages, effectively remedies their cultural displacement. This new self-awareness contrasts sharply with their lack of material goods. Despite the racial, economic, and linguistic disfranchisement by the mainstream structures of race, class, whiteness, and capitalism in America, Laurence Yep's two adolescent Chinese American girl narrators/protagonists are empowered by storytelling. By the end of both books, the protagonists, like the author himself, claim their access to and mastery of the symbolic discourses of the Chinese, American, and Chinese American cultures. These girls transform the traditional Chinese stories and storytelling into Chinese American children's literature while they are being simultaneously transformed. Although Casey and Joan are fictionalized adolescents, the images that Yep has created embody and celebrate the productive Chinese American cultural identity formation within American society.

Our reading of Laurence Yep's construction of Casey's and Joan's Chinese American female adolescent subjectivity fits the powerful conceptualization by Lisa Lowe, a leading Asian American cultural critic, on the "racial formation," "gender formation," and "class formation" of the Asian American adult immigrant subjectivity (*Immigrant Acts* 1–36). According to Lowe, *racial formation,* a term borrowed from Michael Omi and Howard Winant, refers to the American nationalist political, legal, and racialist ideology, which categorizes Asian Americans as the racial "Other" in American-white-bourgeois-middle-class citizenship and nationhood and as racial aliens who cannot, should not, and do not melt in the pot. In Yep's *Child of the Owl,* the vivid image of "the dream soul" of "the walker," who is father to the child of owl and wanders miserably on earth, allegorizes the cultural displacement and uprootedness of Barney, Casey's father. Such a persona also mirrors the homelessness of the Chinese American sojourner male laborers in general. Joan Lee, the Chinese American girl narrator/protagonist in *The Star Fisher,* vigilantly resists the alienating gaze of whiteness in her school and the predominantly white middle-class community of Clarksburg, West Virginia:

> As we were changing, Ann glanced at me. *"You're a little dark, aren't you?"*
> I blinked, looking down at the back of my hand, and suddenly realized that she wasn't referring to my tan but to my skin color. *"You're a little pale, aren't you?"* I shot back. (58–59)

Yep also enables his adolescent female protagonists to learn of the painful "gender formation" (Lowe *Immigrant Acts* 14) and "emasculation" (Chin et al; Chan et al; Chan;

Cheung) of their fathers, Barney and Mr. Lee. According to Lisa Lowe, such "gender formation" of Asian American immigrant masculinity is the materialization of its "racial formation" or racialization (*Immigrant Acts* 12). Yep represents this when Barney and Mr. Lee, like other Asian American immigrant male laborers, are reduced to the roles of femininity in the racially exclusionary American labor market. Barney is deprived of performing the masculine role as breadwinner because the white American employers would only offer jobs to Casey's mother, Jeanie, but not to him (108). Thus, Barney's joblessness for ten years causes him to give up hope and surrender to gambling. Similarly, Mr. Lee in *The Star Fisher* is engaged in the typically feminized profession of the laundry business despite his scholastic training in China prior to his immigration to America.

Yep's literary representation of the gendering or the "racial castration" (Eng) of Chinese American masculinity particularly allows Casey and Joan to link the personal misfortune and marginalization of their fathers and their individual families to their relearned Chinese American history, which is both racialized and gendered. Such historical knowledge is central not only to Casey's and Joan's reconnection with the past history of their fathers and with the past history of the Chinatown community but also to the formation of their own individual adolescent Chinese American cultural identities. Moreover, it allows the readers to historicize and contextualize Yep's powerful stories of Casey's and Joan's remarkable journeys.

Yep's acute literary representation of Mr. Lee's and Barney's racialized sexual politics of effeminization is neither isolated nor accidental. It is based on Yep's firm grasp of the history of the officially institutionalized racialization of Asian American men and women by American exclusionary immigration laws. According to Judy Yung, a leading Asian American feminist historian, the American exclusion of Chinese men started with the Chinese Exclusion Act in 1882, which was the first discriminative immigrant law in American legal history. This exclusionary immigrant act "bans immigration of Chinese laborers to the United States and prohibits Chinese from becoming naturalized citizens; repeated in 1943" (Yung 424). Additionally, Chinese American women have been systematically excluded in the American 1924 Immigrant Act, which led to the production and maintenance of the bachelor Chinatown society. In *Child of the Owl*, Casey learns from old Mr. Jeh's difficult reminiscence that such historically racialized exclusion of Chinese men and women alike has led to the painful formation of the bachelor Chinatown society as well as the sexual dysfunction of her community. The emasculation of Barney, Mr. Lee, and Mr. Jeh is directly materialized by their social and racial outcast positions in the membership of American citizenship. Thus, Casey and Joan learn more of their Chinese American individual selves through learning the racialized and gendered histories of their fathers, their families, and their communities in the racially hostile environment.

Yep's depictions of the extreme poverty that Casey, Joan, and their families endure in the 1960s and 1920s also indicates that a conception of their "class formation" (Lowe) is central to our understanding of their Chinese American adolescent female subjectivity. The hilarious, sad, yet vivid image of "the lettuce sandwich," which Joan and her siblings "crunched . . . noisily" also symbolizes Joan's agonizing yet successful confrontation with poverty in America (*The Star Fisher* 52–62), a land that is far from being the mythical dreamland of the Golden Mountain or melting pot. Both Casey and Joan learn that being

Chinese American means being poor. The jungle of the "dream-soul" of the father of the child of owl metaphorically represents a Darwinist America where an adolescent protagonist must face her family's struggle to survive either in the California Chinatown or in a West Virginia white neighborhood. Both young women must learn to identify with their culture and to recognize the potent Chinese imagery that can sustain their survival. Yep depicts, in violently graphic details, the extreme starvation, the loss of a job, the loss of souls, and death through the owls' vengeful black magic. His duality in representation allows him to allude to the real brutality and terror found in the American economic disenfranchisement of Chinese Americans. However, these Chinese American children of owl and star fisher are reshaped by the allegorical tales they hear. Thus, they learn to survive with strength, courage, furious imagination, and above all, love. Even young Casey and Joan confront the capitalist bourgeois class stratification and the realistic material sufferings of the lack of everything: food, electricity, shelter, clothes, and equal opportunities in America. Such harsh economic conditions of poverty result from the unevenly developed economic logic of the American nationalist capitalism, functioning to mark the Chinese American immigrants as not only the racial and sexual "Other" but also the naturalized and assigned economic outcast from the nation's white middle-class communities.

Yep's fictional narratives powerfully illustrate that the female adolescent Chinese American heroines never live in the traditional Euro-American bourgeois fairy tales. Nor do they fit the "Orientalized" (Said) Euro-American fantasies or stereotypes of Chinese antiqueness, timelessness, and harmony. Rather, they are the girl warriors like Casey and Joan, who must, in their early consciousness and subject formation, battle against cultural disenfranchisement, racial discrimination, gender hierarchies, and economic deprivation to reaffirm a cultural identity of courage and heroism.

Furthermore, Laurence Yep not only enables his young female protagonists to mediate with their paternal/masculinist narrative patterns of the "racialized," "gendered" and "classed" immigrant reality in the American present but also successfully reconnects his female protagonists with the symbolic orders of their maternal/feminist Chinese cultural heritages. The owls' jungle and the star fishers' sky show Casey and Joan that an enriching maternal lineage of recovered legacies can derive from their mothers (Jeanie the owl and star fisher), their mothers'/Other tongue (Chinese), and their mother culture (Chinese culture). The owl's mother Jasmine parallels Jeanie, Casey's mother. Casey and the readers can see the similarities between the legend of the owl and her own family dynamics in a fantastic narrative of the talk-story narrated by Paw-Paw, Casey's maternal grandmother.

Dualism is emphasized as Yep weaves the fantastic legend into Casey's first-person narrative of her contemporary experience. These maternal/feminist cultural heritages and symbolic discourses are equally characterized by paradoxes as the girls' paternal/masculinist ones. For example, the retelling of Jasmine's jungle of the owl and the star fisher's sky allegorize Chinese culture: fantastic and wonderful on one hand, yet remote and unreachable on the other. These complex mythic signs are as enchanting, mysterious, and estranging to the children of owl/star fisher on earth in the legend as the cultures of China (and Chinatown) are simultaneously empowering and alienating to Casey and Joan. The songs of the mother owl and the mother star fisher are paradoxically as incomprehensible to their owl/star fisher–human hybrid children as Jeanie's and Mrs. Lee's mother tongue of Chinese is alien or discomforting to the Chinese American Casey and Joan. Furthermore, the allegorical owl's world is just as imperfect and complex as the jungle world of the "dream-souls" on the earth associated with the walker/Barney and Casey's Chinese American family and community. There is sibling rivalry, disrespect for the aged owl, desertion, and contradictorily, love. Yep allows his readers a glimpse into the confusing messages of both empowerment and imperfection through the legends of owl and star fisher. Casey and Joan are invited to find out the layered truth of their unique female adolescent Chinese American subjectivity as they listen to the talk-story. They can then name and claim their simultaneous Chinese and American cultural homes, just as the children of owl and star fisher can feel comfortably at home both on the earth and in the sky. The final return of Jasmine and the star fisher to their home of the free sky parallels the symbolic and cultural returns of Casey and Joan both to their maternal cultures in Yep's semiotic reconstruction of a distinctive Chinese American hybrid cultural identity formation. As Yep beautifully states, "And suddenly I knew how the star fisher's daughter must have felt: belonging to both the earth and the sky, she must have seen everything through a double pair of eyes" (*The Star Fisher* 72).

The legends of the owl and star fisher allow Yep to take his readers into their subjective reawakenings. They function through the semiotic network with rich imagery and illuminating allegories that take Yep's audience to the very "cultural locations" (Bhabha) where Casey and Joan boldly enunciate their simultaneous cultural belongings at the end of their journeys. Yep's use of narrative talk-stories of owl and star fisher allow him to pinpoint his young female protagonists' needs for confrontation with the mainstream culture and their Chinese heritage. As Casey and Joan learn to recognize the impossibility of escaping the question of their dualistic identity, they rediscover themselves. As they interact with the legends, Yep's female adolescent protagonists learn to articulate their cultural dislocation, linguistic displacement, and emotional isolation and find the joyful possibilities of belonging to both their maternal fantastic Chinese heritage from the past and the realism of their American present. Yep places both fantasy and reality into the worlds of Casey and Joan and allows them to translate the legends of owl and star fisher into their own tales of Chinese American cultural mediation. Yep's careful use of legend within his realistic descriptions of prejudice and difference suggests that Chinese American culture can be inclusive, respectful, and economically successful.

III.

Our analysis suggests that Laurence Yep's work embodies the very essence of what we have called the *rainbow literature:* colorful, powerful, creative, and humanist. As Yep himself states in the preface to his "Golden Mountain Chronicles," "These books represent my version of Chinese America—in its tears and its laughter, its hunger and its fears, and in all its hopes and dreams" (*Dragonwings*). Yep's writings represent the authorial attempts to negotiate with his "Chineseness" (*The Lost Garden* 110) and the rainbow cultures, as do his fictional Chinese and Chinese American adolescent heroines. The creative stories and writing processes enable Yep to grapple with his own contradictory and perplexing identity of being a hyphenated American who is too American to be accepted by the Chinatown "old-timers" and too Chinese to fit anywhere else. Yep's fictional characters are typically created from the people in his community, parts of himself, and his extended family. His use of the first-person narrative in these texts particularly allows the creative artist to "settle into [the] character" (*The Lost Garden* 106). Yep acknowledges that he gains an immense sense of satisfaction and empowerment as he stitches together, in innovative and striking ways, the bits and pieces of "rags" that constitute his unique self (91–92). Therefore, in reading Yep's work, it is important for readers to understand the lived experiences of the author and of those of Asian Americans in general. Readers are reminded that Yep's Chinese and Chinese American stories are almost always about the remarkable rainbow children and rainbow people he encounters, those who often struggle, with dignity, courage, fortitude, and resourcefulness, to survive in the bottom ladder of the "racialized," "gendered," and "classed" societies. Like his colorful fictional personas in the imaginary worlds, Yep discovers that his rainbow people and his Chinese, Chinese American, and American rainbow histories are as heterogeneous, multiple, and diverse as the stories they have nurtured (Afterword, *The Serpent's Children*). Yep acknowledges his ethnic and working-class roots in his engaging memoir, *The Lost Garden:*

> [Our family's] grocery store [. . . gave] me my first schooling as a writer [. . .] Because of the people I met in our store, I came to have little patience with stories about rich and wealthy people. Even before I began selling what I wrote, I was trying to tell stories about characters who survive at a basic level; and now when I look for folktales to tell, I usually look for stories about ordinary people rather than princes and princesses. (28–31)

We advocate a multidimensional approach to reading and interpreting Yep's literature, one that emphasizes simultaneously the feminist consciousness, the critical consciousness, the aesthetic consciousness, the historical consciousness, the multicultural consciousness, and the political consciousness. Our analysis demonstrates that Laurence Yep's texts demand careful, informed, and critical readings because of their complex, rich, creative, and unique nature. In order to genuinely understand and appreciate Yep's work, readers must be equipped with multiple contemporary literary and cultural theories, including feminism, Asian American and Asian diasporic cultural criticism, Marxism, and postcolonialism. Readers are also encouraged to pay close attention to the social, historic, economic, cultural, and political contexts within which Yep's work is situated. Such an approach is both productive and empowering. It allows readers to delve deeply into Yep's work, thereby uncovering themes, issues, and techniques beyond regular plots that would otherwise go unnoticed in superficial readings. Moreover, readers can better appreciate Yep's artistry in literary creation as well as his significant contributions to American multicultural children's literature and to Asian American literature.

The proliferation of "multicultural curriculum" in the past two decades highlights the prominent role multicultural literature plays in the education of our youngsters, the rainbow children. Despite the popularity of multicultural books in the school curriculum, teachers are often ill prepared to engage their students in critical reading and aesthetic appreciation of literature (Fang, Fu, and Lamme). In fact, contemporary pedagogical practices have tended to treat multicultural and multiethnic literature, such as Yep's work, as disembodied texts primarily for the purpose of contextualizing ethnicity within the teaching of traditional reading and language arts skills. As a result, students often do not understand the multiple subjectivities, discourses, and power structures encoded in the multicultural work they read. Nor do they learn to appreciate the true significance of the literary style, devices, and elements in such work. Thus, the production and consumption of multicultural/multiethnic literature in effect function to confirm and perpetuate hegemonic discourses. In the end, what began as a promising and benevolent movement in education has, beyond its well-intended rhetoric, served to reinforce racial stereotypes, cultural hegemony, and social fragmentation. In order to truly realize the goals of multicultural education, it is imperative that teachers are trained to embrace, as well as practice, a pedagogy that promotes students' development of multiple consciousness and perspectives. More specifically, we should, in our reading of multicultural/multiethnic literature, strive to answer Paula Gunn Allen's call for simultaneously "attending to the actual texts being created, their source texts, the texts to which they stand in relation, and the otherness they both embody and delineate" (314). Such a pedagogy has the potential to foster a new generation of informed, thoughtful, and critical readers.

Note

The four title concepts of "rainbow children," "rainbow literature," "rainbow histories" and "rainbow cultures" are inspired by Laurence Yep's *The Rainbow People*. Collaborating on this article, Lingyan Yang wrote the title, the theoretical conceptualizations, introduction, and parts 1 and 2. Zhihui Fang wrote part 3 on pedagogical implications. Both participated in proof editing. We thank Jill May and Darwin Henderson for their guidance and comments.

Works Cited

Allen, Paula Gunn. " 'Border Studies': The Intersection of Gender and Color." *Introduction to Scholarship in Modern Language and Literatures.* Ed. J. Gibaldi. 2nd ed. New York: The Modern Language Association, 1992: 303–19.

Anderson, Benedict. *Imagined Communities: Reflections on the Origin and Spread of Nationalism.* London and New York: Verso, 1983.

Balibar, Etienne. Preface. Etienne Balibar and Immanuel Wallerstein. *Race, Nation, Class: Ambiguous Identities.* London and New York: Verso, 1991.

Bhabha, Homi. *The Locations of Culture.* New York and London: Routledge, 1993.

Chan, Jeffery Paul, et al., eds. *The Big Aiiieeeee!: An Anthology of Asian American Writers.* New York: New American Library/Meridian, 1991.

Chan, Sucheng. *Asian Americans: An Interpretive History.* New York: Twayne Publishers, 1991.

Cheung, King-kok. *Articulate Silences.* Ithaca and London: Cornell University Press, 1993.

Chin, Frank. "Come All Ye Asian American Writers of the Real and the Fake," in Chan et al. *The Big Aiiieeeee!: An Anthology of Asian American Writers.* New York: New American Library/Meridian, 1991.

De Beauvoir, Simone. *The Second Sex.* Trans. H. M. Parshley. New York: Knopf, 1952.

Eng, David L. *Racial Castration: Managing Masculinity in Asian America.* Durham and London: Duke University Press, 2001.

Fang, Zhihui, Danling Fu, and Linda Lamme. "The Trivialization and Misuse of Multicultural Literature: Issues of Representation and Communication." *Stories Matter: The Complexity of Cultural Authenticity in Children's Literature.* Ed. D. Fax and K. Short. Urbana, IL: National Council of Teachers of English, 2003: 284–303.

Kingston, Maxine Hong. *The Woman Warrior.* New York: Vintage, 1976.

Ling, Amy. *Between Worlds.* New York: Pergamon Press, 1990.

Lowe, Lisa. "Heterogeneity, Hybridity, Multiplicity: Marking Asian American Differences," *Diaspora* 1.1 (Spring 1991): 24–44.

———. *Immigrant Acts: On Asian American Cultural Politics.* Durham, NC: Duke University Press, 1996.

May, Jill P. *Children's Literature and Critical Theory.* New York and Oxford: Oxford University Press, 1995.

Mohanty, Chandra Talpade. "Introduction: Cartographies of Struggle: Third World Women and the Politics of Feminism." *Third World Women and the Politics of Feminism.* Ed. Chandra Talpade Mohanty, Ann Russo, and Lourdes Torres. Bloomington and Indianapolis: Indiana University Press, 1991.

Omi, Michael and Howard Winant. *Racial Formation in the United States: From the 1960s to the 1990s.* 2nd ed. New York and London: Routledge, 1994.

Said, Edward. *Culture and Imperialism.* New York: Knopf, 1993.

———. *Orientalism.* New York: Vintage Books, 1978.

———. *The World, the Text, and the Critic.* Cambridge, MA: Harvard University Press, 1983.

Siao, Eva and Rewi Alley. "The Story of the White Snake." *Peking Opera: An Introduction through Pictures.* Peking: New World Press, 1957.

White, Hayden. *Metahistory: The Historical Imagination in Nineteenth-Century Europe.* Baltimore and London: The Johns Hopkins University Press, 1973.

Woolf, Virginia. (1948). *The Voyage Out.* New York: Harcourt Brace.

Wu, Zuguang, Huang Zuolin, and Mei Shaowu. "The White Snake." *Peking Opera and Mei Lanfang: A Guide to China's Traditional Theatre and the Art of Its Great Master.* Beijing, China: New World Press, 1981.

Yang, Lingyan. "Theorizing Asian America: On Asian American and Postcolonial Asian Diasporic Women Intellectuals." *Journal of Asian American Studies* (June 2002): 139–78.

Yep, Laurence. *Child of the Owl.* New York: Harper Trophy, 1977.

———. *Dragonwings.* New York: Harper Trophy, 1975.

———. *Mountain Light.* New York: Harper Trophy, 1985.

———. *The Rainbow People.* New York: Harper Trophy, 1989.

———. *The Serpent's Children.* New York: Harper Trophy, 1984.

———. *The Star Fisher.* New York: Puffin Books, 1991.

Yung, Judy. "Appendix: A Chronology of Asian American History." *Making Waves: An Anthology of Writings by and about Asian American Women.* Ed. Asian Women United of California. Boston: Beacon Press, 1989.

14

"If You Give a Nigger an Inch, They Will Take an Ell"

The Role of Education in Mildred D. Taylor's Roll of Thunder, Hear My Cry and Let the Circle Be Unbroken

Cicely Denean Cobb

In *Song of the Trees,* Mildred D. Taylor first introduced the Logan family. Like Virginia Hamilton, Taylor relied on both social and psychological realism to depict how Blacks attempted to survive in the racist South, circa 1930. She explored such themes as racism, poverty, and family resilience. It is in *Roll of Thunder, Hear My Cry,* and *Let the Circle Be Unbroken* that Taylor highlighted a fourth theme—the Logan family's emphasis on formal and informal education. Encoding education as a primary concern in southern Black families, Taylor's fiction became the first children's literature family saga to address the role that education would take in twentieth-century African American culture. Furthermore, Taylor showed her readers Black adult attitudes about the formal lessons children learn at school and compared them with the informal ones they learned from their elders and neighbors. Taylor was the first African American children's writer to address the importance of this theme. I wish to review the historical realism of Taylor's work, briefly identify the literary roots of her writing, fully discuss *Roll of Thunder, Hear My Cry,* and suggest the relevant subplots in *Let the Circle Be Unbroken* that continued Taylor's emphasis on social and psychological realism.

In his poignant autobiography, *Narrative in the Life of Frederick Douglass,* the Black abolitionist notes his slaveowner's sentiments regarding Blacks and education: "If you give a nigger an inch, they'll take an ell" (45). One hundred years later, the vast majority of southern Whites continued to adhere to the same doctrine. As historian James D. Anderson states in *The Education of Blacks in the South, 1860–1935,* it was difficult for a significant number of southern African American men to achieve an education. Their parents sharecropped; southern society expected that Black boys would also partake in the humiliating cycle (79). Black male adolescents' education revolved around picking cotton and other farm tasks. If some African American boys were able to seek a formal education, it was usually a limited one (55). White northern philanthropists became interested in educating the southern Negro and stated that their primary goal was to "challenge racism," but they fostered its growth by demanding that Black formal education adhere to the doctrines of the Hampton-Tuskegee model (55).[1] This so-called "right" way of educating African Americans benefited Whites by providing them with a "sound investment in social stability and economic security" (79). Thus, a vast majority of these students were incapable of achieving well-paying jobs. Despite gaining education, Black males remained "good field hands" (81). Mildred D. Taylor's series shows that Black males were educated for manual labor.

The Logan men were modeled after Taylor's paternal relatives. While living in Mississippi, Mr. Taylor endured psychological pain from social injustice.[2] Formal education was not an option for him; work would be his key to social and economic mobility. An emphasis was placed on his informal education. This knowledge was derived from the daily experiences of life as a southern Negro. Throughout the Logan series, Mildred D. Taylor suggests that southern Black men who were from her father's generation probably benefited more from informal education than from formal education. These Black men used a wealth of "plain common sense" as they faced prejudice and attempted to survive in such a "racist culture" (Crowe 8).

Within the saga, Taylor demonstrates the importance of education to the southern Black family, and she openly acknowledges the role that Black women played in education. Mary Logan emphasizes the need for her children to receive a formal education. As noted in *The Road to Memphis,* Mama wishes to have each of her children receive the "best education they could afford," and she states, "Sacrifices are necessary in order for children to receive a good education" (36). Throughout the series, Mary Logan is linked to formal education, whereas David Logan is linked to family education.[3] Papa Logan teaches his family that they should be watchful of both present conditions and past episodes that have shaped their experiences. They must have a "wary eye upon the present, but yet another turned toward the past" (Smith 246). The parents' roles suggest a sexual difference in educational possibilities.

Although Mary Logan claims that she and David want each of their children to take the "ell," it becomes evident that the elder Logans view Cassie as their family's future. The boys—Stacey, Clayton, Chester, and Christopher John—are urged to attend school. In *The Road to Memphis,* Mama is outraged when Stacey quits high school in order to work at a box factory. Cassie states that Mama "gone 'round and 'round with Stacey about staying in school" (57). Yet, Mary allows Stacey to leave school because she knows that her sons will be able to fall into their father's footsteps. For the Logan boys, if formal education is not achieved, they will have their legacy to fall back on—the Logan land.

Taylor alludes to the sexual realities of heritage and change through the Logan land, which is not an option for Cassie. Again, Taylor's series reflects the realities of southern history. Although Papa claims that a portion of the land is hers, Mary and Big Ma realize that

Cassie's future lies away from rural Mississippi. Thus, Taylor is true to southern history in her depiction of females and education. In *What a Woman Ought to Be and to Do,* Stephanie J. Shaw argues that, during this era, the only options that were available to the vast majority of Black women were marriage and/or domestic work and teaching (5). Aware that marriage "unequivocally limited women to the home," a small percentage of African American women sent their daughters away from the South in order to receive a formal education (47). They called on the "known" and "unknown" to assist them with their plight (47).

Taylor's adolescent series also fits with earlier fiction written by Black females. Over the years, African American women have been acknowledging this need for formal training and independence in their fiction. For instance, in 1973, Toni Morrison published *Sula.* Morrison, like her literary foremother, Zora Neale Hurston, centers her text on mother–daughter discourse. In her 1939 masterpiece *Their Eyes Were Watching God,* Zora Neale Hurston constructs a conversation between her protagonist, Janie Crawford, and Janie's grandmother, Nanny. Nanny informs Janie that, as a former slave, she was not granted the opportunity to explore "what a woman oughta be and to do" (15). Thus, the Black grandmother is motivated to "take a broom and cook-pot" and "throw up a highway through de wilderness" for Janie (15).

Thirty-four years later, Morrison describes the influence that matriarchs have on their daughters. Critics often focus on the friendship between Sula Peace and Nel Wright—two girls who "come from extremely different family environments"; however, one of the most important relationships found in *Sula* is the protagonist's relationship with Eva and Hannah, her grandmother and mother. It is from these women that Sula learns not to allow herself to be restricted by race, gender, and economics (Taylor-Thompson 706).

In *Sula,* neither Eva nor Hannah stresses formal education to Sula. Instead, the women teach Sula a lesson about what would be detrimental to her development—motherhood. Children have prevented both women from fully developing their selfhood. Motherhood prevented Eva from leaving the Bottom; Hannah, unlike the Old Testament figure, did not desire to become a mother.

Years later, Eva recalls her prior actions and urges Sula to embrace a maternal role:

> "When you gone to get married? You need to have some babies. It'll settle you."
> "I don't want to make somebody else. I want to make myself."
> "Selfish. Ain't no woman got no business floatin' around without no man. [. . .] You need. [. . .] I'm a tell you what you need." (92)

Sula silences her grandmother: "I don't want to make something else. I want to make myself" (92). In ways similar to Hurston's Janie, Sula is able to discover what it means to be colored and a female on her own terms. These women wrote for an adult audience. Taylor's writing addresses these same issues for a younger audience.

In *Roll of Thunder, Hear My Cry* and *Let the Circle Be Unbroken,* Mildred D. Taylor demonstrates the influences that grandmothers and mothers have on their daughters. After reading these novels and Chris Crowe's analysis of Taylor's works, one realizes that Big Ma is modeled after Taylor's maternal grandmothers—the "wise ones"; Mama is modeled after Taylor's mother, whom she describes as "the quiet, lovely one, who urged perseverance" (qtd. in Crowe 26). Thus, Taylor fictionalizes her personal experiences in these novels. She shows how limitations prevented the elder Taylors from accomplishing their goals; they relied on Mildred Taylor to execute them through her education and writing. Taylor reveals how both Big Ma and Mama—two women who were denied the full chance to "bloom"—rely on Cassie, their "strong-willed, plain-spoken and full of energy" granddaughter/daughter, to reject her "fallen dead" role in order to become the "tree" that refuses to be moved (MacCann 95).

In a sense, Cassie becomes these women's—and Taylor's—mouthpiece. This is especially important when looking at Big Ma. Her own daughter died in infancy. Thus, she was unable to preach the "great sermon" to her. Cassie is essential to her. Both of Cassie's matriarchs realize that without an education, Cassie will "have few economic alternatives" (Shaw i). Cassie's two educations enable her to believe that "regardless of the limitations that others might impose on her (due to her race, class, and sex), none of these conditions necessarily determined her ability and aspiration" (i). Cassie's education will allow her to pass a legacy on to her daughters—and she will show them "what [they] ought to be and to do" (3). The roots of their training will allow Cassie to survive, even when she leaves the South.[4] Taylor's young heroine becomes educated and independent within the series, and she is able to define a new position for educated African American women.

A small minority of Black southern women hoped that their children would receive a formal education, especially those female workers who had daughters, in opposition to a statistically significant number of African American women who believed that their daughters, too, would embark on the endless cycle of Black female drudgery. Black mothers who advocated for female emancipation from America's "controlling images for black women" (Collins 45–67) wished to see their daughters formally educated in either the North or the South. Furthermore, some southern African American women used their "community work" as the means to foster the "black women's activist tradition" (143).[5] In 1980, Bonnie Thornton Dill studied domestic workers and their children, and she noted that some southern Black domestics and field laborers viewed their work as enabling their daughters to strive for opportunities that appeared to be unobtainable. Taylor's fiction reflects this urge for formal education found among a small group of southern Black women.

Over the years, scholars have questioned Mildred D. Taylor's motive for writing the Logan family series. When considering the historical events that occurred around the time that *Roll of Thunder, Hear My Cry* was published—events such as busing and school integration that had a tremendous impact on African American children—as well as Taylor's personal childhood, it should be no surprise that Taylor saw the need to create positive images of African Americans who overcame racial adversity as they strived for equality. Taylor had faced a number of racial problems while growing up. At age 8 (the same age as Cassie Logan), Mildred D. Taylor experienced her "first lessons about racism" (Crowe 117). Crowe writes:

> As a young child, she always loved her family's regular trips to Mississippi, viewing the trip itself as a 20-hour picnic. Later, she realized that her mother packed food to take along in the car because after they left Ohio, they wouldn't be allowed to eat in "White Only" restaurants. She realized that they drove straight through because they wouldn't be allowed to stay in "White Only" hotels or motels along the way to Mississippi. She learned that the police stopped her father in the South not for speeding or any other traffic violation but for being a black man driving a nice new car. She saw the signs, "White Only, Colored Not

Allowed" over restroom doors and drinking fountains. On her trips to Mississippi she learned much about her family and her heritage, but she also learned about racial discrimination in the South. (117)

Taylor experienced similar problems when her family took a trip to California. Because they were traveling to the West Coast, Taylor assumed that her family would endure fewer racial problems. She was "partially right" (118). Although the Taylors "saw no signs barring 'Coloreds' from businesses," they were not allowed to stay at certain hotels and restaurants. That trip taught the ten-year-old Mildred D. Taylor that for "black Americans second-class citizenship was not restricted to the South" (118).

Mildred D. Taylor's juvenile fiction accurately records her experiences and memories and emphasizes that Black women were intent on gaining formal education while maintaining informal family education within their southern Black society. In *Roll of Thunder, Hear My Cry,* Mildred D. Taylor explores the lessons that she learned both at school and at home, allowing the Logan children, but especially Cassie, to receive similar treatment.

Cassie is a winsome protagonist who serves as Taylor's astute female narrator.[6] The novel details one year of the Logans' traumas living as a strong and loving African American family in rural Mississippi during the times studied by Anderson and Collins. She aptly shows that southern Black families understood the importance of informal and formal education. When placing Cassie in scenes with her male siblings, Taylor alludes to the differences in male and female perceptions of education. Taylor contrasts Little Man's obsession with his appearance with Cassie's practical attitude. When the children are running late to school, Cassie warns them about the repercussions of being late:

> "You keep it up and make us late for school, Mama's gonna wear you out," I threatened, pulling with exasperation at the high collar of the Sunday dress Mama had made me wear on the first day—as if that event were something special. It seemed to me that showing up at school at all on a bright August-like October morning made for running the cool forest trails and wading barefoot in the forest pond was concession enough; Sunday clothing was asking too much. Christopher-John and Stacey were not too pleased about the clothing or school either. Only Little Man, just beginning his school career, found the prospects of both intriguing. (4)

The student body is composed of children who are needed in the fields from early spring until the cotton is picked. Thus, Great Faith "adjusts its terms accordingly beginning in October and dismissing in March" (16). Each academic year, the student enrollment diminishes.

Cassie's mother is an outsider in this community, and she is outspoken about Black education. Her daughter is also assertive, as is noted in the incident involving Miss Crockett and Little Man. During Cassie's altercation with Gracey Pearson and Alma Scott, one senses that the protagonist's sassiness has caused her to be reprimanded on more than one occasion. When Miss Crockett overhears the girls' argument, Taylor writes, the "yellow and buckeyed fourth grade teacher glares down [at Cassie . . .] with a look that say Soooo, it's you, Cassie Logan" (18). Miss Crockett's other nonverbal gesture—the pursing of her lips—signals that she is exasperated at having Mary Logan's rebellious daughter as her student. Taylor shows regional differences between Cassie's mother and the other teachers when

Cassie refuses to join in unison with her classmates and say, "Yes'm, Miz Crockett" (20). A third incident confirms the teacher's disgust with Cassie's informal upbringing. Miss Crockett announces that each student will receive a textbook. The readers are from the White elementary school. Immediately, Cassie realizes that Little Man is going to be displeased with the conditions of his primer:

> I glanced across at Little Man, his face lit in eager excitement. I knew that he could not see the soiled covers or the marred pages from where he sat, and even though his penchant for cleanliness was often annoying, I did not like to think of his disappointment when he saw the books as they really were. But there was nothing that I could do about it, so I opened my book to its center and began browsing through the spotted pages. (22)

Unsurprisingly, Little Man informs the instructor that the book is "dirty" (23). Taylor's more mature narrator comes to her brother's defense, establishing that Cassie is her siblings' deliverer. Within the confines of the school, Cassie is learning to speak out for what is right, and she is learning the consequences when she does or does not voice her concerns.

In terms of informal education, the Logan children are taught "Caucasia 101" by their parents, Big Ma, and Mr. Morrison. The elders educate them about the ordeals that both their family and neighbors have endured. The various lessons that the children are taught range from the family's rich history to the hardships that are associated with being Negro (e.g., inequality from social institutions—"the judicial system, health and law enforcement agencies"), and that Blacks should not befriend Whites (MacCann 94; Crowe 124).

Although the children have been educated about the consequences that occur when a Black person does not remain in his or her place, none of them has personally dealt with the blunt force of White brutality. While in Mr. Barnett's store, it is Cassie, not her brothers, who is reminded of her subordinate state:

> After waiting several minutes for his return, Stacey said, "Come on, Cassie, let's get out of here." He started toward the door and I followed. But as we passed one of the counters, I spied Mr. Barnett wrapping an order of pork chops for a white girl. Adults were one thing; I could almost understand that. They ruled things and there was nothing that could be done about them. But some kid who was no bigger than me was something else again. Certainly Mr. Barnett had simply forgotten about T.J.'s order. I decided to remind him and, without saying anything to Stacey, I turned around and marched over to Mr. Barnett. (110)

Taylor's main character reacts as any child would if faced with a prejudicial incident. However, when Cassie attempts to inform the storeowner of his error, he reminds Cassie that she is nothing but someone's "little nigger" (11). Despite the fact that her family has owned land in Spokane County for over fifty years, Cassie is merely a child whose mother needs to remind her of her place within southern society.

In *Let the Circle Be Unbroken,* Taylor continues to describe how Cassie is motivated to discover where the "ell" will take her. This novel, like *Roll of Thunder, Hear My Cry,* exposes the Logan family's trials and tribulations. The year is 1934. Taylor focuses on how Cassie Logan, now ten years old, is growing wiser about the ways of the world, especially the "discriminatory world of Mississippi" (Crowe 73). Mildred D. Taylor is more concerned with Cassie's growing awareness of "institutional racism" in *Let the Circle Be Unbroken*. The central drama is T.J. Avery's trial and execution. From that event four subplots evolve: the Blacks' involvement with the AAA, the reunion between Mary Logan and her nephew Bud Rankin, Miss Lee Annie Lees's desire to vote, and Stacey's disappearance. Of the four, the subplots that have the greatest impact on Cassie's development are her relationships with Bud and his daughter, Suzella Rankin, and Miss Lee Annie's desire to vote. These are the events that separate her from the "naïve, innocent" young girl who is found in *Roll of Thunder, Hear My Cry*.

Shortly after T.J.'s trial, Cassie is introduced to Mama's nephew, Bud Rankin. Cousin Bud resides in New York. He is a welcome addition to the Logan family until he reveals that Lydia, his wife, is Caucasian. It is at this moment that Cousin Bud distinguishes himself from the rest of his family. To the Logans, Whites are best left alone. Cassie's statement further summarizes her family's sentiments on Black/White relations. Cassie explains that Papa has told her, "When they entered our lives, they were to be treated courteously, but with aloofness, and sent away as quickly as possible. Besides, for a black man to even look at a white woman was dangerous. A year and a half ago Mr. John Henry Berry had been burned to death, killed for supposedly flirting with a white woman, and his uncle, Mr. Samuel Berry, who tried to defend him and his brother, had lain like a charred log until he had died a few months ago" (162). Befriending a White woman was a dangerous act in the South; marrying one was unthinkable.

Eventually, Cassie meets Cousin Bud's daughter, Suzella. Through her biracial cousin, Cassie becomes aware of the notion that Black beauty is inferior to whiteness. Cassie watches as the boys and grown men boast about Suzella's beauty and listens as her mother explains the history of skin preference:

> Oh, it goes back a long way. We've been taught so long to think we're less than anybody else, many of us have grown to believe it, in some ways if not others. And a lot of us figure the lighter we are, the better we are [. . .] like white people. (254)

Through her association with Suzella, Cassie learns about a concept that is affecting African Americans: passing. Passing is an "act of crossing the socially constructed 'color line' that separates white and black Americans" (Wald 560). Taylor's 1981 novel for young readers introduced her audience to the problems with "passing" and intermarriage for Black women and men. Thus, she opens a conversation not earlier found in adolescent literature.

Within Cassie's relationship with Miss Lee Annie Lees, Mildred D. Taylor addresses the tactics that were once used to prevent blacks from voting.[7] Taylor incorporates this historical event as the background that is needed to discuss Cassie's and Miss Lee Annie's unique relationship. She foreshadows the ideal of Black vote in the South when she introduces Russell, Miss Lee Annie's grandson. Russell is a private in the U.S. Army.[8] He believes he should be allowed to vote because he has served in the army.

By using each of these events—Miss Lee Annie Lees's desire to vote and Russell's ability to serve in combat and inability to vote—Mildred D. Taylor pinpoints how racial discrimination of that time continued to suppress Blacks. Again, Taylor introduces ideas not found in children's and adolescent literature by showing that although White discrimination had been diminished, it was not eradicated. The author uses Miss Lee Annie to comment on how African Americans lost some of the opportunities that were gained after the Civil War. Miss Lee Annie tells Cassie, "My papa voted. Said it was a right fine feeling. He voted and he didn't know no law at all 'ceptin' that he was a free man and a free man could vote. [. . .] I's sixty-four years old [. . .]. And this old body wants to vote" (195–96). In a sense, Miss Lee Annie is preaching *her* great sermon. Although Miss Lees's audience is Cassie, Big Ma, and Mama, it is Cassie who the elderly neighbor wants to "respond" to her "call." Miss Lee Annie seeks the right to vote. When her link to the past is thwarted, Cassie—as the future—must seek and gain suffrage.

Throughout the series, Mildred D. Taylor uses motifs and symbols that are prevalent in Black Aesthetics. For instance, she has a quilting session occur in mid-April, and it is here, in the traditional place of Black women, that Miss Lees announces her plans to vote. This is also during a time associated with Easter and the dawn of spring (rebirth). That April, Miss Lee Annie experiences an awakening in "[her] old age" (196). Most importantly, it is a female descendant rather than a male one who undergoes a rebirth. Miss Lee Annie tells the youngest of the "kissin' friends" that for years she had aspirations that she wanted to accomplish, but Whites prevented her from accomplishing her goals. Miss Lee Annie wants Cassie to develop a willpower that will allow her to do what she wants to do regardless if Whites are displeased. Again, Taylor places a need for Black formal education in her adolescent novel, and she demonstrates its importance to Black families in the first half of the twentieth century.

Cassie becomes interested in the judicial system, and she assists Miss Lee Annie in preparing for the voter's examination. As the test approaches, Mama convinces Papa to allow Cassie to be an active participant. Mama believes that Cassie's participation is important because it is something that could "mean a lot to Cassie one day" (333). Within this subplot, Taylor implies that Black women understand that informal education will not be enough if they hoped to change the prejudices of southern Whites when, at the courthouse, Miss Lee Annie's voice is silenced. After "failing" the exam, Miss Lee Annie merely bows her head and remains quiet. Cassie—and Taylor's youthful audience—sees the implication of White power and realizes that Black women must be willing to work toward change until all Black people can vote.

In essence, Mildred D. Taylor demonstrates how the vast majority of women in southern Black families had to rely on social and psychological networks in order to survive racial discrimination. In *Roll of Thunder, Hear My Cry,* Cassie's need to receive both a formal and informal education is stressed. In *Let the Circle Be Unbroken,* Taylor allows Cassie to embrace Black history and to welcome the opportunity to change Black society. This is achieved by keeping an eye on present conditions while holding on to the history of Blacks in the South. Throughout her series, Mildred D. Taylor shows her youthful readers the trials and heartaches of southern prejudice. She places Black history at the forefront and shows how Cassie "takes an ell" through her informal and formal education. In doing so, Taylor shows her readers how to "be" like Cassie, and, most importantly, how to function effectively in American society.

Notes

1. This model placed an emphasis on industrial rather than classical education.

2. In his critical study of Mildred D. Taylor and her work, Chris Crowe states that Taylor's father fled Jackson, Mississippi, because of a racial incident that occurred at his job. When Taylor was three weeks

old, her father punched a White coworker. Thus, the decision for Wilbert Taylor to leave the South was "essentially made for him." The character, Uncle Hammer, is "patterned after [Taylor's] two legendary great-uncles who had shown great courage growing up in Mississippi" (2).

3. Taylor credits her father for providing her with the informal stories and values (concerning their family) that are found in her novels. Taylor describes her father as a man who "shared with his [family] the wisdom and insight of his own experiences" (qtd. in Crowe 30).

4. Trees are important symbols for Taylor. The title of her first novel is *Song of Trees*. For Taylor, trees are a symbol of resilience. Thus, it is not coincidental that Taylor coins the name "Logan" for her characters.

5. Community work, in Collins's text, refers to participation in organizations such as church groups and quilting bees, imagery that has been used by southern Black female writers.

6. Cassie is drawn from Taylor's family stories. According to Chris Crowe, Taylor used her Aunt Sadie and her (Taylor's) sister Wilma as her model for Cassie (36).

7. At this time, great obstacles were created in order to prevent Blacks from voting. They included poll taxes, "economic reprisals, and physical violence." As noted in *Africana,* even in 1960, only "5% of eligible Blacks were registered to vote" (Gates and Appiah 560).

8. It is interesting to note that Russell can serve in combat but is unable to vote.

Works Cited

Anderson, James A. *The Education of Blacks in the South, 1860–1935.* Chapel Hill, NC: University of North Carolina Press, 1988.

Collins, Patricia Hill. *Black Feminist Thought: Knowledge, Consciousness, and the Politics of Empowerment.* New York: Routledge, 1991.

Crowe, Chris. *Presenting Mildred D. Taylor.* New York: Twayne Publishers, 1999.

Dill, Bonnie Thornton and Maxine Bacca Zinn, ed. *Women of Color in U.S. Society.* Philadelphia: Temple University Press, 1994.

Douglass, Frederick. *The Narrative in the Life of Frederick Douglass.* Ed. William L. Andrews and William S. McFeely. New York: Norton, 1997.

Gates, Jr., Henry Louis and K. A. Appiah. *Africana: The Encyclopedia of the African and African American Experience.* New York: Basic Civitas Books, 1999.

Hurston, Zora Neale. *Their Eyes Were Watching God.* 1937. Urbana, IL: University of Illinois, 1978.

Koblitz, Minnie W. *The Negro in Schoolroom Literature: Resource Materials for the Teacher of Kindergarten through the Sixth Grade.* New York: Center for Urban Education, 1967.

MacCann, Donnarae. "The Family Chronicles of Mildred D. Taylor and Mary Mebane." *Journal of African Children's & Youth Literature* 3 (1991–1992): 93–104.

Morrison, Toni. *Sula.* New York: Plume, 1973.

Shaw, Stephanie J. *What a Woman Ought to Be and to Do: Black Professional Women Workers During the Jim Crow Era.* Chicago: The University of Chicago Press, 1996.

Smith, Karen Patricia. "A Chronicle of Family Honor: Balancing Rage and Triumph in the Novels of Mildred D. Taylor." In *African-American Voices in Young Adult Literature: Tradition, Transition, Transformation.* Ed. Karen Patricia Smith. Metuchen, NJ: Scarecrow Press, 2001. 246–76.

Taylor-Thompson, Betty. "*Sula.*" *The Oxford Companion to African American Literature.* Ed. William L. Andrews, Frances Smith Foster, and Trudier Harris. New York: Oxford, 1997. 706–07.

Taylor, Mildred D. "Acceptance of the *Boston Globe/Horn Book* Award for *The Friendship.*" *Horn Book Magazine* 65.2 (1989): 179–82.

———. *Let the Circle Be Unbroken.* New York: Dial, 1981.

———. *The Road to Memphis.* New York: Dial Books. 1990.

———. *Roll of Thunder, Hear My Cry.* New York: Dial, 1976.

Wald, Gayle. "Passing." *The Oxford Companion to African American Literature.* Ed. William L. Andrews, Frances Smith Foster, and Trudier Harris. New York: Oxford, 1997. 560.

15

Telling Secrets and the Possibilities of Flight in I Hadn't Meant to Tell You This

Paula T. Connolly

About her award-winning book for young adults, *I Hadn't Meant to Tell You This* (1994),[1] author Jacqueline Woodson has written:

> I was inspired to write [the novel . . .] for a lot of reasons. [. . .] I really wanted to write about people crossing racial lines to be friends, and people crossing class lines. I wanted to write about what it meant to be a girl in this society, in a society where self-esteem seems to go down when you reach a certain age. [. . .] A lot of times when I see girls slouching or see them sitting quietly in classrooms, I start thinking, "This person does not like themselves." That's so heartbreaking to me and I think I'm trying to write past that, to show people that no matter who you are in the world, it's okay to be who you are. (Random House publicity)

For Woodson, fiction is a way both to examine injustice and to revision today's world—to offer possibilities for change, alternatives to oppression, and encouragement for those suffering prejudice. Clearly grounding her novels in the contemporary world, Woodson eschews simplistic essentialism on several levels. Neither arguing that one type of prejudice is worse than another nor that one person's experience typifies all others, Woodson problematizes issues of oppression, particularly by exploring—as quoted earlier—how racial, class, and gender oppression is often heightened by the vulnerabilities of childhood.[2]

Keenly situated within feminist theories of identity development, Woodson's characters seek respite and recovery from exploitation through processes of identity development expounded in feminist theory. Finding a safe place away from society's myriad assaults, these characters fight their invisibility in a society that seeks to label and castigate them rather than to understand their uniqueness. In that movement away from the larger society, and in the connections made between apparently dissimilar characters, the ability of these young adults to redefine themselves and to find their own voice[3] stands at the core for the transformation of these "slouching girls."

Woodson is particularly connected with contemporary Black feminists in her rejection of objectification and binary thinking. As Patricia Hill Collins has argued in *Black Feminist Thought,* categorizing people according to their differences—as in White/Black, male/female binaries—fosters attitudes of difference: "One part is not simply different from its counterpart; it is inherently opposed to its 'other' "(Collins 70).[4] In response to such detrimental binary categorizations, Collins scrutinizes the "transversal politics" of Black feminism, arguing that "boundaries are not fixed" within groups (246) and that "effective coalition" (247) between different groups offers real avenues for social justice. It is, Collins writes, "[e]mpathy, not sympathy [that] becomes the basis for coalition" (247). Indeed, Black feminist Barbara Smith has argued, " 'What *I* really feel is radical is trying to make coalitions with people who are different from you' " (qtd. in Collins 232).

This resistance to polarities and objectification underwrites Woodson's fiction. Moreover, the "ethic of caring" (as discussed in Collins 263) and the movement to coalitions through empathy typify Woodson's character development of her main characters as they make friendships with people ostensibly different from themselves. Various other elements in Woodson's fiction connect both to Black feminism and to Black Aesthetics as a whole: her frequent signifying when commenting on the works of Black artists and leaders; her incorporation of music and art as tools of resistance and identity; her use of realistic, complex, and not racially stereotyped characters; her central placement of the Black community; and her belief that literature is a means of social activism.[5] In that regard, Woodson herself notes, "[t]he rest of my life is committed to changing the way the world thinks, one reader at a time" (*Horn Book* 715).

Within her novels, Woodson seeks to examine and break myriad boundaries and stereotypes. In *I Hadn't Meant to Tell You This* and its sequel *Lena* (1999), Woodson explores such taboo subjects as incest, blurs the line between adult and children's literature by incorporating excerpts from poet Audre Lorde's *The Cancer Journals*, and moves beyond constrictive racial prescriptives of authorial/narrative perspectives by writing (in the sequel) through the point of view of Lena who is white. In these two novels, Jacqueline Woodson examines the lives of young girls and the ways they are not only assaulted by a world that defines and castigates individuals on the basis of race, class, and gender, but also the ways they can find the strength to combat that world. As Jacqueline Woodson has written: "I write about black girls because this world would like to keep us invisible. I write about *all* girls because I know what happens to self-esteem when we turn twelve, and I hope to show readers the number of ways in which we are strong" (*Horn Book* 713).

In both *I Hadn't Meant to Tell You This* and *Lena,* Woodson focuses on the ways two girls—Marie, an upper-middle-class black girl and Lena, who self-identifies as white-trash—must navigate a world in which their identities have been prescribed and at times assaulted by others. Both girls must deal with their mothers' abandonment—Marie's mother has left her and her father to travel the world whereas Lena's mother has died of cancer. For each young girl, the loss of her mother has induced a sense of insecurity and emotional atrophy that her father's responses have only exacerbated. Following his wife's abandonment, Marie's father no longer hugs or holds his daughter, although she longs for his affection. Lena's plight is quite different, for she suffers her father's sexual assaults, which began shortly after her mother's death.

To the family, friends, and society that surround them, no two girls could be more different. Marie herself recognizes this as she describes her privilege:

> My father was a college professor. I never had to worry about money or the future. [. . .] My clothes were expensive. [. . .] I looked over at Lena. She was wearing a beat-up-looking sweatshirt and dingy jeans. The clothes looked as though they had never been new. (95–96)

As Marie knows, Lena is the type of girl her "father would say [. . .] didn't look clean" (15). Marie—popular, financially secure, and voted best dressed at her school—clearly epitomizes social success, whereas Lena—poor and friendless—seems her antithesis and the quintessential outcast.

Moreover, and most apparent to the town of Chauncey where the story takes place, the two girls are separated by race. Chauncey is a town that not only categorizes its inhabitants but also does so in binaries—one is wealthy or poor, Black or White. Where one lives in the town, what sports one plays at the school (86), are all defined by one's race. The girls' fathers, too, reify this segregation by categorizing otherness in keenly derogatory terms. Lena's father "doesn't [. . .] like mixing races" and calls the local school a "nigger school" (40); Marie's father is "not too keen on white people. He spreads the word *whitetrash* around pretty freely" (41). Such rigid segregation most clearly defines the social prescriptions that discourage Marie and Lena from transgressing racial and class boundaries to become friends.

Poet and author Audre Lorde, whom Woodson overtly signifies in many of her novels, particularly in *I Hadn't Meant to Tell You This,* castigates such binary categorizations as a direct assault on one's identity:

> Much of Western European history conditions us to see human differences in simplistic opposition to each other: dominant/subordinate, good/bad, up/down, superior/inferior. In [such] a society [. . .] there must always be some group of people who, through systematized oppression, can be made to feel surplus, to occupy the place of the dehumanized inferior. (*Sister Outsider* 114)

In Chauncey, Woodson shows us a world where difference is denigrated— hence, the derogatory name-calling—defined only in antagonistic and mutually exclusive opposition— as Black/White, rich/poor—and becomes the foundation for both psychological and physical assaults on children. Clearly not an easy issue to present in an adolescent novel, incest and the sexual assault of young girls are nonetheless a central part of both *I Hadn't Meant to Tell You This* and *Lena.* It is not, however, the only abuse engendered against young girls here, nor does Woodson allow it to stand alone, isolated from a range of societal abuses against children. Incest is, instead, placed against the context of racism and classism, against a society whose binary oppositions and created "otherness" serve as a backdrop and contributing factor to child abuse.

In *I Hadn't Meant to Tell You This,* Woodson explores the effects of such marginalizations, not only in the way Marie is initially reluctant to befriend Lena, but also in the ways children inculcate derogatory stereotypes into their own sense of identity. When one of Marie's friends calls Lena "whitetrash" (18), Lena reveals how the term has become a part of her:

> "I'm whitetrash," Lena said flatly, as though she had said this a hundred thousand times before or maybe heard it from a hundred thousand people. "Whitetrash," she said again, softer, as if the words were sinking in, finding a home somewhere inside of her. (19)

The insidious effect of derogatory categorization is made clear later when Lena acknowledges how a litany of racist terms—"whitetrash. White cockroach. Cracker"—have transformed her sense of self: "After a while, the names kind of settle inside you [. . .] it's like the names *own* you" (*Lena* 51). In Chauncey, personal identity is dissolved into rigid and single signifiers, not merely of race but also of racist typology. Such language—used against both Black and White people here—is clearly a weapon, and Marie knows from her own experience how "words [can . . .] stab into [you]" (69).

The implications of subsuming such derogatory definitions as one's self-view are clear in the characterization of Lena. Through her, Woodson examines the potentially horrific effects of such an assault on children, particularly by showing how Lena's self-definition and societal placement as "whitetrash" make her more vulnerable to sexual assault. Lena explains to Marie that she fears leaving her abusive father because she feels that "I got to love him. [. . .] Because if I don't, that only leaves me and Dion. And what if somethin' happens to her? Then it's only me [. . .] stupid, whitetrash me" (78). Unable to see herself as anything other than how she's been categorized—that is, as refuse—Lena cannot imagine an identity and existence apart from that and remains with a sexually abusive father.

Lena's self-view is not only a result of social conditioning, but also, of course, of the assaults she has endured. When Marie asks her "[w]hat does it [sexual assault] feel like?" Lena tells her, "Like I'm the dirtiest, ugliest thing in the world. [. . .] Like I'm not worth the water it takes to wash in the morning" (57). Lena's "dirt" is a conglomeration of her self-abhorrence and victim's guilt as well as a physical reality; she hopes that not washing her hair or dressing well will discourage her father's unwanted attention. Furthermore, Lena's social class and poverty—she literally lives near the town dump—as well as the social prescription of "whitetrash" become an overwhelming assault on her sense of worth. Her identity is, thus, vulnerable to being subsumed into external and derogatory categorizations of being worthless and dirty and, as the image of trash implies, of a collapse into total negation.

In Chauncey, some people are so keenly marginalized as to be made invisible. Once a mining town and now an affluent Black suburb, Chauncey is a place where poor White people "moved into the crevices at the edge of town" (4) and those who go to the local schools "don't stay long [. . .] they're gone before [anyone knows . . .] their names well enough to say 'Hey' to them. [. . .] They keep to themselves [. . .] eat huddled around the tables in the farthest corners of the cafeteria, their heads bowed in silence" (4). Living metaphorically like the "cockroaches" they are called, staying only in the crevices of the town, these people function without names, "huddled" "heads bowed" "silence[d]."

This invisibility becomes a sign of Lena's victimization as well. Her vulnerability as a young, poor female is exacerbated not only because she inculcates society's views of her worthlessness, but also because signs of her abuse are ignored by others. Indeed, Lena knows that she cannot tell the truth and be heard: " 'Nobody believes it when you tell them,' she whispered [to Marie].'Everybody says it's impossible' " (42). Lena is, for the most part, right about her voicelessness.[6] When she tells Marie that her father "loves [her] too much" (42), Marie's initial response is a violently accusatory one:

> "I don't want to hear it, Lena!" I said, putting my hands over my ears. "You're probably lying. Nobody really does that kind of stuff. Not to their daughter." [. . .] I wanted to hit her, hard, for lying to me and thinking she could get away with it. "You're a [. . .] dirty liar. You just want attention." (55)

Lena responds not to Marie's typifying her (as does the rest of society) as dirty but instead to what she feels is a more virulent accusation. She confronts Marie: "'You think I want *attention*? That's the last thing I want. I wish I was invisible" (56).

Indeed, Lena's desire for invisibility is one reason for her appearance, and we discover that she keeps herself dirty both as a sign of victim's guilt and because she hopes to avert the attention of her father. Yet invisibility becomes an ironic means of psychological escape for Lena, and she describes how "'When my daddy's touching me, I take off, boom! and I'm gone. Thailand, Colorado, the Blue Ridge Mountains. I think of all the places I've heard of with beautiful names and try to imagine what they look like in real life [. . .] until it's over" (76). Making herself psychologically not present during the assaults becomes a way for Lena to create a temporary disjunction between her physical reality and her damaged psyche. It becomes a way for her to survive and, hence, invisibility simultaneously becomes a refuge for Lena and a weapon used against her.

Lena, hiding within her dirty clothes and emotional withdrawal, is Woodson's "slouching" girl; outward appearances would define Marie as Lena's antithesis. Daughter of a college professor, living in a good neighborhood, and a well-established member of the "in" clique, Marie appears to be a happy and successful young woman. Indeed, it is her visibility—she was voted best dressed at her school two years in a row—that most clearly marks Marie's success. Yet whereas Lena's pain and marginalization are reflected in her outward appearance and, thus, her social invisibility is ironically more apparent, that is not the case with Marie.

When her mother abandoned Marie and her father two years ago, it left Marie feeling as if "half of me had walked away" (25). Bereft, Marie still wonders "how to walk through the world feeling whole" (25) again. Unable to discuss her mother's leaving with either her friends or her still grieving father, Marie feels trapped, alone, and silenced. "Sometimes [she tells us] I wanted to let somebody know what was going on in my head" (51). What Marie does, however, is follow her father's example and learn to grieve in silence:

> I listened to my father and realized that you cry at night when you think no one is listening. You cry with the water running behind a closed door where you can wash your face and pat the red from your eyes. You cry hard and you cry alone. (25)

Left "hanging like laundry on a line" (39), Marie has more in common with Lena than anyone in Chauncey can imagine. Woodson breaks down antithetical binaries by showing what the two girls share; it is their mutual grief that unites Marie and Lena, having them move beyond the prescriptive bounds of race and class. Marie realizes her connection with Lena: "I felt like she had always been there for me, somewhere, a soul mate, another girl floating through this world without a mother" (49). When Marie confronts Lena, asking her, "How come you want to be friends with a black girl, anyway? You should make friends with the white kids at Chauncey," Lena responds, "Because of our mothers. [. . .] There's stuff we can talk about. [. . .] About what it's like. White, black—it shouldn't make no difference. We all just people" (59). The keenly felt grief and loss of her mother has made Lena move beyond socially inculcated definitions of otherness: "When my mama died, I stopped hating. What's the use? [. . .] You can hate all your life and people still gonna die and kill each other and build churches and pray to God and hurt their daughters" (58). As Marie realizes, "Underneath it all, Lena was a lot like me" (58). Sharing their fears and loss becomes a foundation for a friendship that crosses clearly delineated and socially guarded boundaries of race and class.

Describing an interior, creative movement apart from the social restrictions and assaults of the world, Woodson shows how the girls create a "middle place"—distinct from the White and Black sections of Chauncey—a place, Marie describes, "where Lena and I met and came together, it seems, regardless" (1). The "middle place" that they create is both a physical and psychological one, simultaneously real and metaphoric. A movement to interiority and away from the prescriptions and assaults of the world that surrounds them, this "middle place" is a protected and reflective movement in the evolution of self.[7] It is in finding a respite from a world that marginalizes children into social categories that one can still external cacophony and finally listen to oneself. Audre Lorde has described this process for her own child: he "will learn [. . .] how to move to that voice from within himself, rather than to those raucous, persuasive, or threatening voices from outside, pressuring him to be what the world wants him to be" (*Sister Outsider* 77).

Marie's home offers a temporary respite to Lena and her younger sister, Dion. In Marie's home, as Lena sits, happy and safe in a bubble bath, Marie reads from the work of Audre Lorde. A battle cry against the plight of such girls in an antagonistic world and an energizing source of strength for them both, Lorde seems to be speaking directly to them when she writes:

> I have found [. . .] that battling despair does not mean closing my eyes to the enormity of the tasks of effecting change, nor ignoring the strength and the barbarity of the forces aligned against us. It means teaching, surviving and fighting with the most important re-

source I have, myself, and taking joy in the battle. It means, for me, recognizing the enemy outside and the enemy within, and knowing that my work is part of a continuum of [. . .] reclaiming this earth and our power. (102–103)

In Woodson's sequel, Lena recalls the passage, telling her sister, "there was something in it about life and love and work and power that only girls and women got" (*Lena* 54). What these girls *get* from Audre Lorde is an affirmation of their own personhood, despite the conflicts they face. She offers them hope, and, as Marie reads her work aloud to a bathing Lena, Lorde gives them the hope and determination to demand their visibility and self-worth; she offers a reclaiming of power and self-esteem to girls otherwise left "slouching" from the world's assaults.

Eschewing a simplistic essentialist stance, Woodson problematizes the relationship of Marie and Lena, showing that although they share commonality in what they have lost, race and class are still factors that define their lives. In nuanced ways, Woodson acknowledges the difference and contributions of race and class in each girl's life, and those differences are set in complicated balance with what they share. Class is a significant factor. Although each girl has lost a mother, each loss has been different; Marie's mother has left her and her father to travel the world whereas Lena's mother has died from cancer. The secure financial position of Marie's mother had allowed her freedom to travel, whereas the poverty of Lena's mother prevented her from getting medical attention and, in all probability, contributed to her early death. As both girls have lost mothers, though in different ways, both also suffer estrangement from their fathers; unlike Lena's father who loves her "too much," Marie's father cannot show his love in physical embraces. There are clearly elements of their respective lives that the other cannot comprehend: Lena, for example, envies the fact the Marie's father does not touch her, whereas Marie initially envies Lena because her father *does* touch her. As each girl grapples with these differences, they discuss, argue, and strive to understand the other.

Essentialism, "ignor[ing] differences of race, sexual preference, class, and age [. . .] a pretense to a homogeneity of experience" (Lorde *Sister Outsider* 116), becomes yet another way to deny individuality. To Lorde, and clearly to Woodson, difference is not to be ignored or marginalized, but rather appreciated. And it is especially in those moments when people of different races and classes seek to understand the other, that true self-creation occurs. In these novels, Woodson exemplifies Lorde's view that "Difference must be not merely tolerated, but seen as a fund of necessary polarities between which our creativity can spark like a dialectic. [. . .] Only within that interdependency of different strengths, acknowledged and equal, can the power to seek new ways of being in the world generate, as well as the courage and sustenance to act where there are no charters" (111).

Marie and Lena move with few charters into an unmapped territory of alliances between Black/White, rich/poor, into a friendship that acknowledges their differences, shares common grief, and promises a strengthened sense of self. Each girl shares what she has and borrows from the other. To achieve this, both Marie and Lena must look beyond how they are otherwise categorized and see each other as individuals. Although, for example, Marie finds it hard to believe Lena, thinking that "it [incest] couldn't happen to anybody I knew. It happened to sad, foreign girls in Third World countries," when she acknowledges Lena on a personal level—"How could it happen to Lena, the girl I was walking home from school with? [. . .] Lena . . . my friend" (54–55)—she soon does come to trust the secrets she has been told.

As Woodson is neither simplistic nor essentialist in her discussion of race and class, neither is she about gender. Not reinforcing a facilely reductive or structured paradigm of positive mother figure/negative father figure, Woodson's feminism explores the nuances of familial structures and gender roles. Marie's mother, for example, is a problematic character who both suffered keen psychological restraint in her marriage and also determined to "fly" away, an image representing both the freedom the girls desire and the abdication of responsibility that constrains them. When Marie describes how her mother left, she recalls, "When I was ten, I watched her walk away. [. . .] She didn't look over her shoulder. She didn't wave good-bye. I stood with my father at the window, my head pressed against the glass" (24). Yet Marie's mother, although dealing a devastating blow to her daughter, is not neatly defined as the archetypal bad mother. She was a woman also suffering depression and suffocating in an unhappy marriage. And while Marie says she learns to cry in silence from her father, it is a lesson, too, that she has learned from her mother, for Marie knows "my mother hadn't been happy. Some nights, when my father was late coming home from work, I would hear her in the bathroom, crying . . . sobbing, gulping for air, turning the water on thinking I couldn't hear her grieving" (23).

It is important, too, to realize that Marie's mother has left her daughter important gifts. While her father defines the White people who live on the outskirts of town as "trash," Marie's mother had "corrected" him, redefining them as "People [. . .] Poor white *people*" (5). It is the definition of whites as people, not as trash, that stays with Marie and marks her early meetings with Lena, providing a countering voice to the myriad social voices—including the voice of her father—that warn her to stay away from Whites.

The legacy of Lena's mother is also mixed. Her memory offers Lena much strength, and, as the second book begins with Lena and her sister fleeing their abusive father, Lena recalls how "Mama [. . .] used to all the time say to me that no matter what happened, I'd find myself on the other side of it. She'd say 'Don't you be scared none either, Lena, 'cause you got a right to be in the world just like everybody else walking through it' " (*Lena* 1). As the two sisters travel south, trying to find their mother's family, Lena hopes her mother is guiding them on, and she draws pictures of West Virginia because it "remind[s] me of Mama, like maybe that's her inside of all that blue, looking down at us" (2). Moving beyond the simple figure of good mother/bad mother and instead showing a more complex character, Woodson has Lena later realize that because her mother never left her abusive husband, she unintentionally left them more vulnerable to his direct abuse. And in the end, Lena knows that her mother's family will not offer them a home.

What Marie and Lena come to, particularly because they offer each other community, is the strength to release and forgive their mothers. Marie realizes that "I don't love [my mother] because I have to. [. . .] I love her because I know why she had to go away. [. . .] She would have died" (72). When asked if "you hate your mother for dying," Lena responds "It wasn't her fault" (73) and at the end of *Lena* she realizes that, although her mother's family would offer them no protection, her mother's memory had:

> My mama used to always say you can't stop hoping. Even when everything else in the world seemed to be gone, she said that's the thing you got to hold on to. Hope. (102)

The power and role of women in the shaping of their children's lives are clear in both *I Hadn't Meant to Tell You This* and the sequel *Lena,* but despite the abuse by Lena's father, Woodson shows that men, too, can be nurturers. Although Marie's father withdraws from his daughter after his wife's abandonment, he is sensitive to her grief. When he leaves for a date and turns to wave good-bye to Marie, he "saw me [Marie recounts] with my head pressed against the window, that same window I had watched my mother walk away from home, he swallowed [. . .] and turned back for home" (26). Having been a target of racist aggression, he is not pleased that his daughter has befriended Lena and her sister, nor that she has invited the two girls into his home. Yet, after he has met them and despite their dirty appearance, he tells Marie, " 'Those friends of yours [. . .]. They're nice girls. Maybe they'll stay around awhile" (74–75). Lena and Dion do not "stay around" but instead run away from Chauncey, hoping to escape their father. This is a new grief to Marie. Her father knows this and offers his gentle comfort, holding her for the first time since her mother left:

> Each morning my father comes into my room and, taking my face between his hands, asks if I'm okay. His hands are warm and [. . .] gentle as they patted the back of my head, "Go ahead, Marie," Daddy whispered. "It's okay to cry." (114)

Now, offering her both the love she has craved as well as an understanding and acceptance of grief, Marie's father becomes the central nurturer in her life.[8] In the second book, after Lena and Dion have faced the dangers of a life on the road, Marie's father finally locates them and offers them a home. Overcoming the racial and class stratification of Chauncey, Marie's father offers his love and home to two young girls who bear no biological relation to him, and he transcends constrictive notions of nurturer and family.

Marie has played a significant role in the creation of this new family, not only in her friendship with Lena but also in the truths she has told her father. When Lena had first told Marie about the incest she has suffered, she made Marie promise not to tell anyone. Once Lena has left Chauncey, chased out by the fear of more sexual abuse, Marie knows it is time to speak the secret. That morning, Marie tells us, "I knew I would tell. It seemed like Lena was saying, *It's okay now, Marie. Go ahead and tell it. Then maybe someday other girls like you and me can fly through this stupid world without being afraid*" (13).

Finding voice to speak the secrets that have held Lena and Dion captive and abused, when Marie determines to tell Lena's story, she exposes the "stupid[ity]" of a world that categorizes, abandons, and abuses its children. She makes visible those marginalized, as Woodson clearly does in her novels. Marie also shows the hope for "flight" here, for if before they met, Marie and Lena had each been "floating" as if adrift in their mutual grief, they learn to "fly" when they are together. Signifying on images of flight, Woodson shows both Lena and Marie breaking free of oppressive and at times destructive authorities and the social oppressions that define, categorize, and, hence, seek to physically and psychologically trap them. From their swinging ever higher between earth and sky to the final plane flight in the second book when Lena and Dion fly back to Marie and her father, flying becomes, for these girls, an image not merely of escaping oppressive bonds but also of reaching their potential—of moving outside those oppositionalized boundaries to create new social spaces, new possibilities for friendship and family, new possibilities for identity, and ultimately new ways to recreate their worlds.

Notes

1. *I Hadn't Meant to Tell You This* was a Coretta Scott King Honor Book. Also see Patrick Jones, "The Best Best Book for Young Adults in 1994," *VOYA* 18.5 (December 1995): 289–96 for an analysis of why the book can be deemed the "best" book of 1994. More recently, Woodson's *Miracle's Boys* (New York: Puffin, 2000) has received the 2001 Coretta Scott King Award.

2. Patricia Hill Collins, in *Black Feminist Thought,* 2nd ed. (New York: Routledge, 2000), defines discriminations because of race, class, and gender as "intersecting oppressions" (8).

3. For discussions of such development of female voice, see Mary Field Belenky, *Women's Ways of Knowing* (New York: Basic Books, 1986); Carol Gilligan, *In a Different Voice* (Cambridge: Harvard University Press, 1982); and Adrienne Rich, *On Lies, Secrets, and Silence: Selected Prose, 1966–1978* (New York: Norton, 1979).

4. See Thomas Gossett, *Race: The History of an Idea in America* (1963. New York: Oxford University Press, 1997) for an examination of the historical development of race as "other." Also see George Fredrickson, *The Black Image in the White Mind* (New York: Harper, 1972).

5. For a study on signifying, see Henry Louis Gates, Jr., *The Signifying Money* (Oxford: Oxford University Press, 1988); for a discussion of the role of the arts, see Addison Gayle, Jr., ed. *The Black Aesthetic* (New York: Doubleday, 1971) and Lawrence Levine, *Black Culture and Black Consciousness* (Oxford: Oxford University Press, 1977); for a recent discussion of racially stereotyped versus realistic characters, see Collins.

6. For discussions of such voicelessness, see Belenky; Gilligan; Robin Lakoff, *Language and Woman's Place* (New York: Harper and Row, 1975); and Rich.

7. See Belenky; Homi Bhabha, *The Location of Culture* (London: Routledge, 1994); Anna Julia Cooper, *A Voice from the South* (1892. New York: Oxford University Press, 1988); and Walter Ong, *The Presence of the Word* (Minneapolis, MN: University of Minnesota Press, 1981).

8. With the character of Marie's father, Woodson also works against the literary stereotype of the invisible/absent father. Sims identifies "the absent Black father" as the "single most frequently occurring phenomenon in [. . . the] social conscience books" (25) that she evaluates in her study. See Rudine Sims, *Shadow and Substance* (Urbana, IL: NCTE, 1982).

Works Cited

Belenky, Mary Field, et al. *Women's Ways of Knowing: The Development of Self, Voice, and Mind.* New York: Basic Books, 1986.

Bhabha, Homi K. *The Location of Culture.* London: Routledge, 1994.

Collins, Patricia Hill. *Black Feminist Thought: Knowledge, Consciousness, and the Politics of Empowerment.* 2nd ed. New York: Routledge, 2000.

Cooper, Anna Julia. *A Voice from the South.* 1892. New York: Oxford University Press, 1988.

Fredrickson, George. *The Black Image in the White Mind: The Debate on Afro-American Character and Destiny, 1817–1914.* New York: Harper, 1972.

Gates, Henry Louis, Jr. *The Signifying Money: A Theory of African-American Literary Criticism.* Oxford: Oxford University Press, 1988.

Gayle, Addison, Jr., ed. *The Black Aesthetic.* New York: Doubleday, 1971.

Gilligan, Carol. *In a Different Voice: Psychological Theory and Women's Development.* Cambridge: Harvard University Press, 1982.

Gossett, Thomas. *Race: The History of an Idea in America.* 1963. New York: Oxford University Press, 1997.

Jones, Patrick. "The Best Best Book for Young Adults in 1994." *VOYA* 18.5 (1995): 289–96.

Lakoff, Robin. *Language and Woman's Place.* New York: Harper and Row, 1975.

Levine, Lawrence W. *Black Culture and Black Consciousness: Afro-American Folk Thought from Slavery to Freedom.* Oxford: Oxford University Press, 1977.

Lorde, Audre. *The Cancer Journals.* 1980. San Francisco: Aunt Lute Books, 1997.

———. *Sister Outsider: Essays and Speeches.* Freedom, CA: The Crossing Press, 1984.

Ong, Walter J, S. J. *The Presence of the Word.* Minneapolis, MN: University of Minnesota Press, 1981.

Nikolajeva, Maria. "Exit Children's Literature?" *The Lion and the Unicorn.* 22.2 (1998): 221–36.

Rich, Adrienne. *On Lies, Secrets, and Silence: Selected Prose, 1966–1978.* New York: W. W. Norton, 1979.

Sims, Rudine. *Shadow and Substance: Afro-American Experience in Contemporary Children's Fiction.* Urbana, IL: National Council of Teachers of English, 1982.

Woodson, Jacqueline. *I Hadn't Meant to Tell You This.* New York: Bantam Doubleday Dell, 1994.

———. *Lena.* New York: Delacorte-Random House, 1999.

———. *Miracle's Boys.* New York: Puffin Books, 2000.

———. "A Sign of Having Been Here." *Horn Book* 71.6 (1995): 711–15.

16

The Cheetah Girls Series

Multiracial Identity, Pop Culture, and Consumerism

Violet J. Harris

Aperennial idea explored by authors is the question of identity. As a thematic trope, the search for identity can be depicted as an individual quest or interrogated as a group quest through the perspective of an individual. Race is an aspect of identity that can be central for an individual or tangential but rarely absent for those who find themselves categorized as minorities, non-Whites, or the "Other." Historically, race, whether or not one considers it a social construction or biological construct, appeared frequently in American literature often manifested in stock or stereotypic ways. African Americans, in particular, have been an integral presence in American literature, although often unacknowledged as argued by writer Toni Morrison and literary critic Valerie Babb. Morrison and Babb documented the processes by which "whiteness," not white skin color, became the equivalent of American. They explored the hegemonic cultural processes, institutions, and products that were adopted, in ad hoc fashion, to ensure that "blackness" would also embody the dichotomous opposite of whiteness, especially in art forms.

African Americans, then and now, could not control their depictions in various art forms. Consequently, particular images were entrenched in high and lowbrow culture. Literary scholar Sterling Brown identified seven stereotypes of Black characters most often found in American literature as the (1) contented slave, (2) wretched freeman, (3) comic Negro, (4) brute Negro, (5) the tragic mulatto, (6) local color Negro, and (7) the exotic primitive. Gender is an integral component of these literary stereotypes in that some, for instance, the brute Negro, are typically male, and others, the tragic mulatto, are usually female.

The same characters also appeared in Black literature for children.[1] Comparable tendencies to stereotype other racial and ethnic groups were also evident. Asian Americans,

Latinos/as, Native Americans, and women (including women from various racial and ethnic groups) deconstructed their literary images in essays, journal articles, and monographs[2] and identified stereotypes in these literatures as well. For example, Native American males were portrayed dichotomously as the noble savage or the marauding savage but savages nonetheless (see, for example, Seale and Slapin).

The mulatto, well adjusted or tragic, especially the female mulatto, holds a curious fascination for many in literature, as is found in William Wells's 1853 novel *Clotel*. She represents the encounters and clashes of cultures, conquest, desire that is often illicit, and a legal and cultural problem that is particularly emphasized in stratified societies. In fact, historians and legal scholars argue that the institutionalization of color stratification began early in the seventeenth century in Virginia as a convenient way of coping with the biracial children of slave women and questions about White male rape of them.[3] She is *La Malinche* in Latina literature and the subject of much speculation in short stories and novels written by antislavery activists and in current nonfiction.[4] Indeed, Vashti Lewis has argued that individuals who were "near-white black" predominated in literature during the antebellum period. They also populated literature written during the postbellum and pre– and post–Harlem Renaissance periods. For instance, notable postbellum novels *Iola Leroy* written by Frances E. Harper in 1892, Charles Chestnutt's *The House Behind the Cedars* published in 1900, and his 1901 novel *The Marrow of Tradition* contain this representation. Ironically, many African American women novelists, pre– and post–Harlem Renaissance, seemed preoccupied with the tragic mulatto. Thus, Pauline Hopkins, Nella Larsen, Jessie Redmon Fauset, and Dorothy West can be seen using this characterization in their writings.[5] These middle- and upper-class novelists embodied many of the ideals, behaviors, and traits in their tragic heroines: Black/White, intelligent, educated, often in Ivy League colleges, cultured, well-to-do world travelers. Many were light skinned. At the time of their publication, these early works that explored the lifestyles of mulattoes were often considered minor in the grand scheme of literary significance or depictions of race relations. Their recovery and rediscovery have been effected by African American literary scholars such as Mary Helen Washington, Hazel Carby, and Henry Louis Gates, Jr.

The current fascination with Sally Hemings in the American conscience is an example of the way in which issues of literary representation and the existence of the mulatto shape national consciousness and identity. Most historians might accept the fact that Sally Hemings was Thomas Jefferson's slave sister-in-law, but many will question the fact that she was the mother of his slave children. Annette Gordon Reed's *Thomas Jefferson and Sally Hemings: An American Controversy* and *Jefferson's Children* are recent publications that scrutinize this historical episode of miscegenation among American presidents.

Several thought-provoking portrayals of mulattoes or near-white black characters exist in children's literature, both in historic and current publications. Mrs. A. E. Johnson is currently considered the first African American writer of children's fiction. Her first novel, *Clarence and Corinne, Or God's Way,* appeared in 1890. Moral rectitude rather than race dominated her writings. Ironically, her characters appeared to be "White" from her descriptions of their skin, hair, and eye color. Mildred Taylor effectively captured the tangle of emotions felt by these near-white black characters in *Let the Circle Be Unbroken* when she depicts Uncle Hammer's daughter's visiting the Logan family and creating havoc that could result in violence when her potential White suitors discover that she is Black.

As time progresses, the literary depictions shift from involuntary interracial liaisons that result in mulatto or near-white black characters to the conception of such children as biracial or multiracial progeny of legalized or publicly sanctioned unions. This shift in status is important because of the voluntary nature of the relationships among the individuals and the resultant disruption they represent for our constructions of race. Children's literature figures prominently in this literary shift, too. For instance, Arnold Adoff crafted stories about biracial children and their parents that portray a less complicated existence, one untouched by violence, anger, or opposition in picture books such as *Hard to Be Six*. Authorial intentions seem to negotiate the format and result in a text that features a voluntary, loving interracial relationship. Another example is the evocatively named character Ginger Brown created by Sandra Dennis Wyeth. Ginger's paternal grandparents are White. Her maternal grandparents are African American and White; her mother and father are biracial and White, respectively. What, then, is Ginger? In the past, she would have been labeled an octoroon, a historic anachronism. Today this is not so neatly tied together, as Virginia Hamilton shows in her exploration of the intersection of racial, ethnic, and religious identities in *Bluish*. Occasional works of historic fiction such as *Letters from a Slave Girl* by Mary Lyons and *Tempestuous: Opal's Story* by Jude Watson highlight the sexual exploitation of mulattas. Asian American authors have begun to interrogate biracial identity as well. For instance, Lawrence Yep's 1995 novel, *Thief of Hearts,* challenges notions of group solidarity based on racial identity and shows the racial allegiances biracial children are often forced to make. Series fiction has been reinvigorated through the inclusion of characters that are African, Asian, Latino/a, and Native American, as well as those who are gay or evangelical Christians.

Another method for rejuvenating series fiction has been the introduction of characters that represent particular racial or ethnic groups in the "Sweet Valley High," "Babysitters' Club," "Dear America," "My America," and "Pony Pals" series. These representations of biracial and multiracial characters have been published over the past thirty years. Books by African Americans, such as Deborah Newton Chocolate's "Neate," Walter Dean Myers's "18 Pine Street," and Sandra Dennis Wyeth's "Ginger Brown" series, have been released. In addition, Laurence Yep's "Goblin Pearl" series is a humorous mystery series that subverts some assumptions or stereotypes about Chinese Americans such as the computer geek or the sexualized, exotic girl.

Deborah Gregory, author of "The Cheetah Girls" series, attempts to capture a "multiculti vibe" that harkens to the interracial stories in the "Neate" and "18 Pine Street" series, but it is strongly linked to popular culture and consumerism and, possibly, privileges biracial and multiracial identity. The "Cheetah Girls" series is a part of the Jump at the Sun imprint within Hyperion Books, an imprint first under the direction of Andrea Davis Pinkney (1997–2002), now an editor/director of children's book publishing at Houghton Mifflin. She stated some of the purposes of the imprint:

> The mission of Jump at the Sun is to publish books that celebrate the cultural diversity of African Americans. Our books range across the genres—from board books through young adult novels—and the titles are both literary and commercial. The main point is that they

are for all readers—meaning the readership is not exclusive to African Americans. (Darigan 78)

Davis Pinkney has quietly subverted some of the prevailing notions associated with multicultural literature through manuscripts published under the imprint. The "Cheetah Girls" series demonstrates this quality.

Part of the appeal of the "Cheetah Girls" series is its sense of style and the suggestion of a global youth culture linking fashion, music, and friendship with a dollop of social consciousness that is often race or color and class based. Author Deborah Gregory adopts and reinterprets some familiar tropes, such as the introduction to fairy tales and references to *The Wizard of Oz;* clothing featuring animal prints; sprinklings of stars on each cover; and attractive teens posed in ways that suggest the characterization and plots within each book. One might argue that Gregory created a hip-hop series that appropriates the more acceptable and less threatening aspects of the musical genre and promotes a global, deracinated, teen culture, but has she? I wish to concentrate my analysis on the assessment of the racial and ethnic imagery; incorporation of popular culture, especially music; consumerism; and language.[6]

The unexpected racial and ethnic imagery in the "Cheetah Girls" series begins with the cover of the first book, *Wishing on a Star,* published in 1999. Three young girls, Galleria, Dorinda, and Chanel, dressed rather coolly hip in animal prints, wearing makeup that suggests the young, fashionable colors of LORAC and MAC, and having skin colors suggestive of multiple racial and ethnic heritages, are featured on the cover. Indeed, the inside cover echoes a fashion magazine with its credits for clothing and makeup and listing of stylists, makeup artists, and hair stylists. An initial reading of the text requires that the reader refer to the photographs of the characters on the back cover in order to determine who is who based on the descriptions of racial and ethnic mixtures ascribed to the girls. For example, Galleria Garibaldi is an exotic biracial. Garibaldi's father, a garment manufacturer, is an Italian from Bologna, Italy, and her mother, former model and boutique owner/designer, is African American. Her parents' background suggests an aura of cosmopolitanism and sophistication. Chanel Simmons is described as a "blend of Dominican and Puerto Rican on her mother's side, Jamaican and Cuban on her father's side—and sneaky deaky through and through!" (3). She is a representation of biracial identity that encompasses race, ethnicity, language, and geography. The description of Chanel harkens back to the duality of the tragic mulatta: virginity and purity represented by whiteness and eroticism and chicanery represented by darkness. Galleria and Chanel's friendship mirrors that of their mothers who met while modeling in the United States and Europe. In contrast to her description of Chanel, Galleria describes Dorinda Rodgers on the basis of physical attributes. "She is so tiny and pretty. I mean munchkin tiny. She doesn't look like a freshman at all. (She looks about twelve years old. For true). She is also about the same color as Chanel—kinda like mochachino—and her hair is cornrowed in front, then the rest is just freestyle curly" (33). Later, the reader discovers that Dorinda has been skipped twice in school and she *is* a twelve-year old freshman. Presumably, Dorinda is Black, although her skin color and hair texture do not differ markedly from the other two. These descriptions parallel the color, class, and character gradations associated with mulattas in earlier literary history. Dorinda also provides an example of the contradictions inherent in using physical attributes or phenotypes as the basis for racial classifications.

I shared the cover of *Wishing on a Star* with groups of librarians and teachers and asked them to identify the girls based on their physical descriptions. Most often they could not, and they questioned whether the racial and ethnic identity confusion was intentional or whether the girls represented some multiracial ideal of blurred physical characteristics associated with a particular racial or ethnic group. The author might have chosen not to describe Dorinda's parental heritage in book one because she is in foster care and in the plot of the seventh book in the series, *Dorinda's Secret,* Dorinda discovers her biracial identity. Dorinda's White and wealthy birth sister, Tiffany, locates her and Dorinda is momentarily shaken to discover that she is the daughter of a White mother.

> I can't believe this! Here I am, wondering how Tiffany could possibly be my sister if she's not part black—and all the time, I'm half white! Well, so what? I say to myself. Galleria's half white. Chanel's all kinds of things mixed up in one cute cuchifrita. I guess it's okay that I am what I am. I just can't believe I've lived all these years and never known! How could they not have told me any of this? It makes me so furious, I could scream. (78)

Clearly, to appropriate a historic term, racial amalgamation is celebrated.

Characters who are presumably African American are symbolized by twin sisters, Anginette and Aquanette, sometimes referred to by the other girls as the "hot-sauce twins." Cover photographs depict two noticeably brown-skinned girls. The first set of twins whose images serve for that of the characters in books one through four could be described as having skin reminiscent of the color of honey or almonds. Their noses and lips are mid-sized. In contrast, the twins who replace them in books 5 through 12 have darker brown skin and larger lips and noses. They are described as "those fabulous Walker twins from Houston. They are about the same height and size, but one of the twins is a chocolate shade lighter than the other" (Gregory 1999). Other descriptions throughout the series detail them as having "juicy lips," "chedda waves" hairstyles, acrylic nails, and accents that shout their southern origins. Galleria criticizes their clothes as "churchy," their makeup as brash, and their general affect and behavior as comical. One could argue that Anginette and Aquanette serve as comic foils, a bit uncomfortably as their portrayal hints at the comic Negro stereotype of the past. They also hint at a bit of class bias, particularly the references to their nails and hairstyles.

Gregory is a former fashion model, magazine writer, and "girl about town" who challenges the reader to move beyond some, but certainly not all, traditional images of race and ethnicity in America. Perhaps she is a potential member of the group of creative artists labeled as "post-Black" by Thelma Golden, a former director of the Whitney Museum and current deputy director and chief curator of the Studio Museum in Harlem.[7] Post-Black artists sometimes hold aesthetic beliefs that defy the earlier categorization of Black artists as authors who place racial or ethnic identity as the central frame in their stories. Instead, they deliberately and a bit self-consciously play with stereotypes and usurp and subvert their traditional connotations. Their actions are not unlike those of earlier writers Langston Hughes, Bruce Nugent, Wallace Thurman, and Zora Neale Hurston who sought to defy the stodgy middle-class conformity of their "elders" led by W.E.B. Du Bois. Gregory and post-Black artists Glynn Ligon and Kara Walker, as did their predecessors several generations ago, walk a slippery tight rope that could result in a fall that hints of racial and ethnic stereotypes.

The low-key buffoonish comments and behaviors attributed to the girls veer into stereotype. If we give Gregory the benefit of the doubt, we might consider the twins as post-Black comic foils rather than stereotypes. In some ways, their responses to the big city are reminiscent of the characterization on television's *Beverly Hillbillies* series. Anginette and Aquanetta's parents are a part of the American middle class; their mother is a district manager for the Avon cosmetic company and their father is senior vice president of marketing at Avon. Yet, the girls, despite growing up in multiracial Houston, Texas, seem awed by meeting a Dominican girl and another girl who is Italian and African American. Gregory may be subverting our shared notions of racial or ethnic identity because, on the surface, many Dominicans may seem superficially to be Black based on their physical characteristics. As Southerners, the twins might have encountered fewer progeny of inter-racial couples, given the fact that most southern states outlawed interracial marriage until the Supreme Court decision "Love v. the State of Virginia" in the 1960s. Nonetheless, their lack of knowledge about intermarriage is puzzling.

Galleria and Chanel revel in their biracial and multiracial identities. Gregory informs the readers several times about the girls being the product of love relationships between married couples. For instance, Anginette and Aquanette tell how Galleria's parents, Mr. and Mrs. Garibaldi, met through the personal ads in *New York Magazine:* "Lonely oyster on the half-shell seeks rare black pearl to feel complete." The twins, whose parents are divorced, consider the Garibaldi couple the happiest one they know. Chanel's parents are divorced, but they, too, were a loving couple at one time. Chanel's father now dates an Eastern European immigrant whom he assisted financially with the opening of a business; her mother dates a wealthy Saudi Arabian. Any problems or issues faced by these multiracial families and couples stem not from their race and ethnicity but their personalities. New York is positioned as a conglomeration or amalgamation of global cultures in which these pairings are not unusual, or at least not unusual in Chanel's and Galleria's neighborhoods.

Aquanette and Anginette are rarely referred to as pretty or beautiful, but they often characterize Galleria, Dorinda, and Chanel in that way. Slightly problematic are the constant references to the twins' "juicy lips" in several of the books. My response to the term *juicy lips* might suggest a bit of racial hypersensitivity; however, one notorious stereotype of Blacks has been big, usually red lips. I tested my reaction against the phrase with an African American teenager who read a few of the books and had passed it on to at least one of her friends. She suggested that the term might be used to describe nice, full lips males found attractive. Our opposing responses may reflect a generation difference. On the other hand, the teen's response may suggest the author's successful attempt to subvert and reinterpret a stereotype.

Arguments for a reading that suggests Gregory is subverting stereotypes are less convincing in book four, *Hey, Ho, Hollywood!,* as the twins' ready acknowledgment of their vocal talents contrasted to their constant doubts about their physical beauty: "And I *guess* we're kind of cute: Angie and I are both brown-skinned, with nice 'juicy' lips and big brown eyes. Still, we're not *real* pretty, like the rest of the Cheetah Girls" (3). These self-deprecating comments suggest that beautiful Black girls must possess the characteristics of biracial or multiracial females—for example, lighter skin and eye colors and long straight or curly hair—to be attractive. Since the Diaspora, skin color variation and the privileging of light skin and long hair have been major intragroup problems plaguing Blacks. Consider a bit of folk wisdom familiar to many: If you're yellow, you're mellow; if you're brown stick around; if you're black, get back! Other manifestations of color stratification are found among those in the Caribbean and Central and South America in comments such as "dark behind the ears." Perhaps most tragically, the quadroon balls in New Orleans prior to Emancipation highlighted the institutionalization of racial stratification. Numerous literary examples exist in adult literature; Jean Toomer's *Cane*, Charles Chestnutt's "The Wife of His Youth," and Wallace Thurman's *The Blacker the Berry* are just three examples. Children's and young adult literature authors have explored Black responses to skin color variation, specifically dark skin, and its impact. Virginia Hamilton's *Zeeley*, Brenda Wilkinson's *Ludell*, and Rita Williams-Garcia's *Blue Tights* are representative.

The twins' characterizations of their father's girlfriend Abala and her friends highlight their brown or dark brown skin in not so subtle ways that should provoke the reader's unease: "Abala is real dark—darker than *us*—and it makes her teeth look real white. She is real pretty though, and she wears African fabric draped around her body and head" (22). The "but" in this equation is "dark but pretty"—as if the two are not complements. Anginette and Aquanette have begun to internalize the negative perceptions of beauty and who can or cannot fit idealized standards.

Galleria and Chanel mention the twins' looks and skin color in negative ways; Dorinda, however, does not. In one scene, Dorinda scratches numerous mosquito bites, and Aquanette offers a folk medicine remedy. Galleria queries Aquanette in this fashion about the home remedy: "How brown cow?" Bubbles asks, giggling (*Ho* 45). Her mother, Ms. Dorothea, quickly reprimands her daughter, perhaps because she, too, is dark, tall, and plus-sized and is familiar with negative comments about the beauty of Black girls:

> "Darling, that's not funny," Ms. Dorothea says suddenly.
> "What, Mom? I'm just riffing off a *nursery* rhyme!"
> [. . .] "Even so, darling, sometimes you have to give your 'riff' the 'sniff test' before you 'flap your lips'—if you 'get my drift,' Ms. Dorothea says, looking at Galleria like she's not the only one with rhyme power. (45)

Aquanette tries to ease the tension by offering a rationale for Galleria in that she was simply being herself and did not intend any harm, however. Some of Aquanette's reactions may emanate from her adoration of Galleria and her belief that she is unique and wonderful.

Some of my sensitivity about the twins lessens when they become the central focus in book eight, *Growl Power!*, and nine, *Showdown at the Okie-Dokie*. Books eight and nine shift to Houston, the twins stomping ground, and this allows Gregory to foreground their talents, families, and cultural heritage. Racial and ethnic imagery becomes mixed with geographic and regional imagery. Galleria, Chanel, and Dorinda are surprised to see Blacks and Whites dressed in similar ways; for instance, all wear cowboy boots and hats. Curiously missing in the scenes are the Mexicans and Mexican Americans one would expect to find in Houston. In some ways, Gregory fulfills expectations about race read as "black and white" in books eight and nine, but she does challenge assumptions about race and ethnicity through multiracial imagery in her other books.

Equally intriguing is Gregory's use of class and gender. Girls are encouraged to explore their intellectual and artistic interests but are supported in their pursuit of fashion and beauty, especially the acquisition of consumer goods as seen in book two, *Shop in the Name of Love.* These topics are explored in the next section.

Galleria fits the definition of a BAP (Black American Princess), an individual described as a "pampered female of African-American descent born to an upper-middle- or upper-class family. An African-American female whose life experiences give her a sense of entitlement" (see Johnson et al. 2001 for a discussion of this ideal). She lives in a neighborhood located on the Upper East Side, an indication of some wealth. Her wealth is demonstrated in numerous ways: designer clothes—Gucci and Prada, Godiva chocolates, various accoutrements in her bedroom such as computer, telephone, and its decorative elements, and the kinds of treatment accorded her poodle such as regular grooming services. Granted, there are many individuals within the middle class who also possess these material goods, but there is a sense of entitlement emanating from Galleria's casual comments about travel to Europe, allowances, designer clothes, and the fact that she is named for her mother's favorite shopping mall, "The Galleria," in Houston, Texas.

Galleria has adopted many of the ideas her mother shares about being a diva. It is an attitude about the world and how you fit in, a sense of pride, a "fierce" attitude, a feeling of independence, and equal doses of glamour and drama. Additionally, a sense of connection with family and community is emphasized, along with an understanding that the girls should engage in some social action but always be stylishly dressed. Friendship is central too, as the girls attempt to avoid some of the internecine wars among adolescent girls. These attitudes and behaviors are apparent in "The Cheetah Girls Credo" (which appears at the beginning of each book): "All Cheetah Girls are created equal, but we are not alike. We come in different sizes, shapes, and colors, and hail from different cultures. I will not judge others by the color of their spots, but by their character." Galleria attempts to live up to the values espoused in the Credo, but she sometimes struggles because of her desire to be the leader or star.

According to the *BAP Handbook,* Chanel would fit the mold of the Bohemian BAP. She lives in Soho, a neighborhood Galleria finds more "freestyle" than her own neighborhood. By that she means that you could encounter individuals who could be a "Park Avenue lady, or someone with blue hair, a nose ring, and a boom box getting their groove on walking down the sidewalk." Chanel is also a dancer and secretly wants to become a ballerina as well as a famous girl group singer. She faces a dilemma in book ten, *Cuchifrita, Ballerina,* and must choose between continuing to hang out with the Cheetah Girls or attend a prestigious dance school.

Dorinda meets Galleria online in a chat room. The initial conversation centers on attending the same school and deciding on an outfit for the first day of classes. The girls want their clothing to reflect the latest and coolest styles, but Galleria comments on what is also appropriate: "September is the time for the belly button to go on vacation and the brain to come back in full effect. Unless you want Serial Mom to corner you in the girls' room and cut off your top with a rusty pair of scissors, you'd better leave the 'boob tube' at home!" Chanel enters the conversation and it shifts to comments about where Dorinda attended junior high and currently lives. Addresses become identities, and Dorinda identifies her junior high as "uptown" where she has been labeled a "hoodie girl." Chanel considers that okay, and tells her it could be worse if she lived in the suburbs. Chanel self-identifies herself as a "Dominican bap" and Galleria a "boho." Although Dorinda's neighborhood leads Chanel to identify her as a "girl from the hood," she could be middle or working class or poor because of the nature of the neighborhoods located in New York City's Harlem. *Who's 'Bout to Bounce?* centers on Dorinda and allows her to reveal her feelings about living in Cornwall Projects as a child in foster care. She also reveals her fear that the others will discover that she is only twelve years old and poor.

> This is where I get off, I think with a sad sigh. I wish I could invite my crew over to my house for some "Snapple and snaps." After all, I only live six blocks from here [the park where they run]. But after seeing where *they* all live, I'm too embarrassed to let them see my home. I live with my foster mother, Mrs. Bosco, her husband, Mr. Bosco, and about nine or ten foster brothers and sisters—depending on which day you ask me. We all share an apartment in the Cornwall Projects. We keep it clean, but still, it's real small and crowded. It needs some fixing up by the landlord, too—if you know what I'm sayin'. (11)

Eventually Chanel and Galleria visit her home, but they are mindful of her feelings about her neighborhood and poverty and try not to make unkind or thoughtless remarks. Besides, the girls are impressed with the family's ability to live in a small space and on limited income. Dorinda supplements the family's income by working at the local Y. This affords her the chance to wear the latest fashions and pay for treats such as pizza and beverages after school. Thus, she is able to emulate the middle-class lifestyle of her friends to a limited degree.

Gregory inserts several issues related to the working poor and foster care. One, for example, is the education of Blacks who migrated from the South to northern cities. Mrs. Bosco is illiterate and attempts to mask her illiteracy with comments about problems with her eyes or the need for glasses. Dorinda is sensitive to her situation and aids in the masquerade with the other children in foster care. Insightfully, Gregory notes the role of the sharecropping system, school segregation, and differential funding for Black and White schools in the South as noteworthy factors in Mrs. Bosco's illiteracy.

The plight of children in foster care and the difficulties faced by the working poor are depicted poignantly. Mr. and Mrs. Bosco care for the children least likely to find permanent homes through adoption—older Black and Latino/a children, biracial children, HIV positive children, and children with disabilities. Dorinda considers their home a virtual United Nations because African and White immigrant children have also been placed with the Boscoes. Dorinda's thoughts are clear on these matters as are the emotional strains of seeing children placed and removed from the home she shares with the Boscoes. She is hurt and feels unwanted while simultaneously finding some joy in the fact that she provides some comfort and love for the other children. The anger and resignation felt by children in long-term foster care are shown. "See, sometimes the kids in our house go back to their real parents. Once in a blue moon, they even get adopted by new families, who are looking for a child to love. Nobody has ever tried to adopt *me,* though. Sometimes I cry about that—nobody wanting me" (21–22). Clearly, Dorinda hopes to have a family and fulfill her dreams of a multifaceted, artistic career. A family of sorts is possible for her in books seven and eleven, *Dorinda's Secret* and *Dorinda Gets a Groove.* The appearance of a White sister, Tiffany, raises a host of issues for Dorinda.

> "Dorinda," Mrs. Tattle takes over. "Your mother surrendered custody of both her children at the same time. You were eighteen months old, and Tiffany was seven months. You were placed in a foster home, and Tiffany was placed with adoptive parents."
>
> "You're trying to tell me that Tiffany got adopted because she's white, and I didn't because I'm black?" (77).

Dorinda begins crying inconsolably and angrily. Still, she can't fathom that she has a White sister and a White mother. Dorinda's biracial identity is not construed as a marker to separate her from other children considered Black by potential parents, but other questions spring forth: Will her friends continue to accept her when they discover that she is biracial? What kind of relationship will she develop with Tiffany? How will Dorinda and Tiffany bridge racial identity gaps and class gaps? Tiffany is quite musical and wants to join the group. She is willing to share some of her wealth with Dorinda, and they begin a relationship that is less tenuous than what one might expect.

Books seven and eleven might engage the reader in a manner different from the others because the themes explored are less superficial. Gregory does, however, continue to maintain some of the light, hip tone throughout. Often this occurs through the use of music, teen vernacular, and other elements of teen and popular culture.

Music plays an integral role in each book in the series. Gregory signals its importance in several ways. First, the introduction in book one mimics the beginnings of fairy tales, identifying Galleria and Chanel as the princesses who wish to shine as stars in the world of music. Second, a miniature CD is included of a song recorded by a girl group, "After Dark," whose photographs appear on various covers. Third, there are the continuous references to vaguely disguised musical acts of today such as "Kahlua" who suggests Brandi; "Mo Money" who echoes Monica, and "Karma's Children" who resemble Destiny's Child. Fourth, the lyrics or stanzas from various rap songs are referenced throughout. The rap included here is not the "gangster," "bling-bling," sexualized urban vamps, or pseudo pimps of some of today's popular artists. Instead, the songs are "bubble gum" rap with some social consciousness and an infectious beat, if one knows how to rap. Finally, other musical styles, including classical, jazz, R and B, or world music, are mentioned on occasion. For example, Chanel's mother listens to music from her root culture in addition to Middle Eastern music. Galleria's mother often shares "old school" R and B groups such as the Supremes for purposes of providing the girls with lessons in music history and models of artists who exuded class. If that were not enough, Galleria, Chanel, and Dorinda take classes at Drinka Champagne's Conservatory where they are introduced to traditional fine arts. The girls are also members of a social group, the Kats and Kittys, reminiscent of The Links, a social organization for the children of middle- and upper-class Blacks.

Most of the group's songs are written by Galleria and Chanel, and they vie for the rank of head diva in the group. The lyrics often contain references to movies (Anginette and Aquanette named their pet guinea pigs Porgy and Bess and Galleria's dog answers to

Toto, a reflection of Gregory's passion for *The Wizard of Oz*), allusions to current teen pop stars (Brandi and Monica), and a few parodies of pop songs. Gregory calls to mind some aspect of the disco movement in book six when the girls are signed to a recording contract and expand their repertoire with songs such as "It's Raining Benjamins" which hints of "It's Raining Men" recorded by campy disco favorites "Two Tons of Fun."

Suggestions of hard-core gangster rap are found in references to record companies; Def Jam Records is hinted at by the books' "Def Duck Records" and comments about MCs and ruthless producers. For example, Mr. Johnson owns Jackal Management Group, a not so subtle comment about his business practices. The pitfalls for young and talented and not so talented teens seeking stardom are explored in realistic fashion. The girls experience unbridled competition, accusations of plagiarism, and occasional internal strife as they compete in talent shows and showcases in New York City, Houston, and Hollywood. Despite setbacks, they continue to dream of fame and fortune in the entertainment business.

The language featured in the series situates the characters as a part of a global youth culture and reflects the creative linguistic abilities of teenagers. "You know what I'm sayin'" and "aight" have been appropriated. They signal and signify the cool stance of urban youth unabashedly peppered throughout the series. Gregory crafts voices for her characters that are sometimes idiosyncratic, for example, "flipping the flim-flam" (acting or doing something shady) and mostly expected, "wanna-be." Some of the language reflects geographic differences and root languages of immigrants, for instance, "la gran fantasía." Yet, she does not abandon the reader in a linguistic wonderland. Readers unfamiliar with the language of urban youth can access the glossary included in each volume. Some of the language reflects the distinctive spellings found in rap music, such as *duckets* for money rather than ducats. Not surprisingly, there is a gender distinctive tone to the language that seems to incorporate some of the cadences or constructions of baby talk. Perhaps that should be expected given that the Cheetah Girls are teens.

Materialism and consumerism are also integral components of the series. The girls love dressing well and aspire to wear the au courant Gucci and Prada. They are cautioned throughout the series, however, of the need to rein in their expensive tastes and think about some aspects of long-term financial planning. For example, Chanel accesses her mother's charge card number and runs up an exorbitant bill purchasing clothes. As punishment, she must work off her debt. Some of the girls' impulsiveness for expensive clothing is channeled into setting up a business. Galleria purchases a studded dog collar and creates a fashion fad by wearing it. Schoolmates notice the collar and place orders. She and her friends purchase supplies and use Mr. Garibaldi's factory to create the collars. The enterprise is short-lived, however.

Gregory's focus on business, fashion, and music parallels the ways they are connected to hip-hop, pop, and R and B cultures. One style of clothing popular in some hip-hop circles is the "ghetto fabulous" style represented by individuals such as Mary J. Blige. Another is the gangster look with its baggy, oversized jeans, head coverings that resemble do-rags, and oversized diamond and platinum jewelry. Still another is the neo-hippie look. Among some female pop and R and B singers and groups, a more designer look is preferred. The book jackets for the series reflect this objective. The Cheetah Girls have a unique style—animal prints in their clothing from head to toe—that is easily recognized and imitated. Their style is not positioned within any of the usual hip-hop categories, but it reflects the urban sophistication often associated with New Yorkers. In much the same way that rap moguls Sean P. Diddy Combs and Russell Simmons and female singers and rappers such as Jennifer Lopez and Eve have signature styles and clothing lines, the Cheetah Girls desire to shape and influence trends. This is a potentially lucrative goal that has been analyzed in hip-hop magazines *Vibe* and *The Source,* as well as the new business magazine for teens, *Teenpreneur.*

The girls want to look good because they feel good about themselves and wish to project that to the world. The projection of a healthy body image is one of the more positive aspects of their focus on clothing and makeup. They glory in looking good, and they note how appearances affect the women in their lives. Mrs. Garibaldi is a plus-size diva that commands attention in every situation. She does not fret over her large size but instead uses it to her distinct advantage. In contrast, Chanel's mother Juanita constantly frets about her size and exercises constantly to ensure that her weight is comparable to the weight of her modeling days. The twins' mother Mrs. Walker's emotional state is evident to the twins when they notice her less than impeccable appearance. Finally, Mrs. Bosco displays a lack of style, but the girls do not belabor the issue. The variety of female styles and attitudes about bodies are notable aspects of the books. The girls are not obsessive about their bodies. They eat pizza and other foods reflective of their cultures that are not low calorie, exercise regularly, and compliment each other's appearance with the exception of the jokes about Aquanette and Anginette's hairstyles and clothes.

What might one conclude about this series and its role in the lives of potential readers? Gregory achieves a primary goal of writers in creating memorable characters. In some ways, her characters are cutting edge. They imply an emerging trend in children's and young adult literature, the biracial or multiracial character who signifies a possible new societal order. The characters' language represents an unabashed acceptance of urban youth and the pivotal role they play in popular culture. Gregory is probably one of the more successful authors to capture the cadence and rhythms of urban language. The age-old desire to achieve artistic success parallels the lives of earlier girl groups and some current musical stars, for example, the Supremes and Destiny's Child, but lessons are slipped in about the strife that can arise from such associations. Gregory's candor on issues—race, adoption, and poverty—seems somewhat refreshing for series fiction clearly designed to entertain. Perhaps most importantly, Gregory entertains her potential audience.

Notes

1. See, for example, Dorothy Broderick, *The Image of the Black in Children's Literature* (New York, R. R. Bowker & Co., 1973); Rudine Sims, *Shadow and Substance* (Urbana, IL: NCTE, 1982); Violet J. Harris, "African-American Children's Literature: The First One Hundred Years," *Journal of Negro Education,* 59 (1990): 540–55; and Dianne Johnson, *Telling Tales: The Power and Pedagogy of African American Literature for Youth* (New York: Greenwood Press, 1990).

2. Several pioneering analyses appeared in the journal published by the Council on Interracial Books for Children and in volumes such as *Through Indian Eyes: The Native American Experience in Books for Children* (Berkeley, CA: Oyate, 1998).

3. For a more complete discussion of this, see Luther Wright's insightful article "Who's Black, Who's White, and Who Cares: Reconceptualizing the United States's Definition of Race and Racial Classifications," *Vanderbilt Law Review* 48 (1995): 513–69.

4. *Mestiza* identity parallels mulatta identity issues. Gloria Anzaldua and Cherie Moraga explore the representation in Latino/a literature. Writers in the Caribbean also contend with a multiplicity of identities forged by language, geography, and race and are found in the works of Louise Bennett, Derek Walcott, Merle Hodge, and Jamaica Kincaid.

5. Suzanne Bost's 1998 article "Fluidity Without Postmodernism: Michelle Cliff and the 'Tragic Mulatta' Tradition," in the *African American Review* (Winter 1998: 673–89) addresses the works of these authors in more depth.

6. The twelfth and thirteenth books, *In the House with Mouse!* and *Oops, Doggy Dog!*, have been published since the completion of this analysis, and they are not discussed in this chapter.

7. For a discussion of Thelma Golden's remarks, see Ian Parker's "Golden Touch" in *The New Yorker* 14 Jan. 2002: 44–49.

Works Cited

Babb, Valerie. *White Visible: The Meaning of Whiteness in American Literature and Culture.* New York: New York University Press, 1998.

Brown, Sterling. "Negro Character as Seen by White Authors," *Journal of Negro Education* 2 (1933): 179–203.

Chambers, Veronica. *Marisol and Magdalena.* New York: Jump at the Sun/Hyperion Books for Children, 1999.

Darigan, Daniel L. "Sorting Out the Pinkneys," *Language Arts* 80 (2002): 75–80.

Gordon Reed, Annette. *Thomas Jefferson and Sally Hemings.* Charlottesville, VA: University of Virginia Press, 1997.

Gregory, Deborah. *Wishing on a Star.* New York: Jump at the Sun/Hyperion Books for Children, 1999.

———. *Shop in the Name of Love.* New York: Jump at the Sun/Hyperion Books for Children, 1999.

———. *Who's 'Bout to Bounce.* New York: Jump at the Sun Hyperion Books for Children, 1999.

———. *Hey, Ho, Hollywood!* New York: Jump at the Sun/Hyperion Books for Children, 1999.

———. *Woof, There It Is.* New York: Jump at the Sun/Hyperion Books for Children, 2000.

———. *It's Raining Benjamins.* New York: Jump at the Sun/Hyperion Books for Children, 2000.

———. *Dorinda's Secret.* New York: Jump at the Sun/Hyperion Books for Children, 2001.

———. *Growl Power!* New York: Jump at the Sun/Hyperion Books for Children, 2001.

———. *Showdown at the Okie-Dokie.* New York: Jump at the Sun/Hyperion Books for Children, 2002.

———. *Cuchifrita, Ballerina.* New York: Jump at the Sun/Hyperion Books for Children, 2002.

———. *Dorinda Gets a Groove.* New York: Jump at the Sun/Hyperion Books for Children, 2002.

Hamilton, Virginia. *Bluish.* New York: Blue Sky/Scholastic Books, 1999.

Johnson, Kalyn, Tracey Lewis, Karla Lightfoot, and Ginger Wilson. *The BAP Handbook.* New York: Broadway Books, 2001.

Lanier, Sherman and Jane Feldstrom. *Jefferson's Children.* New York: Random House, 2000.

Lewis, Vashti. "The Near-White Female in Frances Ellen Harper's Iola Leroy." *Phylon* 45 (1984): 314–22.

Lyons, Mary. *Letters from a Slave Girl.* New York: Atheneum, 1992.

Morrison, Toni. *playing in the dark.* Cambridge, MA: Harvard University Press, 1992.

Rinaldi, Ann. *My Heart Lay on the Ground.* New York: Scholastic, 1999.

Seale, Doris and Beverly Slapin. *Through Native American Eyes.* Berkeley, CA: Oyate, 1998.

Spodek, Bernard, Rosalinda B. Barrera, and Violet J. Harris. "In Touch with Kids: A Conversation with Jean Marzollo," *The New Advocate* 15 (2002): 91–99.

Taylor, Mildred. *Let the Circle Be Unbroken.* New York: Dial Press, 1981.

Watson, Jude. *Tempestuous: Opal's Story.* New York: Aladdin Paperbacks, 1996.

Wilkinson, Brenda. *Ludell.* New York: Bantam Books, 1980.

Williams-Garcia, Rita. *Blue Tights.* New York: Lodestar Books, 1987.

Yep, Laurence. *Thief of Hearts.* New York: Harper Collins, 1995.

17

Story-Reading, Story-Making, Story-Telling

Urban African American Kindergartners Respond to Culturally Relevant Picture Books

Lawrence R. Sipe and Patricia A. Daley

What could culturally relevant teaching in an urban public school classroom look like? Sonia Nieto (2000) has written eloquently of schools whose distance from students contribute to their disengagement from education, where students learn that "what goes on in school is irrelevant to their lives" (96), and that while "cultural diversity is valuable [. . .] in school it is not as valuable as is the dominant culture" (97). While affirming that children should not study only about themselves and their own communities, Nieto stresses that "curriculum needs to *build on* rather than neglect" what children bring with them into the classroom (96). Can we see the results of such a philosophy in an urban public school classroom, specifically in reference to the use of culturally relevant children's literature?

This chapter is based on a yearlong study that focused on two major questions: What constitutes the literary understanding of a class of African American urban kindergartners as suggested by their oral and written responses to readalouds of picture storybooks by, for, or about African Americans? How is this literary understanding socially co-constructed by children and their European American teacher in a student-centered classroom?

I.

The site for this study was a neighborhood elementary school (grades K–5) serving approximately 700 students (98% African American, 1% Latino, and 1% other) in a large U.S. northeastern urban public school district. This was a high-poverty school, with over 75 percent of the students eligible for free or reduced-price lunch. It was located in a mixed residential-commercial neighborhood characterized by attached housing, small businesses, and churches.

The focus classroom was divided into activity areas, including dress-up and play centers, with group work tables and a large carpeted section for storybook readalouds. Literacy activities and artifacts in the front of the classroom included morning message (co-created with the students daily), word wall (including alphabet posters), and many other informational posters, such as colors, shapes, and the alphabet song. There was a book cart containing books that had been or were about to be read aloud to the students, and three book racks displaying books with their front covers showing. Every available flat surface was covered with literacy artifacts created by the children; artifacts were also hanging in front of the windows on clotheslines.

This was a colorful, rich literacy environment including over 500 picture storybooks. By the end of the school year, the students had participated in over 150 morning message and alphabet activities. They had listened to more than 150 pieces of children's literature in the form of picture books presented in an interactive format (Barrentine 36–37) that encouraged free discussion and response, had written over 150 journal entries, and had heard dozens of other books read to them either by the teacher or classroom aide at various times during the school day.

Enrollment varied between twenty and twenty-five, with a roughly equal number of boys and girls at all times. All were African American. The teacher, Mrs. Martin (a pseudonym, as are all the children's names) was a European American who had taught in the school district for ten years, nine of them at the kindergarten level. She was also a doctoral candidate at a local university. Mrs. Rogers, an African American part-time aide, assisted for three hours every morning.

The research team consisted of the authors of this chapter and one other graduate research assistant, Angela Wiseman. Lawrence and Angela are European American, and Patricia is Asian American. Observations were scheduled for three days each week from the end of September through mid-June. During readalouds, Mrs. Martin sat in a chair next to the book cart in the carpeted area of the classroom. The students were seated on the floor at her feet, close enough to see the illustrations. We audiotaped and transcribed fifty-three of these interactive readalouds. Following each one, students returned to their desks for journal writing, while the researchers talked with and observed individual children. Once students finished writing in their journals, they discussed them with Mrs. Martin. Children could then engage in free reading on the carpet.

The choice of the picture books was based on our desire to provide the children with a rich "literary buffet" (Kristo 59) of a variety of genres and illustrational media and styles while also emphasizing high-quality, recently published books for, by, and about African Americans. Thus, thirty-one of the fifty-three readalouds (about 60 percent) were African

American books. These represented a wide range of genres: ten were contemporary realistic fiction; two were informational books; six were African folktales; six were African American folktales; four were fantasy with African American characters; and three were poem picture books with African American themes. Choices included books by such distinguished African American children's illustrators and authors as Walter Dean Myers and Christopher Myers; Jerry, Brian, and Miles Pinkney; E. B. Lewis; and Donald Crews.

II.

These picture books were experienced by the children as a single multifaceted event that extended beyond the confines of the readaloud itself. Because each readaloud was framed by the teacher in a discussion of what Sipe has referred to as "book as a cultural product" (264)—including interchanges about the dust jacket, front and back covers, endpages, title and half title pages, front matter (such as publisher and location), and dedication—students learned to make meaning of the picture-book experience while using these elements. The children often talked about visual aesthetic considerations and how these contributed to the story's meaning. For example, during the readaloud of Christopher Myers's *Wings,* there was a discussion of the book's endpages and their composition of an abstract blue-and-white, marbleized paper pattern:

> *[unidentified child]:*   That's water.
>
> *Teacher:*   What do you think of these endpages?
>
> *[unidentified child]:*   Wings.
>
> *Kevin:*   I think it's on that, in that, end page, it's uh, it do look like wings, but it, I think it's really water.
>
> *Khalil:*   They broke the tub. They broke the whole tub and then all the water started to come out.
>
> *Martin:*   I think it's water is coming from out the pool.
>
> *Joe:*   I hope I had my swimming trunks on; cause I would, cause I'd jump in there!

Not only was this a marvelous interpretation, to see flowing water in a marbleized paper pattern, but also marvelous that Joe threw himself wholeheartedly into the imaginary world created by Kevin and Khalil.

Later in the year, during free reading, boys could be seen picking up this book, opening to the endpages, holding it over their heads, and pretending to drink the water flowing out of the book. In another example, the students discussed the aesthetics of the African folk tale, *In the Rainfield: Who Is the Greatest?* In a story that depicts Fire, Wind, and Rain having a contest to see who is the greatest, Rain, a female, wins over Wind and Fire, who are males:

> *Teacher:*   Do you remember at the beginning of the story I showed you the end pages and I said, "Why do you suppose the illustrator chose this color?" And I

> remember somebody saying that it was their favorite color? That was a guess. Do you have more ideas about why the illustrator chose this color?
>
> *Naisha:*   Because they liked the color of her body!
>
> *Teacher:*   It's like the color of Rain's body.
>
> *Donna:*   Maybe cause the lady liked the color purple and she put in on there because Rain was the best girl.
>
> *Teacher:*   So you're thinking that the illustrator said, "Well, purple is my favorite color so I'm going to make the greatest [Rain] the color that's my favorite."

This sophisticated statement about the illustrator's method of interpreting the significance of the text occurred fairly early in the school year (second week of November). Later in the year, the children came to expect this part of the discussion and were sometimes impatient about it:

> *Dean:*   You didn't take the dust cover off . . .
>
> *Teacher:*   Oh, I didn't get to that yet. I'm going to take that off in a minute, but first we are looking at the back of this.

The children became so adept at visual meaning-making that they speculated during the discussion of the cover of one book that it was similar to another book because of the similarities in the cover illustrations; in contrast, it took the teacher more than a dozen conversational turns before she made the same connection. The covers of both books (*Something Beautiful* and *Sunday Week*) contained full-face portraits of an African American girl.

By the end of the school year, the children were conversant with most of the standard names for parts of picture books and employed these terms as they constructed coherent interpretations of the books as aesthetic wholes. For example, during the first five minutes of the discussion surrounding *Leola and the Honeybears,* an African American variant of *Goldilocks and the Three Bears,* the children correctly utilized the following terminology on their own: *front cover, back cover, dust jacket, endpages, title page,* and *double-page spread.* These kindergartners had learned much of the metalanguage for talking about picture books, and it functioned as a heuristic tool for their developing literary understanding and response.

The students also personalized the stories. As could be expected, if children encounter culturally relevant literature in ways that encourage their engagement, they should find it natural to enter into the world of what Louise Rosenblatt has called the "poem" (Rosenblatt 126): it becomes the literary work that is created when a reader interacts with a text. In *Max Found Two Sticks,* for example, the children began the readaloud session by looking at the book's cover illustration (a young African American boy sitting on the front porch of his urban house), speculating about the story. Notice how the children immediately began to draw their own lives into a relationship with the illustration:

> *Isaac:*   It's gonna be about a boy in a house.
>
> *Teacher:*   Okay, what do you think, Dawn?

Dawn: I think it's gonna be about, um . . . a boy sitting on the steps because his mom had a baby. . . . Because his mom said he couldn't come in unless he comes into his room.

Teacher: Oh, because why? What did she want him to do?

Dawn: She wanted him to watch . . . if he go in he got to watch TV upstairs in his room.

Teacher: But why can't he come in because the baby is there?

Dawn: Because uh . . . he got uh . . . he's got to clean his room up.

Dawn clearly had no difficulty in advancing an interpretation of the illustration because it portrayed a familiar scene. In this vignette, we can also see how the teacher encouraged Dawn, affirmed her answers, engaged with her in conversation, and did not correct her speech patterns (such as "if he go in"); she responded to her in Standard English without becoming authoritarian. Then the children began to speculate about the title, about what Max might do with the two sticks. Their responses demonstrate a willingness to connect their own lives with the book:

Naisha: I think . . . he's gonna make a stickalou with those sticks. . . .

Teacher: A stickaloon?

Naisha: Like the back of my shoe!

Teacher: Oh, oh, oh, . . . like the back of my shoe . . . like one, two,

Naisha: buckle my shoe! Three, four, shut the door!

Teacher: Right! Right! Five, six, pick up . . .

Class: Sticks!

Teacher: Very good. Okay.

[unidentified student]:   Seven, eight, lay them straight!

The teacher noted and applauded Naisha's whimsical intertextual connection to a familiar rhyme, thereby both encouraging and affirming this type of active relationship to the text. We understand these personal connections to contribute to the "blurring" of story and life, so that the children's lives entered into the stories and the stories entered into their lives. This blurring also occurred during the journal writing immediately following the readalouds. For example, after the readaloud of *Wings,* in which a new African American boy in school is laughed at by teachers and students because he has wings, Shawna drew a picture of unhappy people and dictated as her story, "They are laughing at me." Shawna had inserted herself in the place of the boy with wings.

Culturally relevant stories often provided children with the opportunity to tell stories of their own; this became another way that children engaged expressively with the stories and blurred the distinctions between story and life. For example, during the readaloud of *Black Cat,* Jhalil noticed the graffiti in the illustrations:

Jhalil: It's like bad guys—they be spraying bad stuff.

Teacher: Like spray paint?

Jhalil: Like that stuff—I see it every day and I want to see who's doing it! . . . There's a bad guy house right next to my apartment.

Teacher: So you think the bad guys are spraying that stuff on walls. What do you mean, a bad guy house?

Jhalil: They like stole money from the bank. . . . Me and my mom we was walking me to school. I saw two bad guys. I thought I saw their guns but I didn't. They was going somewhere so they could spray stuff on the walls!

Although it's difficult to tell what details in Jhalil's story are fiction and what actually happened, he is practicing the techniques of story makers by combining his own experience with imagined experience in creative ways.

Of particular pertinence to a multicultural pedagogy is the creation of a space in which to discuss issues of race, gender, and culture. One of Nieto's concerns is teachers' resistance to bringing up difficult or contentious issues in the classroom, "even though these may be central to students' lives"—a stance that simply "reinforces students' feelings that school life is separate and unrelated to real life" (98). In this classroom, the teacher engaged her students with difficult issues as they arose during storybook readalouds. One of these issues was the concept of skin color, the major topic of two books read during the year: *Shades of Black* and *The Colors of Us.* In the readaloud of *Shades of Black,* one child quickly understood the subject of the book:

Teacher: What do you think they're talking about?

Elena: Their color!

Teacher: Their color, thank you, Elena! This little boy is African American too, but his color is. . . .

Several children: White!

Teacher: He's kind of a creamy white. This little boy or little girl is chocolate brown.

At the end of the book, the following exchange occurred:

Teacher: Some of them do look white but remember the title of the book is *Shades of Black.* That means that there are many colors of black. All colors of black. If somebody says you are black and I am white. . . . I'm not white like that shirt, am I? Do white people look white like that shirt?

Several children: No.

Teacher: Come here, stand next to me [speaking to a boy with a white shirt]. Does my skin look like that shirt?

Several children: No.

Teacher: And does your skin look like the black on that rectangle [gesturing to a color chart]?

Several children: No!

Teacher: No, it does not. It's just an easy way to describe people. White and black. And what they are telling you is that there are all different shades and that they are all special.

Here we can see the way in which Mrs. Martin could persistently bring a sensitive topic into her classroom through the open-ended discussion afforded by the readaloud situation.

Shades of Black was read in December. In June, during the reading of *The Colors of Us,* the children became engaged in matching their own skin tones to those of the variety of children of different races and ethnicities in the story:

Katrin: I'm the one with the pink shoes on.

Teacher: Oh, you think this is your shade. Yeah, that does look like you. A pretty dark brown.

Briana: I'm her.

Teacher: Oh, you think you look kind of like her. A little bit lighter brown, like a golden brown. They're all pretty; they're just all different.

Other potentially difficult issues that came up during readalouds included gender issues (such as an illustration of a boy turning the rope for double dutch in the book *Sunday Week,* which sparked a lively conversation, and the question of whether girls play basketball during the readaloud of *Strong to the Hoop*) and race relations (such as a discussion of the significance of Martin Luther King, Jr.'s life during a readaloud of *Young Martin Luther King*).

The image of *flying* as a metaphor for freedom is an important African American cultural idea, embodied in its oral and literary traditions (Walters 4). In *Wings,* Christopher Myers draws on the potency of this metaphor: the main character in this picture-book fantasy is Ikarus Jackson, an African American boy with wings who is derided and ostracized by his teacher and classmates but who overcomes their negativity. The narrator is a young girl who sympathizes with Ikarus. The back cover of this book contains the words, "Let Your Spirit Soar." When Mrs. Martin read these words to the children, Mitchell spontaneously assumed the stance of an African American preacher, proclaiming "Let your spirit soar, my soul! Let your spirit fill my soul!" When Mrs. Martin asked the children what the girl should have said to Ikarus, Alice shouted emotionally, "Keep your soul up and fly!" These responses show the children's strong associations with the image of flying and the ways in which they connected it to freedom and spiritual triumph.

We have shown that the children's responses were rich and varied. They were responding to literature that made them feel comfortable and affirmed, and their stories were read by a teacher who pointed out reasons for such comfort and affirmation. She interacted with them as co-creators of the literary "poem," addressed difficult issues, accepted alternate ideas, and created a space within which they could explore the many ways of understanding literature. It is also important to consider the teacher's stance in sharing stories.

III.

We now turn to a consideration of Mrs. Martin's reading style. There are a number of ways in which teachers read aloud to children. Some view this activity as a type of performance and expect children to wait until the performance is over before discussing it. Other teachers ask frequent questions as they read to ensure that children comprehend the story. Still others encourage students to make spontaneous comments during the reading and are tolerant of children's attempts to link the story with their own lives. Our examination of Mrs. Martin's reading style suggests that she was drawing on a number of traditional story telling techniques.

Theories of storytelling seem particularly relevant because in the field of folklore the study of storytelling focuses on oral performance, which Richard Bauman characterized as a situated activity: "its form, meaning, and functions rooted in culturally defined scenes or events" (3). The classroom storybook readaloud is such an activity, in which the traditional roles of teacher (performer), students (audience), and story (picture book) are combined in a communicative event containing "the potential to rearrange the structure of social relations within the performance event and perhaps beyond it" (3). Both practitioners and folklorists suggest the following elements in storytelling:

- The oral tradition of storytelling is not primarily concerned with word-for-word repetition of a fixed text but is a flexible means of communication (Heckler 22–23).
- Storytelling acknowledges and adjusts to the audience's responses (Birch 107).
- The success of the storytelling depends on the intimacy created between teller and listener (Harley 130).
- The story is something created by both the audience and the narrator (Martin 143).
- Bauman (4) suggests that oral narrative performance is the unity of *text* (the original text, on which the storyteller bases his or her telling); the *narrated event* (what the storyteller says); and the *narrative event* ("the context of situated action," which includes the audience and its responses).
- In some cultures, storytelling is often connected to song, dance, visual elements, and social interaction, becoming a multimedia performance (Price and Price 12–14).

The goal of storytelling is, thus, similar to the goal of developing literary understanding: presenting a story in a way that would encourage children to respond aesthetically to literature, to co-create the world of the story (Rosenblatt 126) not only in conjunction with the author via the text (Iser 61) but also with the teacher, reader, or storyteller. This added dimension of storytelling as part of the readaloud repertoire can enhance our understanding of the ways in which the interactive storybook readaloud helps children develop as engaged readers of literature. It is true, as John Foley observes, that the storytelling experience is an oral performance and much is lost when it is written down in a format that uses only words (17–18). However, according to Foley, within the differing circumstances of each performance (setting, audience composition, and individualized responses within the audience) there is a type of "interpretive contract" in which the performer and audience co-create the work jointly from the text by negotiating what Iser has called the gaps between reader, or audience, and text, or story (45–46). Similarly, within the differing styles of individual teachers and the varying composition of kindergarten classes, we can think of the teacher's interpretive contract to help students bridge the gaps in the picture story-book being read aloud. It is possible to speak of fulfilling this contract with an implied audience (for example, African American students) in a performance tradition (for example, interactively reading picture storybooks aloud to young children).

The readaloud transcripts suggest that, for Mrs. Martin, the picture-book was a text that needed to be "recontextualized 'in motion' " (Price and Price xi) as a dynamic and interactive experience. Mrs. Martin acted as a storyteller in five ways: she was the *teller* of the story; she formed a *bridge* between the children and the story; as a *flexible adaptor* of the story, she let her reading be determined in part by her audience; and as an *extender and multiplier of meaning,* she encouraged different kinds of literary responses.

As the *teller,* Mrs. Martin was relatively unconcerned with a word-for-word rendering of the story, departing in significant ways from the written text. She recreated the text, assuming ownership of the story rather than being simply a mouthpiece for the written word. While the author's words were an important part of the readaloud, this teacher wove her own comments, observations, and interjections into the text. In doing so, she acknowledged that she remained herself in relationship to the tale and its culture, while also engaging the children with the story. Although a storyteller cannot say what it is like to belong to another culture not her own, she can speak of her own understanding of that culture and in that way mediate understanding (Heckler 29). Notice in the following example (from the readaloud of *Something Beautiful,* a contemporary, realistic picture book portraying a young African American girl thinking about her neighborhood) that the words of the text, presented here in boldface, are enmeshed with the teacher's own creative comments. Also notice how the teacher integrates illustration and text:

> *Teacher:*   Well, let's see what she's going to do. I can see her washing something. **. . . and a sponge and some water. I pick up the trash. I sweep up the glass. I scrub the door very hard. When Die disappears, I feel powerful.** She says, "Oh, boy, look what I did! I took that nasty word off my door." And she cleaned up everything. **Someday I'll plant flowers in my courtyard. I'll invite all my friends to see.**

As an emotional *bridge,* the teacher involved the audience of children and also involved herself in the story. She also valorized children's responses by seriously entertaining and engaging them. The following interchange occurred after *Something Beautiful* referred to a woman sleeping in a cardboard carton:

> *Teacher:*   So you think she wants to be living in that cardboard box?
>
> *Naisha:*   How did she live on the ground?
>
> *Teacher:*   She does, she lives in that cardboard box right there on the ground. Do you think she wants to live there, Kevin?
>
> *Kevin:*   No, because every time when me and my mom go to the Dunkin' Donuts we see people on the ground, um, and they be sleepin' and they look like they don't have no food. And this guy is laying on the ground and came in the donut [shop] and he went over in the corner and then laid down in the street.

> *Teacher:*   And how did that make you feel? When you see that, how does that make you feel?
>
> *Kevin:*   It make me sad.

This kind of scaffolding encouraged children to insert themselves into the plot and characterization of the story. They began to insert themselves as well. The following example is taken from the readaloud of *Wiley and the Hairy Man:*

> *Teacher:*   **"No thank you, Wiley. I'll just wait right here till you get tired or hungry."** He's saying, "That's okay, you know I can't climb up that tree, but you are going to have to come down sooner or later and I'm going to be waiting right here!" That's something my mother used to tell me when I was little.
>
> *Katrin:*   My mom used to tell me everyday!

Mrs. Martin is demonstrating here her awareness that storytellers "are compelling when they find their own voice and speak with conviction and with attitudes which can make their points of view springboards for the audience" (Birch 108).

Just as the teacher encouraged the children to engage emotionally with the story as a way to help them connect with it, she also helped them co-create their understanding of the story. The following vignette is from the readaloud of *The Magic Tree: A Folktale from Nigeria:*

> *Teacher:*   Okay. What do you think? How do they treat him?
>
> *Amanda:*   They treat him like a slave!
>
> *Teacher:*   They treat him like a slave. They ask him to do things over and over again, but they're not very nice to him. **Beginning very early in the morning when the first person in the village woke up, it was "Mbi, wake up so you can do this! Mbi, sleepyhead, wake up and do that!"**
>
> *Amanda:*   And they call him names.

The teacher incorporated her own comments and a child's response in with the text. In an example from *Strong to the Hoop,* the story of an African American boy who tries to play in a neighborhood basketball game with some older boys, she inserted her own life into the story:

> *Teacher:*   **I cut through the lane and bump into Marcus. It's like running into a rock.** Oh my goodness! **"You're too small. Get out of here or I'll push you out." I don't like his talking. Why can't he just shut up and play?** They are saying mean things to him too. "You're too small!" And if you go to a real basketball game, and I go to a lot of basketball games, you'll see that the players are talking to each other, "Get him, get him, get him, run over here, guard, guard, guard him!" They are talking a lot of jive talk.

Mrs. Martin is demonstrating that "[i]t is precisely the storyteller's work to explore a story and make a personal relationship with it" (Heckler 29).

As a *flexible adaptor,* the teacher, like a storyteller, let her reading be determined in part by her audience. The following is taken from a reading of *The Adventures of Sparrowboy,* in which a young African American boy sees a sparrow and imagines himself a superhero. In the fantasy, he seems to enter a comic book and acquire the ability to fly from the bird.

Teacher: **RRRRRP!!! IS IT TOO LATE FOR THE SPARROW?** How many think it's too late? (show of hands) Well, guess what? **"Hang on, little guy!"** Here he comes! **"I don't get it. Why can't you fly?"** Why can't he fly . . . he saying to the bird, "I don't get it, why can't you fly?" Why? What is wrong? Why can't that bird fly?

Joe: Because the bird gave him the powers.

Teacher: How many think that's right (show of hands)? I don't know. What do you think, Amanda?

Amanda: It is right because that's a sparrow.

Teacher: He gave his powers to the boy you think?

Amanda: Yes, and he doesn't have any, that's why he can't fly.

Teacher: So what do you think he should do? What is Sparrowboy going to do?

Several children speaking at once: Fly! / he gonna kill him / and sparrow boy gonna give them back so he can get to fly.

Teacher: Okay, let's see . . . you think he's gonna get his powers back; let's see.

In this particular passage, the teacher was engaged with the children in wondering how the superhero power transfer was going to work out for the boy and the bird. Her stance was one of co-wonderer; she followed the children's conversational lead and included herself in their speculations ("Okay, let's see"). Together they built alternate story lines and experimented with the world of the tale. As Rafe Martin writes, "stories must be re-created, not just re-performed. If tellers let technical skills grow out from their own experience, understanding, and inner seeing of the tale, the telling that emerges tends to have the power to move an audience" (146).

As an *extender and multiplier of meaning,* Mrs. Martin encouraged multiple ways of responding, including physical movement, sociodramatic play, dramatic reenactments, and journal writing. She urged the children to be co-creators of the story along with her, recognizing their suggestions even when these seemed unlikely. In the following example, from the readaloud of *Wiley and the Hairy Man,* the teacher and children are thinking about how the boy protagonist, who has climbed a tree, might escape the monster waiting below.

Isaac: If he try to go home and get something to eat he's gonna eat him!

Teacher: That's right, if he tries to go home you are going to be hungry and I'll be waiting for you! You will have to come down sooner or later! And I will be waiting right here. Oooh! **Wiley thought about that Hairy Man down there on the ground, and he thought about his hound dogs back home, and he came up with a plan.** What do you think the plan's going to be? Kevin?

Kevin: The monster . . . the Hairy Man gonna go to sleep, and he ain't gonna hear him, and the boy gonna tippy toe and untie the dog and he gonna wake up and the dog is gonna come and bite him.

Teacher: Oooh! That's a good idea—he could wait for the Hairy Man to go to sleep and he could sneak down and they could come back and bite him! What do you think, Edward?

Edward: I think he's gonna kick him in his face!

Teacher: Gonna kick him in the face! What do you think, Amanda?

Amanda: When the hairy monster is not looking he'll say, "Oh, I'm walking down the street," acting like there is somebody else coming and he'll look back and see and then he'll jump down and he'll go get his dogs and then he'll get back up and try to look to see if he's still there—

Teacher: Oh, so he can act like somebody else is coming, and when he looks away, he'll sneak down?

Amanda: Yes, and then his dogs—then he'll put some fire around his legs and he'll be burning up . . .

Teacher: He'll be burning up, okay—

Amanda: And the dogs will be barking.

In this example Amanda, inspired perhaps by the other children's stories, began to act out her scenario by pantomiming walking down the street, pretending to be occupied and then suddenly lighting out to get the dogs. This kind of dramatic response was not infrequent in the class, particularly among the male students, and it included pretending to fight, dance, swoon, and kiss, as we see later in the same readaloud:

Teacher: **The Hairy Man yelled, gnashed his teeth, and stomped all over the cabin.**

Several children: I told you he was gonna do that!

Teacher: **He grabbed that baby pig and stormed out the door into the swamp, knocking down trees as he ran.**

Katrin: And he stomped his feet, and pulled his hair! (Children stomp their feet)

The alternate stories offered by Kevin, Edward, and Amanda and Mrs. Martin's acceptance of them illustrate folklorist Barre Toelken's point:

Does it really matter after all that a story can have numerous meanings? Not at all, as long as we are ready and willing to deal with the delights of variety, ambiguity, suggestion, nuance, and culturally centered elements of meaning. (41)

The teacher's reading style is significant on several levels. First, it was dialogic in the Bakhtinian sense of allowing for multiple, open-ended, and unresolved points of view in the literary discussion (349). Second, this style encouraged remarkably free and incredibly rich literature responses on the part of lower socioeconomic status African American kindergartners who may not have participated regularly in interactive storybook readalouds prior to entering this classroom. Third, it incorporated elements of a traditional storytelling style, which may have encouraged open participation. This may be, in part, because it is culturally congruent in a way similar to that discussed by McMillon and Edwards (119) in their research on the reasons why a young African American boy who excelled in his culturally congruent Sunday School classes was not successful in his regular school classroom. Culturally relevant teaching honors in a school context what children bring from their own backgrounds (Foster, 1989, 1992, 1995; Ladson-Billings, 1994; Lee, 1993). In this case, Mrs. Martin's readaloud style may have been a key factor in making her classroom culturally congruent to the children's home culture.

The teacher played an active role in scaffolding and enabling the children's developing literary understanding, and this study, therefore, supports those who call for active students *and* active teachers (Cazden 422). One significant aspect of our study lies in its explication of a type of readaloud style that has not been examined in such detail heretofore and that has great potential for engaging children in active literary exploration and interpretation. Children who come from a culture that emphasizes oral language and storytelling (such as some urban African American children) may be more highly engaged when a teacher employs such a readaloud style. We believe our work has significant pedagogical implications for the ways in which teachers read to young children. Sonia Nieto tells us that our curriculum "lets students know whether the knowledge they and their communities value has prestige within the educational establishment" (96). If children believe that what they bring with them is valued by the teacher, they can feel free to apply whatever they know to the making of literary meaning and can develop sophisticated ways of talking about what they read. In the social milieu of a readaloud, they also learn how meaning can be constructed in collaboration with teachers and peers: that they can contribute to the creation of knowledge rather than be passive recipients. If such an outcome can be facilitated with culturally relevant children's literature, then shouldn't we be using more of it in our classrooms?

Works Cited

Bakhtin, Mikhail M. *The Dialogic Imagination.* Austin: University of Texas Press, 1981.

Barrentine, Shelby J. "Engaging with Reading through Interactive Read-Alouds." *The Reading Teacher* 50 (1996): 36–43.

Bauman, Richard. *Story, Performance and Event: Contextual Studies of Oral Narrative.* Cambridge, MA: Cambridge University Press, 1986.

Birch, Carol L. "Who Says: The Storyteller as Narrator." *Who Says? Essays on Pivotal Issues in Contemporary Storytelling.* Ed. Carol L. Birch and Melissa A. Heckler. Little Rock, AR: August House Publishers, 1996. 106–28.

Cazden, Courtney. "Contemporary Issues and Future Directions: Active Learners and Active Readers." *Handbook of Research on Teaching the English Language Arts.* Ed. James Flood, Julie M. Jensen, Diane Lapp, and James R. Squire. New York: Macmillan, 1991. 418–22.

Coy, John. *Strong to the Hoop.* New York: Lee and Low Books, 1999.

Dickinson, David K. and Rebecca Keebler. "Variation in Preschool Teachers' Styles of Reading Books." *Discourse Processes* 12 (1989): 353–75.

Dickinson, David K. and Miriam W. Smith. "Long-Term Effects of Preschool Teachers' Book Readings on Low-Income Children's Vocabulary and Story Comprehension." *Reading Research Quarterly* 29 (1994): 105–22.

Echewa, T. Obinkaram. *The Magic Tree: A Folktale from Nigeria.* New York: William Morrow, 1999.

Foley, John M. *The Singer of Tales in Performance.* Bloomington, IN: Indiana University Press, 1995.

Foster, Michelle. "'It's Cookin' Now': A Performance Analysis of the Speech Events of a Black Teacher in an Urban Community College." *Language in Society* 18 (1989): 1–29.

———. "Sociolinguistics and the African American Community: Implications for Literacy." *Theory into Practice* 31 (1992): 303–11.

———. "Talking That Talk: The Language of Control, Curriculum, and Critique." *Linguistics and Education* 7 (1995): 129–50.

Harley, Bill. "Playing with the Wall." *Who Says? Essays on Pivotal Issues in Contemporary Storytelling.* Ed. Carol L. Birch and Melissa A. Heckler. Little Rock, AR: August House Publishers, 1996. 129–40.

Heckler, M. A. (1996). "Two Traditions." *Who Says? Essays on Pivotal Issues in Contemporary Storytelling.* Ed. Carol L. Birch & Melissa A. Heckler. Little Rock, AR: August House Publishers, 1996. 15–34.

Hickman, Janet. "A New Perspective on Response to Literature: Research in an Elementary School Setting." *Research in the Teaching of English* 15 (1981): 343–54.

Iser, Wolfgang. *The Act of Reading: A Theory of Aesthetic Response.* Baltimore, MD: Johns Hopkins University Press, 1978.

Johnson, Dinah. *Sunday Week.* New York: Henry Holt, 1999.

Katz, Karen. *The Colors of Us.* New York: Henry Holt, 1999.

Kristo, Janice V. "Reading Aloud in a Primary Classroom: Reaching and Teaching Young Readers." *Journeying: Children Responding to Literature.* Ed. Kathleen E. Holland, Rachael A. Hungerford, & Shirley B. Ernst. Portsmouth, NH: Heinemann, 1993. 54–71.

Ladson-Billings, Gloria. *The Dreamkeepers: Successful Teachers of African American Children.* New York: Teachers College Press, 1995.

Lee, Carol. *Signifying as a Scaffold for Literary Interpretation: The Pedagogical Implications of an African American Discourse Genre.* Urbana, IL: National Council of Teachers of English, 1993.

Martin, Rafe. (1996). "Between Teller and Listener: The Reciprocity of Storytelling." *Who Says? Essays on Pivotal Issues in Contemporary Storytelling.* Ed. Carol L. Birch & Melissa A. Heckler. Little Rock, AR: August House Publishers, 1996. 141–54.

Martinez, Miriam and William Teale. "Teacher Storybook Reading Style: A Comparison of Six Teachers." *Research in the Teaching of English* 27 (1993): 175–99.

Mattern, Joanne. *Young Martin Luther King, Jr.: I Have a Dream.* Mahwah, NJ: Troll Communications, 1991.

McMillon, G. T., & Patricia A. Edwards. "Why Does Joshua 'Hate' School . . . but Love Sunday School?" *Language Arts* 78 (2000): 111–20.

Myers, Christopher. *Wings.* New York: Scholastic, 2000.

———. *Black Cat.* New York: Scholastic, 1999.

Nieto, Sonia. *Affirming Diversity.* White Plains, NY: Longman Publishing Group, 2000.

Olaleye, Isaac O. *In the Rainfield: Who Is the Greatest?* New York: Blue Sky Press, 2000.

Pinkney, Brian. *Max Found Two Sticks.* New York: Simon and Schuster, 1994.

———. *The Adventures of Sparrowboy.* New York: Simon and Schuster Books for Young Readers, 1997.

Pinkney, Sandra L. *Shades of Black.* New York: Scholastic, 2000.

Price, Richard and Sally Price. *Two Evenings in Saramaka.* Chicago, IL: University of Chicago Press, 1991.

Rosales, Melodye. *Leola and the Honeybears.* New York: Scholastic, 1999.

Rosenblatt, Louise. "The Poem as Event." *College English* 26 (1964): 123–28.

Sierra, Judy. *Wiley and the Hairy Man.* New York: Dutton, 1996.

Sipe, Lawrence R. "The Construction of Literary Understanding by First and Second Graders in Oral Response to Picture Storybook Read-Alouds." *Reading Research Quarterly* 35 (2000): 252–75.

Smith, Elizabeth B. "Anchored in Our Literature: Students Responding to Multicultural Literature." *Language Arts* 72 (1995): 17–20.

Toelken, Barre. "The Icebergs of Folktale: Misconception, Misuse, Abuse." *Who Says? Essays on Pivotal Issues in Contemporary Storytelling.* Ed. Carol L. Birch & Melissa A. Heckler. Little Rock, AR: August House Publishers, 1996. 35–63.

Walters, Wendy W. "'One of Dese Mornings, Bright and Fair,/Take My Wings and Cleave De Air': The Legend of the Flying Africans and Diasporic Consciousness." *Melus* 22 (1997): 3–29.

Wyeth, Sharon D. *Something Beautiful.* New York: Bantam Doubleday Dell, 1998.

18

Responding to Chinese Children's Literature

Cultural Identity and Literary Responses

Jiening Ruan

The ever-growing cultural and linguistic diversity in school-aged children brought a new call for multicultural education, an ideal advocated by educators such as James Banks and Sonia Nieto in their many publications. Many teachers and educators have worked to develop literacy programs that encourage students to examine their own cultures as well as seek to understand cultures that are different from their own. Defining multicultural literature and its use in education is important.

Barbara Diamond and Margaret Moore have written that multicultural literature is literature that "focuses on specific cultures [in America] by highlighting and celebrating their cultural and historical perspectives, traditions and heritage, language and dialects, and experiences and lifestyles" (43). Furthermore, they argued that multicultural children's literature includes the literature of diverse cultures outside the United States, from which the people of color in this nation claim ancestral heritage. Books about diverse cultural groups in the United States play a significant role in educating youngsters about diversity, while books with characters or descriptions of cultures outside of the United States also provide precious sources for multicultural knowledge.

According to Donna Norton, many goals of multicultural education can be accomplished by exposing children to multicultural literature. Teachers may help young children recognize similarities and differences among various cultures by sharing children's books with them. Many misconceptions and stereotypes about diverse cultures can be overcome when teachers and students read and discuss books that present accurate pictures of those cultures. Furthermore, multicultural children's literature can help children recognize that despite huge differences in physical features, language, cultural practices, and customs, human beings share similar kinds of feelings, emotions, and needs. While children develop a better understanding of their own and other people's cultures, they also become more willing to respect and appreciate the values and beliefs of different cultures, including their own.

There is a great need for introducing well-written and authentic Chinese American children's literature to the elementary language arts curriculum since Asian Americans constitute the fastest-growing minority in the United States. From a historical perspective, Chinese culture has exerted great influence on several other Asian cultures. It is also important to consider how Chinese American children respond to Chinese children's books because this will lead to a better understanding of all children's responses to Chinese literature in particular and to Asian American literature in general. Response theory and methodology make this possible.

In her many writings, Louise Rosenblatt emphasized the importance of examining children's interaction with books from both efferent and aesthetic stances. Such interactions involve not only linguistic resources and linkage but also "personal associations, feelings, and ideas being lived through during the reading" ("Retrospect" 104). Today's children often read both efferently and aesthetically. While they use their cultural knowledge to assist them in understanding new information, they also experience the pleasure that these literary works bring along. At the same time, they may learn about diverse cultures from their readings of multicultural literature. Listening to their more elaborate responses to these books can become possible as they discuss literature with researchers and become familiar with divergent themes and cultures.

Children's interpretation of multicultural literature and their understandings of linguistic texts vary greatly according to their sociocultural backgrounds and prior personal experiences with any particular culture. Trousdale and Harris claim, "A reader's encounter with a text is affected as much by what the reader brings to the experience as by what the written text itself provides" (195). If we closely examine children's responses to the literature that reflects their cultural backgrounds, we will gain new insights into the impact that culture-specific texts can have on children's comprehension of literature and better understand their personal responses to individual texts.

In recent years, within the literary context, research on mulitcultural children's literature has focused on issues of cultural authenticity and literary quality (e.g., Cai 1994). However, Au forcefully argues that those studies have not adequately addressed responses of students either from mainstream or from diverse backgrounds. She concludes that there is a "notable lacking" (97) of research on children's responses in elementary classrooms. Furthermore, most studies have focused on children from African American or Hispanic American backgrounds.

In 1995, Liaw explored several first-generation Chinese American children's reactions to and interpretations of three Chinese American children's books: *Lon Po Po* by Ed Young, *I Hate English* by Ellen Levine, and *Tikki Tikki Tempo* by Arlene Mosel. Liaw found that these children moved beyond literal interpretations, relating the stories to their own personal experiences. She also found that among these Chinese children, responses to the same piece of literature varied according to their age and the amount of exposure to traditional Chinese values they had earlier experienced. Liaw's study contributes to our understanding of Chinese American children's response to Chinese children's books. However, Liaw used subjects of different ages with different amounts of exposure to Chinese culture, and choices of genres were limited. The first two are both folktales whereas the third is a contemporary children's picture book. Finally, parental influence on children's responses was not examined, although it is well known that often young children's sense of identity is shaped by their parents and other family members.

This study explores young Chinese American children's responses to Chinese American children's literature books. The term *Chinese American children's literature* in this study is defined as children's books with Chinese as the main character(s). This study tries to expand on Liaw's study in scope and in depth. It seeks to answer the following questions: (1) How do children with a similar cultural background who are the same age respond to the same piece of Chinese (American) literature? (2) What are some of the response patterns that these children display? (3) How do these children respond to books from different genres? (4) How do parental attitudes toward Chinese children's literature books impact these children's preference when choosing books?

Purposive sampling was used to select samples for this study. Three first-grade Chinese children in a midwestern university town participated in this study. Two of them came to America with their parents, and the other one was born in the United States. Their parents were all seeking master's or Ph.D. degrees at the university. All three children were attending the local Chinese Language School on Saturday afternoons and being instructed with Chinese textbooks also used in China. Because of time constraints, no Chinese children's trade books had been shared with these children other than the stories presented in their textbooks.

These three children had very different life experiences although they shared similar cultural backgrounds. All of them came to the Chinese Language School because their parents wanted them to appreciate their Chinese heritage. Mei was born in the United States. She was a typical American girl in many ways except for her physical attributes. She had many European American friends. She was taking piano lessons, painting lessons, and gymnastic lessons in her spare time. Bing came to America when he was four years old. He had adjusted quite comfortably to life in America, and he spoke English like a native. He enjoyed TV programs and basketball games more than reading English or Chinese. Kang had come to America in the last year, and this was his second semester in the first grade. At the time of the study, he was still in the process of adjusting to American culture, although he was quickly catching up in school.

These children learned Chinese mainly because their parents wanted them to do so. Their parents were very involved in their children's Chinese language studies. The parents brought their children to the school and picked them up after school was over.

I assumed the role of a participant in this study. Before the study was carried out, a good rapport had been established among these children and myself. The children willingly told me what they really thought of the books shared with them in the study. In addition, as a Chinese native, I fully understood the cultural backgrounds of these children, which helped greatly when making interpretations from the data collected.

Three books with Chinese children as main characters were used in this study. These books also represent a wide spectrum of genres, ranging from folklore to stories about the Chinese American experience in North America to informational stories about Chinese language or culture. Of the three books selected—Ed Young's *Lon Po Po,* Sarunna Jin's *My First American Friend,* and Huy Voun Lee's *At the Beach*—the first is a very popular Chinese folktale among American school children; the second is a contemporary story depicting a young Chinese immigrant's experience in the United States; and the third contains information about the Chinese written language.

I met these three children individually and shared the three books with them. Before sharing the books with them, I interviewed them about their general attitudes toward and familiarity with children's books with Chinese characters. After each book had been shared, I did a postreading interview with each child, soliciting responses to each book. In addition, they were also requested to complete a survey after each book was read to them. The survey, which has two major constructs, efferent and aesthetic, allowed me to consider the children's responses to the story structure and understand the pleasures gained from each reading. Some general affective statements were also included in the survey.

Parent interviews explored whether the home environment had an impact on the children's responses to the three books. Research studies have demonstrated that parental involvement is very critical in children's appreciation of literature (e.g., McClain and Stahl 1995). Thus, the parental factor was a very important consideration to this study.

The book-sharing sessions were audiotaped and later transcribed. Notes and personal memos were also taken after the book-sharing sessions. All these helped triangulate my data sources. Children's reactions and responses were constantly compared and patterns were identified from the data. The patterns that emerged from these data allowed me to make general assertions about the children's responses to this literature.

Assertion 1: These children, although they were from the same cultural background, produced different responses to the same stories. I believe that several factors led to the differences in their responses to the same Chinese children's books. First of all, cultural identity did not appear to be the major concern of these children. However, the degree of acculturation they had experienced while in America had a strong impact on their preferences among the books. Surprisingly, none of these children mentioned that they liked or disliked any of the books because the children in the books were from the same ethnic or cultural background as theirs. Throughout the whole study, the children made no associations to the Chinese culture or their own cultural background when they evaluated the three books.

Mei and Bing liked *Lon Po Po* very much because they were used to the Western version of the story. Kang indicated that he had never heard the story of *Little Red Riding Hood*, and he did not care too much about the story. On the other hand, Mei and Bing did not care much about *My First American Friend.* They explained that they did not have any particular feeling about this book. When asked why, Mei explained she could not relate herself to what happened to the little Chinese girl in the book, who had a hard time finding a friend when she first came to America. Bing said the story was boring. He simply said he did not like the book and would not want to make friends with the characters in the book. In contrast, Kang loved this book and named it as his favorite book among the three. He said that he had a similar experience, and he had found it hard to find a friend at school when he first arrived in America. His preference for *My First American Friend* above the other two was closely connected to his personal experience of encountering social difficulties while settling into a new culture. He explained, "When you go to a new place and you don't know anybody, it can be like the story." This second pattern indicates that children's previous experiences and prior knowledge greatly influence their preferences and responses to the books shared. This became obvious through our many conversations.

All three children liked the book *At the Beach.* They liked this book because it concerned writing certain Chinese characters, and they had learned these characters in Chinese class at the Saturday school during the semester. They felt good about themselves because they knew all the characters in the book, and they were amazed that these characters resembled things in nature.

Mei and Bing selected *Lon Po Po* as their favorite because they had heard the Grimm version at school. They enjoyed relating their preferences and comparing the two stories. Mei produced an elaborate account of *Little Red Riding Hood*, and she pinpointed the major similarities and discrepancies between the two stories. She said, in the *Little Red Riding Hood* story, "the wolf ate the grandma and the girl, and in this book, there was no grandma and the wolf was killed by the sisters." *My First American Friend* appealed tremendously to Kang, but he did not enjoy *Lon Po Po* much. He explained that *Lon Po Po* was not real while *My First American Friend* was "real and meaningful" for him.

I found that the children's personalities and personal tastes strongly related to their preference in books. Both Mei and Bing were excited about *Lon Po Po*. They all said that the story was fun and claimed that the children in the story were smart. They explained that they liked smart kids. Bing said, "They are smart, and they killed the wolf." During my interview with his father, I was informed that Bing liked stories or movies that contained lots of action and were sometimes violent. His father joked that *Lon Po Po* was Bing's type of book. Mei said she liked *Lon Po Po* because she enjoyed all sorts of fairy tales. She could retell the story with all the details in *Lon Po Po*. This quiet, sweet little girl had read several collections of *Fairy Tales From around the World,* and she said these were her favorite books. Her mother said that her bedtime stories came from those books. Therefore, Mei was familiar with the plots of fairy tales, and she liked those with happy endings.

In many ways Kang was the most precocious. He was quiet and very serious about his school work, both at the Chinese Language School and his elementary school. His favorite book, *My First American Friend,* is a realistic story with little action. Kang's recent entry into America and his serious personality might have caused him to accept this book as his favorite.

Assertion 2: The children reacted to books from different genres differently. Although the majority of children at this age have been shown to prefer folktales in past studies, books from other genres can be as appealing to some other children.

Mei and Bing both selected *Lon Po Po* as their favorite. It was followed by *At the Beach* and *My First American Friend.* They both loved *Lon Po Po* because of their familiarity to its story structure; they could relate this story to other folktales they knew. They also liked *At the Beach*, which is an informational book. They placed *My First American Friend* at the bottom of their lists. The order of Kang's preferences was reversed: *My First American Friend, At the Beach,* and *Lon Po Po.* When I asked him why he felt this way, he told me that *My First American Friend* was "meaningful." *At the Beach* was "fun because it has lots of Chinese characters that I know how to write." He also commented that *Lon Po Po* was fun but it was not "real." He said he did not like stories that were not real.

The children had developed genre knowledge; their earlier experiences with various genres partially determined the type of books they favored.

Assertion 3: Parental preferences and attitudes about children's literature had significant impact on these children's interest in the particular type of books they liked. While I visited their homes, I browsed through their book collections and talked with the parents. I discovered that parental perceptions concerning the books most appropriate for their children's development partly explained these children's book preferences.

All of these children listened to their parents read aloud to them at bedtime, although the types of books shared were very different. Kang's father was a mathematician. He provided his child access to many factual and informational books. He thought that entertainment was not the major concern of reading. According to Kang's father, the purpose of reading was to obtain knowledge (both cultural and scientific). A good book had to be "meaningful" or having some real-life ramifications. Kang's most favorite books were a series of *Children's Anthology of Science.* Before Kang went to bed each night, he flipped to a page with a topic that interested him and handed the book to one of his parents to read to him.

Mei's mother was in complete charge of Mei's education. There was a big collection of children's books, both in Chinese and in English, in her house. Most of them were folktales of different kinds from different countries. Mei's mother thought that her daughter should be a good, well-behaved little girl and that there were lots of moral lessons that Mei could learn from fairy tales and folktales. She told me that she often used these stories to illuminate her points with Mei, and she found it very effective. Also, she thought that reading books could help her daughter improve her language skills, both in Chinese and in English.

Bing's parents were magazine editors before they came to America. There was also a large collection of children's books in their apartment, but Bing was not interested in reading them. Most of the books were in Chinese. His parents allowed Bing to choose whatever books he liked to read when they went to the county library on weekends. His father thought that good children's books should be entertaining with interesting plots as well as cultural knowledge. He had no intention of curbing his son's interest in certain types of books so long as Bing enjoyed reading. The father told me that so far his son liked books with action and sometimes even "violence."

Assertion 4: Book-sharing experiences help develop positive attitudes toward reading Chinese children's literature for Chinese American children. As I worked with these children, they demonstrated significant changes in their interests in reading Chinese children's books. In the prereading interviews, they all displayed a general indifference to reading Chinese children's books. After the book-sharing sessions, all of them expressed great interest in reading other Chinese children's books in the future in spite of their likes or dislikes for certain books. Kang, commenting on *My First American Friend,* said, "It is nice to see children like us are in the books." Mei stated that she wanted to go back and find some more books with Chinese children and share the books with Kang and Bing.

Furthermore, my interactions with the families created positive changes in the way the parents thought about multicultural children's literature. All of the children's parents told me it had never occurred to them that they should look for depictions of Chinese children in English texts; they had previously limited their search for Chinese children's literature and imagery to books published in Chinese. Mei's mother and Kang's father commented that sharing these types of books would add another dimension to their children's reading. Mei's mother asked me to loan her two of the books to read to her daughter. Bing's father also mentioned that sharing imagery of Chinese children and their culture in English with his son would help Bing adjust better in American society. In addition, at the conclusion of the study, they all agreed that it would be beneficial to expose their children to these books in the future and hoped that these books could help their children develop a stronger positive sense of cultural identity in America.

My study has several limitations. First, my sample size was small. A larger sample size could produce more stable findings. Second, these children come from academic families. Exploring the responses of Chinese American children from different family backgrounds would help us better understand how all Chinese American children respond to literature with Chinese characters and customs. However, this research has several significant findings and important implications. I explored young first-grade Chinese children's literary responses to seeing English-language children's literature with strong Chinese imagery and inquired into family sharing of children's literature within three academic Chinese families living in America, something not earlier studied. My findings suggest that young children respond to their literature in intriguing and unique ways. The children, although all from a similar Chinese sociocultural background, responded to the same books in different ways. These differences were related to their previous experiences, personalities, and parental preferences.

In terms of responding to culturally specific children's books (in this case, Chinese children's books), this study suggests that cultural identity is not the strongest determining factor that underlies young children's personal responses and preferences to the books. Contrary to many previous research studies, I found that cultural identity was not explicitly expressed within the children's responses to the books shared with them. Their previous personal experiences, personalities, and parental attitudes were more relevant to the kinds of responses they expressed. Therefore, I would speculate that the child's age when exploring literature is an important factor in his or her developing understanding and appreciation of cultural literacy. These first graders were in the process of developing their sense of cultural identity. Thus, they might not have reached the stage where they would approach the books from a Chinese cultural perspective. However, my hypothesis needs to be further tested. In fact, my study supports McGee and Purcell-Gates's 1997 contention that we need more distinct studies of cultural identity and its influence on readers' responses to children's literature.

My findings suggest that children should also be exposed to books from different genres. Many times folktale literature is the prominent genre found in a teacher's collection of children's literature. Therefore, young children do not often have opportunities to interact with informational texts or contemporary stories, and information from the studies conducted becomes limited. This current study supports the viewpoint that "Expository text should consume a substantial part of the elementary literacy and language curriculum" (Hiebert 482). Books from different genres have great potential for children from different cultures and with different learning styles.

My research also details the tremendous impact parents can have on their children's preferences for and appreciation of books. Researchers have long recognized that parents sharing books with their young children can lead to their children's better language and literacy development (e.g., Clark 1984; Durkin 1975; Fox and Wright 1997; Morrow 1993). Children who are exposed to literacy activities at home usually develop better knowledge about text structures, linguistic features, and literary conventions. They also have a broader prior knowledge about things and people in the world through their intergenerational conversations. However, few studies have explored parental involvement and children's appreciation of literature when the parents are well-educated immigrants living in America. More studies are needed to help us understand the links between parental preferences and children's preferences of the literature.

Finally, I would argue once again that there is importance in exposing all children to multicultural literature. I observed a tremendous change in these children's attitudes when reading English-language children's literature with Chinese imagery by the end of the study. If we want all children to read multiculturally, we must strive to introduce them to multicultural children's books from all genres at an early age, and we should consider ways we can involve their parents or caretakers in our activities.

Works Cited

Au, K. H. "Multicultural Perspectives on Literature Research." *Journal of Reading Behavior* 27 (1995): 85–100.

Banks, J. A. "Ethnicity, Class, Cognitive and Motivational Styles: Research and Teaching Implications." *Journal of Negro Education* 57 (1988): 446–52.

———. *Multiethnic Education: Theory and Practice,* 3rd ed. Boston: Allyn and Bacon, 1994.

Cai, M. "Images of Chinese and Chinese Americans Mirrored in Picture Books." *Children's Literature in Education* 25 (1994): 169–91.

Clark, M. M. "Literacy at Home and at School: Insights from a Study of Young Fluent Readers." *Awakening to Literacy.* Ed. H. Goelman, A. A. Oberg, and F. Smith. London: Heinemann, 1984. 122–30.

Diamond, B. J. and M. A. Moore. *Multicultural Literacy: Mirroring the Reality of the Classroom.* White Plains, NY: Longman Publishers, 1995.

Durkin, D. "A Six-Year Study of Children Who Learned to Read in School at the Age of Four." *Reading Research Quarterly* 10 (1975): 9–61.

Enisco, P. "Cultural Identity and Response to Literature: Running Lessons from *Maniac Magee.*" *Language Arts* 71(1994): 524–33.

Fox, B. and Wright, M. "Connecting School and Home Literacy Experiences Through Cross-Age Reading." *The Reading Teacher* 50 (1997): 396–403.

Glaser, B. G. and A. L. Strauss. *The Discovery of Grounded Theory: Strategies for Qualitative Research.* New York: Aldine Degruyter, 1967.

Harris, V., ed. *Teaching Multicultural Literature in Grades K–8.* Norwood, MA: Christopher-Gordon Publishers, 1992.

Hiebert, E. H. "Research Directions: Department Editor's Note." *Language Arts* 68 (1991): 482.

Jin, S. *My First American Friend.* Milwauke, WI: Raintree, 1991.

Lee, H. V. *At the Beach.* New York: Henry Holt and Company, 1994.

Liaw, M. L. "Looking into the Mirror: Chinese Children's Responses to Chinese Children's Books." *Reading Horizon* 35 (1995): 185–97.

McClain, V. and S. A. Stahl. "Standing in the Gap: Parents Reading with Children." Paper presented at the Annual Meeting of the National Reading Conference (New Orleans, LA, November 29–December 2, 1995).

McGee, L. and V. Purcell-Gates. "So What's Going on in Research on Emergent Literacy?" *Reading Research Quarterly* 32 (1997): 310–18.

Mikkelsen, N. "Toward Greater Equity in Literacy Education: Storymaking and Non-Mainstream Students." *Language Arts* 67 (1990): 556–66.

Morrow, L. M. *Literacy Development in the Early Years: Helping Children Read and Write.* Boston: Allyn and Bacon, 1993.

Nieto, S. *Affirming Diversity: The Social Political Context of Multicultural Education.* 2nd ed. New York: Longman, 1996.

Norton, D. *Through the Eyes of a Child.* 4th ed. Englewood Cliffs, NJ: Prentice-Hall, 1995.

Pappas, C. C. "Fostering Full Access to Literacy by Including Information Books." *Language Arts* 68 (1991): 449–62.

Patton, M. *Qualitative Evaluation and Research Methods.* 2nd ed. Newbury Park, CA: Sage Publications, 1990.

Rosenblatt, L. M. *The Reader, the Text, the Poem: The Transactional Theory of Literary Work.* Carbonade, IL: South Illinois University Press, 1978.

————. "Retrospect." In Farrell, Edmund J. and James R. Squire eds. *Transactions with Literature: A Fifty-Year Perspective.* Urbana, IL: National Council of Teachers of English, 1990. 97–107.

Sims, R. (1983). "Strong Black Girls: A Ten-Year-Old Responds to Fiction about Afro-Americans." *Journal of Research and Development in Education* 16 (1983): 21–28.

Trousdale, A. M. and Harris, V. J. "Missing Links in Literary Response: Group Interpretation of Literature." *Children's Literature in Education* 24 (1993): 195–207.

Vandergrift, K. *Children's Literature: Theory, Research, and Teaching.* Englewood, CO: Libraries Unlimited, 1990.

Young, E. *Lon Po Po.* New York: Philomel, 1989.

Keeping Current

"Keeping up" is one of those things that we all talk about in the field of children's literature. It is a difficult issue because there are many journals and organizations that talk about children's literature, discuss how we could best use children's literature in our classrooms, and consider the importance of applying good multicultural standards to what we teach. We both like to teach children's and adolescent literature courses best, but Darwin also teaches courses in multicultural education. We share some interests in similar journals, but we also read different sorts of things. Talking with one another helps each of us find some of the many perspectives in the field.

Darwin likes to watch for issues of the *African American Review* that deal with children's literature. In 1998 there was a special issue edited by Dianne Johnson containing articles on a variety of topics, including pieces about Arna Bontemps's *The Lonesome Boy,* illustrated by Joseph A. Alvarez, quilts as a symbol in children's literature by Olga Idriss Davis, and Eleanora Tate's Carolina trilogy, illustrated by Carole Brown Knuth. Darwin has alerted Jill to the issues that dealt with children's literature, and she has read the articles, enjoying the variety of perspectives available. Darwin also watches for issues of *Journal of Children's Literature,* published by the Children's Literature Assembly of the National Council of Teachers of English. Both Darwin and Jill have published in this journal, and they see it as an important place because the editors strive to include both theory about children's literature and issues of classroom practices. Jill likes to read journals that originate in the Children's Literature Association, especially the *ChLA Quarterly,* because it has articles that are theoretical and that emphasize reading with an eye on critical theory.

Still, we know that this is only the beginning of articles that have been written on children's literature, and we rely heavily on our librarians at our university and public libraries to help us find books and periodicals that expand our understanding of culturally diverse texts. We have found that our libraries hold a wealth of information in their electronic databases. For instance, Purdue University has the *MLA International Bibliography.* Jill went to that site and found information about recently published journal articles and books in children's literature. She also could see what dissertations had been published. Browsing this bibliographic database allowed her to see that much is being published about the classics in our field, and that there are also articles and books available that deal with issues of diversity. When she was looking for new sites on internationalism in children's and adolescent literature, she discovered that Azuka Okeke had written the dissertation "The Representation of the Cultural and Social World in Selected Nigerian Children's Literature" and that she could find a full description in *Dissertation Abstracts International*. She discovered that *Style* had a special section devoted to international children's literature in the fall of 2001. And she found that *Radical Teacher* had published Patti Capel Swartz's "Bridging Multicultural Education: Bringing Sexual Orientation into the Children's and Young Adult Literature Classroom" in 2003, an issue that she was also pursuing at the time. *The Children's Literature Comprehensive Database* allows us to find information on featured children's authors and illustrators, recent award winners (and total lists for many of the awards), and book reviews for many books. Both Jill and Darwin believe that this site is an excellent one for colleges and universities to subscribe to because it is an easy reference to topics that college and university librarians may find out of their day-to-day domain. In addition, because we are teaching in schools of education and have lots of elementary education students in our classes, we use ERIC's database to find sources. We have access to the *International Index to Black Periodicals, Contemporary Authors,* and the *Wilson OmniFile* online, so we can ascertain what is being discussed in various fields about children and adolescents and their literature, books that have just been published, and author sketches.

It is important to ask your librarians what electronic sources are available. Libraries and librarians are our compatriots in this study of cultural diversity. They have been the driving forces behind many of the book awards we now find available for us; they have built sensitive contemporary collections; they have fought against censorship; and they have been essential figures in UNICEF and in IBBY. Keeping current depends on keeping libraries free and open for all of us.

Our other ways of keeping current include traveling away from home. When we attend major conferences, we listen to experts speak about the place of literature in the world of the child and the adolescent; we learn about new literary patterns that expand our personal canons of literature; we hear teachers and librarians talk about their successes and failures when they are sharing literature with youthful audiences. We have favorite organizations, but we choose not to mention them here. Rather, we ask that you find out what meetings you can attend first locally, then at the state level, and finally at national and international meetings. Many of the people who are in this volume are professional friends we first met at conferences.

Part III

Defining Cultural Uniqueness: Agency in the Critique of Children's and Adolescent Literature

What History Asks

What history asks of us
is to see both ways at once

like a stereoscope
coming into focus,

union of duality
north and south, say

or mother—daughter, lover—
beloved, merging

like tulips lifting
vivid petals

from under weathered
maple leaves,

spires rising from the prairie,
houses emptied of memory,

a white lowrider filled
with immigrant children

passing horse-drawn
buggies of the Amish

on a mainstreet paved
with bricks, buckling now,

still bearing the name
of the place they were made,

or the quilt hung
in a dark window

that silently repeats
its simple litany

of hands—common
icons of desire.[1]

—*Christian Knoeller*

We have had a long-standing interest in the Harlem Renaissance and its influence on children's and adolescent literature. When we were both teaching at Purdue University, we toyed with the idea of writing a book about the migration of Blacks from the South to the North and its relationship with the Black Arts movement. Once Darwin left for the University of Cincinnati, we never stopped researching the topic.

When Jill was at the Beinecke Library on the Yale University campus, she became fascinated with the correspondence between Arna Bontemps and Langston Hughes housed in the James Weldon Johnson Collection. Bontemps and Hughes were lifelong friends, and they wrote the children's book *Popo and Fifina* together. *Popo and Fifina* was published in 1932; by that time both men were already established writers. With only nine months difference in their ages, they had similar literary interests and attitudes about the possibilities of African Americans in the arts. Throughout their lives, they were occupied by the pursuit of Black literature. Both were active in the Harlem Renaissance.[2] Both were successful playwrights and recognized voices in the artistic community of Harlem. They each had poetry in Alain Locke's *The New Negro,* a significant collection of Black writing that was first published in 1925. Hughes had several poems published in the collection, whereas Bontemps had but one, his award-winning "The Day-Breakers":

> **The Day-Breakers**
> *We are not come to wage a strife*
> *With swords upon this hill,*
> *It is not wise to waste the life*
> *Against a stubborn will.*
> *Yet we would die as some have done.*
> *Beating the way for the rising sun.*[3] (Locke 145)

Both had poems published in the controversial journal *Fire!!* that lasted for one issue only, in 1926.[4] Again, Hughes had several poems published whereas Bontemps had one, "Length of Moon." Ironically, "Day-Breakers" has been continually taught in schools while "Length of the Moon" has disappeared from the canon.

> **Length of Moon**
> *Then the golden hour*
> *Will tick its last*
> *And the flame will go down in the flower.*
>
> *A briefer length of moon*
> *Will mark the sea-line and the yellow dune.*
>
> *Then we will think of this, yet*
> *There will be something forgotten*
> *And something we should forget.*
>
> *It will be like all things we know:*
> *A stone will fail; a rose is sure to go.*

It will be quiet then and we may stay
Long at the picket gate,—
But there will be less to say.[5] (22)

Although Bontemps showed potential as a poet, he chose another route within Black Aesthetics. He married, moved to Chicago, went to graduate school in library science and later became the librarian and archivist at Fisk University. He began to edit collections of other people's works. His edited publications established a running record of the elite Black writers of his time. Bontemps's archival work is significant today because it identified a canon of Black writers who were noteworthy during the Black Renaissance that was situated in Chicago, San Francisco, and Harlem. Furthermore, a close reading of his letters suggests that Bontemps was defining an aesthetic that has often been ignored when discussing children's and adolescent literature.

Bontemps and Hughes remained in close touch via correspondence, and they visited one another throughout their lives. They also edited two significant collections of Black literature together: *The Poetry of the Negro, 1746–1949* and *The Book of Negro Folklore*. During the 1940s Hughes placed all of his letters from Bontemps in the James Weldon Johnson collection. Those letters suggest much about the American literary canon. Their correspondence has allowed us to consider how the literary canon might be judged and expanded by leading Black writers and critics. Using research collections is important to scholarship.

Reading letters and documents by authors who have donated their personal artifacts to archival collections helps literary criticism contextualize the artistic aesthetics of writing at a certain period and lets the scholar evaluate how a particular author fits in his or her period, a practice taken up in New Historicism. Charles E. Bressler argues that New Historicism addresses the question: "Do contemporary issues and the cultural milieu of the time operate together to create literature [. . .] or is literature simply an art form that will always be with us?" (240). As a critic who practices New Historicism, Stephen Greenblatt places textual analysis within the study of culture. He suggests that the creative process of production is linked to material culture. Greenblatt writes:

> Indeed even if one begins to achieve a sophisticated historical sense of the cultural materials out of which a literary text is constructed, it remains essential to study the ways in which these materials are formally put together and articulated in order to understand the cultural work that the text accomplished. (449)

New Historicism places the author's text within the society where she or he lived and suggests that rhetorical language represents or reimagines cultural beliefs and practices.

How did Bontemps and Hughes consider Black representations in the arts? How did their evaluations of cultural aesthetics shape their writing? What did they see that they considered set the pace for future writers? Arna Bontemps's correspondence to Langston Hughes during the first half of 1942 when Bontemps was living in Chicago, attending graduate school, and working for the Chicago Writers Project helps us answer these questions. At that time he was married and his children were students at Du Sable High. While

Bontemps does talk a good deal about his and Hughes's writing, he also mentions children's and adolescent literature that he finds especially noteworthy for their presentations of Black America. Reading his correspondence has allowed us to see how current events and American racial attitudes helped shape Bontemps's commentary in his correspondence to Hughes. It also details his interest in establishing a strong archival collection that would address the writing of Black Americans.

On January 19, 1942,[6] Bontemps mentioned the announcement of Lippincott's new book by Zora Neale Hurston and then he turned to children's book publishing, asking, "Have you noticed that debate in the PUBLISHERS' WEEKLY on Negro dialect in children's books. They have considerable to say about us in each installment." Then he suggested that the articles should be placed in the collection at Yale and added, "I wonder if he [Johnson] has the HORN BOOK for January–February 1940. (I think that's the date.) Anyhow it had much about the Negro in juvenile letters, including an article by me and another one about me by Miss Rider."

Dialect in children's literature and the creation of a strong Black presence in children's literature were important issues for Bontemps. He had just received a contract from Houghton Mifflin for *The Fast Sooner Hound,* a book he was writing with Jack Conroy.[7] Their main character in *The Fast Sooner Hound* talked in dialect, though it cannot be tagged as Black dialect since no identifiable Black characters can be found in the illustrations by Virginia Lee Burton. These illustrations were appreciated by Bontemps, so perhaps he did not see this as a story about a Black railroad worker. Still, there are similarities in *The Fast Sooner Hound* to John Henry's legendary defeat of the steam engine because the dog can outrun any train, and the main character's jobs on the railway resemble those of early Black southern workers who migrated to find better jobs.[8] When applying for a job as a fireman, the protagonist explains, "Last year I shoveled coal on the Katy. Before that I worked for the Frisco line. Before that it was the Wabash. I travel light, I travel far, and I don't let any grass grow under my feet" (2).

Dialect was a hot topic in children's literature circles when Bontemps wrote to Hughes about the controversy. Author Eva Knox Evans explained in her 1941 *Publishers' Weekly* article "The Negro in Children's Fiction" that Black children in her class seemed distraught to hear that her heroine did not talk as Blacks did. Then she argued against using Black dialect and praised Bontemps's dialogue in his recently published children's book, *Sad-Faced Boy:*

> They [Black readers] have been conditioned to expect it, by a tradition in the writing of stories about Negroes. For dialect has become so identified with Negroes that it is easy to understand why authors have hesitated to dispense with this distinguishing characteristic. But Negroes no longer talk like Uncle Remus. They talk much like anyone else, depending on the part of the country from which they come and on the degree of their literacy.
>   [. . .]
>   And just to show how far authenticity and realism can go without the use of dialect, "Sad-Faced Boy" (Houghton Mifflin) conveys fully and effectively the difference in enunciation of the southern country boy from that of the child of Harlem. Arna Bontemps, himself a Negro, has done a beautiful job of showing the rhythm and slur of the southerner as contrasted to the more correct and clipped speech of the northerner. (650, 651)

Knox did not favor a realism that would depict the "problems peculiar to the history of their race in this country" in books for young children, but she conceded that they would be "thrilling plot material" for older children's books. Knox mentioned *Shuttered Windows* by Florence Means as an exemplary story for high school students, and she concluded, "Children like these books I have mentioned" (652).

Two months later, in the October 18, 1941, *Publishers' Weekly,* the editors published an article entitled "Negro Dialect in Children's Books" that included "letters on this subject from a bookseller, a librarian and a famous author of Negro fiction" (1555). Librarian Adelaide C. Rowell of the Chattanooga, Tennessee, Public Library wrote:

> Dialect is something more than the speech of Negroes or Jews or Italians or what you will in Atlanta, New York, or Jackson, Mississippi. Dialect is the folk flavor in the speech of people of all races; remove all this, and replace it with the "King's English," and you will have done away with much of the racy tang of expression among books and people. [. . .] I cannot think of anything worse than a world where people all dress alike, talk alike, and consequently, think alike—a truly standardized set-up. (1556, 1557)

Author Christine Noble Govan argued for dialect writing, commenting,

> If it be legitimate to drop Negro dialect as a means of conveying a part of life, why not all dialect: the soft, burry and expressive Old English terms of the mountaineer; the quaint colloquialisms of New England; the French and Spanish phrases of portions of the "deep South"; American children would grow up ignorant of them all, and consequently unaware of portions of America's rich and varied tradition. It would leave them totally unprepared for the writings of Julie Peterkin or DuBose Heyward or George W. Cable; even for that of the Negro writers themselves, from Charles W. Chestnut, through Langston Hughes, Arno [*sic*] Bontemps, and the others of the 'twenties, to Zora Hurston, Richard Wright and William Attaway, all of whom use dialect freely and beautifully—and effectively. (1558)

Comments within this second article, which suggested dialect was easily emulated, seemed condescending to Black authors, librarians, and teachers, and they brought a final retaliation from a group of Black leaders in libraries and schools, including Georgia Cowen Poole and Charlemae Rollins, in the January 10, 1942, edition of *Publishers' Weekly:*

> [. . . Govan] states further that Langston Hughes, Arno [*sic*] Bontemps, Richard Wright, and others use dialect "freely and beautifully—and effectively." These folkways are a heritage which we Negroes, no less than our white friends, want to have preserved; but the preservation of these values is different from the preservation of illiterate habits of speech which authors of books about Negroes mistake as dialect. The incorrect grammar and "sort of liquid and picturesque speech" of characters in books by Govan, Knox, Garner, and Weaver are not comparable to the very realistic vernacular of Arno [*sic*] Bontemps, which no Negro finds offensive, and to the adult dialect found in Peterkin, Haywood, and Hurston. (105)

Black critics were suggesting that dialect was a natural expression of a people and that it could only be effectively written when authors were familiar with spoken folkways. These authors would understand the difference between expressive "folktalk" and the stilted self-styled written conversations by White authors that suggested there was an accepted standard of illiteracy within a certain group of people.

Two articles in *Horn Book* discussed Arna Bontemps's *Sad-Faced Boy* and his career as an author. Bontemps explained how he and his family had lived in northern Alabama when he wrote this story and had been inspired by three real boys. Librarian Ione Morrison Rider tells of meeting Bontemps at the branch library where she worked when he and his family lived in Los Angeles. Rider explains that the staff recognized him first by his signature because their library owned *God Sends Sunday* and recalls that he became a daily visitor of the library and was well versed on contemporary literature: "He kept in touch with the best current writing, and although reticent shared his views generously when asked" (17). She recalls when he came to talk with the children during story hour, saying he found "not the usual fifty, but about two hundred urchins of different races, including Mexican, Negro, Japanese" (17). Then she describes the afternoon's session:

> They surged in waves around him on the clean linoleum floor. He had to pick his way between grimy hands and bare feet to the corner from which he told the story of Toussaint L'Ouverture and read aloud several of Langston Hughes's poems. [. . .] Whatever is yet to come from his pen we await with anticipation, confident that it will be poetically conceived, and written with distinction. (17, 19)

Langston Hughes was Bontemps's dear friend and mentor. On the bottom of his June 19 typewritten letter, Bontemps scrawled, "Nice poem —*'Still Here!*' " He and Hughes obviously shared their writing with one another. In his letters, Bontemps talked of sending materials to the Yale collection, and he asked if Hughes could come to Chicago and direct a play. Both men already were successful playwrights. Yet, Bontemps's life had taken a turn toward the literary world as one connected with the public institutions of schools and libraries. He read the library journals and edited authors associated with the Chicago Writers Project. Furthermore, he was strongly connected to the world of children's literature. In his letter of June 19, Bontemps informed Hughes about the library scene in Black Chicago: "Mrs. Florence Crannell Means (*Shuttered Windows, Tangled Water,* etc.) was luncheon guest today. She's on her way to be main speaker at the A.L.A. Convention at Milwaukee. Also getting ready to write about Negroes again." His lack of enthusiasm suggests to us that this was not an author whose images were ones he favored, though he knew she was popular with children's librarians. In his next letter, dated July 3, Bontemps again asked Hughes to come to Chicago and stay for the literary activities surrounding the American Library Association meeting. Then he turned again to the visit of Florence Means, adding:

> The Hall Branch had a party for Mrs. Means (a lovely soul), to which all the above [the children's editor for Houghton Mifflin and various children's librarians from around the country] and many other writers of juveniles and ALA-er's came. I was the only man present, and as such I fear I got more than my share of attention. Oh, yes, Brunetta Muzon was there, and the white folks fairly swooned in contemplating her beauty. You should have heard them. She did look her best!

Arna Bontemps's correspondence shows an interest in fiction that honestly depicted American society. He discussed authors who wrote on the cutting edge. He liked the work of Carson McCullers (August 12, 1942) and he enthusiastically discussed the work of Katherine Anne Porter and Leonard Ehrlich, adding, "I can almost quote GOD'S ANGRY MAN. It belongs with a few novels like OF HUMAN BONDAGE, MY ANTONIA, THE GRANDMOTHERS and THE SUN ALSO RISES that I go back to now and again" (August 19, 1942). Yet, when Bontemps comments about Means's visit to Chicago, he does not address her literary contributions. Indeed, the entire ALA convention seems to have been regarded by Bontemps as a place important for its possible connections with publishers and librarians. On July 8, Bontemps wrote again that Hughes should journey to Chicago. Concerning the larger literary world and its recognition of the Black author, he added,

> You said nothing about the mail Knopf is forwarding to you in my care. More came—a magazine from India, commenting of your COMMON GROUND article, "What the Negro Wants," and suggesting that the demands are certainly most reasonable and moderate. [. . .] Running for a bus yesterday, I slipped, fell, ruined a pair of gray pants, damaged my knee and hand and marred a copy of Arthur Koestler's book "Dialogue with Death," which I had just been given for review by the SUN. [. . .] There is to be a big festival of Negro music at Soldier's Home Field Sunday. Reckon I'll go. Murial Rahn will sing, and Canada [Lee] will appear in something or other. Yale will, of course, get a program if I go.

Bontemps's comments about sending the musical program for the Yale collection suggest how important this archival storehouse should be to the Black artistic community.

On September 14, 1942, he wrote to Hughes with reading suggestions:

> Two other swell juveniles you MUST read: ALL-AMERICAN by John R. Tunis (absolutely WONDERFUL treatment of the Negro's problem in a mixed high school; I hope it sells a million) and UNCLE BOUQUI OF HAITI by Courlander (charming little book and a fine companion piece to POPO). HEZEKIAH HORTON by Ellen Tarry and Oliver Harrington (both colored Harlemites) is also tops. The illustrator is art editor of PV. This makes two books this year (the other STEPPIN AND FAMILY), both excellent and both perhaps improvements on the original, which the juvenile book folks seem to think owe something to SAD-FACED BOY. It just happens that the comparison makes me feel complimented in each case.

The first author mentioned by Bontemps was a White writer whose sports stories for young adults dealt with the problems of competitive sports within American society. Thus, Bontemps and Hughes were not simply choosing Black authors when they discussed writers who could create a realistic picture of racial relations, nor were they determining that there was a particular style for Black authors to follow. Yet, in their collection of poetry by Black authors, they chose to include only those poets who have "Negro" ties, whether those ties are from slave times within the United States, the later migration to the North to seek a new kind of freedom, the Blacks who sought social and intellectual freedom in Europe, or the Caribbean Blacks who felt more cultural affinity in their communities. In their "Preface" Bontemps and Hughes maintain there is a difference in Black writing:

> The Negro in Western civilization has been exposed to overwhelming historical and sociological pressures that are bound to be reflected in the verse he has written and inspired. The fact that he has used poetry as a form of expression has also brought him into contact with literary trends and influences. How one of these forces or the other has predominated and how the results may be weighed and appraised are among the questions to which the poetry itself contains the answers. (*The Poetry of the Negro 1746–1949* ix)

Our reading of the correspondence between Bontemps and Hughes has allowed us to consider that a very different American literary canon might exist if divergent voices had been called together to select "the best" books for everyone to read and discuss. What if African American, American Indian, Chinese American, and Japanese American critics had been invited to discuss what aesthetics meant for them? What might our children have read throughout the twentieth century? And what criticism would the adults sharing their literature with them need to read?

In 1977 Peggy Whalen-Levitt posed two questions centered on the child's position in children's literature: "What is the significance of particular aesthetic experiences to particular children or groups of children? [. . . W]hat are the functions of these experiences in the lives of children?" (17). In 1986 *The Children's Literature Association Quarterly* ran a special section devoted to children's literature and society. Guest editor Tony Manna concluded that by looking at "children's literature in and of its time, and in relation to the values of its producers and its audiences, both the literature and specific features of an era can come into sharp focus" (58). New Historicism has presented us with new critical challenges. We must ask: Is this literature art? Or, is it simply a social commentary? Who controls what is considered exemplary children's literature?

Students at all levels are best drawn into literary experiences when they are encouraged to explore the personal and historical significance of the artist's work. Furthermore, a cultural understanding for all artistic work—whether in print or media format—is firmly established when the audience appreciates the use of symbols and motifs particular to cultural expression. As one of the early and important critics in Black Aesthetics, Houston A. Baker, Jr. called literary criticism of Black writing "spirit writing," and he commented on his personal need to revise his stance from deconstruction to reconstruction, alluding to the historical and literary significance of earlier Black writing. Language, Baker has asserted, is what privileges experience within cultural boundaries. It has been the "white folks' way" of controlling community; words such as "sambo" and "mammy" have caused Blacks to be labeled rather than listened to and understood. Stereotypes that subconsciously control literary appreciation have caused readers to meet literature about the Black community with certain unspoken biases. Nancy Tolson earlier spoke to this issue in "The Black Aesthetic within Children's Literature." Using a Black feminist stance, she suggested that the best positive Black images for children have been written through the lens of the Black Aesthetic.

Often the stories of culture in America have been written with an eye toward the White press and its ability to censor ideas it deems controversial. In order to be "heard" and published, culturally diverse groups have developed a secondary language that is controlled by the rhetoric of selfhood and pride. Even when published, these authors have found their works criticized by the White press for its imagery, focus, and language. Most criticisms are based on White canonical standards, and they fail to consider the writer's experience in America. Furthermore, critics have been loath to take into account divergent cultural aesthetics and their representations within the larger frame of American literature. Thus, ethnic texts have often been categorized as failing when judged by the standards set in the White press. In 1949, when *The Poetry of the Negro* was negatively reviewed in the *Saturday Review of Literature* for including texts that were not "folk materials" and for exclusively printing Black authors, Arna Bontemps felt compelled to write:

> The rub of the whole review is an even stranger point. It is the suggestion that Negro poets are out of place when they work within the traditions of other English and American writers, that their appropriate vein is expressed in the quotation "I sees Lawd Jesus a-comin/ a rain-bow roun' his shoulder." Well, however attractive such lines may be, however appealing to some the concept of the Negro as a quaint, unassimilated visitor from a far country, this is a lost cause. The Negro will be, if he is not already, an American of this common garden variety. Everything he reads or sees or experiences will combine to make him that way. It is not a matter of election or choice. It is inevitable. [. . .] There is no need of wincing. (James Weldon Johnson Mss Collection, Beinecke Library)

Toni Morrison has commented on our inability to read any literature without discerning a White understanding of race. And she has argued that experts in literary analysis must consider how "an American brand of Africanism" based on European cultural hegemony has shaped American literature. She has called for a study of intellectual domination: "how knowledge is transformed from invasion and conquest to revelation and choice; what ignites and informs the literary imagination, and what forces help establish the parameters of criticism" (8). Morrison has argued that Americans will always live in a race-conscious culture, and that within that setting we need to consider how this shapes our reading of fiction. As an author, Morrison has commented that she has always sought to write honestly about Black culture. She has endeavored to write "metaphoric, economical, lunatic, and intelligent at the same time [. . .] and not make it exotic or comic or slumming" (qtd. in Als 73). Her writing, Morrison explained, has come from her need to explore the density of experience in Black life:

> I didn't want it to be a teaching tool for white people. I wanted it to be true—not from outside the culture, as a writer looking back at it [. . .] I wanted it to come from inside the culture, and speak to people inside the culture. It was about a refusal to pander or distort or gain political points. I wanted to reveal and raise questions. (qtd. in Als 73–74)

How does one identify voices that do not pander to their audience, both those within their cultural milieu and those from without? We believe that these final essays can help us consider how we can give agency to those writers whose voices have been disregarded in the literary practice of "making canons." Junko Yokota and Ann Bates, Sarah Mahurt, Beth Burch, and Joan Glazer directly address issues of quality, selection, and the possibilities of sharing literature with youthful audiences in their discussions of Asian American, Caribbean, Jewish, and exploited children. Alisa Clapp-Itnyre suggests that we should reconsider books we have earlier discarded. And, finally, the last three authors take us inside conversations with children's authors, elementary school children, and adolescents. Eve Tal, Lois Campbell, and Leslie Murrill end our conversations with a call for larger audience participation in our discussions. They suggest that further dialogue should be open to the producers of books because they can help us see their dilemmas in writing for a youthful audience. They encourage us to listen to the first audiences of children's and adolescent literature—the young people who can gain agency by knowledgeably reading and discussing culturally diverse literature with us and with their peers.

Notes

1. Reprinted by permission of Christian Knoeller.
2. David Levering Lewis's *When Harlem Was in Vogue* (New York: Knopf, 1981), *Harlem Renaissance: Art of Black America* (with David Driskell and Deborah Willis Ryan. New York: The Studio Museum in Harlem: Harry N. Abrams, 1987) and his edited *The Portable Harlem Renaissance* (New York: Penguin Books, 1994) spurred our interest in the topic. Much of what we found interesting was first defined for us in his writing. For instance, while we knew of and had read works by both Arna Bontemps and Langston Hughes prior to reading Lewis, it was his biographical sketch of Bontemps in *The Portable Renaissance* that first alerted us to Bontemps's continual connection to the James Weldon Johnson Collection at the Beinecke Library. Lewis explains that Bontemps spent his "final years" as the curator of the James Weldon Johnson Memorial Collection of Negro Arts and Letters at Yale (741).
3. Reprinted by permission of Harold Ober Incorporated. From *Personals.* Copyright © 1963 by Arna Bontemps.
4. We quote from Steven Watson's *The Harlem Renaissance: Hub of African-American Culture, 1920–1930* (New York: Pantheon Books, 1995):

> Printed on fine cream-colored paper and sporting a dramatic red and black cover, the magazine *Fire!!* appeared in November 1926. It celebrated jazz, paganism, blues, androgyny, unassimilated black beauty, free-form verse, homosexuality—precisely the "uncivilized" features of Harlem proletarian culture that the Talented Tenth propagandists preferred to ignore. *Fire!!* offered an alternative manifesto to *The New Negro,* undiluted by sociopolitical issues and race-building. (91).

5. Reprinted by permission of Harold Ober Incorporated. From *Personals.* Copyright © 1963 by Arna Bontemps.
6. The Beinecke Rare Book and Manuscript Library offers researchers a wide variety of important manuscripts, rare books, and research materials valuable for scholarship in New Historicism. Letters quoted in this introduction are part of the James Weldon Johnson Manuscript Collection at the Beinecke Library, Yale University. Bontemps's letters to Hughes are housed in the Langston Hughes papers. We have placed the dates for each letter within our conversation.
7. Both Hughes and Bontemps co-authored books with White authors. Hughes's most famous White collaborator was Milton Meltzer. In the summer of 1999, we were able to meet Milton and talk with him about his work with Langston Hughes. Bontemps co-authored a book with Jack Conroy, a folklorist whom Bontemps met while both were working on the Black history writing project for the Federal Writers Project in Chicago (www.macc.cc.us/~conroy/bio.htm, August 1, 2001). They wrote one other children's book together, *Sam Patch,* published in 1951.
8. Ronald Takaki discusses the great Black migration from the South to the urban North that occurred between 1910 and 1920 in *A Different Mirror: A History of Multicultural America* (Little, Brown and Company, 1993) in "To the Promised Land" (340–69). Takaki explains that while Black workers used the trains as primary vehicles to better wages and job security, they also sought escape from Jim Crow laws and segregation.

Works Cited

Als, Hilton. "Ghosts in the House: How Toni Morrison fostered a generation of black writers." *The New Yorker,* October 27, 2003: 64–75.

Baker Jr., Houston A. *Afro-American Poetics: Revisions of Harlem and the Black Aesthetic.* Madison, WI: University of Wisconsin Press, 1988.

Baldwin, James. *The Fire Next Time.* New York: Dial Press, 1963.

Benston, Kimberly W. "Facing Tradition: Revisionary Scenes in African American Literature." *PMLA* 105 (1990): 98–109.

Bontemps, Arna. "Sad-Faced Boy." *Horn Book* 25 (1939): 7–12.

Bressler, Charles E. *Literary Criticism: An Introduction to Theory and Practice.* 2nd ed. Upper Saddle River, NJ: Prentice Hall, 1999.

Conroy, Jack and Arna Bontemps. *The Fast Sooner Hound.* Illus. Virginia Lee Burton. Boston: Houghton Mifflin, 1942.

Evans, Eva Knox. "The Negro in Children's Fiction." *Publishers' Weekly.* 30 Aug. 1941: 650–53.

Fire!!: Devoted to Younger Negro Artists. 1926. Westport, CT: Negro Universities Press, 1970.

"A Further Statement on Negro Dialect in Children's Books." *Publishers' Weekly.* 13 June 1942: 104–05.

Greenblatt, Stephen. "Culture." *Contexts for Criticism.* 2nd ed. Ed. Donald Keesey. Mountain View, CA: Mayfield Publishing Company, 1994: 445–50.

Hughes, Langston, and Arna Bontemps, ed. *The Poetry of the Negro, 1746–1949.* Garden City, NY: Doubleday & Company, 1949.

Locke, Alain. *The New Negro: Voices of the Harlem Renaissance.* 1925. New York: Atheneum, 1992.

Manna, Anthony L. "Children's Literature and Society." *Children's Literature Association Quarterly* 11 (1986): 58.

Morrison, Toni. *playing in the dark: whiteness and the literary imagination.* Cambridge: Harvard University Press, 1992.

"Negro Dialect in Children's Books." *Publishers' Weekly,* 18 Oct. 1941: 1555–58.

Rider, Ione Morrison. "Arna Bontemps." *Horn Book* 25 (1939): 13–19.

Whalen-Levitt, Peggy. "Literature and Child Readers. " *The First Steps: Best of the Early ChLA Quarterly.* Ed. Patricia Dooley. West Lafayette, IN: ChLA Publications, 1984: 17.

19

Authenticity and Accuracy

The Continuing Debate

Darwin L. Henderson

Several years ago, I received a desperate telephone call from a former student. She had been assigned to a new elementary school where the enrollment was predominately African American. She said she wanted to select books for her classroom library that reflected the children's experiences and culture. Despite the fact that she had taken a children's literature course with me, she couldn't think of any books with African American characters. All she could think of, she said, was *Little Black Sambo.* Distressed, I reminded her that *Little Black Sambo* was not a story about an African American child and that the story exemplified the worst kind of stereotypic portrayal of a Black child. I also reminded her of the bibliography I had given each student in class with appropriate titles for elementary children in various genres. In constructing the bibliography, I had carefully selected picture books written from a cultural consciousness, stories told from a cultural perspective, demonstrating a specific cultural worldview or sensibility (Sims 12–13). I reminded my former student of the importance of evaluating and selecting books that maintained literary quality and artistic merit, told stories that were distinctive of a given culture's lived experiences, and likewise, were enjoyable, fresh, and inviting for all readers. Our conversation ended pleasantly; she rediscovered the importance of culturally relevant books and materials for her classroom, and I was able to reinforce, once again, the necessity for books that distinctly depict a culture authentically and accurately.

However, I began to wonder if other teachers found themselves faced with the same dilemma. Were other teachers at a loss when selecting books for their classrooms that were culturally relevant? If those teachers couldn't remember books they had been assigned to read in academic courses that were designated as appropriate texts, would they revert to using books that depicted stereotypes, thus further perpetuating the same distortions and myths to another generation? I also wondered why the stereotypical texts are remembered, considered appealing, and so deeply ingrained in the consciousness of those mainstream readers who select them. Selecting books such as *Little Black Sambo* reveals a sentimentality toward a text, a feeling that suggests that because the text is old, or considered a classic, it can no longer harm or stir controversy. This way of thinking about books ignores the social, political, and cultural milieu in which the text exists (Harris "Using Multicultural Literature" ix). If teachers only select books on "face" value rather than on a clearly understood rationale for evaluation, selection, and purpose, are the books selected really authentic and accurate depictions of a particular culture, and do these teachers understand from whose perspective the books have been written?

One of the most highly debatable issues in multicultural literature today is that of authenticity and authorial freedom (Harris "Continuing Dilemmas" 112). Can an author who is outside a culture write about that culture effectively? Will the author's stories be realistic, accurate, and authentic? These questions have often generated intense discussion and conflict.

The response to these questions is always divided through the center of the political context in which they are asked. Some authors who live within the cultural context of which they write argue against the inaccurate portrayals of characters written by those who do not share the lived experiences of the culture. They argue that the writers tell their stories from an outsider's perspective and not through the cultural traditions of the characters about whom they write. They state that the lack of a cultural matrix produces inaccuracies and, therefore, weakens their stories. However, are the writer's cultural origin and perspective the only elements that make a good story? Can a story be authentic if the writer does not recognize and relate to those cultural traditions that make multidimensional characters?

Authors who write outside their own cultural experiences often cite artistic freedom among their decisions to write such stories. Kathryn Lasky, an author who has written outside her own culture, states:

> [. . .] great stories are told from the inside out but great artists, even those not of a particular culture, can indeed find the real voice. They can go inside out, even if they have not been there before. This is the whole meaning of being a great artist. (5)

Some authors further defend their right to produce such texts by suggesting that if writers were only allowed to write from their own cultural experiences, their productivity and imaginative freedoms would be limited. Again, Kathryn Lasky's remarks illustrate this point of view:

> I attended a private girls' school where I was one of three Jews; the rest were mostly Episcopalians with a scattering of Presbyterians. I spent six years playing the role of a shepherd in the school Christmas pageant because of my dark swarthy looks, and it was assumed that if Jews weren't money lenders or scribes perhaps they had been shepherds. [. . .] Remember I am the daughter of Midwestern Jews by way of Russia. I grew up in shopping malls and dreaming about rock and roll and Jack Kennedy and his New Frontier. But as I said before, I have written about that already and life is too short to tell the same story twice. (1, 7)

Judy Moreillon, a teacher-librarian and author of the picture book *Sing Down the Rain,* initially wrote the text to be performed as a "choral reading at a multicultural parent evening" by fourth graders (127). Although impressed by the students' response to the poem and the ability of struggling readers to participate in the performance, Moreillon remembered previous students she had taught who were Tohono O'odham. She states that her decision to publish her poem about the Sonoran desert and the Tohono O'odham Nation was based on "the lack of children's literature, both fiction and nonfiction, that accurately and authentically portrayed the cultural and spiritual traditions of the Desert People" (129). Although well intended, Moreillon's goal was to fill a gap that existed. Fully aware of the controversy, she felt she could meet the standards for authenticity and accuracy set forth by critics.

> [. . .] despite the warnings I'd heard about outsiders writing about another's culture, I began to pursue publication of the piece [. . .] I don't know if it's right or wrong for outsiders to use their writer's art to tell an insider's story [. . .] I don't know if it's ever possible to be skilled enough or to research thoroughly enough to be able to completely understand "the other." What I do know is that during the year and a half between acceptance and the birth of the book, I had the opportunity to revisit all my fears about writing from the outsider position. (131–32)

Although Lasky and Moreillon crossed literary cultural boundaries for reasons of artistic freedom and the creation of stories where a need existed, W. Nikola-Lisa, a highly successful author of picture books, apparently writes for more personal reasons. He states that his motivation for writing outside his culture is rooted "in some uncomfortable scenes from [his] past" (316). Nikola-Lisa details his growing up in rural southern Texas often staging surprise attacks, with BB and pellet guns, on the Mexican American children who were unarmed and lived on the adjoining property. Reflecting on his behavior, he states that his actions were natural given the southern Texas environment in which he was raised and the strong influence of television Westerns. He also reveals an incident, while in college and hitchhiking with an African American friend on the outskirts of Detroit, in which he stopped short of using the word *nigger* while reciting the old familiar racial epithet "eenie, meenie, miney, moe" (316–17). Nikola-Lisa further explains that his motivation for writing moves beyond the personal relationships he currently has in his life:

> When I look at what motivates me as a writer, especially when I write a text that has multicultural dimensions to it, it is not just the personal relationships I currently sustain but those confrontations with my past that inform and propel my writing. The impressions these experiences have left, moreover, can be distilled into one fundamental idea; that American life is riddled with unparalleled duality—between the books I have published that reflect a multicultural perspective, I see this theme again and again. (317)

Lasky, Moreillon, and Nikola-Lisa indicate a willingness or compelling need to cross literary cultural borders, each for her or his own reasons. However, the crossing of boundaries often heightens tension and further deepens the racial chasm and the debate of who can write about another culture.

Of equal concern in this debate is the question of whether a writer of color has the same freedom to write outside multicultural or racial themes. What constraints are imposed when a writer of color proposes a story from a nonracial perspective? In a 1992 *Booklist* interview with Hazel Rochman, the late Virginia Hamilton discussed the realities of writing outside one's culture as an African American writer:

> But it's very difficult when you're a black writer to write outside of the black experience. People don't allow it; critics won't allow it. If I would do a book that didn't have blacks, people would say, "Oh, what is Virginia Hamilton doing?" Yet, a white writer can write about anything. [. . .] I feel the limitation. I'm always running up against it and knocking it down in different ways, whichever way I can. But I know that it's there and will always be there. I mean there were people who said in the middle of my career, "Now Virginia Hamilton has finally faced who she is." Well, how dare they? (Rochman 1021)

Supporting the argument of African American writers are the statistics about the books written in a given year by African American writers. The Cooperative Children's Book Center (CCBC), a research library of the Schools of Education and Library Science at the University of Wisconsin-Madison, receives and reviews nearly all of the trade books published in English in the United States yearly. Among the responsibilities of the CCBC staff is the recording of statistics regarding multicultural titles by ethnic groups. The CCBC reported that in 2001 "approximately 201 books specifically about African and/or African American history, culture, and/or people" were published (Horning 9). However, 99 of those 201 books were written and/or illustrated by African Americans.

The CCBC statistics also place the issue of authenticity within a political context when questions of who controls the editing, marketing, sales, and publication of multicultural books arise (Harris "Continuing Dilemmas" 115). Thus, it appears that those outside African American culture wrote and illustrated slightly more than half of the books reviewed by the CCBC in 2001. Those at the helm of the publishing world, who are most likely not of African descent, and who determine what is published, appear to act as gatekeepers of the kinds of stories and images representing African Americans (Sims Bishop 42). Walter Dean Myers addressed the editorial aspect of the issue:

> The publishing world touts itself as very liberal, but I keep challenging people to name five books written over the last 20 years by blacks that are on non-black subjects. So when you have a black writer who says, "I've got this great idea about space monkeys that talk," he or she is turned down. And what they are allowed to write about very often reflects the editor's opinion. [. . .] So, what I'm suggesting is that when a black person approaches a publisher, the ideas that are accepted are normally ones that the editor can see as recognizably black (qtd. in Sutton 27).

Jacqueline Woodson, a novelist and author of picture books, has successfully written novels with principal characters who are not African American. Woodson is skillful in the juxtaposition of race, class, gender, and societal issues that create richly textured and compelling stories. Woodson's characters often experience complex issues of adolescence and young adulthood such as isolation, feelings of being misunderstood, and invisibility.

However, Woodson feels that she must bring something of herself when she creates non–African American characters:

> When I write of people who are of different races or religions than myself, I must bring myself to that experience, ask what is it that I, as a black woman, have to offer and/or say about it? Why did I, as a black woman, need to tell this story? [. . .] I cannot step directly into my character's experience [. . .] but I can weave my experiences of being black in this society, a woman in this society, [. . .] around the development of my character and thus bring to the creation [. . .] a hybrid experience that will, I hope, ring true. (37)

However, when Woodson considers the question of Whites writing outside their culture, she is perplexed by the numbers of books written about African Americans by White writers (38). She recalls meeting a woman at a conference who had written a book about a family of color. When asked a question about knowing a family of color, which indirectly questioned the writer's knowledge about such families, the woman replied that the story was based on a family who had worked for her family. Woodson's response to the woman's remarks support the argument of the African American writers who feel that only they can tell their story. Woodson questioned how the writer could craft a story about a family of color without knowing the language used in their home at the end of the day, the expressions used among themselves and close friends, their personal experiences, and their feelings of joy and pain. Finally, Woodson asked, "And most of all, why was it this woman needed to tell this story?" (38).

While the argument continues, it is important to ask what constitutes an authentic, accurate depiction of a culture? Are there criteria an author or illustrator must meet, qualities he or she must possess that indicate how an individual could be qualified to write or illustrate a book outside his or her own culture? Nina Mikkelsen maintains that an authentic text has several critical features that effectively "inscribe" readers, inviting them into the world of the story in specific ways (35). She asserts that because some readers may feel challenged or alienated by books that do not reflect their own culture, readers must be involved in "the usual way," through a cultural initiation into the character's world and perspective. This is achieved through the reader understanding the history, values, beliefs, and traditions of the culture depicted.

How the writer achieves this initiation depends on each individual, but Mikkelsen implies that the writer may be most successful in the process if the character(s) become initiated along with the reading audience (36). Thus, Mikkelsen makes a distinction between surface plot and deep story structure. She defines surface structure as that which attends to observable details and facts, whereas deep structure refers to attending to the values, beliefs, perspective, or worldview of a culture (36). One might infer, then, that writers who are successful in telling another culture's story not only report observable details but also have a sensitivity to the lived experiences and cultural matrix of history, values, beliefs, and traditions.

The debate of authenticity is not new. Thirty years ago, the Council on Interracial Books for Children in its bulletin, *Interracial Books for Children,* published Ray Anthony Shepard's comparison of the books written and illustrated by Jack Ezra Keats and John

Steptoe. Shepard felt strongly that Steptoe's representations of urban African American life were more authentic. His argument, framed in the context of the early 1960s and the civil rights movement, asserts that Keats characters were simply "colored white kids" (3). Shepard implied that Keats's early books that presented Peter, the young Black child character who appeared in seven picture story books, reflected an integrationist's point of view that mirrored the political and social thinking at that time (3).

In the discussion, Shepard stated that by 1968 the Black Power movement was at the forefront of the struggle for racial equality and Keats's books began to reflect a darker color palette. In summarizing Keats's books, Shepard felt the color of the characters was irrelevant. That is to say, although appealing in their universality of Peter's various adventures in the stories, they reflected no aspects of the African American culture in which he lived. In comparison, Steptoe's books were seen as more harmonious as language style, narrative, setting, characterization, and illustration complemented each other, creating a sense of wholeness, and representing the lived urban experiences of an African American child (3).

Curious about the ways in which writers craft stories, especially those that represent cultural groups, I asked two highly acclaimed authors and an illustrator to share with me their understanding of what it means to cross cultural boundaries. One of the writers I spoke with was Sonia Levitin. Best known for the Platt Family trilogy, young adult novels based on her own family's experience of the anti-Semitism of Nazi Germany, she is also the author of the novel *The Return.* The novel is based on the actual experiences of the Ethiopian Jews who were secretly airlifted by the Israeli military to their new home in Israel. The Black Jews of Ethiopia, who had observed Jewish religious traditions for centuries and had faced continued discrimination because of their beliefs, suddenly found themselves refugees in a new land.

When Levitin heard about this extraordinary story, she postponed her other writing projects and began the research for the novel. When I asked her to respond to how she prepared for writing *The Return,* she replied:

> The research was very extensive. When I wrote *The Return,* I saw every piece of film that I could find and at the time there was not a whole lot of film. There was one short film done by a Canadian, which I saw over and over and over again. Then I had to find out what plants grew in Ethiopia, what the people ate. I interviewed everybody that I could who'd been there. I interviewed the anthropologists and religious leaders. I went to an Ethiopian synagogue. I talked with many individuals from there. I have to know these things and have to respect it before I can write about it with real understanding.[1]

In response, I remarked that she had been very successful in the depiction of characters who were not of her own racial background but who did share her religious beliefs. I asked how comfortable or difficult that experience had been for her. She stated that she realized that she could not come to her writing from her perspective and the beginning of this realization:

> At least [I have to] recognize the fact that I am white, that I'm living better than most probably, as far as I'm never hungry, I'm never cold, I have every need met. [. . .] The problem

is a lot of people will approach other cultures with words like interesting and quaint. I think that's too bad. Because they see themselves as the one dominant and higher culture, and everything else as less.

An important factor in Levitin's perspective is no doubt the impact of the experience of entering this country as an immigrant while in her childhood. She states that the family's exile in Switzerland, surrounded in a mountain setting by pines and watching plants and animals grow, heightened her senses and is a vital part of her childhood memories. The experience of being uprooted from a stable upper-middle-class existence has profoundly influenced her worldview and appears to have allowed Levitin the opportunity to open herself to the extraordinary life experiences of others who are different from herself.

I also talked with Alan Schroeder, the author of several picture books that feature historical figures in African American history or entertainment. Schroeder's best-known work is *Minty: A Story of Young Harriet Tubman,* for which he was given the Christopher Award in 1996. Nearly all of Schroeder's work has been recognized by critics for its moving, accurate depictions and fascinating use of language. Schroeder has a vivid memory of the childhood experiences that influenced him later as a writer.

Although he remembers many sensory experiences in his childhood, he especially recalls the role of sounds and images. He stated, "It certainly dictates the sort of work I'm attracted to. Sounds and images are the most important in my memory." Schroeder's Danish grandparents read to him the stories of Hans Christian Andersen at an early age. He says that he was attracted to those stories for their emotional honesty and because they were so different from other children's stories. Understanding that stories progressed from beginning to middle to end, he quickly read the Nancy Drew books and moved on to Agatha Christie while still in grade school. As a teenager, Schroeder became interested in how directors told stories through film. He began to understand how movie sets were arranged, how dialogue was written, how each craft in the film-making process was used to create a perfect story:

> I was about 12 or 13 years old when I saw the film *Cabaret.* Bob Fosse was the director of that film. To this day the film still takes my breath away; the perfection of many of the images. In several of the sequences, you realize every single detail has been thought out. The perfection of so many of the images in that film really, really inspired me to want to become a perfectionist in my own work. [. . .] When I was 16, I went to an evening of two silent films. [. . .] One was a Charlie Chaplin film. And I was just knocked out, not only by the level of artistry, but the level of pathos. [. . .] That's something I would love to continue to incorporate into my writing, a certain element of pathos.

Simultaneously, he discovered how music, mostly ballads sung and played by such singers and instrumentalists as Pearl Bailey and Louis Armstrong, could also be a source of storytelling. However, it wasn't any story that attracted his attention. It was stories, whether literature, music, or film, representing the past, evoking a feeling of history, and depicting real people facing tremendous challenges that inspired him.

Although Schroeder's interests in literature, music, and film may seem irrelevant to the discussion of authenticity and accuracy, he revealed that his interests placed him "outside" the world of his peers. "All my life I've seen myself as an outsider, very, very much out of step with other people my age, when I was growing up." Schroeder's self-proclaimed outsider status seems simplistic as an explanation for his success of writing about African Americans; however, the practice of "slipping under the skin of other people," as he expressed it, began while in a college writing class. He wrote a first-person narrative from a woman's point of view, which outraged the class when they discovered he had written the story. "They did not feel that I was playing by the rules. And I thought, what rules? How can you possibly be laying down rules on the creative experience?" Alan Schroeder contends that it is very easy for him to slip into the skin of African Americans to depict the African American experience. He stated that African American stories contain a great deal of drama:

> African Americans had to succeed in the face of blistering oppression, of terrible racial discrimination, of poverty, of geographical difficulties, of slavery. [. . .] I love that quality of being able to slip into somebody's skin, however briefly, and empathize with their concerns, with their needs, with their wants, their hurts, their loves, their fate. [. . .] I am attracted by their emotional lives, their unusual situations, the drama of their situations.

Alan Schroeder's interests sustained him through his childhood; he was an artistic child experiencing and exploring literary themes through a child's emerging adult sensibility. The memory of early sensory experiences, an awareness of his own "otherness," and the ability to "slip under the skin" of other people have given Alan Schroeder the ability to successfully create stories about African Americans. Obviously, this extraordinary ability is not only due to research about the subject but also includes an emotional sensitivity that especially guides the dialogue in all his stories.

Finally, I had a conversation with Jerry Pinkney, an acclaimed illustrator of outstanding picture books for children. A nominee for the Hans Christian Andersen Award for illustration, Jerry Pinkney has been illustrating children's books for nearly forty years and is the recipient of numerous citations, including the Caldecott Honor Award, the Christopher Award, and the Coretta Scott King Award. In our conversation, he remarked that the success of his depictions of the African American experience in illustration lies in the extensive research required for each book project. Knowing the style and color of the clothing worn, the architecture of the specific time period, the indigenous plant and animal life of the region in which the story is set, and the various items owned and used by each character becomes vitally important. In a separate, unrelated interview he talked about the detailed research for *Minty:*

> I worked with the National Park Service in Harper's Ferry, West Virginia, which aided me even with the simplest of details. For instance, I needed to know what the slave holders drank with their evening meals. Other writers suggested that there would be a pitcher of milk on the table, but that didn't sound right to me. When I informed the people at the National Park Service that *Minty* was set in Virginia in the 1840s, they told me that people back then would be drinking cider or beer with their meals. There are so many little specific things like that, which you have to know in order to make the pictures accurate. (Henderson and Manna 28)

Pinkney's statement suggests that his successful depictions do not rest merely on him being an African American. As an artist, he has to know specific details that inform him how to visually depict African American cultural experience accurately. He states that research gives an authenticity to his work, which actually allows him to speak, visually, more clearly. Given his success with African American themes, I asked Jerry Pinkney how comfortable or difficult it was for him to illustrate a manuscript outside his own culture. He responded that he found it more challenging. "At this point, I'm becoming more comfortable with feeling uncomfortable about entering into a space where it's going to challenge my sensitivity towards that particular culture." When he began illustrating *Journeys with Elijah,* a book of tales about the ancient prophet, he admitted that he felt overwhelmed by the task and how little he knew despite his research for the project. "I was really over my head because of the eight different stories, the eight different time periods, and some of them dealing with that part of Jewish culture and religion that I knew nothing about. I had to be extremely sensitive." He hired an assistant for the project who helped him understand his research about Judaism and culture, talked with him about the importance of the prophet in each setting and each time period. Armed with a new perspective borne of time to reflect, he felt a sense of clarity and confidence in his knowledge, which became a path for the completion of the project. The success of *Journeys with Elijah* appears to have afforded other opportunities for Jerry Pinkney to illustrate outside his culture. He has adapted and illustrated Hans Christian Andersen's fairytales *The Little Match Girl, The Ugly Duckling,* for which he was awarded the Caldecott Honor Medal, and *The Nightingale.* I asked him what additional influences, other than hiring assistants and the extensive research necessary for the completion of each assignment, made it possible for him to write and illustrate beyond the African American experience. Interestingly, he stated that his very early influences were N. C. Wyeth, Howard Pyle, and Arthur Rackham because of their ability to paint imaginatively, yet realistically. Later, he became interested in Charles White, Jacob Lawrence, and Romare Bearden for their own unique narrative styles. However, he attributes his earliest awareness of the uniqueness of people to the neighborhood where he lived as a child.

> Our neighborhood was African American, but the surrounding communities were Jewish and Italian. So, in order to go to the store, to school, or any place, I would walk through other neighborhoods that were quite different from mine. Rather than just move through them, I was always interested in how other people lived. You could tell that by how they kept their houses, whether in fact they hung out on the steps or on a porch. All those things, very early fascinated me. [. . .] I attended an all African American elementary school, all the teachers were African American. I had a good foundation there in terms of early role models. Maybe that, in a sense, allowed me to feel secure enough to be curious about other cultures. Writers often keep written files or notes, my file was a visual file. [. . .] Interesting enough, I didn't know at the time that that curiosity would be somehow stored away, and it would find a way to express itself.

The sensory experiences of Levitin, Schroeder, and Pinkney are compelling in the remarkably similar importance they place on the influences of their early development and the shaping of an openness to cultural difference during childhood. Although these experiences significantly shaped their perspectives, it is obvious that their willingness to cross cultural boundaries in their writing and illustration was greater than collecting facts to tell and paint their stories.

Reflecting on my conversations with Levitin, Schroeder, and Pinkney, I sense a deeply held desire to connect with humanity, a sense of compassion, and a willingness to "slip under the skin" of someone whose lived cultural experience is different. These qualities appear to be in accord with the opinion of Henry Louis Gates, Jr., the noted African American literary critic. Gates believes that "no human culture is inaccessible to someone who makes the effort to understand, to learn, to inhabit another world" (30). He rejects the argument that one cannot write outside one's cultural experience.

Although the debate of authenticity and accuracy continues with many unanswered questions, one important issue remains at the center of the argument: the responsibility of the writer. If the literature selected for children is for the purpose of socialization, change, and insights into human experience, then it is the writer's responsibility to accurately and authentically depict characters who reflect a culture's values, beliefs, customs, and worldview (Bishop, Multicultural 42–43). It is the writer's responsibility to not merely write about characters who just happen to be among those of any given ethnic American population but also to fully contextualize those characters according to the cultural matrix in which they are living. Eloise Greenfield, the recipient of numerous awards for poetry, fiction, and biography, reflecting on the responsibilities of writing for children, stated:

> A book that has been chosen as worthy of a child's emotional investment must have been judged on the basis of what it is—not a collection of words arranged in some unintelligible but artistic design, but a statement powerfully made and communicated through the artistic and skillful use of language. (21)

Because the argument no doubt will continue, it is the writer's responsibility to craft stories with a sensitivity to illuminate and reflect life as it is lived culturally, to infuse stories with multidimensional characters, and to assist children in their developmental journeys.

Notes

1. The interviews with Sonia Levitin, Allan Schroeder, and Jerry Pinkney were held by telephone during July 2001.

Works Cited

Andersen, Hans Christian. *The Little Match Girl.* Illus. Jerry Pinkney. New York: Penguin Putnam, 1999.
———. *The Nightingale.* Illus. Jerry Pinkney. New York: Penguin Putnam, 2002.
———. *The Ugly Duckling.* Illus. Jerry Pinkney. New York: Penguin Putnam, 1999.
Bannerman, Helen. *The Story of Little Black Sambo.* 1899. New York: Harper and Row, 1923.
Bishop, Rudine Sims. "Multicultural Literature for Children: Making Informed Choices." *Teaching Multicultural Literature in Grades K–8.* Ed. Violet J. Harris. Norwood, MA: Christopher-Gordon Publishers, 1992. 39–53.
———. "Selecting Literature for a Multicultural Curriculum." *Using Multiethnic Literature in the K–8 Classroom.* Ed. Violet J. Harris. Norwood, MA: Christopher-Gordon Publishers, 1997. 1–19.

Gates, Henry Louis, Jr. "Authenticity, or the Lesson of Little Tree." *The New York Times Book Review* 24 Nov. 1991: 1, 26–30.

Goldin, Barbara Diamond. *Journeys with Elijah: Eight Tales of the Prophet.* Illus. Jerry Pinkney. San Diego, CA: Gulliver/Harcourt Brace, 1999.

Greenfield, Eloise. "Writing for Children—A Joy and a Responsibility." *The Black American in Books for Children: Readings in Racism.* Ed. Donnarae MacCann and Gloria Woodard. Metuchen, NJ: Scarecrow Press, 1985. 19–22.

Harris, Violet J. "Continuing Dilemmas, Debates, and Delights in Multicultural Literature." *The New Advocate* 9:2 (1996): 107–22.

———, ed. *Using Multiethnic Literature in the K–8 Classroom.* Norwood, MA: Christopher-Gordon Publishers, 1997.

Henderson, Darwin L. and Anthony L. Manna. "The Wrinkle of Skin, The Fold of Cloth: Conversations with Jerry Pinkney." *Art & Story: The Role of Illustration in Multicultural Literature for Youth: The Virginia Hamilton Conference.* Ed. Anthony L. Manna and Carolyn S. Brodie. Atkinson, WI: Highsmith Press, 1997. 19–31.

Horning, Kathleen T., et al. *CCBC Choices 2002.* Madison, WI: Cooperative Children's Book Center, 2002.

Lasky, Kathryn. "To Stingo with Love: An Author's Perspective on Writing Outside One's Culture." *The New Advocate* 9:1 (1996): 1–7.

Levitin, Sonia. *The Return.* New York: Atheneum, 1987.

Mikkelsen, Nina. "Insiders, Outsiders, and the Question of Authenticity: Who Shall Write for African American Children?" *African American Review* 32:1 (1998): 33–49.

Moreillon, Judy. *Sing Down the Rain.* Illus. Michael Chiago. Sante Fe, NM: Kiva Publishing, 1997.

———. "The Candle and the Mirror: One Author's Journey as an Outsider." *The New Advocate* 12:2 (1999): 127–40.

Nikola-Lisa, W. "Around My Table Is Not Enough: A Response to Jacqueline Woodson." *The Horn Book Magazine* May/June 1998: 315–18.

Rochman, Hazel. "The *Booklist* Interview: Virginia Hamilton." *Booklist* 88:11 (1992): 1020–21.

Schroeder, Alan. *Minty: A Story of Young Harriet Tubman.* Illus. Jerry Pinkney. New York: Dial Books, 1996.

Shepard, Ray Anthony. "Adventures in Blackland with Keats and Steptoe." *Interracial Books for Children* 2:4 (1971): 3.

Sims, Rudine. *Shadow and Substance: Afro-American Experience in Contemporary Children's Fiction.* Urbana, IL: National Council of Teachers of English, 1982.

Sutton, Roger. "Threads in Our Cultural Fabric: A Conversation with Walter Dean Myers." *School Library Journal* 40:6 June 1994: 24–28.

Woodson, Jacqueline. "Who Can Tell My Story?" *The Horn Book Magazine* Jan./Feb. 1998: 34–38.

20

The Aesthetics of Caribbean Children's Literature

Sarah F. Mahurt

Picture books are an important part of Caribbean children's literature today, although it has taken a long time for this to develop. The foundation of the picture book genre in the Caribbean is built on the oral tradition from Africa; slaves brought tales to the region when they were transported to the area. These stories were handed down through generations, typically through storytelling sessions in an island village. The tales taught morals, traditions, and historical heritage (Honeyghan 411). They evolved into their own form as the diverse cultural groups in the Caribbean interacted. As Cheryl Robinson has suggested, Latino/Latina children's literature in the Caribbean in the 1950s contained the oral tradition.

Though artists abound in the Caribbean, very few of the first picture books had color illustrations due to cost and limited opportunities for printing in color. In addition, because of the small population of the region, major publishers did not support this work. At first, and continuing today, children's books were published by individual authors or by writers' groups, such as the Children's Writers Circle in Jamaica, on the various islands.

Many of these books remain local selections. People from different islands are aware of the books in other areas of the Caribbean, but they often find it difficult to obtain them. In the United States, these locally published books were virtually unobtainable. However, Internet resources are currently making some of these locally published books available throughout the world.

In recent years, as part of the contemporary emphasis on multicultural children's literature and the increase of Caribbean peoples in the United States, Britain, and Canada, major publishers have begun introducing Caribbean picture books in these countries. Modern Caribbean picture books include the folktales of the trickster, animal tales, and supernatural tales collected from oral storytellers. They also encompass an expanded scope of topics and genre, such as realistic fiction, alphabet and counting books, poetry, and art and music collections. The newer titles are colorfully illustrated in a variety of styles and media. Although it is still difficult to get a wide variety of Caribbean children's literature, there is a trend to publish more books from the area (Pratt and Beaty 134).

What makes a good Caribbean picture book? Neither illustrations nor text alone can be considered without looking at the significance of the interrelationships created between the illustrations and the text (Keifer 75). Thus, the picture book must be looked at as an "aesthetic whole" (Horning 93), with the text, the illustrations, and the successful integration of those two parts taken into consideration. When defining quality in multicultural picture books, I find there are several layers that must be added to successful integration of text and illustration. Cultural sensitivity and authenticity are critical features that need to be included in any discussion of multicultural children's books, including Caribbean ones. I find it important to consider the text, illustrations, and their interaction within the added elements of historical information, cultural details, and regional authenticity. These are vital issues in Caribbean children's literature. Before decisions about quality in Caribbean picture books can be made, the critic must develop an understanding of the Caribbean's historical, cultural, and physical contexts that honestly reflects this area and its people.

The region's historical development fostered a heritage of rich diversity through the intermingling of the indigenous Arawaks and Caribs, Africans, Chinese, East Indians, and Western Europeans. After gaining independence from European colonialism, each island nation has developed an individual culture that has maintained African traditions while building unique folkways ("Caribbean Culture" Mahurt and Dixey 25). There is diversity throughout the region, but there are factors that can be considered as part of a broader Caribbean culture due to the dominant African influence (Bello 247). There can be a broad definition of the Caribbean picture book that is inclusive of the various island nations, although each country maintains its own literary traditions.

The importance of the extended family is part of this broader culture and is seen in children's picture books such as *My Little Island* (Lessac) when a young boy returns to his island home to visit relatives. This is seen again in *My Grandpa and the Sea* (Orr), as Lila interacts with her grandfather to learn about living with the sea. In *Gregory Cool* (Binch), an "All American" boy who thought he knew it all visits relatives in Tobago and learns about island life through his extended family.

In Caribbean children's literature, there is the theme of surviving through ingenuity and creativity that grew from resistance to slavery and colonial oppression (Bello 248). This is seen in the Anansi tales in which Anansi uses his wiles to survive. In *Tiger Soup: An Anansi Story from Jamaica* (Temple), Anansi tricks Tiger into leaving his soup for him to eat and later tricks Tiger into believing that the monkeys ate the soup. Folktales such as *Tukama Tootles the Flute* (Gershator) also show survival through ingenuity. Tukama not only learns a lesson in listening to elders, but also he cleverly outsmarts a hungry giant.

Within the Caribbean region, views differ concerning the ideal of good children's literature. Some scholars and teachers feel that only positive stories from Caribbean authors are acceptable whereas others feel sensitive portrayals by authors outside the culture are suitable if authentic. Still others are pleased to find children's books about the region and are willing to accept them regardless of their faults ("Tropical Gardens" Mahurt and Dixey 63). These issues are also seen in the broader field of multicultural children's literature; critics have argued that authors and illustrators must be from the culture they depict (Feelings 46; Mikkelsen 17). Other authorities have argued that cultures can be accessible to those who make efforts to learn and understand them (Gates 30; Rochman 138). Writers and illustrators may not need to be culturally or ethnically bound in their representations.

Social and political issues of power, ethnic ownership, and cultural definitions of aesthetics also come into play when looking at authenticity, quality, and cultural sensitivity. This is especially true when colonialism, with inherent problems of power relationships, becomes an intervening issue. Thus, I would argue against trusting authors from former colonial powers when they write about the culture where they resided. Additionally, tourists who visit the islands may feel they can use a Caribbean setting for text and/or illustrations, but they often lack in-depth knowledge about the culture. Nina Mikkelsen argues for an understanding of the "deep and surface features" (7) within a culture that natives possess, giving them deep understandings of the values and beliefs. For her, an outsider may misrepresent those values and beliefs while attending to the surface details and facts: Literary perspective comes with an inner understanding developed through personal experiences within a culture. Although the outsider may do thorough research, his or her view is clouded by his or her own lens and limited experiences with the other culture (Mikkelsen 5).

Yet, it is difficult to evaluate authenticity within a Caribbean picture book; either the author or the illustrator may or may not be native to the area. Many of the picture books with Caribbean themes and illustrations that are published by the large publishing houses have either an author or illustrator who is not from the Caribbean. For example, author/illustrator Frane Lessac (*Caribbean Alphabet; Caribbean Canvas; Caribbean Carnival* by Burgie; *My Little Island; Not a Copper Penny in Me House* by Gunning; *The Chalk Doll* by Pomerantz) lived in Montserrat for years but is an American now living in Australia. Illustrator Caroline Binch lives in England and has traveled to the Caribbean. Two of the Caribbean books she illustrated (*Down by the River* by Hallworth and *Hue Boy* by Mitchell) have been written by Caribbean authors. She authored and illustrated another, *Gregory Cool,* after conducting research in Tobago. Brian Pinkney, an award-winning African American illustrator, has illustrated the Caribbean folktale books *The Faithful Friend* and *Cendrillon* for author Robert San Souci, an American author. Marie Lafrance, a Canadian, illustrated books written by Caribbean authors Lynette Comissiong and Ricardo Keens-Douglas (*"Mind Me Good Now!"* and *La Diablesse and the Baby*). Lynn Joseph, a Trinidadian living in New York, has written a variety of picture books (*Coconut Kind of Day; An Island Christmas; Jasmine's Parlour Day; Jump Up Time*), but they are illustrated by artists who have no Caribbean roots. As can be seen by this short listing of some widely published picture books about the Caribbean, there are relatively few (e.g., *Calypso Alphabet*) that have both author (e.g., John Agard) and illustrator (e.g., Jennifer Bent) with insider perspectives.

Even when living within a culture, people have differences of opinion about authenticity and cultural sensitivity when their culture is portrayed in a book. For example, although John Agard is a Caribbean author and Jennifer Bent a Caribbean illustrator, readers from the Caribbean do not agree on the sensitivity of *Calypso Alphabet*'s portrayal of Caribbean culture. Yahaya Bello considers it an excellent book, describing Agard as being "true to his West Indian roots" (258). However, I have had personal conversations with teachers and parents who feel that parts of the book painted an old-fashioned picture with its depictions of donkeys in cane fields and burying navel string. They thought the "z for zombie" (unpaged) showed a stereotypical superstition. Still others fondly remembered the personal scenes and could recount events such as the spot where their navel string was buried and being told stories of zombies during their childhood. I have found that even when a book is culturally authentic there can be disagreements as to its sensitivity both by people of the culture and outside the culture.

It is important to analyze authenticity and cultural sensitivity in the portrayal of characters and theme within the text and the illustrations. This can be a real issue when an illustrator has not experienced the Caribbean. There are concerns about flora and fauna, such as that seen in *One Smiling Grandma,* a text by Barbadian author Ann Marie Linden that was illustrated by Lynne Russell. There are authenticity issues within the illustration for "[t]en sleepy mongooses" (unpaged) because the mongooses have stripes and are a charcoal color rather than brown. Caribbean children, when shown these illustrations, have asked me if the artist was depicting raccoons, an animal they have rarely seen. Also, the children noticed that the "[n]ine hairy coconuts, hard and round" were unusual because the outer green husks of the coconuts that are present as they grow in the tree were missing in the illustration. The fuzzy brown coconut seen in grocery stores is hidden inside the green shell when it is growing on the tree. Russell's "hairy coconuts" appear to be placed on top of the palm fronds rather than hanging from stems as they really do, adding to the inaccuracy of her presentation.

Tom Feelings has discussed the importance of harmonizing imagery in illustrations of African American characters (48). He sees this as an important part of African American heritage that preserves the knowledge of a people. He feels strongly that the artist must be a member of the culture represented for the portrayal to be a valid depiction (47). In *One Smiling Grandma* (Linden), identity is lost. The diversity and differences seen in Caribbean people are not represented. The characters also show little emotional response or involvement in the scenes, something atypical of Caribbean people.

Unfortunately, very few of the artists are from the Caribbean culture, and the list of picture books available to Caribbean children would dwindle to almost nothing if this standard was enforced. Therefore, until there is an abundance of picture books created by Caribbean artists and authors that can be available for Caribbean children, we must look for those that are the best of those available. Children of the Caribbean need to see themselves and their surroundings in colorful and well-illustrated picture books (Mahurt 10). Negative portrayals are problematic in multicultural picture books, but being entirely left out of literature and, thus, becoming invisible can also have a significant negative effect on children (Roethler 3). The islands are usually seen on world maps and globes as small dots, so Caribbean children sometimes have difficulty seeing their importance in the larger world. They need to see themselves in the same type of colorful picture books as those they read about children from other cultures. They should not be invisible in the picture book world.

It is a difficult process to determine what makes a good Caribbean picture book. Ideally, the Caribbean picture book should be one that is of interest to Caribbean children and is written by people from that cultural designation. Because Caribbean people are scattered throughout the world, the author or illustrator may be living outside the region. Many writers and illustrators who have emigrated to the United States, Canada, and England are writing Caribbean picture books. They would be ideal authors and illustrators for authentic representations. Along with this group of authors and illustrators, there are recently published books of quality that can be considered Caribbean picture books when using a broader definition. I would include authentic and culturally sensitive books about the Caribbean or with Caribbean scenes. For instance, there are award-winning books that are well researched and well illustrated, such as *The Faithful Friend* (San Souci) and *La Diablesse and the Baby* (Keens-Douglas). These picture books are not written and illustrated by people of the Caribbean culture, but they are sensitive portrayals in both text and illustration. I include these because they fill a need until there is a larger group of published authors and illustrators either living in the Caribbean or from that culture originally. Caribbean children should be exposed to representations of themselves. They need books that help them identify with their unique culture and surroundings.

Five award-winning picture books can serve as models. The Americas Award presented by the Consortium of Latin American Studies Programs (CLASP) focuses its prize on Latin American children's books; the judges include the Caribbean as part of Latin America and choose books for their high literary quality. Good integration of text, illustration, design, and cultural contextualization is expected of the winners. This prize is a useful indicator of quality in a Caribbean picture book.

Sweet, Sweet Fig Banana, a realistic fiction book written by Phillis Gershator and illustrated by Haitian artist Fritz Millevoix, is on the 1996 Americas Award commended list. This book pairs an author who has lived in St. Thomas for many years with a Haitian illustrator. *Sweet, Sweet Fig Banana* is a story of a boy named Soto who grows his own fig banana tree. The first part of the book chronicles the growth of the tree and shows a child's impatience when waiting nine months for the fruit to grow. The author places local dialect within the conversations throughout the book: Soto asks his mother, "When the bananas comin'? When the flower comin'? When the bananas gettin' yellow?" (unpaged). Finally, the figs are cut to save them from marauding thrushes and tree rats. Soto and his mother leave home to go to the Market Square where his mother sells most of them. Soto gets permission to share some of the sweet, sweet fig bananas with three special town friends, the hat maker, the fraico seller, and the librarian. While rich, vibrant illustrations of Haitian-born artist Fritz Millevoix add authentic visuals to the Caribbean language used by the characters, I find disconcerting the change of illustrative style in the middle section of the book when Soto and his mother go to the marketplace. At the beginning of the book there are fully colored pages with the text placed in the double-spread vibrant illustrations. When the format changes, the text is boxed on white pages while white-bordered illustrations are placed on the opposite page. Near the end of the story, fully illustrated double-spread pages again appear, but the style switches once more on the last page to the boxed text with a smaller illustration. For me, this lack of format continuity detracts from the overall aesthetic design of *Sweet, Sweet Fig Banana.*

Another book recognized by CLASP is *Down by the River: Afro-Caribbean Rhymes, Games, and Songs for Children* (Hallworth). It was awarded the Americas Award for 1996. This wonderful book is a collection of childhood activities. In her introduction, Grace Hallworth talks about her Trinidadian childhood and explains how the ethnic diversity of Trinidad built a unique Trinidadian culture. While researching the rhymes, songs, and games, Hallworth traced them to European, African, and American roots. She presents this information as proof of "the interrelationship of different cultures" (unpaged). *Down by the River* is organized chronologically; activities go through a child's day. The rhymes are grouped by topic and cover a range of activities and topics such as "Wake-Up Time," "Friendships," "Going Shopping," "Taunts and Teases," and "Time for Bed." The book closes with two traditional Caribbean storytelling endings, "Fall on de wire/De wire bend/And that's the way/The story end" and "Cric crac/Monkey break he back/For a rotten pomerac" (unpaged).

The realistic watercolor illustrations that accompany these rhymes, songs, chants, and games show active children playing and singing in all types of weather and in places such as the school yard, in town, at home, and at the beach. The weather is varied and the characters are individually depicted. Varying moods and emotions are displayed as the children gleefully play or pensively prepare for bedtime. Caroline Binch's illustrations also record the diversity of people who make up Trinidad. Although she is not from the Caribbean, Binch spent time in Tobago, the sister island to Trinidad, while researching *Gregory Cool,* a Caribbean picture book she both wrote and illustrated in 1994. Her attention to Caribbean culture can be seen in her use of vibrant colors, characterization of the children, and authenticity of the cultural details in the illustrations.

An alphabet book, *Fruits: A Caribbean Counting Poem* (Bloom), has won recognition both in the United States and in Britain. It was awarded the Nestle Smarties Prize by the Book Trust (United Kingdom) in 1997 and it won honorable mention for the Americas Award. In addition, it was short listed for the Mother Goose Prize for Illustration, an award also given by the Book Trust. Valerie Bloom, a Jamaican living in London, first published *Fruits* without illustrations in *Duppy Jamboree* (*Fruits* unpaged), a collection of her poetry. The paintings of British illustrator David Axtell propelled the poem into an award-winning picture book. In this poetic picture book, Bloom shares a day in the life of a greedy young girl. She teaches children a life lesson about greed without being didactic. Her parable is a hallmark style in Caribbean tales. It is obvious from the text and illustrations that the young girl has been told not to eat the fruit seen around the house. In the illustrations, she hides from adults and quiets her younger sister who is watching with great interest. In the end, she suffers the aftereffects of her disobedience and gets a stomachache from counting and eating too many fruits. She says, "Mek me lie down on me bed, quick./Lawd, ah feeling really sick" (unpaged).

The author's language leads the reader into the Caribbean setting: "One guinep up in the tree/Hanging down there tempting me./It don' mek no sense to pick it,/One guinep can't feed a cricket" (unpaged).[1] To help young readers understand the localized names of fruits and specialized words, a short glossary on the frontispiece lists "some words you may not know" (unpaged). By the second page, we realize that the Caribbean language is an important aspect of Bloom's poetry. In this excellent picture book, the words and illustrations work together to develop the book's tone. The combined poem and humorous illustrations spring to life. Because he adds details not found in the poem, David Axtell's realistic illustrations help to develop the plot while adding a layer of meaning not possible with words alone.

Folktales are the mainstay of Caribbean children's literature, and recent publications of folktales in picture books have also won awards. *The Faithful Friend,* written by Robert San Souci and illustrated by Brian Pinkney, was recognized for its quality as a Caldecott Honor Book and as a Coretta Scott King Illustrator Honor Book. It is also listed as a commended book for the 1995 Americas Award. Pinkney and San Souci have also collaborated on a Caribbean version of Cinderella, *Cendrillon.* While working on the project, they shared period pictures and research information ("Weaving") to add to the authenticity of their work. San Souci and Pinkney are not from the Caribbean, but their work is enhanced by their research. San Souci gives a description of the story's basis and his research, along with an explanation for his blending of folktale motifs, in *The Faithful Friend.* This is a trademark of his other folktale retellings. *The Faithful Friend* is based on a tale from Martinique that contains elements of European tales and variants from Africa, South America, and Puerto Rico.

In San Souci's adaptation of *The Faithful Friend,* two friends set out on a quest to court the beautiful Pauline. Clement has fallen in love with her. When he journeys to meet Pauline and ask her for her hand in marriage, his close friend Hippolyte decides to accompany him. Pauline's guardian, Monsieur Zabocat, forbids her to marry Clement, but Pauline defies her guardian, and the three set out on an exciting journey back to Clement's home. The story contains elements of the Islands: Monsieur Zabocat is a quimboiseur or wizard; his curse will stop Clement and Pauline from their marriage; three zombies are set to do his bidding. However, Hippolyte's unwavering friendship with Clement causes Hippolyte to protect his friends, and in the end all are rewarded except for Monsieur Zabocat. Pinkney's distinctive scratchboard illustrations lend themselves to the intrigue and magic found in this folktale. Pinkney uses strong lines and authentic scenes to provide a shadowy setting for this intriguing tale. His composition and style are a good fit with San Souci's retelling of this romantic Caribbean tale.

Another recent folktale retelling published in Canada has been honored by *Storytelling World,* an international journal. *La Diablesse and the Baby* (Keens-Douglas) was chosen for a 1995 honor award. It was also a finalist for the Canadian Governor General's Award and won the Alcuin Society Design Award. Ricardo Keens-Douglas was born and raised in Grenada. He is an author and actor who carries on the tradition of Caribbean storytelling on Canadian radio. In introductory notes, Ricardo Keens-Douglas describes La Diablesse, a woman with one human foot and one cow foot (unpaged). She is known within the oral storytelling tradition throughout the Caribbean and is sometimes called the goat-foot woman. Keens-Douglas see this archetype—the creature who steals away children—as common in a variety of cultures, but he explains it is particularly well known in the Caribbean through storytelling.

La Diablesse and the Baby has the rhythms of an oral tale that is being told to the family, friends, and neighbors for years. It holds characters and events that can be found in Caribbean folk literature. The grandmother sings to soothe a fussy baby upset by thunder and lightning strong enough "to wake the dead." A glamorous stranger comes to the door looking for shelter and is allowed into Granny's home. When this beautiful stranger asks to hold the baby two times Granny grows suspicious. La Diablesse always asks the same question three times, but since Granny knows all about La Diablesse she saves her grandchild: "if Granny had given her the baby to hold, she would have disappeared like lightning, and I would not be here to tell this tale" (unpaged). Marie Lafrance, the Canadian illustrator, uses an expressionistic, folk art style. She blends size, color, and distortion to help the reader enter the stormy world of the grandmother and baby. Her illustrations are eerie and colorful depictions of the supernatural in this tale. The right-hand pages contain strong visual representations of La Diablesse's world and add authenticity to the tale.

These are quality picture books that could be classified as Caribbean children's literature when using a broad definition that includes books with authentic portrayals of the Caribbean experience. Historical and cultural themes are represented in the texts and complemented by authentic illustrations. Although there will be continual controversy concerning the ability of authors and illustrators from outside the culture to authentically characterize the Caribbean, we must make good choices from the books that are currently available. My ideal definition of cultural integrity cannot always be met because there are not many Caribbean picture books created by both an author and illustrator from the culture. We must develop sensitivity when choosing Caribbean picture books by developing an understanding of the culture. Adults choosing books must read widely within the culture's literature and be more selective. Rudine Sims Bishop has suggested that evaluators of ethnic literature must be familiar with a body of work about a people. They should read a wide range of books to develop an awareness of that culture. Furthermore, Bishop believes that authors and illustrators from a community will help those outside develop a deeper understanding of life experiences, beliefs, and values of the culture (39). Horning and Kruse suggest that adults who select and share books for children set goals beyond accumulating multicultural books and search diligently for outstanding literature (9). I believe these guidelines apply to the Caribbean picture book. It is no longer good enough to accept all books written about the Caribbean regardless of their quality. There are more books available. Access to books through the Internet has opened a wider market. Therefore, it is important to be more critical of the Caribbean books written for children. Books must be judged for their integration of text, illustration, and cultural representation. Positive, accurate, and aesthetically pleasing books should be valued for their authentic portrayals of the people and their Caribbean culture.

Note

1. From *Fruits: A Caribbean Counting Poem* by Valerie Bloom. Copyright © 1992 by Valerie Bloom. Reprinted by permission of Henry Holt and Company, LLC.

Works Cited

Agard, John. *Calypso Alphabet.* Illus. Jennifer Bent. New York: Henry Holt, 1989.

Bello, Yahaya. "Caribbean American Children's Literature." *Teaching Multicultural Literature in Grades K–8.* Ed. Violet J. Harris. Norwood, MA: Christopher-Gordon, 1992. 243–65.

Binch, Caroline. *Gregory Cool.* New York: Dial, 1994.

Bishop, Rudine Sims. "Evaluating Books By and About African-Americans." Ed. Merri V. Lundgren. *The Multicultural Mirror: Cultural Substance in Literature for Children and Young Adults.* Fort Atkinson, WI: Highsmith, 1991. 31–44.

Bloom, Valerie. *Duppy Jamboree.* Cambridge, UK: Cambridge University Press, 1992.

———. *Fruits: A Caribbean Counting Poem.* Illus. David Axtell. New York: Henry Holt, 1997.

Burgie, Irving. *Caribbean Carnival: Songs of the West Indies.* Illus. Frane Lessac. New York: Tambourine, 1992.

Comissiong, Lynette. *"Mind Me Good Now!"* Illus. Marie Lafrance. Toronto: Annick Press, 1997.

Feelings, Tom. "Transcending the Form." Ed. Merri V. Lundgren. *The Multicultural Mirror: Cultural Substance in Literature for Children and Young Adults.* Fort Atkinson, WI: Highsmith, 1991. 45–57.

Gates, Henry Lewis, Jr. "'Authenticity,' or the Lesson of Little Tree." *The New York Times,* 24 Nov. 1991: 1, 26–30.

Gershator, Phillis. *Sweet, Sweet Fig Banana.* Illus. Fritz Millevoix. Morton Grove, IL: Albert Whitman, 1996.

———. *Tukama Tootles the Flute.* Illus. Synthia Saint James. New York: Orchard, 1994.

Gunning, Monica. *Not a Copper Penny in Me House.* Illus. Frane Lessac. Honesdale, PA: Boyds Mills Press, 1993.

Hallworth, Grace. Illus. Caroline Binch. *Down by the River: Afro-Caribbean Rhymes, Games, and Songs for Children.* New York: Scholastic, 1996.

Honeyghan, Glasceta. "Rhythm of the Caribbean: Connecting Oral History and Literacy." *Language Arts* 77 (2000): 406–13.

Horning, Kathleen T. *From Cover to Cover: Evaluating and Reviewing Children's Books.* New York: Harper Collins, 1997.

Horning, Kathleen T. and Ginny Moore Kruse. "Looking into the Mirror: Considerations Behind the Reflections." Ed. Merri V. Lundgren. *The Multicultural Mirror: Cultural Substance in Literature for Children and Young Adults.* Fort Atkinson, WI: Highsmith, 1991. 1–13.

Joseph, Lynn. *An Island Christmas.* Illus. by Catherine Stock. New York: Clarion, 1992.

———. *Coconut Kind of Day.* Illus. Sandra Speidel. New York: Lothrop, Lee & Shepard, 1990.

———. *Jasmine's Parlour Day.* Illus. Ann Grifalconi. New York: Lothrop, Lee & Shepard, 1994.

———. *Jump Up Time.* Illus. Linda Saport. New York: Clarion Books, 1998.

Keens-Douglas, Ricardo. *La Diablesse and the Baby.* Illus. Marie Lafrance. Toronto: Annick, 1994.

Keifer, Barbara. "Visual Criticism and Children's Literature." Ed. Betsy Hearne & Roger Sutton. *Evaluating Children's Books: A Critical Look.* Urbana-Champaign, IL: University of Illinois, 1992. 73–92.

Lessac, Frane. *Caribbean Alphabet.* London: Macmillan Education, 1989.

———. *Caribbean Canvas.* New York: Lippencott, 1989.

———. *My Little Island.* New York: Lippencott, 1984.

Linden, Ann Marie. *One Smiling Grandma.* Illus. Lynne Russell. New York: Dial, 1992.

Mahurt, Sarah. "Virgin Islands Children's Literature: From the Oral Tradition to the Modern Picture Book." *TELLing Stories: Theory, Practice, Interviews, and Reviews* 4. (2000): 4–10.

Mahurt, Sarah and Brenda Dixey. "Caribbean Culture." *The Five Owls* 10 (1995): 25–32.

———. "Tropical Gardens: Caribbean Children's Literature." *Journal of Children's Literature* 21 (1995). 63–68.

Mikkelsen, Nina. "Insiders, Outsiders, and the Question of Authenticity: Who Shall Write for African-American Children?" *African American Review* 32 (1998) 19 p. 15 Dec. 2000. www.findarticles. com/cf_1/m2838/n1_v32/20610470.

Mitchell, Rita Phillips. *Hue Boy.* Illus. Caroline Binch. New York: Dial, 1993.

Orr, Katherine. *My Grandpa and the Sea.* Minneapolis: Carolrhoda, 1990.

Pomerantz, Charlotte. *The Chalk Doll.* Illus. Frane Lessac. New York: Lippencott, 1989.

Pratt, Linda and Janice J. Beaty. *Transcultural Children's Literature.* Upper Saddle River, NJ: Prentice-Hall, 1999.

Robinson, Cheryl. "Through a Child's Eyes: A Select Bibliography of West Indian Literature for Children." Fourth Caribbean Regional Conference of the International Reading Association, St. Croix, VI. 7 April 1989.

Rochman, Hazel. "And Yet . . . Beyond Political Correctness." Ed. Betsy Hearne & Roger Sutton. *Evaluating Children's Books: A Critical Look.* Urbana-Champaign, IL: University of Illinois, 1992. 133–48.

Roethler, Jacque. "Reading in Color: Children's Book Illustrations and Identity Formation for Black Children in the United States." *African American Review* 32 (1998): 13 p. 15 Dec. 2000. www.findarticle. com/cf_1m2838/n1_v32/20610476.

San Souci, Robert. *Cendrillon.* Illus. Brian Pinkney. New York: Simon & Schuster, 1995.

———. *The Faithful Friend.* Illus. Brian Pinkney. New York: Simon & Schuster, 1995.

———. "Weaving the Common Thread: Heroism, Pride and Freedom in Children's Literature." Teachers Employing a Love of Literature Conference, West Lafayette, IN. 11 Nov. 2000.

Temple, Frances. *Tiger Soup: An Anansi Story from Jamaica.* New York: Orchard Books, 1994.

21

The Power of Women, the Power of Teens

Revisioning Gender and Age in the Nancy Drew and Hardy Boys Mystery Series

Alisa Clapp-Itnyre

Yellow- and blue-backed copies of the Nancy Drew and Hardy Boys books, respectively, can be found throughout American homes today, and yet few people realize that these are not original stories; they are 1960s' revisions of 1930s' stories. Contemporary children's literature experts today condemn these revisions as bowdlerized "shadows" of the original 1930s books; I will argue that these revisions stand as an important cultural icon to their teenage readers of the 1960s. Ultimately, both versions of the Nancy Drew and Hardy Boys books—those originals begun by Edward Stratemeyer and the revisions issued by his daughter Harriet Stratemeyer Adams thirty years later—hold important, though different, cultural values for their audiences of yesterday and today.

Perhaps no single author of this century has been as popular with adolescents as was Edward Stratemeyer, though very few would even recognize his name. He was born in 1862 in New Jersey when popular fiction was taking publishing companies by storm. Stratemeyer wrote various stories and novels before turning to series fiction with the Rover Boys (1899–1926). This series would be followed by some incredibly popular novel collections for both boys and girls: Dorothy Dale (1908–1924), the Motor Girls (1910–1917), Tom Swift (1910–1941), the Honey Bunch series (1923–1953), Ruth Fielding (1913–1934), and his longest-running series, the Bobbsey Twins (1904–1992), all published under various pseudonyms. As scholar Carol Billman points out, two ingenious marketing strategies were used by Stratemeyer to increase the interest in his series fiction: first, he convinced his publishers to sell them at over half the cover price and, second, when even his incredibly fast pace of writing could not keep up with demand, he established the Stratemeyer Syndicate and hired ghostwriters to take his plot outlines and write the novels (21). Both strategies worked. By 1927, 80 percent of books purchased by young adults were Stratemeyer series books (Kismaric and Heiferman 125). Early twentieth-century adolescents flocked to buy these cheap, thrilling, up-to-date adventures that contained teens like themselves propelling the adventure; girls were especially excited to have heroines who did everything boys did, not surprising given that 1920 saw women's right to vote finally come to fruition.

Stratemeyer's last two series were his greatest achievement: in 1927 he launched the Hardy Boys Mystery Series under the pseudonym Franklin W. Dixon, and in 1930 started its female counterpart, the Nancy Drew Mystery Series authored by Carolyn Keene. As always, Stratemeyer sketched the outlines, then hired ghostwriters to write the actual stories. Canadian Leslie McFarlane was Franklin W. Dixon from 1926 to 1946, and Mildred Wirt Benson, as recently discovered,[1] was the first Carolyn Keene (1930–1948). Nancy Drew's popularity is substantiated in the Christmas season sales of the Depression year 1933: Macy's sold six thousand titles, making it the first series to outsell a boys' series (Billman 3, 7). Sales continued unabated despite Stratemeyer's death in 1930; his daughter Harriet Stratemeyer Adams managed to keep the Syndicate afloat, writing outlines herself to farm out to changing ghostwriters. Her decisions were not always popular; she and Benson often clashed, Adams wanting Nancy to be more "lady-like" than the adventure-loving Benson was writing her;[2] and when Adams reduced Benson's salary from $125 to $75 to meet Depression problems, Benson quit for three volumes, returning to write number eleven.

However, due primarily to the usurpation of TV as primary teen entertainment, sales of the Stratemeyer series began to falter throughout the late 1940s and 1950s, and seven of the sixteen series died during these decades. Outmoded stories from the 1930s could not appeal to 1950s' sensibilities, and even the Nancy Drew and Hardy Boys books were vulnerable. As Carole Kismaric and Marvin Heiferman point out, "As satellites circled the earth, suburbia seduced families away from cities, and teenagers took over American culture, Nancy, Frank, and Joe were no longer the coolest teens around" (101). By 1959, Adams faced a crucial decision regarding the Hardy Boys and Nancy Drew series: retain them and watch sales slip further or try to modernize them to suit newer audiences. Adams's decision, still controversial among literary purists, was to revise and update all the older volumes while continuing to add new volumes to the collection. Helped by Andrew Svenson, ghostwriter for the Happy Hollister series and Adams's partner (1961–1975), and a few other writers, Adams began the immense, eighteen-year task of revising over thirty books in each series. Adams had a penchant for claiming to be Carolyn Keene anyway, and with the revisions, she was able to claim sole authorship.[3] In some cases only minor plot changes were made, but in others the stories were entirely rewritten with only the title linking them to the original. Adams and her helpers sometimes shortened the books, trimming them from twenty-five to twenty chapters and from about 210 pages down to about 175 pages, so that the books read faster for their busy teenage audiences. Dated words (like "roadster") were changed, and vocabulary was simplified ("said" replacing words like "chortle" and "retorted"). Though seemingly deceptive and certainly "un-literary," these changes met the market demands: sales again rose and the Hardy Boys and Nancy Drew became the most popular series characters to a whole new generation of readers. As Kismaric and Heiferman argue, "whether driven by concern for the Syndicate's health, social conscience, or her own ego, it's clear that if Adams hadn't had the guts and the smarts to refashion the Syndicate's classic characters, there would have been no more cliff-hangers for Nancy, Frank, and Joe. They would have died a sad, slow, death and contributed three more tombstones to the graveyard of children's series literature" (107).

Today, many readers are critical of the revisions and interested enough in the originals that Applewood Books has found a profitable market for the reprinted originals, their promotional reading "They're Back Again . . . Just as You Remember Them." Many people do not remember the originals, however, and are shocked to discover that their favorite yellow- or blue-bound books *are* revisions. Phil Zuckerman, who led Applewood's republishing efforts, describes first reading the blue-cover *The Mystery of Cabin Island* to his son and discovering "something was missing for me. It didn't seem like the same book. [. . .] But then I discovered that the book had, in fact, been rewritten since the time when I had read it" (41). Robert L. Crawford protests the Syndicate's "unprecedented scheme to reissue the books in reduced and 'modernized' formats but under the original titles" (10). John M. Enright complains that the 1967 *The Mark on the Door* "trims action scenes down to the bare bones" and falters in other literary ways (41).

Children's literature critics and feminist scholars have been equally as vocal in their responses to the revised Nancy Drew books. Betsy Caprio catalogued the various Nancy personalities in *The Mystery of Nancy Drew: Girl Sleuth on the Couch* (1992) and found the "Classic" Nancy Drew of the 1930s and 1940s, created by Mildred Wirt Benson and color-illustrated by Russell H. Tandy, more admirable than "Two-Dimensional Nancy" of the later 1950s through 1970s, so termed because "interior line drawings of Nancy and her friends deteriorated into caricature, stick-figures, as if to say these stories were but parodies of the original Nancy Drews" (23). According to Caprio, Nancy becomes the "watered-down [. . .] creation" of Harriet Adams who "set about to make [Nancy] more gentle, send her off to church regularly, and generally dispel Nancy's larger-than-life mystique" (22). Similarly, Diana Beeson and Bonnie Brennen studied the revisions to *The Hidden Staircase* and discovered that the revised Nancy "is depicted as far less independent and self-confident and relies far more heavily on officials for help and guidance" (196). Roberta Seelinger Trites, in *Waking Sleeping Beauty* (1997), suggests that Nancy Drew is still "subjected to societal subjugation" (11). Carolyn G. Heilbrun, in her keynote address at the first-ever Nancy Drew Conference of 1993, spoke for many when describing "the original Nancy Drew [. . . as] a moment in the history of feminism" (11) to be undone by the apparently *anti*-feminist, revised Nancy: "All the changes point to the original Nancy Drew as a true feminist adventurer, while her more recent avatar makes her more of a Barbie doll conforming to that ideal of femininity dear to the radical right" (15–16). Bemoaning the condensed plots and inferior writing of the revisions, Robert Crawford ultimately ponders, "Why then did professional librarians and practitioners in the fields of children's literature and popular culture not arise in outrage at the Stratemeyer Syndicate's publication of altered, revised, and even rewritten versions?" (10).

One obvious reason may be that readers of the 1960s felt the books *were* more relevant to their culture. Consider what was occurring during the years of the revisions (1959–1960s): in 1959 Fidel Castro took control of Cuba, increasing Cold War fears, with the famous Bay of Pigs scare following in 1961. In 1962, James Meredith registered at the University of Mississippi amidst protests, escalating the civil rights movement of the 1960s, and Martin Luther King, Jr. led various demonstrations from Birmingham to Chicago. From 1965 to 1968, Lyndon Johnson sent more and more troops to Vietnam; by 1967–1968 antiwar protests had reached an all-time high. Betty Friedan's highly influential feminist treatise, *The Feminine Mystique,* came out in 1963, leading to the formation of the National Organization of Women in 1966. Significantly, teens were at the forefront of many of these movements, contributing to both the military support of and the public protest against the Vietnam War. They also fueled both the civil rights and women's movements, with people like James Meredith and Elizabeth Eckford (the latter one of nine teenagers to integrate the high school in Little Rock, 1957) becoming key players. The Stratemeyer revisions would never make overt references to such headline-grabbing events, yet their underlying messages typically urged teenage involvement in the highest level of political intrigue.

I would suggest, then, that one reason we "deplore" the changes made to the books of the 1920s and 1930s is because we view the books as *literature,* as many of the preceding scholars' comments reveal. Scholars condemn the abbreviation of text, simplification of vocabulary, reduced descriptions of character, increased dialogue over action scenes, and replacement of full pictures with line drawings. What does not guide these complaints is an exploration of the revisions as important cultural bridges between the traditional views of the 1930s' society and the soon-to-explode 1960s' society.

By closely examining the first books of each series and then six more randomly chosen originals (written between 1927 and 1934) alongside their revisions (revised between 1959 and 1968),[4] I will argue that both originals and revisions are valuable, not for their literary value but for their *cultural* revelations. Because so many people contributed even to these eight books (Walter Karig wrote *Nancy's Mysterious Letter;* and, as earlier mentioned, Harriet Adams had help with the revisions), these series books—like all ghostwritten series books—reflect broad cultural ideologies, in this case, ideas about young adults and their roles in society. Exploring those literary elements most criticized by scholars— the series' plots, minor characterizations, and protagonists—from a cultural perspective, I will suggest how each element in the revisions empowered 1960s' young adult audiences. First, plots became unrealistically complex, but they also revealed the more complex roles teens played in 1960s' society. Second, minor characterization was reductive, but it was also less culturally stereotypic and more empowering because it depicted teens interacting with all classes and genders on an equal footing, thus reflecting progress made by the racial and gender battles of the 1960s. And, finally, Nancy, Frank, and Joe grew up in these thirty years, literally from 16 to 18, and 15 to 17, but also symbolically in their power relationships with other adults and their parents, thus suggesting a new model for 1960s' teens. Indeed, as Trites argues in *Disturbing the Universe,* "power is even more fundamental to adolescent literature than growth" (x) and, though she does not include either series books in her analysis, I would argue that the revisions, especially, exemplify the issues of power she describes—young adults' negotiations with social institutions, parents, and selves.

Though Nancy's plots often suffer from midcentury marriage propaganda, I disagree that her aggressive character falters, as many critics claim—and for a reason we tend to overlook: though launched in the conservative late 1950s, the changes were mostly made during the 1960s when the feminist movement was gathering momentum (the eighth volume of Nancy Drew that I will examine was rewritten as late as 1968).[5] I would argue that despite a conservative Adams at the helm, the Syndicate's need to appeal to the youth of the day would have dictated that the series continue, not diminish, the pluckiness of their female heroine. In other words, any consideration of Nancy's feminism and the series' value must take into account not only gender but also the *age* of both the protagonists' maturity and the social epochs in which the books were written. By examining the cultural value of the revisions in terms of those literary elements often considered "weakest" (plot, minor characters, and protagonist development), I would begin the process of privileging cultural considerations over literary ones.

Plots of series books have always been faulted for being formulaic and unrealistic, but the revisions' plots are especially criticized for becoming unnecessarily complicated. Yet these plots hold fascinating cultural signification. From the beginning, the Stratemeyer Syndicate had dictated that books be free of cultural specifics that would date them. But cultural ideologies infiltrate both series on every level. A clear gender bias driving the Hardy Boys books of the late 1920s and early 1930s was that of boyish adventure—adventure, ultimately, to prepare men for the real world, such as seen in 1930s' magazines for high school boys like *Scholastic,* which told boys: "Every day brings nearer the time when you will be living and fighting for a career in a competition that is keen, as remorseless, as subtle as you will ever know" (qtd. in Palladino 19). In their first adventure, *The Tower Treasure* (1927), Frank and Joe compete with Detective Smuff and even their dad to find the thief of Mr. Applegate's jewels, exonerating their friend Slim's father and, thus, saving the entire family from financial ruin. In Book Four, *The Missing Chums* (1927), they must use cunning to save themselves and Chet and Biff from kidnappers. In Book Seven, *The Mystery of the Caves* (1930), the boys find and reunite a temporarily deranged professor with his twin sister by living in a cave for a week, narrowly escaping death from climbing accidents and the deranged man's gunshots. Finally, in Book Eight, *The Mystery of Cabin Island,* the Hardy Boys and friends also live by their own wits in an isolated cabin, capturing a crook and finding Mr. Jefferson's missing stamp collection in the cabin's chimney.

In the 1960s' revisions of these four books, Cold War fears underline the boys' adventures. In 1959, James B. Conant published a report insisting that schools increase academic rigor and produce future leaders to compete technologically with "the communist menace" (Palladino 171). These contemporary themes were embedded in the revisions of *The Tower Treasure* (1959), *The Missing Chums* (1962), *The Secret of the Caves* (1964), and *The Mystery of Cabin Island* (1966). These rewritten stories not only contained pointed references to college (Slim's family needs to be rescued now so Slim can attend college; the boys visit Kenworthy College in *Secret of the Caves*), but also boasted "up-to-date methods used by police" (qtd. in Crawford 10–11), such as the binoculars and telephoto cameras the boys now use in *The Mystery of Cabin Island.* Social deviants and foreign infiltrators were everywhere in these books published during the end of the McCarthy era. For instance, the Hardy Boys' 1962 *The Missing Chums* mystery now involves the disappearance of Chet and Biff only as it is entangled in the case of bank robbers whereas in the 1964 *The Secret of the Caves* the professor has now been abducted because of his knowledge of international spies. When Joe and Frank find him, they not only to reunite a brother and his sister but also rid our country of "foreign" (never nationally identified) spies. And *The Mystery of Cabin Island* revision adds a new character, a "ghost" in a turban haunting Cabin Island, a Middle Eastern ambassador for king "Shah Ali" who is looking for what is now a missing *medal* collection. Stolen stamps become stolen medals whose recovery is not merely a personal matter but also an international one. The Cold War paranoia of the era might make us uncomfortable now, but the capability invested in the Hardy Boys—who move from solving local cases to international ones—clearly empowered its 1960s' teenage readers.

Nancy's mystery plots also reflect their respective eras. The Nancy Drew series actually began and ran unabated during the Depression—with Nancy emerging, as Deborah Siegel writes, "as a kind of Robin Hood for the 1930s, one who restores wealth and property to the temporarily disenfranchised" (176). In those books I studied, original Nancy restores Josiah Crowley's legacy to deserving benefactors in Book One, *The Secret of the Old Clock* (1930); reunites Laura Pendleton with her true guardian in Book Three, *The Bungalow Mystery* (1930); restores an inheritance to Nancy Smith Drew in Book Eight, *Nancy's Mysterious Letter* (1932); and returns twin babies to their biological mother in Book Eleven, *The Clue of the Broken Locket* (1934).

Often Adams's more refined sensibilities, reflecting proper 1950s' and 1960s' etiquette,[6] prompt small details to change in the revisions of these books. For instance, Nancy's friend Allie Horner in the original *The Secret of the Old Clock* used the inheritance money to buy more chickens to raise whereas Allison Hoover of the 1959 version will use the money to become a professional singer, a much more acceptable and cultured occupation for a woman of the late 1950s. Similarly, the Nancy Drew 1960s' plot revisions often focus more on marriage: not surprising when, by 1960, 24 percent of women Nancy's age were already married (Palladino 169). For example, the revision to *Nancy's Mysterious Letter* reveals that the other Nancy is engaged to the duplicitous thief *midway* through the novel instead of at the end. Thus, Nancy's search for the other Nancy is not simply to unite her with her fortune but also to prevent an unfortunate marriage to a dishonorable man. Marriage is highlighted in other revised books, too: Helen Corning, Nancy's friend of the early books, is engaged by Book Three (*The Bungalow Mystery*) of the revised series. And *The Clue of the Broken Locket,* almost completely rewritten in the 1965 revision, changes from a story of finding baby twins' true parents to one of helping a young woman find her family's lost treasure so that she can marry her fiancé. Notably, as is true with the Hardy Boys, the new Nancy is engaged in more socially influential cases such as Lonely Hearts Clubs and record counterfeiters. And in *The Bungalow Mystery* revision of 1960, not only does Nancy unite Laura with her true guardian but she catches bank robbers as well.

Although the focus on marriage increases, marriage is cautiously viewed in the revisions, as shown by the 1968 Nancy Smith Drew plot. The other Nancy had placed her dreams on marriage, but our Nancy comforts her by saying, "as soon as the shock is over, you will be grateful that you were saved from a very unhappy marriage" (171), a lesson reflecting women's late 1960s' liberation. When updating *The Clue of the Broken Locket,* the Syndicate replaced the entire plot about the babies whom Nancy and Bess mothered with current 1960s' teenage interests in singing stars. Thus, the plots of the newer Nancy Drew books, though identifying with their young, romantic audience, still empower young women to become more socially minded and less centered on marriage and families.

Besides their drastic plot changes, the Stratemeyer revisions have also been criticized for their reliance on stereotypic, one-dimensional minor characters. The originals actually came under large attack in the 1950s for their caricatured portraitures of various races: a shallow Jewish boy Phil Cohen and a silly Italian Rocco of the first volume of the Hardy Boys, and a drunken African American Jeff Tucker found in the first Nancy Drew books are representative. In 1970, Gerard O'Connor was still concerned that in the revisions "the essential nature of the Hardy Boys world has not really changed at all. Mr. Rocco is still selling fruit and he still has an accent. Patrolman Riley is still an Irish cop pounding a beat" (240).[7] Nevertheless, in those revisions I studied, ethnic friends were either omitted (*The Secret of the Caves*) or went undescribed except by name (*The Missing Chums*), and Italian Mr. Rocco has been made sympathetic, not silly, in *The Tower Treasure.* The character of the uncultured, inebriated African American Jeff Tucker found in Nancy Drew's first volume, *The Secret of the Old Clock,* garners Donnarae MacCann's well-deserved condemnation: "His so-called comic nature works as a demarcation line between two cultural worlds, one of which is irrevocably inferior" (132). The 1959 revision makes Jeff an older Caucasian gentleman, still speaking in colloquialisms ("Yes, ding it" 119), but who is not inebriated and who is helped by Nancy, not scolded, as she puts in a good word so he will not lose his job. Yet, MacCann points out that the erasure of all African Americans in the revisions is no solution, leaving "the series book literature [. . .] largely all-white literature" (134). This expunging of race seems to be a move reflecting societal events and current attitudes. After all, the United States was embroiled in the civil rights movement during the 1960s, as the country debated racism not only in societal customs but also in popular culture portrayals—and erasing the problem, rather than overtly addressing it, may have seemed the safest solution to Adams.

Also in reaction to social trends, gender stereotypes somewhat improve. Bobbie Ann Mason and others have always been quick to note how Bess and George take on stark contrasts of femininity with Bess prone to diet and romance and George more boyish and athletic (53–56). But these stereotypes began as early as the 1932 *Nancy's Mysterious Letter,* where Bess is introduced as a plump woman "who loved good things to eat" while George is "boyish" (2). The revisions simply carry on the "unfortunate" tradition of labeling young women. However, these depictions also suggest more possibilities for girls: that one can be "chubby" or "boyish," neither fitting the "ideal woman" image, and still be a heroine is certainly a feminist stance. Unfortunately, unflattering portrayals of women also exist in the Hardy Boys books—such as the meek, mild girlfriends Callie Shaw and Iola Morton who sit at home and applaud their boyfriends' success—only to be counterbalanced by equally bad stereotypes of the Hardys' male friends—chubby, food-loving Chet Morton and athletic but rather dim Biff Hooper. Perhaps the minor character to make the most "improvement" in the Hardy Boys' revisions is opinionated, domineering Aunt Gertrude who now is described as "actually a great favorite with the boys despite her tart tongue and frequent predictions of dire mishaps overtaking her sleuthing nephews" (*The Secret of the Caves* 60). As with Hannah Gruen, Nancy's "older housekeeper," Aunt Gertrude is no longer the butt of jokes, and both women contribute their own small share of aid to the young sleuths in the revisions.

Original books also contained elitist attitudes in their depiction of minor characters, as when Nancy suspects the *nouveau riche* Blairs right away in *The Clue of the Broken Locket.* By the 1960s' revisions, occasional elitist attitudes still appear, but in general the revisions avoid stereotyping *people* of various classes. Now any class can be totally trustworthy or highly suspicious. For example, in the 1962 *The Missing Chums,* two newly introduced lower-class characters, Alf and Sutton, become the friend and the villain, respectively, to the Hardy Boys. The Middle Eastern man added to *The Mystery of Cabin Island,* though initially suspected of being a crook, turns out to be a sincere, polite ambassador. These "egalitarian" alterations affect even women who are no longer simply annoying actresses and aunts, but now are the criminals, as is the case of newly added characters Mrs. Aborn (in the 1960 *The Bungalow Mystery*) and Mrs. Driskell (in the 1965 *The Clue of the Broken Locket*). The hegemony of the early 1960s' world would dictate that people be more alike than different; hence, cultural stereotypes are less important, but so, too, are personality distinctions, as is seen with the depiction of Aunt Gertrude. Deviance makes one not an annoyance but a villain now, especially when it comes to women. It is much to Frank, Joe, and Nancy's credit, though, that they no longer judge criminals based on class, gender, or race demarcations; anyone—poor or rich, male or female, from any ethnic group—may be a criminal or a friend in the revisions.

The three protagonists themselves—Nancy, Frank, and Joe—have tended to elicit the most debate among critics. Yet it is with these characters that the social implications for teenagers become most pronounced. While their reading audience is becoming younger and younger, these youth become older: literally, of course, as Frank grows from 16 to 18, Joe jumps from 15 to 17, and Nancy also ages from 16 to 18. Perhaps they have aged so they can drive a car, but this aging also allows these youth to interact with the adults around them in more uncompromising ways. Maturity is most striking for Nancy, making her an important feminist role model for her 1960s' readers.

Various critics note the increased presence of authority figures, particularly police, in the revisions, and this is often argued—as Beeson and Brennen argue in "Translating Nancy Drew"—to imply that youth has a growing dependence on adults. For instance, whereas originally Joe and Frank only accidentally make contact with the police (*The Secret of the Caves*) or tend to isolate themselves away from worldly help (*The Mystery of Cabin Island*), the new Hardy Boys are continually contacting the police or aided by police who deliver messages and arrest culprits. Likewise, the revised Nancy Drew consistently checks in with the police whenever a clue is discovered, no matter what town she finds herself in, an important enough step that illustrators capture it in *The Mysterious Letter* (73). Beeson and Brennen suggest the cultural significance of such reliance on authority: "Postwar American society, with its conservative political and economic agenda, focuses on cooperation, law, and conformity. Individuals are continually urged to obey the rules, respect the law, and find legal solutions to problems rather than to take the law into their own hands" (197). They suggest that Nancy's independence is much diminished by this newly acquired reliance on legal authority figures and conformity to the law.

I would argue another way of reading both Nancy's and the Hardy Boys' increased interaction with the police: the police, in fact, always trust and support the work these young people are doing. Never do they question the reliability of these youth, work without informing them of any clues they may discover, or speak condescendingly to them. By the Book Seven revision, Chief Collig is calling the Hardy Boys to help *him* with a case (1). Nothing seems more empowering of a teenager than to be treated as an adult, a powerful message to send to 1950s' and 1960s' youth, as historian Grace Palladino reminds us: "They may have been rebels, as their critics charged, but they were not rebelling against the adult world, they were chafing at the bit to move into it—to get out of school, get a job, get married" (164). These books show teenagers neither as rebels nor as childish and incapable but as "teenagers [who] are celebrated for being just who they really are—indefatigable and independent do-gooders who keep the world safe" (Kismaric and Heiferman 8). Given the increased rebellions from youth in the civil rights movement and soon the Vietnam protests, Nancy's, Frank's, and Joe's complicity with authority may have been questioned by the more rebellious flower children of the mid to late 1960s; most readers, perhaps, identified with these youthful characters for their authority and by their ability to work within the system, garnering more power of their own.

The Hardy Boys are more mature and confident in the rewrites. In the originals, they are engaging as they play practical jokes on each other and their friends, but they are clearly making themselves young—perhaps even younger than their 15 and 16 years—when they do so (consider the tricks they play on a lazy farmer and unsuspecting Rocco in *The Tower Treasure,* both scenes that are deleted in the revision). Furthermore, many of their clues are discovered accidentally when out on boys' romps to the swimming hole. The revisions make these searches more intentional and less "boyish." Joe and Frank are unwittingly caught when they attempt to rescue their friends Chet and Biff in the original *The Missing Chums;* in the revision, they intentionally let themselves be kidnapped by the culprits in town so they can lead the police to the crooks' hangout. A means of enforcing adultlike behavior on 1960s' kids prone to pranks, these literary tropes also assure youth that they can do more than they had first believed of themselves.

The original Hardy Boys are especially anxious to fill their father's shoes. Because he is such a well-known detective, they feel inadequate. They get lectures from him about developing their detective skills: "Your powers of observation have not been trained. A good detective has to school himself to remember all sorts of little facts like that" (*The Tower Treasure* 36). Of course, the adventures in this first book are set up to be training ground for later sequels, but in many ways this feels like rites of passage. In fact, Fenton Hardy sets himself up as their competition in *The Tower Treasure:* "you can't ask me to help you any more than I've done. [. . .] So, from now on, you are part of my opposition" (83). One whole chapter switches points of view to that of Fenton Hardy as he flies to New York City to track down the owner of the red wig. The boys wait anxiously at home. Their reasons to solve the case, in fact, are very telling: "It'll clear Mr. Robinson—" "We'll get the reward—" *"Dad'll be proud of us"* (italics added 193). In the revision, the boys' goals have changed: "Now Mr. Robinson's cleared for sure! [. . .] That's the best part of solving this mystery" (168). Their dad still sets himself up as competition in a chapter now entitled "Rival Detectives" but the angst is gone. He is more diplomatic when talking to the boys and even invites them to New York to help with the detective work. This empowerment will infiltrate the rest of the new series: in Book Seven's revision, Fenton actually gives the boys the case he has been hired to do (find Mr. Todd) so he can work on the government case, which the boys end up solving as well.

If the revisions sanction the boys as an equal to their father, they empower Nancy, for she does not have any rival detective in the family whom she needs to live up to. Carson Drew in both series is present and supportive but never a rival; in fact, Nancy is most invasive in a case of his in *The Clue of the Broken Locket,* which, when rewritten, takes Nancy far away from River Heights and involves her in a case clearly of her own finding. Furthermore, Nancy matures even more than the Hardy Boys in the revisions, which, I would suggest, does even more to help the feminist cause. Original Nancy may have spunk, but she is also childish, impulsive, and impatient, as opposed to the sedate and responsible 18-year-old of the revisions. The first volume, *The Secret of the Old Clock,* is a case in point. Beeson and Brennen make much of the fact that in the original, "Nancy frequently works outside the law, [whereas] the new Nancy is a law-abiding citizen" (196), a point that applies to this mystery when Nancy hides a clock from the police as she gives an officer a ride back to town. In contrast, the revised Nancy decides, "I'll just have to 'fess up [. . .] and take the consequences!" (143). What is notable, however, is that revised Nancy still "keeps" the hidden notebook from inside the clock, thinking to herself that, after all, the police "were not involved in locating Mr. Crowley's missing will" (144). The original Nancy is also duplicitous with her friends and rather rudely tells her friend Helen Corning that she has to leave camp early because "There's something I must attend to at once" since "she knew that Helen and her friends would not leave her alone for a minute" (119–20). The revised Nancy more kindly appeases Helen by telling her she's "had a wonderful time" and that she'll "try to get back" (100). More impatient with others, original Nancy is always hard on herself too, the authors pointing out her mistakes in the process: "How foolish of me to take this road" (28) and "It was foolish of me to take time to look at the clock" (168). In the revisions, such self-effacing statements are deleted and setbacks are explained simply as a part of sleuthing.

Plunkett-Powell feels that the "earliest Nancy Drew simply did not feel fear. She had spunk and she had concern, and that was enough" (61). My reading shows otherwise. In the original *The Secret of the Old Clock,* Nancy gets timid when facing criminals: "The look on the robber's face frightened her" (130) whereas the very same juncture in the revised volume reads instead "But she steeled herself not to show any of her inward fears" (108)—proactive as opposed to reactive. Thus, Billman's comment seems particularly relevant to the revisions: "For preteens, unsure of their footing in their own surroundings, Nancy's ability to triumph over wicked, grown men and emerge from dangerous encounters unscathed is as reassuring and confidence-inspiring as it is thrilling" (120).

The 1930s' Nancy in *The Mysterious Letter* also changes by the 1960s' revisions. Original Nancy is more impatient ("wrathful" 101) and rude with the annoying Mrs. Sheets whereas new Nancy, though "furious," quickly "bursts into laughter" when the woman leaves (101–02). These characteristics also spill over into her treatment of innocent little boys. To Tommy, who has seen the mail thief, she replies impatiently, "Oh, Tommy, don't say 'well' all the time. It's far from well" (13), whereas revised Nancy exclaims, "Oh, Tommy, you've been a wonderful help to me" (8) and she brings him candy and a badge for his services. In this same original volume—interestingly, written by Walter Karig—original Nancy is continually reminded that a woman's place is in the home by the many "cross people" (79) in the story such as Mrs. Sheets: "When I was a girl, girls stayed home and learned to cook and sew and mind their own business, not to go gallivantin' around in swell autos and waited on hand and foot" to which Nancy replies, "If you have come here to lecture me, would you mind waiting until I have finished my luncheon?" (63)—an answer at once plucky and yet revealing the same class condescension Mrs. Sheets resents. The quote serves to remind readers that Nancy—as a girl and as a teenager—is breaking social customs. By the 1960s, writers seemed unable to even register what a girl's job might be; at any rate, Nancy and her friends run around as if this is the norm for girls without ever encountering a surprised or surly person.

Nancy's feminism is often seen to hinge on her relationship with boys. For instance, Carolyn Heilbrun writes that "what Nancy once did for herself is done by her boyfriend Ned in the revised version[s]" (16). Bobbie Ann Mason, clearly reading the originals, exalts in Nancy's control over Ned—"Nancy has Ned under her thumb, and she must keep him there if she is to protect her purity" (63)—and Nancy's general nonchalance, even deceit, when it comes to boyfriends: "To the extent that a girl sleuth is a sneak, some of her wiliest sleuthing involves deceiving her boyfriends or leading them on a merry chase" (62). I would suggest this "feminist" nonchalance continues to be the case in the revisions, too. For instance, in *Nancy's Mysterious Letter,* original Nancy's attempt to fit the polite, sought-after girl extends as far as her trying to make a good impression on Ned's parents who will drive her to Emerson College to watch Ned play in the football game. After writing a thank-you note, she sighs, "Perhaps it is a little stiff, but it is better to be somewhat formal than too eager" no doubt displaying appropriate etiquette for the 1930s (94). Though Nancy drops Ned quickly enough to run after the thief, she still takes Mr. Nickerson with her for help and protection. In the revised version, all polite etiquette, romantic interest, and reliance on men are extinguished: Ned's parents are deleted, and just when Ned is finally in the limelight in his own right for making the winning touchdown, Nancy spots the thief and exclaims, "Oh, I don't want to take away any of the glory from the celebration [. . .] but I just saw a man over there who looks like Edgar Nixon!" and immediately everyone leaves Ned to dash after the culprit (135). Nancy is hardly reliant on Ned; in fact, her career as detective always comes first over Ned's football and academic career. In the revised version of *The Bungalow Mystery,* Nancy has another boyfriend, Dan, whom she manages to push off onto her new friend Laura so she can go to the bungalow and do some sleuthing. And though in many of the revisions, such as *The Clue of the Broken Locket,* Ned, Dave, and Burt (Bess and George's boyfriends, respectively) may appear more frequently, their presence only seems to mean three more people whom Nancy may unwittingly show up with her quick mind and brave strategies.

In conclusion, both the Hardy Boys and Nancy Drew mature with the revisions. It is a maturity that comes with experience, with a relationship to the adult world in all its many guises, pleasant, authoritative, and villainous. The Hardy Boys scoot around on their motorcycles and boat, working with the adult world but pretty much single-handedly tackling gangs of thieves, kidnappers, and international spies. Nancy is even more impressive, driving around the country in her dark blue convertible, associating with male *and* female villains, doing what it takes two boys to do, and making detective work her own unique career without any competitive residue that the Hardy Boys feel for their father. The illustrations may dwindle down to stick figures and the dialogue may dilute down to colloquial phrases, but I do not think the revisions should be condemned. The 1960s needed a stronger kind of youth and a stronger kind of woman to face the wars, social unrest, and the feminist movement shortly on this country's horizon. Perhaps the Hardy Boys and Nancy Drew books—blue-backed and yellow-backed, respectively—in a small way prepared youth to believe in their own political power: the power of teens *and* the power of women. One contemporary Nancy Drew reader, as quoted in a 2000 Gannett News Service newspaper article (picturing a girl fondly holding a yellow-backed Nancy Drew book) sums it up best:

> What I learned from Nancy Drew is to never trust the obvious, to not be afraid to take risks, that we can do more than we think we can, that it is great to have a best friend who generally accepts you no matter what the circumstances, that women can do all the things boys can do and without their help.

A truer statement of teen and women empowerment has probably never been written.

Notes

1. For the intriguing mystery behind the Nancy Drew authorship, see various articles in Dyer and Romalov's *Rediscovering Nancy Drew,* including Geoffrey S. Lapin's "Searching for Carolyn Keene" (52–58), Mildred Wirt Benson's own "Fulfilling a Quest for Adventure" (59–65), and Karen Plunkett-Powell's *The Nancy Drew Scrapbook* (Part 1, 1–52). Harriet Adams for many years claimed to be the real Carolyn Keene.

2. Adams had said that she found the original Nancy "too bold and brassy" (qtd. in Kismaric and Heiferman 113). During the court battle *Grosset and Dunlap v. Gulf and Western,* 1980, Mildred Wirt Benson testified that "Mrs. Adams was an entirely different person; she was more cultured and more refined. I was probably a rough and tumble newspaper person who had to earn a living, and I was out in the real world. That was my type of Nancy. Nancy was making her way in life and trying to compete and have fun along the way. We just had two different kinds of Nancys" (qtd. in Johnson 37).

3. Lapin was an early defendant of Mildred Wirt Benson, asking why "this Adams woman [was] being touted as the author of those books" (54). Tracking down Benson, Lapin discovered that Adams could make this claim because of the contract Benson and other ghostwriters signed, relinquishing all authorship rights to the Syndicate.

4. I will be using the following Hardy Boys books: *The Tower Treasure,* number one, 1927, rev. 1959; *The Missing Chums,* number four, 1928, rev. 1962; *The Secret of the Caves,* number seven, 1929, rev. 1964; and *The Mystery of Cabin Island,* number eight, 1929, rev. 1966. Of Nancy Drew books, I will be using *The Secret of the Old Clock,* number one, 1930, rev. 1959; *The Bungalow Mystery,* number three, 1930, rev. 1960; *Nancy's Mysterious Letter,* number eight, 1932, rev. 1968; and *The Clue of the Broken Locket,* number eleven, 1934, rev. 1965.

5. Heilbrun refers to the "terrible fifties" as a time when things took a turn for the worse with the Nancy Drew series (17) while Caprio calls the revised Nancy "not unlike Barbie" and "the vapid, baby-doll movie heroines of the 50s and early 60s" as reflecting "the regression in the status of women during

the decades after World War II" (22). I suggest that there is some confusion in linking the revisions with the post–World War II 1950s because the revisions *began* in 1959 and continued through the 1960s. It would seem more natural to link them with the newly inaugurated women's movement.

6. Emily Post, in her preface to the tenth edition of *Etiquette: The Blue Book of Social Usage* (1960), writes that "What was once considered the tradition of gracious living of the few has in these times of plenty rightly become the heritage of us all. [. . .] I do think that Americans today are drifting toward, not away from, finer perceptions and good taste" (xxvii), suggesting the increased pressure on Americans during the early 1960s to conform to established social rules. Americans' penchant for etiquette takes on great global power when she writes, "At a time when the whole world looks to America for leadership, our country is still youth personified" (xxviii), with the obligation to socially conform resting squarely on the shoulders of youth.

7. Gerard O'Connor adeptly chronicles the "world of prejudice" of the Hardys' WASP world where Italian Tony Prito and Jewish Phil Cohen speak in muddled English, fun is made of Italian vendor Rocco and Irish policeman Con Riley, and villains turn out to be Asian Louie Fong and African American Luke Jones: "The influence of the Hardy Boys stories on American thought is as inestimable as their readers are incalculable. [. . .] Millions of minds, my own included, have been irrevocably warped by the taken-for-granted caste system" (239).

Works Cited

Beeson, Diana and Bonnie Brennen. "Translating Nancy Drew from Print to Film." *Rediscovering Nancy Drew*. Ed. Carolyn Stewart Dyer and Nancy Tillman Romalov. Iowa City, IA: University of Iowa Press, 1995. 193–207.

Benson, Mildred Wirt. "Fulfilling a Quest for Adventure." *Rediscovering Nancy Drew*. Ed. Carolyn Stewart Dyer and Nancy Tillman Romalov. Iowa City, IA: University of Iowa Press, 1995. 59–65.

Billman, Carol. *The Secret of the Stratemeyer Syndicate: Nancy Drew, The Hardy Boys, and the Million Dollar Fiction Factory*. New York: Ungar, 1986.

Caprio, Betsy. *The Mystery of Nancy Drew: Girl Sleuth on the Couch*. Trabuco Canyon, CA: Source Books, 1992.

Crawford, Robert L. "Rewriting the Past in Children's Literature: The Hardy Boys and Other Series." *Children's Literature Quarterly* 18.1 (1993): 10–12.

Enright, John M. "Hardy Boy Notes—the Epic: Rebels and Mystical Men." *The Dime Novel Roundup* 59.3 (1990): 41–43.

Gannett News Service. "Nancy Drew Inspires Generations." *Palladium-Item,* Richmond, Indiana. 28 Nov. 2000: B4.

Heilbrun, Carolyn G. "Nancy Drew: A Moment in Feminist History." *Rediscovering Nancy Drew*. Ed. Carolyn Stewart Dyer and Nancy Tillman Romalov. Iowa City, IA: University of Iowa Press, 1995. 11–21.

Johnson, Deidre. "From Paragraphs to Pages: The Writing and Development of the Stratemeyer Syndicate Series." *Rediscovering Nancy Drew*. Ed. Carolyn Stewart Dyer and Nancy Tillman Romalov. Iowa City, IA: University of Iowa Press, 1995. 29–40.

Kismaric, Carole and Marvin Heiferman. *The Mysterious Case of Nancy Drew and the Hardy Boys*. New York: Simon and Schuster, 1998.

Lapin, Geoffrey S. "Searching for Carolyn Keene." *Rediscovering Nancy Drew*. Ed. Carolyn Stewart Dyer and Nancy Tillman Romalov. Iowa City, IA: University of Iowa Press, 1995. 52–58.

MacCann, Donnarae. "Nancy Drew and the Myth of White Supremacy." *Rediscovering Nancy Drew*. Ed. Carolyn Stewart Dyer and Nancy Tillman Romalov. Iowa City, IA: University of Iowa Press, 1995. 129–35.

Mason, Bobbie Ann. *The Girl Sleuth: A Feminist Guide*. Old Westbury, NY: The Feminist Press, 1975.

O'Connor, Gerard. "The Hardy Boys Revisited: A Study in Prejudice." *Challenges in American Culture*. Ed. Ray B. Browne, Larry N. Landrum, and William K. Bottorf. Bowling Green, OH: Bowling Green University Popular Press, 1970. 234–41.

Palladino, Grace. *Teenagers: An American History.* New York: Harper Collins, 1996.

Plunkett-Powell, Karen. *The Nancy Drew Scrapbook.* New York: St. Martin's, 1993.

Post, Emily. *Etiquette: The Blue Book of Social Usage.* 10th ed. New York: Funk and Wagnalls, 1960.

Romalov, Nancy Tillman. "Children's Series Books and the Rhetoric of Guidance: A Historical Overview." *Rediscovering Nancy Drew.* Ed. Carolyn Stewart Dyer and Nancy Tillman Romalov. Iowa City, IA: University of Iowa Press, 1995. 113–20.

Siegel, Deborah L. "Nancy Drew as New Girl Wonder: Solving It All for the 1930s." *Nancy Drew and Company: Culture, Gender, and Girls' Series.* Ed. Sherrie A. Inness. Bowling Green, OH: Bowling Green State University Popular Press, 1997.

Trites, Roberta Seelinger. *Disturbing the Universe: Power and Repression in Adolescent Literature.* Iowa City, IA: University of Iowa Press, 2000.

———. *Waking Sleeping Beauty.* Iowa City, IA: University of Iowa Press, 1997.

Zuckerman, Phil. "Publishing the Applewood Reprints." *Rediscovering Nancy Drew.* Ed. Carolyn Stewart Dyer and Nancy Tillman Romalov. Iowa City, IA: University of Iowa Press, 1995. 41–46.

22

Teaching Holocaust Literature

C. Beth Burch

Teaching the Holocaust is daunting, unnerving. Even thinking about approaching Holocaust texts gives us pause, and decisions about what to teach and how to speak of the unspeakable that is the Holocaust can be nearly paralyzing. There is nothing like the Holocaust, and there are no precedents for teaching it or agreements about how to proceed. And whatever you do or however you do it, you will likely have second thoughts about what you taught and how you taught it. Nevertheless, we must teach the Holocaust: Our citizens are obligated to know about this terrible part of the past that actually is not past but that resonates even now. From my research and teaching of Jewish writers and the Holocaust, here are some suggestions for your study and teaching of the Holocaust, some ways to begin thinking about the subject.

Approach the Subject with Respect and Understand That the Holocaust Is Unique in History

The Holocaust is not just another example of extreme prejudice. It is *sui generis,* unique in the Western experience, what James Farnham has called a "rupture" in Western civilization (65), where the entire fabric of modern life has been rent by the systematic, technological, and single-minded murder of 6 million Jews of Europe as well as gypsies, gays, retarded people, and other "undesirables." We cannot compare the attempted genocide that was the Holocaust to anything else in history. Because of this and because of the magnitude of death and suffering it engendered, we must approach the Holocaust with awe and respect and the understanding that the Holocaust is not something we can hope to comprehend or even articulate. It is not something that should be cheapened by platitudes or moralizing or by attempts to "understand" it or find some redeeming value or moral lessons in it; its evil is too enormous for human comprehension. We realize this all too well when we read Elie Wiesel's *Night,* Tadeusz Borowski's *This Way to the Gas, Ladies and Gentlemen,* Primo Levi's *Survival in Auschwitz,* Aharon Appelfeld's *Badenheim 1939,* Paul Celan's poetry, diaries by Chaim Kaplan or Israel Lichtenstein, or the Oneg Shabbat archives hidden in the Warsaw ghetto for the world to find. All that we can really do in the face of the Holocaust is to listen to the survivors and witnesses, be grateful for their survival, and remember the dead with a sense of vigilance.

Respect the Survivors

The survivors are our means to memory, our link to the past. We must read their diaries and memoirs and watch their videotaped accounts with respect and attention. Survivor testimony is primary, the first order of approach to the Holocaust and the place where we begin our study and our teaching; their words must be approached with awe, respect, fear, trembling, outrage, and compassion (Wiesel *A Jew Today* 165 ff.).

We are fortunate that some survived. Some victims endured and lived to witness for those who came after, to tell the unspeakable degradation and murder of the Holocaust, the inarticulable life of extremity, a "condition from which there is no escape, no place to go except the grave" (Des Pres 7). Some held on in defiance of dehumanization, in determination to overcome silence, to remember the dead, to remain, quite simply, alive. They came through a life of extremity, as Terrence Des Pres has written in *The Survivor,* "to keep a living soul in a living body" (7). Anyone preparing to teach the Holocaust should read Des Pres's study of survivors of extremity and should simultaneously read extensively in the diaries and memoirs. And anyone teaching the Holocaust should know that witnessing the Holocaust allows survivors to commemorate the victims, find some modicum of present peace, document what happened for posterity, and put on trial the perpetrators of evil (Tager 267). This last point, the hope that the murderers will be exposed, is extremely important to psychological health. When Primo Levi learned in 1959, for example, that a German publisher had purchased translation rights for his memoir *Survival in Auschwitz,* he "felt overwhelmed by the violent and new emotion of having won a battle" (qtd. in Tager 281). His witness was his weapon against the ignorance and the denial of the Germans vis-à-vis their past.

There are certain aspects of surviving that we on the other side of that experience need to understand. We need to know, for instance, that we do not have the ability to judge survivors, nor should we be permitted to. Students do in fact frequently judge survivors and victims harshly—ironically more harshly than they judge the Nazis. They expect Nazis to be evil, selfish, diabolical, and arbitrary, and they expect victims to be innocent, compliant, forgiving, and true to stereotype. They find difficulty in accepting survivors' behavior born out of the sheer will and instinct to stay alive, behavior that may seem, according to current ways of thinking, selfish, cold-hearted, even cunning. Somehow we who teach the Holocaust must find ways to help students know how ethical behavior depends on traditional cultural support and how the Holocaust was a world unto itself, nothing like the world the survivors, who could not choose their fate, left or the one that we now inhabit. Helping students conceptualize this means, James Farnham argues, redefining ethical behavior as "not necessarily obedient behavior, not merely conformity to an external set of values. Rather, it is acting in a way which, according to one's best lights at the time, contributes to the freedom of other persons" (65).

What also needs redefining is the meaning of survivors' resistance, for there is the misconception that armed resistance like that of the Warsaw Ghetto Uprising is the only kind of resistance. Writing a diary was resistance, singing was resistance, praying on Shabbat was resistance, maintaining dignity in the face of those whose primary aim was to dehumanize was resistance. Simply surviving was resistance because it thwarted the Nazi design to murder the Jews, at least temporarily and as long as one Jew remained. Remaining alive became a victory, for surviving was an unimaginable struggle that destroyed the body and tortured the mind. Hear, for instance, a bit of Gisella Perl's account of extremity, of the dehumanizing filth of existence of life in Belsen Bergen:

> Everybody in the block had typhus [. . .] it came to Belsen Bergen in its most violent, most painful, deadliest form. The diarrhea caused by it became uncontrollable. It flooded the bottom of the cages, dripping through the cracks into the faces of the women lying in the cages below, and mixed with blood, pus and urine, formed a slimy, fetid mud on the floor of the barracks." (Dawidowicz *Holocaust Reader* 171)

And here is part of the last testament of Israel Lichtenstein, who assembled and then hid the Oneg Shabbat archive materials from the Warsaw Ghetto, records assembled surreptitiously and at great risk to all those in the archive group. Lichtenstein risked his life and those of his wife and child to ensure that a record of the Nazis' murders and crimes remained behind for the world to find. In his simple yet plaintive last testament written just before he and his family were transported on July 31, 1942, in what Lichtenstein knew was really an "annihilation action," we can hear his sorrow as he acknowledges his fate and expresses a desire to be remembered—not just himself, but his artist wife, Gele Seckstein, and his baby daughter as well. "I want my little daughter to be remembered," he wrote:

> Margalit, 20 months old today. Has mastered Yiddish perfectly, speaks a pure Yiddish, at 9 months began to speak Yiddish clearly. In intelligence she is on a par with 3- or 4-year-old children. I don't want to brag about her. Witnesses to this, who tell me about it, are the teaching staff of the school at Nowolipki 68. I am not sorry about my life and that of my wife. But I am sorry for the gifted little girl. She deserves to be remembered. (Dawidowicz *Holocaust Reader* 296–97)

These accounts speak to why we must go to the survivors' documents when we first begin to read about and teach the Holocaust. Scholars repeatedly point out the similarity in the diaries and memoirs, how the events described are eerily alike from memoir to memoir and how the tone is consistently one of stark simplicity, clean narration, emotion expressed but typically held tightly in check (see Des Pres 30–50; Rosenfeld 37–61). Survivors' experiences were remarkably the same, as their testimonies indicate, even though they were "selected," taken from their homes and businesses, rounded up, and put on trains and trucks, and, from all over Europe, transported to many different destinations. Together, their accounts constitute a complex and compelling historical record of the disaster, necessary reading for those who teach it.

Ground the Study in History and Testimony

If we then listen first to the survivors and begin our study with the survivors' accounts and with the documents and recorded history of the Holocaust, we ground our students' knowledge and concepts of the Holocaust in the most reliable information possible. This way, students' knowledge about the Holocaust is honest, even if their education about the Holocaust is truncated. This is exceedingly important because of the strategies of Holocaust deniers, whose strategy is often to try to engage in a "debate" about the Holocaust and to enjoin those who are listening to "hear the other side." This notion of "another side" is a spurious argument, a false appeal to rationality. About the Holocaust and its facts, there is no other side, nor can there ever be "opinions" about this. The Holocaust happened. Stretched end to end, the written records and documents verifying the Holocaust go on for miles, and many of them were prepared by the Germans themselves, who meticulously and precisely recorded details of round-ups, "selections," gassings, medical experiments, and "actions" (see Dawidowicz's *The War Against the Jews 1933–1945* for extensive documentation). Using history and testimony as the first choice of teaching materials also helps students be clear about what happened and what did not. Younger students especially may not be able to make generic distinctions between novels and diaries, particularly at first; they frequently describe everything they read as "stories." Indeed, some Holocaust educators prefer to teach only history and testimony. Rebecca Welch Johnson, for instance, teaches exclusively from nonfiction; she centers her instruction on *The Diary of Anne Frank* and on Elie Wiesel's *Night,* which together Johnson says offer a "clearer perspective of what really happened during those years" than fiction (70). Using history, memoir, and other nonfiction as the main staple of the curriculum creates a consistency of materials that is important, especially for students in middle school and younger.

Indeed, fiction about the Holocaust can present problems, particularly for these younger readers. Jane Yolen's *The Devil's Arithmetic,* for example, is a work of fiction in which the protagonist travels through time to experience the Holocaust and then miraculously ends up herself again, safe at home in America decades after the Holocaust. Although this plot permits children to read the book and keep intact their feelings of personal security while still allowing them to imagine themselves in a situation similar to that of the protagonist, it may also engender a sense that the Holocaust, like time travel itself, is of the exotic fabric of fantasy. It is quite possible that this plot strategy sows the seeds of doubt and denial alongside those of Holocaust awareness. Using fiction to approach the Holocaust may subvert, most likely unintentionally, the real, lived experiences of the Holocaust, for a work of fiction can always be dismissed as an invention, regardless of its basis in empirical reality. Even Cynthia Ozick, who has written a novella about the Holocaust, *The Shawl,* argues for the primacy of history and fact in Holocaust studies: "Scholars may not agree on what happened," she argues, "but they do consent to an actual happening. Your Napoleon may not be my Napoleon, but the fact of Napoleon is incontrovertible. To whatever degree, history is that which is owed to reality" (1). Perhaps the question is whether we educators *need* to use the fiction; one thing to consider is that no matter how interesting or absorbing the fiction is, the facts of the Holocaust are more compelling by far.

If You Use Fiction, Evaluate It Carefully

Elie Wiesel, defining literature as text that is imaginative or fictive, believes that there is "no such thing as Holocaust literature—there cannot be. Auschwitz negates all literature as it negates all theories and doctrines; to lock it into a philosophy means to restrict it. To substitute words, any words, for it is to distort it. A Holocaust literature? The very term is a contradiction" (*A Jew Today* 175). Indeed, how can fiction possibly convey life in the camps? In the Warsaw ghetto? How can the absolute terror of living through the Holocaust be recreated through the imagination? And if we teach fiction about the Holocaust, do we disrespect the truth of the experience as evidenced in the testimonies? The teacher who decides to use fiction about the Holocaust or fiction set during the Holocaust must address these concerns. Nevertheless, many educators do believe that there are good reasons to choose fiction for teaching the Holocaust.

Educators who embrace the teaching of fiction make the case that fiction helps them teach beyond the history to the moral imperative of the Holocaust. Rachel Baum, for instance, argues that although historical knowledge is "essential to any understanding of the Holocaust, Holocaust literature teaches us, in part, how to feel about the historical facts" (45). Although it is true that we can never grasp what the victims or survivors felt, perhaps it is possible that fiction appeals to certain readers whose empathy can be aroused from the effort to imagine themselves in the plot. Erhard K. Dortmund explains why fiction is important to his Holocaust course at Western Oregon State College:

> Still, there is a way to help make the truth of the Holocaust take hold, to make possible in the classroom those moments of clarity and astonishment that, at their best the liberal arts make possible. I am thinking of certain works of fiction. Chastened and inspired by the works of historians, storytellers free the factual from its dead weight. Their novels, short stories, and poems are our classroom guides to the far side of the literal, where stones bleed and the dead speak. (B2)

Dortmund further argues that using fiction makes possible more than simply "covering" the Final Solution; fiction helps students realize that the "Holocaust's brutal intrusion into modern life was something long in the making" (B2). From this initial realization among his students, Dortmund exposes the long history of anti-Semitism, considers issues of resistance and the Allies' response to the Holocaust—altogether "the interconnective sweep of historical events, that one thing does indeed lead to another" (B2). In short, he uses Holocaust fiction as an avenue for approaching Holocaust history.

At minimum, educators who use fiction in a study of the Holocaust must choose this fiction carefully. Joel Shatzky evaluates Holocaust literature using three criteria: (1) historical accuracy, (2) literary quality, and (3) intellectual integrity (105). Most important, Shatzky is committed to historical accuracy: the literary work should be "free of distortions and outright fabrications that could create in the reader's mind a false impression of the historical record of the Holocaust," he argues (105). He points out that for many people, the novel is the chief avenue for learning about the Holocaust, yet Holocaust fiction is not like most historical fiction with characters like Mary Queen of Scots who can be recreated from imagination. Shatzky is aware that even nonfiction Holocaust narratives can inadvertently misrepresent facts (through misperception or transmuted memory, for example) but believes that "as long as the author makes an honest attempt to follow the known historical record, such works should not be faulted for minor inconsistencies" (105).

For the second criterion, that of literary quality, Shatzky imposes stringent artistic restrictions. The notion of literary quality applied to Holocaust literature means for Shatzky the same judgments that apply to other literature: considerations of plot, characterization, language, structure, effective and appropriate use of symbolism, and other literary elements. Just because a work is historically accurate does not mean that it is well written, and the shortcomings of Holocaust literature, like those of other works, should not be ignored, Shatzky argues: We should not teach works that are shallow or written poorly.

Alvin Rosenfeld defines and judges Holocaust literature quite differently than Shatzky. Defining Holocaust literature as the entire scope of texts written about the Holocaust and including testimonies and memoirs, Rosenfeld correctly argues that the basic function of Holocaust literature is to "register and record the enormity of human loss" (27). Listen:

> The only knowledge we are left with, then, [after the Holocaust] is this: in our own day, annihilation overleapt the bounds of metaphor and was enacted on earth. Is it possible to make poetry out of that? [. . .] The answer, clearly, must be yes. Poetry [. . .] survives to remind us of all that has been destroyed. And also to remind us of what has not been destroyed, for while it is true that Holocaust literature is nothing if not language in a condition of severe diminishment and decline, it is still capable of articulating powerful truths—if none other, then those that reflect life in its diminishment and decline. We have lost so much, but not yet the power to register what it is that has been taken from us. (27)

Because Holocaust literature expresses the abject horror of the destruction, for which there are no adequate symbols or representations, it is chiefly nonsymbolic and directly narrative. Rosenfeld argues that Holocaust literature uses received forms and literary texts to refute, repudiate, and deny "not only [. . .] an antecedent literary assertion but also [. . .] its implicit premises and explicit affirmations" (31). Literature of the Holocaust turns commonly held ideas about literature upside down and creates a literary landscape that is a shadow text, a dark evocation of an ur-text. Common logic dictates that we cannot have the same expectations of Holocaust literature that we do of "regular" literature because it comes from a universe where the world as we know it has been destroyed. In the universe of the Holocaust, no rules apply, all bets are off, there is no *why*.

Shatzky and Alvin Rosenfeld agree, however, in objecting to works of literature that sensationalize the Holocaust or exploit it for any reason, particularly for sexual purposes or for voyeuristic entertainment (Shatzky 105; Rosenfeld 162–67). Elie Wiesel calls this "Holocaust kitsch" (characterized by sentimentality, suspense, a bit of sex, and voiceover about the silence of God) ("Art" 38). Shatzky and Rosenfeld both criticize novels like William Styron's *Sophie's Choice,* whose Polish protagonist and survivor of Auschwitz Sophie is presented as a sex object, the desirable "Mutilated Woman" (Rosenfeld 164), thus making the book an example of horror-tinged erotica (in spite of the fact that nearly all Holocaust diaries and memoirs are uniformly, decidedly, and particularly sexless).

Shatzky's third criterion, intellectual integrity, refers to the "ways in which the artistic elements of a work conflict with the moral demand upon them" (qtd. from Ostvath and Satz 201), and here Shatzky approaches the heart of how we should think about Holocaust texts. He means that works that trivialize, demean, or diminish the Holocaust or calmly incorporate it into an aesthetic framework should be rejected. Also relevant to a work's integrity is whether the issues of the Holocaust are central to the work or merely tangential, symbolic, used to represent some other human malevolence or malignity. If the Holocaust is not the center of the literature, then the integrity of the Holocaust is "compromised" in that work (107), Shatzky maintains; he abjures the "borrowing" of the Holocaust as a symbol for something else. Particularly unsettling is the attempt to appropriate the Holocaust for a moral lesson, the effort to see some good coming out of it.

Avoid Placing the Holocaust on a Continuum with Problems of Intolerance and Prejudice

Don't make the Holocaust relative or representative or symbolic of something else. Many well-intentioned educators, particularly those for whom the Holocaust is relatively new territory and especially those who know little about Jews and Jewishness, feel compelled to analogize the Holocaust, to compare it to history's atrocities, and to create relationships among them. Sometimes these kindly educators say they teach the Holocaust to help ensure that it never happens again. They frequently want to show how the Holocaust was the result of a long history of intolerance and prejudice. This approach is simply wrong; it relativizes the Holocaust, pretending that it is on a prejudice-intolerance continuum, that what happened to six million Jews is just prejudice run amok. But prejudice is not the same as the systematic killing of the Holocaust. We must study the Holocaust in the context of nothing else but the Holocaust. We may address the long history of Christian anti-Semitism as a corollary, perhaps, but there is no other comparable experience against which the Holocaust can be framed. To do so suggests an inadequate knowledge of the Holocaust or disrespect for its survivors. To teach young children about prejudice and tolerance is an admirable thing, but we should not confuse this aim with Holocaust study.

Especially problematic is literature depicting Holocaust terror as metonymy, symbolic of someone's personal pain, a metaphor for something else, which diminishes its impact and significance. This kind of literature distances readers quite far from the suffering of survivors by appropriating aspects of the Holocaust experience. Here is Rosenfeld on the subject:

> There are no metaphors for Auschwitz, just as Auschwitz is not a metaphor for anything else. Why is that the case? Because the flames were real flames, the ashes only ashes, the smoke always and only smoke. If one wants "meaning" out of that, it can only be this: at Auschwitz humanity incinerated its own heart. Otherwise the burnings do not lend themselves to metaphor, simile, or symbol—to likeness or association with anything else. They can only "be" or "mean" what they in fact were: the death of the Jews. (27)

To compare the Holocaust to anything else desecrates the memory of all those it consumed. This is why Rosenfeld and others have deplored, for instance, some of Sylvia Plath's poetry for its occasional use of Nazis to symbolize overweening authority and power gone awry and for its conflation of death and sexual desire. Rosenfeld describes poems like Plath's "Daddy" as "suicide portrayed as a big striptease" (106).

Lawrence Langer is especially unflinching in his dismissal of those who try to make the Holocaust into an exemplar of suffering or write about "moral life in the camps" or about "the light of human community emerging from Holocaust darkness" (*Atlantic Monthly* 115):

> I feel no impulse—not the slightest—to reclaim meaning from Holocaust atrocity or to embrace a Lincolnesque rhetoric seeking to persuade us that "the horrible experience of the camps will not have been in vain." There is nothing to be learned from a baby torn in two or a woman buried alive. [. . .] If Jewish experience in the Holocaust can be made to "stand for" something else, some "larger human experience" [. . .] then the intolerable may seem more tolerable through the sheer invocation of patterns or analogies. Whatever the intention, the result is to dilute or diffuse the particularity of mass murder. (112–13)

There is simply no way to soften, mitigate, or understand the Holocaust. It is dishonest to pretend otherwise.

In a similar distortion of the Holocaust, some readers have appropriated it, perhaps inadvertently, to represent Jewishness in the twentieth century, thus reducing the whole of a more than five-thousand-year-old religion and a vibrant culture to the sum of six million victims. That is, all of what many readers know of Jewish culture, Judaism, and Jews is that they were the primary victims of the Holocaust and that six million of them perished at the hands of the Nazis. Sandra Stotsky has made this point with poignancy. She surveyed the contents of six leading literature anthologies for grades 6–12 and six leading elementary reading series and was "appalled" to discover that the Holocaust has come to stand for the Jewish experience in the literature because that is, for the most part, all of Jewish culture that is represented there (58). This, too, is an injustice to the survivors, whose diaries and testimonies inevitably hark back to the richness of life before the Holocaust and, like Lichtenstein's proud recounting of his daughter's linguistic ability, celebrate life.

Know Your Students and Consider Their Ages as You Select Teaching Material

Today the Holocaust is being taught to younger and younger students. Or at least the makers and teachers of Holocaust curricula claim that they are designing Holocaust studies to children as early as kindergarten. The New Jersey Commission on Holocaust Education, mandated by the state to develop a Holocaust curriculum, published and distributed the curriculum guide *Caring Makes a Difference, K–8*, which has been called a Holocaust curriculum and which has been distributed to all New Jersey school districts, along with funds for teacher training on the subject (Sepinwall P6). Harriet Sepinwall notes that "books recommended for use with K–4 generally do not provide graphic details of the horrors of the Holocaust" but instead include stories relating to strained or lost friendships, hidden children and their rescuers, even life inside concentration camps, separated families, or life as a survivor

(P7). The Holocaust Human Rights Center of Maine has also developed a curriculum guide for grades kindergarten through four, which teachers can use to develop a Holocaust curriculum (Sepinwall P6). Yet how can we honestly teach kindergartners—and even 10-year-olds—about the Holocaust? Putting aside the psychological questions about teaching the Holocaust, can we assume that even a 10-year-old has the *cognitive* ability to understand such concepts as state-directed, institutionalized murder? Do we honestly believe that young children can understand and respect the survivor's dilemma? Is it wise to expose 10-year-olds to the brutal, dispiriting, arbitrary nature of *l'univers concentrationnaire*?

I worry about the Holocaust's being taught to elementary children, even when the teachers are obviously well intentioned and capable. Vickie Zack has written about her teaching of *The Devil's Arithmetic,* which she presented to her fifth-grade students in Montreal as a featured text from the class library. She had not intended to deal in depth with the Holocaust, she notes, but three children in class chose to read *The Devil's Arithmetic,* which Zack did not assign. Her students chose it voluntarily. In fact, quite a few of Zack's students straightforwardly did *not* choose to read it, declining because of the subject matter; others read a bit of it and decided it was too much for them. The three who completed the book read it because, as Zack reports, they "wanted to know"; the book had a profound effect on them, both "compelling and repelling" (43). She describes their last reading conference session for *The Devil's Arithmetic,* where she discussed the selection process and the "extermination procedure":

> The children's faces looked strained, and one child's head was face-down on the carpet while listening, not able to meet my eyes as I told them of the selection, of families being separated, of some going directly to their death, usually children and the elderly. They responded: "It was not that way in this book." I did not go beyond the details of this book *in any other way* [emphasis added]. There were enough hard lessons for the time being. (46)

Clearly, Zack knew her students and capably guided them through this introduction to the Holocaust, and the students were not alone in their reading. Clearly all three were motivated to read this book: one, a Jewish child, had relatives who perished in the Holocaust; another told Zack that children "should know" about the Holocaust and said that she did want to know, despite the fact that adults might be afraid such reading would "scare" children; a third simply thought it was "a good book" (43). Yet this entire teaching/learning scenario is fraught with dangers, particularly because of the students' ages.

In 1990, the late Lucy Dawidowicz, historian whose seminal study of the Holocaust, *The War Against the Jews 1933–1945,* is an important work in the study of the Holocaust, published an essay in *Commentary* about the teaching of the Holocaust. There Dawidowicz approvingly refers to 15 as the age when Holocaust education typically begins. High school students are more intellectually prepared than younger students to handle Holocaust knowledge; they are also often preoccupied by ideas of fairness and justice. During secondary school, students also have the benefit of more sophisticated experience in history, language, and literature that can be brought to bear on the topic. In many respects, this is the best time, perhaps, to introduce the Holocaust because students are able to read and understand intellectually (at least) the history and the eyewitness accounts. The Holocaust should definitely be studied by this time, lest some students drop out of school and know nothing of it at all.

Recently, a colleague confided that she did not force any of her university students (minimum age: 18) to read the Holocaust literature or watch the Holocaust films that were part of her syllabus because she was afraid of their vulnerability. Although I am sympathetic with professors' desires to protect their students' emotional health, I disagree with her (except in rare and plain cases of psychological distress). University students should know about the Holocaust. We should not avoid the Holocaust with them, and we should not water down their curriculum by throwing a couple of novels at them without any historical background. If students leave university (or exit high school) without a clear understanding of the Holocaust, we risk creating an "educated" populace ignorant of the Holocaust or harboring grave misconceptions about it.

We should not, however, assign Holocaust literature without preparing our students. Preparing students to read about the Holocaust requires deliberate effort from the teacher. Jeffrey Berman, professor of English at the State University of New York at Albany, points out that "young people who come to our classrooms today are more at risk for depression and even suicide than they once were" ("Syllabuses of Risk" B9) and that difficult texts such as those encountered in a class studying Holocaust literature can contribute to anxiety and depression in students, female students particularly. Berman, whose book *Surviving Literary Suicide* chronicles his extensive experience with literature and trauma, argues that we should give more thought to how we frame "emotionally charged texts"; he does not argue that we should not teach such texts. Berman prepares his students for such reading by first "alert[ing] them to the possibility that some of them might respond to a classroom reading or writing assignment in a way similar to how some people react to a flu vaccination: namely, by developing symptoms of the illness against which they have been inoculated" ("Syllabuses of Risk" B9). Students need to know that they may be at risk from the reading, and to warn them of this directly and honestly is Berman's first order of business. He also suggests that instructors teaching emotionally charged texts should watch for symptoms of distress from students, who may be so indirect as to say they are simply "having problems" with a writing or reading assignment. Berman recommends confronting such revealing hints directly and immediately and believes that we should make ourselves available to students who are disturbed by a reading or writing assignment. We teachers should also be prepared to make appropriate referrals to counseling services.

Realize the Enormity of the Holocaust and Its Impact Throughout Our Time

What the Holocaust destroyed was not only the Jewish community of Europe but also contemporary humanity's psychological grounding in a just world. Terrence Des Pres writes that we live "in the unrest of aftermath and we inherit the feeling that something has been taken that cannot be restored. I am not speaking of the victims, whose lives and world are indeed gone, but merely of ourselves and the impact of the Holocaust upon the way we think and feel. We are infected by a sense of terminal defilement" (106). He argues that our age has never been able to assimilate the implications of what the Holocaust wrought; we cannot recover innocence after Auschwitz. What has made the difference in us and in our collective thinking is simply the fact that the Holocaust occurred. Des Pres believes that to turn what we know of the Holocaust into knowledge, we must confront its events again and again; this means we must hear the survivors again and again. Until this process of confronting is complete, our "spiritual condition will be characterized by deep unrest" (109). He describes our responses to the Holocaust as progressing through three approximate stages: the first two of these, denial and obsession, indicate that the spirit feels compelled to work through events not only for which it feels responsible but also events by which it feels polluted and maimed. Denial is the spirit's refusal to confront the events that trouble it. Obsession is "despair, nihilism, madness": the spirit is "stuck" (110). In the third stage, which Des Pres believes is emerging in our time, appears a new kind of conscience, constructed through memory in action, through knowledge of the Holocaust, through witness, through "allowing the demise of innocence to be the birth of vigilance" (110). Thus, we return, always, to the importance of the survivors' witnessing.

This witnessing is a complicated endeavor. Michael Bernard-Donals and Richard Glejzer uniquely differentiate *witnessing* from *testimony;* witnessing is seeing an event, and testimony is a movement from witnessing into discourse, a passage that "tears the fabric of the language of testimony and manifests itself in stutters, silences, and nearly uncontrollable fits of violent speech" (xv). They present a compelling case for a special witnessing, a "redemptive" witnessing, one that is, however, not redemptive in the commonplace way. According to most traditions of Judaism, redemption creates a product resulting from a human-to-Other transaction—that is, the negotiation between the person and the world or the person and the community ultimately "generates" something that exists beyond the human and beyond the worldly, something that advances the person or the community in its search for perfection of the world. Bernard-Donals and Glejzer note that "what is produced—in prayer, in the encounter between human and divine in the work of the world—exceeds the work itself and also exceeds our human capacity to describe it" (5). Thus, representations of the Holocaust in fiction, in narratives, on video, can be redemptive in this particular sense because they produce a "sublime excess" that "troubles testimony and narrative and forces the reader to confront the horror of the limit rather than (in conventional terms) the presence of the object or the event itself" (5). As Bernard-Donals and Glejzer consider the implications for a pedagogy of the Holocaust, they return to their distinction between witness and testimony; a witness is in a position of "non-knowledge, of not knowing or understanding, only seeing." The person testifying or offering testimony is in a position of "bearing the burden of not knowing by attempting to know" (173). This understanding leads them to the idea that what we need to teach about the Holocaust is *that what we are supposed to know we do not know.* The most important things about the teaching are not the readings, exams, quizzes, or lectures. Rather the lessons remain in the "gulf that surrounds" the material, that which the specific details naturally silence. These are difficult concepts, but they point us to the extreme complicatedness of undertaking this teaching.

Thus, in our teaching of the Holocaust, we rely on witness and testimony to somehow illustrate and open up a vast emptiness. This testimony, whether presented through memoir, diary, poem, or in some instances transcribed faithfully into novelistic form, is fluid, continuing, enduring; it defies any would-be commodification of the Holocaust. Testimony rejects closure; it will not allow us to feel satisfied or smug or content that we understand or know. Holocaust testimony and witness absolve us of the impulse to compartmentalize the Holocaust, to wrap it up and seal it off forever; we do not have to, nor can we ever, make sense of its dis-ease. The poets of witness regard memory as the biblical watchword from Deuteronomy: *Zakhor*—Remember! This is not a call to historiography; it is the excavation of the ruin of an event. Paul Celan's poem "There Was Earth Inside Them, and they dug" uses the metaphor of excavation with the extended repetition of the verb *dig*. All the poem's characters are digging a grave so massive that it never seems completed; all they have time to do, it seems, is to dig. The poet explains in a series of negative phrases what the characters did not or could not do, for having to dig constantly: grow wise, praise God, invent a song, think up language. The people were consumed by an idea of death so commodious that it adhered to everything they did and thought. The poem begins in past tense then shifts to present tense in the third stanza to suggest that the digging—the horror—never ends, that there can never be an understanding or a conclusion to or a reason for the deaths from the Holocaust. The only purpose for digging is to put away the dead, and the only reason for excavating the ruin of this event and for speaking this poem is to engage, to record, indeed to witness, this putting away that never ends.

The witnesses make possible an open and infinite discussion. Carolyn Forché, in her monumental anthology *Against Forgetting: Twentieth-Century Poetry of Witness,* writes that the poem (and by extension all survivors' reports) exists as testimony, as artifact, trace of the original disaster, evidence (31–35). Her statement of ethics articulates what it means to read Holocaust literature in this way: "Ethical reading of such works does not inhere in assessing their truth value or efficacy as *representation* but rather in recognizing their evidentiary nature: here language is a life-form, marked by human experience, and is also itself material evidence of that-which-occurred" (1).

This, then, is how we can think about and, therefore, teach the Holocaust.

Works Cited

Baum, Rachel. "'What I Have Learned to Feel': The Pedagogical Emotions of Holocaust Education." *College Literature* 23.3 Oct. 1996: 44–57.

Berman, Jeffrey. "Syllabuses of Risk." *The Chronicle of Higher Education* 15 Feb. 2001: B7–B9.

Bernard-Donals, Michael, and Richard Glejzer. *Between Witness and Testimony: The Holocaust and the Limits of Representation.* Albany: State University of New York Press, 2001.

Dawidowicz, Lucy S. *A Holocaust Reader.* New York: Behrman House, 1976.

———. "How They Teach the Holocaust." *Commentary* Dec. 1990: 25–32.

———. *The War Against the Jews, 1933–1945.* New York: Holt, Rinehart, Winston, 1975.

Des Pres, Terrence. *The Survivor: An Anatomy of Life in the Death Camps.* New York: Oxford University Press, 1976.

Dortmund, Erhard K. "Teaching Students to Confront the Holocaust's Brutal Intrusion into Modern Life." *The Chronicle of Higher Education* 28 June 1989: B2.

Farnham, James F. "What Is the Value of Teaching the Holocaust?" *The Journal of General Education* 41 (1992): 18–22.

Forché, Carolyn, Ed. *Against Forgetting: Twentieth-Century Poetry of Witness.* New York: W. W. Norton, 1993.

———. "The Question of Language and Ethics." Unpublished essay. 2000.

Johnson, Rebecca Kelch. "Teaching the Holocaust." *English Journal* 69.7 Oct. 1980: 69–70.

Langer, Lawrence. "Pre-empting the Holocaust." *The Atlantic Monthly* Nov. 1998: 105–15.

Ostvath, Zsuzanna and Martha Satz. "The Audacity of Expressing the Inexpressible: The Relation Between Moral and Aesthetic Considerations in Holocaust Literature." *Judaism* 34 Spring 1985: 197–210.

Ozick, Cynthia. "The Rights of History and the Rights of Imagination." *Commentary* 107.3 Mar. 1999; www.findarticles.com/cf_0/m1061/3_107/54098045/p1/article.jhtml?term=cynthia+ozick.

Rosenfeld, Alvin H. *A Double Dying: Reflections on Holocaust Literature.* Bloomington, IN: Indiana University Press, 1980.

Sepinwall, Harriet Lipman. "Incorporating Holocaust Education into K–4 Curriculum and Teaching in the United States." *Social Studies and the Young Learner* 11.3 Jan.–Feb. 1999: P5–8.

Shatzky, Joel. "Creating an Aesthetic for Holocaust Literature." *Studies in American Jewish Literature* 10.1 Spring 1991: 104–14.

Stotsky, Sandra. "Is the Holocaust the Chief Contribution of the Jewish People to World Civilization and History?: A Survey of Leading Literature Anthologies and Reading Instructional Textbooks." *English Journal* 85.2 Feb. 1996: 52–59.

Tager, Michael. "Primo Levi and the Language of Witness." *Criticism* 35.2 (1993): 265–88.

Weisel, Elie. "Art and the Holocaust." *New York Times* 11 June 1989: 2: 1, 38.

———. *A Jew Today.* New York: Random House, 1978.

Zack, Vicki. " 'It Was the Worst of Times': Learning about the Holocaust through Literature." *Language Arts* 68.1 Jan. 1991: 42–70.

Works Consulted

Abrams, Rebecca. "Showing the Shoah." *New Statesman* 17 July 2000.

Bosmajian, Hamida. "Doris Orgel's *The Devil in Vienna:* From Trope into History." *Children's Literature* 28 (2000): 112–31.

Braham, Randolph L., ed. *Reflections of the Holocaust in Art and Literature.* New York: Columbia University Press, 1990.

———, ed. *The Treatment of the Holocaust in Textbooks: The Federal Republic of Germany, Israel, the United States of America.* New York: Columbia University Press, 1987.

A Cybrary of the Holocaust. Project ABE. Joseph Korn. 9 June 2001 http://remember.org/index.html.

Davies, Ian, ed. *Teaching the Holocaust: Educational Dimensions, Principles and Practice.* New York: Continuum, 2000.

Des Pres, Terrence. *Writing Into the World: Essays 1973–1987.* New York: Viking, 1991.

Fridman, Lea Wernick. *Words and Witness: Narrative and Aesthetic Strategies in the Representation of the Holocaust.* Albany, NY: SUNY Press, 2000.

Garber, Zev, Alan L. Berger, and Richard Libowitz, ed. *Methodology in the Academic Teaching of the Holocaust.* Lanham, NY: University Press of America, 1988.

Goertz, Karein. "Transgenerational Representations of the Holocaust: From Memory to 'Post-Memory.' " *World Literature Today* 72.1 Winter 1998: 33–38.

Gorrell, Nancy. "Teaching Empathy through Ecphrastic poetry: Entering a Curriculum of Peace." *English Journal* 89.5 May 2000: 32–41.

———. "Teaching the Holocaust: Light from the Yellow Star Leads the Way." *English Journal* 86.8 Dec. 1997: 50–55.

Hirschfield, Claire. "Teaching the Holocaust: A Conceptual Model." *Improving College and University Teaching* 29 Winter 1981: 24–27.

Holocaust and Jewish Studies Sites. Virginia Wesleyan College, Norfolk, VA. Dr. Dan Graf. 7 June 2001. 10 June 2001. www.vwc.edu/library_resources/wwwpages/dgraf/holocaus.htm.

Holocaust/Shoah—Educational Projects and Resources. Ed. David Dickerson. 10 Dec. 1999. 10 June 2001. www.igc.org/ddickerson/education.html.

How to Teach Holocaust (*sic*). Ed. Arnošt Lustig, Marta Vančurová. 29 May 1998. The Jewish Museum in Prague. 10 June 2001. www.jewishmuseum.cz/english/aholocaust.htm.

Kelly, David. "Using Literature to Teach History: an ERIC/ChESS Sample." *OAH Magazine of History* Winter 1999: 53–55.

Kessler, Kate. "Teaching Holocaust Literature." *English Journal* 80.7 Nov. 1991: 29–32.

Kettel, Raymond P. "Reflections on *The Devil's Arithmetic* by a Holocaust Survivor: An Interview with Jack Wayne—B8568." *The New Advocate* 9.4 Fall 1996: 287–95.

LaCapra, Dominick. *History and Memory after Auschwitz.* Ithaca, NY: Cornell University Press, 1998.

Lang, Berel, ed. *Writing and the Holocaust.* New York: Holmes and Meier, 1988.

Langer, Lawrence L. *The Age of Atrocity: Death in Modern Literature.* Boston: Beacon, 1978.

———. *Preempting the Holocaust.* New Haven, CT: Yale University Press, 1998.

Leak, Andrew and George Paizis, ed. *The Holocaust and the Text: Speaking the Unspeakable.* New York: Macmillan, 1999.

Lipstadt, Deborah. *Denying the Holocaust: The Growing Assault on Truth and Memory.* New York: Free Press, 1993.

Morse, Jonathan. "Words Devoted to the Unspeakable." *American Literary History* 5.4 Winter 1993: 715–34.

Museum of Tolerance Online. The Simon Wiesenthal Center. 1997. 8 June 2001 http://motlc.wiesenthal.com/resources.

Penkower, Monty Noam. "Shaping Holocaust Memory." *American Jewish History* 88.1 March 2000: 127–32.

Ponomareff, Constantin V. "The Aestheticization of the Holocaust." In *In the Shadow of the Holocaust and Other Essays.* Constantin V. Ponomareff, ed. Atlanta, GA: Rodopi, 1998. 23–32.

Rosenfeld, Alvin, ed. *Thinking about the Holocaust After Half a Century.* Bloomington, IN: Indiana University Press, 1997.

Rothberg, Michael. *Traumatic Realism: The Demands of Holocaust Representation.* Minneapolis: University of Minnesota Press, 2000.

Schwarz, Daniel R. *Imagining the Holocaust.* New York: St. Martin's, 1999.

Sherwin, Byron L. and Susan G. Ament, ed. *Encountering the Holocaust: An Interdisciplinary Survey.* Chicago: Impact Press, 1979.

Steiner, George. *Language and Silence: Essays on Language, Literature, and the Inhuman.* New York: Atheneum, 1967.

A Teacher's Guide to the Holocaust—Literature. Florida Center for Instructional Technology, College of Education, University of South Florida. 2000. 9 June 2001. http://fcit.coedu.usf.edu/holocaust/arts/lit.htm.

Tritt, Michael. "Methods and Strategies: Teaching Holocaust Literature." *English Quarterly* 17.3 Fall 1985: 26–33.

United States Holocaust Memorial Museum. United States Holocaust Memorial Council. 11 June 2001. www.ushmm.org.

The Yad Vashem International School for Holocaust Studies—Educational Guidelines. Yad Vashem The Holocaust Martyrs' and Heroes' Remembrance 2001. 9 June 2001. www.yad-vashem.org.il/education/home_education.html.

Zack, Vicki. "Nightmare Issues: Children's Responses to Racism and Genocide in Literature." *The New Advocate* 9.4 Fall 1996: 297–308.

Zehavi, Alex. "Reaching Out: Israeli Holocaust Literature for Children and Youth." *Modern Hebrew Literature* 8 Spring 1992: 40–42.

23

The Mill Girls in Fiction

Exploited Children or Independent Young Women?

Joan I. Glazer

Child labor, such as the use of young girls in the mills of New England in the mid-1800s, has been an issue worldwide and over time. The Roman consul Cato the Elder, after his retirement, bought many people the Romans had captured in war, but especially children whom he could purchase cheaply, train, and then sell at a considerable profit. In the early years of the American colonies, homeless children were shipped to the United States from Britain to be used by the planters as laborers (Meltzer 7–8). Today particular attention is being paid to the sweatshops of India, Afghanistan, and Pakistan where children as young as age 5 work long hours, producing clothing, carpets, and sports equipment. This is not to say, however, that child labor is not a problem within developed countries as well (McKechnie and Hobbs 89–100).

In all of the instances, there have been differences of opinion about the efficacy and the morality of using children as laborers. Many rationales are offered in support of children as workers: They have small fingers and can tie threads quickly; they are the right height to pick crops; they learn quickly. They are the most inexpensive workers available. Poor children are better off working in a factory than they would be roaming the streets looking for food. This is one way children can contribute to the well-being of their families. If these children were not working in factories, they would have to do some other, even worse, kind of work to get enough money for them and their families to eat. So go the arguments for keeping young children in the workforce, whether paid or not.

On the other side are those who look at the long hours and inhumane treatment of many of the children working in factories or on farms. They are not educated. Their health suffers. They are separated from their families. They have no freedoms. They become ill and suffer permanent disabilities as a result of the working conditions. They are taken advantage of because they have no political influence. The United Nations' International Labor Organization in Geneva, Switzerland, has estimated that there are at least 73 million child laborers in the 10 to 14 age bracket and up to 200 million working children of all ages (Clark 11). These workers have been described as the "invisible" children, the small hands behind many of the carpets, athletic shoes, soccer balls, toys, and chocolate candies that find their way into developed nations.

We might expect that such children would be written about and serve as protagonists in fiction for children, but this is rarely the case. Although there is a body of work for children and adolescents that focuses on children in the Holocaust, there are few books that focus on children working in factories or as slaves in households, farms, or factories. The serious books addressing the issue in contemporary times are nonfiction. Milton Meltzer, in *Cheap Raw Material,* presents a history of children in sweatshops up through the 1990s. In his introduction, he says that in attempting to understand and explain why American children can be exploited in this way, he used statistics:

> [. . .] used numbers—hundreds, thousands, millions—to give some statistical measure of the seriousness of what this book deals with. But such figures rarely touch the heart. If readers could only *see* each young worker, if they could *know* that boy or this girl, then they would be able to grasp the meaning of the large numbers. This is why, wherever possible in telling this story, I have let young people who work tell their story in their own words. (2–3)

Susan Kuklin, in her nonfiction book *Iqbal Masih and the Crusaders Against Child Slavery,* uses photographs as well as direct quotations to tell the story of Iqbal Masih, a child in Pakistan who was given away by his family when he was 4 years old to a factory owner in order to obtain a loan. Iqbal became a "debt-bonded laborer," expected to work until the debt, as well as interest and expenses, were paid. When he was 10 years old, he attended a freedom day rally and learned that there were laws in Pakistan to protect child laborers and that all debts such as his family's had been canceled. After getting his freedom for himself, Iqbal began a campaign to free all such child workers and became known internationally before a laborer on his uncle's land killed him when he was 14.

Both of these books, as well as others such as *Kids on Strike!* by Bartoletti and *Good Girl Work: Factories, Sweatshops, and How Women Changed Their Role in the American Workforce* by Gourley, use specific examples within the larger context of social conditions, laws, and economic forces taking place as children became part of the workforce. Teachers exploring the topic in classrooms frequently use these books. They note also that the United Nations Convention on the Rights of the Child ratified a document in 1989 that included the provision Article 32, 1:

> Parties recognize the right of the child to be protected from economic exploitation and from performing any work that is likely to be hazardous or to interfere with the child's education, or to be harmful to the child's health or physical, mental, spiritual, moral or social development. (Convention 11)

Videos and Web pages that identify good nonfiction sources can also be good sources, but they are not always aesthetic experiences for youngsters. For instance, when Bill Bigelow, in his article describing a full social studies unit on global sweatshops, suggests two pages worth of articles, videos, organizations, and Web pages, he does not list a single book of fiction (116–17). The children who are "invisible" as workers are also nearly invisible as protagonists in fiction for children and adolescents in classroom instruction.

The exception to this is the use of young girls in the mills, particularly those in New England, in the 1800s. Fiction writers have researched the practice of using young female workers in the mills, read about activists such as Lucy Larcom, Harriet Hanson Robinson, and Sarah Bagley (Selden), and incorporated this background into fiction books that contain strong protagonists, bringing the issue of child labor alive through characters who can be known by the reader as individuals, with the possibility of, in Meltzer's words, "touching the heart."

Katherine Paterson's *Lyddie* presents the reader with a character who is typical of the mill workers in many ways. Lyddie Worthen is a farm girl from Vermont who moves to Lowell, Massachusetts, in 1845 for the express purpose of getting a job in a mill. She is proud to be earning her own money, interested in becoming literate, distressed by the level of noise in the weaving room where she works, ill at times from the heat and lint and lack of fresh air in the factory, tired from the thirteen-hour workdays, and accepting of the rules of the mill and of the boarding house where she lives.

Paterson presents Lyddie as a three-dimensional personality with her own special needs and traits. The story opens on the farm in Vermont where Lyddie, her mother, her brother, and her two young sisters live. We immediately see Lyddie as quick thinking and brave. It is she who herds the family into the loft when a bear wanders into their cabin after the door has been left ajar and she who comforts their frightened mother. It is Lyddie who tries to keep herself and her brother Charlie together when their mother takes the two younger children and moves to her sister's and brother-in-law's home. Lyddie survives her work at the Cutler Tavern, where she has been sent because her mother is using her labor to pay off the family debts, and it is Lyddie who, when dismissed by the mistress, says, "I'm free. She's set me free. I can do anything I want. I can go to Lowell and make real money to pay off the debt so I can go home" (45).

Once at the mill, Lyddie learns quickly, eventually watching four looms at once and clearing $2.50 a week above the $1.75 subtracted for room and board. She debates whether to sign the petition for a ten-hour workday, eventually deciding to do so more because of her friendship with a girl who favors it than for her own beliefs. The lessening of work hours will result in a reduction in pay, and Lyddie's focus is on earning enough money to pay off the family debts. She cares for her younger sister when their mother is committed to an asylum, yet lets that sister go to live with Charlie when it is in the younger girl's best interests. The echo of "I'm free" resounds later when Lyddie reacts to the words of the overseer, "You're my prize girl" with her own thoughts, "I'm not your girl. I'm not anybody's girl but my own" (109).

Paterson once described her decision to write about the mills in Lowell:

At a workshop I had heard some letters read aloud that were written by Vermont farm girls who had gone to the factories in Lowell and in Manchester, New Hampshire, to work. Those letters sent a thrill up my spine. "Why hasn't anyone written a novel about these wonderful women?" I asked myself. I found out later—fortunately much later—that several people had or I wouldn't have had the nerve to try myself. (qtd. in *Book Links* 52)

The contents of the letters from many of these workers and the courage shown by the young leaders in the battle for better working conditions give a picture of many of the these early child and adolescent factory workers as independent young women, striving to improve themselves. Often they were sending money home to help their families. Many engaged in educational activities, attending the lectures that were given specifically for women mill workers, or were even, as in *Lyddie,* hiring their own teachers to come to the boarding houses once or twice a week. These young women were not victims.

Yet, there is another side to the factory work, and it is also portrayed in *Lyddie.* Work began at five in the morning, with a half hour break at seven for breakfast and another break for lunch, and ended thirteen or fourteen hours later in the summer, somewhat earlier in the winter when there was less light. The work was dangerous for those who could not maintain their concentration. Many became ill and died from breathing the lint-filled air. The overseers were given bonuses if "their" girls produced increased amounts of fabric, and thus there was constant pressure to watch more looms. Newspapers of the day sometimes described these workers as slaves. Lyddie rejects this: "She *wasn't* a slave. She was a free woman of the state of Vermont, earning her own way in the world. Whatever Diana, or even Betsy, might think, she, Lyddie, was far less a slave than most any girl she knew of" (94). Lyddie could make decisions for herself, unlike the American slave. She might be working long hours in difficult conditions, but she had chosen this employment and could leave whenever she chose.

The mill workers in Lowell in the 1830s and 1840s had a better life than do the child laborers in the factories of third world countries today; yet many of the issues are the same. The mill workers were cheap labor, and using them was justified by saying that this allowed young women and children who might otherwise be idle to be usefully employed. Today's child workers are also cheap labor, and their work is justified by saying that this allows them to earn some money for their financially strapped families. In both cases, the corporate world with ideals of profit has overpowered individual rights, and in both cases, the customers for the products were or are unaware of or unconcerned about how or who is involved in producing the goods they purchase.

Writers of fiction portray their protagonists as having the inner strength to cope with the challenges and inequities that life may bring and the background and skills necessary to succeed. Lyddie is a farm girl, used to working all day and proud of her physical strength. She is accustomed to long hours of hard work. The switch from farm worker to factory worker is doable for her.

Amanda Videau, the protagonist in Ann Rinaldi's *The Blue Door*, another mill story set in the same time period, has lived all her life on the family plantation on St. Helena's Island in South Carolina where they raise cotton for northern mills. Her mother owns four plantations and two-hundred and fifty slaves. When her grandmother decides to make peace with her own father—Amanda's grandfather—who is a mill owner in Lowell, she decides to do so by sending Amanda north to the mill. Through a series of mishaps and adventures, Amanda ends up taking the identity of another girl and arrives in Lowell to be a mill girl rather than granddaughter of the owner.

Her background makes her reactions very different from those of Lyddie. For her the breakfast at the boardinghouse is "mush," the weather is "ungodly cold," and as she leaves for lunch on her first day at the mill, she feels "like a drum fish, running in our creek during spring migration, being pushed along by the other drum fish who were all swimming the same way. Because if they didn't, they might lose their lives" (141). Yet she also has the inner resources to cope with this change in status. She learns about the life of the mill girls and sees the differing outlooks, particularly about working conditions, with some of the mill girls publishing in the *Operatives Magazine* and others in the *Lowell Offering.* She divides the girls into two groups, those "who worked because they had to earn a living and those who came to Lowell because they wanted independence. Or to get out of their far-flung New England villages, to a place where there were libraries, lectures, and social and literary clubs" (163). Eventually she becomes an activist for better working conditions.

When Amanda compares mill work to slavery in a letter, she argues that her family treated their slaves in South Carolina better than the mill owners treat their workers. She never accepts the working hours, though she does see how one can advance one's standing. In the end, Amanda returns home, knowing much more about her family. The story is part of a trilogy that gives the history of several generations in one family, and relates the events and characters of *The Blue Door* within a larger structure.

Both Lyddie and Amanda work in the mills after the first unsuccessful strikes, or turnouts, and just before the second push for a ten-hour workday. The idea of a strike is not new, but both discover a worker still risks dismissal if she participates in any activities that are critical of the mills and their owners. The workers are mostly young girls and women who are seeking independence or need the money for their families, but many are willing to take the risk to improve their working conditions.

A change in the background of the workers was beginning in the time period of these two novels, with more and more immigrants arriving. By the 1850s, the mill workers were no longer primarily American-born but were mostly immigrants, especially immigrants from Ireland whose families began fleeing the famine that had overtaken their country. The American workers complained that the immigrants were less educated and willing to work for lower wages (Gourley 30). The jobs the girls from Vermont and Massachusetts left were quickly filled by the new arrivals.

This change in the workforce shows in *So Far from Home: The Diary of Mary Driscoll, an Irish Mill Girl* by Barry Denenberg, also set in Lowell, this time in 1847. The protagonist is a young girl from County Cork, Ireland. Therefore, the story opens in Skibbereen with the famine in full force where Mary is dreaming of going to America and sending money home to her parents. Her sister Kate is there already, working as a maid for the wife of a mill owner. When her Aunt Nora, also in America, sends her a ticket and tells her about the work available, Mary thinks, "I would like to work in the mills. 'Tisn't for me to be someone's servant, like Kate. A day's pay for a day's work, that's what I say" (11). As in *Lyddie,* the protagonist sees herself as independent, as taking this job because it will let her be her own person.

Told in diary format, the narrative goes from Mary's life in Ireland, where English landlords are evicting the Irish renters daily, through Mary's month-and-a-half crossing of the Atlantic, her arrival in Boston, and finally her work in the mill at Lowell. Early on, the reader learns that the mill owners are eager to replace the "complaining" Yankee girls with Irish girls. Mary discovers that she will be taught her job by another girl, the hours are long and the room is noisy, and she is to abide by the strict rules of the mill. Like Lyddie—unlike Amanda—she is impressed with the amount and the quality of food provided when she visits one of the boardinghouses. She lives in the Acre, a very poor area inhabited by Irish immigrants. When she begins work in June, Mary knows it is difficult. By October, her diary reads:

> I am worn. Standing all day has caused my feet to ache terribly. Nothing relieves the pain. Weariness has crept into my bones. My eyes feel as if they will burst from my head thanks to the endless noise. The lint flies everywhere. Breathing itself is a burden. At night my chest heaves painfully. I wake as tired as when I lay down. (133–34)

Denenberg shows the realities of Irish immigration in his narrative. Mary leaves the mill, not because of her health or the work, but so she can provide bail money for a friend who has been imprisoned in Boston. She leaves with the understanding of her aunt's philosophy that when one gate closes, another opens. Mary might not have been able to send the money to her parents before they died, nor to save the young blind girl she met on shipboard, but she can help her friend Sean.

Even though Lyddie, Amanda, and Mary have very different backgrounds, their stories as told in these historical fiction novels have similar patterns. Each author begins by introducing the main character as she moves to Lowell to work in the mills, and each shows the protagonist to be independent, strong-minded, and eager to learn. All three girls have strong family relationships, and their concern for their families is one of the central factors in the decisions they make. Work in the mill is a route to better times. Lyddie uses the money she has earned to go to Ohio and attend Oberlin College; Amanda returns to her family with a stronger understanding of the ties that hold them together; Mary goes to help her friend.

The setting of the mill as workplace allows the authors to introduce a variety of characters. All of the authors show that the girls in the mill have different purposes and different outlooks. Some favor the strike; others do not. Some learn all they can, spending money on books and time at lectures. Others are more interested in the clothes they can buy. As the protagonists come into a setting already populated with people who know one another, they must make friends and make judgments. They try to fit it. All three are concerned about the way they speak. Lyddie's Vermont accent shows her to be from out of state and to be uneducated; Amanda doesn't speak because her accent will show that she is from the South and is not the person she is pretending to be; Mary's Irish accent shows her to be an immigrant and, thus, poor.

It is not surprising that these personal attributes and concerns should dominate the stories. May, in writing about realism and moral attitudes in children's literature, notes "Fiction authors often want to entertain their readers more than they want to instruct them about life and they become involved in the story they are telling. As they write, the events come alive, the characters take on new shape. [. . .]This means that a story created around a good idea may seem less didactic because a good author will not allow a didactic theme to dominate" (114–15). In fact, it is through characterization rather than with a dominating didactic theme that these authors entice readers into their stories.

Having introduced the protagonists in their home settings, each author then has reason to give a full explication of the conditions in the mills, the new setting in which the characters find themselves. This aspect of living conditions shows clearly the negativity of mill work. All three of these authors have done careful research. Their descriptions are accurate and consistent with one another. The workday is thirteen hours; the factories are noisy and air hot and filled with lint; children are injured regularly, sometimes they have hair or fingers caught in the machinery, sometimes they are hit by a loose shuttle; children get coughs and other respiratory ailments and die; no water buckets are allowed in the work rooms; workers who are late are locked out and docked pay. It is basically the setting that provides the conflict for the protagonists, what Lukens and others would term a conflict of person against society (68). While the characters may be arguing with other workers or worried about family members, the societal norms of that time and place are what allow them to be workers in factories at the age of 13 or 14, forced to accept the conditions.

These historical details help the authors envision the women and young girls as useless economically and, thus, to see work in the mills as one way to rectify their idleness. This historical society allows an overseer to earn more if those under his supervision produce more, providing a logical rationale for extended hours and higher productivity from each worker. The plight of the Irish immigrants, who were willing to accept even less pay and work longer hours than the American laborers, made these workers first easy prey for corporations, and then a target of derision from their coworkers, again, all within societal norms. Yet, each of the characters copes with class discrimination, learns to read better and to write, attends lectures, makes friends, and takes a stand on issues.

The protagonists in these stories are strong females. The books meet the six basic criteria for positive gender role models as presented by Heine and Inkster. Heine and Inkster suggest examining the personal traits of the character, the issues important to the character, how the character solves problems, the character's relationships with others, how the character departs from traditional stereotypes, and whether the character provides a voice for those who are often unheard in children's literature (429). Under each of these topics are questions to guide the analysis, with each focusing on the character's independence of mind, willingness to address significant issues, and ability to take action herself rather than relying on others. These characters particularly provide unique voices for the child factory worker, voices seldom heard in literature for children and adolescents. Yet this is a voice from the past, a voice of competence, a voice from a setting that had more positive elements for the individual than do today's factories that employ children.

Novels that explore child labor in contemporary settings, which will bring the invisible children to the forefront, will be novels whose conflicts again are concerned with personal struggles against society. As Woodhead and Myers have asserted, authors whose characters face the conditions known to occur with child labor have much to give as they explore the effects of work on the child through three-dimensional characters who are as compelling as the fictional Lyddie, as resilient as the actual Iqbal.

It also means that authors not only must thoroughly research the specific setting, noting how child labor fits into a complex political/social reality globally, but also acknowledge that different countries have different concepts of childhood that underlie their attitudes toward child labor. Adding to the complexity are the economic relationships.

Businesses in developed nations may choose to have their manufacturing done in undeveloped nations where child labor laws are not enforced because this reduces the cost of production and, thus, increases their profits. Undeveloped nations may allow this to happen, explaining that this is a better life for the children than they might have otherwise and charging that stopping production in their countries cuts them out of the world economy and undermines the livelihood of their citizens. Just as readers learn in *The Blue Door* that northern textile manufacturers had an interest in maintaining southern slavery because it allowed them to purchase cotton more cheaply, so readers can learn that the desire for profit and the workings of the global economy affect an individual worker in today's world.

Marian Koren argues that since "all human beings are inhabitants of this global world," then "universal rights must be formulated" (243). These rights declare that a human being is educable, capable of dignity, and can "live and act non-destructively" (243). Koren believes these rights extend fully to children. It may be that books showing children not having these rights will help to create an awareness of the conditions under which some children live and the reasons that such conditions exist. If it is important that students think about how issues in historical fiction "resonate in their own lives," as Kelly Chandler has proposed, then it is equally important that they see how contemporary issues resonate and relate to their own lives. Programs devoted to the concepts of social justice work toward having students develop critical perspectives toward their own experiences and then turn toward the society at large with the goal of effecting positive change. Literature has the potential to contribute to the goal of nurturing a more just society: When a good writer shows how individuals react to and change their own circumstances based on a set of values and presents these characters so compellingly, the issues the characters face will indeed resonate in the lives of the readers. Thus, new novels about children working in factories are important because they allow the "invisible" children to become visible.

Works Cited

Bartoletti, Susan Campbell. *Kids on Strike!* Boston: Houghton Mifflin, 1999.

Bigelow, Bill. "The Human Lives Behind the Labels: The Global Sweatshop, Nike, and the Race to the Bottom." *Phi Delta Kappan* 79:2 (1997): 112–19.

Chandler, Kelly. "Considering the Power of the Past: *Pairing Nightjohn* and *Narrative of the Life of Frederick Douglass.*" *United in Diversity: Using Multicultural Young Adult Literature in the Classroom.* Ed Jean E. Brown & Elaine S. Stephens. Urbana, IL: National Council of Teachers of English, 1998. 103–10.

Clark, Charles S. "Child Labor and Sweatshops: An Overview." *Child Labor and Sweatshops.* Ed. Mary E. Williams. San Diego: Greenhaven Press, 1999. 10–20.

Convention on the Rights of the Child, U. N. Document A/44/49 (1989). www1.umn.edu/humanrts/instree/k2crc.htm.

Denenberg, Barry. *So Far from Home: The Diary of Mary Driscoll, an Irish Mill Girl.* New York: Scholastic, 1997.

Gourley, Catherine. *Good Girl Work: Factories, Sweatshops, and How Woman Changed Their Role in the American Workforce.* Brookfield, CT: Millbrook Press, 1999.

Heine, Pat and Christine Inkster. "Strong Female Characters in Recent Children's Books." *Language Arts.* 76:5 (1999): 427–34.

Koren, Marian. "Human Rights of Children: An Emerging Story." *The Lion and the Unicorn.* 25:2 (2001): 242–59.

Kuklin, Susan. *Iqbal Masih and the Crusaders Against Child Slavery.* New York: Holt, 1998.

Lukens, Rebecca J. *A Critical Handbook of Children's Literature.* New York: HarperCollins, 1995.

May, Jill. *Children's Literature & Critical Theory: Reading and Writing for Understanding.* New York: Oxford, 1995.

McKechnie, Jim and Sandy Hobbs. "Child Labor: The View from the North." *Childhood: A Global Journal of Child Research* 6:01 (1999): 89–100.

Meltzer, Milton. *Cheap Raw Material.* New York: Viking, 1994.

Myers, William E. "Considering Child Labour: Changing Terms, Issues and Actors at the International Level." *Childhood: A Global Journal of Child Research* 6:01 (1999): 13–26.

Paterson, Katherine. *Lyddie.* New York: Dutton, 1991.

———. "*Lyddie.*" *Book Links.* 5:6 (1996): 52–55.

Rinaldi, Ann. *The Blue Door.* New York: Scholastic, 1996.

Selden, Bernice. *The Mill Girls.* New York: Atheneum, 1983.

Wade, Rahima C. "Social Action in the Social Studies: From the Ideal to the Real." *Theory into Practice* 40:1 (2001): 23–28.

White, Ben. "Defining the Intolerable: Child Work, Global Standards and Cultural Relativism." *Childhood: A Global Journal of Child Research* 6:01 (1999): 133–45.

Williams, Mary E. *Child Labor and Sweatshops.* San Diego: Greenhaven Press, 1999.

Woodhead, Martin. "Combatting Child Labour: Listening to What the Children Say." *Childhood: A Global Journal of Child Research.* 6:01 (1999): 27–50.

24

Asian American Literature

Voices and Images of Authenticity

Junko Yokota and Ann Bates

The time is right for a reexamination of the ways in which the contemporary, diverse Asian American community is represented in the literature used in classrooms today. Currently, Asian Americans account for approximately 4.6 percent of the school age children in the United States, a number that has increased by over 50 percent since the 1990 census. Meanwhile, new issues and questions regarding the role of multicultural literature in the curriculum are emerging. The importance and value of using a variety of texts, including multicultural literature, to teach about cultures are widely acknowledged by professional organizations in education. But the number of Asian American students in our classrooms underscores the need to add another dimension to this goal: to develop curricula that address these students' particular needs as they "navigate through western education" (Ching 23). Above all, students need access and introduction to highly engaging reading materials that enlighten, entertain, and inform. Before getting into the heart of this chapter on Asian American literature, we first wish to present some disclaimers about our process. We have chosen to use the umbrella term *Asian American,* but we do recognize the potential problems involved in using a term that groups together people from such a wide range of cultural similarities because they come from a geographically contiguous region. Thus, we wish to point out the important concept of "intragroup diversity" or "within-group" variations noted in the *Dictionary of Multicultural Education* (151–52), which indicates that there is considerable variation even *within* a cultural group.

The first important variation in defining Asian ethnic groups is by their country of origin (Japan, China, Laos, etc.). The second important variation is differences in "place of birth, generations in the US, age, level of income, educational achievement, etc." (Grant and Ladson-Billings 151). Finally, in certain instances Asian children may have been adopted by non-Asian families, and this affects ideas of ethnic identity. These variations cause us to raise the issue of the role played by heritage as opposed to that of upbringing in defining children's cultural identity. In addition, we see a further issue of heritage versus upbringing arising when we consider how others view people who are obviously of Asian heritage by birth but who have been raised within another cultural setting. Clearly, for us, the use of the term *Asian American literature* cannot refer to a diverse body of literature without offering both convenient and difficult summations.

We define Asian American literature as representing Americans of Asian heritage and including stories set in America as well as in Asian countries. Annual publications statistics maintained by the Cooperative Children's Book Center indicate that between 1994 and 2001, children's books by and about Asian Americans accounted for an average of only 67 out of approximately 5,000 published annually in the United States. In 2001, there were 96 books by or about Asian Americans published; nine were middle grade novels. Three of the nine novels were written by Asian Americans; one, *A Single Shard* by Linda Sue Park, won the Newbery Award; and another, *A Step from Heaven* by An Na, was the winner of the Printz Award.

We believe it important to consider the many books of Asian origin (including those created by Asian Americans) whose content does not reflect Asian or Asian American heritage. For example, notable Japanese author and illustrator Mitsumasa Anno's books are stellar in many ways, but they focus on mathematics or reflect his journeys throughout the world rather than address specifically cultural or Asian issues. Likewise, Asian American author/illustrator Keiko Kasza's picture books depict animals in situations that reflect children's interests and concerns, and Norbert Wu's *Fish Faces* is an informational book about fish. Such books, although excellent, are excluded from the present discussion because they do not specifically relate to Asian culture.

I.

Although literature has always held a special place in the lives of children, its importance in the school curriculum has increased in the past two decades. Once employed in classrooms primarily to delight and entertain, children's literature is now widely used to teach concepts and skills, generate discussion about curriculum topics, facilitate reflection about the world around children, and promote self-discovery. Sharing literature in "thematic ways" began as a grassroots movement, and teachers shared trade books they used as part of reading instruction. Children's literature is now mainstream, with all current basal reading series including it as the central reading material of their programs. The statement "Literature is the means by which children come to understand the stories of others and learn to embrace the diversity in our schools" (Pang et al. 217) speaks to the promise that multicultural literature is expected to fulfill: Students can learn about cultures—even their own—through literature. If, indeed, this is the primary reason for including multicultural literature in the curriculum, then issues such as accurate representation, cultural authenticity, and sensitivity to stereotyping become critical in the process of selecting books, planning instruction, and facilitating discussion. It is also important to emphasize that, although literature may hold the potential to accomplish these ideals, the actualization of these goals depends on teachers' sensitive and knowledgeable selection and engagement of the text as they share it within their classrooms.

It is equally important for Asian American students to see images of their particular culture and ethnic history portrayed in their literature and for non-Asian students to glimpse images of people different from themselves. Asian imagery used in the curriculum should represent many backgrounds so that all readers, regardless of cultural background, can see themselves in what they are required to read. The universality of themes and the similarity of experiences across cultural groups, as well as the unique depictions of details from diverse groups, need to be included. Another important need is books that contain contemporary realistic depictions of people and, thus, establish a sense of the cultural "here and now."

Prior to the 1970s, most books focused on Asian Americans were written by non-Asians, presented themes and illustrations focused on exotica, and perpetuated common stereotypes. These books often reflected the limited expectations held by the larger society that Americans were lucky and should take pity on the unfortunate others and charitably help them out. As Chu and Schuler have observed, illustrations in the books of these years often featured "Fu Manchu Mustaches, short, straight cereal bowl haircuts, buck teeth, myopic vision, and clothing that were cruelly and offensively indicative of ancient ways" (94). Asians were depicted as different from the mainstream American population but strangely similar to each other: They were yellow skinned and slant-eyed. These books now serve as artifacts from another era, a time when accurate understanding of Asian cultures was not particularly valued. Asian American children's literature that goes beyond stereotypes has a relatively short history, and the number of books representing Asian Americans is relatively small considering the population growth of this diverse group.

In the 1960s, first-generation immigrants Taro Yashima and Kazue Mizumura created several picture books set in Japan. Their texts realistically represented the countries and time periods portrayed, and they were based upon firsthand knowledge of the countries. However, the illustrations, limited by the printing process available, show people who are abnormally yellow. Also published during this time period were Yoshiko Uchida's stories, based on her personal experiences as a child in the Japanese American internment camps.

The work of the Council of Interracial Books for Children during the civil rights era helped to raise public awareness of the need for change in how people outside the mainstream were depicted, and by the late 1980s, more Asian American authors were writing stories based on their personal experiences. This coincided with the inclusion of multiculturalism as a curricular theme in American schools. A genuine need was realized for materials that were appropriate, accurate, and sensitive in their depictions of Asian people and cultures. Authors such as Sook Nyul Choi, Lensey Namioka, and Yoko Kawashima Watkins contributed new voices to the already established ones of Laurence Yep, Allen Say, and Ed Young.

II.

The first wave of Asian American writers and illustrators came mostly from Japan and China; today increasingly more Koreans are creating books for children. Although a few books now available are set in Vietnam or Thailand, virtually no representation of the Philippines or other Pacific Islands can be found in children's books published in the

United States. A handful of books represent India, and Afghanistan has recently been depicted in books for children, but many other Asian countries are yet to be represented at all. Despite the huge increase in the Hmong student population in the United States, very few books represent their culture, a group whose story patterns are virtually unknown to the Western world. Clearly, there is a need for more widespread representation of Asian diversity in children's books.

Children of biracial backgrounds are commonly found in the school population. They face different challenges from other children. One of the earliest portrayals of a biracial child was in *How My Parents Learned to Eat,* a story about the courtship and marriage of a Japanese woman and her American military husband. It attempted to depict the child's negotiation between two different backgrounds as noble. But many of its cultural details were problematic. For example, the image of a Japanese teenager in a school uniform dating a uniformed American military man in that postwar era is inaccurate. Japanese schools, especially of that time period, were strict about appropriate behavior of their students, particularly when in school uniform. Moreover, it is clear that the girl comes from a fairly affluent home, and their endorsement of their school-age daughter dating and marrying a foreign soldier is unimaginable in this postwar era when most meeting and marrying was done through arrangements made by parents and elder relatives. More recent portrayals of biracial children can be found in Lawrence McKay, Jr.'s *Journey Home* and Janet S. Wong's *The Trip Back Home,* showing biracial children accompanying their mother to her homeland, far from the everyday home of the children. These are more realistic situations, with their depictions of the biracial child's opportunity to visit one half of her ethnic and historical heritage (Yokota and Frost 53).

The overall impression of Asians represented in the body of children's literature available today continues the feeling of "long ago and far away." Historical fiction and folklore abound, with extremely limited numbers of contemporary realistic stories. "The near absence of the modern Asian world in children's literature is a puzzling phenomenon" (MacCann 66).

The historical fiction in print tends to focus on limited topics such as wartime stories and portraying victims (of the atomic bomb, internment camps, or forms of racial oppression). "Citizens as victims" is a common theme in wartime stories set in Asian countries, too, so Chinese and Korean wartime stories portray Japan as victimizer of the Chinese and Koreans in their homeland. Well-known picture books that are emotionally intense war-related experiences include *Hiroshima no Pika* (Maruki), *Shin's Tricycle* (Kodama), *Baseball Saved Us* (Mochizuki), and *Faithful Elephants* (Tsuchiya). Novels such as *So Far from the Bamboo Grove* (Watkins and Fritz), *Sadako and the Thousand Cranes* (Coerr), and *When My Name Was Keoko* (Park) also focus on wartime victimization. Although not set during wartime, another example of victimization and survival is found in *Dragon's Gate* (Yep), which depicts the Chinese labor on the building of the transcontinental railroad.

In a study of how the Chinese and Chinese culture were portrayed through books available in libraries, Cai found that folktales accounted for 70 percent of the titles, an overrepresentation that corresponds with publication figures of books about Chinese and Chinese culture ("Images" 169–70). Folktales can be a source of information about another culture, but, as Cai points out, they do not portray contemporary life, culture, or value systems and may indeed perpetuate stereotypes, especially if this is the only experience students have with literature featuring Chinese and Chinese Americans. Even the picture book stories in the survey that featured contemporary Chinese and Chinese Americans were ineffective in presenting current issues and themes, relying instead on such predictable and overworked subjects as festivals, kites, dragons, and life on boats (180–81).

There is a need for historical fiction focused on more diverse themes such as *The Ghost of the Tokaido Inn* (Dorothy and Thomas Hoobler) or *The Den of the White Fox* (Lensey Namioka), which are mysteries that are also adventure stories. *A Single Shard* by Linda Sue Park is set in twelfth-century Korea, but the theme of "work hard to rise beyond your adverse circumstances" is universal.

In order to overcome the sense that Asians cultures are remote and ancient, contemporary images are necessary to balance the "long ago and far away" sense that the overabundance of folklore and historical fiction bring about. Kazumi Yumoto's novel about modern sixth graders pondering the meaning of friendship, life, and death in the book *The Friends* offers contemporary descriptions of everyday life in Japan. Stories such as this afford American students today opportunities to make comparisons of contemporary life in another country to their lives.

A major problem plaguing the image of Asian Americans is the endorsement of erroneous images created by those who are outside their cultural group. Disney's film presentation of the legendary Chinese folk heroine Mulan is an example of how difficult it has been for Asian themes to be interpreted accurately when the goal is to appeal to Western audiences rather than inform or challenge them. Mo and Shen (129–33) illustrate how, in the Disney movie, motives of Mulan to fight in her father's place are filtered through a Western lens of self-fulfillment and personal growth rather than the more accurate (but less familiar to mainstream American audiences) theme of filial responsibility and respect for elders. One way for teachers to combat such inauthentic interpretations is to seek culturally authentic book versions of a story depicted in popular media. For example, Jeanne M. Lee's picture book version, *The Song of Mu Lan,* presents the beautifully illustrated story in traditional poetic song. Illustrations are true to authentic cultural images. Additionally, *Fa Mulan* by Robert San Souci is illustrated by Jean and Mou-Sien Tseng; *The Ballad of Mulan,* illustrated by Song Nan Zhang, is published bilingually by a small Asian publisher as is *China's Bravest Girl: The Legend of Hua Mu Lan,* retold by Charlie Chin and illustrated by Tomie Arai. Obtaining such an authentic bilingual book requires looking up the publisher information on the copyright page and contacting the publisher directly, but this type of effort pays off in providing a cultural gem, authentic in its storytelling.

Despite the misinformed images and misinterpreted stories that exist, many culturally authentic books about Asian Americans are available, and they should be lauded. In particular, books created by cultural insiders and individuals who have done extensive research to offer culturally responsible images should be promoted. Most prolific in this category are Allen Say and Ed Young, who grew up in Japan and China, respectively, and emigrated to the United States as young adults. Say's artwork at times seems almost photographic in its realism, and his texts accurately and sensitively portray the country of his youth. His images are predominantly from a few decades ago, perhaps indicative of the years when he resided in Japan. His picture book *Grandfather's Journey* was awarded a Caldecott Medal.

In addition to historic family-based stories set in Japan, he has a number of modern-day stories reflecting Asian Americans. Young's work, although focused on Chinese images, also encompasses books set in Japan as well as in other non-Asian cultures. His Chinese rendition of the Red Riding Hood tale, *Lon Po Po,* was awarded a Caldecott Medal.

These two author-illustrators are joined in creating authentic Asian American books by Japanese American author and illustrator Sheila Hamanaka, Chinese American illustrators Jean and Mou-sien Tseng, Korean American illustrators Yumi Heo and Oki Han, and Korean illustrator Chris Soenpiet. Janet Wong's poetry addresses her mixed Asian heritage. People of Asian descent are also writing culturally authentic books and publishing them outside the United States, in other English-speaking countries. Junko Morimoto's books were originally published in Australia; Paul Yee's books were first published in Canada. Earlier authentic portrayals in novels written by outsiders include the historical fiction books by Erik Haugaard and Katherine Paterson. Insider voices present in both historical and contemporary novels for children include Laurence Yep, Kyoko Mori, Linda Sue Park, Lensey Namioka, and An Na. Their books explore how the stories and lives of their ancestors form their heritage and roots and consider contemporary, day-to-day experiences as well as serious questions about identity.

III.

Two general categories of critical issues related to Asian American literature deserve attention. The first encompasses the creation of high-quality literature that more accurately represents Asian American cultures. The second focuses on the evaluation and selection of quality literature and its use in classrooms.

The importance of creating high-quality literature that accurately represents Asian American cultures is related to Zipes's point about the power that children's literature can exert over the thinking and developing tastes of young readers: "books for the young [. . .] have always been used as weapons or instruments to train and cultivate taste, to help children to see distinctions and distinguish themselves" ("Sticks and Stones" 66). Adults largely control the selection and purchase of books for use in schools and libraries and for placement on recommended and required reading lists. Therefore, a group of educated adult readers influences what is being written for children and who is doing the writing in interesting ways. When it comes to Asian American literature, we must consider if these adult readers are concerned with cultural accuracy and authenticity, or if they focus only on the visual or narrative presentation, the skills of author or illustrator, an award, or simply the nostalgia associated with a classic or an old favorite. The issue of "outsiders" is relevant here because commercial and market demands may become more significant in motivating a writer to produce or publisher to solicit a work about an unfamiliar culture than attention to accuracy and authenticity. Teachers need to understand how market issues affect what's available—but they can also take a role in influencing what gets published because of their collective buying power.

Respect for another culture is reflected through authentic representation of themes as well as accuracy of cultural details. Cai explains that certain aspects of Asian American culture do not translate precisely into familiar Western concepts, and efforts to reshape them can compromise the true meaning ("Can We Fly" 6). In *The Happy Funeral,* for example, Eve Bunting attempts to depict the joy that is present at the funeral of an elderly Chinese person who has lived a full, fortunate life. Leung believes that a more appropriate way of depicting this cultural belief, however, is as a "smiling" funeral, a subtle but important difference.

The concept of cultural responsibility implies that those who create images of culture have a responsibility to represent it authentically. A demand for accuracy is taken for granted in the creation of a scientific book. Likewise, cultural responsibility should demand that those who create images of culture do so in some documentable way to indicate how authentically the culture is being represented. Philip Lee, co-founder and publisher of Lee & Low Books, discussed with Glenna Sloan how the lack of diversity in publishing personnel impacts the level of cultural sensitivity, as well as promotion and sales to particular audiences.

It is important to consider the impact a book has on the reader's images of the culture portrayed. "In the United States, multicultural literature revises traditional Eurocentric beliefs about history and challenges monocultural social models" (Grant and Ladson-Billings 185–86). If so, this call for revision must include eliminating from school curricula books that reflect that no longer appropriate images. Often nostalgia and sentimentality supplant rational thinking: "I loved that book as a child." But to native people of a culture, books that outsider adults remember fondly from their childhoods may embarrass, put down, or offend children about their heritage in untrue ways.

There are several important criteria to keep in mind when selecting and evaluating Asian American literature. First and foremost, the books must be of high quality in all traditional ways of evaluating good books; they must adhere to the high standards of literary criticism. Beyond that, the key point is to seek culturally authentic literature that is also culturally specific. The following questions can serve as guidelines in evaluating books:

- Do the author and illustrator present insider perspectives?
- Is the culture portrayed multidimensionally?
- Are cultural details naturally integrated?
- Are details accurate and interpretation current?
- Is language used authentically?
- Is the collection balanced? (Temple, Martinez, Yokota, and Naylor 101)

Many have called for culturally authentic images in books for children (e.g., Cai and Sims Bishop; Harris; Tomlinson; Yokota). Yet we must also be aware that this call for authenticity does *not* imply that there is one standard image for a culture—there is no such thing as *the* Asian American experience. However, there are experiences that fall within the range of what would ring true to people of Asian American heritage. Whereas authentic images align with possible experiences and offer valuable insights, misinformed images only offer false portrayals. The increase in the number of native writers and illustrators has given rise to more authentic depictions; yet, stereotyped and erroneous images also continue to abound. The author or illustrator who creates from "outside" Asian cultures still exists, and their contributions are still debated. Some maintain that with extensive research and integrity of purpose, non-Asian authors and illustrators can successfully depict a culture that is personally unfamiliar to them. Others claim that research, observation and imagination can only take one so far, that the nuances of a culture are not easily understood or portrayed, but are very easily misinterpreted.

Early attempts to be inclusive with respect to children's literature often produced images that lacked cultural clarity. The resulting composite image was so vague that other than recognizing the character as being non-Caucasian, the darker "unirace" child with indistinct facial features and generic clothing lacked markers specifically identifying a culture. In the setting of a book one might find a mixture of many different cultural aspects that were vaguely grouped together as "African" or "Latin American." Many who previously asked why illustrators should be denied the right to "artistic license" have begun to understand that mishmash images created in the name of artistic creativity often show confused depictions of a "composite culture."

The perspective of the author or illustrator in creating a book has often been categorized as "insider" or "outsider." This distinction refers to the ability of the creator to offer a perspective as a member of the culture or as a person outside the culture. The insider perspective is held with different views: Some believe that only those born into the culture can offer a native perspective. Others believe that through study and life choices, some people gain an insider perspective and that some are born into a cultural group but have no desire to understand or represent their own heritage with the insider perspective. The other distinction in the insider/outsider debate is that one is not better than the other at all times. They offer different kinds of understandings—and, depending on the circumstances, it is interesting to note the outsiders' views of a people that insiders may not recognize as being different or interesting to outsiders. Nuances of authenticity, however, are typically instantly recognizable to insiders.

Whether illustrations are authentic or not varies on several dimensions: overall impression, despite the details that may be accurate; details that are missed, despite the overall image that appears to be authentic. What matters? Everything matters, from overall to specific, even colors and clothing styles, signs on the buildings, and so forth. Pictures have the power to convey a lot of information and are often visually imprinted in our minds in ways that allow readers to recall images that are impressionistic. For example, Mingshui Cai, a native Chinese, when shown a picture book with a blue creature that the text identified as a dragon, asked, "What is *that*?" As a result of growing up Chinese, he knew that Chinese dragons had very specific physical features that were not part of the illustration—the details that were wrong resulted in an unrecognizable image. In another book, the illustrator's lack of knowledge led to lanterns being depicted with the country's flag as the motif, and the logos of popular electronics companies being placed on people's traditional clothing.

IV.

Classroom teachers and librarians have significant influence on what and how students read, discuss, and think about literature. In fact, how students perceive culture as portrayed in literature is related in part to how teachers respond to cultural values and beliefs present in the literature. Because of this powerful influence, there is a need for culturally authentic materials as well as learning activities that enhance student understanding of culture.

Finally, teachers and librarians can expand their understanding of their own cultural background as well as that of cultures beyond their own if they make a commitment to be "teachers as readers" (Temple, Martinez, Yokota, and Naylor 114–15).

When selecting literature for classroom use, teachers must strive to achieve a balance of representation. They must be vigilant in the search for accurate representations and sensitive to the problems with the extensive use of folktales to represent a culture. This could mean "weeding out" certain old favorites as well as a genuine effort to find titles that explore the contemporary issues of ethnicity as experienced by students in our classrooms.

Teachers are responsible for selecting books that help students appreciate and understand cultures—their own as well as those unfamiliar to them. This calls for a collection that offers sensitive, accurate portrayals through a balance of folktales, realistic fiction, and nonfiction. Acquiring and maintaining such a collection requires a close look at certain "favorites" that do not meet the current criteria. For example, in spite of well-publicized criticism regarding the lack of cultural authenticity in *Tikki Tikki Tembo* and *The Five Chinese Brothers,* the books remain on many classroom and school library bookshelves. Why is this the case, and what can be done to remedy it?

The Five Chinese Brothers had to look very much alike in order for this story to work. But in the original version of this tale (Bishop), not only do the brothers look alike, but all the townspeople also look alike, and the entire town moves and sways to the same degree and appear identical in physical features and clothing. Phoebe Yeh describes the process by which her publishing company went about looking for the right person to reillustrate the story (as *The Seven Chinese Brothers*) in the late 1980s. Jean and Mou-Sien Tseng, spent months doing meticulous research on "hairstyles, clothing, even footwear and arms carried by warriors of the period" (70).

Award-winning books such as *Tikki Tikki Tembo* (Caldecott Honor) and *The Funny Little Woman* (Caldecott Medal) are still being favorably reviewed on the websites of major book vendors. For example, Amazon describes *Tikki Tikki Tembo* as "a perfect book to read aloud," with students chanting along, "Tikki tikki tembo-no sa rembo-chari bari ruchi-pip peri pembo." A review from *Publishers' Weekly* states that "Beautifully expressive drawings enhance the book's Oriental feel." The story emphasizes the nonsensical and nonnative sounds of Chinese names, and the illustrations depict a vague image of "Oriental." Noted Chinese children's literature critic Mingshui Cai states that he does not see any connection to Chinese reality in *Tikki Tikki Tembo.* "The name does not sound like Chinese, ancient or modern" ("Images" 185). In addition, the illustrations do not reflect Chinese style. The standards for selection of books used for classroom instruction must transcend those of the marketplace.

Reader comments on the Amazon website indicate considerable cultural confusion among teachers: they recommend reading the Japanese tale *The Funny Little Woman* as an introduction to "Oriental culture" and "Good to read at Chinese New Year." Teachers often defend books such as *Tikki Tikki Tembo* or *The Funny Little Woman* because their students respond positively to them. But that may be because such books represent all that has been offered to the students. This is an example of the critical role that teacher knowledge plays in the book selection process. Teachers need experience and exposure to quality Asian American literature so that they can think critically so new and better favorites can emerge to replace the old and problematic.

MacCann cites the "continuing obstacle to intelligent, challenging multicultural work" as the lack of cultural understanding exhibited through the awarding of children's literary prizes (66). The impact of winning an award on the cultural acceptance of what is sold, read, and remains in publication is tremendous. Although most literary awards do not include cultural authenticity as a criterion for evaluation, awards such as the Coretta Scott King Award or the Pura Bélpre Award are based on cultural images as well as on quality of literature. It is worth noting that the Asian Pacific American Library Association is currently in the process of establishing a permanent literary award focused on Asian children's literature. However, in 2004, it had only been presented once, in 2000, considering books published during the three years preceding that time.

In many elementary schools, literature is presented primarily in basal anthologies used for reading instruction. Editors of these textbooks have responded to the need for cultural and ethnic diversity in their selections. Do these represent a variety of genres in Asian American literature, or is the folktale, which seems to illuminate cultural differences and thereby reinforce stereotypes, still chosen over works that portray contemporary Asian American life?

A set of basal literature anthologies by Scholastic designed for classroom reading instruction was examined to determine the proportion of folktales to stories that feature examples of contemporary Asian or Asian American life. There are six anthologies for each grade level in this series, each of which contains approximately ten to twelve selections. In addition, each anthology is accompanied by four trade books that complement the anthology's particular theme. The series contains fourteen titles by Asian or Asian American authors: four folktales, five contemporary stories, two photo essays, and three biographies. Not all of these are culturally specific, however: two of the contemporary stories, one of the biographies, and one photo essay do not have ethnicity as a theme. This balance among genres in the series reflects the work of a series' selection committee.

Thus far, we have proposed ways in which teachers can evaluate and select good Asian American books that are culturally authentic depictions. We have also presented issues of importance for teachers to consider while reflecting on the literature. Now let us consider ways that teachers can scaffold students' reading experiences and extend them in order to maximize the cultural understandings that children develop. First, there are many ways that teachers can take advantage of the cultural connection to storytelling. Because storytelling originates with the oral tradition, it is grounded in ways that cultures shared stories from one generation to the next. One example is the Japanese storytelling form known as *kamishibai* that uses a stack of large, illustrated cards. (*Kamishibai* literally means "paper theatre" and refers to the way in which the cards were placed within a wooden stage that faced listeners.) The storyteller reads the text printed on the back of the card at the end of the stack while showing the illustration on the front of the stack of cards. After reading each card, the storyteller flips the back card to the front and repeats the process after reading each card. Teachers can adapt the use of these cards to have a "reader's theater" type of experience for students, converting the text on the cards into dialogue format.

In addition, students can benefit from being introduced to Asian American literature through effective book displays, inviting book talks, engaging read alouds, and extension activities whereby literature is connected to the classroom curriculum. The unfamiliarity of some Asian cultures can be scaffolded by introducing foreign vocabulary, background information, and information about the authors and illustrators. Books on tape, especially when read by an Asian person who believably sounds like a member of the culture (the audio version of An Na's *A Step from Heaven* is a good example) can make the story come alive (Yokota and Martinez). Pairing an Asian American book with a book that may seem more culturally familiar can also help bridge cultures (Stan 27–35). One such pairing could be *Chibi: A True Story from Japan* with *Make Way for Ducklings*. Both are about ducks and their ducklings crossing busy city streets in order to find new, safe homes. One is set in the Japanese Imperial Palace moats, and the other in Boston Public Gardens.

Multicultural literature can teach about equity and social justice by prompting students to question their perceptions of others. Henkin uses the inclusive inquiry model to "integrate multicultural, cross-cultural curriculum with literacy in a holistic way [. . . to] provide a framework for critical questions to arise" (89–93). The inclusive inquiry cycle is guided by students' questions; these questions can be inspired by themes presented in literature or by certain aspects of the literature itself. Students explore their questions through reflection, personal engagement, research, collaboration, and social action. Henkin suggests that teachers expand their students' thinking by encouraging them to ask difficult, critical questions and to create classrooms where all student voices are heard.

V.

The first two National Standards for English Language Arts, authorized by the National Council of Teachers of English, address both variety and purpose in text selection. They state that students must read from a wide range of texts including fiction and nonfiction, classic and contemporary works, and literature from many periods and in many genres in order to build understanding of texts, themselves, the cultures of the world, and the many dimensions of human experience. Additionally, students are expected to read for information, to respond to the needs and demands of society and the workplace, and for personal fulfillment. These standards offer clear directives for the range of material we must offer students and the purposes we need to set for the reading of those texts. Along with the stated purposes, perhaps students, too, will make a personal commitment to reading a wide range of material.

Jack Zipes, in his speech at the 2001 International Board on Books for Young People Regional Conference, cited his three personal complaints of the world: intolerance, ignorance, and globalization. His call for teachers and students to engage with literature in ways that combat such attitudes requires activism on the part of teachers. At the same conference, author Carololivia Herron described the call and response of African storytelling tradition, insisting that the audience participate and be included. She explained, "this is not in our blood; this is learned behavior." Likewise, "learned behavior" about being tolerant, informed, and a person who reflects deeply can stem in part from what students take from the books they have the opportunities to read.

Works Cited

Appleby, Arthur. *A Study of Book Length Works Taught in High School English Courses*. Albany, NY: Center for the Learning and Teaching of Literature, 1989.

Bishop, Claire Huchet. *The Five Chinese Brothers.* Illustrated by Ken Wiese. Coward—McCann, 1938.

Brenner, Barbara and Julia Takaya. *Chibi: A True Story From Japan.* New York: Clarion/Houghton, 1996.

Bunting, Eve. *The Happy Funeral.* Illus. Vo-Dihn Mai. New York: Harper and Row, 1982.

Cai, Mingshui. "Can We Fly Across Cultural Gaps on the Wings of Imagination? Ethnicity, Experience, and Cultural Authenticity." *The New Advocate* 8:1 (1995): 1–16.

———. "Images of Chinese and Chinese Americans Mirrored in Picture Books." *Children's Literature in Education* 25:3 (1994): 169–91.

———. "TikkiTikki." E-mail to author. 21 Aug. 2002.

Cai, Mingshui and Rudine Sims Bishop. "Multicultural Literature for Children: Towards a Clarification of a Concept." *The Need for Story: Cultural Diversity in Classroom and Community.* Ed. A. H. Dyson and C. Genishi. Urbana, IL: National Council of Teachers of English, 1994. 57–71.

Chang, Maragaret. "Daydreams of Cathay: How Pat Images of China Influence Modern American Children's Books." Speech given at Global Connections: International Board on Books for Young People Regional Conference. San Francisco, CA. 14, Oct. 2001.

Children's Books by and About People of Color Published in the United States. 2001. Cooperative Children's Book Center, University of Wisconsin, Madison. 8, Oct. 2002. www.soemadison.wisc.edu/ccbc/pcstats/htm.

Chin, Charlie. *China's Bravest Girl: The Legend of Hua Mu Lan.* Illus. Tomie Arai. Emeryville, CA: Children's Book Press, 1993.

Ching, Stuart H. D. and Jann Pataray-Ching. "Memory as Travel in Asian American Children's Literature: Bridging Home and School." *The New Advocate* 15:1 (2002): 23–34.

Chu, E. and C. V. Schuler. "United States: Asian Americans." *Our Family, Our Friends, Our World: An Annotated Guide to Significant Multicultural Books For Children and Teenagers.* Ed. L. Miller-Lachman. New Providence, NJ: R. R. Bowker, 1992. 93–120.

Coerr, Eleanor. *Sadako and the Thousand Paper Cranes.* Illus. by Ron Himler. New York: Putnam, 1977.

Friedman, Ina R. and Allen Say. *How My Parents Learned to Eat.* Illus. by Ana R. Friedman. Boston: Houghton Mifflin, 1984.

Grant, Carl A. and Gloria Ladson-Billings, ed. *Dictionary of Multicultural Education.* Phoenix, AZ: Oryx Press, 1997.

Harris, Violet J., Ed. *Using Multicultural Literature in the K–8 Classroom.* Norwood, MA: Christopher Gordon Publishers, 1997.

Henkin, Roxanne. *Who's Invited to Share? Using Literacy to Teach for Equity and Social Justice.* Portsmouth, NH: Heinemann, 1998. 89–93.

Herron, Caraolivia. "Images of African American Culture in Books for Children." Speech at Global Connections: International Board on Books for Young People Regional Conference. San Francisco, CA. 14, Oct. 2001.

Hoobler, Dorothy and Thomas Hoobler. *Ghost of the Tokaido Inn.* New York: Philomel, 1999.

Kodama, Tatsuharu. *Shin's Tricycle.* Illus. by Noriyuki Ando. Trans. Kazuko Hokumen-Jones. New York: Walker, 1995.

Lee, Jeanne M. *The Song of Mu Lan.* Arden, NC: Front Street, 1995.

Leung, Marilyn. Personal interview. 21 Aug. 2002.

MacCann, Donnarae. "Illustrating the Point: A Commentary on Multicultural and Stereotypic Picture Books." *The New Press Guide to Multicultural Resources for Young Readers.* Ed. Daphne Muse. New York: The New Press, 1997. 62–67.

Maruki, Toshi. *Hiroshima No Pika.* New York: William and Morrow, 1982.

May, Jill P. *Children's Literature & Critical Theory.* New York: Oxford, 1995. 11–12.

McCloskey, Robert. *Make Way for Ducklings.* New York: Viking, 1941.

McKay, Jr., Lawrence. *Journey Home.* Illus. Dom Lee and Keunhee Lee. New York: Lee & Low, 2000.

Mo, Weimin and Wenju Shen. "A Mean Wink at Authenticity: Chinese Images in Disney's Mulan." *The New Advocate* 13:2 (2000): 129–42.

Mochizuki, Ken. *Baseball Saved Us.* Illus. Dom Lee. New York: Lee & Low, 1993.

Mosel, Arlene. *The Funny Little Woman.* Illus. Blair Lent. New York: Dutton, 1972.

———. *Tikki Tikki Tembo.* Illus. Blair Lent. New York: Henry Holt, 1988.

Myers, Christopher. "Panel of Illustrators." Speech at Global Connections: International Board on Books for Young People Regional Conference. San Francisco, CA. 14, Oct. 2001.

Na, An. *A Step from Heaven.* Asheville, NC: Front Street, 2001.

Namioka, Lensey. *Den of the White Fox.* San Diego: Browndeer Press/Harcourt, 1997.

National Council of Teachers of English. *Standards for the English Language Arts.* Urbana, IL: NCTE, 1998–2001.

Pang, Valerie O., Carolyn Colvin, MyLuong Tran, and Robertta H. Barba. "Beyond Chopsticks and Dragons: Selecting Asian American Literature for Children." *The Reading Teacher* 46:3 (1992): 216–24.

Park, Linda Sue. *A Single Shard.* New York: Clarion, 2001.

———. *When My Name Was Keoko.* New York: Clarion, 2002.

Rathbun, David. "Ways of Knowing a Curriculum: Literature by Asian Americans." *Teaching the Humanities* 1:1 (1995): 37–48.

Reimer, Kathryn Meyer. "Multiethnic Literature: Hold Fast to Dreams." *Language Arts* 69:1 (1992): 14–21.

San Souci, R. *Fa Mulan: The Story of a Woman Warrior.* Illus. Jean and Mou-Sien Tseng. New York: Hyperion, 1998.

Say, Allen. *Grandfather's Journey.* Boston: Houghton Mifflin, 1993.

Scholastic, Inc. *Scholastic Literacy Place.* New York: Scholastic Instructional Publishing, 1996.

Sloan, Glenna. "Multicultural Matters: An Interview with Philip Lee of Lee and Low Books." *Journal of Children's Literature* 25:1 (1999): 28–33.

Stan, Susan, ed. *The World Through Children's Books.* Lanham, MD: Scarecrow Press, 2002.

Temple, Charles, Miriam Martinez, Junko Yokota, and Alice Naylor. *Children's Books in Children's Hands,* 2nd ed. Boston: Allyn and Bacon, 2002.

Tomlinson, Carl M., Ed. *Children's Books from Other Countries.* Lanham, MD: Scarecrow Press, 1998.

Tsuchiya, Yukio. *Faithful Elephants: A True Story of Animals, People, and War.* Illus. Ted Lewin. Boston: Houghton Mifflin, 1988.

Watkins Kawashima, Yoko and Jean Fritz. *So Far from the Bamboo Grove.* New York: Lothrop, Lee & Shepard, 1986.

Wong, Janet. *The Trip Back Home.* Illus. Bo Jia. San Diego: Harcourt Brace, 2000.

Wu, Norbert. *Fish Faces.* New York: Henry Holt, 1993.

Yeh, Phoebe. "Publisher's Perspective." *The Multicolored Mirror: Cultural Substance in Literature for Children and Young Adults.* Ed. Cooperative Children's Book Center. Fort Atkinson, WI: Highsmith Press, 1991. 67–73.

Yep, Laurence. *Dragon's Gate (Golden Mountain Chronicles).* New York: HarperCollins, 1993.

Yokota, Junko. "Asians and Asian Americans in Children's Literature." *Encyclopedia of Children's Literature.* Ed. B. E. Cullinan and D. G. Person. New York: Continuum, 2001. 44–45.

———. "Issues in Selecting Multicultural Children's Literature." *Language Arts* 70:3 (1993): 156–67.

———. "Read the World-USBBY Regional Conference in San Francisco." *Bookbird* 40:2 (2002): 50–52.

———, ed. *Kaleidoscope: A Multicultural Booklist for Grades K–8, 3rd ed.* Urbana, IL: National Council of Teachers of English, 2001.

Yokota, Junko and Miriam Martinez. "Authentic Listening Experiences: Multicultural Audiobooks." *Book Links* 13:3 (In press, 2004).

Yokota, Junko, and Sharon Frost. "Multiracial Characters in Children's Literature." *Book Links* 12:3 (2003): 51–57.

Young, Ed. *Lon Po Po: A Red Riding Hood Story from China.* New York: Philomel, 1989.

Yumoto, Kazumi. *The Friends.* Trans. Cathy Hirano. New York: Farrar Straus and Giroux, 1996.

Zhang, Song Nan. *The Ballad of Mulan.* Union City, CA: Pan Asian Publications, 1998.

Zipes, Jack. *Sticks and Stones.* New York: Routledge, 2001.

———. "The Multicultural Contradictions of International Children's Literature: Three Complaints and Three Wishes." Speech at Global Connections: International Board on Books for Young People Regional Conference. San Francisco, CA. 14, Oct. 2001.

25

Walking the Tightrope

A Consideration of Problems and Solutions in Adapting Stories from the Oral Tradition

Eve Tal

> There is a kind of death to every story when it leaves the speaker and becomes impaled for all times on clay tablets or the written and printed page (Sawyer 59).

OR

> [T]here are three kinds of folk stories: the oral, the transcribed and the literary or art tale. No one kind of a story is better than the other; there is no contest since there are no set or even settable standards (Yolen 4).

The argument has been raging for years: Traditionalists like Ruth Sawyer hold that once a story is taken out of the oral tradition, it loses its vitality and becomes forever frozen on the printed page, sometimes in a form that bears little resemblance to the original. Writers and storytellers are accused of "spiritual colonialism" (Heckler 20) and "stealing" other cultures' stories, allowing the reteller to profit while the original tellers and their cultures receive nothing in return. Questions are raised about the moral right of an outsider to tell the stories of another culture and about the authenticity of such a retelling.

Set against these arguments are the voices of writers who make every effort to research the background of their stories for cultural accuracy, consult with traditional tellers, or even spend years living in the culture they are telling about. Writers like Chinua Achebe who grew up in oral cultures contend "if we can no longer maintain the environment for storytelling [. . .] then the best we can do is to try and translate some of the energy of the folk stories into the written stories" (as qtd. in Baker and Draper 7). Even more persuasive is Joseph Bruchac when he asserts that at one time there was a feeling in the Native American community that writing something from the oral tradition weakened and removed it, to the extent that Native tellers refused to tell their stories. Today, however, there is an awareness that "writing down a traditional story from one's own tradition will ensure that it is told in a better and more respectful way and also help to pass it on to future generations" (100).

Proponents of both sides of the argument stress the necessity for an authentic, sensitive retelling of the story, but few guidelines have been proposed to make the task easier for the individual writer. Jewell Reinhart Coburn and Duong Van Quyen stress that when translating a story from one culture to another (both oral to written and Asian to Western in their case), appropriate considerations should be given to authenticity, universality, informational and educational value, captivating writing style, and accurate visual style (179). Jennifer Sergi submits that the form of the retelling must suggest the original oral telling (2). Roderick McGillis (252) and others emphasize the importance of the narrative voice in providing a direct link between the oral and written tale. Probably the strongest proponent of narrative voice is Julius Lester, who writes, "without the voice there would be only summaries of stories, and a story is not merely plot. [. . .] It is the voice of the story teller that maintains our interest as readers" ("The Storyteller's Voice" 71). Narrative voice can take the form of a relatively simple controlling device, a voiced personality with the narrator's opinions and attitudes coloring the story, or a full-blown character like Uncle Remus who is actually identified as the storyteller (Muller 3–4).

Yet these are no more than preliminary guideposts, raising as many questions as they answer. I will explore the question of whether there are standards or rules governing contemporary adaptations, standards writers may be using without conscious awareness. In an attempt to answer this question, I have analyzed the techniques of three contemporary children's writers, William Miller, Jane Kurtz, and Julius Lester; all three have adapted tales from the oral tradition into children's books. To further understand their motivations for choosing specific techniques, I conducted personal phone and e-mail interviews with the authors and supplemented these with their published materials. I discovered that no easy answers emerged. Adapting from the oral tradition is a process. The author is forced to walk a tightrope between the desire to remain true to the original and the need to create a story that will appeal to contemporary children and, sometimes more importantly, contemporary editors. In the process, the resulting published story may bear little resemblance to the original one told orally.

I chose William Miller's *The Knee-High Man* for an intensive textual analysis because the original source of the retelling is available for comparison in Langston Hughes and Arna Bontemps' fascinating compilation *The Book of Negro Folklore* (19). No details are given about the origin of Hughes and Bontemps's version of "De Knee-High Man," but the fact that the entire story is enclosed in quotation marks indicates that it is a transcription. "De Knee-High Man" shares many of the characteristics of oral tales. The Knee-High Man is a flat character with one characterizing trait; he was "alwez a wantin' to be big 'stead of little" (19). He approaches three animals in the swamp where he lives and asks them how he can become as big as they are. When he follows the advice of the horse and bull to eat the same food they eat, he gets a stomachache. The foolish little man then approaches a hoot owl, who wonders why he wants to be big and sensibly suggests that he climb a tree if he wants to see far away. The humorous story ends with the owl's put-down line: "you ain't got no cause to be bigger in de body, but you sho' is got cause to be bigger in de BRAIN" (20). Many elements of the oral tradition are immediately recognizable: the setting of the woods, the use of three animals, the animals' unexplained ability to speak, the protagonist as underdog—all elements retained in Miller's retelling. The Hughes/Bontemps narration makes frequent use of repetition, as when Mr. Horse advises the Knee-High Man to "eat a whole lot of corn and den you run round and round and round" (19). The Knee-High Man tries, but "de corn make his stomach hurt, and runnin' make his legs hurt and de trying make his mind hurt" (19). Much of the humor of the story lies in the language, which is repetitive without becoming tiresome. The entire story runs to about 500 words.

The first striking difference between the two versions is the mention in the second paragraph of the Knee-High Man's fear of the other animals in the woods where he lives. Miller's Knee-High Man wants to be bigger because he is afraid. It is fear that motivates him to seek out the animals' assistance. The second major difference is the Knee-High Man's relationship with the owl, who calls him by name, indicating some mysterious link between them. Like the original owl, this one points out that because the Knee-High Man has never been attacked by other animals, he has no reason to be bigger than they are. He, too, suggests that the Knee-High Man climb a tree to see faraway places. When he reaches the summit and looks down, the Knee-High Man discovers that "[n]o creature was the biggest, the loudest, the meanest from up here. All creatures were the same" (unpaged). In the third major departure from the original, the owl offers the Knee-High Man a ride home. A double-spread illustration shows the Knee-High Man riding on the owl's back high above the forest. The owl assumes mythic proportion while the Knee-High Man himself becomes a godlike creature who reaches heights no ordinary animal can dream possible. The story comes full circle when the Knee-High Man returns home, having learned to accept his own size while at the same time recognizing his ability to transcend his limitations. In addition, he has overcome his fears of the other animals and made a new friend, themes not present in the prototype.

Unlike the dialect of the original, the picture book version of *The Knee-High Man* is in standard English and is told from the third-person point of view; the narrator makes no use of distinctive personal voice. Even the traditional storytelling opening "once" is discarded for a straightforward opening sentence. The only uses of repetitions are structural: "He jumped at the sound of rabbits and toads. He hid beneath his bed when the bear strolled by" (unpaged). These repetitious sentences serve a rhythmic purpose, but the story is no more repetitious than those usually found in picture books for young children. The humor in Miller's version comes from the situation, the illustrations, and, in smaller part, from the dialogue: " 'That's the last time I'll ever listen to a horse,' says the Knee-High Man, exhausted after eating buckets of corn and running for miles" (unpaged).

I interviewed William Miller and asked about the differences in the two versions. Miller explained that because he considers *The Knee-High Man* a story about childhood he emphasized the element of fear to add motivation and drama he felt was lacking in the original. For Miller, the pint-sized Knee-High Man represents childhood, and, like a child, he suffers from a sense of powerlessness. By the time the story closes, the Knee-High Man has learned to be satisfied with his own size, a theme familiar from many children's books but not inherent in the original tale.

In Miller's version, the owl becomes a mentor to the Knee-High Man. While the horse and the bull give childlike advice, the owl is clearly an adult. He takes the Knee-High Man under his wing and tells him the truth. Miller chose to add the element of "mythic flight" to provide action and additional motivation for the Knee-High Man's new, mature perspective on the world. In fact, Miller preferred to end the story on this note, but his editor favored the closure of a "warm cozy" ending, with the Knee-High Man safe at home.

Miller self-consciously determined to use a neutral narrative voice, rather than creating a "storyteller's voice," because he is not a member of the African American culture and did not want to appropriate or imitate the voice of that culture. In some of his other books about African American culture, Miller does use dialect, but only when this is appropriate for a specific character.

When I asked Miller the question of who has a "right" to tell a particular tale, he admitted that being a White author writing about African American culture is definitely a problem. He avoids any attempt to "be Black" and is honest about the difficulties involved. Miller grew up in a culture he calls "poor White southern," which he believes has much in common with the comparable African American culture because these two groups share traditional folklore, religion, language, and food. Miller also is a university professor with a strong record of teaching African American literature. He terms his book a "multicultural project," combining a southern White male writer, a female Jewish editor, and an African American illustrator.

I put similar questions about their personal methods of adaptation to Jane Kurtz and Julius Lester. Both responded by e-mail. I have supplemented their answers in my discussion by using several of their published articles and speeches.

Jane Kurtz grew up as the daughter of White missionaries stationed in Ethiopia. Many of her picture books are retellings of traditional Ethiopian stories, although she has set original stories in modern Ethiopia and written about other cultures. *Pulling the Lion's Tail* is a lyrical retelling of a traditional tale. In this and other stories, Kurtz's original intention was to preserve the tales in versions close to their original. Through trial and error, she realized that the American editors she worked with were not interested in authenticity. According to Kurtz, "they only cared about things like [. . .] having a strong story, having a story U.S. kids could care and relate to, and, yes, having a story that would be considered 'appropriate' for kids. At first I resisted but ultimately realized if any of my stories were going to see the light of day, I would have to adopt those guidelines as well" (e-mail 5).

The original tale does not have a child as the main character. When she was searching for a realistic conflict that would provide the motivation for a young girl to undertake the frightening task of pulling hairs from a lion's tail, Kurtz hit on the idea of the conflict between Almaz and her new stepmother. She was inspired by a conversation with an Ethiopian friend.

Almaz is not the flat character of folktales. Kurtz develops her character's motivation through a series of actions appropriate for a village girl. When we first meet Almaz, she is cooking for her widowed father, and she lacks the patience to let the batter rise long enough. When her father brings home a new bride, Almaz tries to win her love but is too impatient to heed the advice of her wise grandfather who tells her, "Much of what is good comes slowly" (*Lion's Tail* unpaged). Only when all else fails does she follow his advice.

Her grandfather promises to reveal the secret after Almaz brings him hair from the tail of a lion. Accomplishing this mission requires patience and bravery. After Almaz feeds the lion and wins his trust, she is able to pluck the hairs from his tail. By then she has also learned the secret of patience and won her new mother's love.

Kurtz writes that she did not set out to particularize the cultural details in her story as much as eventually happened; she was largely fueled by the details provided by her Ethiopian friend: "Things like her encounter with the lion were hold-overs from my original telling of the story—where I tried to capture tension and immediacy—but the rest became more the story of a real child because I had the real child [. . .] in my mind" (e-mail 3). Kurtz strengthened characterization motivation, thus creating a stronger relationship between cause and effect in the plot. She also "tried to follow the first commandment of written stories (not oral tales): show, don't tell" and worked to create a character who changed internally (e-mail 5). Her other stories are "truer to the oral tradition of having a character that [*sic*] may be changed in circumstances but who hasn't internally changed from beginning to end" (e-mail 6). Narrative voice is not an important consideration in Kurtz's work, perhaps because she is retelling translated stories in English. She utilizes the formulaic "once" to set her retellings in the folklore tradition, but the narrative is standard third-person English, with the addition of a few Ethiopian words that are contextually explained.

Because she is writing about a culture unfamiliar to American readers, Kurtz stresses the importance of illustrations in conveying both the basic feeling of place and portraying culturally authentic details. Getting the details right is the responsibility of the illustrator, but, from Kurtz's experience, publishing houses will not pay for a trip to the location itself. Illustrators are forced to do their own research, which can lead to inaccuracies and the perpetuation of cultural stereotypes. Ethiopia, for example, while known as the "Switzerland of Africa," is often portrayed as a dry wasteland, a portrayal deeply offensive to Ethiopians ("Multicultural" 40).

When asked outright whether she has the "right" to tell Ethiopian stories ("Finding" 71), Kurtz is unable to give a straightforward answer. In referring to another author's retelling, which she dislikes because it sounds Americanized, she writes, "it's a mistake to dismiss the differences that language and environment bring to one's world view [. . .] dismissing those things leads to too pat answers [. . .]" (e-mail 7). Kurtz believes in doing research to ensure the tale has as much cultural authenticity as possible, but she points to the need to balance cultural authenticity with the demands of the dramatic story ("Multicultural" 40). In the end, she asks much the same questions posed by William Miller and other sensitive writers:

> I comfort myself with the observation that all writers transcend self. Men write as women, women as men. If I write a story from another culture, am I committing a worse transgression than when I write a novel in the voice of my son? Is it worse than nobody telling the stories at all? We are each, in the end, a minority of one. ("Finding" 71)

Jane Kurtz particularizes her characters to make them multidimensional and avoid cultural stereotypes. In contrast, Julius Lester particularizes the narrative voice to add universality and an oral storytelling dimension to his work. Whereas Jane Kurtz is concerned with adapting stories from non-English-speaking cultures, Julius Lester adapts from the traditional African American culture for his modern children's books.

It is interesting to compare Lester's version of the Knee-High Man with the two other versions discussed earlier. Both Miller and Lester used the same source. The plot of Lester's retelling exactly follows the transcribed version. The story makes extensive use of dialogue, but the characters speak standard English. Except for the traditional "once upon a time" of the opening, there is no attempt to create the storyteller's voice. This story was published in 1972 in a collection of tales of the same name; the book also includes a few Brer Rabbit stories, and in Lester's versions he is referred to as "Mr. Rabbit." Mr. Rabbit also speaks standard English, although he occasionally uses idiomatic phrases (*The Knee-High Man and Other Tales*).

In his later retellings of African American folklore, Lester developed a unique voice. Comparing a passage from the 1972 stories with a later one reveals several differences:

> "How're you today, Mr. Rabbit?" Mr. Bear said.
> "I got trouble, Mr. Bear," Mr. Rabbit replied, shaking his head. (*Knee-High* 5)

In 1988, the scene reads:

> "Brer Fox! How you doing today?" Brer Rabbit called up.
> "Busy. Ain't got time to be flapping gums with you." (*Uncle Remus* 4)

The language of the second passage uses the natural speech rhythms and humorous language of African American oral tradition absent from the earlier book. It is Lester's contention that the story resides in the voice:

> Without the voice there would be only summaries of stories, and a story is not merely plot. The Uncle Remus stories scarcely vary in plot. They are trickster stories in which one animal tricks another. It is the voice of the storyteller that maintains our interest as readers. ("Storyteller's Voice" 71)

Although Lester has titled his more recent retellings "Uncle Remus" stories, Uncle Remus appears only as the narrative voice. Thus, Lester has changed the stories' perspective and tone. Unlike the earlier stories by Joel Chandler Harris, there is no characterization of Uncle Remus in Lester's tales. Rather, it is Uncle Remus's voice the reader hears in his mind as he reads the stories. In our personal correspondence, Lester wrote:

> [. . .] when people read me, they are not as aware that they're reading as they are that they are listening. I think one thing that distinguishes my retellings from those of others is that I do not write in the disembodied voice of a storyteller. My storyteller has a personality. He puts in comments about himself, his likes and dislikes, etc. What I try to do in print is recreate the storytelling experience as a relationship between teller and listeners. I see writing as a way of creating relationship(s) so through voice I think I overcome the limitations of print. (e-mail 3)

Lester changed details rather than the plots of the Uncle Remus tales "because I thought it was important to bring the traditional tales into the present, so my innovations had to do with how the stories were told, but I did not change any of the story lines" (e-mail 2). Lester has also discussed the difficulties he had with his editor over the contemporary references in his Uncle Remus tales. His Brer Rabbit eats "ham, pork chops, mince pie, fried chicken, hamburgers, and french fries" (*More Uncle Remus* 53) and dreams about buying a red truck (60). When he goes into town, he buys his wife a "coffeepot and a copy of Paris Vogue, and he got the children the tin plate, tin cups, and some Star Wars underwear" (62). Defending his choices, he states that there are contemporary references in the original Chandler tales, some recognizable today, some not: "That is the paradox: the universality of the stories is only revealed if the voice of the stories is specific, if it is immersed in the blackness of yesterday and today. The way to the universal is through the particular" ("Storyteller's Voice" 73).

Lester chooses his stories based on several criterion, the most important being whether he likes the story; only then will he want to share it with others. Next, he asks whether he can do a good job of retelling, and finally, whether the story will communicate to contemporary children. In all three cases he has no rules but relies instead on his instinct (e-mail 2).

In a 1998 speech to the International Reading Association, Lester questioned why race and ethnicity are equated with personal identity. There are African Americans who believe only they are capable of writing African American literature and women who argue that men cannot write about female characters. Lester finds a "small truth" in this, stating that having grown up in the South with a minister father enables him to tell the Uncle Remus tales with "a certain voice and with a certain rhythm" ("Authentic" 2). Yet he does not claim exclusive ownership of these stories or the right to decide that someone else's telling is not authentic. By taking the story out of the traditional context and writing it down, he recognizes that he, too, is no longer true to the original culture. "Putting a story into a book freezes it" (2).

Authenticity for Lester is multidimensional:

> As a writer it is my responsibility to research thoroughly, to provide notes that tell what my sources were and how I may or may not have changed the material and why. As a writer it is my responsibility to write in such a way that I show respect for the culture from which the stories come. And I am also responsible to the story as an expression of the heart's drama. My way of doing this is not necessarily more "authentic." The authenticity lies in telling the story with love and joy for the story as well as love and joy for those to whom the story is being told. ("Authentic" 3)

Careful research, respect for the original culture, an attempt to maintain the balance between the original oral tale and the demands of contemporary readers—these are the themes running through all three authors' comments. Yet there is clearly a third force at work that makes the balancing act all the more difficult: editorial intervention. Miller changed his story's ending to suit the editor's taste for closure. Kurtz rejected authenticity to create protagonists editors considered suitable for American children. Only Lester resisted his editor and refused to eliminate contemporary references, holding that they were essential to the narrative voice and an authentic part of the folk tradition. Lester is the only author who is from the culture. Perhaps he and his editor feel more comfortable with his decisions about voice and authenticity. When forced to weigh fidelity to the original story against the chance to be published, other writers with the best intentions may sacrifice principle to public.

Yet, as we have seen, modern children's book authors do not take their task lightly, no matter what the pressures of the market. They are aware of the oral tradition and make use of many of its conventions to lend authenticity to their work. At the same time, they develop their own individual methods of storytelling based on their personal responses to a particular story. William Miller adds character motivation and imaginative additions. Jane Kurtz retains the premise of the original tale, while creating child characters that are empathetic for American children. Julius Lester invents a unique voice that embodies the authenticity of the past and the relevance of his readers' modern culture. There are no formulas. Each writer develops his own unique method. Still, these authors share a common purpose. We can argue about cultural authenticity, who has the right to tell a story, and even whether an oral story should be written down, but for these authors, it is the story itself that remains the central focus. Whether oral or written, the final question is always "was it a good story?" As Lester states so well:

> Learning about other cultures belongs to the realm of information. There are books that tell about the foods, customs, dances, music, etc., etc. of various cultures. But the primary purpose of story is not the transmission of information. The *primary* purpose of story is one heart touching another. ("Authentic" 3)

Works Cited

Baker, Rob and Ellen Draper. "If One Thing Stands, Another Will Stand Beside It: An Interview with Chinua Achebe." *Parabola* 17.3 (1992). Online. EBSCOHost. 13 July 1998.

Bruchac, Joseph. "The Continuing Circle: Native American Storytelling Past and Present." *Who Says? Essays on Pivotal Issues in Contemporary Storytelling.* Ed. Carol Birch and Melissa A. Heckler. Little Rock, AR: August House, 1996. 91–105.

Coburn, Jewell Reinhart with Duong Van Quyen. "Methods of Translating Folk Literature from One Culture to Another." *A Sea of Upturned Faces: Proceedings of the Third Pacific Rim Literature Conference on Children's Literature.* Ed. Winifred Ragsdale. Matuchen, NJ: Scarecrow, 1989. 178–87.

Heckler, Melissa A. "Two Traditions." *Who Says? Essays on Pivotal Issues in Contemporary Storytelling.* Ed. Carol Birch and Melissa A. Heckler. Little Rock, AR: August House, 1996. 15–34.

Hughes, Langston and Arna Bontemps. *The Book of Negro Folklore.* New York: Dodd Mead, 1958. 19–20, 345–47.

Kurtz, Jane. E-mail to the author. 17 July 1998.

———. "Finding a Place to Call Home." *Writer's Digest* 74.4 Apr. 1994: 71–72.

———. "Multicultural Children's Books: The Subtle Tug of War." *School Library Journal* 42.2 (1992): 40–41.

———. *Pulling the Lion's Tail.* New York: Simon, 1995.

Lester, Julius. E-mail to the author. 18 July 1998.

———. *The Knee-High Man and Other Tales.* New York: Dial, 1972.

———. *More Tales of Uncle Remus: Further Adventures of Brer Rabbit, His Friends, Enemies and Others.* New York: Dial, 1988.

———. "The Storyteller's Voice: Reflections on the Rewriting of Uncle Remus." *The Voice of the Narrator in Children's Literature: Insights from Writers and Critics.* Ed. Charlotte F. Otten and Gary D. Schmidt. New York: Greenwood, 1989. 69–73.

————. "What Makes Stories Authentic?" Speech to the International Reading Association. May 1998.

McGillis, Roderick. "Reactivating the Ear: Orality and Children's Poetry." *The Voice of the Narrator in Children's Literature: Insights from Writers and Critics.* Ed. Charlotte F. Otten and Gary D. Schmidt. New York: Greenwood, 1989. 252–59.

Miller, William. *The Knee-High Man.* Salt Lake City, UT: Gibbs Smith, 1996.

————. Personal interview. 23 July 1998.

Muller, Carrel. "Point of View in Children's Books." *The Writer* 110.9 (1997) Online. EBSCOHost. 13 July 1998.

Sawyer, Ruth. *The Way of the Storyteller.* 2nd ed. New York: Viking, 1962.

Sergi, Jennifer. "Storytelling: Tradition and Preservation in Louise Erdich's *Tracks.*" *World Literature Today* 16.2 (1992). Online. EBSCOHost. 13 July 1998.

Yolen, Jane. *Favorite Folktales from Around the World.* New York: Pantheon, 1986.

26

Students' Construction of Knowledge about Native Americans through Children's Literature

Lois M. Campbell

A passage is read. A question is asked. What has the learner understood about the text? As a teacher-researcher, I have found this "routine" of understanding a child's text comprehension to be somewhat meaningless from both the learner's and teacher's point of view. Furthermore, I see these actions as promoting a view of learning that is diametrically opposed to my understanding of how children learn from their world about them. Therefore, I will present the reader-educator with the process I utilize in my classroom to discern a learner's knowledge of text comprehension. I wish to specifically focus on my students' understanding of Native Americans and determine how their knowledge of Native Americans evolved as a result of classroom instruction of children's literature. It is my hope that as you read about my experiences, you will hear the voices of the children attempting to make meaning from the texts in order to develop an understanding of Native Americans. First, I give a bit of background about my teaching and research philosophy.

The constructivist view of learning has at its center the epistemology of the German sociologist and economist Max Weber who pointed toward the importance of "meaning as constructed by individuals in their attempt to make sense of the world" (Driver and Oldham 106). Driver and Oldham have suggested that "making sense" not only depends on the situation in which the individual is involved but also on "the individual's purposes and active construction of meaning" and that prior knowledge affects the way phenomena are "perceived and interpreted" (106). Nussbaum and Sharoni-Dagan observed that learners "tend to construct meaning of their direct observation of physical phenomena as well as of socially transmitted accounts of physical phenomena" (99). In their work, Driver and Oldham also indicated that learners construct meaning through their natural world—much of their "meaning" has been constructed long before formal classroom instruction.

In 1989, Fosnot defined constructivism through four principles: (1) knowledge consists of past constructions; (2) constructions come about through assimilation and accommodation; (3) learning is an organic process of invention rather than a mechanical process of accumulation; and (4) meaningful learning occurs through reflection and resolution of cognitive conflict and, thus, serves to negate earlier, incomplete levels of understanding. Thus, learners make sense of their worlds through past ideas that transform, organize, and interpret the learner's experiences. As Fosnot states, "cognitive development comes about through the same processes as biological development—through self-regulation or adaptation" (19).

The learning model established earlier by Piaget (1977) coincides with Fosnot's second principle: "[the] logical framework or scheme we use to interpret or organize information" (19) allows us to assimilate and accommodate new information; if that framework is contradicted or put into disequilibrium, the learner accommodates or adapts old concepts to develop a higher level theory or logic. This contrasts with the empiricist view of learning as accumulating facts. Teachers who adopt empiricist research usually accept a preplanned curriculum of the content area or skill that divides knowledge into subparts and sequences skills from the simple to the most complex. Such methodology suggests that learning can be programmatically planned.

This empiricist philosophy does not allow learners to actively construct meaning. Rather, the learners are "passive, in need of motivation, and affected by motivation" (Fosnot 18). Such a model would not support Fosnot's third principle: learners must have experiences that will allow them to develop new constructions of meaning. Fosnot implies that the learner must take an active role in the learning process, and he further maintains that learners construct meaning from the contradiction or cognitive conflict encountered. Through his four principles, Fosnot outlines the natural process of constructing a method that will challenge the students' past construction of meaning.

This idea has also been termed "frameworks, cognitive structures, belief systems, and conceptualizations," and seems "to refer to situations in which students are attempting to make sense of relatively large bodies of organized conceptual public knowledge or using the knowledge that they have internalized to generate explanations of their experiences in the world" (Pines and West 584). Taba et al. present concepts as highly generalized abstractions that have the "power to organize and synthesize large numbers of specific facts and ideas" (12). Throughout my work for this study, concepts were defined as the ideas that learners constructed concerning text as they participated in and with literature in a fourth-grade classroom.

My classroom study may be best defined within the theoretical framework of phenomenology and constructivism. German philosopher Edmund H. Husserl argued that phenomenology addresses the question, "What is the structure and essence of experience of this phenomena for these people" (Patton 69)? Tesch has suggested that the purpose of phenomenological research is to "probe into the richness of the human experience and to illuminate the complexity of individual perception" (5). Yet, to understand this human experience, it must be described, explained, and interpreted: "phenomenologists focus on how we put together the phenomena we experience in such a way as to make sense of the world" (Patton 69). Therefore, the responsibility of the phenomenologist is to utilize an empathetic understanding of the participant's point of view in the process of interpretation. Thus, in order to "grasp the meanings of a person's behavior" (Bogdan and Taylor 14), the phenomenologist must attempt to "reproduce in one's own mind the feelings, motives and thoughts behind the actions of others" (13). I have used these principles in an attempt to reproduce my fourth-grade students' understanding of Native Americans as they constructed knowledge concerning Native Americans through the literature presented in their elementary classroom environment.

As the door of my classroom is opened to you, the reader, you will find a room devoid of desks and the "standard" classroom arrangement of desks. As a constructivist educator, I am a firm believer that children construct knowledge from their environment and from the activities in which they participate. Part of my belief system also holds to the idea that children are better able to construct this knowledge through interactive learning with fellow learners. I have found this interactive learning to be constrained by the imposed structure of classroom seating arrangements, particularly desks. I, therefore, have developed an open environment where children are free to move about but have places and spaces that they might utilize as they develop their understanding and meaning of concepts focused on throughout the day.

Given that children are in need of their personal space, children do have assigned "cubbies" in closets where they can store their materials. They also have assigned table areas when we are in need of large group instruction. I have purposely assigned these areas so that I become accountable for the children's presence in my classroom and so that I "force" learners to develop social/educational interactions with their peers throughout their time in my classroom. To encourage the children to move about the room, I have provided them with plastic "shoe boxes" for their supplies. These boxes are stored nightly in their cubbies, but in the morning are brought with them to the table area or any other work space area where they are engaged in work on a project. Thus, children are not constrained by their desks; on the other hand, they have the opportunity to maintain their privacy within their supply boxes.

As I attempt to provide a constructivist setting for my students, I have attempted to be aware of their various academic and socioeconomic backgrounds. This class was "labeled" as a pull-out room; children who are in need of extended resource room support participated in my class during the content areas of science, social studies, music, art, and physical education. Given my double license in elementary and special education, I usually have children placed with me who have much difficulty with their academics, particularly in reading and mathematics. Perhaps due to my understanding of academic accommodation, I often have children from the gifted and talented program placed in my classroom as well. In this particular classroom (where the research took place), there were three children labeled as gifted and talented, two children labeled as pull-out, and three children labeled as learning disabled who were meant to be provided with educational support by the resource room throughout the day. Additionally, there were three children who were "in line" to be tested for resource room services and two children with diverse ESL skills. In addition to these varying academic levels, these children were also diverse in their socioeconomic levels. Approximately two-thirds of the twenty-five students enrolled in my classroom were supported through some variation of the government-subsidized housing and food program. Of this two-thirds (approximately seventeen students), twelve of the students received both "free hot breakfast and lunch" through the government program. The remaining children in my classroom ranged from middle to high socioeconomic status for this suburban/rural area of north central Indiana. With the view of the classroom in mind, we can consider literature as it is taught in my classroom but particularly with regard to a thematic view of Native Americans.

As an elementary teacher of many years, I have been exposed to a variety of teaching methods for utilization during reading instruction. Over the years, as I have refined and developed my personal understandings of pedagogy and have persevered through the "latest" techniques; I have attempted to help children make meaning from texts. In 1999, I was fortunate to have a team teacher in literature. Her graduate work had been in children's literature, and she had been trained in the Four-Block Method (see Cunningham, Hall, and Defee) of reading instruction. As a team, we began to develop action plans or lessons in ways that we felt (pedagogically) would help children have better experiences with text and able to construct deeper meaning from text.

Throughout our first year of instruction, we developed themes that we used during the year. These themes centered on other themes being utilized simultaneously in science and social studies. Our plan was simply to provide students with experiences with text, based on a theme, and further develop that theme through writing activities. The initial year of implementation went well with the children providing a great deal of writing about their experiences with text; however, I was concerned the children were not "reading enough" literature through their experiences.

In the second year of implementation, the year of the study I am now discussing, I had a different partner for team teaching. Though I was concerned about the lack of continuity, I felt that our combined experiences would allow for appropriate instruction and a continued effort in my pedagogical endeavors. As the school year began, I was fortunate to attend a Four-Block Method conference led by Patricia Cunningham. Through that experience, I was further able to explore my understanding of this approach to reading as well as interact with other educators who were concerned about literature and reading instruction. Based on all these experiences, I developed the method of instruction used in my classroom for this study.

During this study, we again chose themes that would be coordinated with our social studies and science topics throughout the school year. In fourth grade, the state-provided focus for social studies is on Indiana history, so we were easily able to weave a theme of Native American literature throughout the school year. Having done this, we then designed our "technique" of instruction based on experiences with children, professional literature, and pedagogical beliefs. Our basic method of instruction was as follows—utilize a primary text for instruction on the theme. We would then surround that text with a variety of support literature on various reading levels so that students could have multiple experiences with texts on the same theme. Finally, we provided a variety of methods in which students could interact with the text and other children about their understanding of their reading. This might include partner reading, small group reading, reading with the teacher, or individual reading. No matter the text or theme, students were expected to reread the selections many times throughout the week(s) spent with a particular primary text. Furthermore, students were always called on to write about their reading in some manner, for example, through journals, pop-up books, or informational posters. Throughout the entire process, the main idea of our instruction was to provide students with multiple experiences using a variety of texts, discussions of the texts, and activities with the texts. In doing so, we were attempting to help the children construct a deeper understanding of the shared text than in their previous experiences with basal readers or "literature circles" supported by worksheets.

Having spent a number of years as a special education teacher on the Navajo Indian Reservation, I am acutely aware, perhaps more so than my other colleagues, of the misunderstandings and incorrect information presented to and understood by many children in classrooms throughout the United States. I have felt the constant battle of trying to help learners conceptually understand the lives of Native Americans without the constant reference to Thanksgiving; "how it used to be" when Indians and Europeans first encountered each other; misrepresentations of Indian dress and conduct. My personal experiences have caused me to be concerned with the lack of respect and understanding of Native American culture often afforded through mainstream society in the United States and the lack of appropriate instruction in schools. With this in mind, I attempted to provide the students in my classroom with a broader view of Native American cultures and traditions from my understandings and experiences. Therefore, as I began that year, I attempted to ascertain my students' initial understandings of Native American culture.

As I introduce myself each year to my students, I provide them with a "brief" life history of myself, including my years in the Southwest. As I have documented my students' initial thoughts and beliefs concerning Native Americans, I have rarely been surprised by their initial view of the Navajo tribe. Such views are documented in this transcript from the opening week of school.

S: So, you taught on an Indian reservation?

T: Yes.

S: What was *that* like? Do they still wear feathers?

T: No, feathers are only worn for ceremonial purposes. And, what was it like? Well, I really enjoyed teaching out there.

S: What do the kids wear to school?

T: They wear the same things that you wear.

S: You're kidding!

—Transcription of classroom conversation, 8/2000

In assessing their prior knowledge of Native Americans, I am often struck by my students' limited understanding of Native American culture. Note in the transcript the student's reference to "feathers" and what the children might wear. As I have further probed my students' understanding of Native Americans, I have found that it is limited to their understanding of early history in the United States and usually focuses on tribal names such as Sioux, Cherokee, or Apache. (Note that none of these tribes were located in Indiana where this study took place.) Furthermore, their understandings of these tribal names are in name only; they have no understanding of tribal history, geographical location, or current status in the United States. Additionally, their knowledge of Native Americans has been sadly limited to their education through the educational system, via Thanksgiving celebration or the Anglo-Saxon view of Native peoples' early encounters with explorers to the "New World."

During the first two weeks of school, I wanted to provide my students with a variety of experiences so that I could discern their abilities to work together as we explored literature in a variety of ways. Science and social studies were focused on the geological formations of Indiana and the first peoples of Indiana. This allowed me a wonderful avenue for the introduction of Native American literature. In our initial experiences with text, I provided the students with a wide variety of authors, both Native and non-Native Americans, so that students might understand various viewpoints concerning Native Americans. I also chose texts that would demonstrate Native American historical stories, informational texts on various tribes, as well as fiction selections set in various tribal locations throughout the United States. For the initial experience I provided my twenty-five students with over eighty pieces of literature.

During my introduction to this material, I referred the students to our initial understandings of Native Americans in Indiana. I then explained that we were going to spend time exploring our understanding of Native Americans through the different books we had available to us. Furthermore, since I was not aware of their "reading levels," I opted to have the students work in small groups. Please note that I was aware of one student's academic struggle with reading and wanted to create a safe environment for him to explore text in his first encounter with me during our literature time. Therefore, I selected what I felt was the "safest" avenue for initial exploration of the text.

Each table group was provided with a variety of texts concerning Native Americans at different reading levels. Students were encouraged to take time to explore the various texts with their table groups and then select a text with which they were comfortable in reading. Because I wanted to supplement my understanding of my students' ideas about Native Americans, I provided my students with an "exploration page" where they could read the text and jot down their understandings of the text and its content. Furthermore, students were able to tell me their initial ideas about Native Americans and their beliefs about Native Americans after they had read the text. The results of this initial experience demonstrate my students' early views of Native peoples and their understandings of text in a dramatic manner.

As inexperienced readers and writers, these students initially struggled with determining themes of text, as well as text summaries. Students would often provide brief lines from the text or a "generic" theme that was loosely tied to some sections of the story. For example, many children selected pieces by Paul Goble that were retellings of Native stories. Throughout the students' interpretations of the themes of these texts, students would provide brief explanations of the text such as "always go for your dreams" or "never give up." When I tried to have the children explain these themes further, I found their under-standings of the text limited, but, more so, their ability to explain the text was limited by their previous experiences with literature discussions. With my co-teacher, I tried to solicit different responses from the children by asking questions such as, "Why do you think the author wrote this story?" or "Why do you think this book was written?" These questions provided a little deeper although limited view of the students' thoughts about the text. Such explanations are as follows (please note that this text contains students' writings, includ-ing spelling and grammar mechanics):

- "The book was written because the auther might of liked Indians, and wanted to write a book about a Indian tribe."
- "Because he thought it would be a good story, and it was stuck in his head mabe."
- "Because he likes Indians and buffalos and he wanted to write something enterest-ing and something that would be fun for kids."

—*(students' writings, September 2000)*

An initial view of students' understandings of Native Americans was also reflected in these early writings. Students appeared to view all the texts as historical and felt Native Ameri-cans are no longer present in our contemporary society. Therefore, students' texts were often in past tense with references made to Native Americans as couched within myths of Native American culture.

- "Because the Indianas where kind to the nachter. They made special midicens. One indian heald a muskrat."
- "This book is to learn us what they do for a living. It teaces us how they servive."

—*(students' writings, September 2000)*

As my co-teacher and I planned the remainder of the school year, we discussed ways we could help children develop deeper meaning from their texts. We were determined to help the children "move away" from their previously held beliefs about Native Americans and construct a more accurate view of Native Americans, their culture, and traditions.

For the remainder of the year, my colleague and I focused on providing the students with multiple experiences with a variety of texts. Because some students had limited abili-ties, we wanted to afford a variety of opportunities in which students would read a text mul-tiple times. Our pedagogical knowledge informed us that multiple experiences with text in a variety of reading opportunities (individually, small group or with a teacher) would be ben-eficial for all students. Students with limited abilities were able to hear the text many times and were able to practice reading and interpreting the text with strong support and guidance. Students with higher abilities found the multiple experiences with text and time for them to reread the stories for details stimulated their intellectual abilities. Furthermore, they were allowed opportunities for individual exploration of related texts on similar themes.

As the year progressed, our teaching team worked along the themes provided within the social studies historical context as we selected other texts. For example, as we studied Indiana's involvement in the Civil War, we read a variety of books, fiction and nonfiction, about the Civil War and the Underground Railroad. As we moved into the period of immigration in Indiana, we selected media that focused on the theme of immigration in the United States. In an attempt to maintain our goal of helping children construct a more accurate knowledge of Native Americans, we often referred to the historical "happenings" of Native Americans in Indiana during these time periods as well as Native Americans throughout U.S. history. As we completed the school year, our themes were beginning to center on "Indiana Today." With this, we explored the changes Indiana had experienced over time and the status of the state today. We again connected to the theme of Native Americans, both in Indiana and throughout the United States. In an attempt to come full circle in our understanding of Native Americans, we opted to provide a final project for the students. This project, like the first project of the year, would utilize a variety of literature. Students were involved in creating posters to demonstrate their understanding of the text and understanding of Native American culture.

During the final months of school, our themes were focusing on environmental issues in science and the historical changes in the environment in our area, particularly our local river. We utilized a variety of literature with this, including Lynn Cherry's *A River Ran Wild* and Jean Craighead George's two ecological mysteries. We were addressing themes of traditions and honoring these traditions, and so we utilized *Totem Pole*. My colleague and I, again, chose to address the theme of Native Americans throughout this time period; both *A River Ran Wild* and *Totem Pole* focused on Native Americans and were used as central texts. As a culminating Native American project, we provided the students with approximately ninety books about Native Americans. However, this time, we chose to select primarily nonfiction texts to help children with their understandings of Native American life and culture. The project required the students to work together in small groups and to focus on one Native American group assigned to them. We purposefully selected "lesser" known groups as well as the more prominent tribes in Anglo-Saxon culture, such as Sioux (Lakota) and Navajo.

Students worked in table groups and surveyed the variety of materials available to them. Based on their readings of the various books, students were asked to put together final projects (posters) that described their understandings of their Native American group. Students were required to address informational questions on geography, as well as questions concerning a brief history of the people and their current status and lives in the United States. The final projects provided some interesting interpretations of Native Americans today. In their final projects, students were able to fairly accurately define some of the broader historical points of the Native Americans whom they studied. It was interesting to hear the various comments as they researched the historical context of their tribes. Though I could see that their ideas were changing with the ongoing experiences with text, I noticed that students were still holding on to some fairly strong mythical views of Native peoples, as noted in my remarks to their displays:

- "Hey—guess what? Did you know that these guys never really lived in tipis?"
- Dr. C (viewing a poster): "[. . .] the Seminoles really started as much bigger groups of people. But, I still don't see why they wear these outfits like this."

- "This is interesting how the Inuit people survived in the Arctic. Do you think they still live in igloos?"

—(Conversations with students, April–May 2001)

One should note that students' views of Native people still hold on to some strongly held views and beliefs about clothing and housing. Despite a yearlong effort of dispelling myths, students were having difficulty moving beyond their previously held concepts. Furthermore, the students struggled with keeping historical evidence separate from their cognitive belief systems.

The strongest evidence of the lack of change in students' belief systems occurred when they attempted to define their understanding of Native Americans and their lives today. Though some of the children were able to make changes in their belief systems and could fairly accurately describe life today, many children still held strongly to their personal beliefs about Native Americans. This is evidenced in their descriptions of earlier Native American life (which are historically accurate), and their use of present-tense verbs, suggesting that such past descriptions are accurate by today's standards.

- "The Navajo still live on reservations in the southwest. They believe that they should not leave the Sacred Mountain area."
- "The Seminole are known for their colorful clothing, which they still wear today."
- "Many of the Sioux Indians used to participate in the Ghost Dance. They still believe that the shirts they wear can prevent them from being hurt by arrows."

—(Excerpts from text of final projects, May 2001)

As a teacher-researcher, I was interested in the students' use of present-tense verbs, suggesting that at the end of our study their cognitive understanding still held to historical misunderstandings of the Native peoples. Such texts caused me to question the students' view of Native Americans as "reality" in contemporary America. My interpretation of their final projects suggests that students culturally group Native Americans without regard to individuality (i.e., ALL Indians believe that . . .). Furthermore, my students' perceptions of dress still suggested that they believe Native people wear traditional dress on a daily basis (see foregoing quote on the Seminole).

After a year of applied effort to develop students' thoughts and beliefs about Native Americans, I was somewhat, admittedly, frustrated with the end results. My classroom research strongly suggests that learners hold to their belief systems and have difficulty assimilating new information into those already embedded beliefs. Just as Driver and Oldham indicate, learners construct meaning about the natural world; much of the meaning of these students had been constructed long before formal classroom instruction. Pines and West had earlier described learners holding strongly to their views despite teacher interventions, resulting in a clash of ideas between the instructional presentation and popular culture's views. They concluded, "The difficulty is evident in any conflict situation. [. . .] If the teacher is not aware of this, then the best that can be achieved will be that students will continue to hold their previous beliefs about the world and the way it works" (589).

We need to consider ways in which children view their construction of knowledge. For many children, schooling has become a place where knowledge is acquired. Ideas are not necessarily constructed. Driver and Oldham have argued that making sense not only depends on the situation in which the individual is involved but also on "the individual's purposes and active construction of meaning" and the effect prior knowledge has on the way phenomena are "perceived and interpreted" (106). Perhaps the children's personal understandings of knowledge construction were also affecting their understanding of Native Americans.

Finding ways for children to develop a more correct view of their knowledge of Native Americans provides a challenge to teachers and researchers. This study suggests that further explorations in children's conceptual understanding of literature are needed, as well as cultural studies of Native people in their literary representations and studies of students' willingness to revise their perceptions based on their readings of multicultural literature. My reflective practice as a researcher suggests that my colleagues and I need to explore the expansion of our pedagogical and content knowledge in the area of children's literature. These thoughts and decision-making strategies were suggested by Wilson, Shulman, and Richert's description of pedagogical content knowledge in 1987. Perhaps nothing has changed. Teachers need to utilize research information about content and pedagogy as they design an active instructional program that combines best practices and literature for learners involved in constructivist learning. Teachers must reflect on their understandings of content knowledge and, perhaps, restructure their content knowledge to provide learners with opportunities for constructivist activities. Further explorations in both teacher and learner knowledge will provide teacher-researchers with avenues to investigate children's understanding of literature and to ascertain how youngsters develop more accurate meanings of Native Americans as they share literature in the curriculum.

Works Cited

Bogdan, R. and S. J. Taylor. *Introduction to Qualitative Research Methods*. New York: John Wiley, 1975.

Cherry, L. *A River Ran Wild: An Environmental History*. San Diego: Harcourt Brace Jovanovich, 1982.

Cohen, C. L. *The Mud Pony: A Traditional Skidi Pawnee Tale*. New York: Scholastic, 1988.

Cohlene, T. *Little Firefly*. Vero Beach, FL: Rourke Corporation, 1990.

Cunningham, P. M., D. P. Hall, and M. Defee. "Nonability Grouped, Multilevel Instruction: A Year in a First Grade Classroom." *Reading Teacher* 44 (1991): 566–71.

———. "Nonability Grouped, Multilevel Instruction: Eight Years Later." *Reading Teacher* (1998): 51.

Driver, R. H. and V. Oldham, "A Constructivist Approach to Curriculum Development in Science." *Studies in Science Education* 12 (1986): 105–22.

Fosnot, C. T. *Enquiring Teachers, Enquiring Learners: A Constructivist Approach for Teaching*. New York: Teachers College Press, 1989.

George, J. C. *The Case of the Missing Cutthroats: An Eco Mystery*. New York: HarperCollins Publishers, 1999.

———. *The Fire Bug Connection: An Ecological Mystery*. New York: HarperCollins Publishers, 1993.

Goble, P. *Buffalo Woman*. Scarsdale, NY: Bradbury Press, 1984.

———. *The Gift of the Sacred Dog*. Scarsdale, NY: Bradbury Press, 1980.

———. *The Girl Who Loved Wild Horses*. Scarsdale, NY: Bradbury Press, 1978.

———. *Iktomi and the Ducks: A Plains Indian Story*. New York: Orchard Books, 1990.

———. *Star Boy*. Scarsdale, NY: Bradbury Press, 1983.

Goldin, B. D. *The Girl Who Lived with the Bears.* San Diego: Harcourt Brace, 1997.

Hoyt-Goldsmith, D. *Totem Pole.* New York: Holiday House, 1990.

Landau, E. *The Sioux.* New York: Grolier Publishing, 1991.

Lund, B. *The Cherokee Indians.* New York: Capstone Press, 1997.

Lund, B. *The Chumash Indians.* New York: Capstone Press, 1997.

Kavasch, E. B. *Lakota Sioux Children and Elders Talk Together.* New York: Rosen Publishing Group, 1999.

Nussbaum, J. and N. Sharoni-Dagan. "Changes in Second Grade Children's Preconceptions about the Earth as a Cosmic Body Resulting from a Short Series of Audio-Tutorial Lessons." *Science Education* 67 (1983): 99–114.

Patton, M. D. *Qualitative Evaluation and Research Methods.* 1st ed. Beverly Hills, CA: Sage, 1980.

Piaget, J. *The Development of Thought: Equilibration of Cognitive Structures.* New York: Viking Press, 1977.

Pines, A. L. and L. H. T. West. "Conceptual Understanding and Science Learning. An Interpretation of Research within a Sources-of Knowledge Framework." *Science Education* 70 (1986): 583–604.

Taba, H., M. C. Durkin, J. R. Fraenkel, and A. H. McNaughton. *A Teacher's Handbook to Elementary Social Studies: An Inductive Approach.* Reading, MA: Addison-Wesley, 1971.

Tesch, R. *Phenomenological Studies: A Critical Analysis of Their Nature and Procedures.* Paper presented at the Annual Meeting of the American Educational Research Association, New Orleans, LA, 1984.

Wilson, S. M., L. S. Shulman, and A. E. Richert. "150 Different Ways of Knowing: Representations of Knowledge in Teaching." *Exploring Teachers' Thinking.* Ed. J. Calderhead. Sussex: Holt, Rinehart, and Winston, 1987. 104–24.

27

Do Young Readers Need Happy Endings?

Leslie Murrill

"The prince and his bride rode off into the distance on the white stallion . . . and they lived happily ever after." The End.

As a child growing up in the 1960s and early 1970s, I read and listened to many stories with happy endings. Whether the books included a prince and his bride or contemporary children, the characters in my stories rose beyond conflicts and danger to resolve their problems and look toward a bright future. This happy ending convention in books for the young is confirmed by others in education and literary criticism as well. Walter Pape writes that traditional children's books "end happily, however badly they bite" (179). Suzanne Reid describes her expectation when approaching a text for young readers: "because this was a novel for young adults, the main characters would prevail and their problems would be solved in the end" (10). At least for my generation and the generation of my parents, the frequent occurrence of happy endings in books for young people has led many of us to expect them. Because of this, an important consideration is whether or not we perceive happy endings to be the appropriate "norm."

Because children's literature has the unique status of being written and critiqued *by* adults *for* children, it necessarily means that adults have the power to determine what will be made available to young readers; what is "appropriate" for them. This positioning allows authors, editors, critics, teachers, and parents to have a "say so" in prescribing what their children should read—and whether or not happy endings should be requisite of the stories that children and adolescents read. Perusal of most young adult public library collections today reveals that alternative endings, as well as happy ones, have been made available to readers for the past twenty years. Opinions of literary critics, English educators, and authors of young adult works differ concerning the acceptability of alternative endings for today's young readers. Some hold that exposure to less than happy endings can impact a child toward a bleak view of the world. Others maintain that reading about characters who encounter difficulties and work through them is an important point of identification for young adolescents particularly. Additionally, there are those who purport that young readers should have access to endings that satisfy the themes in the literature itself, whether the conclusions are necessarily happy or tragic. Although I want to examine these suppositions, I cannot start until I consider the child reader's expectations.

Peter Hunt argues that "the adult eye is not necessarily a perfect instrument for discerning if a children's book has value or not" (57). As well intentioned as any adult may be, we oversimplify the child's mind if we claim to know all that the child needs. Jill May, in her consideration of reader response, writes, "I discovered that the children had very definite tastes that often conflicted with the adults who read to them" (160). The "real readers" of children's books are children themselves. For me to fully consider whether or not children "need" happy endings, I need to look at what children themselves have to say about alternative story endings. To do this, I have collected reader responses from seventh- and eighth-grade students who have read *Park's Quest* or *Tuck Everlasting.* Their reactions provide a window into the attitudes, wants, and "needs" that are part of who they are. But first, let's begin with the opinions of professionals working in children's literature.

Perspectives represented in the professional literature range from those who view happy endings as a necessary element of books for the young to those who are equally supportive of alternative endings to stories. The former speak of hope as an inherent quality of the children's literature genre. One author writes, "Hope—or optimism—is what art and literature is about. It's certainly what children's literature is all about" (Terris 17). Others maintain that the desire for happy endings to stories is linked to a child's desire for security in the midst of a chaotic world (Pape 181). While these perspectives speak toward the need *for* an element of happiness, there are others who speak *against* any ending which is other than happy. Representative statements in this realm come from teachers, parents, and critics alike.

Marvin Hoffman, a high school English teacher, quotes a parent of three children who has asked him, "Why are all the books you read in school so dark and gloomy? Isn't there something less bleak you can expose the kids to?" (14). Donald Gallo reports that a high school social studies teacher told him, "The endings of *The Chocolate War* and *I Am the Cheese* have depressed me to such an extent that I will not read another book by [Robert Cormier . . .] unless I read the ending first so that I will know if it's safe emotionally" (34). Writer Karina Worlton maintains that "negative literature tends to foster negative attitudes" (488), holding that reading this type of literature creates unpleasant feelings and that children should be given "positive, uplifting literature" (488). Finally, Caroline Hunt writes that adolescents are particularly vulnerable to depression and dark thoughts and cites experts in psychology and children's and adolescent literature who look for what Lynne Rosenthal calls "images of hope to help young readers negotiate the transition to adulthood" (qtd. in "Dead Athletes" 244).

Running through all of these remarks is the perception that children and adolescents "need" to be uplifted by what they read—to find positive, hopeful messages in their literature. This perception is not shared by all, however. Other critics, authors, and teachers have cautioned that providing young readers with exclusively happy stories oversimplifies a child's sense of reality. Elizabeth Law states that "writers for children often forget to respect their audience," speaking against condescension in literature and "dumbing down" to the young reader (15–17). Children who are old enough to read, and particularly adolescents, are not only surrounded by the "real world" on a daily basis but are also aware of the many "negative" aspects of life. Suzanne Reid comments on the work of author Cynthia Voigt who, "like most other writers of young adult literature since the 1960's, recognizes that childhood as a time of innocence and safety is a fiction available only to a privileged few" (157). Kathy Headley, an education professor, quotes author Robert Cormier who defends the harsh look at reality in his books: "Kids know the language they hear and what's going on in the locker rooms and the school buses. They know my books are mild in comparison" (34). If young readers are provided only with happy endings, they will soon realize that their literature does not mirror the realities in their lives. Ellen Howard, the author of *When Daylight Comes,* reflects on her own hesitancy to include reference to physical abuse in this book for adolescents. She writes:

> I told myself it was an unsuitable thing to put in a book for children. I was certain I made the right decision. And I felt, and I feel to this day, like a liar. Here I suppose is where I made a decision about writing for children. I decided I believe in telling children the truth, even when the truth is unpleasant. I believe that children have a right to know about their world. I believe they cannot learn to recognize and rise above evil if they are not taught it exists. But I decided these things *after* I had written and published *When Daylight Comes.* In that book, I did not tell the whole truth, and the leaving it out was a lie. (8–9)

Howard's commentary includes a rationale for sharing the "unpleasant" with children for the purpose of shaping their values and beliefs about good and evil. Others hold to similar lines of thought, all in some way related to the idea that children can benefit from exposure to "heavy" issues. Several speak of the importance of young readers identifying with literary characters who experience personal growth in the face of tragedy or difficulty.

In literature that follows this pattern, often the unfolding story events serve as the frame for the underlying theme—character growth. Jill May describes this occurrence:

> As readers grow older, they are faced with main characters who act in less than heroic ways. Characters are most believable when they face an unusual situation, learn how to cope, and develop an understanding about why things happened as they did. Then the plot's drama evolves around the author's main character and becomes most effective when the story's audience identifies with the main character. (46)

Thus, even if story events end tragically, the reader is exposed to the development of the character in response to the hand that fate has dealt him or her.

This pattern is particularly characteristic of young adult books about death. Susan Beth Pfeffer is the author of *About David,* a story in which teen-aged David kills himself and his parents. Pfeffer writes of the book, "*About David,* of course, isn't about David at all. It's about Lynn (his oldest friend). It's not about death. It's about living" (7). The same is true of what Caroline Hunt refers to as "dead relative" books. In these stories, the hero or heroine learns to deal with someone else's death. She describes this phenomenon: "As the victim's condition grows steadily worse, the narrator changes for the better part; as the parent or sister literally shrinks from disease, the protagonist grows into maturity and responsibility" (243). In these books, the central character learns that facing darkness and difficulty is painful, but that he or she can survive and go on with new understanding of life.

For some, a reader's identity with such a character is attached to an additional purpose. Several who read, teach, and write about children's and adolescent literature maintain that through reading these books children can learn to cope with emotions and experiences in their own lives. Some refer to the appropriateness of providing literature for young adolescents that deals with the emotional pain involved in "coming of age." Patricia Liddie writes of *Jacob Have I Loved* as a novel that is "appropriate to the older junior high student. At a time when vision of self is all-important, ninth graders are relieved to discover that most of us take years to find self and to accept the self that we find, that such acceptance is not an easy passage, and that, very often, the self we find is not the one we expected" (52). Katherine Paterson, author of the novel, argues that young readers look to fiction to "understand others, to rehearse the experiences that someday they may live out in the flesh" (as qtd. in Agee 179).

Others view books about death as psychologically important for young readers. Gibson and Zaidman write that "literature about real and fictional people satisfies a desperate need to comfort children who are justifiably bewildered and fearful about death" (233). High school teacher Marvin Hoffman shares an account of a former seventh-grade class of English students. Just weeks after his students had read and discussed *Bridge to Terabithia,* they encountered a face-to-face confrontation with death when a classmate was killed in a bus accident. Hoffman writes, "these fictional encounters with death had prepared them in some small way for the real deaths that touched everyone in the group" (16). Hoffman viewed the book as a bridge between fictional tragedy and real-world tragedy.

Hoffman's position contains strands of bibliotherapy, as does the viewpoint of Ellen Howard. Three years after publishing *When Daylight Comes,* she wrote *Gillyflower,* a book which dealt with a father's sexual abuse of his daughter. Howard decided to publish the book, "with the hope that someday, somewhere, some child may see in Gilly a girl like herself with the strength and courage to tell [what was happening to her]" (11). When used for "therapeutic" reasons such as Howard's, the purpose for reading becomes empowerment, comfort, and the building of healthy coping skills.

Many books such as *Gillyflower* have been dubbed "problem novels," and they have been published in significant numbers since the late 1960s. Representative of this phenomenon, author Susan Terris reflects on the variety of "problem" topics that she has written about, including "pyromania, autism, polio, death of a parent, kidnapping, chronic depression, alcoholism, being handicapped, adoption, eating disorders, teenage pregnancy, sibling rivalry, and—yes—even murder" (15). Some literary critics have remarked on the "shallowness" in problem novels, particularly in the realm of literary value. Marilyn Apseloff, in her essay on suicide novels for adolescents, discusses the characteristics of several works that typify this form of literature. She notes that although the books follow psychiatric guidelines closely, making them "sociologically acceptable as a form of prevention or bibliotherapy," the novels are flawed by characterization and plot that "are too manipulated" (237–38). In her opinion, the literary value is sacrificed for sake of the "issues message." There are exceptions, however. Robert Cormier is frequently identified as an author whose works effectively integrate contemporary issues within sophisticated literary frameworks. In an interview with author Robert Cormier, Roni Natov commented of his book *The Chocolate War:* "The story is very intense and I think that's what makes it feel authentic. It doesn't feel like the typical young adult novel, sort of trumped up to air issues or to solve problems" (DeLuca and Natov 111). Cormier's characters do face "problems"—within a richly layered context.

Perhaps the difference between Cormier's work and that of the typical problem novelist is his intent. Cormier writes realistically but not didactically. His central themes are not alcoholism, premarital sex, drug use, divorce, or disabilities, although problems such as these may be elements within his texts. The overlying focus within his novels, however, is the struggle between individuals and institutions (Headley 34). Furthermore, Cormier develops this theme within rich, powerful contexts. The complex layers within his texts are not "weak" in characterization or plot. Macleod describes the meanings that Cormier's novels evoke:

> [Cormier] is far more interested in the systems by which a society operates than he is in individuals. His novels center on [. . .] the political context in which his characters, like all of us, must live. [. . .] He has evoked a political world in which evil is neither an individual phenomenon nor a personality fault explainable by individual psychology, but a collaborative act between individuals and political systems which begins when the individual gives over to the system the moral responsibility that is part of being human. Perhaps the message can be summed up as what you fail to understand about your world can destroy you, either literally or as a human being (as qtd. in Campbell 44).

Cormier has frequently been attacked for the disturbing endings which are characteristic of his novels. Representative of these attacks are statements made by W. G. Ellis and Rebecca Lukens. Ellis writes that "evil is not conquered in Cormier's novels. His heroes are more tragic than not" (52). Lukens states, "The effect upon the reader is not merely fear, but often sheer terror [. . .] the effect once again is that life is filled with sinister elements—government-related at that. There is no hope for the honest citizen in today's society. The forces of evil prevail, and despair is the winner" (40).

Cormier has defended his endings with two important statements: First, as he stated in an interview, he has provided his works with endings that satisfy "what the books dictate" (qtd. in DeLuca and Natov 130). Cormier reflected on a time when he faced a publisher's request to change the ending of *The Chocolate War* in order to gain publication support, saying, "It was tempting to say, 'Well, let me see about it.' But I knew that in my mind the curve of the story was to build and then go down. [. . .] I believe in this sense of inevitability. And when I'm bothered by a book that I read that doesn't ring true, I wonder whether the author, playing God, didn't tamper somewhere, by not following the natural outcome" (114). Cormier's works reveal the ending's function as described by several literary critics. D. A. Miller maintains that an ending "completes the meaning of what has gone before" (xi). John Stephens relates the ideas of Frank Kermode who "observes that a common expectation of narrative is that it should be a wholly concordant structure, whose end is in harmony with its beginning, and the middle with both. The end resumes the whole structure" (Stephens 42, Kermode 6). Cormier brings his stories to their aesthetically inevitable conclusions; his endings are defensible in a literary sense—as the natural results of the stories as a whole.

Additionally, although Cormier admits that the physical endings to his works are both tragic and disturbing, he does not view them as hopeless:

> As long as what I write is true and believable, why should I have to create happy endings? My books are an antidote to the TV view of life, where even in a suspenseful show you know before the last commercial that Starsky and Hutch will get their man. That's phony realism. Life just isn't like that . . . If you're going to fight this kind of thing, you've got to be collectively good. There is hope—but we must create it for ourselves. (qtd. in Campbell 56)

In Cormier's work, the graphic endings are necessary tools for taking the reader to a deeper level of reflection that extends beyond self-centered concerns. Donald Gallo has observed that Cormier's novels are often characterized as having "uncompromising endings." He goes on to say that "although the phrase 'uncompromising endings' has, unfortunately, become a euphemism for *unhappy, negative, downbeat*—meaning 'the good guys lose.' I prefer to see those endings as plausible, realistic, real-life endings . . . endings that make readers think far beyond the covers of the book" (35).

Cormier is not the only author for children and adolescents whose stories have received literary praise, yet whose endings have been characterized as disturbing or less than "happily ever after." Katherine Paterson's *Bridge to Terabithia,* although perceived by some as a "death" book, is not characterized by the formula plot and characterization that plague many problem novels. However, Paterson, although not entirely opposed to recommending a book to readers with special problems, is wary of bibliotherapy. She writes: "The first time I was told that *Bridge to Terabithia* was 'on our death list,' I was a bit shaken up. There follows, you see, the feeling that if a child has a problem, a book that deals with that problem can be given to the child and the problem will be cured. [. . .] If we look at life as a series of problems needing solving, it is hard not to offer nicely packaged, portable solutions, preferably paperback" (*The Spying Heart* 31). Joel Chaston, when writing about *Bridge to Terabithia,* stated that in this novel Paterson refrains from turning the character's story into a prepackaged set of solutions. Paterson does not ask the reader to dismiss the pain of death or to forget about it. Grief is not wiped away but is respected (240–41). Nor does Paterson dictate to her readers, through her story's resolution, how they should respond. In *Gates of Excellence,* Paterson writes, "I have no more right to tell my readers how to respond to what I have written than they have to tell me how to write it" (24). As with Cormier's novels, the ultimate conclusion for the reader is his or her decision.

A third author whose work exemplifies the nontraditional ending that satisfies story themes is Natalie Babbitt. In *Tuck Everlasting,* her main character does not drink the water that would have allowed her to live forever but instead chooses to live as a mortal and ultimately die. While the external plot portrays the story of a family's escape from exploitation, the inherent themes confront a reader's perceptions about life and death. Norma Bagnall has reflected on her experience at a Children's Literature Association conference when Natalie Babbitt was answering questions after speaking to an audience of college students and children's literature specialists, and she recalls her surprise when a young woman in the audience asked Babbitt why Winnie in *Tuck Everlasting* did not drink the magic water and, thus, live forever. Bagnall writes:

> The question surprised me. I had just finished a four-week study with fifth graders in St. Joseph, Missouri, with *Tuck Everlasting*. [. . .] In all of the reading, questioning, dramatizing and discussing, not one child asked why Winnie didn't drink the water. It was almost as if the children knew that because of the way Babbitt had structured the story such an ending was impossible. (144–45)

As with the work of Cormier and Paterson, Babbitt's ending leaves the reader with something to think about.

Critics, educators, authors, and parents often closely examine the role of the book as a "lesson" in determining what a story will mean for an adolescent or child. If we approach story meaning from a holistic viewpoint, however, it becomes apparent that the book is only one element that is impacting the meaning of the story; a young reader "creates meaning" when engaging with a story. Peter Hunt suggests that literary critics should consider two elements when looking at a children's novel: both the reader and the text (3). Whereas the book brings to the reader its own plot, characterization, tone, and narration, the reader brings to the book qualities such as his or her attitudes about life, knowledge, experiences, cultural background, race, class, age, gender, and prejudices. Following Hunt's depiction, story meaning is made when reader and text interact (70).

Hunt's statements about story meaning align closely with reader response theory, a stance that maintains that literature studies must focus on the reader's response to what is being read. Each reader's experiences and points of view shape his or her understanding of a text. One idea that has been discussed in conjunction with reader response theory is the notion of an "implied reader," or "the readership for whom the book is written" (Hunt 46). In order to determine who the "implied reader" is for a novel, critics look for subtle clues within the text, such as the attitudes and ideals that the characters portray and the focalizing character with whom the reader is led to identify. In literature marketed for children and adolescents, the protagonists are typically young people, as is the case with many of the books by Cormier, Paterson, and Babbitt. Adults maintain that these books are written "for" adolescents and preadolescents, but it would be foolish to claim that anyone can predict what the actual responses of these young people will be when they individually engage with texts and create meanings based on their own experiences, ideals, backgrounds, and needs.

Several authors have discussed generally accepted perceptions of being "adolescent." C. David Lisman quotes an article by A. Seig that defines adolescence as "the period of development in human beings that begins when the individual feels that adult privileges are due him which are not accorded him, and that ends when the full power and social status of the adult are accorded to the individual by his society" (qtd. in "Yes" 15). Susan Pfeffer claims that rule number one of basic teenage life is "I am the one true outsider," and that this rule, among others, is the basis for an adolescent's connection with characters in literature (5–7). Rebecca Lukens also writes about adolescents connecting with the books they read, basing her statement on her own experience reading *The Catcher in the Rye* as a teenager:

> *The Catcher in the Rye* took reading Americans by surprise. The book said what adolescents were feeling, and what they thought no one knew about themselves: "Surely," adolescents

think, "no adult can put into words our anxiety about our most intimate concerns. Further-more, my concerns aren't quite like other people's. No one else is as troubled as I." (38)

Whether or not adolescents are experiencing the anxieties and self-doubts that these adults describe, they are, of course, experiencing their own unique blend of thoughts, feelings, and questions. They bring all of this into their encounter with literature. This "baggage" will im-pact the meaning that they make of story characters, story events, and story endings.

Without listening to the response of "real" young people, it would be impossible for me to say whether or not adolescents and preadolescents "need" a happy ending or whether or not they like alternative endings to a story. Do their opinions align with those who claim that books for young people must include strands of hope and promise? Do they like to read about characters who encounter problems and tragedies but grow personally through the process? Do they want story endings that satisfy the themes in the stories themselves and provide them food for thought considering larger issues?

Because there is no "generic" adolescent whose opinions can stand for all, my con-sideration of young people's responses to story endings will be individual in nature. I have found out a great deal, however, by listening to the reactions of seventh- and eighth-grade students who have read *Tuck Everlasting* by Natalie Babbitt and *Park's Quest* by Kather-ine Paterson. Although I was not able to talk with readers who had recently read *Bridge to Terabithia* or the works of Robert Cormier, many of the responses to *Tuck* and *Park* speak to the questions raised by those novels as well.

As part of a research project, I observed English classes at a middle school. In one of the class sessions, ten middle school students were asked by their teacher to discuss their responses to *Park's Quest,* a novel by Katherine Paterson that they had just completed, which focuses on an 11-year-old boy's search for answers to his questions about his father, a casualty in the Vietnam War. His quest reveals past events in the lives of his parents that are both enlightening and disturbing, and these raise even deeper unanswered questions.

When the classroom teacher asked students for their general responses to the novel, several stated that they liked it. One said the author tells the story in such a way that "keeps you irritated [. . .] and keeps you reading." When asked to describe their reactions to the ending, however, the general consensus was that the close of the book did not leave them "happy." When asked why, one explained, "It leaves you wanting to know what happened." Another added, "I want a sequel!" Their comments support Jill May's assertion in *Chil-dren's Literature and Critical Theory:* "the uncertainty in the text causes the reader to be slightly uneasy" (125). The students in this classroom told their teacher that they "wanted to know" the specific events in the lives of Park's mother and father that Paterson alludes to but doesn't flesh out. They wanted to know what would happen to the crow that Park had accidentally wounded but whose healing had begun as Park and Thanh nurtured it. The book had left them with unanswered questions.

Stephens, in *Language and Ideology in Children's Fiction,* maintains, "as readers, we learn to look for some sense of completeness, both aesthetic and thematic, over and above the bringing of a series of events to a close." He goes on to argue, however, that "when a physical ending exists but a thematic ending does not, young readers can't always detect this" (42). The students in this classroom may, in a sense, represent a parallel per-spective to what Stephens describes. They definitely looked for a sense of completeness of the physical events in this story in their case; however, they did not sense a thematic ending provided by the author. One student alluded to his individual analysis of a theme layered into the text. He commented that Paterson's mention of the tales of King Arthur and the Holy Grail in Park's imaginings "kind of make the book clearer [. . .] but you have to figure that out for yourself."

Their discussion only briefly focused on the book's ending during that class session. A significant portion of the conversation reflected the students' appreciation of the characterization in the novel. Many remarked on the relationships between Park and his mother, as well as Park and Thanh. Some felt that Park's mother should have told him the truth about their past at an earlier age; many agreed that his mother's hesitance to do so was connected to the concepts of image and protection—both of herself and of Park. The students recognized that the relationship between Park and Thanh was impacted by the different worlds—both physically and emotionally—that they came from, and that their relationship changed when they learned they were related. Students during this portion of the discussion were engaged and personal. One student reflected on her understanding of Park's mother, stating, "My grandparents weren't married when they had my Mom. Sometimes they don't like to tell people that." As the discussion closed, the teacher asked whether or not each student liked the novel. Unanimously, the students responded "yes." Apparently, though many were not fully satisfied with the book's ending, these students did find value in the book, many connected personally with the development of relationships in the novel, and many wanted to follow the story's characters further.

Through a separate research project, I was able to obtain the responses of adolescents to *Tuck Everlasting.* Six eighth-grade students volunteered to correspond with college-level pen pals, writing about their responses to the novel. No specific prompts were established by the teachers involved in the project; rather, students were to react freely. The comments I have included here were taken from the letters that the eighth graders wrote. Many of the students began their letters with general evaluations of the novel as a whole. One wrote, "*Tuck Everlasting* was one of the best books that I have ever read." Another stated, "It was a good book that raised some interesting questions." A third wrote, "I thought it was quite suspenseful." Another explained the difference that she experienced reading the novel at this point in her life than when she had read it at a younger age: "Before this year, I had read about half of *Tuck Everlasting,* but I didn't really read it. I just skimmed the pages and couldn't really get into it. When I read it this year, it was such a good book that I couldn't put it down. It was one of those stories that really gets you thinking."

Throughout their letters, students remarked that the book caused them to think—not only about the story events but also about life and death. Some talked about life and death in terms of Winnie's experience with the Tucks. Others talked about their own personal perceptions. One stated, "I think Winnie would have wanted to live forever in a way because of all the things she would've experienced and lived through. But, the one experience that she wouldn't have been through was dying [. . .]". Another wrote, "I would like to have eternal life *at first,* but then I would probably regret it." A third said, "I believe *Tuck Everlasting* helps us to understand how our fondest wish, that of eternal life, can end up our worst nightmare." In every one of their letters, the students described death as a necessary part of living. As one student put it, "I agree that life makes sense whether we understand it or not. We can't change it worth nothing."

In *Tuck Everlasting,* Natalie Babbitt provides one thing for the reader that Katherine Paterson does not do in *Park's Quest.* Babbitt adds an epilogue that allows readers to find out the eventual conclusion that answers many questions about the "physical" story line. In her epilogue, the reader finds out that Winnie chose living and dying, rather than life everlasting. In so doing, she denied herself the opportunity to marry Jesse—whose tender offer of marriage at 17 had stirred Winnie's emotions. Thus, Babbitt's conclusion does not follow the "happily ever after" marriage convention but instead provides an ending that satisfies the theme of the story.

Students' responses to the epilogue were mixed. One wrote, "I liked this book, but I didn't enjoy reading the epilogue. In my heart I wished she had drank it and lived forever with the Tucks. That would've been *my* happy ending. But, as everybody knows, life doesn't always have a happy ending." Another comment spoke of the ironic tragedy that acceptance of Jesse's proposal would have meant for Winnie: "I think it would've been hard to have been faced with the opposition that Jesse presented to her. In a way he was asking her to give up her life in two ways." A third respondent also spoke about the mixed feelings that the ending evoked for her: "I thought the ending was sad because she didn't drink the water, but I thought it was *happy* too. [. . .] When the spring was destroyed at the end I was happy, because living forever wouldn't be fun." Yes, some of the eighth graders admit to their desire for happy endings, but all of them believed that the story ended "as it had to." And although the novel did not connect with typical teenage "problems" like alcoholism, teen pregnancy, or drug abuse, it connected with a larger human issue—the inevitable cycle of living and dying.

How can these adolescents' responses to literature better inform adults, particularly those who will, in turn, provide these young people with literature to read? Authors, publishers, educators, parents, and critics are all in some sense involved in providing "good" books for young readers. But readers alone can determine what works they themselves evaluate as "good" books. Peter Hunt remarks, "The literature *of* the child may not be the same as the literature *for* the child [. . .] mismatchings are inevitable" (58). Perhaps by listening to adolescents talk about literature, adult providers can glean understanding of what the literature *of* a child is, including what a child makes of endings to stories—whether happily or alternatively interpreted.

It is critical to remember that the literature of a reader is just that—the literature of *that particular* reader. Hugh Crago makes enlightening comments concerning the absurdity of generalizing about books that appeal to the young:

> They [adults who claim to know which books all children should be exposed to] talk as if the same body of literature will have broadly similar "results" for all children, yet common sense tells us that this is highly unlikely to be the case. Large scale surveys of "what children like to read" are intentionally couched at the level of generalization and offer us little illumination. [. . .] Over the past fifteen years, reader-response studies have amply demonstrated what common sense would always have indicated: Each reader brings to every book an enormously complex set of memories, assumptions, and organizing schemas rooted in her or his individual personality. [. . .] The process by which readers [child and adult alike] connect with, and find meaning in, particular books is more than simply a matter of the formal qualities of the text or the decoding skills of the reader; rather, it is a matter of emotional investment. (278–79)

Crago's remarks, which align with reader response theories, take into account not only the fact that a reader is a "child" or an "adolescent" but also that he or she has unique attitudes about the themes in personal explorations. Individual readers will inevitably bring to their readings of books such as *Park's Quest* and *Tuck Everlasting* their own beliefs, concerns, and questions about relationships, life, and death. Frank Kermode places a quotation by Blake in *The Sense of an Ending* that has to do with the final judgment of mankind: "its vision is seen by the Imaginative Eye of Everyone according to the situation he holds" (qtd. in *The Sense* 2). So, a reader brings "the situation he holds" into his personal interpretation of a book.

With this in mind, it is not surprising that individual reader responses to *Park's Quest* and *Tuck Everlasting* were not identical. Even so, there were common strands that ran across a significant number of the responses. I would like to consider what these commonalities might offer as "food for thought" to adults who take part in book provision for young adolescents. Although I would not say that these strands apply to all young readers, I would propose that just considering examples of what some young readers have said about books with alternative endings may allow adults the opportunity to challenge generalizations about children's and adolescent reading needs.

Many of these adolescent readers have revealed an appreciation of the rich characterization that Babbitt and Paterson provide in their novels. They have expressed considerations of the backgrounds the characters bring to the events within the story, their values and worries, what confuses them, what comforts them, and how they see the world. Particularly with the readers of *Tuck Everlasting,* many were able to articulate their considerations of not only the physical story events or personal problems dealt with in the novel but also the broader themes about life that the book stimulated them to consider. And with those who read *Park's Quest,* the theme of relationships was extended by the readers to connection with personal experiences—and new understandings of the emotional "baggage" that plays a part in personal decisions.

Perspectives of these readers on the alternative endings provided by the authors are also thought provoking. Several related their sense of "sadness" when completing their book. Others admitted that they wished for happy endings. Interestingly, though, those who read *Tuck Everlasting* revealed a collective awareness that the ending had to be as it was—that it needed to satisfy the story theme. For most who read *Park's Quest,* however, the unanswered questions that remained at the end of the reading left them with an unsettled sense of closure. One remarked that Park's quest paralleled the knight's quest for the Holy Grail, but his comments were not followed up. Paterson ends her story with the following depiction of Park, Thanh, and their grandfather together drinking spring water from a coconut shell:

> "Now," she [Thanh] ordered. "Now. All drink."
>   Then they took the Holy Grail in their hands and drew away the cloth and drank of the Holy Wine. And it seemed to all who saw them that their faces shone with a light that was not of this world. And they were as one in the company of the Grail. (148)

Not once was this concluding paragraph mentioned throughout the class discussion. Most stated, however, that they were frustrated with the ending and wanted to know more about what happened.

The responses of these adolescent readers suggest several things to those in the business of finding books for adolescents. First and foremost, these readers send us the message that what young people read does not necessarily have to be simple in characterization, theme, or plot. For some adolescents the complex, the richly layered, and the provocative furnish grounds for deep thought. In addition to the problem novels widely available to adolescents during the past two decades, books with broader human themes can indeed "connect" with young readers. This would suggest that books we define as written for youthful audiences cannot justifiably be "put in a box." As adults, we would be pretentious to say that any work is right for all adolescent readers. Also dangerous is the practice of necessarily "writing down" to children—whether through use of language or simplistic ideas. For some readers, books that appear to have controlled vocabulary and ideas may seem uninteresting. A growing number of authors, including Cormier, Babbitt, and Paterson, have recently extended to young readers books that "depict life with an honesty and complexity fuller than has generally been available in the genre" (DeLuca 125). If we, as parents and educators, are afraid to offer these to our children and teenagers, we may be robbing them of rich interactions with literature.

The adolescent responses in my study have also revealed much about whether or not young readers want or need "happy endings" to the books they read. Perhaps the contrast between the responses to *Tuck Everlasting* and *Park's Quest* is an important one to consider. Those who read *Tuck* were evidently well aware of the development of the theme within the story; in fact, their collective responses to the book dealt very little with the actual story events and very much with the overlying theme. In contrast, those who read *Park* focused largely on characters and story events in their subsequent discussion of the novel. The themes of quest for truth, honor, and connection received very little focus. They did not allude to Arthurian literature in their responses. Because they were not centered on the quest, they found little satisfaction in a conclusion that symbolically brought Park to knowledge of the truth and connection with those who were part of who he was. Perhaps as educators and parents, we would do well to raise questions for young readers that might spark their consideration of story themes. Although each reader will ultimately come to his or her own conclusions, offering all participants tools for considering literature in a variety of ways may open up their opportunities for contemplation about stories that do not end happily ever after.

Finally, a young person's response can tell us something important. Our position as listeners is not to criticize or discount these real readers' responses, but to learn from them. We can find out more about what ideas and experiences they bring to the books they read and also what tools they use for interpreting story meanings. We can offer them tools that may not only enrich their contemplations of books but also allow them the freedom to ultimately create meanings that are uniquely theirs.

Do young readers "need" happy endings? If anyone answers this with an unequivocal "yes," then perhaps they haven't really listened to "all" young readers.

Works Cited

Agee, Jane M. "Mothers and Daughters: Gender-Role Socialization in Two Newbery Award Books." *Children's Literature in Education* 24:3 (1993): 165–83.

Apseloff, Marilyn F. "Death in Adolescent Literature: Suicide." *Children's Literature Association Quarterly* 16:4 (1991–1992): 234–38.

Babbitt, Natalie. *Tuck Everlasting.* New York: Farrar, Straus and Giroux, 1975.

Bagnall, Norma. "It Was *Real* Exciting: Adults and Children Studying Literature Together." *Children's Literature Association Quarterly* 12:3 (1987): 144–46.

Campbell, Patricia J. *Presenting Robert Cormier.* Boston: Twayne Publishers, 1985.

Chaston, Joel D. "The Other Deaths in *Bridge to Terabithia.*" *Children's Literature Association Quarterly* 16:4 (1991–1992): 238–41.

Cormier, Robert. *The Chocolate War.* New York: Dell Publishing Co., 1974.

Crago, Hugh. "Why Readers Read What Writers Write." *Children's Literature In Education.* 24:4 (1993): 277–89.

DeLuca, Geraldine. "Taking True Risks: Controversial Issues in New Young Adult Novels." *The Lion and the Unicorn* 3:2 (1979–1980): 125–48.

DeLuca, Geraldine and Roni Natov. "An Interview with Robert Cormier." *The Lion and the Unicorn* 2:2 (1978): 109–35.

Ellis, W. G. "Cormier and the Pessimistic View." *The ALAN Review* 12:2 (1985): 10–12, 52–53.

Gallo, Donald R. "Robert Cormier: The Author and the Man." *The ALAN Review* 9:1 (1981): 33–36.

Gibson, Louis Rauch and Laura M. Zaidman. "Death in Children's Literature: Taboo or Not Taboo?" *Children's Literature Association Quarterly* 16:4 (1991–1992): 232–33.

Headley, Kathy Neal. "Duel at High Noon: A Replay of Cormier's Works." *The ALAN Review* 21:2 (1994): 34–35.

Hoffman, Marvin. "Death in the Classroom." *The ALAN Review* 21:2 (1994): 14–17.

Howard, Ellen. "Facing the Dark Side in Children's Books." *The Lion and the Unicorn* 12:1 (1988): 7–11.

Hunt, Caroline C. "Dead Athletes and Other Martyrs." *Children's Literature Association Quarterly* 16:4 (1991–1992): 241–45.

Hunt, Peter. *Criticism, Theory and Children's Literature.* Cambridge, MA: Basil Blackwell, Inc., 1991.

Kermode, Frank. *The Sense of an Ending: Studies in the Theory of Fiction.* New York: Oxford University Press, 1967.

Law, Elizabeth. "'Yes, but I'm Eleven': An Editor's Perspective on Condescension in Children's Literature." *The Lion and the Unicorn* 17:1 (1993): 15–21.

Liddie, Patricia A. "Vision of Self in Katherine Paterson's *Jacob Have I Loved.*" *The ALAN Review* 21:3 (1994): 51–52.

Lisman, C. David. "Yes, Holden Should Read These Books." *English Journal* 78:4 (1989): 14–18.

Lukens, Rebecca. "From Salinger to Cormier: Disillusionment to Despair in Thirty Years." *The ALAN Review* 9:1 (1981): 38–42.

May, Jill P. *Children's Literature and Critical Theory.* New York: Oxford University Press, 1995.

Miller, D. A. *Narrative and Its Discontents: Problems of Closure in the Traditional Novel.* Princeton, NJ: Princeton University Press, 1981.

Pape, Walter. "Happy Endings in a World of Misery: A Literary Constraint between Social Constraints and Utopia in Children's and Adult Literature." *Poetics Today* 13:1 (1992): 179–96.

Paterson, Katherine. *Bridge to Terabithia.* New York: Harper Collins Publishers, 1977.

———. *Gates of Excellence: On Reading and Writing Books for Children.* New York: Dutton, 1981.

———. *Park's Quest.* New York: Dutton, 1988.

———. *The Spying Heart: More Thoughts on Reading and Writing Books for Children.* New York: Dutton, 1989.

Pfeffer, Susan Beth. "Basic Rules of Teenage Life." *The ALAN Review* 17:3 (1990): 5–7.

Reid, Suzanne Elizabeth. *Becoming a Modern Hero: The Search for Identity in Cynthia Voigt's Novels.* Doctoral Dissertation. Blacksburg, VA: Virginia Polytechnic and State University, 1993.

Stephens, John. *Language and Ideology in Children's Fiction.* New York: Longman, 1992.

Terris, Susan. "Major Themes: Minor Themes." *The ALAN Review* 20:1 (1992): 14–17.

Worlton, Karina. "The Case for Happy Endings." *The Freeman: Ideas on Liberty* 43:12 (1993): 487–88.

Continuing Our Conversations

We wish to end this book with some conversations that we had with our writers as we considered the commentary of the manuscript reviewers and then turned to our dear professional friend Dianne Johnson for one final discussion about issues of cultural diversity and multiculturalism. We begin with comments by Eve Tal and Richard Van Dongen.

When one of the reviewers asked Eve, "How can one walk on a tightrope? What rights do authors and illustrators have?" She wrote back to us that she had been thinking about this for some time. As a writer of fiction and poetry and a critic of children's literature who was born in America and now lives in Israel, Eve has written Hebrew stories and poetry published in Israel. As a scholar of children's literature, she attends conferences on many continents and has delivered many papers on the aesthetic values of children's literature. Eve wrote us that she cannot find an easy answer for these questions:

> A number of years ago, I worked on a collection of folktales of the Beta Israel, the Ethiopian Jews who began arriving in Israel in the 1980s. I reasoned that they had unique stories, but lacked English speakers to tell their stories to the English reading public. At the Israel Folktale Archives of the University of Haifa, I read written transcriptions of oral tales. I also visited with an Ethiopian rabbi, Josef David, who generously told me several tales, allowing me to record and transcribe them. The stories he told orally were fascinating: he responded to my reactions and was encouraged by my laughter, curiosity, and empathy. In my work on the transcribed stories in Hebrew, I was greatly hampered by not knowing Amharic. The storytellers did not have a good command of Hebrew, so the language lacked drama. As written, no one would have published them.
>
> So I changed them. I constructed an opening, middle, and climax. I added dialogue. I gave them shape and form, depending on the age level I was writing for. Sometimes I thought the stories worked, but many times I felt unsure. Did I have the right to reshape the stories into literary form? Do I have the right to retell stories that are not mine? I still have no answers to these questions.
>
> The stories have never been published, but the process taught me a great deal. I researched the life and history of the Beta Israel. I discovered links between their stories and the folktales of other cultures. I met Josef David and listened to the story of his life. I believe we all need exposure to other cultures, and that this exposure should begin in childhood. But

when we take the stories of others and reshape them to fit the concepts and models of our own culture, we commit a double transgression: we close the window on another culture and merely provide one more mirror to our own.

Richard is Associate Dean of Graduate Programs and Faculty Development in the College of Education at the University of New Mexico. However, we revere him as a scholar of children's literature. He has long studied children's literature, and he has been active in many organizations that we, too, have called home, including the Children's Literature Association, the National Council of Teachers of English Children's Literature Assembly, and the International Board on Books for Youth. One reviewer asked Richard, "How do teachers develop the skills of reading that you are employing?" Richard wrote back:

You ask, "How do you try to learn to read multiculturally across borders?" I would say that it is always a work in progress. I would say to someone to read and read and read in literature, in literary theory, and in cultural studies broadly defined. At the same time try to live a life that deliberately and authentically [which] sometimes uncomfortably places you at a boundary edge or even crosses a boundary of culture, and stay very much alive in your intellectual community as this happens. Always resist early judgments.

Reading multiculturally for me is like being invited to a Pueblo Indian wedding. You can't join in something that begins early in the morning and continues on late into the evening in this village context without crossing boundaries. You shape each conversation and each introduction according to the orientation of the person you are greeting. A Navajo visitor may engage in a handshake with no shake and no grip and acknowledge this clasp with a Navajo greeting; an Hispanic visitor is greeted with a hug and close embrace. In the village there are church events, a mass; there are home events. There is food and an order as to when one is served. There are sessions where advice is given to the couple by the elders and others who have been so honored to be asked. In all of this there are no refusals. The event may seem to never end and every step crosses cultural manners from one culture to the next.

Nothing could be worse than not to attend or not to participate if invited. So you plunge in and move ahead. This is the stance for reading multiculturally; not to refuse or dismiss the invitation. Always, however, resist early judgments as you plunge fully into the unknown territory of the text.

In the end, we turned to our trusted colleague Dianne Johnson, a scholar who has written much about African American children's literature, published the critical biography *Presenting Laurence Yep* (Twayne 1995), and has been asked to address issues of multicultural literature with many professional groups. Dianne has made her academic goal the recovery of lost or forgotten African American children's literature and the recording of its history. As Dinah Johnson, she has begun a second career, writing children's books. Her first book, *All Around Town* (Henry Holt 1998), is a narrative that is accompanied by the photographs of Richard Samuel Roberts, an early twentieth-century South Carolina photographer. She has also published *Sunday Week,* illustrated by Tyrone Geter (Henry Holt 1999), *Quinnie Blue* (Holt, 2000), and *Sitting Pretty: A Celebration of Black Dolls* (2000). We asked Dianne, "What is best said to our readers who have just finished reading this

book? How can we encourage them to consider the aesthetics of culturally diverse literature and to find new ways to define multiculturalism?" Dianne leaves us all with some
provocative and profound thoughts:

> Many consider "multiculturalism" a buzzword of the eighties and nineties. But in reality,
> multiculturalism is of ongoing concern and importance. This is true not only because of the
> changing demographics of America, but because of the change in the U.S. and global cli-
> mate following September 11. Unfortunately, some elements of the American population
> have an ever narrowing conceptualization of who "real" Americans are. And American chil-
> dren have little understanding of how Americans are viewed around the world and why, or
> of how people outside of this country live. Multiculturalism has to be interpreted in terms
> of the cultural and linguistic diversity of the United States and of the world.
>
> In this context, I'm thinking about multicultural children's literature, like any litera-
> ture, as a cultural product that can help people to think about their own humanity as indi-
> viduals and as members of small and large communities. That said, my strong contention
> is that the purpose of reading multicultural literature should *not* be to teach tolerance. Who
> wants to be tolerated? I bring up this word because, inevitably, someone throws it into the
> conversation. But we really need to reconsider its implications. We should think about
> words such as appreciation and understanding.
>
> More importantly, I feel that one of the major purposes of sharing this literature is to
> help young people develop an appreciation of good literature in all of its forms and con-
> texts. The sharing of *good literature*. Too often, this concern is overlooked. I agree, for ex-
> ample, that seeing images of oneself reflected in literature is important for children. But I
> do not think that the major goal for writers should be to produce material that boosts the
> self-esteem of readers. This might be one of the wonderful by-products—and there are
> many—of reading good literature, but not the major "purpose."
>
> Another issue that we all grapple with is the double-edged sword of awards. Though
> people don't admit it easily, my suspicion is that there are jurors whose thinking goes some-
> thing like: "Well, the black people and the latinos have their own awards. Why should we
> consider them for the Caldecott?" Of course, people can now point to a writer such as
> Christopher Paul Curtis and the recognition he has garnered. But the politics of the chil-
> dren's book world are still nasty and deep. The statistics suggest that Anglo-American par-
> ents and book buyers are not, for whatever reasons, consciously or not, purchasing books
> with images of non-white characters. Too many people still do not understand that we all
> are diminished as readers and as human beings when we don't open ourselves to a diver-
> sity of stories and share those stories with children.
>
> Finally, cultural diversity is inclusive. It shouldn't mean everything other than "white"
> or mainstream literature. A college student shouldn't point to a book by a black writer and
> call it a "multicultural book." Rather, that student, ideally, should develop a multicultural
> approach to thinking about literature and culture and living. Multiculturalism is a rich, em-
> powering, revealing lens in the exploration of children's literature. It is an idea that should
> be celebrated and embraced.

Index